8·25·93

D1126166

Troubleshooting and Repairing Personal Computers

2nd Edition

Art Margolis

Windcrest®/McGraw-Hill

Notices

Apple®	Apple Corporation	**Multisync**®	NEC Corporation
Atari®	Atari, Inc.	**Mylar**™	E.I. duPont
Commodore™	Commodore Corporation	**NEC**®	NEC Corporation
Compaq®	Compaq Computer Corporation	**Radio Shack**®	Tandy Corporation
Heathkit™	Heath Company	**RCA**®	Radio Corporation of America
IBM®	International Business Machines Inc.	**Sony**™	Sony Corporation of America
		Tandy®	Tandy Corporation
IBM PC®		**Texas Instruments**™	Texas Instruments Incorporated
Intel®	Intel Corporation		
Motorola®	Motorola Corporation	**TRS-8**	Tandy Corporation
Multiscan™	Sony™ Corporation of America	**Zilog**®	Zilog Corp.

SECOND EDITION
FOURTH PRINTING

© 1991 by **Windcrest Books**, an imprint of TAB Books.
TAB Books is a division of McGraw-Hill, Inc.
The name "Windcrest" is a registered trademark of TAB Books.

Library of Congress Cataloging-in-Publication Data

Margolis, Art.
    Troubleshooting and repairing personal computers / Art Margolis.-
-2nd ed.
      p.   cm.
    Rev. ed. of: Troubleshooting and repairing the new personal
computers. 1st ed. c1987.
    Includes index.
    ISBN 0-8306-2187-3 (hard)   ISBN 0-8306-2186-5 (paper)
    1. Microcomputers—Maintenance and repair. I. Margolis, Art.
Troubleshooting and repairing the new personal computers.
II. Title. III. Title: Personal computers.
TK7887.M37 1991
621.39'16—dc20   91-14381
                                    CIP

TAB Books offers software for sale. For information and a catalog, please contact TAB Software Department, Blue Ridge Summit, PA 17294-0850.

Acquisitions Editor: Roland S. Phelps
Book Editor: Bert Peterson
Director of Production: Katherine G. Brown
Book Design: Jaclyn J. Boone
Cover Design: Sandra Blair Design

Contents

Introduction

BACK IN THE LATE 1970s, A FEW LOCAL MICROCOMPUTER BUFFS BEGAN bringing their microcomputers into my TV repair shop when they developed electronic breakdowns. I was able to scrounge up sets of service notes and replacement parts from some of the cooperative manufacturers, and we were able to fix the things.

My technicians and I had a much more difficult time with the little digital computers than any of the analog equipment we routinely serviced, such as TVs, radios, and audio equipment. The difficulty we had was caused by microcomputers being mostly digital. Digital electronics is a different ball game than analog electronics. My employees and I spent decades on analog electronic failures. The digital breakdowns were a new strange set of problems. To help fill the need, I researched the subject, worked on many microcomputers, and wrote a book called *Troubleshooting and Repairing Personal Computers*, published by TAB Books (#1539). Perhaps you have a copy.

Back in those days, before IBM entered the microcomputer market in a big way, about the only micros that were around in any number were home computer enthusiast models such as Radio Shack's TRS-80s, Heathkit's H-59, Commodore's VIC-20, and a few others. They were all 8-bit types and used microprocessors such as the 8085, Z-80, 6500, and 6800. Normal memories were relatively tiny, such as 4K or 16K RAM. Most of the machines were single-board types with no more than 30 – 40 chips on the board. The chips were installed in *DIPs* (dual inline packages). A lot of the DIPs were installed in convenient DIP sockets and could easily be replaced like vacuum tubes before them.

As a result of this simplicity, once we developed an acquaintance with the digital theory and operation, the computer circuits became easy to troubleshoot and repair. In that early book, I covered these 8-bit machines. Response to the book was good.

In the early 1980s, microcomputer development proceeded at a breakneck pace. The Commodore 64 sold in the millions. Radio Shack did a great job with their color computers and other machines. Other manufacturers surfaced, and there were many 8-bit computers on the market. Then in 1981, IBM introduced their PC series of small computers. That introduction created the IBM world. As one rival company president put it, "IBM is not a competitor, they are the environment." The IBM PC, while enjoying some home computer market sales, really took off in the business market. They quickly convinced the business market that a computer system is a must. Without a computer, a business would never be able to compete with a competitor who was so equipped.

IBM sales went wild, and all the other manufacturers went into producing IBM compatible clones. The clone sales also went wild. As it turned out, many of the clones were just as good and often better than the original IBM PC—and cost less. However, the important positive event that took place was that standardization took hold. The standardization is still in place, and today clone sales are as good as they have ever been, if not better. Millions of the original computers in the IBM PC family and clones have been made. A software base for these machines was developed and builds continually.

When IBM went gung-ho for the business market, Apple, in order to compete, went after the scholastic market, in addition to its home market and business market. They promoted the Apple IIe at a very reasonable price for teachers and educators. They have managed to tie up a large chunk of the school market and have continued this effort in a successful manner. Apple also came out with their Macintosh unit that, at that time, had superior abilities in graphics. It was a big hit with users who worked with graphic-intensive applications.

My original book, as a result of the explosive development of computers, became out of date. I proceeded to write a sequel to the original called *Troubleshooting and Repairing The New Personal Computers* (TAB book #2809). It turned out to be even more popular than the first book. A lot had happened since the first book. In addition to the old 8-bit 8085, Z-80, 6502, and 6800 family processors, some 16-bit processors appeared in the IBM PC and clones, in the Commodore Amiga, and in the Macintosh. The 8086 and 8088 processors were in the IBM machine, and the 68000 showed up in the Amiga and Macintosh. In addition, *RAMs* (random-access memories) had developed to a point where 640K and 1 Mb became commonplace. In the old days, the 4116, a 16K RAM chip was impressive. Then the 4164, a 64K chip and the 41256, a 256K chip became the norm.

It is now 1991. The computer market is still explosive and shows no signs of slowing down. It is said that the computer industry will become the largest business in the world. No one appears to doubt that statement. To cover the improvements and advancements of the past five years, so you might intelligently be able to fix troubles with ease, I wrote this book, *Troubleshooting and Repairing Personal Computers, 2nd Edition* (TAB book #3677).

Although the operation of the new computers is much better than in years past, repairing them has become more complex. Instead of having a single board with a few dozen socketed DIPs, they have motherboards with a hundred or so chips. Instead of having all the *I/O* (input-output) circuits and connectors on the main board, the I/O circuits are usually mounted on adapter circuit board cards that plug into the motherboard. Very few of the chips are socketed, because the large chips tend to creep out of their sockets during operation. Instead of only using DIPs in the machines, new types of chip packages are used called *SMD* (surface mount devices). Both the IBM and Macintosh families of machines use many new processors. There are many new circuits, faster clocks, gigantic amounts of memory, and so on. A whole new computer world has emerged.

Don't get discouraged. To repair the equipment, new or old, it is not necessary to know the way it works from the design engineer's point of view. It is only required to have a technician's way of looking at the machine. In addition, the repairs do not require expertise in computer programming. It is, of course, useful to know as much as possible about computers, but the important thing is electronic repair knowledge in digital and analog, which is covered in this book. You need a combination of tools, technique, and technician-level theory of operation. The theory of operation is both general and specific as shown in the book. You should know somewhat how something works in order to figure out how it fails.

In this book, while covering computers from their beginnings in the late 1970s, specific emphasis also has been placed on the IBM and clone machines, the Apple and Commodore computers, and other things. The book starts off with chapter 1, *Diagnosing symptoms of computer trouble.* In this chapter, the typical symptoms that appear when trouble strikes are illustrated. The probable chips or circuits that could cause each trouble are also indicated. Chapter 2 covers the latest test equipment arsenal. These test pieces are the instruments you need in addition to your own five senses. The chapter discusses the correct way to bring these test pieces into action on the problem. In chapter 3, the nuts and bolts of taking the computer apart and putting it back together again without any screws left over is shown. After that is chapter 4, *Common troubles and repairs.*

In chapter 5, the use of chip location guides is discussed. The layout of common motherboards and their important service-connected usages is shown. From there a general discussion of what the large chips on the board are doing, followed by coverage on the RAM and *ROM* (random-access memory) chip insides, brings you up to date on today's new memory chips.

Actual repair procedures are shown in chapters 9, 10, and 11, *Manual fault dictionary techniques, Using diagnostic programs,* and *The latest chip-changing techniques.* Desoldering and resoldering of the common DIPs and the SMDs that are found in computers are in the chip-changing chapter. After that comes chapter 12, entitled *Block diagram of the typical personal computers.* Chapter 12 makes sense of the computer operation.

Then the chip circuits are discussed. Chapter 13, called *Clocks,* is first. Following that is the first microprocessor, chapter 14, *Those older 8-bit processors.* Next, chapter 15 covers 16-bit processors. It discusses the ever-popular 8088-8086 and the 68000. After that is chapter 16 on the 80186, 80286, 80386, and the 68020. Finally there is a full chapter on the new 80486 (chapter 17).

Once past the processors, bus lines and slots are covered in chapter 18. Their importance as test points is shown. Chapter 19, *Memory Map Residents*, clears up any mysteries you might have in this area. Included in the chapter is an explanation of how a memory map is designed.

Then there are chapters on the I/O systems, digital-to-digital, and digital-to-analog, (chapters 20 and 21). Chapter 22, *Display monitor interfaces*, has a lot of new information. In the past five years, video output adapter cards with much improved resolutions and larger numbers of gray scales and colors have become commonplace. There are so many with so many different characteristics that confusion can reign. This chapter will clear the confusion. There is also an in-depth discussion on the important popular *VGA* (video graphics adapter). The audio systems found in computers rounds out this chapter.

To match up with these new video systems are new kinds of TV display monitors. Chapter 23, new in this series of books, covers TV monitors. In a long chapter called *Video display repair techniques*, not only are the older monochrome and color monitors discussed, but the new VGA and Multiscan monitors are covered. This chapter is a condensed TV display monitor repair booklet.

Next in line is an expanded disk drive maintenance and adjustment chapter (chapter 24). It covers 5-1/4 and 3-1/2 inch floppy drives and disks. It also covers typical hard disk drive troubles and fixes. Chapter 25 goes into some detail on troubleshooting computer power supplies. The book finishes up with chapter 26, *Safety first*. Whenever you work on electronic or electrical equipment, there is always a danger. This chapter should give you the guidelines that will help you avoid problems of life and limb.

One extra bonus you will receive from being able to do computer troubleshooting and repairs is a knowledge of the computer innards from a hardware perspective. This information goes a long way toward helping you master your own and other computers. If you comprehend the hardware, you will find you'll become more adept at conceiving and running programs in high-level as well as machine and assembly language.

1
Diagnosing symptoms of computer problems

IF YOU READ A TYPICAL COMPUTER AD, YOU'LL USUALLY SEE A LIST OF the features in the machine. Some of the goodies that will get you excited are one of the latest processors, a hard drive, a 3½-inch floppy drive, a 5¼-inch floppy drive, a 1Mb RAM expandable, a VGA card, a 14-inch Multi-Sync color monitor, expansion slots, serial and parallel ports, professional keyboard, 200 W (watt) power supply and other things. This list can make you drool. These features can make your computing job easy and fun. The only problem is, every now and then that great computer goes down because one or more of these convenient features conks out.

The problem could be a simple adjustment or some cleaning or maintenance ailments and be quickly dispatched. On the other hand, the problem could have its source deep in the microcircuits. Some microscopic transistors or connections could have shorted together, broken apart, or began to cook. These types of troubles take place in germ-size components and are completely invisible. Whatever the trouble, it must be rooted out and remedied if you or another owner of a computer is to get back to work.

After the fact

When you are charged with the responsibility of troubleshooting and repairing a down computer, you start the job after the fact. The failure has already taken place. The computer system is sick or dead. Your job: fix it! Like a detective looking for clues or a doctor examining and taking tests, you as the repair person must carefully analyze the failure, and by logical means piece together all the clues, make electronic tests, work the repair puzzle out, and finally identify the source of the trouble. That is the troubleshooting part of the job.

The repair part corrects the trouble you identified. If adjustments, cleaning, or other maintenance is needed, with the appropriate materials and test equipment the job is executed. Should a component show up as defective, you must either repair the component or change it with a good replacement part.

There are no *ifs*, *ands*, or *buts* with a trouble. In most cases the computer cannot repair itself as the human body can. You must clean the right area, make the correct adjustment, or replace the actual defective component. The computer won't work until you do.

When a problem has occurred, the computer develops symptoms. These symptoms are valuable information. If you can read the symptoms correctly, they will point out the general section of the computer where the seat of the problem is likely to be found. In this chapter, there is a gallery of illustrations that represent a lot of the common symptoms that will appear. Fortunately for troubleshooters, computers have TV displays. Quite often the symptom appears clearly in the display. If you analyze a display that deviates from the norm and determine what is different, you've come up with a valid symptom. If you find the symptom in the gallery illustration, read the caption of the illustration for information on the probable source or location of the problem. Then, refer to the chapter covering those topics to solve the troubleshooting puzzle and bring about the repair.

The process of elimination

The step-by-step process of any troubleshooting job is a process of elimination. The first step is to look at all the symptoms, eliminate those that bear no resemblance to the symptom at hand, and focus on the symptom or symptoms that do apply. For example, if your text display suddenly goes wild and shows all kinds of mixed up words as shown in Fig. 1-1, you have a common condition that servicers call *garbage*. You would, of course, refer to the text about the garbage illustration and turn to the chapters covering the topics referenced in the text. None of the rest of the symptom illustrations would get your attention.

On occasion there is more than one clear symptom displayed. In those cases you'd try to classify the symptoms as primary and secondary symptoms. You must keep an open mind though, because what you think is a secondary symptom could actually be the primary, and vice versa. When there are multiple symptoms, classify them and begin your investigation promptly on the primary. If you find the symptom is not applicable, then you have eliminated it and its indicated circuits as a suspect. This is part of the process of elimination. From there you go on to the next symptom.

Once you have analyzed the symptom, thumbed to the chapter indicated as containing the information to aid you in the repair, and briefed yourself on how the circuit is designed to work, then you are ready to try to figure out the puzzle of how it failed. Each circuit examination requires certain pieces of test equipment, service notes, and diagnostic programs. It is a good idea to assemble them immediately and have them at your fingertips. The assembling of your attack weapons, the test equipment, service notes, and diagnostic software, reinforces the briefing

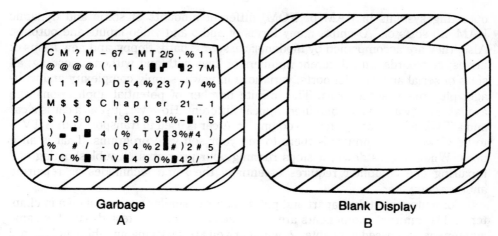

Garbage
A

Blank Display
B

1-1 The classic computer trouble system is called *garbage*. With garbage, the display suddenly locks up and fills with random characters, symbols, numbers, and blank spaces both dark and light as in A. One variation of the same condition exhibits a blank screen as in B. The problem, when it is hardware related, is usually found in the circuits containing the processor, ROM, RAM, or I/O chips.

you gave yourself from the indicated chapter material.

The next step in the process of elimination is to test the circuit carefully. One of two things will happen. One, the entire circuit will check out perfectly. When it does, regardless of your symptom analysis that indicated the circuit as a prime suspect, the circuit is given a clean bill of health and is eliminated as the troublemaker. You must then go back to square one and analyze the symptoms again. However, you must keep in the back of your mind that there is always the possibility the circuit might actually be the source of trouble but for some weird reason checks out fine. In those cases you'll give those circuits another look see the next time around.

Or second, the situation is not as tough and the testing does find a defect in the circuit. You are then able to pinpoint the source of the problem. Once the problem is pinpointed by the process of elimination, you are ready to conduct the actual repair. The puzzle is solved and the job can be completed.

The actual repair, which typically could be changing a chip, eliminating some tiny short circuit, or resoldering a single open connection, is the easier, manual-dexterity part of the job. The pinpointing of the cause of the trouble is the difficult bottleneck and requires understanding the way computer hardware works. Finding the defect in a computer is the uncertain and trying part of the job. That is what most of this book is about, finding the fault.

Typical personal computer system

From a hardware troubleshooting and repair point of view, one personal computer system is quite like another. A computer is a computer. They do come with monochrome or color displays, 8-bit, 16-bit, and 32-bit processors, simple and fancy operating systems in RAM or ROM, different amounts of static and dynamic RAM, all sorts of I/O chips, many forms of audio and video inputs and outputs. Also, they are accompanied by modems; cassettes; hard, floppy, and new forms of drives; keyboards with different numbers of keys with and without encoding; all sorts of serial and parallel ports; variations in power supply complexity and wattage; plus many accessories. The infinite number of potential applications and available software make computers appear different. However, just as a car is a car and a TV is a TV, a computer is a computer. A car is used to transport you. A TV is to be viewed. A computer is there to run your software programs. That is all it does. When it goes down, it stops running your programs. Troubleshooting and repairing one computer requires essentially the same techniques as repairing another computer.

Computers are taken apart and put together in similar ways as shown in chapter 3. The internal components are quite the same and are tested with the same equipment, discussed in chapter 2, whether you are servicing an 8-bit single board or a 32-bit motherboard with daughterboards. The common, everyday problems as discussed in chapter 4 are universal. Although a chip location guide, as covered in chapter 5, varies from computer to computer, the use of the guide remains the same, just as a traveler uses a map in the same way in different locations. The component-changing techniques, covered in chapter 11, are identical in all computers. One personal computer after another, of all different sizes and shapes, can be repaired on the same bench with the same techniques. The play remains the same, only the ailing computers change.

A typical personal computer system, in addition to a power supply, consists of five general sections as shown in Fig. 1-2. At the center of everything is the *MPU* (microprocessing unit), also known as the *processor*. The processor is the heart of the machine. It beats at a certain frequency and does all of the actual computing. Chapters 6, 14, 15, 16, and 17 cover the work that MPUs perform.

Most of the work the processor does is moving data back and forth between itself and three other sections. First of all, the processor receives new data from the various inputs. Second, it moves data back and forth to the memory. Third it delivers finished data to the outputs. Typical inputs that put fresh data into the processor are the keyboard, disk drive, cassette, modems, light pen, joysticks, mouse, Koala pads, analog-to-digital circuits and other items. Usual memories inside the computer are *RAM* (random access memories), *ROM* (read only memories), *PROMs* (programmable read-only memories) and *EPROMs* (erasable programmable read-only memories). The familiar devices that receive outputs from the processor are the TV display, the printer, cassette, disk drives, modems and others.

Between the inputs and outputs and the processor are interface circuits called I/O (for input/output). For example, there are special I/O chips that interface the keyboard to the processor. There are other special video I/O circuit boards that interface the processor to the TV display. These circuits must be used to convert the outside input data signals to forms that the internal processor can use and convert back the data to forms the output devices can work with.

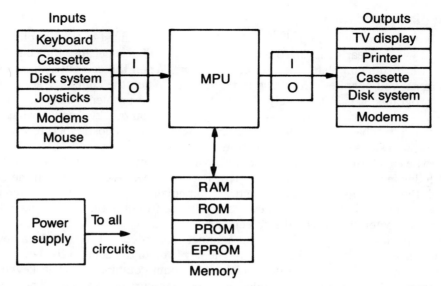

1-2 A typical personal computer consists of these components. The MPU receives data from the inputs via the I/O circuits. The MPU then works with the memory to process the data. The finished data is then sent to the outputs through the I/O.

Memories do not necessarily need I/O circuits to communicate with the processor. The memories are inside the computer with the processor. They both live in the internal digital computer world and both use the same language. The memory and the processor can be wired together directly.

In general, a personal computer operates in the following way. You start typing on a keyboard, which is an input device. The keyboard outputs a coded signal to the input section of an I/O interface chip. The I/O chip in turn sends the signal to the processor. The processor receives the signal and, according to the program running in the computer, processes the signal. The signal as it is processed is passed back and forth with the memory. Once the signal is completely processed, the MPU sends it to the output part of the I/O chip. In the I/O circuits the information is sent to places like the printer where hard copy is made, disk drive or cassette where the data is stored, and the complex video I/O circuits. The video chips and components act as TV stations and generate television pictures of the characters you press on the keyboard in monochrome or color. The picture information is then connected to a form of TV receiver, the display monitor, where it appears on the screen. If there is any audio accompanying the picture, it is converted to sound and emanates from a speaker.

All computers have one section that is common to all the circuits. That section is the power supply. There are many types of power supplies in computers. Their job is to supply all the chips and transistors with a well-regulated *dc* (direct-current) voltage.

The diagnostic display

The beauty of today's computer is, when trouble strikes, most of the symptoms of trouble will be clearly displayed on the TV monitor. This is because the computer system is also a complete closed-circuit TV unit. When the computer is running programs, you operate in response to the display. When the computer stops running programs, it is immediately obvious to you that a problem exists. In lots of cases, if you analyze the troubled display properly, you quickly realize what circuits are in trouble. The display is a powerful symptom diagnostic tool. It is a window to the insides of the digital computer world.

To be exact, the display is a window into a section of RAM called, video RAM. The following is what a typical video RAM section does. As you type on the keyboard, the letters and numbers you strike immediately appear on the TV screen. However, a lot of lightning speed events take place from the time you strike a key till the character appears on the screen.

A typical keyboard is wired in the manner illustrated in Fig. 1-3. As a key is struck, a switch is able to short the row the key is on to the column the key is also wired to. Each key has its own special row-column combination. The keyboard generates an individual signal coded for the character on that key. The signal enters the digital world, is passed through an I/O circuit, and continues on to the processor. The processor, in turn, sends the code to the section of RAM set aside as video RAM. The code is stored in a byte of video RAM. As more characters are struck, they follow the same path and are stored in subsequent bytes.

There is a direct relationship between the bytes in video RAM and the TV screen. For instance, as seen in Fig. 1-4, suppose your display is arranged to show text that has 32 characters across and 16 characters down. The display could just as easily show 40×25 or 80×25. This example is 32×16.

The 32×16 designation means there are 512 blocks to show 512 characters and spaces. One character or space can be stored in RAM in eight bits or one byte. To correspond with the designated 512 blocks on the screen, 512 bytes of RAM are set aside to store key strike, byte-sized character and space codes. This means the video RAM in our example, when in the alphanumeric mode, is 512 bytes long.

The first video RAM location stores the byte for the upper left hand corner of the display and the 512th byte stores the character byte for the bottom right corner. All of the rest of the video RAM locations store the rest of the bytes in numerical order.

Meanwhile the processor is doing a special job. It is scanning the video RAM bytes over and over. It is checking the contents of the video RAM. When the processor, as it examines each video RAM byte, encounters one that contains a character code, it takes a copy of the code and forwards it to the video output circuits. These circuits in turn, convert the code to a video character. The character is then sent on to the TV monitor. The monitor places the character into the numbered block on the screen that matches up with the numbered byte in video RAM. The processor keeps updating the video RAM all of the time the computer is on. As you type, each key strike causes its character to end up in a block on the screen.

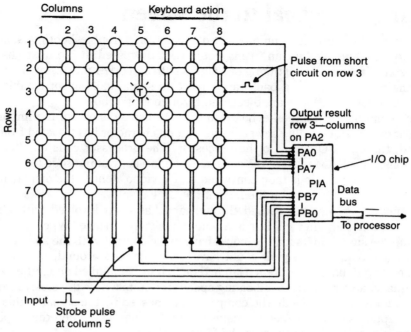

1-3 A typical keyboard is wired with a separate switch for each key. The switches are located at individual intersections of a row-column matrix. Each individual key strike generates a special code for that particular key.

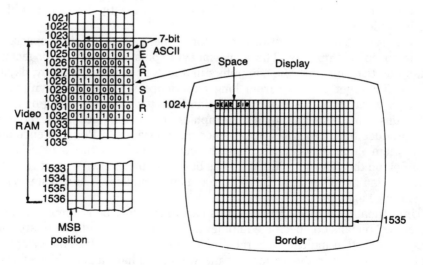

1-4 A section of RAM is set aside to store key strike generated ASCII code. Each byte in this video RAM area is given a one-to-one relationship with the character blocks on the display. Each byte holds the code for its assigned block and is able to cause the key character to be displayed.

Tracing the signal to the screen

One of the most important techniques used in electronic troubleshooting is, signal tracing. A computer technician, using equipment discussed in the next chapter, starting sometimes at the beginning of a signal path and other times starting at the end of the path and working backwards, traces a signal looking for trouble sections. The actual techniques are discussed throughout the book.

The signal path from the keyboard to the TV display is one of the important paths that can be traced. The key strike generated character has traveled from the keyboard, through I/O chips, to the processor. The processor calls on ROM for instructions, uses RAM to store the code, and sends a copy of the code to the video output circuits. The code is then converted to TV video, sent to the display monitor and is scanned into light on the face of the CRT display.

Because the signal has passed through and has been involved with almost every important computer chip, it is a valuable signal to trace. When trouble is occurring, the signal, in its travels, could have made contact with the source of the trouble. As a result, the signal could have been changed around, chopped up, shrunk, enlarged, have interference latched on to it or been killed altogether. All of these signal changes are clues indicating specific circuits where the elusive trouble could be hiding. If a trouble in the computer has messed up the signal in this way, whatever appears on the screen indicates the fault. That way, when the display is incorrect, it becomes a symptom of the fault.

In general, there are about a dozen symptoms that are common when chips or other computer hardware give up the ghost. There are many, many other symptoms that can appear when software becomes faulty, but those troubles are grist for a different software trouble book. This book is mostly concerned with hardware breakdowns.

Besides the common hardware symptoms, there are many other special symptoms in specific computers. These special symptoms are reserved for technicians working on the same specific computers in a factory service company, day in and day out. They get to know from long experience what specific symptoms are caused by what parts. For instance, take an IBM technician working on a PC. He or she runs some tests and finds the graphics are working good, but the machine won't produce text. From past experience on thousands of PCs and encountering this problem a number of times, the technician might know that a 74LS174, a hex D flip-flop on the color/graphics card has burnt up internally. Without further ado, the technician gets one from the stock room and installs it. The PC starts producing text once again.

Unfortunately, a quick repair of this nature can only be accomplished by specialized technicians on specific equipment. Fortunately though, there are the general symptoms that indicate general circuit areas. If you analyze the symptom and find its counterpart in the symptom gallery, you will have a good idea of what circuits are under suspicion. Then if you brief yourself by reading the chapter that discusses those circuits and perform the tests that are provided, odds are good that you will find a circuit fault. The fault location could be indicated as you find a poor logic reading, a wrong voltage, a bad oscilloscope picture, or it could be picked out with diagnostic software.

Armed with these facts, you will be able to find out what chips or other circuit components could possibly contain the fault. Once you pinpoint the bad part, you can turn to chapter 11 which tells you how to purchase replacement parts and perform soldering on the print board.

The symptom gallery

1. Garbage display (Fig. 1-1). The best known computer symptom is called *garbage*. Technicians recognize garbage when the display, instead of showing text, suddenly fills up with incoherent characters, dark and light spaces and other nonsensical figures. When you strike a character on the keyboard, the correct character might or might not appear. Either way this condition is still garbage.

   Remember, what you are seeing is only the contents of the video RAM. There could be all sorts of other wild happenings going on inside the machine that you can't see on the screen. However, the garbage is enough of a symptom. The garbage symptom is being caused by the processor running crazy without directions from the operating system program in the machine. The processor is filling the video RAM with nonsense instead of correct text.

   When garbage is the symptom, the trouble can be caused by any of the circuits that are involved in getting a character from the keyboard to the video output circuits. They all interact, and a fault in any of the chips could intercept the instructions from the operating system to the processor. Without instructions, the MPU runs but makes no sense.

   The main suspects are the I/O chips between the keyboard and the processor, covered in chapters 7 and 20, the MPU itself covered in chapters 6, 14, 15, 16, and 17, the RAM and ROM chips in chapter 8. Any of the chips in those areas could have faults and cause garbage.

   Most garbage symptoms will be found in the above circuit areas. One important way garbage shows up could be that the instructions from the operating system to the processor are not getting to the MPU. Some operating systems are installed in ROM chips and are found on the print board. Other systems are placed in RAM from a disk. Whatever the method, the circuits where the *OS* (operating system) is installed become suspects. When the MPU does not receive its OS instructions, it runs wild and stores just any characters into the video RAM section. The video RAM contents become meaningless. The suspected chips must be tested one by one until the bad one is found and replaced.

   Another way garbage can appear is due to encoded and unencoded keyboards, discussed in chapter 12. Encoded keyboards contain circuits that could have ROMs containing coded characters. This is in contrast to unencoded keyboards, shown in Fig. 1-3, that are simply switches that can short circuit. When shorted, they could cause garbage. The encoded keyboards, when a key is struck, generates an actual code that can be placed into video RAM after a trip through I/O and the processor. If failure occurs in the encoded keyboard circuits, the wrong coded bits could be generated. These wrong bits would find their way to video RAM and appear as garbage on the screen. In either case, the encoded or unencoded keyboard must be replaced or repaired.

Another way garbage could appear is when a defect in the video output circuits generates incorrect characters. The applied code byte does not produce the character that is displayed. This is because the code bytes stored in video RAM do not produce a character directly. The circuits operate in a much more complex manner. The code byte in video RAM is only an address. The address is found in a ROM or RAM chip that is holding bit patterns of the character. The video RAM byte simply addresses the section that contains the bit pattern of the desired character.

Figure 1-5 shows a monitor TV face. The closeup shows one character block. This example has 12 horizontal brightness scan lines in the block. Each scan line has 8 light dots. Each light dot can be turned on or turned off. Each dot is controlled by a bit in the character pattern stored in memory. A high bit turns a dot on, and a low bit turns a dot off. In the character storage area at each address is a group of bits that turn light dots on and off so that a selected character is displayed (that is, unless the character bit patterns have been disturbed and have become incorrect). In those cases garbage could appear. There is more detail on this process in chapter 22.

2. Brightness-only; no video display (Fig. 1-6). A brightness-only display on the monitor could be a variation of the garbage symptom, or it could be an entirely different symptom. When it is a garbage variation, the trouble is being caused by the computer. When it is not computer trouble, the *CRT* (cathode-ray tube) display itself is the culprit. The trouble must be isolated to one of these two main pieces of hardware.

The easiest way to determine which unit has the trouble is to substitute either the computer or the monitor with another known good piece. If you try a good monitor and the blank brightness remains, odds are the computer contains the trouble. If you substitute the monitor and the correct display returns, the old monitor is proven to be the culprit and needs repair. There is more about monitor diagnosis and repair in this chapter and in chapter 23.

When the computer is indicated as the brightness-only troublemaker, the first step is to check out the video output circuits. Some computers have the video output circuits integrated onto the motherboard. In these instances, the indicated circuits must be checked out with the techniques discussed in chapter 22. Other computers have the video circuits contained on plug-in cards. All you have to do for a checkout is replace the suspect card with a good video card. If the trouble disappears, the fault is on the

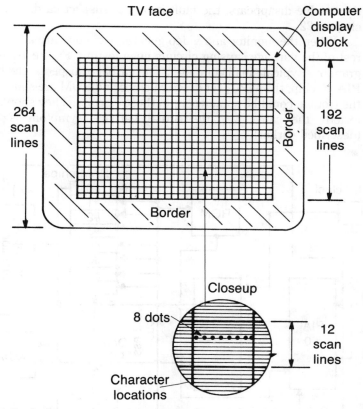

1-5 A closeup of a character block shows it is made up of a number of scan lines. Each block line is composed of light dots. In this example there are 12 lines with 8 dots to a line, producing 96 dots in a block. Each dot can be turned off and on. In ROM there are bit switches for the dots. A high turns a dot on, and a low turns it off. The bits are arranged in character patterns and can form the characters on the display.

1-6 When the video disappears from the screen, only the brightness is left. The loss of video is usually caused by problems in the video output circuit or card in the computer or the monitor itself. The first step is to determine which one has the trouble.

the trouble disappears, the fault is on the suspect card, also discussed in chapter 22.

When the monitor and video generator circuits are all exonerated, the rest of the garbage causing circuits need testing. Figure 1-7 is a block diagram of a typical small computer. The garbage suspects, the keyboard, the PIA #0 chip, the MPU, set of RAM chips and ROM are shown. The seat of the trouble could be somewhere in those circuits. They should be tested in exactly the same way the actual garbage symptom is checked out (described earlier).

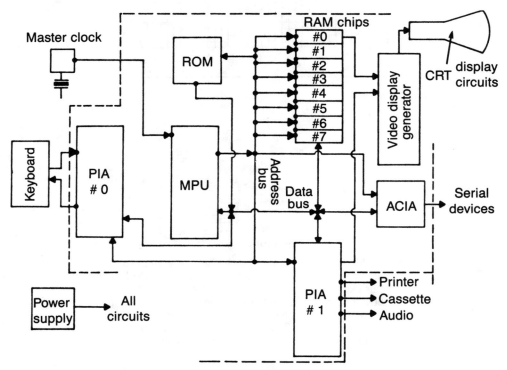

1-7   This block diagram of a typical computer system produces video from key strikes. A character is generated in the keyboard, enters an I/O chip like *PIA* (parallel interface adapter) #0, and is sent to the MPU. The MPU and ROM generate the *ASCII* (American standard code for information interchange) code and stores it in video RAM. The code is also sent to the video display generator and causes the picture tube dot patterns to be displayed. When necessary the code can be output through the *ACIA* (asynchronous communications interface adapter) to a modem or out the PIA #1 to a printer or other peripheral device.

There is one other test measure that can be used with this brightness-only symptom. If the computer under test has an audio circuit, you can use the audio to help separate the suspects. Run a test to find out if the audio is still in operation. This test is covered in chapter 22.

In general, if the audio is operating, the MPU is usually working fine. This means the operating system is o.k. too. The trouble is most likely in the video generator and video output circuits. All of this is discussed in chapter 22.

3. Sync troubles. This is a general category of display troubles that include vertical rolling, picture whipping off into horizontal lines, picture jitter, picture bending, and the like. The computer generates the computer display composed of dots placed onto specific spots on the screen. These dots are supposed to hold still and not stray from their designated positions. If they do move off their spot, in any way, the picture is exhibiting sync trouble.

Computer-generated video, shown in Fig. 1-8, whether it be text or graphics, are still pictures, like photos. This is different than a TV station's moving pictures. The computer simply generates a set of dots on the monitor face. The dots can be turned off and on in monochrome or color. Text is arranged with one keyboard character shown in a character block. Graphics are displayed with individual or groups of dots. When movement is shown in graphics, it is affected by turning dots off and on in ways that make the objects in the display appear to move. When the computer circuits cause sync problems, the dots are not holding in their designated spots.

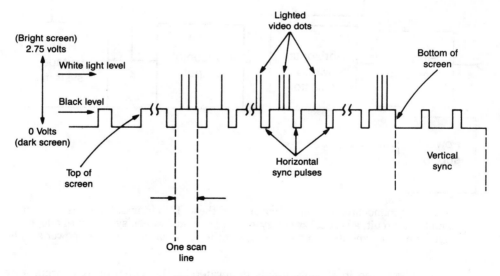

Video signal, one screenful of light

1-8 The video signal generated by a monochrome system, from a voltage point of view, looks like this on a scope. The scope shows voltage vertically. In this example, the vertical parameter is 0 to 2.75 (volts). The brightness varies with the voltage. The higher the voltage, the brighter the picture. One square wave represents one scan line side to side in the display. The scan line is not lit. The dot voltage spikes mounted on the scan line cause dots to light. Note the top of the screen and the bottom with all the scan lines between. There is a horizontal sync pulse after every scan line. There is a vertical scan line after every screenful of light or field.

On the other hand, Fig. 1-9, a typical block diagram shows the computer monitor is a form of TV receiver. It has the same type of sync, horizontal, and vertical circuits that any ordinary TV set has. When the monitor circuits fail, you'll see the picture roll up and down, flop over sideways or whirl off into horizontal lines. These are the same symptoms you've seen on your home TV over the years.

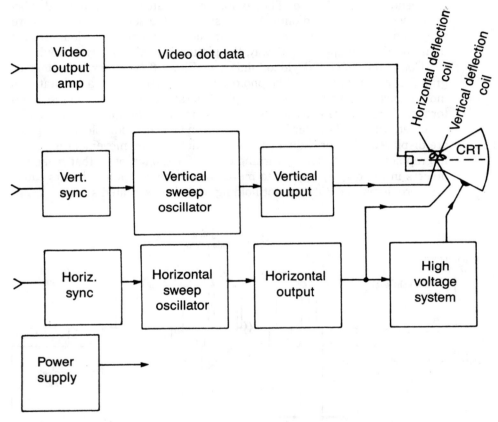

1-9   A typical monochrome monitor consists of these TV circuits. There is a video dot amplifier circuit, a vertical sweep system, a horizontal sweep system with a high voltage by product and its own power supply, different than the computer power supply.

The video in a computer is generated in the video output circuits or video cards. Part of the total video signal are horizontal and vertical sync signals as in Fig. 1-10. These signals are fed to the horizontal and vertical sweep circuits in the monitor. The job of sync signals is to lock the oscillators at specific frequencies. Therefore, when the symptom is sync trouble, the prime suspects are the sync generators in the computer and the oscillator circuits in the monitor. There is much more detail on these circuit areas in chapters 22 and 23.

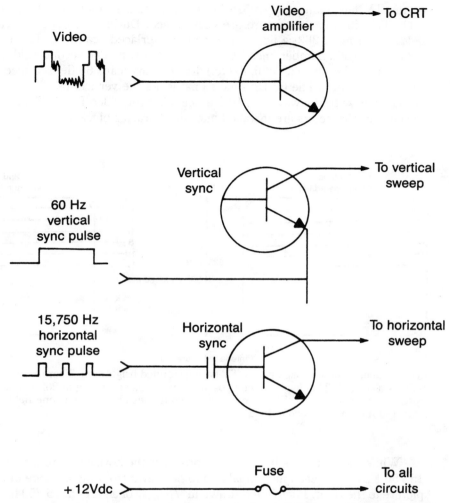

1-10 There are three types of monochrome signals that are applied to the monitor. There is the video, the vertical sync pulses, and the horizontal sync pulses.

The first quick test is to substitute the monitor. If a new monitor works fine, then the old one has the fault. If a new monitor shows the same sync trouble, then the trouble is in the computer. If the computer has a video card generating the sync, try a new card. If the computer has the video circuits integrated onto the motherboard, troubleshooting techniques will have to be used.

Older computer monitors used the same horizontal and vertical frequencies as commercial TV. Vertical oscillators in a home TV run at a frequency of 60 *Hz* (Hertz). Horizontal oscillators run at 15,750 Hz. With these frequencies, a *raster* (the brightness pattern on the display), is drawn on the TV face composed of 525 lines, 30 times a second, shown in Fig. 1-11. The lines in the picture are easy to see. During each second, two fields are drawn, 262½ lines each, called interlaced scanning. The first field has the odd number lines (1, 3, 5, 7, etc.) drawn. The second field has the even number lines (2, 4, 6, 8, etc.) drawn. This scans 60 fields a second over the TV face. The 60 Hz sync signal locks the vertical oscillator into perfect step with the way the MPU is scanning the video RAM. That way the correct characters are installed into the character blocks.

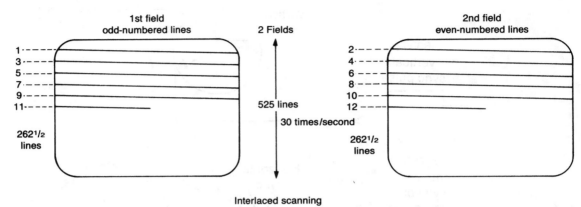

Interlaced scanning

1-11 A conventional monitor display uses TV-type generated brightness. There are 525 scan lines drawn 30 times a second. The display is composed of two fields consisting of 262½ lines each. The fields appear 60 times a second. First the odd numbered lines are drawn as one field and then the even numbered lines as the second field.

While the vertical is ticking away properly, the horizontal frequency of 15,750 Hz causes each individual line to be drawn from the left side of the picture to the right. Each line is drawn in $1/15,750th$ of a second. 15,750 lines/60 fields equals 262.5 lines/field.

In newer computers, a lot of effort has been made to get rid of the obvious lines the picture is made of. The poor resolution of the picture is disturbing in a lot of applications. Fine picture detail becomes blurred. As a result, the frequencies have been altered somewhat in order to make the lines less obvious and produce better resolution.

First of all, the horizontal frequencies have been increased. Instead of the conventional 15,750 Hz, the frequency has been increased. In different systems you'll find frequencies above 30,000 Hz. The higher the frequency, the more lines per second are drawn. If the frequency is doubled, there will be about 1100 lines on the screen instead of 525. Some monitors have raised their frequencies so that 2000 lines are on the screen. At this rate, the lines are almost invisible.

To accommodate the increased number of lines, the vertical frequencies have also been altered. Typical new monitors have vertical frequencies that range between 45 and 75 Hz. Chapters 22 and 23 go into these new frequencies in greater detail. Whatever the frequencies, when these circuits fail, you could have a sync troubleshooting job on your hands.

4. TV monitor-only troubles. When the TV display monitor proves to be the only source of trouble, the following considerations should be reviewed. The monitor bears a strong resemblance to a home TV. Inexpensive monochrome and color monitors are actually nothing more than half a home TV. They have picture tubes and the circuits to drive the picture tube.

Because computer TVs are part of a closed-circuit system with video circuits in the computer, they do not have to be tuned to a transmitted signal as a home TV does. Therefore the tuner, i-f strip, video detector, etc., are not needed in the monitor. The only circuits required are those shown in the Fig. 11-9, block diagram.

The monochrome monitor picture tube in Fig. 1-12 needs the following voltages and signals to drive it. First of all, the electron gun requires filament voltage to heat it up, cathode and control grid bias voltages and input video signals, a dc potential on the screen grid and a variable voltage on the focus grid. Next there is a high dc potential at the high voltage button on the bell of the tube. The circuits that generate these voltages are discussed in chapter 23.

Next the picture tube needs horizontal sweep and vertical sweep signals injected to the sweep coils in the deflection yoke around the CRT bulb neck. Figure 1-13 shows the components. The signals, also discussed in more detail in chapter 23, cause the electron beam from the gun to be swept in the desired patterns across and down the face of the tube faster than the eye can see. The electron beam paints a brightness rectangle on the CRT face that is called a *raster*.

The horizontal sweep signal grabs hold of the cathode ray as it passes through the neck of the bulb and draws a line of light from the left side of the screen to the right, at the home TV frequency of 15,750 lines a second. At the same time, the companion vertical signal, also connected at the bulb neck in the yoke, takes hold of the cathode ray and draws it down and then up 60 times a second. The results of the two signals pushing and pulling the electron beam is the screenful of light consisting of $262^1/_2$ lines of light on the face of the CRT 60 times a second.

The two sweep signals are locked into step with the computer video output by the horizontal and vertical sync signals derived from the computer clock circuits.

Inexpensive TV monitors were the norm up to the mid 1980s. Since then, in order to increase display resolutions, a large number of more expensive monitors have been developed. These newer monitors have increased horizontal frequencies so more horizontal lines can be drawn, increasing resolution. These better monitors also have more versatile

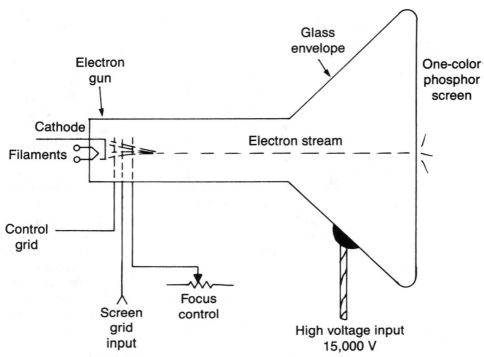

1-12   A monochrome picture tube consists of a glass bulb, an electron gun full of electrodes, and a layer of white, amber, green, or some other color phosphor, on the face panel. The CRT will fire a cathode ray at the phosphor screen to produce light when the filaments are heated, the cathode receives video, the control grid gets a bias voltage, the screen grid gets an acceleration voltage, the focus grid gets a fixed high dc, and a high voltage around 15,000 volts is applied to the HV (high-voltage) input button.

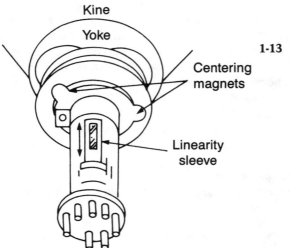

1-13   Around the neck of the CRT are electromagnets and permanent magnets. The electromagnets receive the sweep signals that move the cathode ray across and down the screen to produce the brightness. The permanent magnets can move the ray to effect good centering and linearity.

inputs. However, as far as troubleshooting and repairs go on the newer monitors, they are still serviced in the same way. These newer monitors are also covered in chapter 23. Whether the monitors are old and inexpensive or new and expensive, the general symptoms of trouble remains essentially the same (Fig. 1-14).

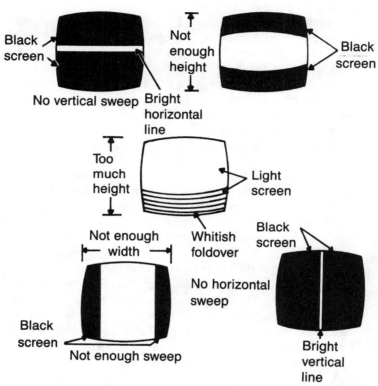

1-14   These sweep symptoms are called no vertical sweep, not enough height, too much height, not enough width, and no horizontal sweep.

(a) Vertical sweep. When the vertical sweep circuits in a monitor develop faults, the symptoms can vary according to which component or circuit section has failed. Remember, the vertical sweep circuit does nothing but draw the electron beam down and back up again and again. Faults can first of all reduce the amount of sweep producing a vertically shrunken raster. This condition produces a display with black areas at the top and bottom of screen. A different fault can cause too much sweep and spread the vertical out too far. A circle displayed on the screen would look like an egg. In addition the sweep could fold over at the bottom of the screen at the same time. Then there are the cases where the vertical sweep fails altogether. When this happens the sweep collapses into a bright white line across the center of the screen. The sweep signal is unable to draw the beam either up or down. When the raster collapses into a bright horizontal line in this way, it is good practice to turn the brightness down. That way the phosphor on the face panel won't be burned by the repeated scanning of the electron beam across the center of the screen.

(b)   Horizontal sweep. Problems in the horizontal-sweep circuits cause similar symptoms but turned 90 degrees. There can be the condition of not enough horizontal sweep with black spaces on the sides of the screen, too much sweep that produces a wide, nonlinear picture or no horizontal sweep, producing a bright vertical line from top to bottom.

The horizontal sweep circuits perform a second important job in addition to drawing the beam across and back on the screen. It must also generate the dc high voltage that is applied to the button on the side of the CRT bell, as shown in Fig. 1-12. The way the sweep signal is able to develop this 15 kV is the following.

In the monitor, Fig. 1-9, there is a special high voltage circuit. The circuit is based around a high voltage transformer called the *flyback*. A portion of the horizontal sweep signal is tapped off and applied to the primary of the flyback. Due to the high frequency of the horizontal sweep signal, as the ac signal rises and then suddenly falls or flys back, an instantaneous high voltage is developed at the primary. This voltage is then stepped up at the secondary of the transformer. The action produces an ac (alternating current) high voltage. A high voltage rectifier then converts the ac to dc. The dc in turn is applied to the button on the CRT bulb. The high dc potential can then strongly attract the electron beam and cause the electrons to forcefully hit the phosphor creating light. There is more detail on the HV generating in chapter 23.

When the horizontal sweep circuit fails, it could kill the HV and brightness will disappear, Fig. 1-15. This is a fairly common trouble.

Black screen

No brightness

1-15   When the brightness disappears from the monitor, it could be caused by the horizontal high-voltage system or the monitor power supply. The first step is to determine which circuit is at fault.

No brightness could also be caused by the monitor main power supply. However, you can tell the difference. If a no brightness condition is caused by the sweep or high voltage circuits, the rest of the monitor would still be running. For instance, if the computer has audio circuits, determine whether the monitor can sound off. If it can, then the trouble is loss of high voltage. Should the audio also be gone, then the condition is probably being caused by the low voltage power supply that is common to both the audio and high voltage circuits. For more detail on these conditions read chapters 23 and 25.

(c) Video troubles. The next input the monitor needs is the video output signals from the computer. The computer acts as a tiny TV transmitter. The computer generates a TV signal. It doesn't send the signal out over the airwaves. It simply connects the video output, by wire, to the monitor. Some computers have the video output circuits integrated onto the motherboard. Other computers use video output cards that plug into slots. Chapter 22 discusses the various video output procedures. Whatever the mode of transmission, whether the video is called composite TV, digital, analog, or what have you, as far as troubleshooting goes, video is video. The video enters the monitor at a video amplifier stage and is then routed to the electron gun of monochrome monitors or to the three guns of color monitors.

The video signal then modulates the electron beam or beams. When the video signal develops troubles, the following symptoms could appear on the monitor face. There are three general video monitor symptoms.

- No video. First of all, there is the case where the video signal leaves the computer o.k. but does not make it to the electron gun and does not modulate the cathode ray. The brightness could disappear completely or appear on the screen with no display. The trouble can be found anywhere along the video signal path from the computer output cable through the monitor video circuits to the destination CRT. The electron gun in the CRT is also a suspect. Chapter 23 contains the techniques to pinpoint the actual troublemaker.

- Weak video. This symptom is simply a variation of no video. When the video output signal exits the computer circuits, it is normally in a weakened condition. In the monitors there are complete video amplifiers and video output circuits just as in any home TV. These circuits process the video, maintain frequency response, and amplifies the video till it is strong enough to drive the electron guns in the CRTs. Usually a weak video display trouble will be caused by a fault in these video amp and output stages.

- Smeary video. This is a rare type of trouble but when it happens it is easy to diagnose. The picture looks like a rag has been wiped over it from left to right. The display smears in that direction. The smearing could happen due to the high frequencies required to display video. The video that is applied to the electron gun has frequencies in the megahertz range. This is in comparison to audio frequencies that are applied to speakers. They are in the kilohertz range.

In order for a spot in a display to change sharply from black to white or white to black, the frequency must be about 4 MHz. If it is lower, the spot change will smear rather than be a clean change. In the video amplifiers there are special resistors and peaking coils that are supposed to maintain the video frequency response. If these components or other video parts fail, the signal applied to the electron gun will not be fast enough to turn the beam off and on at the required frequencies.

As one or more of these video components conk out, the frequency response drops off in the amplifiers and the picture appears to smear. If the amplifiers and other circuits check out o.k., the picture tube itself can also cause this trouble when the gun develops open or shorted electrodes.

5. Power-supply symptoms. There are many variations of power supplies in personal computers and their peripherals. In the early days of microcomputers, there were many units that integrated the computer motherboard with the display monitor. The power supply that came with these units had to take care of the computer and the TV display. There aren't too many of them around anymore in personal computers. Monitors have become devices on their own and now usually have their own power supply. This change simplifies supplies because monitors require TV type supplies which are quite different than the microcomputer supplies. Both the monitor- and computer-type supplies are covered in chapter 25.

Power supplies that only have to energize a computer and not peripherals such as displays and disk drives only need to generate small voltages. Typically, such a supply, shown in Fig. 1-16, only produces dc voltages like + or − 5 volts and + or − 12 V. The main requirement for these small drive voltages is, they must be carefully regulated. That is, they are not permitted to drift up or down in voltage. They must hold that 5 or 12 V steady or else the computing could get messed up.

When these supplies fail, the common symptom you'll encounter is a dead computer. The off-on switch won't turn the computer on. The pilot bulb could be lit or off according to what part failed in the supply. These small supply failures are one of the most frequent types of breakdown. They are usually among the easiest to trace out and repair. There is no complex computer theory required to solve these power supply failures. Chapter 25 covers a typical small supply and provides the repair techniques in detail.

When the supply must not only energize a motherboard, but also provides operating voltages for cards plugged into board slots, the supply, by necessity, is larger. The wattage requirements rise. The supplies become more complicated. When these supplies act up there could be other symptoms besides the classical dead set symptom. For example, a disk drive could quit, a plug-in modem might stop transmitting or receiving, a plug-in FAX (facsimile) system stops operating, etc.

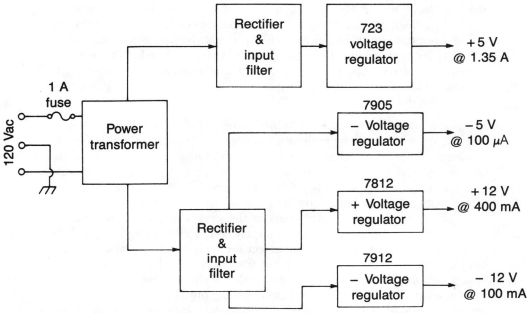

1-16 A small computer only needs + and − 5 V, and + and − 12 V to operate. Its power supply is able to convert the wall socket 120 V ac to those dc voltages.

In the computer monitor, the supplies are feeding TV-type circuits. As a result, when the monitor acts up, television receiver troubles could appear on the screen. The two following symptoms on the monitor face indicate monitor power supply breakdown.

(a) Shrunken display (Fig. 1-17). If the supply is energizing the horizontal and vertical circuits and the supply output voltage loses some of its power, these two sweep circuits weaken and can put a shrunken picture on the display. The picture won't sweep out to the sides of the picture tube or to the top and bottom. This could make the picture appear to shrink on four sides. A variation of this trouble is two sided shrinking.

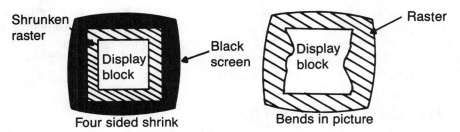

1-17 The common symptoms of power supply failure, besides the dead computer and blown fuse are four-sided shrinking of the display, with or without bending.

(b) Visible hum (Fig. 1-17). When the supply simply loses a degree of power, as above, the picture could shrink, but the sides and/or the top and bottom shrink in but are otherwise o.k. Not so when the picture exhibits visible hum. In those cases, the picture bends. The bending could be fixed or the bending could travel through the picture along with thick black horizontal stripes. The techniques to cure this condition are discussed in chapter 25.

6. Peripheral device symptoms of troubles. When a peripheral device develops trouble, quite often the symptoms are obvious. The ailing peripheral stops working. Other times when the peripheral becomes faulty, the symptoms are not so obvious. The peripheral could develop a short circuit. Because the peripheral is connected to the motherboard in one way or another, the short could make the entire computer go down.

For example, an electrical short in the keyboard could short out the power supply and blow a fuse in the supply. When something like this happens, the first steps to take is disconnect the peripherals one at a time and turn on the computer each time. If the trouble is indeed a short in the keyboard, when you disconnect the keyboard, the short is not attached to the supply anymore and the fuse will stop blowing out.

The same goes for all the other peripherals, especially the ones that have cards plugged into slots on the motherboard. If the computer goes down, pull the cards out of the slots one at a time. Should the computer come back to life once again, odds are good the card is defective and needs a new one or a repair job.

On the other hand, sometimes a bad part in the computer can make a peripheral shut down. For instance, take the case of an AT compatible that comes on for a few seconds and then shuts down the hard disk that was about to boot the machine for action. It turned out that there was a bad RAM chip in the first 128K of the memory map. The computer couldn't pass the first memory test. It shut down the hard disk. Replacing the bad chip on the motherboard allowed the computer to once again boot and the disk stayed on.

You must keep your eyes and mind open for troubles such as these, but for the most part, when a peripheral conks out, the peripheral itself has the trouble. The best test, of course is to install a known good peripheral in place of the one under suspicion. If the new peripheral restores the computer, the old one is definitely defective. If the new peripheral also refuses to work and exhibits the same symptoms of trouble, then the problem is in the computer and not in the peripheral.

Diagnostic programs

The question always arises: if the computer is so good, how come it can't diagnose its own symptoms and then print on the screen the identity of the part causing the trouble? As a matter of fact, it can. However, the situation is not quite that simple.

The big limitation with diagnostic test codes is, if the computer is not working properly, it often can't run the diagnostics. It can only perform the tests, for sure, when the computer is operating as it should. So what good is that?

Despite the fact the diagnostic won't help much when the computer is very sick, it does have some valuable uses when the machine is ailing but still limping along. There are many faulty parts a diagnostic will pinpoint for you.

Sometimes one RAM or ROM chip will go down. A diagnostic could be able to test all the RAMs and ROMs and pick out the defective chip. Other times a video output chip, sound circuit or other I/O chip will develop faults and the diagnostic will test the chip and find the exact trouble. Another area the diagnostic is valuable in is peripheral difficulties. The test code can discern the trouble and let you know if the condition is being caused in the peripheral or in the I/O circuit that is supporting the peripheral. The test programs are not perfect and should be used only in cases where they will work. They become particularly valuable when you use them and you are fully aware of their limitations. In the final analysis of a repair, a component has failed, must be pinpointed, repaired or replaced. Use test codes as part of your arsenal when the opportunity arises and don't depend on it too much.

Most personal computers, as you turn them on, routinely run a few diagnostic tests on the memory and other areas. This procedure is to ensure the fact that the computer is working properly and you do not go to work and hours later find out the machine is faulty and your hard-gained efforts were for naught. There will be more about diagnostics in chapter 10.

Although there are many routine step-by-step procedures to guide you through a repair, at a certain stage, you must use your own common sense and initiate your own troubleshooting moves. Part of your arsenal of service weapons must be little diagnostic software moves that will check out the processor, memory, I/O chips, address and data bus copper lines, video circuits, audio chips, and other items. As you study this book, you'll find hints on using these tricks in the chapters that cover those circuits.

2
The latest test-equipment arsenal

THE MOST IMPORTANT TEST EQUIPMENT IS THE TROUBLESHOOTER'S brain. Your brain is limited, however, in its ability to check out the vital signs of the ailing or dead electronic circuit. Your brain has to rely on only a pair of eyes, ears, sense of touch, smell, and taste. The brain needs some additional pieces of test equipment that are able to read voltages, current, resistance, frequencies, capacitance, and so on. These extra test units then provide the values of the electronic vital signs so the brain can puzzle out which part has the fault.

All electronic circuits, including computers, contain the same components, and these units all fail in the same way. In circuits there are transistors, diodes, capacitors, resistors, switches, connectors, and other components. A lot of the components are microscopic and contained in chips. Others are discrete and are distributed over the print boards of the computer. When a circuit goes down, usually there is only one fault, either microscopic or discrete. Sometimes that single fault will cause damage to a nearby component. However, most of the time, you are looking for just one cause of circuit death. It can occur, but odds are against having more than one trouble happen at the same time.

The way electronic components fail are not complicated. As shown in Fig. 2-1, when a transistor or diode gives up the ghost, a piece of their semiconductor material either breaks, shorts through, or changes its basic chemical composition. A capacitor loses life when its dielectric material burns up, shorts through, or otherwise loses its insulating qualities. Resistors die when the resistive element cracks, burns, or disconnects from the leads. Transformer windings can disconnect or smoulder their insulation off. Fuses blow, plugs corrode, switches break, connections come apart, and copper traces on print boards develop shorts between close spaces or break apart. These faults are ways electronic parts become defunct. It doesn't matter whether the components are microscopic and encased in a chip or

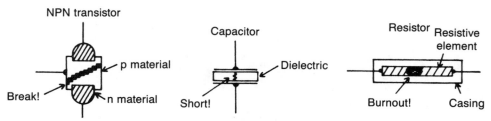

2-1   Transistors fail when their semiconductor material breaks or somehow changes its chemical composition. Capacitors develop faults in their dielectric material. Resistive bodies can crack or burn.

are relatively large, discrete units and are soldered to a print board. They pass away in the same way. When they do, they can bring the entire computer down with them.

When you begin to troubleshoot a sick computer, sometimes you are lucky and you can see breaks or charred parts. Other times you can hear arcing inside a component. On occasion you'll smell overheating or smoke. There could be times when you'll feel a part and it is cool when it should be warm or hot when it should be cool. Your natural senses in those cases become the test equipment that pinpoints the fault. However, most of the time, your senses fall short of doing the job. You must add to your troubleshooting arsenal the pieces of test equipment that will read the circuit's vital signs and indicate where the source of the trouble is located.

Troubleshooting is puzzle solving. In order to figure out what part is bad, you must accumulate a number of clues, and then by deduction come up with a list of prime suspects. Test equipment is the medium by which you obtain your electronic clues. Once you have your suspect list, the parts under suspicion can then be tested one by one until the culprit is identified. After the component with the fault is pinpointed, the troubleshooting part of the job is finished. The actual repair portion of the job can take place. The repair can be the replacement of the dead part, the reconnection of a break in the wiring, the disconnection of a short circuit or whatever it takes to relieve the problem the fault has caused.

The pinpointing of defective components can often be accomplished satisfactorily with just a few pieces of test equipment. You can use a voltmeter, logic probe, and a low voltage continuity tester for a lot of repairs. On occasion you'll find it useful to have your old TV service scope to check out some video readings. Another useful item is a logic clip, Fig. 2-2, which is little more than a device that clips onto a chip and extends the tiny legs of the chip, which are valuable test points where readings can be made.

There are lots of other supplementary test pieces such as logic pulsers, current tracers, frequency counters, and multitrace scopes. There are also some really fancy, expensive units that substitute external processors for the circuits under test.

Another type of test equipment is diagnostic software. The big drawback with software is that it is useless for repair jobs where the computer is not operating.

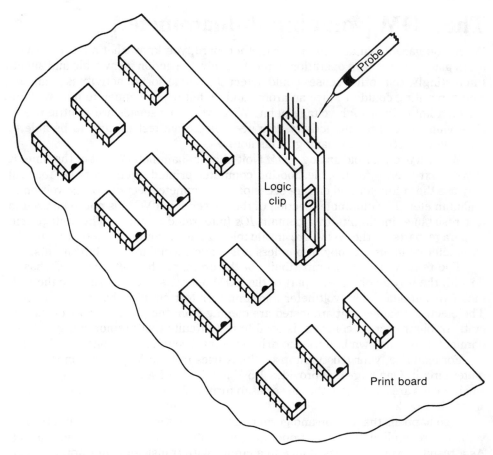

2-2 A logic clip is little more than a handy extension of the pins on a chip. Instead of burrowing into a print board to test tiny pins, use the clip to extend the pins out into the open where they are easily tested.

However, once you get a computer running, the software is invaluable to check the machine out before putting it back into service. Software diagnostics has its greatest value when you need to exercise a working computer.

Software can also come in handy when you are working on some subtle trouble that is causing incorrect results in a computer that otherwise appears to operate properly. There are times when the troubleshooting question becomes: is the problem due to a breakdown in the hardware or a glitch in the program you are running? Diagnostic software can often help you answer that question. You can exercise the hardware with the diagnostics. If the hardware works o.k. when driven by the diagnostics, then the hardware is exonerated as the troublemaker. The suspect software needs checkout.

The VOM (volt-ohm-milliammeter)

When you gaze down at a computer motherboard, you know that a lot of activity takes place while it is in operation. Unfortunately, the action is invisible and silent. Interestingly, your other senses could detect that some sort of activity is going on. The computing could produce an aroma and be felt if you happen to put your finger on a hot chip or high voltage point. Whatever, your senses are of little use in observing the computing activity. You need electronic test devices to be able to examine the action in a meaningful fashion.

You will use your old analog *VOM* (volt-ohm-milliammeter) most of the time. It is your sixth sense for troubleshooting computer printed circuit boards. You will only use the voltmeter and on rare occasions the ammeter sections of the volt-ohm-milliammeter. The ohmmeter section of the conventional VOM is not to be used to test resistance in circuits that contain *ICs* (integrated circuits). The voltage and amperage parts of the VOM are invaluable to check computer activity, but the ohmmeter contains a booby trap unless it is made special to test chip circuits.

The reason for the incompatibility of the ordinary ohmmeter with ICs has to do with the way an ohmmeter part of the VOM operates in comparison to the voltmeter or ammeter. The voltmeter and ammeter test circuits that are energized. The electrical values that are tested are coming from the power supply of the circuit. An ohmmeter, in contrast, is used to test circuits that are not energized. An ohmmeter uses its own batteries to drive current through a component under test.

For example, your trusty Simpson 260K uses five 1.5 V batteries in the ohmmeter circuit. One large cell provides 1.5 V for the R × 1 and R × 100 ranges. Four smaller cells are added together in series to furnish 7.5 V for the R × 1000 range, as shown in Fig. 2-3.

It so happens that silicon and germanium junctions in transistors turn on when voltages are applied. They start operating with applied voltages well under a volt. As a result, if you test a resistance in a circuit with transistors, you would be getting confusing readings as the tiny transistors in the silicon chips began operating. Even worse, the voltage could cause puncturing of glassy insulators on the transistors, killing the chip. This would induce additional troubles into the board, confusing you to no end, slowing the repair, and jacking up the cost of the repair. Of course, this worse-case scenario might not happen, but why not do the job correctly? Use a low-voltage continuity tester. Figure 2-4 describes a typical tester. If you can't buy one, build it.

The voltmeter and ammeter part of the VOM is quite safe and convenient. There is no battery output. The unit under test supplies the electrical energy. The voltage test is made by connecting the probes in parallel with the circuit to be tested. The analog voltmeter is simply a sensitive meter movement and has its needle moved as a tiny amount of current comes out of the computer circuit and courses through the movement winding. The range scale processes the incoming current through precision resistors and deflects the needle safely for both meter and computer. You use the ammeter tests amperes or milliamperes by installing the meter in series with the circuit under test. Most of the time, during computer testing, the voltmeter of the VOM is used. The ammeter is used rarely if at all.

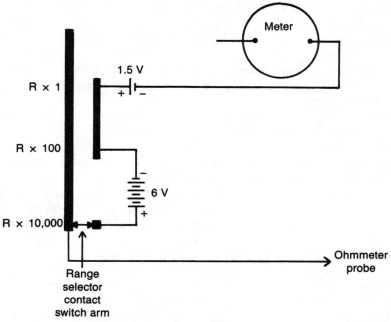

2-3 Older-style ohmmeters were not designed to test chips. The batteries supply too much voltage.

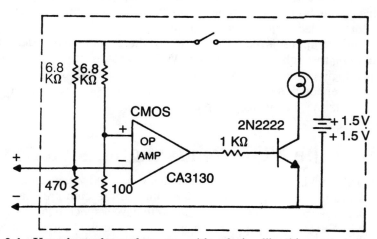

2-4 Use a low-voltage ohmmeter with a design like this one to test resistance in circuits with chips.

This section discusses the logic probe. Quite often the VOM, with either an analog or digital readout, can be used instead of a logic probe. Different technicians develop different test habit patterns. There are pro and con arguments for both units. For instance, the VOM has a one-lead advantage over the logic probe.

The logic probe requires you to connect two leads to the circuit under test. If the logic in the circuit is +5 V for a logic 1, or as it is called, a high, and zero volts for a logic 0, or a low, two leads must be connected—one to a +5 V test point and a second lead to the zero test point, which is usually ground. A third lead is then used to make the actual touchdown for the reading. During each test, one or more of a number of *LEDs* (light-emitting diode) will light or not according to the logic state on the test point.

The VOM, on the other hand, only has one lead connected to the circuit. That lead is attached to zero volts, which is usually ground. There are many obvious ground connections all over the board. Any of them will do, although it is good practice to find a ground in the circuit under test. The second lead is used for the touchdown. The VOM will then read the actual voltage, either by means of a needle pointer in an analog VOM or a digital readout in a *DMM* (digital multimeter). Typically, when either meter reads +5 V that is equivalent to the logic probe high or *H*. When the voltmeter reads near a low of zero volts, that means the same thing as a logic probe showing a low or *L*.

In addition to being able to make digital circuit tests, the VOM will also read analog circuit voltages. A logic probe is not designed to read analog circuits. With the VOM, you also have the capability to quickly test voltages in the power supply, both sides of a digital-to-analog converter, the video output display circuits and others, that the logic probe cannot. The VOM can make all of these tests without changing any connections and only need to turn the range switch as needed. Do not assume the logic probe is not needed; it is. It too has its strengths as described later in this chapter. The logic probe is able to make some tests the VOM cannot. They are both needed in your weapons inventory.

While your computer is operating normally, there can be five different types of signals coursing through the circuits. The VOM is able to let you "see" four of the signals. The logic probe gives you a view of the fifth signal. The logic probe also shows you its version of some of the other signals. The signals are the logic highs, logic lows, tristating, no signal, and pulse signals.

The way the VOM reads digital signals

When you are checking out a digital chip with a voltmeter, you interpret the needle movements in the following way. The bare pins on the chip are the test points. Each pin, under normal operation is supposed to have a specific logic signal coursing through it. You test the chip to make sure that prescribed signal is present. If it is there, that pin, to all appearances is operating properly. Should the signal be missing or incorrect, that is a clue that indicates trouble.

To test *TTL* (transistor-transistor logic) chips, the range switch on the VOM is set so that +5 V can be seen easily. You can set the range switch on the 10 V scale. That way, when +5 V is encountered on a pin, the needle swings up about halfway on the scale. The +5 V is immediately apparent.

The negative probe is connected to a convenient chassis ground. Next, if it is easy to do, attach a logic clip. A logic clip, as shown in Fig. 2-2, is simply a device that extends the tiny leg test points so that the pin readings are made in an easier fashion. It is a test point adapter. If the clip does not fit quickly onto a suspect chip, don't bother with it—test the actual pins.

As shown in Fig. 2-5, a TTL chip, a logic high or H is any + dc voltage that reads from + 2.5 to + 5 V. A logic low or L is any + dc voltage between 0 and + 0.8 V. Any voltage that lies between these limits, that is between + 0.8 and + 2.5 V, is not a valid logic signal. This in-between voltage is called *tristating* or *three stating*. Some technicians call it *floating*.

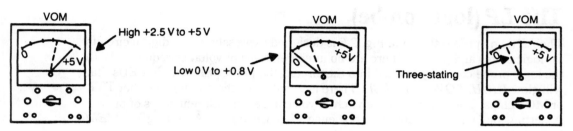

2-5   The VOM can quickly test for highs, lows, and some tristating.

A tristating test point means the test point is shut down as far as logic signals go but is still connected into the circuit. A high impedance builds up, and static voltage in the circuit develops at that point due to circuit noise. The voltmeter responds to the meaningless static charge. The VOM reads voltage whether it is static or intelligent signals.

If you find such a voltage, you can double check it with the logic probe. The logic probe shows nothing during tristating. If perchance the logic probe does show a high or low, then the voltmeter reading is misleading and the pin is not tristating but is actually a high or low as the logic probe indicates.

The other important form of chips, the *MOS* (metal-oxide semiconductor) type, acts in a similar but not exactly the same way as a TTL, during VOM testing. Both the TTL and MOS chip types are discussed in greater detail throughout the book. An MOS chip high is any voltage of + 4.2 V or higher. A low is any voltage of + 1.8 V or lower. The voltages between + 1.8 and + 4.2 V are the tristating voltages.

Tristating is tricky during troubleshooting. The chip might be tristating according to circuit design, or it might be tristating because the chip has died. Check your service notes to determine whether the chip is in fact designed with tristating ability. If it does have tristating circuits built in, the condition could be normal. If it is not designed to tristate, then if you find it doing so, the chip could be defective.

The above tests are the ones that are used the most when testing digital chips. Later on in the book, there are discussions on service notes called *logic charts*. These are lists of all the pins on all the chips in a computer that shows the logic states, highs, lows, or tristating that should be present under normal operation.

The technique to use these service charts is to test pin after pin and compare the results to the charts. Any deviation from what the charts say should be on the pins indicates that trouble could be nearby.

After a bit of practice, you can test pins quickly with a VOM and tell if chip readings are normal or not. The logic probe also gives you the capability to test the same pins to "see" the same signals. The way the logic probe displays the signals is quite different than the VOM. You must learn to take these readings in both ways.

The *LP* (logic probe)

The *LP* (logic probe) shown in Fig. 2-6 is designed expressly to test digital circuits for logic states and pulses. There are no interpretations of voltages required. With the logic probe correctly hooked into the circuit, the probe will turn on LEDs that will glow *HIGH, LOW,* or *PULSE.* There is a switch for the reading of either TTL or MOS chips. There is a second switch so you can detect different types of pulses. A setting on pulse indicates the presence of pulse trains. A setting on *MEM* locates a one-shot pulse and stores it.

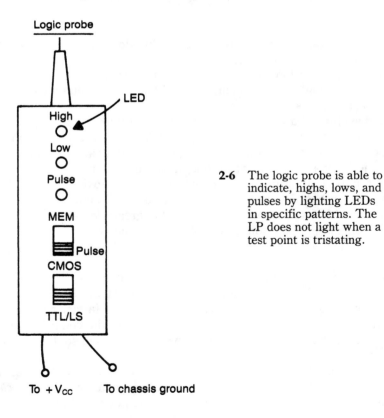

2-6 The logic probe is able to indicate, highs, lows, and pulses by lighting LEDs in specific patterns. The LP does not light when a test point is tristating.

As mentioned, the logic probe needs two connections before its probe will read logic states. It requires two connections because it must be attached across the type of voltage under test. Most of the time chips receive about +5 V as drive voltage. When testing a +5 V leg, the probe must be connected to the +5 V input. Other times the circuit could be powered with +15 V. When testing a +15 V leg, the probe must be attached across +15 V. Should you connect the probe to the wrong voltage source, the resulting logic readings will be incorrect. The LP will be seeking out highs and lows that are proportional to the wrong voltage source.

When you hook the two power probes into the computer, the logic probe becomes a circuit of the computer and is energized by the computer power supply. If you connect into the +5 V leg, the LP is a +5 V device tester. Connected to +15 V, the LP is a +15 V tester.

A typical logic probe glows through LED indicators. Some LPs, in addition to the LEDs, also have some sort of audio tone indicator. With the audio tones, one distinctive tone for a high and another tone for a low, you can keep your gaze fixed on the tiny test pins and not have to glance over at the LED readings. That is faster and also safer. Your fingers are less likely to slip and cause an accidental short in the energized circuit.

There is usually one LED and separate tones for HIGH and LOW. Note there is no indication for tristating. If a pin is in a tristate condition, the probe will not light or sound off. As mentioned earlier, the probe will double check an apparent tristate condition a VOM might detect. However, the logic probe is the final word. Should a VOM read what looks like a tristating pin, but the logic probe says it is a high or low, the logic probe is final. Only when the probe will not light will the VOM tristate finding be confirmed. When the logic probe shows a HIGH, LOW, or PULSE glow when the VOM indicates tristating, then believe the logic probe.

Typically an LP has three LEDs. The lights can assume one of seven combinations during a test. Table 2-1 shows the meanings of the seven combinations. Go through these important test conditions one by one. The first combination shows all three lights off. This will happen if the probe is not connected properly to an otherwise energized computer. This also happens if the test point has broken away from the circuit. Another possibility is the test point is tristating. There could be some static voltage buildup but the voltage is not defined for the logic probe. The probe can't detect such an illogical voltage. The VOM will recognize it because the VOM is responsive to any voltage analog, digital, defined or static. The logic probe cannot.

The second LED condition happens when the probe touches down on a test point with a HIGH. The HIGH LED goes on. This is a clear indisputable indication that a HIGH is on the test point. There is no signal movement. There is a HIGH voltage duration holding steady on the test node.

The third indication is the one where only the LOW LED lights up. There is a definite LOW on the test point. Like the HIGH reading, there is no pulsing signal going on, just the LOW duration of the signal wave holding steady on the test point.

**Table 2-1. A typical logic probe is able to form
seven patterns that indicate the condition that exists at a test point.**

	LEDs			Signal	Explanation
	High	**Low**	**Pulse**		
0	○	○	○	None	Probe not attached Test point dead Test point three-stating
4	☀	○	○	5 V ⌐̄ ⌐̄	Test point held high
2	○	☀	○	5 V	Test point held low
5	☀	○	☀	High duration Pulses	High with pulse
3	○	☀	☀	Low duration	Low with pulse
1	○	○	☀	⎍⎍⎍⎍⎍	Square wave more than 100 kHz
	☀	☀	☀	⎍⎍⎍	Square wave less than 100 kHz

The next indications are combinations of PULSE and logic state conditions. If the HIGH and PULSE LEDs both light, it means there is a wave train at the node, with positive going durations between pulses. When the LOW and PULSE LEDs are both lit, it means there is a wave train at the node with negative going durations between pulses.

In the past few paragraphs the words *duration* and *pulse* were mentioned. In a graph of a square wave cycle, as shown in Fig. 2-7, the bottom of the wave is typically at zero volts, a low, while the top of the wave is at +5 V, the high. The

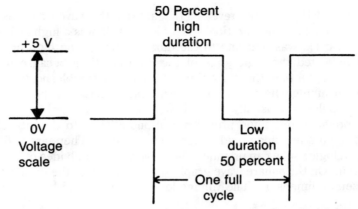

2-7   In a square wave, the highs and lows are called *durations*.

amount of time, measured in nanoseconds (billionths of a second), the wave stays at a high or low is called the *duration*. In a true square wave, the high and low durations are equal. They are each said to have *duty cycle* of 50%. This is the nature of a true square wave.

When the square wave changes its duty cycle from 50% to some other percentage, the wave is no longer square. For example, if the high duty cycle is 75% and the low is 25%, then the wave is no longer square. When this happens, the high with its longer time stretch still retains its identity as a duration, but the low with the shorter time elapsing is transformed into a pulse. Figure 2-8 illustrates negative going and positive going pulses.

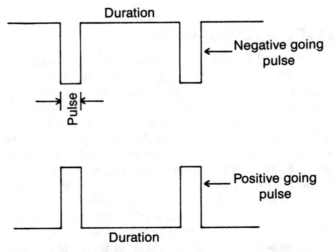

2-8   When a high or low takes up less than 50% of a full cycle time, they are called *pulses*.

The last LED possibility revealed the fact that the wave train was not a square wave but a PULSE. The duration time of each cycle was a high or low. The pulse time of the cycle was opposite to the duration time. The high or low the LED revealed indicated the logic state of the duration time because it has a much greater duty cycle than the pulse time. Actually for troubleshooting, the probe is simply determining whether or not there is a pulse on the test point. The highs and lows of the pulses are usually ignored.

The previous five logic probe indications all had to do with checking test points to see if a test node read a high, low, or pulse. There are two more indications that a logic probe can provide. They give you a rough idea of the frequency of a wave train. On the square wave graph, the frequency or the timing of the wave is the horizontal dimension. The voltage level is represented by the vertical dimension.

The three LEDs will light in certain patterns to designate the approximate frequency of a true square wave on a test point. If the wave is less than 100 kHz all three LEDs will light. A square wave has a 50/50 duty cycle so both the high and low LEDs plus the PULSE LED will light. When indeed all three LEDs light, then you know that you are dealing with a wave train that has a frequency of less than 100 kHz. This, of course, is not a precision result but it can be useful in some go/no go test situations.

When the frequency is above 100 kHz, as it is in most computer circuits, then the durations are happening so fast that the ordinary logic probe can't respond by lighting the high and low LEDs. The PULSE LED though will respond and light brightly. This test indication definitely tells you that a wave train on a test node is present and is above 100 kHz. That is the limitation of the inexpensive logic probe. This pulse test is an important one and will be covered in more detail in later chapters.

A TV service oscilloscope

The ordinary, inexpensive TV repair oscilloscope can't be used to display computer-generated wave shapes all over the unit, but it can be very valuable in some of the sections. The computer is one part of a closed-circuit TV system. The computer puts together a television-type signal, places the computed data bits into the signal, and then transmits the completed signal to the TV display monitor. Inside the monitor are TV circuits and a picture tube. An ordinary TV repair oscilloscope is able to display practically all of these TV signals. It is a valuable piece of test gear for your arsenal. Examine an ordinary scope, usually called an x-y.

It's called x-y because it displays a picture on its CRT in the form of an x-y graph. The graph has a horizontal x dimension that shows frequency or timing. The vertical y dimension illustrates voltage levels according to the height of the wave shape input. The typical TV scope is restricted to displaying signals up to about 100 kHz. You can set the horizontal sweep of the display from 0 to about 100 kHz. Once set, the scope starts drawing a green line across the black screen at the frequency you set it at.

This horizontal line that can be adjusted to draw green light across the screen at any frequency between 0 to 100 kHz, can be set to match the frequency a suspect circuit is running at. For example, suppose your video display in a PC disappears and you decide to trace the video from the video card to the display monitor. You know that one line of video on the screen is drawn at the rate of 15,750 Hz. Therefore you set the horizontal time base x part of the scope graph to the horizontal frequency of 15,750 Hz. This matches the frequency you want to take a look at.

The y part of the scope graph represents the voltage level of the frequency you want to test. The voltage level is obtained by taking the scope probe and touching down on a test point. The peak-to-peak voltage at that point will be sampled and injected into the scope vertical circuits and expand the horizontal line in accordance to the amount of *P-P* (peak-to-peak) video voltage that is on the test point. Figure 2-9 shows what one line of video looks like on the scope. There is more about this video in chapters 12, 22, and 23. If the voltage is large the vertical height of the line will be great. Should the voltage be small the line will not expand very much.

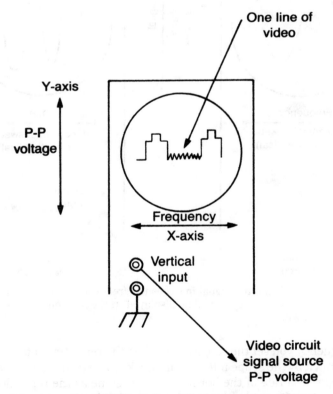

2-9 An ordinary TV repair oscilloscope can provide valuable graph pictures of the video display circuits.

For example, suppose you want to take a look at one cycle of the 60 Hz sine wave coming out of your 110 V wall socket. You'd set the scope horizontal frequency at 60 Hz. Next you would take the scope probe and touch down on the hot side of the line. A voltage of 110 V ac then enters the scope's vertical input and expands the horizontal line 110 volts P-P. On the screen will be displayed sine waves as shown in Fig. 2-10. The sine wave is shown as rising and falling P-P voltage. When the voltage is at a peak it will expand the vertical y line to a maximum. When the voltage is at a null the vertical y line collapses to minimum. The amount of voltage makes the scope vertical sweep rise and fall according to the instantaneous voltage of the moment. This test shows full wave cycles of the power company's output.

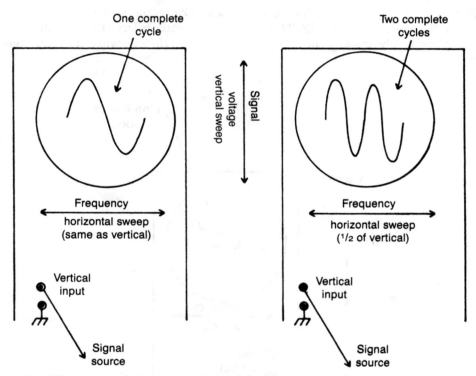

2-10   When the vertical input signal matches the frequency of the internal horizontal sweep in a scope, one cycle will be displayed. If the horizontal is ¹/₂ the vertical, two cycles will show.

The frequency you set the scope on is called the repetition rate. The horizontal line that is drawn by the scope internal circuits keeps repeating itself over and over. When the repetition rate of the horizontal is the same as the repetition rate of the signal applied from an external test point to the vertical input, one complete cycle of the signal being tested will be displayed on the scope face. If the repetition rate is half the vertical, two cycles will appear. Should the repetition rate be one-tenth the input signal frequency, ten cycles will be shown. If you take a scope picture of a 1 MHz clock signal in a small computer, with the scope running at 100 kHz it will display 10 cycles of the computer clock, which can be discerned easily.

As the frequencies of computer clocks increase, as you test for the clock with an x-y scope, the number of cycles that will be displayed increases. Suppose your computer operates with a 4 MHz clock. This is 40 times the top operating frequency of the scope. You can't get these scopes to show one cycle of this 4 MHz signal. However, you can take a scope picture and you will see 40 cycles displayed. The 40 cycles will appear as one picture and will be in the form of an envelope, as in Fig. 2-11. The appearance of the envelope therefore is proof positive that the clock is running. This is important servicing information during troubleshooting and after a repair.

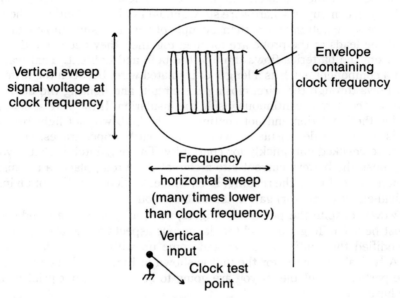

2-11 When the vertical input is many times the internal horizontal, an envelope appears.

In addition to the clock circuit itself, the clock signal is applied to many of the circuits and travels over address and data bus lines. The inexpensive x-y scope is able to give you a quick look see throughout the computer and provide you with all sorts of information. In high-frequency circuits you might not be able to obtain the frequency the circuit is operating at but you will know if it is running or not running.

Besides being able to test computer generated video signals, the complete video monitor and clock frequencies, the x-y scope is also useful in mouse circuits, joysticks, inputs and outputs to audio circuits, and other low-frequency areas. If you must know the exact frequency a circuit is operating at, then you must employ a frequency counter and an expensive multiple-trace, high-frequency scope. These specialized pieces of equipment are covered in this chapter.

Continuity testing

One of the most important pieces of test equipment is the simple continuity tester. Earlier in this chapter the VOM was discussed. In the VOM is an ohmmeter that has restricted uses in computer troubleshooting because it can cause confusing readings and possible damage to chips, because of its excessive battery voltage. In addition, an ohmmeter is a device that, as it pumps some of its own battery current through a component to be tested, then provides the actual number of ohms in the component. A continuity tester, in contrast, does not give an ohms number. A continuity tester simply tells you whether a circuit or component has a dead short or an open. A dead short is a resistance near zero ohms and an open circuit is shown as an infinite number of ohms. The test is a go/no go type.

In addition to the ohmmeter as a continuity tester, an ordinary continuity tester that you can buy in a hardware store should not be used either. The garden-variety testers are nothing more than a couple of batteries and bulb contained in a probe. If the leads of the probe are touched together, they become a dead short, current from the batteries flows through the bulb and lights it. That way, if you connect a component, such as a length of insulated wire, between the tester leads, current flows through the wire, closing the circuit, and lighting the bulb. The lit bulb proves the wire is continuous inside the insulation. If the wire should be broken inside the insulation and not continuous, the bulb will not light because the circuit is open. Besides insulated wire, print board copper traces, connections, etc., can be checked out quickly for continuity. The only hitch is that if you accidentally push the battery current into a chip at the wrong place, a transistor can get turned on, confusing the reading. Even worse, a silicon junction or an insulated *FET* (field-effect transistor) gate could be blown out.

However, despite the potential dangers, continuity testers are indispensable and must be used. To get around the dangerous aspects of the tester, technicians have modified the continuity tester and come up with a low-voltage continuity tester. A typical schematic for the unit is shown in Fig. 2-4. The circuit is simple and the parts are available. If you are going to be checking out print boards it's best to have one.

The circuit can be built and installed into an ordinary hardware type tester. Just remove the old circuit and use the case. The circuit uses the same batteries and bulb, in most instances. The additional components are an NPN transistor such as a 2N2222 and a CMOS comparator like a CA3130.

The NPN transistor acts as a switch for the bulb. The batteries, bulb and transistor are all in series. When the transistor turns on it lights the bulb. The *op amp* (operational amplifier) controls the conduction of the transistor. The op amp connection is attached to one of the tester leads. The other lead is attached to the emitter of the transistor and the biasing resistors of the op amp. When a short circuit is between the leads, the op amp output goes high and turns on the NPN, which lights the bulb. Should an open circuit be between the leads, the op amp output goes low, turns off the NPN, and the bulb will not light.

The battery puts out + 3 V. This is enough voltage to power the CA3130 when it is wired as shown in Fig. 2-4. The + 3 V will also light the pilot bulb and energize the 2N2222 transistor. The resistor values shown biases the op amp so the input voltage to the component under test cannot exceed 0.2 V. This is not enough voltage to accidentally turn on a silicon junction that needs 0.6 V to conduct. This small voltage also will not rupture an insulated gate. It is safe to check out chips made of silicon with this short-open tester.

Logic pulser

There are many ways to test computer circuits as you will learn in the next two chapters. The voltmeter, logic probe, ordinary x-y scope, and continuity tester are used to conduct most of the troubleshooting tests. There are some other pieces of equipment that also find use, though not as often as these pieces. One such unit is a signal injection device, the logic pulser. It is usually made in the form of a probe. It connects to the circuit in the same way the logic probe does. There are two connections that go to +5 V and chassis ground.

The pulser is able to generate a square wave cycle. While the computer is energized, the pulser probe is touched to a test point. There is a button on the pulser. At the correct time the button is pressed. The probe then injects one complete square wave cycle to the test point. A square wave, starting with a high, falling to a low and then going high once again enters the circuit under test.

This injection of one square wave cycle is able to make a test point that is in a high state momentarily go low. On some chip pins, this low will turn on the test point. This activity could tell the troubleshooter whether or not the circuit is operating.

The major difficulty with this technique is that you must be very familiar with the circuit under test. For instance, if you have a service manual of the unit you are working on and you are following a diagnostic flowchart, the chart might instruct, "pulse the test point." If the circuit turns on, it will mean follow the flow to the left. Should the circuit not respond then it means follow the flow to the right.

Tests like these are often needed on the service bench of a manufacturing plant. It is used for product design, quality control and assembly line troubleshooting. If you are a kit builder or hobbyist the pulser could be a welcome addition to your test equipment arsenal.

Current tracer

Another probe-type device is the current tracer. This is a unit that can pick out spots on a print board where ac current is coursing due to a short. It has a tiny coil in its tip. When you touch down on a test point, the pickup coil will by electromagnetic induction, detect an ac (not dc) current. The coil will pick up the magnetic waves of a wave train as it goes from high to low and back to high. It will not respond to any movement from a steady dc current. When the tracer detects an ac current, it has a pilot bulb that will light.

Current tracers usually have a sensitivity control. The settings could be, for instance, between 1 and 8. The settings do not show any electrical characteristic, they are just there to show a range between 1 and 8. The setting at 1 is the most sensitive, and 8 is the least sensitive. When setting 1 lights the bulb, that shows there is at least 300 μA of current flowing at the test node. If there is more than 300 μA, for instance 1 mA, the bulb will light somewhat brighter. Should the current be as much as 3 mA, the bulb will light even brighter.

The angle at which the current tracer is placed on the test point is critical. In order to detect an ac flow the coil in the tip must cut the electromagnetic lines of force at the correct angle. If the current path is 90 degrees out of phase with the pickup coil, the tracer will not detect the current flow. When you use the tracer, always rotate and move the position of the tracer around the test point. As you use a tracer you will quickly get the feel of it and will use it correctly.

There is one very trying type of short circuit that the tracer can be found to be worth its price many times over. That is when a continuity tester isolates a short that has developed in a circuit that has a lot of parallel branches. In computers there are many such circuit networks. One example is shown in Fig. 2-12. When a short develops in these circuits, the actual fault can be in one of the many lines. In order to pinpoint the leg with the fault, the usual technique is to disconnect one leg at a time and check the freed leg with a continuity tester for a short.

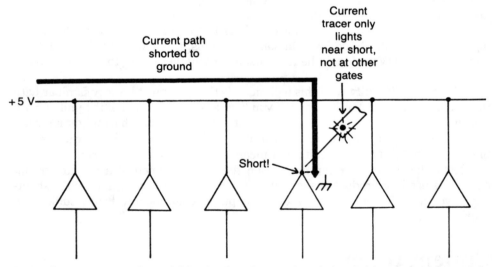

2-12   A current tracer is useful in circuits where a short is located in a group of parallel legs. It can often pick out the leg with the fault.

This can be a time-consuming, tedious procedure. All the legs will test o.k. except the one with the fault. Without the current tracer, you must cut or desolder each leg in turn and check the disconnected leg with the continuity tester. Then when it checks out o.k., you must resolder the connection and disconnect the next leg. In tiny circuit areas, this can result in causing more troubles with the knife or soldering iron.

With the current tracer, you can avoid all the cutting and soldering. All you have to do is energize the circuit, touch down on each leg test point in turn, and measure the relative amounts of current that is coursing through each leg.

In a TTL circuit with a normal high output, current flow should measure a miniscule 40 μA. The TTL circuit with a low output should show a current of 1.6 milliamps. However, when a TTL has a short the current could rise to as much as 55 mA. While the normal current of 40 μA will not be noted by the tracer, the fault current of 55 mA will light the bulb brightly, indicating a short circuit at that point.

The fault finding is therefore easy. Without any cutting or soldering the current tracer is touched down at all suspect parallel leg test points one by one. The short, which is causing a fault current of 55 mA to flow only in the one bad leg, will light the bulb as the test node at that leg is probed. None of the other test points at the other legs will light the bulb at all. The leg with the fault is found. That one leg can be then tested and the short found and remedied. In this actual instance a gate was shorted and replaced to effect the repair.

The frequency counter

Probably every large computer servicing shop has a frequency counter. They are relatively expensive instruments. They are vital in a design lab or manufacturing quality control and troubleshooting section, but they are rarely used in daily personal computer troubleshooting and repairing.

Frequency counters for typical computer repairs can perform one important job—they can measure the exact frequency of the clock crystal. However, a good oscilloscope, discussed next, will also do the same job. Most of the time, in troubleshooting, it is not of much practical use to learn the exact frequency of the clock. The main test is to determine if the clock is running and if it is ticking away around its prescribed frequency. This technique is easily performed by other means as discussed in chapter 13. If you are into design or doing hobby work, the frequency counter could be a welcome addition to your test equipment shelf but for straight servicing or maintenance it has little or no use.

Should you have a counter, it is advisable to use a pickup loop rather than connect the counter directly into the circuit under test. A direct connection will often load the circuit somewhat and cause incorrect readings. The inductive pickup loop, for the most part, avoids this complication.

If you do perform work in servicing that does require the use of a frequency counter, there are some facts that could be important to you. First of all, ordinary counters are only accurate when testing high frequencies. If you test low frequencies, the counter becomes increasingly inaccurate the lower the frequency becomes. However, when testing clocks that are running in the megahertz range, those frequencies read out very accurately. Should you need great accuracy at low frequencies, you'll need to get a very expensive counter that is built around microprocessor circuits that operate as reciprocal counters.

A second fact to understand has to do with the counter oscillator. In counters only quartz crystals are used. There are different qualities of quartz crystals. The less expensive your counter is the lower the crystal quality will be. If your application is not too critical you could get by with a lessor quality crystal.

In addition, crystals age. As they get older they lose some of their stability and are affected by normal changing temperatures in their environment. What you'll notice is that the crystals experience some frequency drift. Usually you can restore the crystals and compensate for aging somewhat with recalibration of the counter.

Frequency counters have a front end where the signal being tested is injected. The front end circuits have a certain input sensitivity, should have a flat frequency response and have a good noise immunity. Naturally the more expensive the counter, the better the front end will be.

Multiple-trace oscilloscopes

If you look at a factory service manual, you'll find scope pictures to go along with the computer schematic and alignment notes. The scope pictures show you what voltage waveforms should look like at specific test points. To utilize the scope pictures, such as Fig. 2-13, you need a scope that can take more than one picture at a time. For example there are many scopes that take two pictures at the same time. There are two separate input connectors, each equipped with its own probe. You can touch down at two separate computer test points. Channel A will be displayed on the top half of the screen, and channel B will be seen at the bottom half of the same screen.

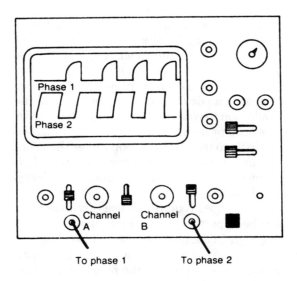

2-13 An expensive dual-trace oscilloscope is useful to view two wave shapes operating at high frequencies at the same time.

The two pictures can be taken using the same horizontal frequency and lined up with each other. They can then be compared to each other. They also can be compared to the prescribed picture of what they should look like, in the service manual. If the scope pictures match up with the service manual photo or sketch, then those test points are operating correctly. Should the pictures on the scope not match up with what is supposed to be on the test points, that could be a clue to trouble.

As mentioned in this chapter, the waveforms have two parameters, one horizontal and the other vertical. The horizontal shows the frequency of the wave, and the vertical shows the voltage. In the inexpensive x-y scope discussed, the horizontal frequency was described in hertz or cycles per second. In these more expensive multiple trace scopes, the horizontal frequency is described by telling how much time it takes for the wave shape to travel through one graticule division (those little blocks). The divisions are shown as little squares in Fig. 2-14. The scope picture is labeled with the timing. It takes the wave shape 10 microseconds to travel one division. This timing is about equivalent to the 15,750 Hz frequency description used for the inexpensive x-y scopes.

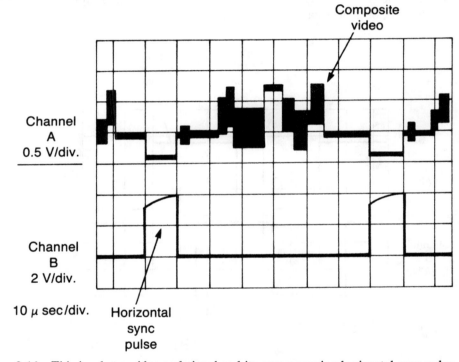

2-14 This is what a video and signal and its accompanying horizontal sync pulse looks like on a dual-trace oscilloscope. The scope is set to view a relatively low horizontal sweep frequency.

The vertical axis is described in terms of voltage. Channel A measures 0.5 V peak-to-peak for every division. It can be seen that the vertical sweep in channel A measures a bit more than two graticule blocks or near 1.5 V peak-to-peak. The waveform from channel B measures two graticule blocks. Because the channel B voltage is 2 V per division, the peak-to-peak is about 4 V.

These two scope pictures are taken in the video output circuits of a small computer. Channel A is showing the composite color TV signal the computer is generating. Channel B, attached to another test point, is showing the horizontal sync pulse that goes along with the composite TV signal. Note how the horizontal sync pulse in B is moving along in step with the sync pulse in A. These two signals are what should be at the designated test points. If they appear on the scope and match up with this prescribed picture, then these circuits are performing properly. Any deviation from this service manual picture could mean trouble is nearby.

Figure 2-15 shows a typical dual-trace oscilloscope taking pictures of a computer clock signal running at 1 MHz. The two test points are at different places in the computer where two clocks are working, an E clock and a Q clock. The top wave is connected to channel A, and the bottom wave is connected to channel B. You can see the two wave shapes are both running at the same frequency, but they are out of step, or as it is called, out of phase.

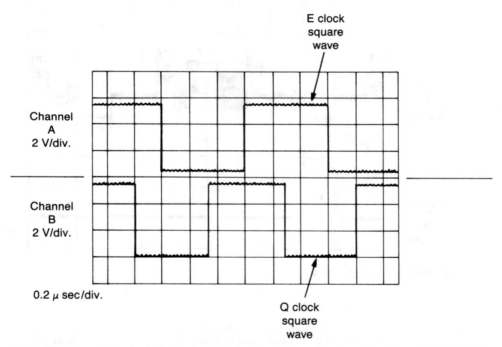

2-15   This is what a dual-clock signal looks like. The scope is set to view relatively high digital signals.

In this case, the vertical sweep measures 2 V per graticule division. The horizontal sweep is running at 0.2 microseconds per division. Note that one full clock cycle consisting of a low and a high take up about five or six divisions. Five divisions of 0.2 microseconds multiplies to about one microsecond or one millionth of a second. In one second there would be a million full cycles. That means the clock is running at one megahertz. This is one square wave cycle every one millionth of a second. Because the scope is set at two millionth of a second, (0.2 microseconds × 10 graticule divisions = 2 microseconds), two one-millionths of a second, square waves appear on the screen.

These two parameters, frequency (or timing) and peak-to-peak voltage are usually all you'll ever see on service notes. If you are very experienced, you might want to observe rise and fall times of wave shapes and sometimes pulse widths. However, this information is rarely, if ever, needed for normal troubleshooting and repair of existing equipment that has suddenly failed.

The dual-trace oscilloscope can be useful somewhat in the service shop, but it is needed more for design work and manufacturing. It uses a split screen approach to compare wave shapes, one wave above the other. The comparison thus becomes easy to observe and pick out flaws. Note how easy it is to see the two sync pulses in Fig. 2-14, and observe they are in sync with each other. In Fig. 2-15, it is immediately obvious that the two clocks are running at the same frequency and are out of phase with each other, which is the desired operation.

The major advantage a good dual-trace oscilloscope has over the x-y oscilloscope is its frequency range. The x-y oscilloscope cannot display the clocks except as an envelope. The dual-trace can show the clocks individual pulses. However, this ability to show higher and higher frequencies is accompanied by higher and higher prices.

Specialized troubleshooting

If you get a job that requires special troubleshooting measures, there is a world of test equipment available. For example, suppose you find yourself working on a service bench at a large company, repairing defunct motherboards that are based on the 286 processor. Every morning you are faced with a stack of defective boards that came in from all over the world. You obviously can't get up any volume of repaired boards with the routine test equipment discussed so far in this chapter. You will need all those pieces, but in addition you'll need specialized test equipment that will aid you in getting the boards repaired in volume.

First of all you could use chip testers that you can plug the large chips into and have the tester tell you if the chip needs replacement or not. Secondly you would need large special logic chips that would attach to the big chips and give you easy access test points. You would of course require well-written service manuals for the boards.

The most important service techniques are signal injection, signal tracing, and component substitution. There are many specialized signal injection devices, signal tracers, and component substitution equipment. Of great importance in factory board repairing are special test jig machines that allow you to substitute for the processor on the board and run tests with service software. Used properly, these test jigs pinpoint bad components quickly.

3

Taking computers apart

IN THE EARLY DAYS OF PERSONAL COMPUTERS, THAT IS, THE LATE 1970s and early 1980s, when computers needed maintenance, repairs and upgrading, taking them apart could be tricky, as shown in Fig. 3-1 and 3-2. The Tandy CoCo 1 had a screw hidden under a label. The Commodore 64s and 128s required some desoldering. Computer users were not encouraged to take them apart. Warning signs abounded, warranties were threatened if you dare to open the case.

Computer manufacturers were not really that anxious for you to get into their machine. As a result, they gave you a little obstacle course before you could see the print board, chips, disk drive mechanism and other working parts.

About the time the IBM PC came out in 1981 and 1982, the manufacturers came to the conclusion that maybe computer users were not that inept and perhaps could solve a lot of problems if they had easy access to the computer innards shown in Fig. 3-3. After all, car manufacturers gave drivers a hood latch that let them look under the hood and take care of many maintenance and easy repair jobs. Computer users could possibly do the same thing.

Peripheral slots

The Apple and IBM machines were then equipped with motherboards that had peripheral slots. These slots are discussed in detail in chapter 18. The slots were a giant step forward.

In early computers, and in fact in some recent computers, all of the computer circuits are integrated onto a single board. For a small computer with 64K or 128K of memory that is accessed by an 8-bit microprocessor and has a single board containing 40 or 50 chips, this design is fine. However, when 16- or 32-bit processors are used to access large amounts of memory, integrating all the circuits onto one board is not the best way to go. The board could end up with chip counts in the hundreds.

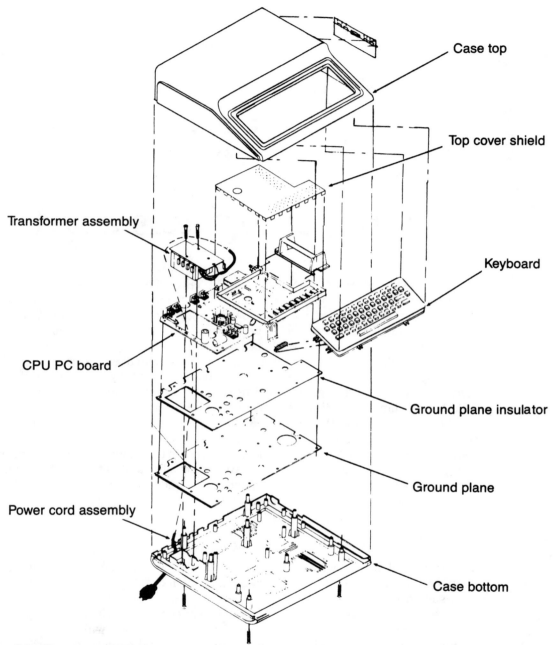

3-1 Factory service manuals are the best source of specific service information such as this exploded view of a Tandy Color Computer.

CABINET REMOVAL

Whenever you need to remove the cabinet top:

- Refer to the inset drawing on Pictorial 3-1, insert the blade of a small screwdriver into the notch in the latch plate, and then, as you lift upward on the front, slide the latch plate toward the front of the Computer about 1/4".

- Likewise, open the latch plate on the other side of the cabinet top.

- **WARNING:** When the line cord is connected to an **ac** outlet, hazardous voltages can be present inside your Computer. See Pictorial 3-1.

- Carefully tilt the cabinet top back.

- Unplug the fan.

- When the top is tilted straight up, carefully lift the hinges out of the rear panel.

Simply reverse this procedure to close and lock the cabinet top back on the Computer.

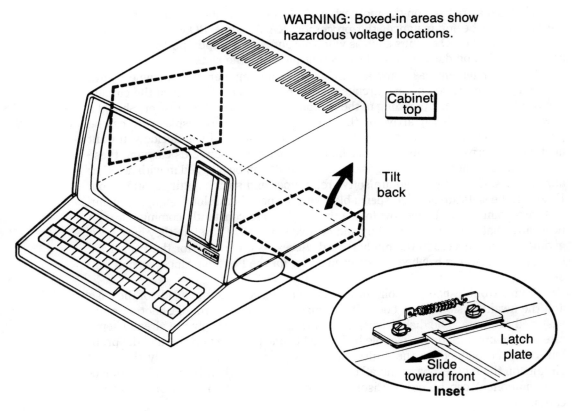

WARNING: Boxed-in areas show hazardous voltage locations.

Cabinet top

Tilt back

Slide toward front

Latch plate

Inset

3-2 Be careful taking computers apart if they are built together with a TV monitor.

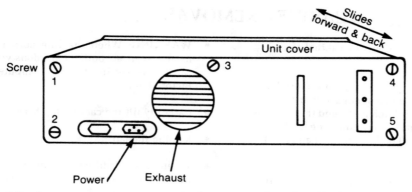

3-3 An easy access computer case lets you get in to install adapter cards, cleaning, and easily maintain.

When slots are used on the motherboard, the only circuits that are attached to the board can be for instance, the processor, RAM, some ROMs, and support chips. Most of the I/O circuits such as video output, audio output, ports, and others can be installed on daughterboard cards that plug into the slots.

This arrangement has many advantages over a computer with a single board. With only the basic computing circuits on the motherboard, the rest of the circuits can be quite versatile. Upgrading of the computer becomes an easy matter. Should a new type of video display arrive on the market, the old type of display card can be pulled, and a card with the new design plugged in its place. If you decide you want another disk drive, modem, FAX machine, or what have you, cards carrying these devices can be plugged into empty slots. Some cards can be plugged in with no other adjustments. Other cards require software, jumper and switch settings, and so on. However, the slots are now indispensable. With the peripheral slot design, the manufacturers want you to know how to use them. They are constantly coming out with new cards that they want you to buy and be able to install. Therefore they have been giving you easy access to the motherboard. Access is quite easy for the PC-XT-AT type systems. Access has been made even easier for the PS/2 machines, seen in Fig. 3-4.

From a troubleshooting point of view, this easy access to the inside of the case and the awaiting slots are a boon. It has made preliminary troubleshooting quite easy and accurate. The disk drives, keyboard, and power supply are already separate plug-in units. Should a trouble be located in one of those peripherals, the problem could be blamed on the faulty one quickly. In addition with only the basic circuits on the motherboard and all of the rest of the peripherals on cards, a defective component can be quickly isolated to either the motherboard or one of the cards.

Zenith and Kaypro have carried this modular approach one step further. They not only have slots for the peripherals but they have broken up the motherboard into a group of smaller boards. For example, the processor has its very own board.

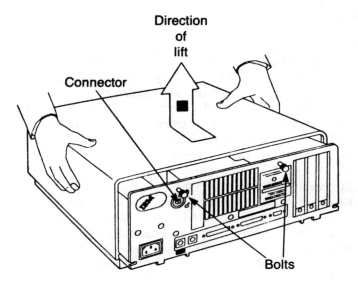

**Direction
of
lift**

Connector

Bolts

**PS/2 Models 50 & 70
lifting the cover**

3-4   The IBM PS/2 smaller models open like the PCs but easier.

If you have a board with a 286 and you desire to have a 386, you could pull the 286 board, buy a card with a 386 and plug it in.

When the computer is composed of a main board with very little on it except for slots, and all the circuits come on separate cards, it is known as a *backplane*. Comptuers with the backplane design are very convenient to repair. The plain slot design is also easy to troubleshoot and repair.

Board swapping

Due to the advent of slots on motherboards and cards that plug into the slots, a great percentage of repairs have become as routine as vacuum tube changing was in oldtime TV sets. All a computer repair person needs on service calls is a stock of boards, in the same way a TV repair person carried a stock of tubes.

The computer servicer, then analyzes the symptoms of trouble, isolates the problem to one of the boards and changes the entire board. This works out fine for backplane computers. For computers with motherboards, the technique is just as convenient. If the trouble is on a card, the job is completed by plugging in a new card. However, when the problem is on the motherboard, the replacement is easy, but the motherboard is expensive.

Motherboards can often be traded in. The boards are then repaired in the service shop and become good replacements once again.

Different style computers

Personal computers are constructed in a lot of different ways, but typically there are five general encasements. First of all, as in Fig. 3-1, there are the old, smaller 8-bit types that have the keyboard and a single integrated board in one case. These computers connect to monochrome or color monitors. Many of them are equipped with an RF (radio frequency) amplifier circuit that lets you hook up to channel 3 or 4 of a home TV set. Examples of these computers are the old Apples, the Commodores, VIC 20, 64s and 128s, Ataris, TRS-80 CoCos and other single board computers. Most of these computers are now orphans, but there are still millions of them around being used by devotees.

Secondly, there are the many portable computers. They come complete in one case that includes a flat panel display. They are able to operate anywhere with batteries or can be plugged into an electric outlet. They can be simple little monochrome devices or more complex, expensive units that are as powerful as a desktop computer. Small ones have miniaturized keyboards, medium-size ones can have larger, almost full-size keyboards, and large ones have keys with no restrictions. The flat-panel displays, for the most part, are not as satisfactory as a monitor, although recent developments promise displays that will be as good as any typical monitor.

A third style of computer has the CRT display built right into the case along with the computer and disk drive, as in Fig. 3-2. This is an old type style and is found in computers like the TRS-80 Models I, II, III, and IV and in the Macintosh computers. They are also common in dedicated word processors and other such units.

A fourth style, presently the most popular (Fig. 3-5), had its start in the IBM PC and was continued in the XT and AT. The same style is found in most of the IBM compatibles. These are built to be friendly to the user who wants to upgrade the unit and to the troubleshooter. The print boards, disk drives, and power supply are all packaged into a flat, strong, metal box. The keyboard is separate. The monitor is separate too and can be placed safely on top of the metal boxed unit.

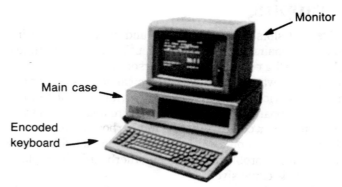

3-5   The most popular computer configuration is the familiar IBM PC family and their clones.

The fifth type of computer casing, Fig. 3-6, is found in the units that stand on one end of the floor and are called *towers*. The high end of the IBM PS/2 models and their clones have adopted this style. Besides saving space on the desk, they are made with doors that swing open and give easy access to the slots and boards.

PS/2 Models 60 & 80
opening the case

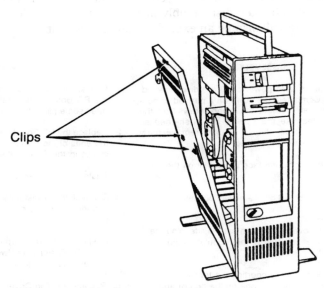

Clips

3-6 The IBM PS/2 larger models have access doors that open easily to the main components.

Until recently, the last two years, the keyboard and single board in one flat case was the most popular personal computer. It sold well at very low prices. There were more than twenty million of them sold. They were made well and the majority of them are still in use. Some of them are used in business but the great majority are in the homes.

The other styles of personal computers are all much more expensive than the single-board types. Portable computers are relatively expensive and are popular with traveling business people, journalists on the move, students, and similar users. Computers that have the CRT enclosed with the computer boards have specialized uses as so-called transportables. Most of these are dedicated word processors.

By far, the great majority of the computers being bought and used today are the IBM and IBM compatibles. They have more than 80% of the personal computer market with Apples taking about 7%.

Step-by-step disassembly

When you want to take a computer apart, it's best to have a set of disassembly instructions. They save a lot of fumbling, removing the wrong screws or bolts, taking too much of the machine apart, not being able to get all the screws back in, and even causing troubles that did not exist in the machine before you started monkeying with it.

For your particular computer, you should own a copy of the technical reference manual that was written specially for your computer. In the manual, hopefully, there should be step-by-step disassembly instructions on the order of Fig. 3-7. If you are lucky, there will also be an exploded view of the unit.

DISASSEMBLY

1. Make sure all cables (also power cord) are disconnected. Place the Color Computer face down on a padded or non-scratching surface and remove the seven screws from the Case Bottom. (Because the screws are positioned so deeply, you may not be able to actually remove them until the Computer is turned face up.)

2. Carefully place the Computer face up and lift off the Case Top and set it aside.

3. Carefully lift the Keyboard off the plastic bosses and remove the Keyboard Cable.

4. Remove the Top Cover Shield and set it aside. You may have to remove the top cover of the modulator (U5) to get the shield off.

5. Remove the three screws supporting the transformer assembly (two on transformer, one on the board) and disconnect all jumper cables.

6. Remove the ten screws fastening the CPU PC Board and lift the Board off its plastic bosses.

7. Remove the Ground Plane and Insulator from the back of the PC Board by using a screwdriver or other small, thin tool to pry off all sixteen fasteners from the rear of the Board.

REASSEMBLY

1. Replace the Ground Plane and its Insulator on back of the PC Board and install the sixteen fasteners. You may need some pliers to close the tips together and then insert.

2. Replace the PC Board onto the plastic bosses. Be sure that the ends of the Power Cord are pulled through the square cutout in the Board where the transformer is positioned.

3. Fasten the PC Board in place using ten No. 6 × 1/2" screws.

4. Connect the transformer jumper cables, E1 through E4 and the Power Cord jumpers, E6 - white, E5 - green, and E7 - black.

5. Position the Transformer assembly and attach jumper cable E8. Fasten using two No. 6 × 1 1/2" screws (on Transformer) and one No. 6 × 1/2" screw (on board).

6. Replace the Top Cover Shield.

7. Reconnect the Keyboard Cable and Cable Shield if used. Replace the Keyboard onto the plastic bosses in the case bottom.

8. Replace the Case Top onto the Case Bottom and carefully turn the entire unit over (face down).

9. Replace the seven screws in the Case Bottom (Two No. 6 × 7/8" toward the front and five No. 6 × 1 1/4" toward the rear). **Do not put the longer screws in the front positions, it could dent the Computer Case Top.**

10. *Don't forget to put on the Radio Shack authorized seal to maintain the warranty.*

3-7 Step-by-step disassembly instructions carefully show the way to dismantle your computer successfully and then put it back together again.

As far as the IBM compatible computers go, the manufacturers are anxious for you to be able to take the case off and further have the ability to remove and insert the various adapter cards. Usually, in the user's guide that comes with the machine there will be instructions and illustrations on how you can do it.

These valuable service notes must be carefully followed. It is easy to find most of the screws and connecting cables without these aids but there is always one screw or wire that gets placed in an out-of-the-way location that will cause you disassembly troubles. Following the detailed instructions though, will clue you right onto that one oddly placed bolt that is stopping the case from coming apart.

Besides pinpointing wayward mounting hardware, the disassembly instructions go far beyond just taking the unit apart and then reassembling it. A computer repair, from beginning to end, consists of a finite number of service moves. Each individual move can be counted like the step-by-step disassembly instructions are numbered. If you were a service manager and you assigned the same repair job to two different technicians, one will probably make more service moves than the other. All things being equal, the one who produces the fix with the least moves is the more expert repairer. Every repair is like working your way through a maze. The technician who consistently takes the shortest possible path from beginning to end and avoids the most dead ends is the better repairer.

One of the areas where a lot of moves can be bypassed is disassembly. An expert servicer will rarely take the entire computer apart. Most of the time all that is needed is to get the motherboard out in the open.

The more you take apart, the more you will have to put together once the repair has been made. The more screws you remove, the more cables you disconnect, the more chips you take out of sockets, and the more desoldering you perform, the more possibility of inducing additional trouble there is. Good technique dictates that you take apart only what is required to pinpoint the defect and then repair or replace the fault. Further dismantling is not only a waste of time but is an invitation to problems that otherwise would never have occurred. The trick to safe and efficient disassembly is to brief yourself carefully on the disassembly and plan your moves before picking up the screwdriver.

While the computer is open

When you must take your computer apart, you have the opportunity, while the machine is open, to perform some important inspecting and cleaning. There are a group of service moves you can run through. Do not take your computer apart ever unless there is a problem you must cure. However, when you must take it apart, make a thorough visual inspection and a careful cleaning. Sometimes just the visual inspection and cleaning will pinpoint the trouble and the repair can be completed right then.

Most of the time though, you won't be that lucky, for the repairs are not that simple. The inspection and cleaning however, gives you a quick familiarity with the machine. This allows you to be a lot more comfortable and help you avoid inducing additional troubles.

Once the computer has its print boards out in the open, you can examine the board for various types of short circuits. In the exploded view of a single board computer in Fig. 3-1, it is shown that the print board is put together in layers. Beneath the board is an insulator, the same size as the board, that covers the entire foil side of the board. Beneath the insulator is a metal tray called the ground plane.

It covers the entire insulator. The insulator keeps the foil side of the board from contacting the components on the board. The foil on the board that is supposed to be ground level is connected at spots through the insulator to the ground plane. All the rest of the foil and components on the board are not permitted to contact the ground plane. If they do, you have a short circuit on your hands.

If you are working on a board of this nature, one of the first service moves you should make is to visually inspect the three layers. On occasion a capacitor, resistor, or other component can have an extra long lead sticking out of the bottom of the print board. Over time, the lead will puncture the insulator and make contact with the ground plane. When that happens, you have a short to ground and it could cause a problem, perhaps even the problem that made you take the computer apart in the first place. In such an obvious case, when you clear the short by snipping the excess lead, you will also have completed the repair.

Another quick check should be made at all the IC chips that are socketed. A very common trouble that happens with chips in sockets is, they have a tendency to gradually creep out of the socket. Some of the little legs could stop making contact with the metallized holes the legs are residing in. This creates an open circuit and could kill the action of the chip.

The IC socket creep condition can be confusing and cause you to replace a chip that tests bad but is actually fine. The chip simply lost contact at one or more of its legs. Then when you test it by direct replacement, the computer starts working again. You assume the chip was bad. This isn't too much of servicing error when the chip is inexpensive. However, if the chip costs a few hundred dollars, the error is more serious.

To avoid assuming chips are bad when they have simply crept out of the socket, make sure all socketed chips are firmly seated in their sockets. The socketed chips are usually the ones that either would be very difficult to change, chips that need to be changed every now and then, or chips that have a relatively high failure rate.

When a chip has more than a couple dozen pins it can be a desoldering headache. Chapter 11 goes into the details of changing chips correctly. Examples of chips that occasionally need to be changed for upgrading reasons are ROMs, numeric coprocessors, and RAMs. Chips with higher failure rates than other types are RAMs, clock controllers, and all the chips that run fairly hot and require heat sinking. Heat sinks tend to peel off the chips, and the chips burn up. You should be on the lookout for these visual conditions.

Another quick check should be made on the IC sockets. On occasion a socket can get bent under instead of being soldered into its board hole during manufacturing. It passes inspection because it still makes a pressure contact. During its active customer use, the contact eventually loses contact and the circuit opens up at that point. If you examine the board under a bright light you can spot the bend under the pin. Moving the pin into its assigned board hole and a drop of solder produces a quick fix.

There are many other board problems that yield to a close visual examination. Over the board are many sets of parallel copper etch lines, as Fig. 3-8 and 3-9 show. These can be address lines, data lines and control lines. All of these lines must be continuous from one end to the other. If any of the lines, at any spot, are shorted together or broken open, chances are the computer will not work properly. These etch trails are the source of a good percentage of troubles. It is good practice to give all the copper etch lines a close look at the beginning of every repair. If you do any soldering during the repair, inspect the area around the new solder junction carefully once the repair is finished. Often solder drips or forms little balls. Slivers of solder could attach themselves and cause a short between copper traces. The heat from the solder could loosen nearby connections. While the case is open, take a few seconds and double check your work.

Another service move that reaps dividends while the computer is apart is strategic cleaning. As time goes by and your computer gets use, it gathers dirt. Luckily most dirt and dust is an excellent insulator and as such won't short out the print board or components. The big problem with dirt is ventilation. Most of the new computers need good ventilation fans to keep air circulating through the unit. As the chips run, they generate heat. If your machine is using 100 W of energy it is creating heat in the same way a 100 W light bulb would. Ventilation fans keep air moving. The hot air is expelled, and cool air enters continually. If the fan didn't ventilate, the heat would build up till some sensitive chip overheated and died.

When dust enters the machine and lodges around the ventilation holes, it restricts the circulation of air. In addition, dirt can restrict the movement of the keys on the keyboard, the access to the slots and cartridge holders, ports, plugs and other moving parts. Dust is especially bad when it gets into the disk drive area and other peripherals that may be installed inside the computer. When you do get an opportunity to dust and clean your machine it is wise to do so.

There are all sorts of devices to clean the various sections of the computer, from small special-purpose vacuum cleaners that can suck dust or blow it away. There are devices that will spray chemicals to clean sensitive areas. If you browse in an electronic supply store there will be plenty of cleaning units to choose from.

A simple way to remove the dust inside the computer is with a few different size, clean paintbrushes. The dust removal must be performed slowly and carefully. Be especially careful around the RAMs and other MOS chips because they are susceptible to static electricity. The most dangerous times are on cold, dry days when sparks can fly from your hands to a doorknob after you walked across a thick rug. It is always a good idea to ground the paintbrush with a jumper wire to an earth ground. Safe grounding techniques for protection against static electricity is covered in chapter 11. It should also go without saying, be sure the computer and its peripherals are disconnected from one another and that none of them are plugged into electricity during any disassembly, visual inspections, cleaning, or reassembly.

Furthermore, do not use any water or cleaning solution on the print board. The idea is not to make the board good looking, all you want to do is eliminate obvious physical problems that are causing troubles, provide adequate air circulation, and a clear view of the circuits in case more advanced troubleshooting is needed.

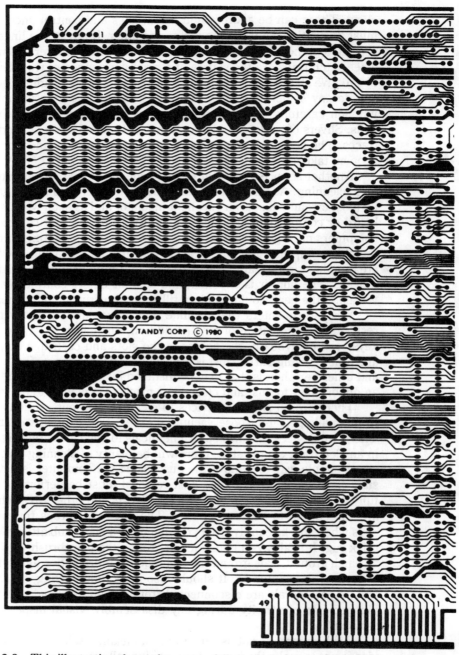

3-8 This illustration shows the copper foil wiring on the bottom side of a print board. It can serve as a roadmap of the chip connections.

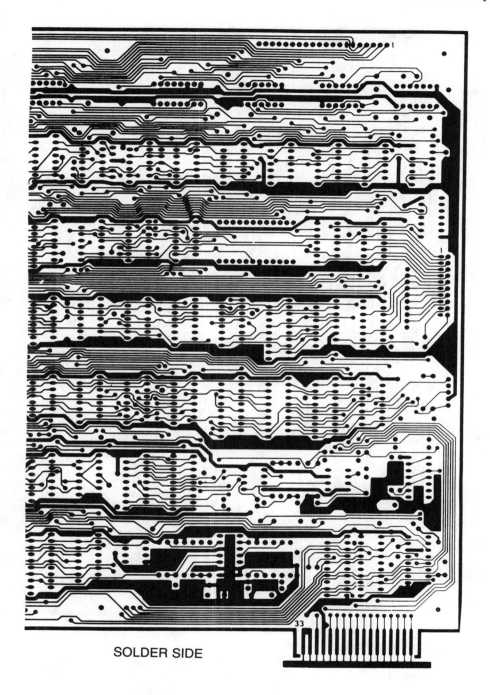

SOLDER SIDE

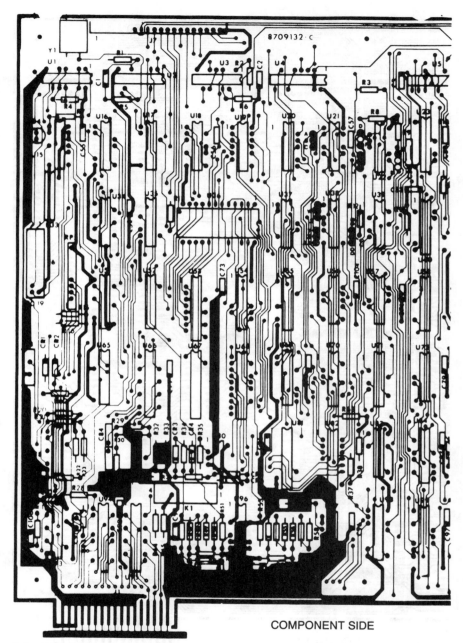

COMPONENT SIDE

3-9 This illustration shows the components and chips on the top side of the print board. The component leads are poked through holes in the board and soldered to the copper foil connections as seen in Fig. 3-8.

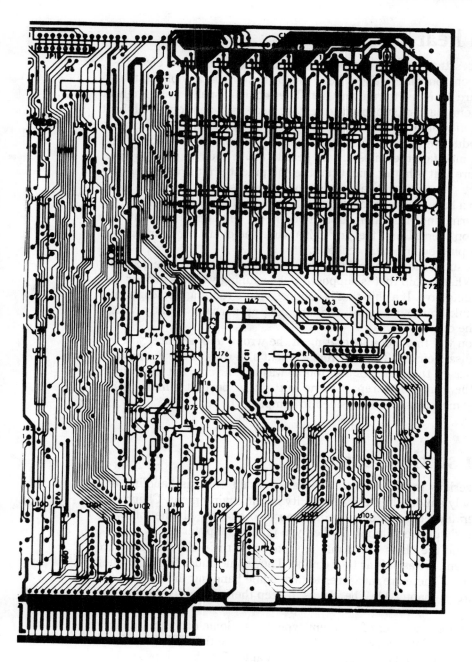

A word on heat

The two main forces that can kill perfectly good chips are heat and electricity. There isn't too much you can do about heat except to work in a cool, ventilated area. Some chips are designed to run very hot. These chips usually will have heat sinks pasted on them that are supposed to remove heat as it develops. The heat sinks can stand up in ventilated air streams or be made to touch the metal chassis through a heat-conductive paste. Either way, when the computer is well designed, the heat sinks will maintain the chips at safe heat levels. If the computer is operated in a temperature that is hotter than what the equipment is rated at, chances of a chip giving up the ghost due to heat prostration increases.

This brings up a little heat-test technique that can be quite useful. Some chips run cool, others warm, and still others, hot. If you know what chips do what, you can run a feel test on them. Don't feel any chips while the computer is energized! Be sure to pull the plug before every feel test.

If a chip that is supposed to be cool is running warm or hot, odds are good the chip is defective. When a chip that is supposed to be running warm is cool or hot, that chip could be defective. If a chip that is supposed to be running hot, especially those with heat sinks, is found to be running cool or perhaps slightly warm, chances are that the chip is bad.

On occasion you will find a chip operating at the wrong temperature, you will replace it, and be disappointed. The new replacement also runs at the wrong temperature. In those cases, the source of the trouble was not the chip but the circuits that are driving the chips. The repair turns out not to be that simple. More advanced servicing measures will be needed to complete the repair.

A word on static electricity

One of the most serious problems with integrated circuit chips is handling and operating them safely amidst the static electricity in our environment. Chapter 11 deals with the overall problem in detail. Until you read chapter 11, the following are a few facts you should keep in mind when you take a computer apart.

First of all, while the chips are firmly ensconced in their circuits, they are grounded correctly and are as safe as they can be. They come under fire when they are out of the circuits. There are measures to take while handling them out-of-circuit. The details are in chapter 11. The idea is to keep them grounded properly at all times.

Secondly, there are a number of different type chips. Some of them are fairly rugged and can resist all but heavy static charges. These are the TTL (transistor-transistor-logic) chips. The TTLs are discussed in chapter 7. Other chips are very susceptible to static charges. These are the MOS (metal-oxide semiconductor) chips. These are discussed in chapters 6 and 7. They are very sensitive, and unless you follow the professional techniques of handling these chips, every now and then you will destroy one. If it is an expensive chip that you waited weeks for, losing it from a static charge can be quite aggravating.

There are a number of ways a static charge can slip by your defenses and kill a chip. The most common way is for you to carry the death charge. At humidity levels of 40% or lower you can, just by moving around, build up a static potential in your body of hundreds of volts. If during routine chip replacement you accidentally ground yourself with a chip in your hand, the spark will course through the oxide insulators in the chip and puncture the oxide. If that happens the chip becomes useless.

To avoid this problem as you handle chips, you must keep yourself and everything else that contacts the chip grounded safely to earth. There are special anti-static kits available that will ground you safely. Don't just ground yourself, that could be dangerous. Use one of those kits as described in chapter 11. The kits have special series resistors in the grounding lines to keep you safe from accidental electric shock.

Checkout before reassembly

Once you have pinpointed the trouble, relieved the short, open, or leak, or installed the known good replacement, the time has come to reassemble the computer. It is good practice to always check out the machine thoroughly while it is apart. There is always the possibility that during the reassembly something will go awry and the machine won't work when back in the case. If you know that it was working fine before you put it together then you can be fairly certain that something went amiss during the reassembly. This is valuable service information.

For example, suppose you repaired a garbage problem by locating a break in the board that disconnected some bus lines and resoldered them. Once all the computer voltages matched up with the prescribed voltages on a test chart, like the ones in chapter 9, around the trouble area, you hooked the cables up, with the motherboard still out of the case. You then energized the unit and ran off the diagnostic program for the machine. The computer passed every test in good fashion. You were then satisfied that the trouble had been found and fixed.

You replaced the motherboard and closed the computer. As a final measure, you ran the diagnostic again. This time the garbage returned. Your heart sinks, but you stand a chance because you had the unit working fine. That was, until you put it back together. You start to retrace the disassembly looking for some simple trouble. Aha! You notice one of the screws holding the motherboard is not seated properly and is bending the board. You loosen it and note that it is stripped. You install a new screw and it seats correctly. The board is on longer bent. It lies flat.

You try the diagnostic once again. The computer runs like a charm. You figure the bent board must have been touching something and causing a short circuit. The original repair was still o.k. The reassembly had induced a new trouble that was easy to dispatch because you suspected something like that had happened because the open chassis check had been good.

Not having parts left over

Just as the trick to trouble-free disassembly is knowing where the screws are, the knack of reassembly is not having any parts left over. If you happen to repair an old computer, often you'll find most of the screws or bolts are missing. About the only ones left are the ones in the corners. This indicates a previous worker with sloppy techniques. In the close quarters of computer connections, a technician like this will usually cause plenty of induced troubles as he or she goes about daily work.

The idea of good reassembly is to put the machine back together so that it is hard to tell that any repair work was ever done at all. This can be done if you take care and use good work habits.

A flawless repair can go like the following. Suppose one day striking keys on your keyboard does nothing. The screen stays blank. You carefully disassemble the computer. Good technique has you taking the case off the computer and laying all the cables, bolts, cards, and other dismantled parts out on a large piece of paper in the neat order you removed them.

After a while, you diagnose the interface chip between the keyboard and the processor as being defective. You have to order a new one. The computer is apart all over the workbench.

You order the chip and they give you a delivery date of about two weeks. There is other work you want to do on the bench so you must gather up the computer sections and store them. It is good technique then to take some cellophane tape and secure all the screws, shields, and other mounting hardware pieces to the sheet of paper they are layed out on rather than just dumping them together on the chassis. The better you arrange the hardware, the easier the reassembly will be a few weeks later when you have forgotten where and how some of the hardware goes. Then when the part finally arrives, is installed, and the reassembly begun, it will proceed smoothly step-by-step and there will be no parts left over.

4

The common problems and repairs

THE MOST COMMON RESPONSE A PERSON MAKES WHEN HIS PERSONAL computer quits is to check the fuse. This reaction has been ingrained in everyone from past experience with all types of electrical and electronic equipment. It often cures the trouble. Unfortunately, even though computers do possess fuses (Fig. 4-1) most of the time its replacement does not provide the fix.

Most of the time this first service check yields the fact that the fuse is fine. Should the fuse in fact actually be blown, installing a new replacement and turning on the machine usually blows the new one too. The fuse is placed strategically to blow when a serious short circuit happens that would otherwise burn up a lot of components and wires. Don't ever defeat a fuse. Should you put the wrong fuse into a computer circuit you could cause a great deal of circuit damage.

There might be some rare instance where the fuse itself will fail and is not opening due to a short. Then the fuse replacement will cure the failure, but don't count on being so lucky. The fuses most of the time blow for some other reason. Should you encounter a fuse failure and a new replacement also blows, then the repair is out of the realm of easy jobs and the scope of this chapter. For more advanced repair information on this condition turn to chapter 25.

Don't be disheartened about the bad fuse news, for there are many other common repairs that you can take care of with relative ease.

The two types of repairs

There are two distinct kinds of computer repairs. One requires that you comprehend the general workings of the computer. That way you can examine the symptoms and puzzle out, in general, what section of the computer contains a troublemaker. Number two type of computer repair demands that you really

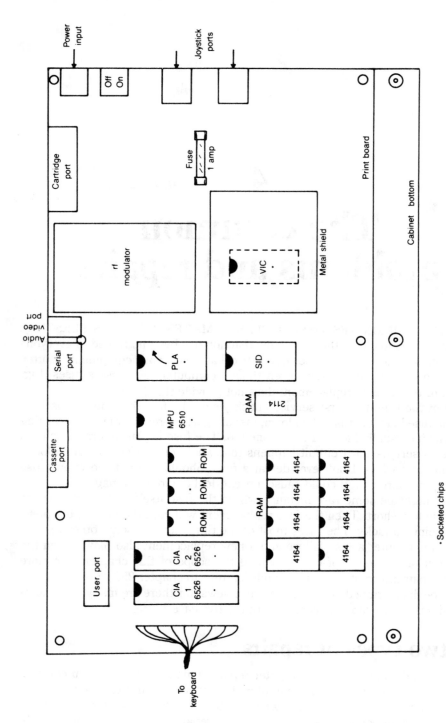

· Socketed chips

4-1 As you glance over the real estate on a computer print board, the most recognizable component you will find is the fuse. This board has one located at right center. The various input and output ports are located at the back and right side of the board.

understand the hardware of the machine, and from the knowledge of how it works, figure out how it fails. You must be able to read the schematic diagram and service notes. You must also be able to use test equipment like the logic probe, voltohmmeter, and oscilloscope.

Chapters 1 – 7 cover the easy repairs. The rest of the book goes into considerable detail on the harder troubleshooting and repairs. Percentagewise the frequency of easy and hard repairs are about evenly split. That is, when trouble strikes chances are 50-50 as to whether you are going to have a simple quick fix or you must resort to more complex troubleshooting measures.

The rest of this chapter goes into the really easy repairs that you can handle without any understanding of how your computer works.

The ports

Your personal computer connects to a myriad of input and output peripheral devices through a variety of ports around the back sides and sometimes even the front of the case. Different computers use different types of ports according to need. Figure 4-1 shows a lot of different port configurations. A port consists of the connector on the computer and the cable that plugs into the connector.

The older 8-bit, single-board computers typically have input ports for the keyboard, joysticks, light pens, mice, etc. There are output ports for TV monitors, printers, special mechanical devices, and so on. Then there are input-output ports for the peripherals that send to and receive from the computer. Typical peripherals are the disk drives, cassettes, and modems. The ports are familiar. They can have pins, holes, and edge connectors of many sizes, shapes, numbers and configurations. In these smaller 8-bit computers, the port connectors for the most part are wired right onto the print board. In order to remove and replace them, tricky soldering must be performed.

In the larger bit-size computers, instead of soldering these connectors onto the main board, slots have been devised. Cards have been designed to plug into the slots. Chapter 18 goes into detail on the electronics the slots provide for the computer. In this chapter you are only concerned with the physical problems that might befall the slots and cards that plug into the slots.

Although the slot itself is sometimes thought of as a port, it really is not. A port is the initial input or final output of the computer. A slot is an interim connector in the computer system. The slot is a handy device that permits new circuits to be connected and disconnected easily to and from the motherboard.

The actual ports are wired onto the card. In contrast, in the smaller computers, the ports are wired onto the main board. Wherever the ports are wired, they come under close scrutiny by the troubleshooter because they are subject to a lot more stress than other circuits. They develop more problems than other circuits. Every time a peripheral is connected and disconnected from a port, some wear takes place. The ports are parts that are physically stressed. To make the problem more hazardous, most of the pins and holes are tiny and fragile. Great care must be taken during connection and disconnection moves.

The symptoms of trouble are obvious. Erratic symptoms could appear on the screen or in the audio. Sometimes after a connection is made, a section of the computer will stop working. On occasion during a disconnection, a pin will dislodge or bend. All these problems and others can and do happen often.

Fortunately, the problems can often be found quickly by using your five senses. For example, if your printer starts acting erractically, and you find the erratic behavior will stop if you hold the plug tightly in place, you know you have a poor plug connection.

If nothing is loose, the problem is usually due to corrosion. The fix typically consists of cleaning the corrosion off the plug system. You can use a liquid similar to that used to clean corrosion in TV tuners. Spray some solution on a paper towel and wipe all the contacts carefully. If there are any hard to get to areas spray some solution on a cotton swab and reach those corroded spots. Do not leave any lint. The corrosion should wipe right off.

If you find a connection is loose, examine it under a bright light and figure out mechanically what the trouble is. If you can repair it easily and permanently, do so. However, should the connector be worn or broken, buy a new exact replacement plug or cable. Don't fool around with plugs or cables that do not repair easily. Replace them. You want a permanent, guaranteed repair. If a repair should not take and a failure occurs when the machine is back in operation, you could be in for a lot of frustration.

Keyboards

Your keyboard (Fig. 4-2) is a complex piece of equipment and has a lot of moving parts. Each key is seated on a piece of rubberlike material that in turn sits on a miniature switch. The switch sits on a print board. When you strike a key, you press the key onto the rubber seat. The seat moves and presses the switch onto a connection on the keyboard. As the connection is made, a circuit is closed and a digital signal is generated. Then when you let up on the key, the rubber springs back and lets the switch disconnect. The digital signal stops.

4-2 Each key on the keyboard is an individual switch with moving parts that are subject to mechanical failure.

All these moving parts are subject to wear and corrosion. Each part is miniature in nature. It doesn't take too much dust or corrosion to foul a key. The first thing that must be done with a keyboard is to keep it clean.

A good rule is to expose the keyboard only when it is being used. Just as a secretary in an office puts a cover on her typewriter every night, you should keep the keyboard covered whenever it is not in use. Any type of dust cover will do. This preventative maintenance is mandatory if you want the keyboard to last.

Should your keyboard build up some dust anyway, it is easy to clean. Cotton swabs are excellent little cleaners. Take an extra minute or two and pick out all the dirt that collects between keys. Do not use any cleaning solutions on the keyboard. Perhaps you could wipe the top of the keys with a damp cloth but be careful.

On occasion one of the keys will stop working and you can feel that it is broken. It won't bounce when you strike it. This is a mechanical failure. If you take the keyboard apart you could probably see what broke and either fix the mechanical malfunction or replace the broken key section.

Before you attack such a job there are some facts that you should consider. First of all, the key parts are miniature and very touchy to handle. Unless you are used to working with tiny parts and have some jeweler's screwdriver tools, don't do it. You'll cause more trouble than you began with. Secondly, make sure that replacement parts are available. Should you find a bad part but not be able to purchase a replacement, you have wasted your time and will have to put the keyboard back together. A service shop is not going to be kind to you if you bring the keyboard in to them in pieces.

Should you have good hands and can get parts, go ahead. The keyboard mechanical repairs are rather easy if you have no problems with the above hurdles.

Socketed chips

All the chips in your machine are attached in one of two ways. Number one, the little package with tiny sets of pins has the ends of the pins soldered to the print board. The fact that the chip is soldered to the board represents a major repair problem. The job of desoldering a chip and then resoldering it or a replacement back in the print board holes is difficult to say the least. Chapter 11 goes into the various techniques needed to change chips correctly.

The second way chips are mounted is in sockets. The sockets are soldered to the print board and its chip is plugged into the socket. The pulling of a chip out of a socket and then plugging it or a replacement back in the socket is a minor job. However, it is still a job and requires some care and attention. The chips and sockets are miniature devices and do not work as easily as a tube and a tube socket.

The best test of a chip is to remove it from the print board and install a known good replacement. If the computer trouble disappears then odds are good the old chip was bad. With the new chip installed the repair is complete. This is, of course, the same type of repair job that is so popular with vacuum tubes.

The chip replacement test is very difficult with soldered-in chips. The techniques used with those chips consist of taking test readings, running diagnostic software tests and then from the results of the tests trying to conclude which chips are suspects. The suspects are then desoldered and new chips tried. These techniques are all highly advanced and take time and skills. Chapters 12–22 are devoted to these techniques.

With socketed chips the whole situation changes for the better. When trouble strikes, if you have replacement chips for the ones in sockets, you can try new chips one at a time. You can gingerly pull out an old one, perhaps with the aid of a chip puller (Fig. 4-3) and plug in a new one (Fig. 4-4). Each socketed chip can be tried one at a time. Chances are good you might find the bad one in that way. Chapter 11 goes into detail on the proper way socketed chips should be unplugged and plugged. You should brief yourself before attempting the chip changing. It is not too difficult if you do it according to the rules.

4-3 You can avoid a lot of grief when removing a socketed chip by using one of these specially designed chip pullers.

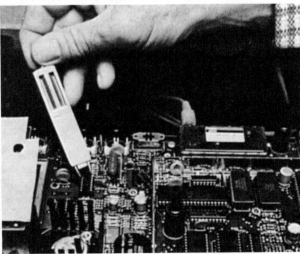

4-4 To insert a chip into a socket, there are available chip inserters like this one that can be grounded for the insertion.

Burned components

If you ever see smoke coming out of your computer, obviously something is burning. Where there was smoke there will be charring. A close visual inspection could reveal a burnt part. On some occasions, you will spot the bad part.

Even if there was no smoke a visual inspection could turn up a charred component. The bad part could be a chip, resistor, capacitor, or even a length of wire. If a part is charred it was electrocuted either on its own or some short circuit in the machine was drawing a lot of current and the part was unfortunate enough to be in the path of the current.

If you find a charred chip it probably shorted internally and started cooking on its own. When a resistor is found to be blackened it could be either way. The resistor could have had its resistive element lose resistance and started drawing a lot of current or it could just be in series with a different short circuit. Capacitors, when they burn, usually do so because they change from a capacitance to a resistance due to shorting in their dielectric.

When a part chars and becomes useless, it must be replaced. Chip changing is covered in chapter 11. If a resistor or capacitor needs changing, it can be easily done. The first trick is do not desolder the component. Instead snip the component off the board. Make your cut at the body of the part. Leave the leads soldered to the board and sticking up in the air. Turn over the end of the lead. That way the old leads act as a terminal strip to connect the new part to.

When you solder the new part to the old leads use a heat sink as shown in Fig. 4-5, so the heat from the connection does not loosen the old leads connection to the print board. The soldering iron must not be larger than 30 W.

4-5 When changing a discrete component on a print board, it is good technique to leave some of the old leads intact and solder to the leads rather than the boards. In addition always use a heat sink to avoid overheating or loosening leads on the board.

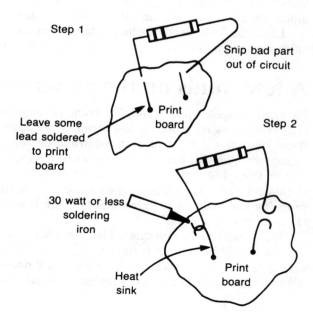

Step 1

Snip bad part out of circuit

Leave some lead soldered to print board

Print board

Step 2

30 watt or less soldering iron

Heat sink

Print board

If the part that is replaced is a transformer with loose leads, use the same approach. Do not desolder the leads from the print board or terminal strips. Snip the leads leaving plenty of slack. Then connect the new replacement leads to the old. Solder them and tape up the solder connection.

Built-in disk drives

Chapter 24 goes into detail on maintaining and repairing disk drive systems that are installed in the computer case with the rest of the circuits. However, you can conduct some quick checks on the physical layout of the drive and often find the reason for troubles. The quick checks are quite simple and can yield results.

The first moving part a disk encounters is the front panel. It is attached to the case. Make sure it is secure and not loose. If it is loose, tighten it down. A loose front panel can cause problems.

Next check the front latch. It should open and close easily. Watch the arm that holds the read-write head. On many built-in drives, as the door is opened, the arm should rise. If it doesn't, the drive won't accept a disk. If the arm won't rise try to figure out why. Oftentimes, the reason is an easily located physical failure that is quickly remedied. Your mechanical ability should permit you to determine a cure.

The next thing to do is rotate the drive hub. It should rotate freely. If it can't rotate, find out why it is stuck and try fixing it. However, do not get into a situation that is over your head. Drives are ticklish devices. Refer to chapter 24 for more detail on the drive hubs.

There are one or more print boards that control and interface the drive to the computer. Make sure they are secure. Drive systems do a lot of rotating and arm movement. The various parts including the print boards could loosen and cause problems. If a board or connection is loose, tighten it.

Last, check the head carefully. There must not be any debris or other material lodged around it. The cleaner the disk system is, the better it will perform.

A few words on the power supply

Personal computer power supplies come in many configurations. The keyboard-only computers only need a few small dc voltages to operate. The supplies for these machines consist of a step-down transformer, some rectifiers, and filter capacitors. The VIC 20 and Commodore 64 computers use an external transformer system (Fig. 4-6) that is nothing more than a large calculator style ac adapter. It should get warm when it is plugged into a wall socket. If it doesn't warm at all it is probably bad and needs replacement. There is some more repair information on these items in chapter 25.

Other keyboard computers, like the TRS-80 Color Computer, use the same type of supply but mount it right in the keyboard case. When it is operating the case gets warm at its location. Here again if it doesn't warm, the supply is probably not working. It is not easily replaced though like the external adapter supply.

4-6 Power supplies are usually separate devices and not part of the main board as discussed in chapter 25. This one is not even in the computer case. It plugs into the side of the case.

The little portable computers can be run on batteries or be plugged into the wall. Obviously keep track of the battery output and as they weaken, replace or recharge them as indicated. The portables have a plug-in supply like the keyboard-only types. Feel around the power transformer and find out if it is warming. If it is not, that is a clue and could indicate a defective supply.

The larger computers have larger supplies. Some supplies not only have to feed the computer itself but also a built-in disk drive and perhaps even the built-in TV display monitor. These supplies must turn out heavy currents and can get very complicated. They require considerable troubleshooting skills when they stop putting out the strictly regulated dc voltages. Chapter 25 goes into the advanced techniques that are required to fix them.

Do not try to troubleshoot these heavy-duty supplies unless you are well briefed and have the proper test equipment. One of the most important pieces of equipment is an isolation transformer with a rating of at least 500 VA. This is a transformer with separate primary and secondary windings. The primary connects to the wall socket and the secondary to the computer input plug. That way, if you should contact a voltage in the computer you are isolated from the heavy current the electric company supplies and you will not get hurt.

5
All about chip-location guides

THERE ARE THREE LEVELS OF TROUBLESHOOTING AND REPAIRING personal computers shown in Fig. 5-1. One is called *board level*. The second is *chip level*. The third is known as the *circuit level*. Each type has as its objective the pinpointing of the defective component or connection and then the replacement or repair of the defect. Board-level repair is the changing of an entire system. It is expensive. Chip-level servicing can be likened to tube changing techniques in older TVs. All that was needed was a tube location guide and a set of replacement tubes. Circuit-level troubleshooting is exactly like TV bench servicing that requires schematic diagrams and test equipment.

This chapter deals with the TV-tube imitative, chip-level servicing. Unfortunately though, chip-level servicing is not quite as simple as TV tube swapping techniques are. First of all, only a few chips on a computer board are in sockets in comparison to tubes, which are 100% socketed. The chips that are soldered-in are a chore to replace. Secondly, it is not easy to obtain and keep a complete set of spare chips on hand. Without a set of replacement chips the direct-replacement test cannot be easily used. You must try to puzzle out which chips are suspects, buy those chips, and install them one at a time until you replace the bad one.

Despite the difficulties, you can succeed in pinpointing a few chip suspects for a trouble, replacing them, and completing a satisfactory repair. It is not as easy as tube swapping but it is not that hard either. Examine the way the pros work at the board and chip level.

Board swapping

When a computer goes down and a user calls a repair person, the user does not care why the machine conked out, he or she wants it back on line at once. Computers are used in every avenue of our lives. In many applications and especially in

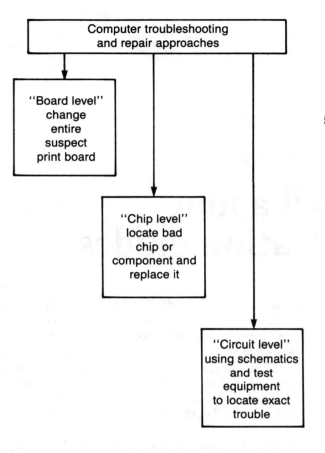

5-1 There are three general troubleshooting and repair approaches for computer boards. The easiest approach is to simply replace an entire board once the fault is determined to be on the board. Next is to change suspected part after suspected part till the bad one is found. The hardest is to locate the exact defect with the aid of service equipment and then replace only the bad part.

a sensitive area there can be no delay or else great harm can occur due to the breakdown.

In order to get a computer back on when time is of the essence, a technique called *board swapping* is used. These repair people carry spare computer boards with them. On a vital field call on a single board computer, the repair person quick checks a computer to see if the seat of the trouble could be on the single print board among the 100 or so chips. If he or she suspects that one of the chips or board components is bad, without further ado, he or she disconnects the old board, removes it and installs a known good new board. If the trouble disappears, the field repair is over. The repairer transports the bad board back to the repair shop and gives it to a technician to fix. Once the board has been repaired and checked out carefully it goes into inventory as a replacement board. This technique is expensive and aptly named *board swapping*.

The technique can be carried one step further. If the computer that goes down has multiple print boards, such as an IBM PC or one of its clones, the board swapping is a bit more complicated.

In a PC-type machine, there could be six or more boards. They could be the main board and plug-in cards. In these cases the field troubleshooter has to pinpoint the trouble to one of the many boards. The repairer must diagnose the symptoms and come to a decision on which board has the troublemaker. He or she then replaces that board. If the condition disappears then the repair is complete. If not, he or she makes a second diagnosis and board swap. He or she keeps doing that until he changes the bad board.

Table 5-1 is a board-swapping trouble chart for a typical IBM PC with a main board, four cards, and the keyboard printed circuit board. When a trouble befalls a print board in such a machine the symptom will appear as one of those listed in the chart. An experienced field repairman can quickly learn which board is indicated as holding the trouble. If he is carrying a set of boards with him, he can swap the indicated board. The boards are as follows in Fig. 5-2.

**Table 5-1. Each board in a computer produces its own symptoms.
By analyzing the symptoms, the defective board is often indicated.
Swapping the board for a known good one can produce an instant repair.**

Typical IBM PC style boards	Troubles board can cause
Main board	Dead computer Garbage
Color/graphics card	No color or poor color No video Garbage Loss of graphics Cursor missing No horizontal sync No vertical sync
Monochrome adapter card	No video Garbage Loss of graphics Cursor missing No horizontal sync No vertical sync
Keyboard circuit board	Wrong character Garbage
Disk drive adapter card	Both drives have trouble reading or writing
Disk drive analog circuit board	One drive will not read or write

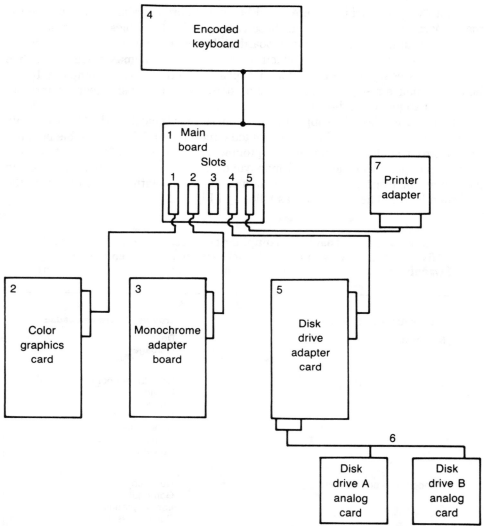

5-2   A typical five-slot motherboard can have adapter cards like these plugged into the slots.

1. The *main board* that holds about 100 chips with various pin counts.
2. The *color/graphics card* that is a board with about 60 chips.
3. The *monochrome adapter board* also holding about 60 chips.
4. The chips contained in the encoded keyboard.
5. The disk-drive adapter card.
6. The disk-drive analog cards.
7. The printer adapter card.

There are specific symptoms that point to a particular board or two. For instance, if the TV display starts rolling up and down or sideways, or loses vertical or horizontal sync in any way, two cards are indicated as containing the trouble. They are the monochrome adapter card and the color/graphics card. They should be replaced one at a time and hopefully the sync trouble will cease. If it doesn't the trouble is probably not in the computer but in the monitor. The board swap in that case becomes a test measure rather than a cure. It isolates the trouble to the monitor.

Another type of symptom that is specific to these two display cards is the loss of either low-resolution or high-resolution graphics. This symptom calls for these cards to be swapped. If a cure occurs, then the old card has a defect among its many chips.

When a symptom such as, no text but the graphics are o.k., then the trouble could be in the color/graphics card since it is in charge of selecting either the text or graphics mode and it stopped selecting the text mode. A whole new card cures since it installs the one new chip that was bad on the old card.

Another symptom that can be blamed on the color/graphics card is, no color or poor color. It produces the color. If a new card does not restore the color then the color monitor could be a problem.

The keyboard circuits could cause keyboard style troubles. For example, you hit keys but the wrong character shows up on the screen. Perhaps the uppercase is working but the lowercase is not or vice versa. The keyboard PC board is a tiny computer in its own right and has its own processor and some ROM. Changing the board could cure these symptoms.

There are two boards devoted to interfacing a disk-drive system to the computer. When troubles occur in these boards they appear as disk read-write troubles or they prevent the computer from accessing the drives.

A thoughtful analysis of the symptoms can indicate which of the two cards has a troublemaker in this particular system. For example, if one drive will not read or write, then its disk-drive analog card has problems. Should both drives not be capable of reading or both drives not be able to be written to, then the disk-drive adapter card has a defect. If the drives can't be accessed at all, then both cards are suspect.

Besides these specific troubles there are the general symptoms such as garbage and no display at all. These type symptoms can, unfortunately, originate in any of the boards except the two disk drive cards. They make the board swapper check out the keyboard, main board, and the two display boards.

Although board swapping is very expensive, it is necessary in many instances at this stage of the game. You might find yourself in a position where you can utilize the technique. Perhaps you can be able to diagnose a bad board and take it to a service outlet for swapping or repair. At any rate, the technique is easy and you might be able to use it under certain circumstances.

Chip-level servicing

If you think of a print board as a little electronic town then the chips are the houses in the village. When trouble strikes it usually happens in only one of the chips or other support components. The hardest problem of the repair is finding out which chip or component is harboring the defect.

From careful examination of the symptom, a particular chip is indicated. Each chip is there because it is assigned a job to do. The jobs are simple or complex, but each one is vital to the operation of the computer. As you look at the print board and see many dozens of chips laid out on the board, it appears impossibly complex. It is quite complicated but only because there are so many circuits. Each circuit, by itself can be comprehended without too much difficulty.

Back after WWII, a computer system took up complete floors of office buildings and cost millions of dollars. The equivalent to these giant computers now sits on a desk. The systems today are not much different than those gargantuan devices, they are simply shrunk in size. All those circuits and more have been changed from vacuum tubes to microscopic transistors. Fortunately, you do not have to concern yourself with individual transistors on a chip. All you need to know is what signals are going in, what in general happens to them inside there, and what signals come out. This is plenty of information to get broken computers fixed.

All those chips on a board are laid out in a carefully designed manner. For chip-level servicing, all that is really needed are charts of the chips that show the trouble a chip causes when it malfunctions. Then when a chip fails, the symptom is indicated and a chart shows you which chip matches the symptom.

Once you know which chip or chips are the suspects from the trouble charts, the next job is to find the indicated troublemakers. A chip-location guide will do that for you. A chip-location guide is the most used piece of service information used by print board repairers. Now the guide can take many forms. Any one of them will do. The important thing is to have your directory map of the little village populated with chip structures.

The guide should provide the following information. It should show the physical location of the chips on the board, the generic number of each chip, the keyway of the chip so the pin numbers can be counted and any important landmarks on the board. Landmarks are interface port locations, fuses, the off-on switch, and other useful items.

The guide could be a sketch, photo, designer board layout, or even the board itself. The easiest type guide to handle is a sketch without any extraneous chip location information.

The ideal chip-location guide

A chip location guide for a single board computer like the Commodore 64 (Fig. 5-3) and the Radio Shack Color Computer (Fig. 5-4) is not too complicated. These home computers only have 30 or 40 chips mounted on the board. A set of guides for multiple board computers such as the IBM PC (Fig. 5-5) and Apples (Fig. 5-6) are more complex since some boards have 60, 80, and 100 chips. Whatever the chip count, the guides are a must when you are seeking out a chip or group of chips. Also see Fig. 5-7.

A servicing chart that features trouble symptoms and then lists the suspect chips that could be causing the symptoms, is only doing the first half of the job.

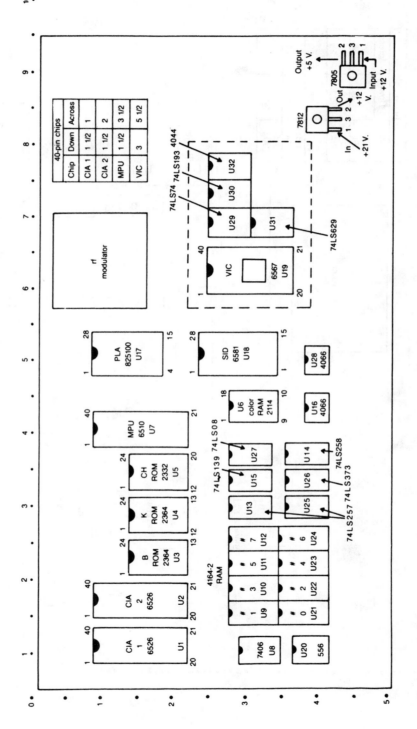

5-3 A single board like this Commodore 64 has its chips laid out neatly and easily found with a chip location guide such as this one.

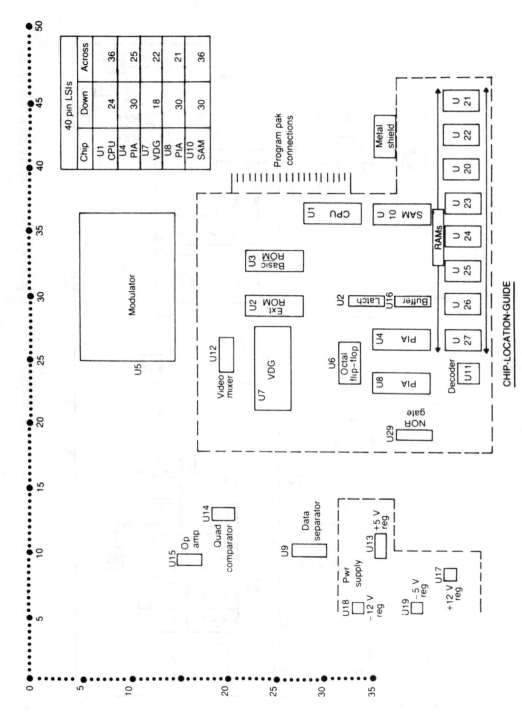

40 pin LSIs		
Chip	Down	Across
U1 CPU	24	36
U4 PIA	30	25
U7 VDG	18	22
U8 PIA	30	21
U10 SAM	30	36

5-4   This color-computer location guide reveals the power supply is inside the computer case and could be causing overheating.

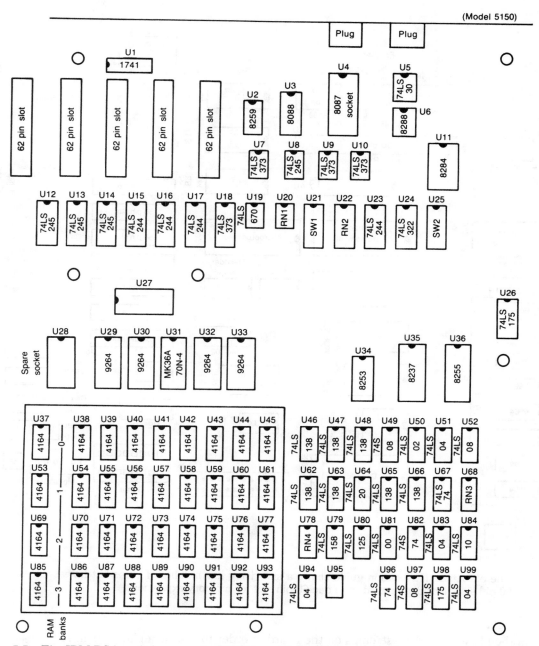

5-5 The IBM PC board shows a set of 90 chips with the U numbers laid out to read from left to right.

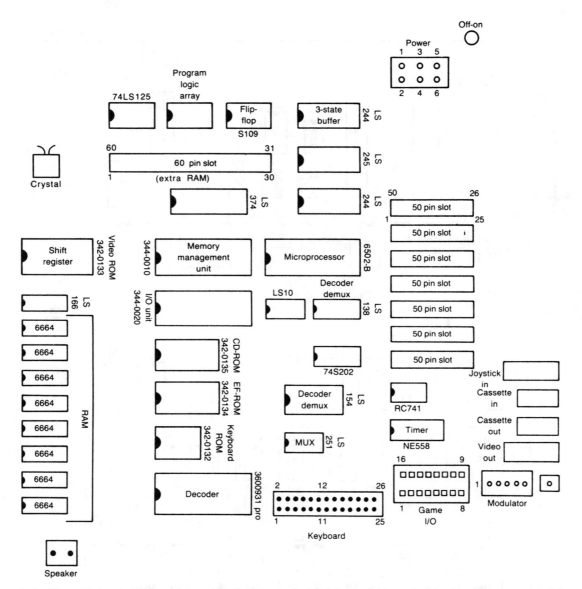

5-6   The old Apple IIe location guide shows a surprising low number of chips but has seven useful 50-pin slots for adapter cards and one 60-pin slot for memory expansion.

You then have to find those chips on the board in order to test or replace them. A guide that quickly points out their physical location is needed. Besides just pointing them out, a guide should have some other service information to aid in the repair. There is enough mystery in puzzling out the trouble without complicating the search by having to figure additional details. A good location guide should provide the following information.

1. The location of every chip.
2. The approximate size of each chip in relationship to the rest of the chips.
3. The U number of each chip. The letter U is the conventional way that chips are listed in the parts list, just as resistors have R numbers and capacitors have C numbers.
4. The location of the chips keyway on each chip. The keyway is a paint dot or notch that is placed on one end between the first and last pin numbers. From the top, pin 1 is to the immediate left of the keyway and the last pin is to the right. Pins are counted from pin 1 counterclockwise to the last pin. For example, on a 40-pin chip, the top left pin is 1, the bottom left pin is 20, the bottom right pin is 21 and the top right pin is 40.

   It is the usual practice to line up all the keyways to point in the same direction, if at all possible. On single boards with a few dozen chips, they will all be pointed in the same way. On larger boards this might not be possible. However, the designers make this effort. It tends to make testing easier.
5. Some chips are socketed and others are soldered right onto the board. It is useful if the location guide shows the socketed chips. Then if there are no socket designations you can know the chip is soldered in place.

   During troubleshooting, if you find that all the suspect chips are socketed then you can test the chips by direct replacement. If the suspects are soldered into place, then you can't easily use direct replacement and must prepare yourself to use more difficult techniques.
6. Besides chips there are many other components mounted on the board. If there are any transistors, it is useful to have them shown on the guide. This includes power supply regulators that resemble the transistor. Transistors should be marked to show the names of the leads such as emitter, base, collector, source, gate, or drain. Power supply regulators on the guide are especially handy when they show the voltages on the pins.
7. If there are any metal shields on the board their location should be shown. Any chips or transistors beneath the shield are drawn in dotted lines.
8. A board has landmarks. Main boards are usually screwed to a ground plane or the case. The holes for each screw should be shown. They are good landmarks to help you zero-in on a small chip on a large board. Main boards have all sorts of interface ports. These should all be shown on the ideal location guide.

Other items that would be useful without cluttering up the guide are fuses, plugs, off-on switches, reset buttons, an rf modulator if one is mounted on the board, power supply components, and other special devices. A card is plugged into a bus in the machine. An important landmark on a card is the position of the connector that plugs into the bus.

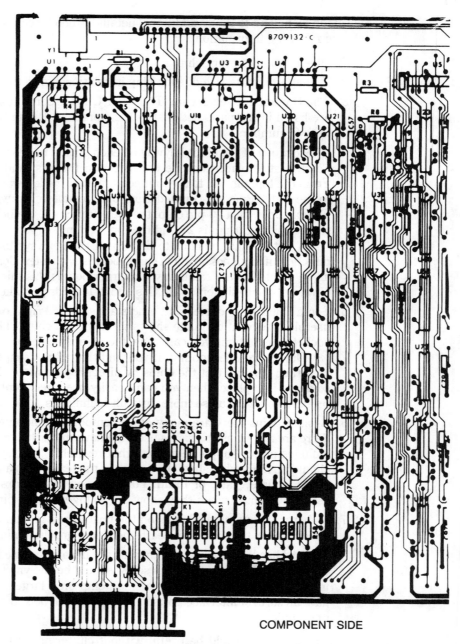

COMPONENT SIDE

5-7   This is a more detailed manufacturer's rendering of a location guide. It shows every component and connecting wire on the print board. It is harder to read than a chip location guide but provides much more location information.

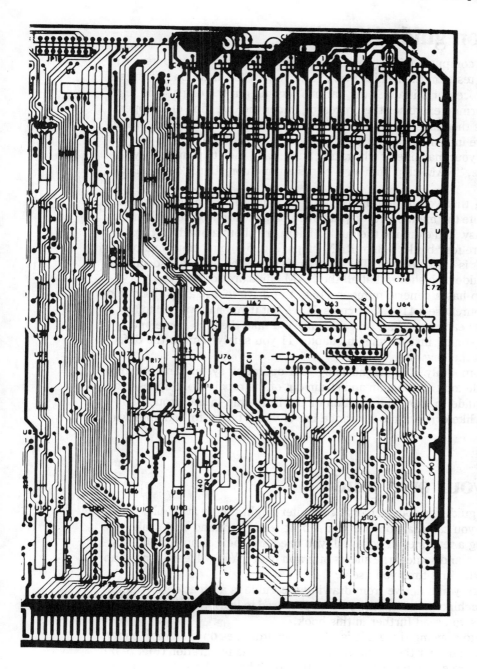

The location guide in action

A typical personal computer failure can happen like this. Lots of computers run internal diagnostic tests on their chips every time you switch them on. The tests are made as the processor initializes the various registers in the chips. The tests are simply little warmup exercises the processor, under the direction of the operation system, makes the chips perform. If a chip can't perform the exercise a flag goes up and you are informed via the TV display.

As you turn on your machine, it whirrs and buzzes and then to your dismay, the display says in code, "RAM chip number 4 of system memory Bank 2 has failed." What can you do?

The first thing that you do is remove the case from the main section of the IBM clone and locate the main board. If you have a chip location guide of the main board the rest is easy. You examine the guide. There are about a hundred chips on the board. There are four banks 0-3, of RAM chips (Fig. 5-5) nine chips to a bank. The number 2 bank is easily located. The number 4 chip of the bank is also quickly pinpointed. The guide also shows that all the RAM chips are socketed.

The RAM chip has a generic number 4164. You drive to a nearby electronic supply house and purchase a 4164. One costs $1.99, but if you had wanted to buy a set they would have each been half that amount. You take the chip home and following the chip changing instructions in chapter 11 you safely remove the defective one and install the new one.

The job went smoothly. The diagnosis by your operating system and the map location of the guide took all the pain and strain out of the repair job. Suppose you did not have the guide to show the location of the little chip in the group of 100 chips? It would be like driving into a strange big city and trying to find your way without a map.

Drawing your own guide

The chip-location guide for your personal computer might not be available. When you can't get one, you can draw one for yourself. It is not hard and won't take any longer than writing a few lines of code. All you need are some simple school supplies, a pencil, ruler, and some large sheets of graph paper. You will easily make up the drawing time the first time you use it.

Another benefit you'll derive from drawing the guide is a great deal of familiarity with your machine. In addition, you'll be prepared to learn the block diagram of your machine as you read further in this book.

The first step to drawing the guide is to mark coordinates on the graph paper. All that means is to number the blocks on the paper. In the illustration (Fig. 5-3) I have the numbers across the page going from 0 to 10. The numbers down the left side of the page go from 0 to 5. That way every spot on the page has a location. You can locate every chip on your page quickly.

As you draw each chip onto the guide you can make a list of the chips and record its position on the guide. For example, the RAM chip you needed to locate earlier will have coordinates. Once you know them it is easy to relate to the actual RAM position on the print board.

Once you have the coordinates laid out, you can draw in the chips. The sketch need not be exact. The shape of the chips does not have to be proportional rectangles. The location of the chip does not need to be on their precise coordinate. You do not have to put the manufacturer's part number on a chip. You do not even have to put as much information on your guide as shown, in order for the guide to save you lots of time.

I usually place the graph paper alongside the exposed board and start drawing the RAMs. There are usually at least eight RAM chips in a small single board computer and typically 36 in four banks of nine each on a motherboard in a larger machine. The illustrations show guides for a Commodore 64, an IBM PC, and others. Perhaps your personal computer is among the group and you won't have to draw your own.

The eight RAM chips on the Commodore 64 single board have the generic number 4164. The 41 designates a dynamic RAM and the 64 means there are 64K bits, not bytes, of dynamic storage. You'll hear dynamic RAMs called DRAMs. The eight chips are in a clump at the left bottom of the board. They are surrounded by a group of other chips. The other chips can be drawn in next.

If you notice, all of the chips are oriented in the same direction. That is, the keyway notches are all at the top of the chips. Draw the keyways in, the pins on the chip can be located in reference to the keyway.

On the chips, in the printed nomenclature, is printed something that indicates the generic number of the chip. Place the generic number of each chip inside or near its rectangle that you drew. When you purchase a replacement chip, you will place the order with the generic number. The chip can be made by many manufacturers. Each different maker will have their own nomenclature on their chip. The generic numbers however, all remain the same. A 4164 made by Texas Instruments works the same as the one made by Motorola.

On the IBM board (Fig. 5-5) there are four sets of eight RAM chips plus a RAM parity control chip for each bank. That means 36 chips. On our example board, IBM also uses 4164 chips. The 36 chips are located in the bottom left of the motherboard. They can be drawn in as shown and occupy most of the bottom left quadrant of the board. A keyway and 4164 should be placed on each chip.

When print boards are made by large manufacturers, besides printing the copper traces on the board, they also print a lot of service information. One of the important pieces of information are the U numbers. On the Commodore 64 board, there are numbers U1 through U32. The IBM main board has U1 through U99.

Examine the IBM board closely. U1 starts at the upper left-hand corner. The U's then proceed like writing, scanning across to the right, then back to the left and so on. U99 is at the bottom right-hand corner.

When you make up your location guide you should enter the U numbers as you draw. Then make up a U parts list. The U parts list (Table 5-2) is shown for the IBM main board. With the location guide and the chip list you give yourself a lot of quick service information. This can avoid a great deal of confusion during an actual troubleshooting and repair job.

**Table 5-2. The U numbers are convention for chips.
These are the chips on the IBM PC board. When you find a
defective chip, this list will tell you what the generic name of the chip is.**

U Numbers on IBM Main Print Board			
U#	**Chip Type**	**U#**	**Chip Type**
U1	MC1741CP	U51	74LS04PC
U2	P8259A	U52	74LS00PC
U3	P8088	U53-U61	MK4564N-20
U4	8087	U62	74LS158PC
U5	SN74LS30N	U63	74LS38PC
U6	D8288	U64	74LS20N
U7	74LS373PC	U65	74LS138PC
U8	SN74LS245N	U66	74LS138N
U9, U10	74LS373PC	U67	74LS74AN
U11	UPB8284AD	U69-U77	MK4116N
U12-U14	74LS245N	U79	74LS158PC
U15-U17	SN74LS244N	U80	74LS125AN
U18	74LS373PC	U81	74S00PC
U19	74LS670PC	U82	74S74PC
U23	74LS244N	U83	74LS04PC
U24	74LS322AN	U84	74LS10PC
U26	74LS175PC	U85-U93	MK4116N
U27	74LS02PC	U94	74S280N
U29	5000017	U95	2979DRAEB
U30	XE5000021	U96	74LS74AN
U31	XE5000022	U97	74S08N
U32	5000023	U98	74LS175PC
U33	1501476	U99	74LS04N
U34	8253-5		
U35	8237A-5		
U36	8255A-5		
U37	MK4564N-20		
U38-U40	MK4564N-15		
U41	MK4564N-20		
U42	MK4564N-15		
U43	MK4564N-20		
U44	MK4564N-15		
U45	MK4564N-20		
U46-U48	74LS138N		
U49	DM74S08N		
U50	74LS02N		

After the RAM chips are drawn in your guide, the next chip to be drawn is the processor. The Commodore 64 uses a 6510 and the IBM has an 8088. The processors are larger chips than the RAMs. The 6510 is found as U7 on the 64's print board. The 8088 is U3 on the motherboard. Once the processors are drawn in it is a good idea to draw in some landmarks. On the 64's guide, the two metal shields, the fuse, the ports and the off-on switch location will give good perspective. For the IBM, five card slots and the two plugs will make the guide resemble the board.

Once these important chips and landmarks are on the guides, the rest of the chips can be drawn and entered on the U list. While drawing a proper guide can be a bit tedious it has important and in many cases vital value. There will be many repair jobs that will be easy to complete that would present many complications without the guide.

The block diagram

Drawing the guide of your machine gives you an intimate understanding of the physical construction of the computer. You will be able to go to the RAMs, processor and other items confidently when the need arises. The guide is the beginning step of eventual mastery of the hardware in your machine. When more information is needed during a repair job, the next information step is a block diagram (Fig. 5-8). The location guide tells you where the chips are and the block diagram shows the way the chips are wired together and, in general, how they process the signal that you input.

The location guide with trouble charts points out the possible suspects. It is strictly a rote method like a multiplication table. When a certain symptom appears, the trouble chart lists the possible suspect chips from the experience of the person who devised the chart. The location guide then pinpoints the actual chips under suspicion on the board. As long as the trouble is in one of the indicated chips, the rest of the repair consists of changing the chips one by one until the bad one has been replaced.

The block diagram is the first step away from the rote method and to a logical puzzle-solving procedure. The block diagram of a personal computer shows an overview of the computer at work. The block diagram fills in a lot of information that the location guide fails to provide. The block diagram, while it can stand on its own in a general way, refers to your very own location guide in a unique manner. Since most computers are pretty much the same, a block diagram refers to a lot of computers. However, if you read the block diagram and refer it to your location guide you'll have specific servicing information for your machine.

You'll find in later chapters that the block diagram lays out computers in general and shows how they work. With the aid of the location guide you drew you'll be able to follow the way your computer works. If you can look at the location guide and visualize it in terms of the block diagram you will take a giant step from the rote fixing of your machine to a logical analysis of troubles. From understanding in general how it works (block diagram style) you puzzle out why it failed and which chips could cause the trouble.

Schematic diagrams

While the block diagram provides an overview of the operation of your computer, the schematic diagrams, like Fig. 5-9, of the circuits at a chip level. Inside the chips (Fig. 5-10) are many thousands of individual circuits. These internal circuits are microscopic. Also, they are internally wired and the connections between the resistors, capacitors, and transistors, for the most part, do not enter or exit the chips at the pins. They cannot be easily tested and do not play a part in normal

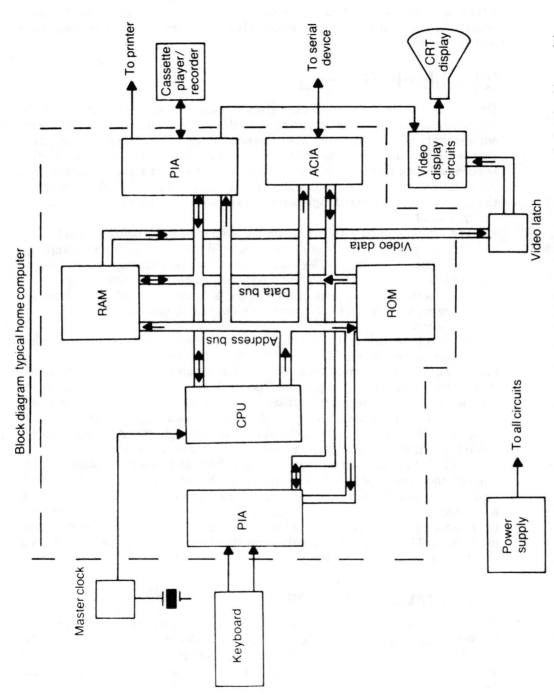

5-8 A block diagram of the print board and peripherals provides the signal flow and makes some sense of what the chips are doing. The block diagram does not show chip location information and should be used as an adjunct to the location guide.

servicing procedures. As a result, the internal wiring of most chips is ignored during routine servicing. The chip-level servicing that is conducted deals with the inputs and outputs that are connected to the pins of the DIP. Most of the chips that are in computers are called DIPs, that stands for *dual in-line packages*. Note the dual rows of pins that are all in a line (Fig. 5-11).

When tests are made at a pin a schematic diagram (such as Fig. 5-12) is needed unless you are so familiar with the diagram that you memorized the pins. In the chapters after this one you will find schematic diagrams and block diagrams. Just remember they represent the same circuit areas but the schematic diagram shows exactly what is on the print board.

The most prominent parts on the board are the chips. As mentioned they are labeled with U's. Resistors and capacitors are designated with R's and C's (Fig. 5-9). There could be inductance coils with L's. These letters are fairly standard. Other components are labeled accordingly. Throughout the book there will be typical examples.

The invisible internal wiring of chips (Fig. 5-10) will not be found on ordinary computer schematics. They are invisible on the schematic too. However, there are block diagrams and internal wiring, schematics for some of the chips that will be discussed in the book. If you ever need the internal wiring of a chip, you must contact the manufacturer of the chip and make a request. Maybe you'll be able to locate the information in a library but it is difficult to come by.

The location guide, the block diagram and the schematic diagram are all different views of the same circuits. The location guide shows you the physical location of all the chips and some landmarks. It can be used for quick checks that will repair a computer in about 50% of breakdowns.

The block diagram makes sense out of the location guide. Without the block diagram the location guide has limited use. With the block diagram and the location guide, actual diagnosis can be performed and produce about 20% more repairs.

The schematic diagram fills in the detail of the block diagram. All of the servicing information usually needed will be found in a combination of the three types of service notes. With the three, a servicer can make a diagnosis, locate a suspect chip, and then make test readings on the pins. However, the chips drawn on the schematic (Fig. 5-12) are not the same shape as an actual chip. The pins can be any place on the rectangle or block that represents a chip on the schematic.

As a result, when you take a tester, like a logic probe, and seek out a pin to touch down on, you must relate the odd schematic chip to the actual dual in-line chip package. This one step in your mind can be confusing and you could accidentally touch down on the wrong pin and draw the wrong conclusion.

To help you avoid this there are a number of test point charts of common chips throughout the book (see Fig. 5-13). These charts though, have the actual top view of the pins shown in their actual positions (Fig. 5-14). Alongside each pin is the predicted logic state with its predicted pulse condition when the machine is energized and sitting at standby with cursor blinking.

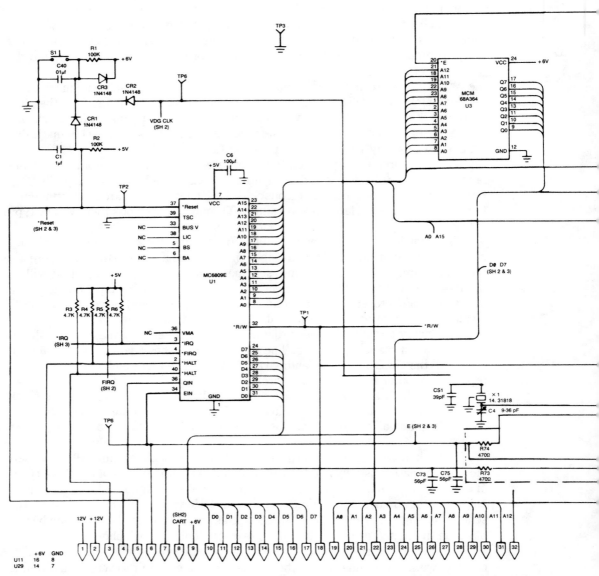

5-9 The schematic diagram brings you down to the actual design of the computer. It provides exact circuit wiring information in electronic language. It requires expertise to read the schematic and then relate it to the actual print board.

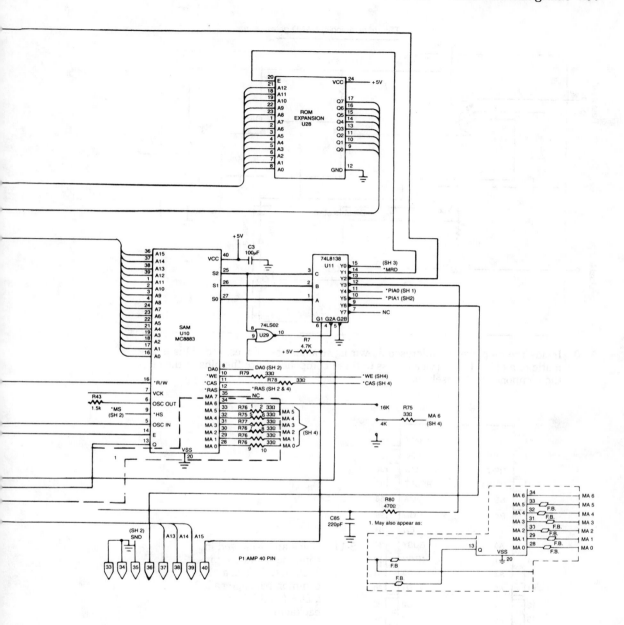

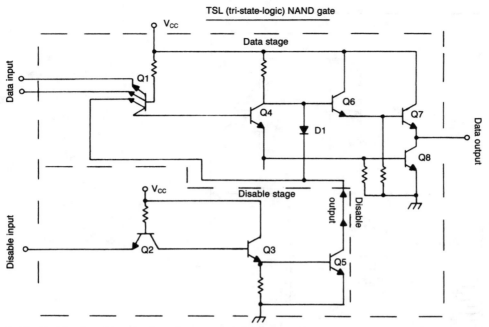

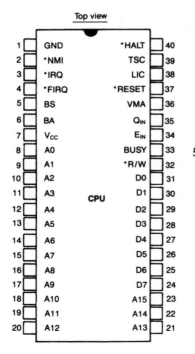

5-10 Inside the chip are the microscopic wiring, transistors, diodes, etc. This is a schematic of a chip. The service access to these components are the pins of the chip not the components themselves.

5-11 Chips are packaged in containers and the pins stick out. This is a common package called a *DIP* (dual inline package).

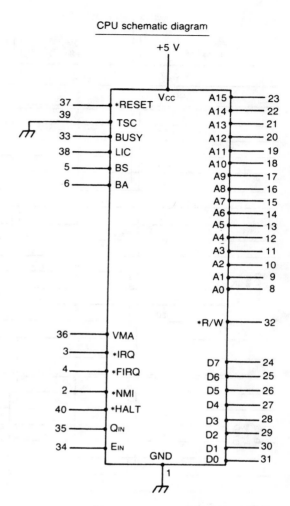

CPU schematic diagram

5-12 This is a schematic diagram of a chip package. Note that the pin layout is different. You must learn to relate the numbers on the chip package actual pinout to the numbers on the schematic representation of the package. They are usually not the same.

The test technique is to take a reading of each pin and compare it with its predicted state and pulse condition. If the reading is not as it should be, that is a clue. A trouble could be nearby. If you find an incorrect condition then you must puzzle out why. You will learn all about these techniques as you proceed through the next chapters.

Pin Number	VOM Reading	Logic Probe		
		High (1)	Low (0)	Pulse
Vcc 7	+5 V	✓		
GND 1	0 V		✓	
8				✓
9				✓
10				✓
11				✓
12		✓		✓
13				✓
14		✓		✓
15		✓		✓
16	2.4 V - 4.0 V	✓		✓
17		✓		✓
18		✓		✓
19				✓
20				✓
21		✓		✓
22				✓
23		✓		✓
				✓
24				✓
25				✓
26				✓
27				✓
28				✓
29				✓
30				✓
31				✓
•Reset 37	+5 V	✓		
•Irq 3	+5 V	✓		✓
•Firq 4	+5 V	✓		
•Nmi 2	+5 V	✓		
•Halt 40	+5 V	✓		
QIN 35	+2.4 V			Blinking
EIN 34	+2.4 V			Blinking
•R/W 32	+5 V			✓

Label: 16 Address Lines A0-A15 (pins 8–23)
Label: 8 Data Lines D7-D0 (pins 24–31)
Label: Clock (QIN 35, EIN 34)

5-13   There are various forms of voltage and logic state service charts available that allow you to test actual voltages and states. The test results can then be compared to the charts to look for deviations from the norm.

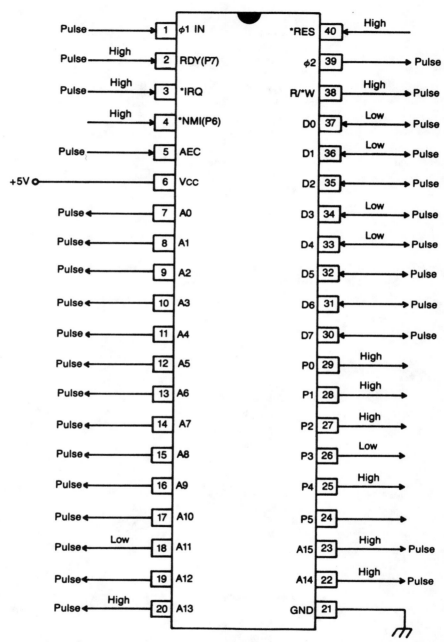

5-14 A service chart that shows the actual pinout of the chip with the prescribed logic states or voltages saves one step in your mind relating pins on a chart to the actual chip.

6

Testing large chips with lots of pins

AT THE CHIP LEVEL, YOUR PERSONAL COMPUTER CAN HAVE A BOARD WITH 100 or more chips on it. If you look closely at the pins you will see that most of the DIPs have 30 or less sticking out in the neat two-pin lines. Every here and there on the board you'll see a larger chip. These larger chips are often not DIPs but chip packages with other configurations. For instance, they could have pins sticking out from all four sides of a squarish package. When you count the number of pins on the larger chips you find that some have 40 pins, others can have 64, 68 and higher. Figure 6-1 illustrates the pin layout of an 80386 processor with 132 pins. These are the high pin-count chips. They are said to be in the class of *LSI* and *VLSI* (large- and very large-scale integration).

Down at the microscopic circuit level in the chips, a typical LSI is considered to possess about 1,000 or more individual germ size circuits. As mentioned, once these circuits have been cast in silicon, they become, from a troubleshooting point of view, one component. If one of the tiny transistors should fail and destroy the operation of the chip, because there is no way to test and repair that individual transistor, the entire chip with the 1,000 circuits must be discarded. Fortunately the large chips have proven to be quite reliable. However, on occasion, like any other electronic component, some of them will fail. The defective large chip is usually not too difficult to pinpoint and replace if you are briefed properly. This chapter will acquaint you with the servicing know how for these large chips.

Gaining access

The only way to gain access to the minute circuits in the chip is through the many pins that stick out of the large chip package. The pins connect internally to groupings of the little circuits. For example, a 40-pin chip contains about 1,000 circuits.

105

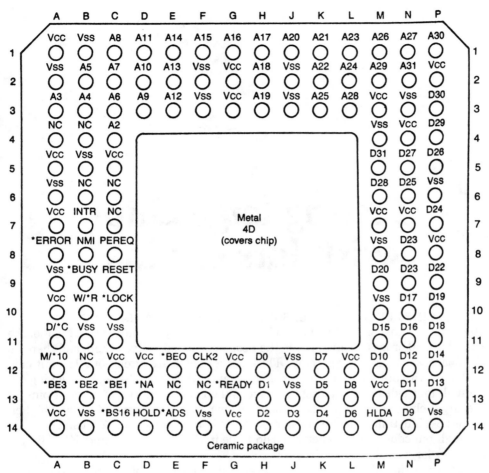

6-1 The 80386 is representative of the way chips are becoming larger and larger. It has a complicated layout of 132 pins.

That means, on an average, one pin connects to about 25 transistor circuits. Each transistor circuit operates with about 10 input-output leads. This means each pin connects to about 250 internal nodes. Unfortunately, you cannot test each of these nodes. There is no access to these individual nodes. You are limited to a single pin that then connects to 250 nodes.

That is why, during testing, you must practically ignore the internal circuitry of the chip and consider the legged packages as a single component. A 40-pin package thus has 40 available pins sticking out of a black box. Only 40 pins can then be used as test points for your logic probe, VOM, scope, continuity tester and other equipment. Only the creator of the chip knows what it contains down to the last detail.

In this chapter, you will take an overview of these large integrated chips, some of which are diagrammed roughly in Fig. 6-2 and possibly found in your personal computer or on one you are called upon to fix. They are the various 8-bit, 16- and 32-bit processors, parallel and serial I/O chips, special kind of addressing chips, and typical video and audio I/O devices. The discussions are on the chip level and do not consider the internal microscopic transistor circuits.

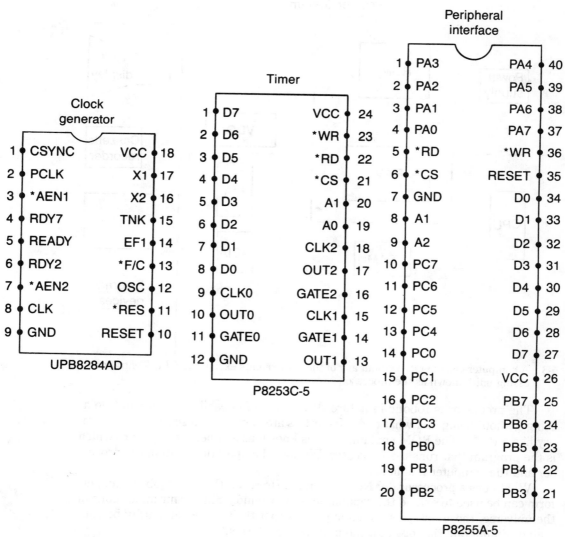

6-2 Typical support chips are becoming more complex. These are diagrams of a few of them.

Processors

A computer (Fig. 6-3), is a computer because of the microprocessor, more commonly referred to simply as the *processor*. Without the processor, there is no computer. A processor can be a computer all by itself without any other circuits. It is the heart of any computer.

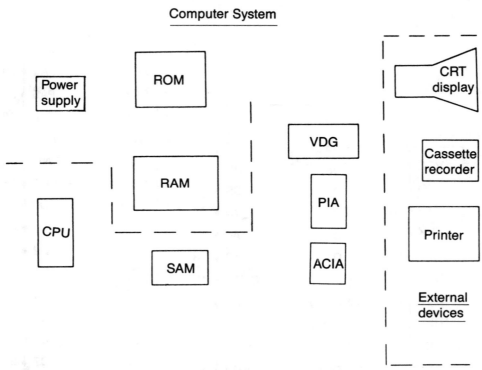

6-3   A computer can operate without any of the components except the *CPU* (central processing unit) known as the processor.

The processor is robotic in nature. It has lots of capability but it can't do a thing without being told what to do. Its orders are contained in some sort of memory like a ROM. The ROM contains what is known as an operating system, which is the program that runs the processor. Without the operating system the processor and the computer it is in is helpless.

What does a processor do? Not that much. However, those few jobs it can perform can be used to extend the capabilities of our minds. Since your minds control the universe, those few jobs are so important that their value can hardly be estimated. Enumerate the jobs that the processor performs.

First of all, the processor is able to store digital bits in memory registers (Figs. 6-4 and 6-5). This is called writing to memory. Then once the bits are in memory,

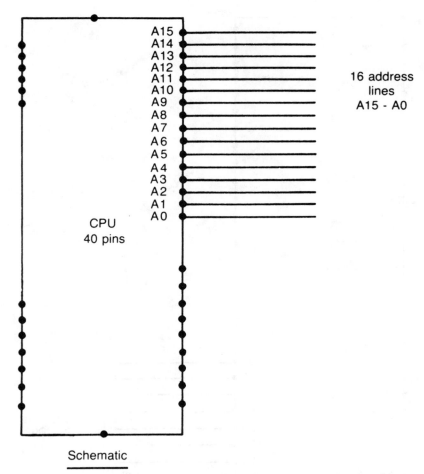

Schematic

6-4 A processor is given a number of address lines. It sends out combinations of bits that unlock and access every memory location.

the processor is able to obtain a copy of the bits and load them back into its own registers. This is called reading from memory.

Besides writing the bits to memory, the processor can write those bits to an I/O chip. When it does this the I/O chips in turn can output the bits to a peripheral like a printer or disk drive. The processor can also read bits from an I/O chip. When it does that the I/O chip can take in bits from a peripheral like a keyboard or cassette player.

The reading and writing of bits (Fig. 6-6) works just like your mind. You can read information into your head through your input mechanism, your eyes. Then you can write information back out of your head through your fingers. You can also talk information out of your head through your mouth.

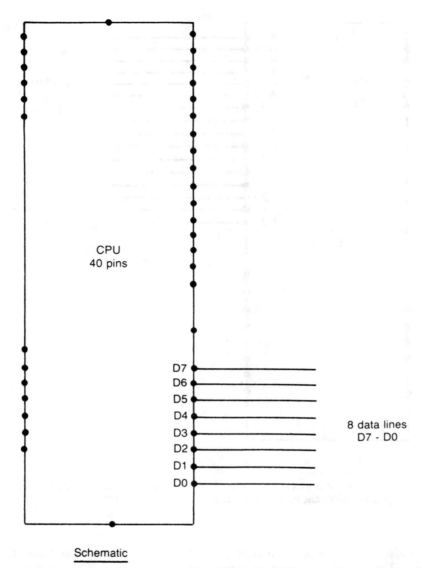

CPU
40 pins

D7
D6
D5
D4
D3
D2
D1
D0

8 data lines
D7 - D0

Schematic

6-5 A processor is given a number of data lines. It can write combinations of bits to addressed locations or read bits out of the locations.

If you sit and think you are able to read information stored in your memory banks in your head and then write any conclusions you have arrived at back into your memory. The computer is simply aping your normal mental activity. Your personal processor in your head conducts this work continually.

In addition to reading and writing the computer processor must process the digital bits while they are in its grasp. In the processor is a group of circuits that

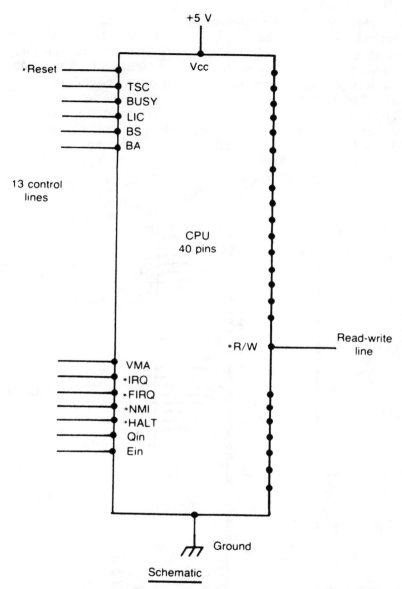

+5 V

Vcc

•Reset

TSC
BUSY
LIC
BS
BA

13 control
lines

CPU
40 pins

*R/W

Read-write
line

VMA
*IRQ
*FIRQ
*NMI
*HALT
Qin
Ein

Ground

Schematic

6-6 The rest of the lines send or receive control bits that perform the various control functions. For example, the read-write line controls the direction the bits travel on the data lines.

can do mathematical and logical manipulations to the digital bits. There is nothing spectacular in these manipulations. You can do them with pencil and paper. What is spectacular and what makes the computer so valuable is one thing. The *speed* at which the computer performs the calculations. It can do calculations in a few moments that would take you months with pencil and paper. The computer makes moves that are measured in billionths of a second. Fortunately, troubleshooting and repair techniques do not get involved very often with these blinding speeds. Most tests are made while the computer is either turned off or sitting idly.

A typical 40-pin processor, at first glance, appears formidable. It seems to be very complicated. However, a closer look shows many pins doing exactly the same thing. For instance, in the example schematic diagram of a processor (Fig. 6-7) there are eight pins labeled, D7 – D0. These are the data bus pins. They are the lines that transfer a byte of eight digital bits to and from memory registers and I/O registers. There are D7 – D0 connections on all the memory and I/O chips. That takes care of eight of the 40 pins on the processor.

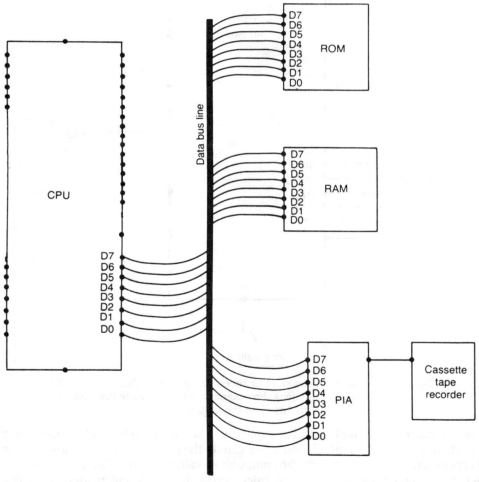

6-7 On the chips in the memory map, which have registers, are data bus connections that lead to the processor.

Also on the schematic (Fig. 6-4) there are 16 pins labeled A15 – A0. These are the address bus pins. They connect to the same chips the data bus pins do. The address pins carry the memory or I/O chip address in two bytes of digital bits. The address bus opens up the addressed register, and leaves all the rest of the registers closed tight. That way the data bus bits can travel to or from the one byte sized register that the address bus opens up. Between the two bus lines 24 of the 40 processor pins are accounted for.

Two more of the pins are needed to energize the processor. Typically + 5 V is applied to one of the pins and the other is connected to the chassis ground. Often some of the rest of the pins are not used. If you figure that four pins are unused, then we are left with 10 more pins not accounted for. These pins are used to control certain aspects of the processor operation.

The pins are made up of two or three interrupt pins and two or three that are connected to the operation of the clock. Others are for special controls to turn the processor on and off and to let the processor turn distant devices off and on. Lastly there is usually some sort of reset pin to reset the registers in the processor on certain occasions. Specific details on these operations are found in this chapter and in chapters 13, 14, 15, 16, and 17.

A word on bits and bytes

The processor operates with bits and bytes. A byte is nothing more than a collection of eight bits. Note that the data bus was composed of eight lines and was able to carry eight bits at the same time over parallel lines. The 16-bit address bus is able to send out from the processor two bytes at the same time. You'll see buses on larger processors with more lines. A processor is usually called an 8-bit type when its data bus is eight bits and its address bus is 16 bits. A 16-bit processor usually has 16 lines in its data bus. Theoretically, a 16-bit processor has 32 address lines, but not many of them actually do. However, they do appear often with 24 address lines. There is a lot more about this subject in chapters 14, 15, 16 and 17.

Computers usually work in terms of bytes (Fig. 6-8). The processor might be a 4-bit (^{1}/$_2$ byte), an 8-bit (one byte), a 16-bit (two bytes) or even a 32-bit (four byte) type. They are all forms of bytes.

A binary bit is known as a 1 or a 0 by machine language programmers. The same bit is thought of as a high or a low by engineers and technicians. What is a bit in reality? It is a dc voltage level (as seen on a scope face in Fig. 6-9). It can be measured with a voltmeter. The meter will read a voltage near + 5 V when it touches down on a high or a 1. The meter will read zero volts when its probe touches a low or a binary 0.

There is no in between with highs and lows. A bit is either a high or a low (Fig. 6-10). The two conditions are called logic states. This is what digital logic is, a high + 5 V or a low 0 V, with nothing in between. This is in comparison to analog states. If we use the same range of 0 to + 5 V in analog, all the voltages between 0 and + 5 V are taken into account. There are an infinite number of voltage levels between 0 and + 5 V in the analog world (as Fig. 6-11 shows). In the digital world there are only two levels, the low level and the high level.

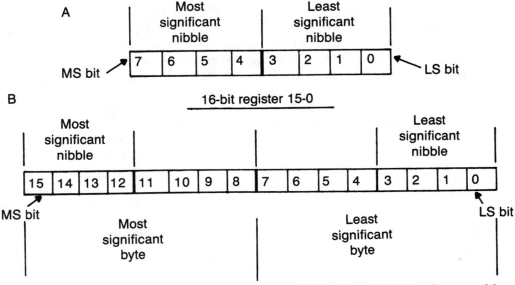

6-8   Computers are designed to work with collections of eight bits called *bytes*. A group of four bits is a *nibble*. A set of 16 bits is known as a *word*. 32 bits is a *double word*.

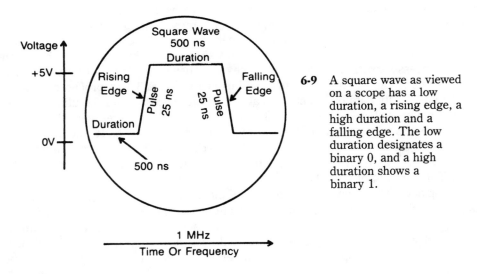

6-9   A square wave as viewed on a scope has a low duration, a rising edge, a high duration and a falling edge. The low duration designates a binary 0, and a high duration shows a binary 1.

To confuse the issue, if a voltage level between 0 and +5 V should appear in a digital circuit, it is called the third digital state (Fig. 6-12). This is a state of no state. When the digital level three states, it has left the digital world and become an analog voltage. It has no meaning in the world of bits and bytes. It is as if it is turned off. What happens in a circuit is, the digital level is cut off, the circuit is still energized and goes into a high impedance state. If you take a voltmeter reading of the pin it will read somewhere in the middle of 0 and +5 V. This three-state effect

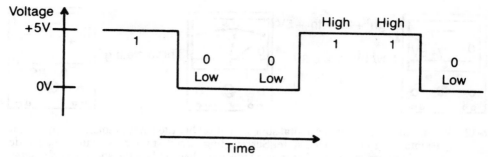

6-10 These six bits are part of a digital wave train full of high and low bits. The rising and falling edges between bits do not count.

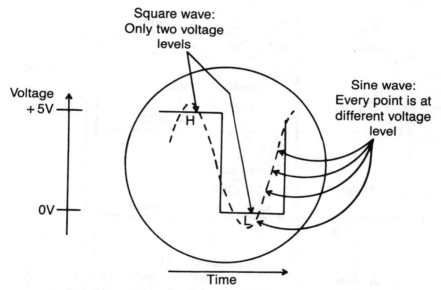

6-11 The digital square wave shown with solid lines only has two voltage levels, high, and low. The analog sine wave shown with the dotted line, can have an infinite number of voltage levels. There is one at every point on the wave shape.

is very important in computers. It is a form of off-on switch (Fig. 6-13). It turns a digital signal off and switches an analog signal on that the digital computer is able to safely ignore. There will be more about three-stating later on in the various chapters. It has a lot of test importance.

The processor's work consists of moving the bits and bytes from place to place and changing them around. When a bit enters the input of a circuit it can turn the circuit on or turn it off, according to the state of the bit and the configuration of the circuit. That is really about all that is going on in digital circuits. The processor makes bits and bytes travel from place to place turning circuits on and off.

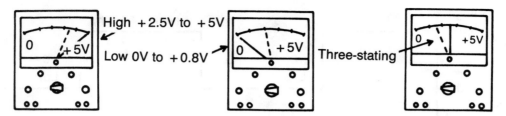

High +2.5V to +5V

Low 0V to +0.8V

Three-stating

6-12   When a data wave train or digital state is shut off but the circuit remains energized, it goes into a high impedance state. Surrounding circuit static noise can develop a dc voltage level somewhere in between a high and a low. This is the so-called *third state*, *tristate* or *three state*. This condition can be an important symptom during troubleshooting.

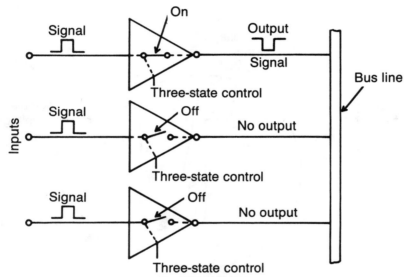

6-13   A tristate condition is required during normal operation to keep all circuits off except desired ones. A troubleshooter must know which circuits are supposed to be off and which ones on. During problems, tristating could also be a symptom of a circuit that stopped working.

Ranges of bits and bytes

The bits and bytes are code numbers. If you enter a single decimal digit at the keyboard, the number is coded into four bits. If you enter a 7 it is coded into low-high-high-high. That is binary for 7. Table 6-1 shows the binary codes for 0 – 15. That is the range of four binary bits. Four bits are called a nibble, which is half of a byte.

When you put two nibbles together to form a byte, they can form binary codes for the range of 0 – 255.

**Table 6-1. Each four bit nibble can code
16 decimal or hexadecimal numbers.
Two nibbles joined together to form
a byte can code 256 decimal or hex numbers.**

Hex-Binary Code Table	
Decimal	Hex / Binary
0	0 / 0000
1	1 / 0001
2	2 / 0010
3	3 / 0011
4	4 / 0100
5	5 / 0101
6	6 / 0110
7	7 / 0111
8	8 / 1000
9	9 / 1001
10	A / 1010
11	B / 1011
12	C / 1100
13	D / 1101
14	E / 1110
15	F / 1111

The data bus is able to transport a full byte of data. Each binary byte it carries then can be any decimal code number between 0 and 255 (like the numbers in Table 6-2). It is all according to the arrangement of the highs and lows.

**Table 6-2. This handy conversion chart
shows the coding of one byte in decimal, binary, and hex.**

Decimal	Binary	Hex	Decimal	Binary	Hex
0	0000 0000	0 0	41	0010 1001	2 9
1	0000 0001	0 1	42	0010 1010	2 A
2	0000 0010	0 2	43	0010 1011	2 B
3	0000 0011	0 3	44	0010 1100	2 C
4	0000 0100	0 4	45	0010 1101	2 D
5	0000 0101	0 5			
6	0000 0110	0 6	46	0010 1110	2 E
7	0000 0111	0 7	47	0010 1111	2 F
8	0000 1000	0 8			
9	0000 1001	0 9	48	0011 0000	3 0
10	0000 1010	0 A	49	0011 0001	3 1
11	0000 1011	0 B	50	0011 0010	3 2
12	0000 1100	0 C	51	0011 0011	3 3
13	0000 1101	0 D	52	0011 0100	3 4
14	0000 1110	0 E	53	0011 0101	3 5
15	0000 1111	0 F	54	0011 0110	3 6
			55	0011 0111	3 7
16	0001 0000	1 0	56	0011 1000	3 8
17	0001 0001	1 1	57	0011 1001	3 9
18	0001 0010	1 2	58	0011 1010	3 A
19	0001 0011	1 3	59	0011 1011	3 B
20	0001 0100	1 4	60	0011 1100	3 C
21	0001 0101	1 5	61	0011 1101	3 D
22	0001 0110	1 6	62	0011 1110	3 E
23	0001 0111	1 7	63	0011 1111	3 F
24	0001 1000	1 8			
25	0001 1001	1 9	64	0100 0000	4 0
26	0001 1010	1 A	65	0100 0001	4 1
27	0001 1011	1 B	66	0100 0010	4 2
28	0001 1100	1 C	67	0100 0011	4 3
29	0001 1101	1 D	68	0100 0100	4 4
30	0001 1110	1 E	69	0100 0101	4 5
31	0001 1111	1 F	70	0100 0110	4 6
			71	0100 0111	4 7
32	0010 0000	2 0	72	0100 1000	4 8
33	0010 0001	2 1	73	0100 1001	4 9
34	0010 0010	2 2	74	0100 1010	4 A
35	0010 0011	2 3	75	0100 1011	4 B
36	0010 0100	2 4	76	0100 1100	4 C
37	0010 0101	2 5	77	0100 1101	4 D
38	0010 0110	2 6	78	0100 1110	4 E
39	0010 0111	2 7	79	0100 1111	4 F
40	0010 1000	2 8			
			80	0101 0000	5 0

Table 6-2. Continued.

Decimal	Binary	Hex		Decimal	Binary	Hex	
81	0101 0001	5	1	128	1000 0000	8	0
82	0101 0010	5	2	129	1000 0001	8	1
83	0101 0011	5	3	130	1000 0010	8	2
84	0101 0100	5	4	131	1000 0011	8	3
85	0101 0101	5	5	132	1000 0100	8	4
86	0101 0110	5	6	133	1000 0101	8	5
87	0101 0111	5	7	134	1000 0110	8	6
88	0101 1000	5	8	135	1000 0111	8	7
89	0101 1001	5	9	136	1000 1000	8	8
90	0101 1010	5	A	137	1000 1001	8	9
				138	1000 1010	8	A
91	0101 1011	5	B	139	1000 1011	8	B
92	0101 1100	5	C	140	1000 1100	8	C
93	0101 1101	5	D	141	1000 1101	8	D
94	0101 1110	5	E	142	1000 1110	8	E
95	0101 1111	5	F	143	1000 1111	8	F
96	0110 0000	6	0				
97	0110 0001	6	1	144	1001 0000	9	0
98	0110 0010	6	2	145	1001 0001	9	1
99	0110 0011	6	3	146	1001 0010	9	2
100	0110 0100	6	4	147	1001 0011	9	3
101	0110 0101	6	5	148	1001 0100	9	4
102	0110 0110	6	6	149	1001 0101	9	5
103	0110 0111	6	7	150	1001 0110	9	6
104	0110 1000	6	8	151	1001 0111	9	7
105	0110 1001	6	9	152	1001 1000	9	8
106	0110 1010	6	A	153	1001 1001	9	9
107	0110 1011	6	B	154	1001 1010	9	A
108	0110 1100	6	C	155	1001 1011	9	B
109	0110 1101	6	D	156	1001 1100	9	C
110	0110 1110	6	E	157	1001 1101	9	D
111	0110 1111	6	F	158	1001 1110	9	E
				159	1001 1111	9	F
112	0111 0000	7	0				
113	0111 0001	7	1	160	1010 0000	A	0
114	0111 0010	7	2	161	1010 0001	A	1
115	0111 0011	7	3	162	1010 0010	A	2
116	0111 0100	7	4	163	1010 0011	A	3
117	0111 0101	7	5	164	1010 0100	A	4
118	0111 0110	7	6	165	1010 0101	A	5
119	0111 0111	7	7	166	1010 0110	A	6
120	0111 1000	7	8	167	1010 0111	A	7
121	0111 1001	7	9	168	1010 1000	A	8
122	0111 1010	7	A	169	1010 1001	A	9
123	0111 1011	7	B	170	1010 1010	A	A
124	0111 1100	7	C	171	1010 1011	A	B
125	0111 1101	7	D	172	1010 1100	A	C
126	0111 1110	7	E	173	1010 1101	A	D
127	0111 1111	7	F	174	1010 1110	A	E

Table 6-2. Continued.

Decimal	Binary	Hex	Decimal	Binary	Hex
175	1010 1111	A F	216	1101 1000	D 8
			217	1101 1001	D 9
176	1011 0000	B 0	218	1101 1010	D A
177	1011 0001	B 1			
178	1011 0010	B 2	219	1101 1011	D B
179	1011 0011	B 3	220	1101 1100	D C
180	1011 0100	B 4	221	1101 1101	D D
181	1011 0101	B 5	222	1101 1110	D E
182	1011 0110	B 6	223	1101 1111	D F
183	1011 0111	B 7			
184	1011 1000	B 8	224	1110 0000	E 0
185	1011 1001	B 9	225	1110 0001	E 1
186	1011 1010	B A	226	1110 0010	E 2
187	1011 1011	B B	227	1110 0011	E 3
188	1011 1100	B C	228	1110 0100	E 4
189	1011 1101	B D	229	1110 0101	E 5
190	1011 1110	B E	230	1110 0110	E 6
191	1011 1111	B F	231	1110 0111	E 7
			232	1110 1000	E 8
192	1100 0000	C 0	233	1110 1001	E 9
193	1100 0001	C 1	234	1110 1010	E A
194	1100 0010	C 2	235	1110 1011	E B
195	1100 0011	C 3	236	1110 1100	E C
196	1100 0100	C 4	237	1110 1101	E D
197	1100 0101	C 5	238	1110 1110	E E
198	1100 0110	C 6	239	1110 1111	E F
199	1100 0111	C 7			
200	1100 1000	C 8	240	1111 0000	F 0
201	1100 1001	C 9	241	1111 0001	F 1
202	1100 1010	C A	242	1111 0010	F 2
203	1100 1011	C B	243	1111 0011	F 3
204	1100 1100	C C	244	1111 0100	F 4
205	1100 1101	C D	245	1111 0101	F 5
206	1100 1110	C E	246	1111 0110	F 6
207	1100 1111	C F	247	1111 0111	F 7
			248	1111 1000	F 8
208	1101 0000	D 0	249	1111 1001	F 9
209	1101 0001	D 1	250	1111 1010	F A
210	1101 0010	D 2	251	1111 1011	F B
211	1101 0011	D 3	252	1111 1100	F C
212	1101 0100	D 4	253	1111 1101	F D
213	1101 0101	D 5	254	1111 1110	F E
214	1101 0110	D 6	255	1111 1111	F F
215	1101 0111	D 7			

The address bus of 16 lines can in the same manner pass 16 bits from the processor to the chips. Sixteen bits can be arranged in 65,536 ways. Each arrangement is a different decimal code. Therefore the range of a 16-bit address bus is 65,536 different addresses. This is known as 64K.

It can be seen that an 8-bit processor that has 16 address lines is able to form 65,536 different addresses, starting with address number 0 and going up to address number 65,535. In a 16-bit processor, there could be a possible 32 address lines on a chip with 64 pins. If a processor does have 32 lines it is able to form an astounding 4,294,967,296 addresses. This is known as 4 gigabytes.

At the present time there are only a few address buses that can conduct 4 gigabytes of registers. Typically the highest number of address lines in personal computers is 24. Twenty-four address lines are able to contact 16,777,216 addresses. This is normally an adequate amount of memory a processor needs to address.

If you are wondering how these amounts of addresses are calculated, it is easy. One address line is able to contact two addresses. An address is nothing more than a turned off electronic circuit that has a combination of highs and lows input to it. The right combination of logic state bits will activate the circuit, otherwise it remains turned off. If an address bus has one line it can be attached to two addresses. A low will turn one address on and a high will turn the other address on. Otherwise the addresses remain off.

If you add a second address line, the two-line bus can be attached to four addresses. There are four possible combinations of bits that two lines can purvey. They are:

> low-low
> low-high
> high-low
> high-high

Each address circuit can be wired to turn on in response to one of the four different bit combinations.

If you add a third line to the bus, the number of bit combinations possible will double. They are:

> low-low-low
> low-low-high
> low-high-low
> low-high-high
> high-low-low
> high-low-high
> high-high-low
> high-high-high

Every time another address line is added the number of possible bit combinations is doubled. Each bit combination will open up a different address. Table 6-3 shows the possible addresses of processors with address buses that range from 16

**Table 6-3. Each additional address line
doubles the number of register
locations a processor is able to access.**

Address Lines	8-Bit Locations
16	64K
17	128K
18	256K
19	512K
20	1024K
21	2058K
22	4096K
23	8192K
24	16 MBYTES
•	
•	
•	
32	4 GIGABYTES (BILLIONS)

to 24. In personal computers you will not normally encounter address buses with less than 16 lines nor more than 24.

Data bus lines are normally either one byte, two bytes or four bytes wide. In the 8-bit computers a data bus is 8 bits or one byte wide. The 16-bit computer features a data bus that is 16 bits or two bytes wide. The 32-bit computer can have a data bus that is 32 bits or four bytes wide.

The registers in memory and on I/O chips are, for the most part, only one byte wide. When we speak of the number of registers in memory we are normally referring to one byte for each address. There are many schemes to combine the byte sized registers, but the memory chips are usually designed as byte sized, not two or four bytes wide. If a 16-bit computer is addressing 16 bits it is addressing two byte sized registers.

Fetch and execute cycle

When your processor is running a program, more than 70% of the instructions it follows are the reading and writing of memory and I/O that has been mentioned. The other 30% of instructions are mostly the processing of the data the processor is transporting back and forth over the data bus.

The entire operation has been dubbed that familiar term, *fetch and execute*. Here is what happens in all computers as a program is run.

When the processor is told to RUN by you it is built to address the first location in memory. If the processor is an 8-bit type it has 16 address lines. It sends out bits LLLLLLLLLLLLLLLL. This combination of bits opens up decimal location 0 (Fig. 6-14). Note that the address only goes to memory and does not return, ever. The address bus is therefore a collection of one-way lines, from the processor to the addressed location.

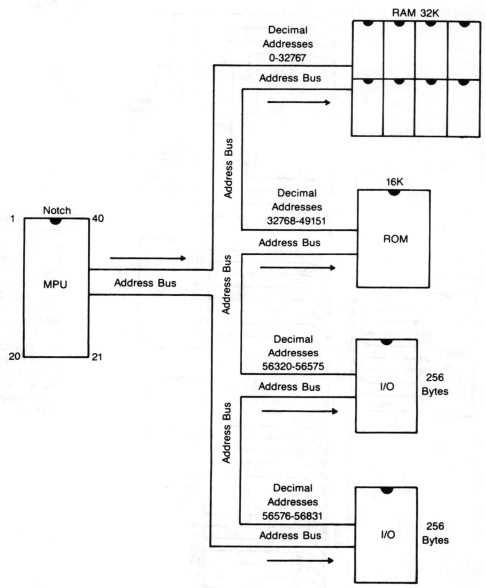

6-14 A processor is built to automatically address every memory map location, in sequence, beginning with 0. The processor will encounter these chips as it sequences from 0 to 65,535.

A typical instruction is the command to read the contents of the location. The location in memory is a byte-sized register. The eight bits of the register is connected to the 8-bit data bus lines (Fig. 6-15). When the location is addressed it opens up. As it is commanded to be read it places a copy of its eight bit contents

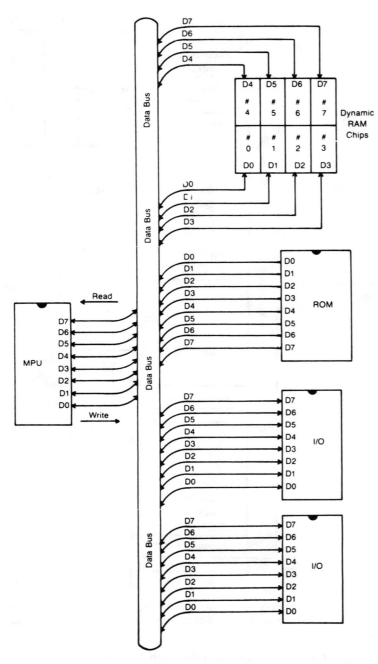

6-15 Each register in an 8-bit computer has bits D7 – D0. These bits are in turn connected to data bus lines D7 – D0 that emerge from the processor. Note the set of eight RAM chips each connect to one data bus line. Each RAM chip contains only one set of bit holders. For instance on the #7 chip are all the D7 bits, on the #6 chip are all the D6 bits, etc.

onto the data bus. The copy then flashes over to the data pins of the processor. The bit information then enters the processor.

Note that the data traveled from the memory to the processor over the data bus, during this read operation. If it had been a write operation the data would have traveled from the processor to the memory location over the same data bus lines and been stored in the memory register. The fact that data can go both ways makes the data bus a collection of two-way lines between the processor and the memory locations. The eight data lines are connected to all locations. The locations are all eight bits wide. Each location has a D7, D6, D5, D4, D3, D2, D1, and D0 connection. All like connections are joined together. All locations are closed until one is addressed. Then that one opens and can be read or written to.

Once the beginning byte has been fetched, it is in the processor. This first byte is an *instruction*. The processor is built to follow its designed instructions. A processor is able to follow the instructions in its *instruction set*. An instruction set can have between 50 and 100 instructions. The number varies according to different processors. There will be more detailed information on instruction sets in chapters 14, 15, 16 and 17.

The instruction, by means of its 8-bit combination code, tells the processor what to do. Typically, the bytes, in locations following the instruction byte, is data, or an address where data can be found. The instruction is followed by the processor. It might be a simple instruction such as, load the data in the next byte into the Accumulator register.

In accordance, the processor will address the next byte, decimal 1, with LLLLLLLLLLLLLLLH. This fetches the next byte, which is data. It executes the instruction and loads the data into the Accumulator register. That is what *fetch and execute* is all about.

Other instructions

The processor besides spending so much time addressing locations and transporting data in and out of storage does some internal work. In the processor are a number of special-purpose registers and a section called the *ALU* (arithmetic logic unit). Your pocket calculator is mostly an ALU. As the name implies the ALU processes data by means of arithmetic and logic.

Although the processor uses the read and write instructions more than 70% of the time, the rest of the instructions deal with data being processed in the special purpose registers and the ALU. There are many more of these instructions than there are read and write instructions, even though the read and write ones are used more.

Even though an instruction set might have 75 specific instructions, there are only about two dozen actual instructions. There is a lot of repetition of instructions with the use of different registers. For instance, a read instruction can be made to read data into four different registers. That would require four separate combinations of bits, one for each register.

The types of instructions break down into three categories. One, is addressing instructions. These instructions all cause certain kinds of addresses to be output from the processor. Two, there are a number of data moving instructions including the read and write types. Three, there are about a dozen data processing instructions. These include the arithmetic and logic instructions. Table 6-4 lists the different types. There is more detail on them in chapters 14, 15, 16 and 17.

Table 6-4. Processor instructions come in three categories.

1- Addressing Instructions	2- Data Moving Instructions	3- Data Processing Instructions
Branch	Store	Add
Jump	Load	Subtract
Call	Move	Multiply
Return	Exchange	Divide
Halt	I/O	AND
		OR
		Exclusive OR
		Shift
		Rotate
		Clear
		Complement
		Increment
		Decrement

To sum up, a computer is able to process binary logic states. The logic states are binary codes for data to be processed. It is worth your while to take the time to code your data into binary bits because the computer can process those bits at blinding speeds. The binary results of the processing can then be decoded back to the data you understand.

The processor, as its name implies, does the processing in its calculator section, the ALU. The processor is also able to address I/O chips and thus control the input and output of data through the I/O chips. The processor is also able to address memory locations and thus be able to move data in and out of memory storage as required during the processing. Chapter 14 describes the 8-bit processors you are likely to have in your personal computer. Chapter 15 covers the most popular 16-bit processors. Chapters 16 and 17 cover the 80386 and 80486 processors.

I/O chips

The processor is inside the computer. It works with the memory chips. The processor and memory cannot be contacted directly by peripherals. They are in a world of their own (Fig. 6-16). They communicate with each other transferring data back and forth over the data bus. The processor is in control because it decides what memory registers it wants to contact by means of its address bus.

The processor is also able to communicate with the I/O chips because the data bus connects to them too. The processor, in addition, connects up to the I/O chips with some lines from the address bus. The processor allows the I/O chips to connect to its private little computing world. However, the I/O chips also connect to the outside world. The I/O chips are ports of entry and exit. While one side connects to the processor's data and address lines, its other side connects to a plug

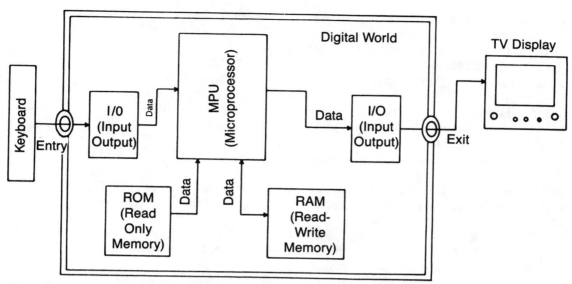

6-16 Actual computing only takes place in the digital world. The I/O chip forms the interface to the outside world.

that can receive inputs from peripherals such as the keyboard, joysticks, cassettes, and disk drives. The plugs can also output signals to peripherals like the printer, cassettes, disk drives, TV displays, audio systems, and so on.

There are all sorts of I/O chips. They normally have high pin counts. Some of them can have 28 pins and others 40 pins. Chapters 20, 21, and 22 cover them in detail. In chapter 20 digital-to-digital I/O chips are discussed. The I/O chips must deal with two types of signals, analog and digital.

Digital signals are those that are composed of logic states. That is either on or off with no in between. Analog signals are composed of a varying signal that can rise to a peak, and can fall to bottom with plenty of activity in between. For example, an off-on switch on your wall is a digital device. It can switch the electricity on or off, 110 V or zero V. There are no other output voltages possible when the switch is operating o.k.

On the other hand, if you install a dimmer switch instead of the off-on switch, you have converted the digital output to an analog one. With the dimmer switch you can have output voltages of 110 and zero but also all the voltages in between are also available.

Inputs

The processor-memory world is a digital one. The outside world also has digital devices but many peripherals output a signal that is analog in nature. The common devices that a computer uses as peripherals provide both digital and analog outputs and need digital and/or analog inputs. For example the keyboard is a digital device. When you strike a key it is either on or off. This digital signal is then transferred to the processor in a digital-to-digital manner.

On the other hand a joystick has an analog voltage output. As you twirl the stick you are varying a potentiometer from high to low and back. It doesn't click from high to low, it smoothly moves from high to low. For example the high is +5 V and the low is 0 V. As the stick is moved, the voltage can slide from 0 V on up to +1, +2 and so on to +5 V. This analog output must be converted to digital before the processor can handle it.

The input from a cassette is also analog in nature and must be converted to digital before the processor-memory digital world can work with it. A cassette tape is not able to store digital signals as is. A cassette tape is built to store audio frequencies. When digital signals are stored on tape they must be coded into audio first.

The code is simple. A digital high is coded as a 2400 Hz audio tone. A low is made into a 1200 Hz tone. The tones are stored on the tape. If you listen to a tape with digital data on it you'll hear a conglomeration of these tones.

In order for the digital world to make sense out of an input from a tape, the analog audio tones must be converted to the original bit and byte structure. This is accomplished in special I/O circuits and chips that are covered in more detail in chapter 26.

Outputs

Once the digital world finishes processing the bits and bytes that are passed through it, the digital information must exit the processor-memory area and come out to be used in our world. The finished bits exit through the I/O ports. One type of output the computer produces is an analog composite TV signal to be seen on the display. There are special video chips that build this signal and send it on to the TV display system.

Another set of bits the I/O chips provide an exit for is the output for the printer. The printer is a computer in its own right and needs a digital input. In the computer the digital input is converted to the proper signals to drive the print head and mechanisms.

The computer then does not need to convert the output that goes to the printer to an analog form. It can simply make a digital-to-digital transfer. However, the printer requires the bits to be lined up in a specific way and have a number of control bits interspersed throughout the bit structure.

There are many other forms of outputs the computer must produce. The cassette tape is loaded with audio tones from a computer output. The disk drive has its floppies and hard disks filled with computer outputs. Sound outputs from computers must be converted from the digital creation of the sound to an analog arrangement before it can be heard over the computer's speaker. Chapters 20 and 21 cover these I/O systems.

Series and parallel

According to the needs of a peripheral device, the inputs and outputs of the computer can either be considered series or parallel. In the processor-memory digital world, for the most part, data is moved in a parallel fashion. In an 8-bit computer, the data bus consists of eight copper lines that run parallel to each other over the board. When the memory sends a byte to the processor during a read operation, all eight bits in the byte travel abreast over the eight lines. They leave the memory register together and arrive at the processor D7–D0 pins together. This, of course, is a parallel transfer of bits (Fig. 6-17A). When a write operation takes place a byte is transferred the other way over the data bus but the bits still move in a parallel fashion.

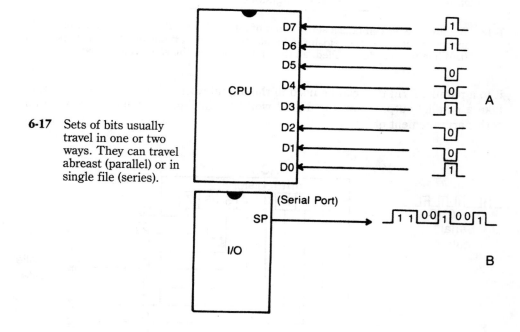

6-17 Sets of bits usually travel in one or two ways. They can travel abreast (parallel) or in single file (series).

This arrangement is fine inside the digital world. On the outside, the parallel movement of bits is not quite so perfect. For instance, the disk drive stores bits on a disk one at a time not eight at a time. In order to store a byte, the bits must be rearranged. The eight abreast bits of the bytes must be made to halt, each one makes a left turn and continue on in single file. That way the bits change their arrangement from parallel movement to series. Instead of trying to enter a disk eight at a time, which is not possible, the bits can enter one at a time (Fig. 6-17B).

It is easy to change a byte from parallel movement to series or vice versa in a circuit called a *shift register*. The shift register is a staple item in I/O circuits. A shift register can take a series input from a peripheral (as in Fig. 6-18) and change

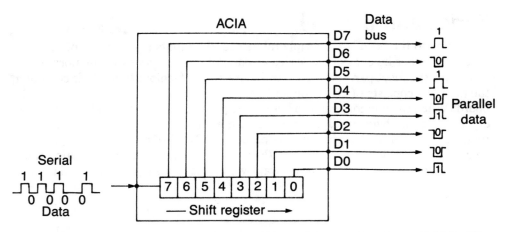

6-18   A shift register can take a series input of bits and convert them to parallel bits. The incoming bits enter the register in bit position 7 and shift one bit at a time to position 0. When the register is filled, all the bits can exit at the same time in parallel.

it to a parallel form that can be used in the digital world. A shift register can also take a parallel output from the digital world (as in Fig. 6-19) and change it to a series arrangement of bits.

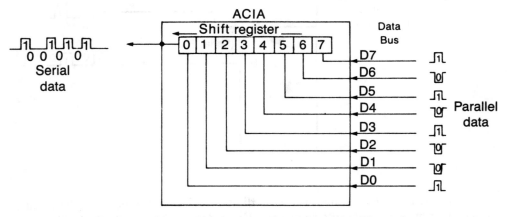

6-19   A shift register can also change a parallel bit input to serial. The register can receive the bits all at once and shift them out of bit position 0 one at a time.

When a byte of bits is in parallel form, it can move for the most part without any additional control bits being interspersed among them. When a byte is moving in series form though, it requires the careful insertion of start, stop and other bits, as shown in Fig. 6-20.

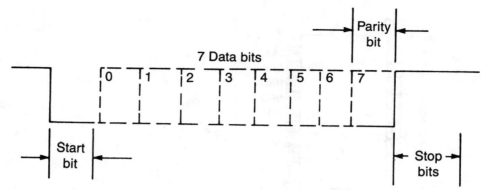

6-20 When bytes are transferred over a data bus, they match the circuits they traverse. When bytes move in serial file, they do not match up and require packaging with start bits, stop bits, and parity bits. The start bit alerts the circuit of the beginning of the serial byte, the stop bit of the end, and the parity of the byte validity.

Interface adapters

There are a number of 40-pin interface adapters that act as I/O ports to pass signals from peripherals to the processor-memory world and then back out to the peripherals after processing. One common chip is the *PIA* (peripheral interface adapter) (Fig. 6-21) and the *CIA* (complex interface adapter) (Fig. 6-22). Both of these chips, and others like them, are quite similar.

A PIA, known generically as a 6820 or 6821, has 40 pins with 24 of them devoted to inputting and outputting data directly. Connected to the D7 – D0 data bus lines inside the digital world are eight pins. Connected to plugs that go to the peripherals are two sets of eight pins each. The data bus pins are labeled D7 – D0, like the data bus lines. The pins that connect to the plugs are called PA7 – PA0 and PB7 – PB0, for Port A and Port B pin connections.

The processor is able to write data for export to the PIA or read data that is imported from the PIA. In order to read and write over the data bus, the processor must be able to address the PIA. It is easy to address the PIA because it only has four addresses. There are only four registers that must be addressed in comparison to the thousands upon thousands that are found in ROM and RAM.

Only five lines of the address lines need to be used to contact a PIA register, because there are only four addresses. Chips like PIAs, when they only need a few address lines to access them, use a few pins as *chip selects*. A chip select is a circuit that is empowered to keep the total chip in a three-state off condition except if the chip is enabled. The word *enabled* means *turned on*.

When the correct enabling bit arrives at a chip select pin, the circuit behind the pin will turn on. All chip selects must be enabled in order to turn on the chip. One or two chip select signals won't do it, all three chip selects must have the correct bits applied to the enabling circuit.

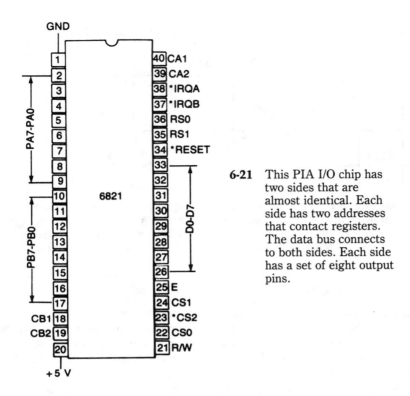

6-21 This PIA I/O chip has two sides that are almost identical. Each side has two addresses that contact registers. The data bus connects to both sides. Each side has a set of eight output pins.

In the PIA there are chip select pins called CS0, CS1, and *CS2. Note that CS2 has an asterisk (*) before the letters. When there is an asterisk or a line over top of the letters like CS, that is code for the fact that, the enabling signal must be a low. A high will not turn on *CS2. There are no asterisks in front of CS0 and CS1. The missing asterisk is also code. It means that the enabling signal must be a high. Therefore in order to select the PIA chip three address lines must send highs to CS0 and CS1 and a low to *CS2. When that happens the PIA turns on. What about the choice of one of four registers?

There are two register select pins also connected to address lines. They are called RS0 and RS1. With two register select pins, one of four registers can be selected. As discussed earlier, two bits can form four different combinations. They are low-low, low-high, high-low and high-high. In the PIA each register input circuit can be enabled by a different one of the four bit combinations. Therefore, once the PIA is selected with three address bits, the register desired can be selected with two more address bits.

Between the eight data bus pins, the 16 port A and B pins, the three chip selects and the two register selects, 29 pins are accounted for. The +5 volt power and the ground are two more. There are nine more pins to examine. Four of them are called CA1, CA2, CB1, and CB2. These are four more I/O pins that connect to the outside world like the port pins do. They do complex jobs and are discussed in more detail in chapter 18.

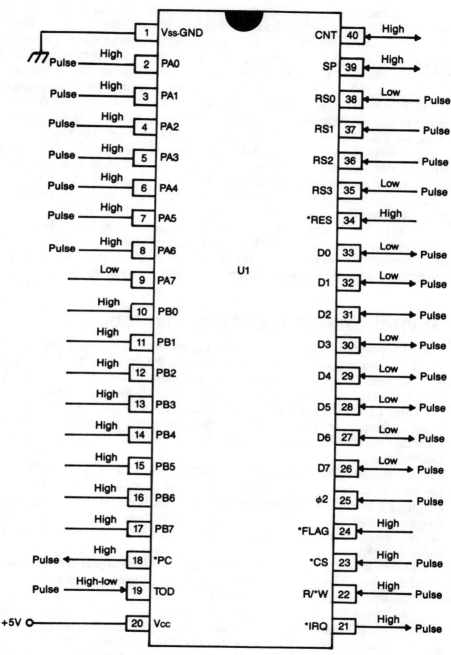

6-22 A CIA is like a PIA but is used with a different family of chips. This is a test-point chart that shows the direction of signal flow and the type of signal that should be present during normal operation.

The remaining five pins are all connected in the digital world. The E pin is another enabling signal that syncs the PIA into step with the beating of the system clock that is covered in chapter 13. The *RESET pin works when a low arrives at the pin from the processor. All the resetting operation does is reset the PIA registers to the initial bit positions it had when the computer was first turned on.

The two pins *IRQA and *IRQB, the interrupt request pins, are outputs from the PIA to the processor. At certain times the PIA needs to interrupt the operation of the processor. At those moments the PIA sends a bit over these lines and the processor gets the bits as an input. The interrupt can then take place.

The final PIA pin is called R/W. This means read and write. The processor, when it addresses the PIA and accesses a register has to tell the register to either send data or get ready to receive data. A read bit signal, which is a high, means send data. A write bit signal, which is a low, means get ready to receive data. The processor sends the read or write bit to the PIA over the R/W line.

CIAs and other similar chips all have pin usages like the PIA. The pins are out in the open and can be tested with the various kinds of test equipment to determine if the correct bits are present on the pins. What happens inside the chips to place the highs, lows and pulses on the pins is discussed in chapter 20.

Asynchronous interface adapters

The PIA interfaces peripherals to the digital world over eight-line data buses. These are parallel connections as all eight bits of a data byte get to travel abreast over the lines. The PIA can connect to peripherals that output parallel bytes of data and is used to transfer a byte at a time rather than a bit at a time.

The PIA is also capable of transferring a bit at a time, if the need is there. However, its primary purpose is to handle bytes rather than bits. There are other chips that are made expressly to handle a bit at a time. These are the shift registers mentioned earlier.

In the heading of this section, the word *asynchronous* is used. In the computer the transfer of data is conducted by the beat of the system clock, as discussed in chapter 13. When the PIA transfers data it is called *synchronous* because the PIA operates to the beat of the clock. In these shift register chips the data to and from the peripheral is in serial form, and as such, is not in sync with the clock. It is called *asynchronous*.

The shift register is able to act as either a serial-to-parallel converter when serial data is received from a peripheral or a parallel-to-serial converter when serial data must be transmitted to a peripheral.

The 24-pin DIP, shown in Fig. 6-23, is a typical asynchronous shift register chip. Connected to the digital world are the usual D7 – D0 pins to the data bus. On the port side only one line is needed to carry the serial data. There is one line for transferring serial data from the chip to the peripheral (TX, transmit data) and one line to transport data from the peripheral to the chip (RX, receive data).

The eight data pins and the two peripheral connections take up ten of the 24

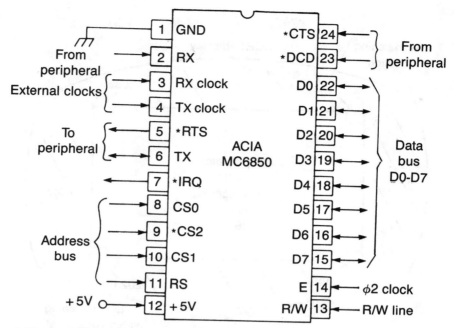

6-23 An ACIA is another type of I/O chip. It has serial port lines that connect to a peripheral. Inside are shift registers that convert the serial data to parallel. The parallel bytes can then make contact with the data bus.

pins of the chip. The +5 V power and ground use two more. Five more lines connect to the peripheral circuits. When an external clock is needed there are two pins the clock can be connected to. One is for the transmitter and the other for the receiver. There are three more peripheral connections to control the flow of data.

The address bus from the processor connects to four pins. There are three chip selects and one register select. The three chip selects are CS0, CS1, and *CS2. A set of high, high, low will select the chip. The single register select can make one of two register selections. There will be more about the operation of these shift registers in chapter 20.

Video-display generators

There are many schemes to convert the data that gets processed in the digital world, into an analog signal that can be seen clearly on the TV display. The computer must be able to construct the signals that can be applied to the TV monitor and produce the monochrome or color picture. A common picture that is constructed is one that shows 40 characters across and 25 down, for a total of 1000 characters. A character code can be stored in RAM in one byte (Fig. 6-24). Therefore this computer will use 1000 RAM addresses to store the display. Each character block in the display features the contents of one RAM address.

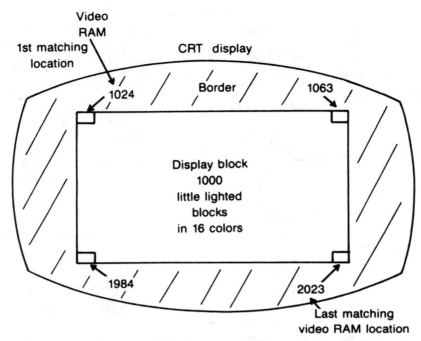

6-24 This display contains 1,000-character display blocks in a 40 × 25 matrix. Inside the computer 1,000 bytes of RAM is assigned to handle the video that will appear in each block. There is to be one byte of code for each block in the matrix. The RAM is at addresses 1024 through 2023. Appropriately this RAM area is called *video RAM*.

The monitor (Fig. 6-25) will light up the screen without any help from the computer. It has its own brightness and contrast controls like a TV. The computer must supply the character for the block. The computer must also supply the synchronization for the characters so they will be at their designated phosphor positions all the while the computer is on.

The characters on the screen, in order to stay in place, must emerge from the computer continually. A circuit in the computer must scan the video RAM again and again, extract a copy of the contents, and send the TV picture information onto the monitor on a continual basis. If the scanning is stopped the characters will disappear from the screen just as if a TV program goes off. A typical scanning frequency is 60 Hz since it matches the typical 60 Hz TV field rate (Fig. 6-26).

Character pointers

The character bytes in the video RAM are called *character pointers* (Fig. 6-27). A pointer is a collection of bits in a byte. In computerese, a pointer is an address in memory. The address points to a register in memory. The character pointers are aimed at a ROM storage area in memory that contains the character bit information to place a particular character on the TV screen.

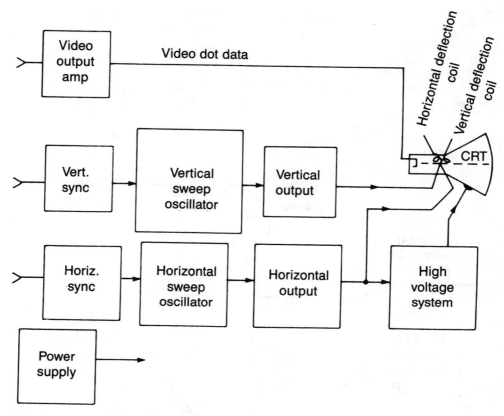

6-25 A computer TV monitor is a separate entity from the computer. All it needs from the computer are video dot data to display in the little blocks and sync signals to keep the blocks locked on the face of the monitor. The monitor produces a screenful of light with a high voltage system and sweep circuits. Chapter 23 has details.

For example, in Fig. 6-28, a character block on the TV screen could contain 64 dots in a matrix of 8 × 8. By turning on and turning off particular dots in the matrix any keyboard character can be made. All that is needed is to know what dots are to turn on and which ones should be turned off.

In the character ROM, in eight registers of one byte each, is a corresponding set of dots to match a character block on the screen. In the eight registers of eight bits each are highs and lows. The highs turn on a dot and the lows turn a dot off. The character ROM contains a complete set of information for every character that needs to be displayed.

The character pointers in video RAM, every time they are scanned by the processor, put their pointer bits out on the data bus. The processor then takes each pointer and addresses the character in the ROM that is pointed to. The 8 × 8 matrix information is then sent to the video display generator circuits.

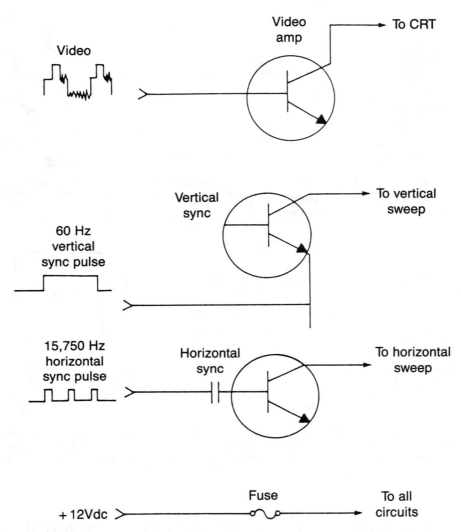

6-26 The monitor requires signals like these to put the computer information on the screen. There is a video signal, vertical sync pulses, and horizontal sync pulses.

In the video output chip, this dot information is changed to a series stream of analog video signals (such as in Fig. 6-29). The video signals are then sent on to the video circuit of the monitor where they are routed to the electron gun of the CRT. In the electron gun the signals that were digital highs light dots while digital lows extinguish dots.

Besides sending video dot information to the monitor, the video circuits might have to send sync signals too, so the video turns the correct dots on and off. Some personal computers package up the sync information with the video. Others like

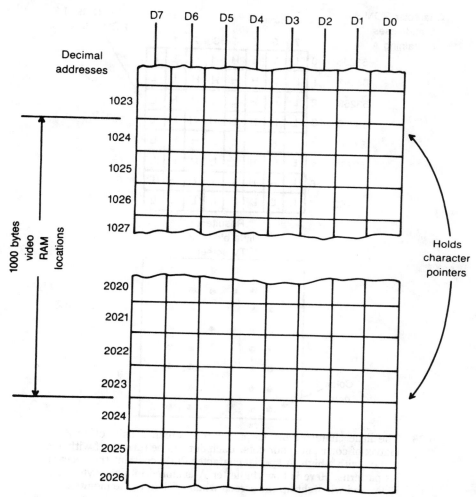

6-27   These addresses in memory are typical of the video RAM locations. They are filled with addresses known as pointers. The pointers tell the processor the address of a ROM storage area that contains the character pattern bit information that will place a character on the TV screen.

the IBM PC have separate sync circuits and the video circuits only send video. Chapter 22 goes into more detail on these different video processing methods.

Typical video generator

A typical video generator has the job of converting digital bits to TV pictures consisting of characters or graphics. This is a digital-to-analog conversion. The generator must take the high and low voltages, change them to continuous voltages and then get them in the synchronized form to be displayed.

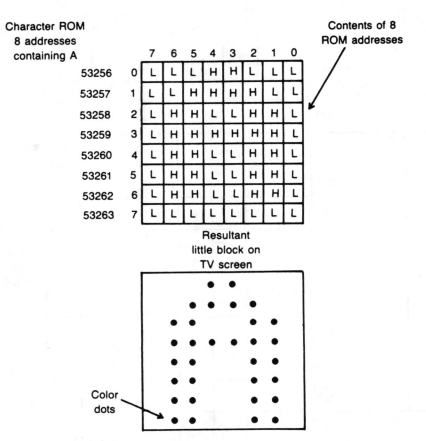

6-28   The little character blocks on the TV screen consist of an 8 × 8 matrix of color phosphor dots. Each dot can be turned off with a low and on with a high. A special character ROM contains the necessary bit patterns. Here is how the letter A is stored in eight bytes of the ROM and will light up the screen when applied to the monitor.

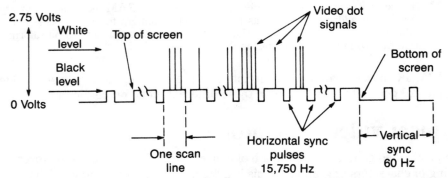

6-29   This is a typical video output from a computer. Note the video dot signals mounted on the other sync and scanning signals. This signal is discussed in chapters 22 and 23.

Inside generator chips are a number of registers and possibly ROM circuits. The registers are connected to circuits that perform video output jobs. The ROM circuits contain character matrixes. The characters could be alphanumerics, graphics, and mixtures of the two. The registers in the generator can normally be addressed and accessed by the processor, like any register location. The generator system is also the video and sync output port.

In Fig. 6-30, a typical video generator chip schematic is shown. The inputs are on the left and the outputs are on the right. The processor can send data bits to the generator over the data bus. The registers in the generator can also be read by the processor over the same two-way data bus.

The processor decides which register it needs to access and sends the address over lines in the address bus. The read/write line from the processor controls the direction the data goes. During a read the data goes from a generator register to the processor. If the processor is writing to the generator, the data goes to the generator.

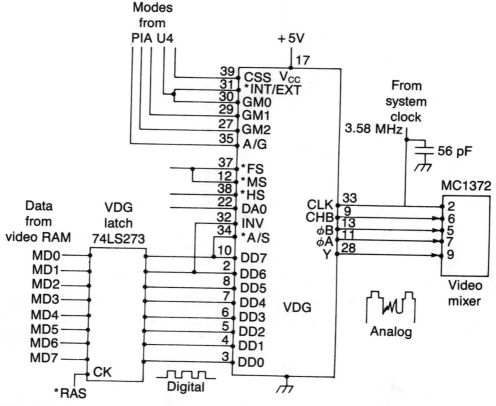

6-30 This is the schematic diagram of a video-display generator circuit. The different computer inputs are inserted on the left and an analog video signal exits on the right.

In this generator, the sync signals are input to the generator from the system clock. The sync signals and the video bits are processed in the generators.

The generator chip has the output on the right. The output is called Y. This is the video dot information to turn the phosphor dots on the TV screen off and on. The dots are also emerging at a specific rate at a particular time. The input sync signals determine exactly when and how fast the serial stream of dots should leave the generator. They are made to appear at the electron gun at precisely the time that the cathode ray from the gun is scanning the point the dot is supposed to turn on or turn off.

7

Checking the low pin-count chips

IF YOU LOOK AT A TYPICAL MOTHERBOARD, IN ADDITION TO ALL THE high pin-count chip packages, there are many smaller size packages with fewer pins. You'll find pin counts as low as 12, 14, 16, and other low pin-counts in abundance. The chips in these smaller packages are primitive in comparison to the sophistication of the high pin-count types. If you hook up a large group of primitive chips, you can do a job that one large chip can do. In fact, a large chip is nothing more than groups of primitive chips cast into silicon.

In older computers, before the advent of the high pin-count chips, the various computer jobs were performed with multitudes of primitive chips. As time goes by more and more high pin-count chips are appearing and making many low-pin count chips obsolete as individual units. However, for the foreseeable future, the primitive chips will continue to play their part in the design of computers.

These basic small chips that support and connect the large chips together have very simple although vital jobs. About all they accomplish is the manipulation and storage of high and low bits. Some of their general names are *gates, buffers, inverters, drivers, multiplexers, decoders, counters, shift registers, latches, flip-flops, triggers*, and *arithmetic-logic functions*. Actually, once you understand how these small chips and their circuits work, you will have a good understanding of the electronics of computers. These simple circuits are the basis of all digital computers.

The chips are built with internal microscopic transistor circuits. The circuits are constructed with two general transistor types. First there are the bipolar transistors depicted in Fig. 7-1. Secondly there are the insulated gate transistors shown in Fig. 7-2. The bipolar transistors are made up for the most part as TTLs, discussed in the next section. The insulated gate transistors, which are MOS types are discussed later in this chapter also. The TTL chips have generic numbers that begins with 74. Fig. 7-3 shows some common price lists of these types. The MOS

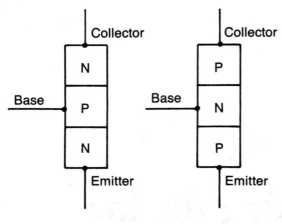

Collector

Base

Emitter

Collector

Base

Emitter

Schematic symbols

7-1 A bipolar transistor is nothing more than pieces of P and N semiconductor material fused together forming two pn junctions. According to the materials a PNP or NPN is made. The schematic symbols indicate the type used.

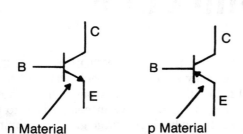

n Material

p Material

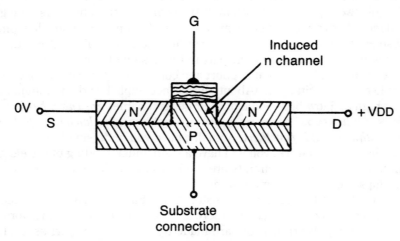

7-2 An insulated gate transistor also uses pieces of P and N semiconductor materials fused together forming junctions. In addition G (gate) electrode is insulated from the P and N material by some metal oxide material.

74LS00

74LS00	.16	74LS165	.65
74LS01	.18	74LS166	.95
74LS02	.17	74LS169	.95
74LS03	.18	74LS173	.49
74LS04	.16	74LS174	.39
74LS05	.18	74LS175	.39
74LS08	.18	74LS191	.49
74LS09	.18	74LS192	.69
74LS10	.16	74LS193	.69
74LS11	.22	74LS194	.69
74LS12	.22	74LS195	.69
74LS13	.26	74LS196	.59
74LS14	.39	74LS197	.59
74LS15	.26	74LS221	.59
74LS20	.17	74LS240	.69
74LS21	.22	74LS241	.69
74LS22	.22	74LS242	.69
74LS27	.23	74LS243	.69
74LS28	.26	74LS244	.69
74LS30	.17	74LS245	.79
74LS32	.18	74LS251	.49
74LS33	.28	74LS253	.49
74LS37	.26	74LS256	1.79
74LS38	.26	74LS257	.39
74LS42	.39	74LS258	.49
74LS47	.59	74LS259	1.29
74LS48	.69	74LS260	.49
74LS51	.17	74LS266	.39
74LS73	.29	74LS273	.79
74LS74	.24	74LS279	.39
74LS75	.29	74LS280	1.98
74LS76	.29	74LS283	.59
74LS83	.49	74LS290	.89
74LS85	.49	74LS293	.89
74LS86	.22	74LS299	1.49
74LS90	.39	74LS322	3.95
74LS92	.49	74LS323	2.49
74LS93	.39	74LS364	1.95
74LS95	.49	74LS365	.39
74LS107	.34	74LS367	.39
74LS109	.36	74LS368	.39
74LS112	.29	74LS373	.79
74LS122	.45	74LS374	.79
74LS123	.49	74LS375	.95
74LS124	2.75	74LS377	.79
74LS125	.39	74LS378	1.18
74LS126	.39	74LS390	1.19
74LS132	.39	74LS393	.79
74LS133	.49	74LS541	1.49
74LS136	.39	74LS624	1.95
74LS138	.39	74LS640	.99
74LS139	.39	74LS645	.99
74LS145	.99	74LS669	1.29
74LS147	.99	74LS670	.89
74LS148	.99	74LS682	3.20
74LS151	.39	74LS683	3.20
74LS153	.39	74LS684	3.20
74LS154	1.49	74LS688	2.40
74LS155	.59	74LS783	22.95
74LS156	.49	81LS95	1.49
74LS157	.36	81LS96	1.49
74LS158	.29	81LS97	1.49
74LS160	.29	81LS98	1.49
74LS161	.39	25LS2521	2.80
74LS162	.49	25LS2569	2.80
74LS163	.39	26LS31	1.95
74LS164	.49	26LS32	1.95

7400/9000

7400	.19	74147	2.49
7402	.19	74148	1.20
7404	.19	74150	1.35
7406	.29	74151	.55
7407	.29	74153	.55
7408	.24	74154	1.49
7410	.19	74155	.75
7411	.25	74157	.55
7414	.49	74159	1.65
7416	.25	74161	.69
7417	.25	74163	.69
7420	.19	74164	.85
7423	.29	74165	.85
7430	.19	74166	1.00
7432	.29	74175	.89
7438	.29	74177	.75
7442	.49	74178	1.15
7445	.69	74181	2.25
7447	.89	74182	.75
7470	.35	74184	2.00
7473	.34	74191	1.15
7474	.33	74192	.79
7475	.45	74194	.85
7476	.35	74196	.79
7483	.50	74197	.75
7485	.59	74199	1.35
7486	.35	74221	1.35
7489	2.15	74246	1.35
7490	.39	74247	1.25
7492	.50	74248	1.85
7493	.35	74249	1.95
7495	.55	74251	.75
7497	2.75	74265	1.35
74100	2.29	74273	1.95
74121	.29	74278	3.11
74123	.49	74367	.65
74125	.45	74368	.65
74141	.65	9368	3.95
74143	5.95	9602	1.50
74144	2.95	9637	2.95
74145	.60	96S02	1.95

74S00

74S00	.29	74S163	1.29
74S02	.29	74S168	3.95
74S03	.29	74S174	.79
74S04	.29	74S175	.79
74S05	.29	74S188	1.95
74S08	.35	74S189	1.95
74S10	.29	74S195	1.49
74S15	.35	74S196	1.49
74S30	.29	74S197	1.49
74S32	.35	74S226	3.99
74S37	.69	74S240	1.49
74S38	.69	74S241	1.49
74S74	.49	74S244	1.49
74S85	.95	74S257	.79
74S86	.35	74S253	.79
74S112	.50	74S258	.95
74S124	2.75	74S280	1.95
74S138	.79	74S287	1.69
74S140	.55	74S288	1.69
74S151	.79	74S299	2.95
74S153	.79	74S373	1.69
74S157	.79	74S374	1.69
74S158	.95	74S471	4.95
74S161	1.29	74S571	2.95

7-3 The TTL chips have generic numbers in the 7400, 74S00 and 74LS00 families of chips. This is a price list of some of the common chips available.

chips have generic numbers that begins with 74 too, but can also be found with generic part numbers beginning with 40, as seen in Fig. 7-4. Examine some of these chips.

TTL chips

TTL stands for transistor-transistor logic. These TTLs are all composed of bipolar transistors. The bipolar transistor is the old one that first came out and replaced the vacuum tube. It is very stable and does not require extra special handling like the more sensitive field-effect transistor discussed in the next section.

HIGH SPEED CMOS

A new family of high speed CMOS logic featuring the speed of low power Schottky (8ns typical gate propagation delay), combined with the advantages of CMOS: very low power consumption, superior noise immunity, and improved output drive.

74HC00

74HC: Operate at CMOS logic levels and are ideal for new, all-CMOS designs.

74HC00	.59	74HC148	1.19
74HC02	.59	74HC151	.89
74HC04	.59	74HC154	2.49
74HC08	.59	74HC157	.89
74HC10	.59	74HC158	.95
74HC14	.79	74HC163	1.15
74HC20	.59	74HC175	.99
74HC27	.59	74HC240	1.89
74HC30	.59	74HC244	1.89
74HC32	.69	74HC245	1.89
74HC51	.59	74HC257	.85
74HC74	.75	74HC259	1.39
74HC85	1.35	74HC273	1.89
74HC86	.69	74HC299	4.99
74HC93	1.19	74HC368	.99
74HC107	.79	74HC373	2.29
74HC109	.79	74HC374	2.29
74HC112	.79	74HC390	1.39
74HC125	1.19	74HC393	1.39
74HC132	1.19	74HC4017	1.99
74HC133	.69	74HC4020	1.39
74HC138	.99	74HC4049	.89
74HC139	.99	74HC4050	.89

74HCT00

74HCT: Direct, drop-in replacements for LS TTL and can be intermixed with 74LS in the same circuit.

74HCT00	.69	74HCT166	3.05
74HCT02	.69	74HCT174	1.09
74HCT04	.69	74HCT193	1.39
74HCT08	.69	74HCT194	1.19
74HCT10	.69	74HCT240	2.19
74HCT11	.69	74HCT241	2.19
74HCT27	.69	74HCT244	2.19
74HCT30	.69	74HCT245	2.19
74HCT32	.79	74HCT257	.99
74HCT74	.85	74HCT259	1.59
74HCT75	.95	74HCT273	2.09
74HCT138	1.15	74HCT367	1.09
74HCT139	1.15	74HCT373	2.49
74HCT154	2.99	74HCT374	2.49
74HCT157	.99	74HCT393	1.59
74HCT158	.99	74HCT4017	2.19
74HCT161	1.29	74HCT4040	1.59
74HCT164	1.39	74HCT4060	1.49

74F00

74F00	.69	74F74	.79	74F251	1.69
74F02	.69	74F86	.99	74F253	1.69
74F04	.79	74F138	1.69	74F257	1.69
74F08	.69	74F139	1.69	74F280	1.79
74F10	.69	74F157	1.69	74F283	3.95
74F32	.69	74F240	3.29	74F373	4.29
74F64	.89	74F244	3.29	74F374	4.29

CMOS

4001	.19	14419	4.95
4011	.19	14433	14.95
4012	.25	4503	.49
4013	.35	4511	.69
4015	.29	4516	.79
4016	.29	4518	.85
4017	.49	4522	.79
4018	.69	4526	.79
4020	.59	4527	1.95
4021	.69	4528	.79
4024	.49	4529	2.95
4025	.25	4532	1.95
4027	.39	4538	.95
4028	.65	4541	1.29
4035	.69	4553	5.79
4040	.69	4585	.75
4041	.75	4702	12.95
4042	.59	74C00	.29
4043	.85	74C14	.59
4044	.69	74C74	.59
4045	1.98	74C83	1.95
4046	.69	74C85	1.49
4047	.69	74C95	.99
4049	.29	74C150	5.75
4050	.29	74C151	2.25
4051	.69	74C161	.99
4052	.69	74C163	.99
4053	.69	74C164	1.39
4056	2.19	74C192	1.49
4060	.69	74C193	1.49
4066	.29	74C221	1.75
4069	.19	74C240	1.89
4076	.59	74C244	1.89
4077	.29	74C374	1.99
4081	.22	74C905	10.95
4085	.79	74C911	8.95
4086	.89	74C917	8.95
4093	.49	74C922	4.49
4094	2.49	74C923	4.95
14411	9.95	74C926	7.95
14412	6.95	80C97	.95

7-4 The MOS chips get their name from the fact that there is a metal oxide insulator between the gate electrode and the body of the unit. Typical MOS chips are found with generic numbers in the 4000 and 74C00 families. MOS chips are considered slower acting than bipolars. There are however, faster acting MOS chips that have numbers in the 74HC00, 74HCT00 and 74F00 families. This is a typical price list of these type chips.

A bipolar transistor has three electrodes attached to it, an emitter, a base and a collector. A TTL (Fig. 7-5) is so called because it acts like two transistors wired in parallel. The TT is there to denote that the device has two emitters. The L part means the TTL has the job of handling logic, which is the manipulation of highs and lows.

A TTL has certain input and output characteristics. All TTLs have very similar characteristics. They are made this way so they can be made compatible with other chips as they are wired together. The input loading from a previous chip and the output driving of the next chip must be correct or else a mismatch will occur and harm the data bit voltage levels as they are passed from chip to chip.

The old, original TTL products were the 7400 series. The first upgrade to these chips were ones with higher power abilities and much faster speeds. In the 7400 chips, it took the bits about 25 nanoseconds to pass through. This is called propagation time. Then appeared a chip with an H, for instance 74H00 has a lowered bit passage time. The time is about 15 ns but at the expense of having to use much higher power.

The next step of upgrading was the installation of tiny nonsaturating Schottky clamped diodes. This gave the TTLs ultrahigh speed but also reduced the power needs by over 80%. These low-power Schottky TTLs are now the most popular types and are known as the 74LS00 family of devices.

There are a few hundred TTLs in the family of chips. The price lists show the majority of the popular ones in use. Except for the LS characteristics the 7400 series and the 74LS00 series are identical and physically interchangeable. It is good technique though, to change a defective chip with an exact replacement.

The MOS chips

TTL chips were the ones that first became common in computers. In about 1970 a second entry appeared, the MOS chip. MOS stands for *metal-oxide silicon*. These chips use field-effect rather than bipolar transistors. The MOS chips are packaged in a dual in-line format and look just like their TTL companions. All the high pin-count chips discussed in chapter 6 are MOS types.

A series of MOS chips also are made to do the primitive jobs like the TTLs. They are the 4000 and 74C00 series (Fig. 7-4). They are functional equivalents and pin-for-pin replacements for the TTL 7400 series. They are recognized by the C in the nomenclature. The C stands for CMOS. Compared to TTLs, CMOS chip speeds are slower. However, power consumption is lower and noise immunity is high. Recently a high-speed family of 74HC00 MOS chips have appeared (also shown in Fig. 7-5).

MOS chips are made as *NMOS*, *PMOS*, and *CMOS*. N stands for negative channel, P for positive channel, and C means complementary and dual channel. The channels are pieces of silicon in the IGFETs the chip is composed of.

Integrated-circuit components

All the components on a chip are made by layering insulators, conductors, and semiconductors. The insulator can be a piece of glassy silicon dioxide. The conductor can be a piece of metal. The semiconductor is a piece of lightly doped silicon. If a piece of silicon is doped with an impurity like arsenic it becomes N-material. Should it be doped with aluminum it becomes P-material. All the components are constructed with these items. The components are resistors, capacitors, diodes, bipolar transistors, and insulated-gate field-effect transistors.

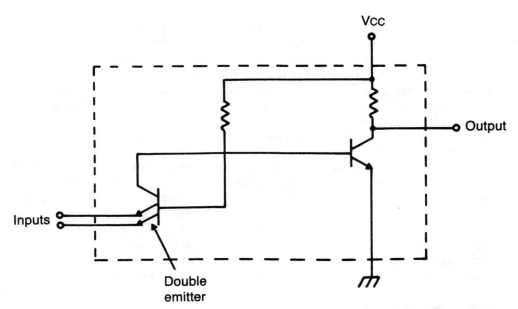

7-5 The TTL chips get their name from the fact that there is more than one emitter at the input bipolar transistor.

A resistor (Fig. 7-6) has a body of resistive material and two leads. A capacitor (Fig. 7-7) has a sandwich of two electrodes or conductors surrounding an insulator or dielectric.

A bipolar transistor (Fig. 7-1) is a sandwich of two pieces of the same semiconductor surrounding one piece of the other semiconductor. Transistors can be called a PNP or an NPN according to the layering.

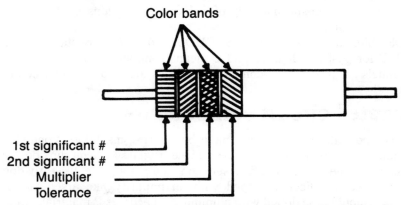

7-6 A resistor is simply a resistive element with two leads. It is color coded with bands on its casing that reveal the approximate ohmage and the percent tolerance of the accuracy of the ohmage.

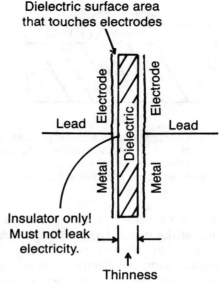

7-7 A capacitor has a dielectric insulator sandwiched between two electrode conductors. Capacitance is dependent on dielectric surface area and dielectric thickness. The more area and the thinner the dielectric, the more the capacitance.

An *IGFET* (insulated-gate field-effect transistor) (Fig. 7-8) is a channel of one type of semiconductor sitting on a substrate of the other. Two leads are attached to either end of the channel. A third lead is connected to the channel but the third lead is insulated from the channel by a piece of glassy silicon dioxide. The third lead is called the *gate*. That is where the name insulated gate comes from.

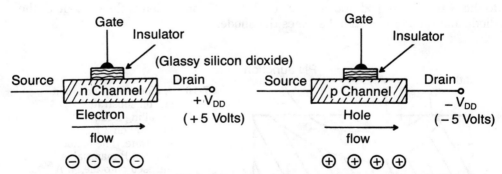

7-8 IGFETs are a channel of P or N semiconductor material connected at both ends to source and drain electrodes. The gate electrode is attached to an insulator on the channel. It is said that negatively charged electrons are on the move in N channels while positively charged holes are moving in P channels.

Silicon chips are constructed on substrates of semiconductor material. A resistor (Fig. 7-9) is installed on the substrate by depositing a resistive element and then attaching two metal leads to the ends of the resistive material. When electric current passes from one lead to the other it must pass through the resistive element. The current is thus controlled by the resistor.

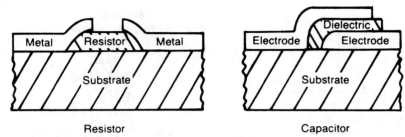

Resistor   Capacitor

7-9 Microscopic resistors and capacitors can be deposited on silicon chip substrates in layers. A resistive element connected at both ends with metal electrodes make up a resistor. A piece of dielectric sandwiched between two electrodes becomes a capacitance.

A capacitor is made by first depositing a metal electrode, then placing a dielectric on top of the metal. Last, a second metal electrode is layered on. The electrodes each exit at different ends of the capacitor. The dielectric is made thin with a controlled amount of dielectric surface area touching the electrodes. The thinner the dielectric and the more the surface area, the more capacitance the miniscule capacitor will have.

The diodes and transistors work due to the action of PN junctions. A PN junction is a place where a piece of P-material is melted to a piece of N-material. For example, suppose a chip has a substrate of P-material. Then a tub of N-material is installed on the substrate. Then another piece of P-material is diffused onto the tub. Figure 7-10 shows how a silicon diode is created. Metal leads can be attached to the N-tub and the additional piece of P. The N-connection is the cathode of the diode and the P-connection becomes the anode.

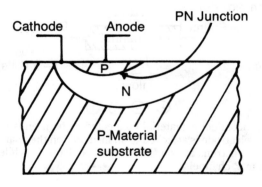

7-10 A diode is formed on a silicon substrate by installing a tub of N material on a P substrate. Then another piece of P material is diffused onto the N. A PN junction is formed, which is a diode.

To produce an NPN transistor, the same procedure is used that made the diode, with one more step. Another piece of N-material is diffused into the top P piece, as in Fig. 7-11. A connection is made to that N piece. This connection is called the *emitter*. A second connection is made to the P. This is the *base electrode*. The connection to the bottom tub of the N is the *collector*.

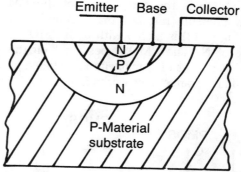

7-11 To form an NPN transistor, the diode is taken one step further. Another little piece of N material is diffused into the top P material.

A PNP transistor is constructed in the same way except the materials are reversed. The substrate must be N-material, the collector P, the base N and the emitter P.

The IGFETs are also made in this manner except the layering is somewhat more complicated. For example in Fig. 7-12, a PMOS has N for the substrate. A strip of P is used for the channel. The P in the PMOS is referred to as P+. The + means it is heavily doped.

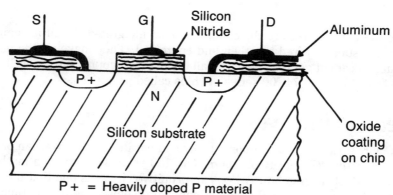

7-12 A MOSFET can be formed on a substrate in a similar manner. This N-channel FET is made on an N substrate. Two small tubs of P+ material (P+ means heavy doping) are installed. The S, G, and D electrodes are then attached.

Also if you notice, the channel is split in two pieces with the N substrate in between. During operation the potential on the two pieces of P+ forces the N material to act like P and connects the two pieces into one channel. You can think of the two pieces of P+ as being one. They act as if they are one.

A connection to the left end of the channel in Fig. 7-12 is called the *source*. The connection at the other end is the *drain*. Between the two is the *gate*. Note that the gate has an insulator between the metal lead and the channel. The gate connects to both sides of the channel.

An NMOS is the counterpart of the PMOS with all the semiconductors reversed. The substrate is P-material and the channel pieces N+ material. The CMOS (Fig. 7-13) is a chip with both PMOS and NMOS IGFETs installed on a substrate of N. The PMOS goes right on the substrate naturally. The NMOS won't, so a pocket of P-material is installed and acts as a sub-substrate for the NMOS. This arrangement works fine.

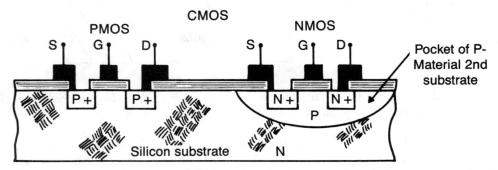

7-13   The *CMOS* (complimentary metal oxide semiconductor) is made with both PMOS and NMOS transistors. This is accomplished by creating a second acting substrate in the main substrate.

These basic structures are the components an integrated circuit is composed of. They are installed, wired together, and energized. They make up the internal wiring that you cannot get to. They form all the high pin-count chips as well as the 7400, 74LS00, 4000 and 74C00 series of chips called primitives.

Boolean primitives

When you wire up a group of components in an integrated circuit, you can produce a Boolean primitive. George Boole more than 150 years ago started a math-logic system called Boolean Algebra. A Boolean primitive circuit is one that uses electronics to solve one of these Boolean Algebra problems. There is nothing new about the way the computer processes binary numbers, it just does it electronically, which is lightning fast.

These circuits are called gates (not to be confused with the gate electrode on an FET). There are only eight types of gates. A gate receives one or more binary bits at its inputs, manipulates the bits in its internal circuits and then predictably outputs one bit. The output can be predicted because a gate operates according to logic. The eight gates are called, buffer, inverter, AND, OR, Exclusive OR, NAND, NOR, and Exclusive NOR.

While you cannot access a gate internal circuitry, you usually can get to a gate's inputs and outputs. These are usually at the pin connections of a primitive chip. If you test a primitive chip, you can tell if it is operating o.k. by checking its inputs and outputs. There is more about these test techniques in chapter 9.

Buffers

A buffer is an amplifier stage. Amplification is an analog function and not a digital one in a pure sense. Buffers are needed in many places in the digital world. For instance the address bits are very weak when they leave the processor. They could never drive open memory locations without some current amplification. There is a buffer in every address line. Each buffer amplifies the current of each transmitted bit. There are also buffers in every data line. In fact there are two buffers in every data line, one for each direciton. The buffers ensure the operation of the address and data bits (discussed in detail in chapter 18).

The logic of a buffer (shown in Fig. 7-14) is the following. Whatever logic state enters the input of the buffer, that same state exits the buffer output. If a high bit enters, a high bit exits. Should a low bit enter, a low bit exits.

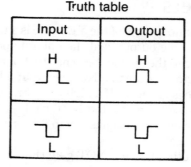

7-14 A YES gate is an amplifier. It is also called a buffer because it is used to condition logic gates for use in circuits. Its distinction is, it outputs the same logic state that is input to it.

Because the logic state does not change as the buffer operates on the input, a buffer is called a YES gate. Every gate has a table that predicts the output of each possible input. The table is called a *truth table*. The YES gate truth table shows two possible inputs, a low and a high. There are only two possible outputs in response to those two inputs, a low and a high.

A common chip (Fig. 7-15) that contains buffers is the 7417. It is called a *hex buffer driver*. Hex means six. There are six little YES gates on a 14-pin DIP. The word *driver* means amplifier. Each little buffer has one input and one output connected to one of the pins. That uses up 12 of the 14 pins. The remaining two pins are the +5 V and ground connections.

When a logic state is input to one of the buffers, it quickly passes through the internal circuit and appears at the output pin with the same state and a higher current level. The state cannot be stored as it is in a flip-flop. A certain amount of time

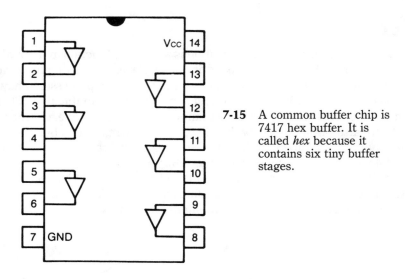

7-15   A common buffer chip is 7417 hex buffer. It is called *hex* because it contains six tiny buffer stages.

does elapse though. The time is called *propagation delay* and takes about 15 nanoseconds.

Inverters

The schematic symbol of the YES gate is a triangle. The input is at the bottom of the triangle and the output is at the opposite pointy end. If you place a little circle on the pointy end the symbol becomes that of an inverter. The inverter is called a NOT gate. The circle is called a NOT circle. If a logic state is passed through a NOT circle, its state is changed. If a high goes through a NOT circle it becomes a low. When a low is passed through the NOT circle it becomes a high. The circle represents internal wiring that changes +5 to 0 V or vice versa. The circle makes a YES gate into a NOT gate.

The truth table of a NOT gate (Fig. 7-16) shows the same inputs as the YES gate but opposite outputs. Inverters, as the triangle symbol indicates, also amplifies the current of a logic state in the same way the buffer does. However, the internal wiring reverses the state of the output.

A common inverter is the 7406 (Fig. 7-17). It is called a *hex inverter buffer driver*. It also is a 14-pin DIP. The six inverter stages each take up two pins for input and output. Power supply needs use up the remaining two pins.

The 7406, as well as many other gates, feature a characteristic (Fig. 7-18) called open-collector. The individual gates on the 7406 chip base their internal circuits on bipolar transistors. Bipolar transistors have a collector as their output electrode. After a gate inverts the state of an input bit, it is ready to output the inversion through the output collector of the stage. With open-collectors the output transistor is made much heftier than the rest of the tiny transistors in the gate. These output transistors are able to put out a relatively large 30 mA of current.

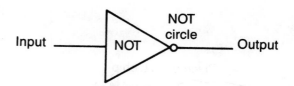

7-16 When a NOT circle is placed on a buffer drawing, it becomes a NOT gate. The truth table shows that when a high is input, a low is output. Should a low be input, a high is output. The NOT circle reverses the state of the output.

Truth table

Input	Output
H ⎍	⎵ L
⎵ L	⎍ H

7-17 The 7406 14-pin DIP contains six NOT gates. It also features an open-collector output.

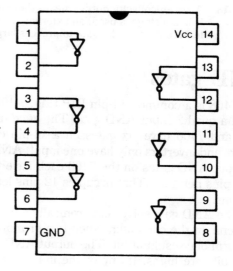

The internal collector resistor normally found in an amplifier is left off in the open-collector circuit. An external discrete pull-up or load resistor is installed on the print board for every open-collector output. That way they can handle extra currents. Inverters often must drive heavy loads like LEDs or relays. The 7406 uses a discrete 1000-ohm resistor for open-collector duty.

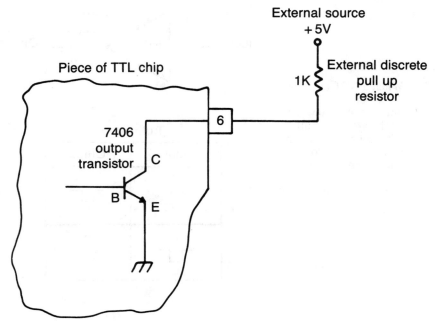

7-18   An open-collector output means there is no pull-up resistors in the chip. When a stage is used, an external discrete resistor must be used. This feature permits the gate to process large amounts of current.

AND gates

The 7408 is a common 14-pin DIP (Fig. 7-19) with AND gates on it. The 7408 is called a quad 2-Input AND gate. The *quad* means there are only four gates. The 7404 and 7406 have six gates on a 14-pin chip. That was allowed because the buffers and inverters only have one input. AND gates can have two or more inputs. The four AND gates on the 7408 each have two inputs and one output requiring three pins per gate. That occupies 12 pins leaving two for +5 V and ground connections.

The AND gate solves electronically a logical AND problem. What is an AND problem? In the computer, when two or more bits are ANDed they will combine and form one resultant bit. The output AND bit will always be a low unless all the input bits are highs. If any of the input bits are low, even one out of many, the ANDed output will be a low. Only when all inputs are high will the output bit be a high.

Figure 7-20 depicts the AND truth table for two inputs. If there are more inputs the results are the same. Only one possible condition exists where the AND will output a high.

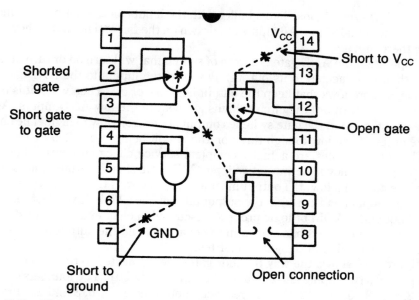

Shorted gate

Short gate to gate

Short to ground

Short to V_CC

Open gate

Open connection

7-19 The 7408 TTL chip is a quad 2-input AND gate. This means there are four gates on the chip, each having two inputs. When gates fail, these assorted shorts and opens are the common reasons.

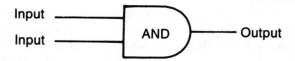

7-20 The AND truth table shows two inputs and one output. There can be many more than two inputs. However, all AND gates will only output a high when all inputs are high. Otherwise the output will be low.

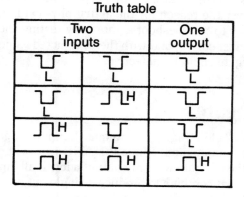

Truth table

Two inputs		One output
L	L	L
L	H	L
H	L	L
H	H	H

The AND symbol looks like a bullet with the inputs on the flat bottom and the output at the rounded top. All inputs are drawn on the flat end no matter how many inputs there are.

In operation the AND gate is a form of switch that will turn on or turn off some circuit that is connected to its output. Typically, the inputs to the AND gate will hold one or more lows that keep the output held low or off. Then when it is necessary to enable (turn on) the circuit, highs are sent to the low AND inputs. As the high enters the input, the gate switches output states from low to high. The change of gate output from low to high turns on the circuit being controlled by the gate.

These truth tables are actually complete service checkout charts. The AND table (Fig. 7-20) shows the way a two input AND gate should output results. When the inputs contain a low, the output must always be low, if the gate is working o.k. When both inputs bits are high, the output bit must be a high. If you test the inputs and output with a VOM or logic probe as discussed in chapter 2, they must correspond with the predicted bits shown in the chart. Should the output not be correct that indicates trouble in the gate under test.

Figure 7-19 shows the way the four gates are connected to the pins of a 7408. Each gate has two inputs and one output on the 14-pin DIP. The four sets of inputs are 1-2, 4-5, 9-10, and 12-13. The respective outputs are 3, 6, 8 and 11. Pin 14 is the +5 V supply and pin 7 is the ground connection.

If the gate connected to input pins 1 – 2 has the output pin 3 reading a high even though one of the two inputs is low, the gate could be shorted. In the gate's internal circuit a PN junction might have shorted or one of the tiny capacitors could have a shorted dielectric. Whatever it is internally the gate shows the short and is defective.

Should you test the gate with pins 4 – 5 the inputs and pin 6 the output, and pin 6 is outputting a low even though both inputs are high, the gate could be shorted to ground as the illustration shows. Suppose you are reading bit states at pins 8, 9, and 10 and the output reads low with both inputs high. A possibility exists that the output pin has disconnected causing an open circuit. Another way the gate could open is internally. Still another type of failure can be a short to the V_{CC} supply line. Whatever the reason for the actual physical failure it is interesting but academic. The way to troubleshoot a gate is by testing the states of the inputs and outputs. They must correspond with their predicted values as commanded in the truth table or the gate could be defective.

OR gates

The 7432 chip (Fig. 7-21) is a quad 2-input OR gate. Logical OR is another way bits can be manipulated. While the AND gate will only output a high if all inputs are high, the OR gate will only output a low if all inputs are low. It too has two or more inputs that combine to produce a single output. However, if any of the inputs are a high the output will be a high. Only when all inputs are low can an OR gate output be a low.

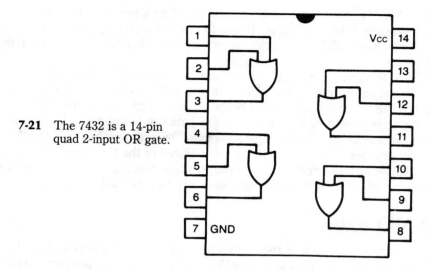

7-21 The 7432 is a 14-pin quad 2-input OR gate.

OR gates are often held high. This is the off position. When it is desired to enable the OR gate, lows are sent to the inputs that are high. The gate will respond by going low. The truth table and schematic symbol are shown in Fig. 7-22.

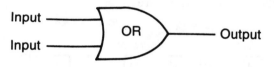

7-22 The OR truth table shows two inputs and one output. There can be many more than two inputs. However, all OR gates will only output a low when all inputs are low. Otherwise, the output will be high.

Truth table

Two inputs		One output
L	L	L
L	H	H
H	L	H
H	H	H

The OR gate schematic symbol resembles the AND gate except it has a pointy output end where the AND was rounded. Also it does not have a flat bottom but one that is gently rounded and comes to a point at either side. The rounded bottom is the input lead area and the pointy end is where the output connection is made.

The 7432 is also a 14-pin DIP and houses four gates. The pins are arranged exactly like the 7408 AND gate. If you find it necessary to test the four sets of inputs and outputs, the 7432 truth table will predict what should be on the pins of a good energized chip.

The NOT, AND, and OR gates are the three main logical functions. There are some others, but they are really a combination of these three. If you combine NOT and AND the result is a gate called NAND. Should you put together NOT and OR a NOR gate is produced. The Exclusive OR gate can be produced by wiring some NAND gates together. Exclusive NOR is made by adding a NOT gate to the EOR gate. These gates even though they are composed of the three fundamental gates are packaged as individual items. During troubleshooting they should be considered as specific gates and their truth tables used as the basis for testing.

NAND gates

At first glance the sketch of the 7400 NAND chip (Fig. 7-23) looks like the 7408 AND DIP. A closer look reveals little NOT circles at each output connection. The NOT circles change the gate to a NAND which is NOT-AND. If you examine the NAND truth table (Fig. 7-24) you'll find the outputs are the same as the AND except for the fact that they are inverted. The AND gate will only output a high if all inputs are high. The NAND gate will only output a low if all inputs are high. All other NAND outputs are highs.

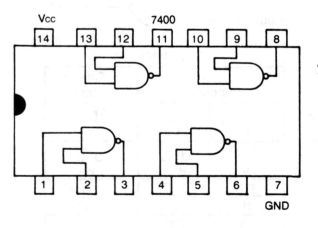

7-23 The 7400 is a 14-pin quad 2-input NAND gate. It looks identical to the AND gate except for the NOT circles on each gate. AND plus NOT equals NAND.

A NAND gate is much more than simply an AND gate plus an inverter. All TTL chips are made from NAND gates. The NAND is the basic logic building block. Any desired type of gate or register can be constructed from the basic NAND gate. The TTL chip is composed of bipolar transistors, diodes and resistors. There are TTL transistors with multiple emitters, ordinary transistors with single emitters, PN junctions acting as diodes, and tiny integrated circuit resistors.

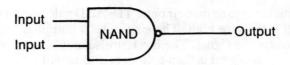

7-24 The NAND truth table shows that the NAND output is an inverted AND output. A NAND gate will only output a low when all inputs are high.

Truth table

Two inputs		One output
L	L	H
L	H	H
H	L	H
H	H	L

The TTL emitters are tied to the input pins of the chip. If a gate has two inputs the TTL has two emitters. Should a gate have three or more inputs, the TTL will provide three or more emitter inputs, whatever is called for. The other bipolar transistors act as inverters or buffers.

The basic NAND itself, that is used in TTLs, consists of five parts (Fig. 7-25), one AND, one NOT, and three YES gates. The AND gate is the multi-emitter one

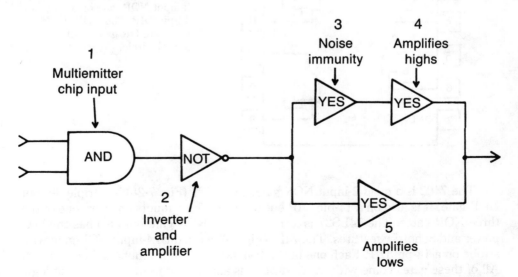

7-25 The NAND circuit is the basis for all TTL chips. The actual circuit in the silicon consists of a multi-emitter AND an NOT gate and three YES gates.

and has two or more inputs. The AND gate of course, will only output a high when all inputs are high. The single AND output is applied to a NOT gate. This gate inverts the signal. The inverter also amplifies the current of the signal.

The signal is then split in two. One pathway has the signal go through a noise immunity YES gate and then into a second YES gate that is built to amplify the signal if it is a high. The second pathway passes the same signal through another YES gate that is built to amplify the signal if it is a low. The final two YES gates are joined together and output their results. It can be seen that the output ends up as an amplified NANDing of the input signals.

NOR gates

The 7402 (Fig. 7-26) is the TTL version of the NOR gate. Just as NAND is an AND-NOT, the NOR is an OR-NOT. The truth table (Fig. 7-27) shows the way a NOR gate is predicted to respond to its inputs. It will only output a high if all inputs are low, otherwise it must output a low. The outputs are the inverted images of the OR gate.

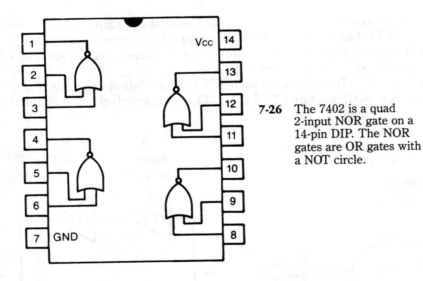

7-26   The 7402 is a quad 2-input NOR gate on a 14-pin DIP. The NOR gates are OR gates with a NOT circle.

The 7402 is a quad 2-input NOR gate. The 7427 (Fig. 7-28) is a triple 3-input NOR gate. It is also on a 14-pin DIP but there are three inputs on every one of the three NOR gates. The 74LS27 is a triple 3-input NOR gate but also has the low-power and Schottky features. The 7425 (Fig. 7-29) is a dual 4-input NOR gate with strobe on a 14-pin DIP. Each one of the two gates has four inputs and one output. All of these gates come with many variations and can be used in all sorts of logic designs. Note that on these 14-pin DIPs it is conventional to assign pin 14 to the +5 V supply and pin 7 to ground.

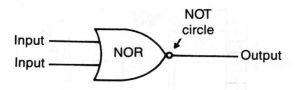

Truth table

Two inputs		One output
L	L	H
L	H	L
H	L	L
H	H	L

7-27 The NOT circle on the NOR gate makes the gate able to output a high only if all inputs are low.

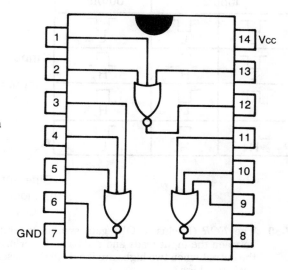

7-28 The 7427 is packaged in a 14-pin DIP. It is a triple 3-input NOR.

Exclusive OR gates

At first glance the Exclusive-OR schematic symbol (Fig. 7-30) looks quite like the ordinary OR symbol. A second look reveals the difference. The input curved base line proves to be twin parallel lines with a space between the lines. The input leads attach to the outermost line. The output though is identical to the OR gate symbol. There isn't any NOT circle.

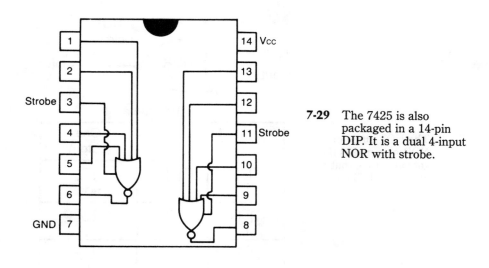

7-29 The 7425 is also packaged in a 14-pin DIP. It is a dual 4-input NOR with strobe.

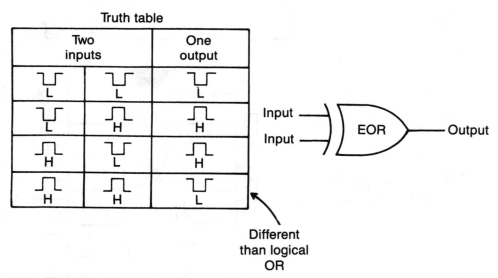

7-30 The *EOR* (Exclusive OR) gate symbol resembles the OR except for the space between the input leads and the base. It performs somewhat like an OR except for the output when two highs are input. In that case, the gate outputs a low while an OR outputs a high.

The truth table starts off with the same results as the OR gate for the first three input possibilities but again a closer look finds a difference. The OR gate specifies that if two highs are input the output must be a high on a good chip. With Exclusive-OR that specification is changed. When two highs are input to an EOR gate a low must appear on the output pin. Only that one output marks the difference between the OR and the EOR.

If you think about it, the outputs of the OR gate do not strictly follow logic. The OR definition is, if one *or* the other of the inputs are high, the outputs should be high. This proves true when the OR inputs are LL, LH and HL. For LL neither input is high so the output as defined, is L. For LH and HL one of the inputs is high so the output must be H. This is also true.

However, in the last possible case HH, both of the inputs are high, not one *or* the other, yet the OR output is still high, which does not follow logically. This is the nature of the OR gate, logical or not.

The Exclusive-OR is the variation of the plain OR that is made to follow the logic. When the four input possibilities of a 2-input EOR gate are considered, they are logically like the OR gate except for the HH possibility. When two Hs are input to the EOR gate the output is logically L. The EOR gate only outputs a high when one *or* the other of the inputs are H, not when both are H. That one input possibility, HH with its low output is the difference between OR and EOR. Incidentally, if you happen to encounter a gate called XOR, it is only another name for EOR.

The 7486 TTL (Fig. 7-31) is a quad 2-input Exclusive OR gate. It is the usual 14-pin DIP these types of Boolean primitive chips are packaged in. The EOR chip can also be obtained in the 74H86, 74LS86 and 74S86 formats.

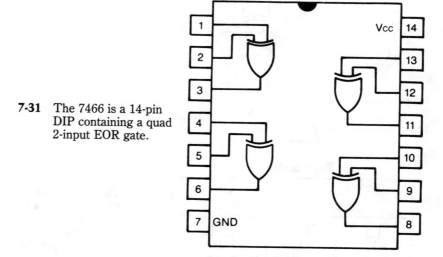

7-31   The 7466 is a 14-pin DIP containing a quad 2-input EOR gate.

Exclusive NOR gates

The *ENOR* (exclusive NOR) gate is like the other inverse gates, an EOR gate with a NOT gate added. The NOT gate appears on the schematic as the NOT circle at the gate output. There aren't too many ENOR gates available. One number that can be obtained (Fig. 7-32) is the 74LS266. It is a quad Exclusive NOR with an open collector output.

It is on a 14-pin DIP. The truth table (Fig. 7-33) shows the final output is the inverted EOR result. While the 74LS266 is available, quite often when a designer wants to install an ENOR gate or two into a circuit, he will fabricate it with other gates. For instance (Fig. 7-34) if the output of an EOR gate from a 74LS86 is fed to the input of an inverter on a 7404, the inverter output will be that of an ENOR. This is common practice.

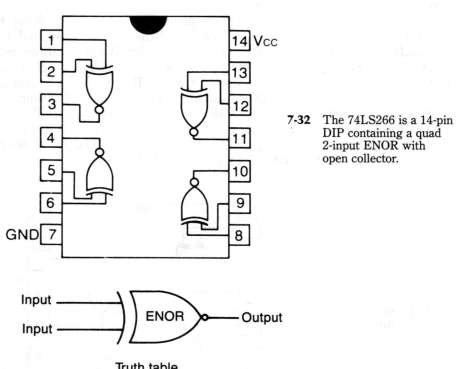

7-32 The 74LS266 is a 14-pin DIP containing a quad 2-input ENOR with open collector.

7-33 The ENOR truth table shows that if the two inputs are identical a high will result. Only when the inputs have mixed states will a low result.

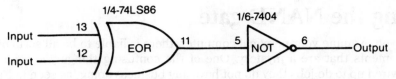

7-34 ENOR gates are often fabricated from combinations of logic. In this case one gate from a 74LS86 EOR gate plus one gate from a 7404 NOT gate are connected in series to form an ENOR.

If you were troubleshooting a fabricated ENOR gate, you would probably ignore the ENOR function and test the two gates as individuals. For instance, you would check the two EOR inputs and then its output. If the output was not what the truth table predicted, the gate could be bad. If the output was correct, then you'd test the inverter input and output. An incorrect reading of course, anywhere along the signal path, could indicate a defect.

ENOR gates as well as other gates can be put together by logically using other chips. For instance (Fig. 7-35) an ENOR gate is made from five NAND gates. Two 7400 chips could provide the five NAND gates with three left over. When gates are left over they must be disabled so they won't interfere with the circuit activity. The inputs and outputs of extra gates can be tied to either +5 V or grounded. The spec sheet that comes with a chip will normally tell you which pins are powered or grounded.

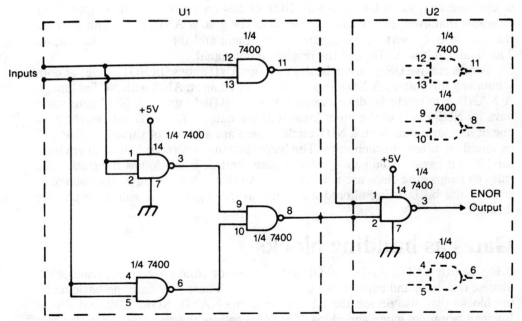

7-35 Another logic combination that can result in an ENOR output can be wired from five NAND sections from two 7406 chips. That leaves three NAND sections unused.

Using the NAND gate

When you examine your personal computer, there is liable to be all sorts of wiring arrangements that are a mystery. One of the confusing things you might see is gates wired up to do jobs they do not have any business doing, as seen in Fig. 7-36. For instance, two NANDs on a 7400 could be wired to be an AND. The inputs are on pins 1 and 2. The output pin 3 is connected to both input pins 4 and 5 of the next NAND. The output is taken at pin 6. Any input injected into pins 1 and 2 ends up being ANDed at pin 6.

This happens because when you short the inputs of a NAND together, it becomes a NOT gate. You are simply changing the two inputs to a single input. That way after the original inputs are NANDed in the first gate it is inverted to an AND by the second gate, which has been made into a NOT gate by shorting its input pins.

To make a NAND OR a couple of inputs, two NAND gates have their inputs made into one. That makes them into NOT gates. The two NOT outputs then are NANDed. The final output is the OR result of the original inputs.

Alternative symbols

On a schematic, the NOT, AND, NAND, and NOR symbols are easily recognized. There also are alternative symbols for these functions (Fig. 7-37). An AND gate might be drawn as an OR gate with NOT circles on inputs and the output. This indicates that even though the total result of the gate is AND, the circuit is doing the job by first inverting the inputs, ORing them and then inverting the output. The final result is ANDing of the original input signal.

An alternative OR gate can be drawn as an AND gate with NOT circles at both inputs and the output. A NOR gate could be found as an AND with NOTed inputs. A NAND gate might be drawn as an OR with NOTed inputs. A NOT gate could have its NOT circle at the input instead of the output. An AND gate might have one of its four inputs with a NOT circle. There are all sorts of variations that will be found on different schematics. The basic drawing is correct. You must envision the bit as it passes from gate symbol to gate symbol. It will follow the truth table rules as long as the chips are not defective. All that is happening is, the voltage or state of the bit is being altered according to the logic of the gate it is passing through.

Gates as building blocks

It is a fact that NOT, AND, and OR gates are made from microscopic transistors, diodes, resistors, and capacitors cast into silicon. These gates are the basic building blocks that also permit the fabrication of the NAND, NOR, EOR and ENOR Boolean primitive gates and chips. The YES gate is the amplifier or buffer that rounds out the eight primitive gates. These gate circuits, except for the buffer, really do not do much more than simply turn on and turn off in predicted sequences, which is what computing is all about.

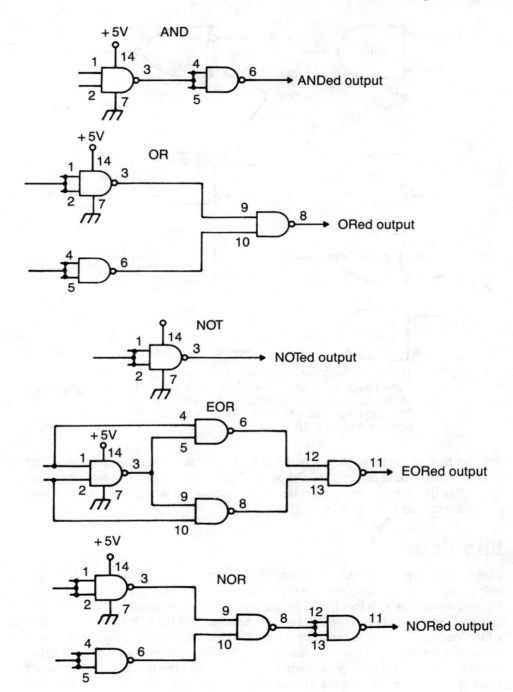

7-36 By combining a group of NAND gates, it is easy to form AND, OR, EOR, and NOR gates.

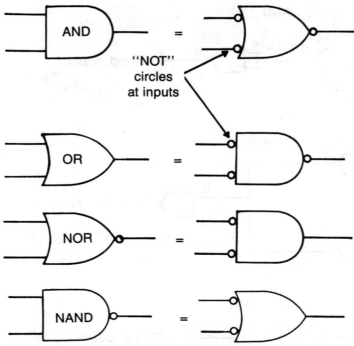

7-37   If you see a NOR gate with two NOT circles at the inputs, it will act as an AND gate. A NAND gate with two NOT circles at the input becomes an OR gate. An AND gate with two NOT circles acts as a NOR. An OR gate with two NOT circles performs as a NAND.

The next step in complexity is the arranging of these eight gates into higher order devices. These devices are also made as low pin-count TTLs and are called names like flip-flops, latches, shift registers, counters, adders, encoders, decoders, multiplexers, and other names.

Flip-flops

There is nothing new about a flip-flop. These circuits were formed with two light bulbs, two vacuum tubes, two bipolar transistors, two FETs, and other devices. You can make one with two NAND gates if you connect them as in Fig. 7-38. The idea is to cross couple the two devices. As mentioned in the chapter on memories, a flip-flop is a circuit that can store a high or a low. It stores the logical bit when one of the two devices, which make up the flip-flop, is turned on while the other one is turned off. It flip-flops, or switches states, when the two devices are forced to switch states. In other words, the one that was on goes off and the one that was off goes on.

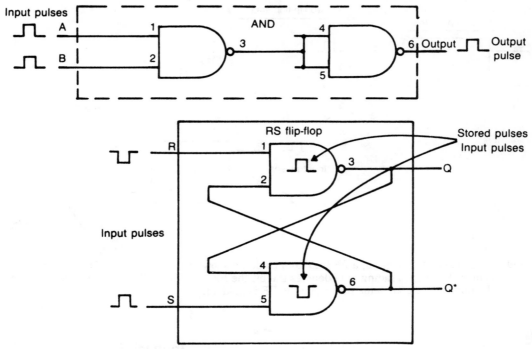

7-38 These two NAND gates can be wired as an AND or a flip-flop. The AND wiring simply accepts two input pulses and passes them to the output without a pause. The only time that elapses is the propagation delay as the pulses pass through the circuits. The flip-flop configuration acts differently. It is a bit holder as found in a static RAM register. The input pulses enter the flip-flop, are stopped and stored.

Figure 7-38 shows two NAND gates wired up as a bit holder. It is called an RS flip-flop. The schematic drawing of an FF (Fig. 7-39) is a square with the letters FF. This RS FF shows two input connections and two outputs. One input, called S for set, is attached to pin 5 of the bottom NAND. The other input, called R for reset, is attached to pin 1 of the top NAND. Output Q is the one that shows the state of the bit. Output *Q will read the inverse of the stored bit. For example, if the FF is storing a high, Q will read H and *Q will read L.

Internally, pin 3 Q is also coupled back to pin 4 of the bottom NAND. Pin 6 *Q is coupled over to pin 2 of the top NAND. The RS FF, therefore, has two inputs and two outputs, unlike gates that also have two inputs but only one output. The truth table (Fig. 7-40) predicts the FF behavior.

The RS is a basic flip-flop circuit. It is known as a bistable FF. The bistable means that one stage will conduct while the other stage is cut off and the two stages will hold that condition continually until an appropriate pulse comes along to change it. Then the stages will switch states and hold that condition in a stable manner until another pulse comes along.

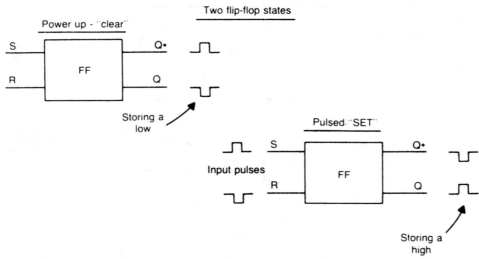

7-39 On a schematic diagram, a *FF* (flip-flop) could be shown as a square with FF in the center. The logic reading at Q denotes the bit the FF is holding. The *Q pin shows the opposite or complementary state the FF is holding.

Truth table		
Inputs		**Output**
S R		**Q**
0 0		Nothing happens
0 1		0 (clear)
1 0		1 (set)
1 1		Nothing happens

7-40 The two inputs of the FF result in four possible outputs. Only an input of mixed states produces a result. When both inputs are the same nothing happens.

The RS FF is the basic type. It simply stores one binary bit. This is in contrast to a gate that passes binary bits. Between the gates and the storage devices digital computing takes place.

Latches

As the name implies, a latch is a place where binary bits are held. The D FF is a typical latch. The D stands for data. The device is a simple latch for data. It, in true FF style, can hold one bit, a high or a low. A group of eight D FFs can hold a byte of data. Figure 7-41 shows the schematic symbol of the D FF. There is one input for data and a second input called Enable, which is the FF's off-on switch.

7-41 The D flip-flop is a typical latch. It has one data input and one enable input. The logic of the bit the latch will be holding can be read at Q. *Q will read the opposite state.

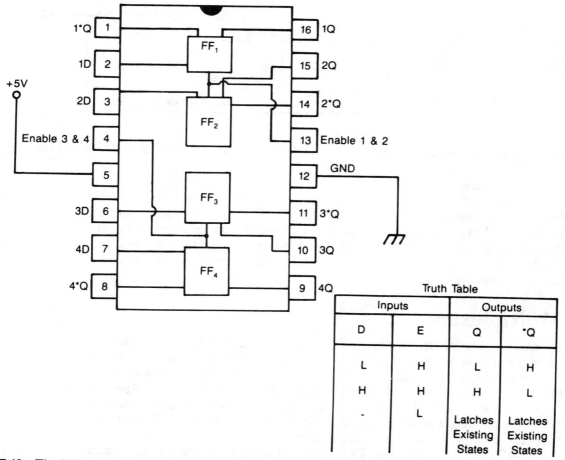

The FF has the two complementary outputs, Q and *Q. Q will output the state of the bit the FF is holding while *Q always outputs the opposite state. The 7475 TTL chip (Fig. 7-42) is a 4-bit Bistable Latch. It can hold four bits in four FF's it contains on a 16-pin DIP. Since one 7475 can hold a nibble, or four bits, two of them working in tandem can hold a byte, or eight bits.

Truth Table

Inputs		Outputs	
D	E	Q	*Q
L	H	L	H
H	H	H	L
-	L	Latches Existing States	Latches Existing States

7-42 The 7476 chip is a 16-pin DIP containing a quad FF with two inputs and two outputs for every FF. This chip can latch a nibble.

Inside each FF (shown in Fig. 7-43) are two AND, two NOTs and a NOR gate. They are wired up so that AND gates are cross-coupled and can store a logic state. The state can be output at Q. When a bit enters the data input it arrives at one of the AND inputs and the NOT input. The second input is the enable bit. When the D input is low and the enable input is high, the AND gate outputs a low. This goes to one of the NOR inputs. The same D bit then passes through the NOT gate and becomes a high. The high proceeds to the second AND gate. This second AND gate has the enable high on its other input. The AND gate as a result outputs a high to its NOR gate.

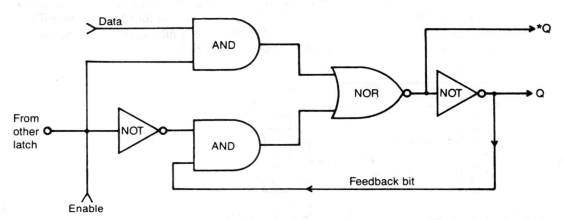

7-43 The internal wiring of one of these FFs is a feedback circuit with two ANDs, a NOR, and two NOTs.

The two AND gates are outputting to Q and *Q but they are also cross-coupled back to each other's inputs. That way, when a data low enters the FF and the enable is high the low appears at the Q output and a high shows up at the *Q. Should a data high enter, a high is on Q and a low on *Q. When the enable is low, the FF shuts off the outputs and stores the data bit that enters. The truth table lists the input-output action.

Multiplexers

A common computer chip is the multiplexer. It is a group of Boolean primitives wired together so that they can control a set of bits that are traveling down a set of bus lines. For example, in an 8-bit computer that is using dynamic memory, a multiplexer can be used in the address bus. An 8-bit personal computer has 16 address lines so it is able to address 64K of dynamic memory. However, the 4164 memory chips only have eight address pins. The sixteen bits must be input eight bits at a time. The multiplexer chip handles that chore.

The 74LS257 TTL chip (Fig. 7-44) is a quad 2-input multiplexer with 3-state capability. That means it has four individual multiplexer sections and can be completely put into a standby three-state condition with a single input bit. Each of

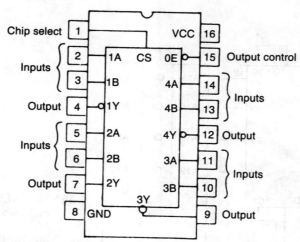

7-44 The 74LS257 chip is a common, multiplexer. It has the capability of receiving eight inputs and coding them into a select four outputs.

these chips can address eight lines. Two of these chips can control the 16 address lines in an 8-bit computer, as in Fig. 7-45.

In Fig. 7-46 each section of a chip contains two AND gates and an OR gate. Each of the AND gates in a section has one input coming from an address line. There are eight address line inputs and four address line outputs assigned to each multiplexer chip.

Examine one section with two AND and one OR gate. Each AND has one input from an address line and one input from the Select pin. However, one of the AND gates has a direct select connection while the other one has its select that is passed through a NOT gate. This makes the two Select inputs have opposite states. That way, when one Select is high the other one is low and vice versa. Therefore, one will select while its opposite will not.

Each of the AND outputs goes to one of the OR gate inputs. The ORs are three state in nature and have their three-state connections wired together. The three-state signal enters at pin 15, the output control. When a high enters at pin 15 the chip outputs go into a three-state high impedance condition and there is no output from any of the OR gates. A truth table will show all the different input and output possibilities.

The chips typically perform in the following way. It is shown in the memory chapter, the 4164 memory matrix is laid out in a grid of 256 rows and 256 columns. Each row needs eight bits of addresses and each column also needs eight bits. The 16 address lines can be connected to the 16 address pins on the two multiplexer chips, eight lines to a chip.

The address bits all arrive at the same time. A select bit also arrives. When it is high, four of the AND gates of the eight on a chip are turned on. Because there are two chips, eight AND gates are turned on and eight bits are outputted through the OR gates. This could address the rows of the 4164 chips.

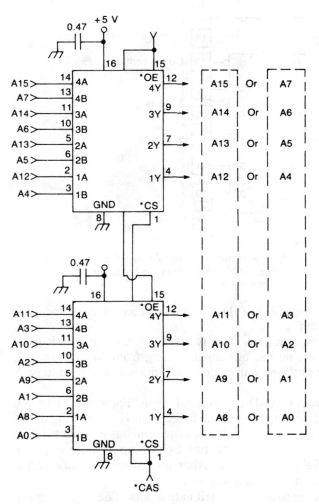

7-45 Two 74LS257 chips can multiplex an entire address bus, A15 – A0, into the needed eight row address bits and the eight column address bits the dynamic RAM needs to operate.

If the Select goes low, the eight AND gates that were on go off and the ones that were off go on. The other eight bits of the 16 address lines are then passed through the OR gate and address the columns of the 4164 chips.

Decoders

A decoder is almost the reverse of a multiplexer. That is why they are also called demultiplexers. While a multiplexer receives a large number of input lines and outputs a smaller number of lines, the decoder inputs a few lines and outputs a lot of lines. For example the 74LS138 has a three-line data input and is able to derive eight individual output lines from the three inputs.

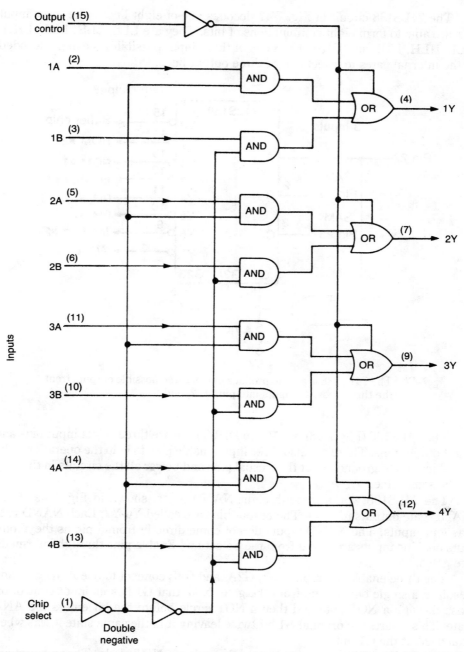

7-46 A low into the chip select pin 1 enables 1A, 2A, 3A, and 4A. A high into pin 1 enables 1B, 2B, 3B, and 4B.

The 74LS138 circuit in Fig. 7-47 decodes one-of-eight lines. The three input bits are able to form eight combinations of bits. They are LLL, LLH, LHL, LHH, HLL, HLH, HHL and HHH. Each one of these input possibilities can be decoded in the internal gates to select one of three output lines.

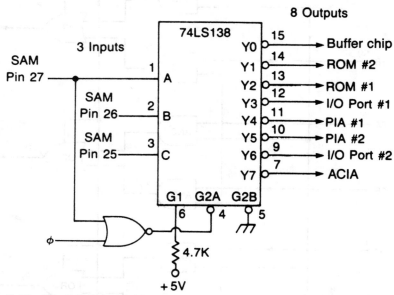

7-47 The 74LS138 is able to produce one of three possible outputs from the three possible inputs into pins 1, 2, and 3.

The 74LS138 (Fig. 7-48) is a 16-pin DIP. There are three select input pins and eight output pins. There are also three input enable pins to help the operation. The +5 V input and ground are at their usual pins and power all the circuits in the chip at the same time.

The 74LS138 works through eight NAND gates, shown in Fig. 7-49. Each NAND gate outputs to a pin. The output pins are called Y0-Y7. Each NAND gate has four inputs. The NAND inputs do not come directly from a pin as the Y outputs do. The inputs are wired from the Select and Enable pins through intermediate gates.

The three enable input pins, G1, G2A, and G2B connect to one AND gate and result in a single enable line from the gate. Note that G1 has its input control bit pass through a NOT gate and then a NOT circle before the bit enters the AND gate. This inverts the original G1 bit twice leaving it in the same state it was when it arrived at the G1 pin.

The G2A and G2B inputs only pass through one NOT circle. Those inputs are thus inverted as they enter the AND gate. As a result the AND gate will only turn on and enable the chip then when G1 is high and the other two enables are lows. Otherwise the chip is off. The output of the AND enabler is connected to one input

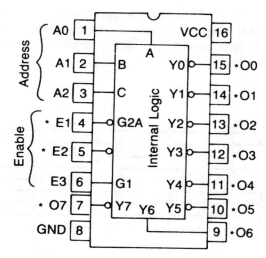

7-48 The 74LS138 chip is a 16-pin DIP. It has three address input bits that choose one of eight chip select outputs.

of each NAND gate. It turns them all on or off at the same time according to the state of the three inputs. To repeat, an H on G1 and Ls on the G2's turns on the chip.

Meanwhile, down at the Select pins, there are a pair of series NOT gates in each select line. As a select bit passes through two NOT gates, it ends up being inverted twice and in the same state it began with. Note that in the output of each series NOT gates are connected to four NAND gates.

There are also connections between each two series NOT gates. A select bit that is tapped off between two NOT gates has its state inverted. Therefore, each one of these tapped lines contains the inverted state on the select input. Note that each one of these lines is connected directly to four of the eight NAND gate inputs.

Each NAND gate then receives four inputs. One input is from the enable AND gate and three inputs are from the select NOT gate configuration. A NAND then can turn on when all four of its inputs are high, the one enables and the three selects. The truth table (Table 7-1) shows which one will turn on when enabled and selected. The NAND gate outputs a low when it turns on. Otherwise it will hold a high state at its output.

Follow one set of inputs (Fig. 7-49) to see how the three selects will choose one Y output. For example, suppose Selects C, B, and A are L-H-L. (The three enables must be H-L-L for any of the eight selections so that this is their states.) When the L at Select C arrives it passes through a NOT gate and becomes an H. The H is immediately passed to Y3, Y2, Y1, and Y0. The H also passes through the second NOT gate where it is inverted into an L. The L is sent directly to Y7, Y6, Y5, and Y4. The L turns them off. The four NAND gates Y3-Y0 though, now have two Hs on their inputs, one H from the Enable inputs and one from the C Select input.

At the same time an H arrives at B Select. The H passes through a NOT gate and becomes an L. The L goes directly to Y5, Y4, Y1, and Y0. It turns them off. They are out of contention. The L though continues through the series NOT gate and becomes an H. The H goes directly to Y7, Y6 Y3, and Y2. Up to this point, all

Table 7-1. The truth table is only operative when the Enable bits are LLH. Then the address bit combination chooses one of eight outputs. The outputs are normally held high. When a low exits, that is the desired chip select.

Inputs						Outputs *0 (held high)							
*E1	*E2	E3	A0	A1	A2	0	1	2	3	4	5	6	7
L	L	H	L	L	L	L	H	H	H	H	H	H	H
L	L	H	H	L	L	H	L	H	H	H	H	H	H
L	L	H	L	H	L	H	H	L	H	H	H	H	H
L	L	H	H	H	L	H	H	H	L	H	H	H	H
L	L	H	L	L	H	H	H	H	H	L	H	H	H
L	L	H	H	L	H	H	H	H	H	H	L	H	H
L	L	H	L	H	H	H	H	H	H	H	H	L	H
L	L	H	H	H	H	H	H	H	H	H	H	H	L

the NAND gates, except Y2 and Y3, have received at least one L, which has turned them off. Only Y2 and Y3 are left. The bit coming in the A select will choose one of the remaining two gates to be the output.

Entering the A select is an L. It passes through a NOT gate and is inverted to an H. The H is then wired directly to Y6, Y4, Y2, and Y0. The only one of these four output candidates without any L's is Y2. Y2 now has four H's on its inputs. There is one H from the enabling pins, one H from C select, one H from B select and one H from the A select. It turns on and outputs a low. All the rest of the Y pins are held high.

That is the way three select inputs can choose one-of-eight outputs. You could trace all eight input bit trios and see how each 3-bit combination will choose one of the Y pins to output from.

Counters

The multiplexers and decoders are clever arrangements of gates to process logic states from place-to-place and to turn circuits on and off. Once a high or low gets into the gates it keeps on moving right on through to the end of the circuit. There are no storage areas. The only time that elapses is the propagation delay, the 15 or so nanoseconds it takes the state to pass through the gate.

If you add storage areas like flip-flops to gates, you can create other digital entities. One such is a counter. For example, if you add a flip-flop to a pair of AND gates, as in Fig. 7-50, the trio can count. It can't count very high but it can count the two binary numbers, 0 and 1 or as you've noted low voltage and high voltage. The two voltages are code for 0 and 1 (Table 7-2).

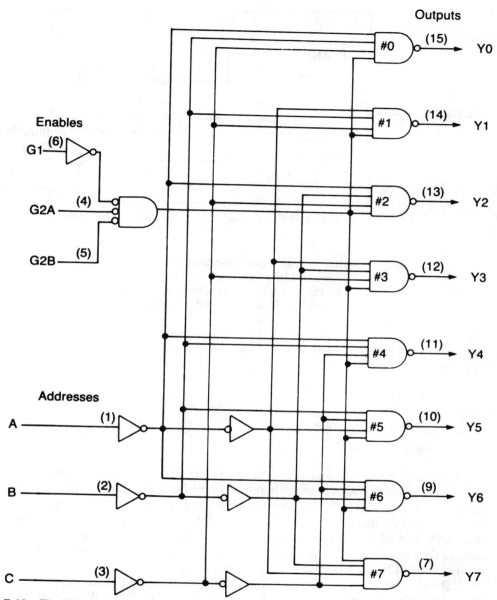

7-49 The three enable bits into the AND gate turns on the chip by connecting to every one of the eight internal NAND gates. The three address bits then choose one of the NAND gates to output according to the three-bit combinations. The output is a form of chip select.

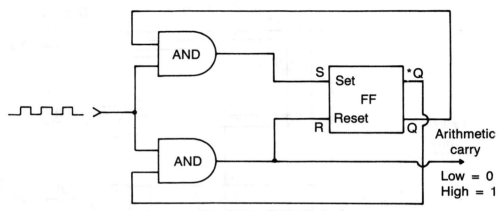

7-50 Two AND gates and an FF can count and produce an arithmetic carry.

**Table 7-2. It is natural for computers to
work in binary because they can
count by turning off and on. These are some
different ways the binary 1 and 0 are described.**

1	0
True	False
High	Low
+ 5 V	0 V
⊓	⊔
Yes	No
Set	Reset
Set	Clear

As expected, the FF and two AND gates are called a *binary counter*. The counter is also able to output an arithmetical carry. Let's examine the way the circuit performs this trick. The FF has two inputs and two outputs. The AND gates output to the FF inputs. The FF outputs are each cross-coupled back to an AND gate input. The other AND inputs on the gates are tied to each other and act as the input to the counter stage. The input consists of either one logic state or a pulse of square waves. The square wave is a steady stream of pulses.

If the counter, after it is powered up is storing a 0, then the following has happened. The *Q output will read a 1 and the Q output will read a 0. With Q low, the stage is considered held at 0. If Q was high the stage is thought of as being held at 1. Whatever Q outputs is the held state.

With the stage being a 0, if a 1 pulse is input from an external source, the pulse causes the stage to flip-flop. Q then changes its output to 1. *Q, always the opposite of Q, outputs a 0. Since Q is now 1 the stage is now considered being held at 1. The count of the stage has just been changed from 0 to 1. The stage has actually counted from 0 to 1 as a result of the input 1.

Looking at the AND gates before they each receive the 1 simultaneously from the external count source, the following was happening. The external input was 0. Q was coupling a 0 back to the gate in front of set. *Q was coupling a 1 back to the gate in front of reset. At that time a 1 arrived from the external source. The 1 made the gate at set have inputs of 0-1. The same 1 makes the gate at reset have inputs of 1-1. The stage flip-flops.

Q goes to a state of 1 and *Q to 0. The stage is now thought of as holding a 1. In addition, if a connection is made at the reset AND gate an output of 1 will emerge. When a stream of square waves enters the stage, at every high the stage will flip-flop. At each change the stage will count 0,1,0,1, etc. Every time the count goes to 1 the stage will output a 1 as an arithmetical carry.

A single FF can't count higher than 1 however it does output a 1 every time it counts to a maximum of 1. If you want to count higher than 1 all that is needed is more of the same type of counting stages (Fig. 7-51). Should you use a second stage, connected to the arithmetical carry output, the second stage will add two more binary digits to the counter. You will be able to count 0, 1, 10, 11. If you add at third stage the count can proceed 0, 1, 10, 11, 100, 101, 110, 111. A fourth stage again raises the count. 0, 1, 10, 11, 100, 101, 110, 111, 1000, 1001, 1010, 1011, 1100, 1101, 1110, 1111 (Table 7-3).

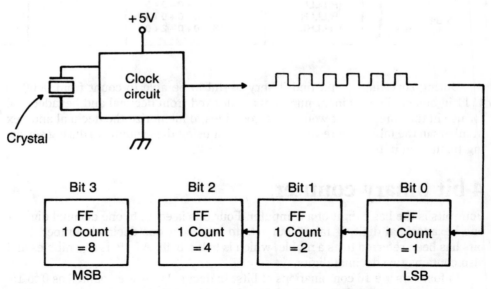

7-51 A four-bit counter goes through a nibble from 0000 to 1111.

If you notice, each additional stage doubles the number you can count to. Also notice that the count consists of the possible combinations of 1s and 0s or Hs and Ls the stages can put together. These two facts are the very core of the relationship between the electronic circuits and computing.

Table 7-3. The nibble counter output can be viewed in many ways. To obtain a result, add the significant values together. The resultant is decimal or can be converted to hex.

	Count in Binary	Significant Values	Decimal Results	Hex Results
Nibble Counter 4 Bits	LLLL	0+0+0+0	0	0
	LLLH	0+0+0+1	1	1
	LLHL	0+0+2+0	2	2
	LLHH	0+0+2+1	3	3
	LHLL	0+4+0+0	4	4
	LHLH	0+4+0+1	5	5
	LHHL	0+4+2+0	6	6
	LHHH	0+4+2+1	7	7
	HLLL	8+0+0+0	8	8
	HLLH	8+0+0+1	9	9
	HLHL	8+0+2+0	10	A
	HLHH	8+0+2+1	11	B
	HHLL	8+4+0+0	12	C
	HHLH	8+4+0+1	13	D
	HHHL	8+4+2+0	14	E
	HHHH	8+4+2+1	15	F
5 Bits	(H)LLLL	(16)+0+0+0+0	16	10
	(H)LLLH	(16)+0+0+0+1	17	11
	(H)LLHL	(16)+0+0+2+0	18	12

During servicing, you'll find it very useful to be able to count from 0000 to 1111 in binary. These binary numbers are derived from decimal and hexadecimal for use in the computer. It would be a good idea to memorize the decimal and hex numbers in the table. There will be more about using these numbers during servicing further on in the book.

4-bit binary counter

Four bits is the basic digit of a computer. Four bits is equal to one decimal digit or one hexadecimal digit. It takes four bits to represent one decimal number. Four bits has been referred to as a nibble, which is half a byte. A byte is two nibbles and also contains two decimal digits.

In four bits are 16 combinations of bits. In decimal they are counted as 0 to 15. 0 is just as much a number as any of the others when referring to computer register contents. You must learn to count from 0 instead of 1 as you have been doing all your life. Often a 1-2-3 in a computer becomes decimals 0-1-2. They mean the same thing.

Computer registers are multiples of four bits. A byte is two decimals, a 16-bit register holds four decimals and a 32-bit register has eight decimals in its bit holders. It is quite easy to convert any computer register contents from the binary in each nibble to its equivalent decimal between 0 and 15.

The hexadecimal, known as hex, is nothing more than decimal plus six. In addition to the digits 0-9, the letters A, B, C, D, E, and F are substituted for 10, 11, 12, 13, 14, and 15. For servicing you need to understand the conversions. They are relatively simple and require no extensive mathematical background.

The reason the comprehension is needed is to perform some signal tracing with binary numbers. If you want to ever write a test set of binary bits to a register, and then read them as a test you need the conversion. Today's personal computers do not accept binary numbers directly even though the binary is the only number system they use. You must enter the binary number through a language like BASIC or assembly language. In BASIC you'd have to convert your test set of bits to decimal.

For example, if you wanted to place a 1101 in binary into a nibble holder through BASIC, you would use decimal 13. Should you be troubleshooting with assembly language, the 1101 could be installed in the nibble holder with its equivalent hex number D. There will be more about all this later in the book.

The 74L93 4-bit binary counter

The 74L93 (Fig. 7-52) is a 14-pin DIP but only uses ten of the pins. The other four pins are unused. Pins 5 and 10 are + 5 V and ground respectively.

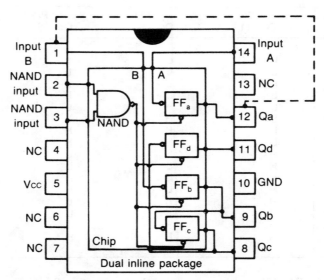

7-52   The 74LS93 is a four-bit binary counter. For routine 0 – 15 counting, pins 12 and 1 are wired together.

The other eight pins are divided equally between inputs and outputs, four of each. Two of the inputs connect to a NAND gate. The NAND gate is the reset for the counter. When both inputs are highs the counter is reset to zero. That is, the four bit holders go to a state of LLLL. Otherwise, the chip is ready to count.

There is only one input needed in a 4-bit counter so input A is used. Input B is then tied to the output of the first bit holder (pin 12) in the group. That keeps the B input from interfering with the count. It also wires the first counter to the second.

Examine the configuration. There are four stages. Each stage can store one bit. Each stage has an output pin. The four output pins are called Qa, Qb, Qc and Qd. The Qa stage receives a 1 at input A, pin 14. It stores the first pulse and shows a 1 at Qa pin 12. Pin 1, input B as mentioned above, is wired to Qa. A second 1 arrives at input A. The connection between Qa and pin 1, input B, carries the Qa output to the next stage, Qb. The carry 1 is stored in Qb.

You can follow the count with the count sequence table (Table 7-4). As each new 1 enters input A the stages store and output highs to the next stage. At the start of a count from 0 – 15 the four bit holders contain LLLL. After the 15 pulses the four bit holders contain HHHH. At the in-between numbers the four bits will hold the binary code for the particular number of pulses that have entered input A and proceeded to work their way from bit stage to bit stage.

Table 7-4. With pins 12 and 1 connected,
inputs at pin 14A will result in these outputs at pins 11, 8, 4, and 12.

	Outputs			
Count	Pin Qd 11	Pin Qc 8	Pin Qb 9	Pin Qa 12
0	L	L	L	L
1	L	L	L	H
2	L	L	H	L
3	L	L	H	H
4	L	H	L	L
5	L	H	L	H
6	L	H	H	L
7	L	H	H	H
8	H	L	L	L
9	H	L	L	H
10	H	L	H	L
11	H	L	H	H
12	H	H	L	L
13	H	H	L	H
14	H	H	H	L
15	H	H	H	H

Two of these 74L93's can be wired together to form an 8-bit counter. The eight bits can count 256 times, from 0 to 255. The 4-bit counter can only count 0 – 15. When two 4-bit counters are wired together to form 8-bits, they form two nibbles. The nibbles are called the *most significant nibble* and the *least significant nibble*.

The LSN is the nibble counter just covered that counts from 0 – 15. The MSN is the second one that allows the count to go up to 255.

After the LSN counts up to 15, it then passes one high to the MSN. The LSN continues to pass one high every time it counts past 15. This allows the MSN to store an additional high every 15 counts of the LSN. The maximum count the two nibbles working together can store occurs when they contain HHHHHHHH. This is the binary code for decimal 255.

If you tie four nibble counters together they continue to count until they reach HHHHHHHHHHHHHHHH. This is the binary code for the decimal number 65,535 commonly known as 64K. In hexadecimal that binary number is known as FFFF. That is because the hex number F is code for HHHH in binary. Four nibbles of HHHH produces four Fs.

Counters are vital in computers. A counter is able to perform all the mathematics a computer must do. It can add with the counter. It can subtract with the counter by using some tricky manipulations called *two's complement*. It can multiply and divide with the counters. Understanding these processes are not needed for servicing computers. I mention them in passing so you'll appreciate the importance of the counters. You can learn more about the mathematical manipulations in books on programming.

Shift registers

Besides counting, bit holders and gates can act as shift registers. A shift register is a group of bit holders that are able to shift their contents to the register on the right or the one on the left. What good can shifting the bits from side to side do? It is very valuable. First of all it solves the problem of converting series streams of data to parallel groups. For instance, if a modem is inputting data into a computer, the data is in the form of a steady serial stream of highs and lows that arrived via the telephone from afar. Inside the computer, the data must be placed on the data bus. The data bus could be eight parallel copper traces running around the print board. The serial stream must be converted to a parallel group. This is accomplished in a shift register.

The shift register is also able to reverse the operation. If a computer has some parallel data on its output that must be converted to a serial stream, the shift register can do this too.

Besides being able to convert serial bits to parallel and vice versa a shift register can perform some multiplication and division operations. For example, suppose you have a byte sized shift register with the least significant bit, the LSB set at 1. The register then reads 00000001. In decimal this is 1. Now shift the 1 to the next most significant bit or in other words, shift the 1 to the left. The register then reads 00000010. In decimal this is 2. Then shift the 1 another bit holder to the left. The register reads 00000100. The register is now coded 4 in decimal. Shift one more and the decimal value is 8 as the register reads 00001000. 00010000 is 16, 00100000 is 32, 01000000 equals 64 and 10000000 is 128. As you can see, shifting the bits higher multiplies the decimal equivalent by 2 for every bit that is moved.

Should you reverse the shifting and go lower, you'll divide by 2 for each move lower. This is one of the ways a computer can multiply and divide. This is an important function of the shift register.

The 8-bit serial shift register

In chapter 5, the series-to-parallel shift register was discussed. It can be contained as part of one of the large chips especially I/O types. This 7491 8-bit serial shift register (Fig. 7-53) does not perform any series-to-parallel conversions. It simply has a serial input, shifts serial data from bit to bit and then outputs serial data.

The 7491 is contained in a 14-pin DIP but only seven pins are used. Pins 5 and 10 are +5 V and ground respectively. Pins 11 and 12 are inputs A and B. Pins 13 and 14 are the final output Q and *Q. Pin 9 is a clock input to drive the serial bits from stage to stage.

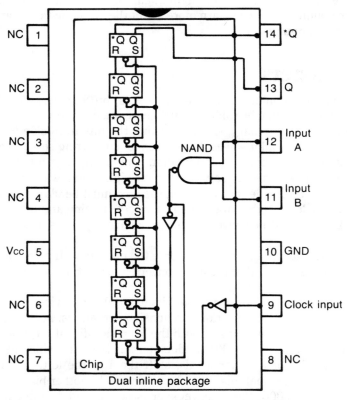

7-53 The 7491 is a 14-pin DIP containing a serial 8-bit shift register.

The truth table (Table 7-5) is simple. If both inputs A and B are both highs, then Q is high and *Q is low. Otherwise, Q is low and *Q is high.

Table 7-5. The truth table shows when the inputs are high. The final output will be a high on Q and a low on * Q.

7491 Truth Table			
Inputs		Outputs	
A	B	Q	*Q
H	H	H	L
L	–	L	H
–	L	L	H

–, Doesn't matter which state H or L

The schematic diagram (Fig. 7-53) also called the logic diagram, shows eight R-S flip-flops wired in series. The clock pulse enters and passes through a NOT gate. It connects to all eight FFs and clocks them all at the same time. Inputs A and B feed a NAND gate. The output of the NAND gate is split and one leg is sent to a NOT gate while the other leg goes directly to Reset of the first FF. The output of the NOT gate goes to the Set connection of the first FF. This makes the inputs at reset and set complementary.

The FFs are wired in series. They terminate at Q and *Q of the last FF. When the clock is running, any input at A and B will pass from FF to FF until it exits at Q and *Q. The data bits move every time the clock pulse has a rising edge.

Test approach for these chips

Understanding all the details on all these chips and others that you might encounter during servicing, can be mind boggling. However, all the details are not needed to suspect a chip, make meaningful quick tests on them, and pinpoint bad ones. The right approach will often have you quickly zeroed-in on the defect.

The first thing to do is look at the chip, even though it is tiny it is an important part of the computer. If there are 100 chips on a board there are 100 separate devices all completely independent of each other. They might be wired together but they are each doing their own job. It is as if you have a giant board with 100 individual TV monitors in a studio. The TVs are wired together but you wouldn't worry about the surrounding TVs if one conks out. You'd attack the bad one and ignore the good ones.

Once you focus in on a chip you are ready to test it. You have access to the chip only through its pins. There are only three kinds of pins (see Table 7-6). First of all there are the power pins. You'll see Vcc, which means + 5 V supply for the collec-

Table 7-6. For most chips doing most jobs, these quick voltage tests will yield results.

Quick Voltage Tests	
Missing Voltage on Pins	**Possible Location of Trouble**
Power pins Vcc, VDD, etc.	Trouble is located before V-input pin in V-supply line
Digital logic input pins	Trouble is located before input pin in signal path
Digital logic output pins	Trouble is located in chip itself

tors of all the bipolar transistors. There might be VDD. This is the + voltage for the drains of field-effect transistors. There might be a pin called VBB or VEE. These could be voltages needed to supply the bases or emitters of bipolar transistors. Then there could be a Vss. This is the voltage for the source of an FET. Then of course there is the ground pin or pins. The supply voltage pins are always the first ones tested. They energize every single transistor on a chip at the same time.

The second type of pins are the inputs. You must know which pins are inputs. If you suspect a chip as defective, you can test the inputs. Should one or more of the input voltages or pulses be missing, chances are the chip is not defective. The chip is probably not receiving the correct input from another circuit. When all the pin inputs are correct then the chip itself becomes an important suspect. A trouble could have occurred in the chip after the inputs were injected.

The third type of pin is the output pins. After a chip is powered properly and is receiving all its input voltages and pulses correctly, it must process those logic signals as it is prescribed to do. If it is not acting according to design, it could be because an internal circuit has failed. This will show up at the output pins. When the inputs are good but an output or outputs are not correct, chances are good there is an internal chip failure.

When a chip fails internally, the best thing to do is replace it with a known good exact replacement. There is little chance of actually figuring out what happened inside the chip and except for purists—who cares? The important thing to do is to get your computer back on line.

The approach therefore is that once you are able to analyze the trouble in a computer and decide on suspects, treat the suspects as individual devices. Test the input power and ground first. Second test the input logic signals. Third test the output signals. In chapter 2, the test equipment and the type of signals you are looking for are discussed. In other chapters the service notes and techniques needed to comprehend your test results are covered. Between these chapters and your understanding of the way the chips perform their jobs, you will be able to perform quite a lot of the troubleshooting and repairing of personal computers.

8

Memory
contained in chips

FIGURE 8-1 IS A BLOCK DIAGRAM THAT DEPICTS THE THREE ESSENTIAL sections of all computers. Two of the three vital circuit sections are the microprocessor and the I/O ports. A flood of information coded into bits and bytes enter and exit the computer and are processed in the processor.

However, the processor and ports are nothing more than dumb machines. They have no brains. The intelligence that directs their every move comes from the computer memory. The memory must be consulted by the processor for every move the processor makes. The processor is completely dependent upon the binary-coded instructions and data that is stored in the memory banks.

The storage areas, in the computer itself, is composed of many chips. This is in contrast to storage areas such as disks and cassette tapes. The disks and tapes are external to the computer and are held in drives and cassettes, which are peripheral devices. The disk drives are discussed in chapter 24. The memory chips are internal to the computer and are connected directly to the processor circuits.

There are two distinct types of memory chips, the well-known RAM and ROM chips. The RAM chips are storage places where the binary bit intelligence is held while the processor is doing its work. About 70% of the work the processor does is to write bits to RAM and read bits out of RAM. The writing bits is actually a move that stores bits in RAM addresses. The reading is the retrieval of the stored bits.

The ROM memory is a storage place where permanent intelligence is installed at the factory. The ROMs are loaded with programs that operate the computer so it can run applications. The ROMs cannot be written to. They are already full of intelligence that is burned into the silicon. The ROMs can only be read and have copies of its intelligence sent to the processor.

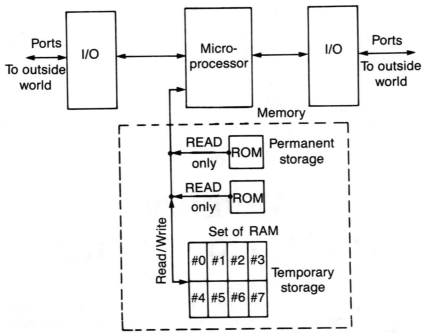

8-1   Inside a personal computer there are a group of chips. Central to all is the microprocessor. The MPU works with a set of RAM storage chips, some ROMs that tell the MPU how to operate, and some I/O ports to interface with the outside world.

The RAM chips are available in many different types, sizes, shapes, and capacities as discussed throughout this chapter. They keep getting smaller in size and larger in the numbers of bits they can store. You'll find them in chip sockets on the motherboard, soldered directly onto the motherboard, or contained in modules called *SIMMs* (single inline memory modules). Figure 8-2 is a recent price list of memory chips. It shows the wide diversity of chip types that are readily available.

RAM stands for random-access memory, which is a misleading name. It is also called read/write memory because the processor can either read from it or write to it. The RAM storage areas, when you first turn on your computer, are empty storage bits arranged in bytes, typically eight bits to an address. The addresses begin with address zero and proceeds according to how much memory the processor is capable of addressing. For instance, a typical 8-bit computer is able to address 65,536 individual bytes. This amount of memory can then be the total storage area, and RAM chips can be wired to hold this amount of bytes for use by the processor.

ROM stands for read-only memory. This is an accurate name because that is all the processor can do with the ROM's burned-in bits. The processor can read

DYNAMIC RAMS

PART	SIZE	SPEED	PRICE
TMS-4027	4096x1	250ns	$ .95
4116-200	16384x1	200ns	.89
4116-150	16384x1	150ns	1.49
MK4332	32768x1	200ns	6.95
4164-200	65536x1	200ns	1.95
4164-150	65536x1	150ns	2.49
4164-120	65536x1	120ns	2.89
4164-100	65536x1	100ns	3.39
TMS4464-12	65536x4	120ns	3.95
TMS4464-10	65536x4	100ns	4.95
41256-150	262144x1	150ns	2.59
41256-120	262144x1	120ns	2.95
41256-100	262144x1	100ns	3.15
41256-80	262144x1	80ns	3.75
41256-60	262144x1	60ns	5.25
414256-100	262144X4	100ns	12.95
414256-80	262144X4	80ns	13.45
1 MB-120	1048576x1	120ns	11.95
1 MB-100	1048576x1	100ns	12.35
1 MB-80	1048576x1	80ns	12.95

SIMMS & SIPS

PART #	SIZE	FOR	SPEED	PRICE
41256A9B-12	256K x 9-BIT	SIMM/PC	120ns	$36.95
41256A9B-80	256K x 9-BIT	SIMM/PC	80ns	49.95
421000A8B-10	1MB x 8-BIT	SIMM/MAC	100ns	109.95
421000A9B-10	1MB x 9-BIT	SIMM/PC	100ns	113.95
421000A9B-80	1MB x 9-BIT	SIMM/PC	80ns	119.95
256KX9SIP-80	256K X 9	SIP/PC	80ns	54.95
256KX9SIP-60	256K x 9	SIP/PC	60ns	64.95
1MBX9SIP-80	1MB x 9	SIP/PC	80ns	124.95

EPROMS

PART#	SIZE	SPEED	VPP	PRICE
1702	256x8	1000ns	25v	4.95
2708	1024x8	450ns	25V	4.95
2716	2048x8	450ns	25V	3.49
2716-1	2048x8	350ns	25V	3.95
TMS2532	4096x8	450ns	25V	5.95
2732	4096x8	450ns	25V	3.95
2732A	4096x8	250ns	21V	3.95
2732A-2	4KX8	200ns	21V	4.25
2764	8192x8	450ns	12.5V	3.49
2764-250	8192x8	250ns	12.5V	3.69
2764-200	8192x8	200ns	12.5V	4.25
27C64	8192x8	250ns	12.5V	4.95
27128	16384x8	250ns	12.5V	4.25
27128A-200	16384x8	200ns	12.5V	5.95
27256	32768x8	250ns	12.5V	4.95
27256-200	32768x8	200ns	12.5V	5.95
27C256	32768x8	250ns	12.5V	5.95
27512	65536x8	250ns	12.5V	7.95
27C512	65536x8	250ns	12.5V	8.95
27C101-20	131072x8	200ns	12.5V	24.95

STATIC RAMS

PART#	SIZE	SPEED	PRICE
TMM2016	2048x8	150ns	3.25
HM6116LP-2	2048x8	120ns	5.49
HM6264LP-15	8192x8	150ns	6.95
HM6264LP-12	8192x8	120ns	7.95
HM43256LP-12	32768x8	120ns	17.95
HM43256LP-10	32768x8	100ns	18.95

8-2   Here is a recent price list of typical memory chips. The SIMMs (single inline memory modules) are becoming popular.

the contents of memory holders in ROM. It just can't write to the ROM because the holders have permanent bits cast into the silicon. If the processor should try to write to a ROM chip, the bits would arrive at the chip but would not be able to gain entrance or be stored.

In the factory, a typical ROM chip could have its bit holders wired with microscopic silicon diodes. A program of operating system bits is burned into the diodes. That is, when a high is desired, the diode is left intact. When a low is required, a special machine blows out the diode. The ROM programs are thus installed permanently into the chip.

Storage bytes

RAM chips are little warehouses where bits can be stored as long as they are energized. When they are turned off the bits disappear. The bits are nothing more than high (H) and low (L) voltage states, for example +5 and 0 V. Each bit circuit is able to store one of those states.

There are two general methods by which the bits are stored, called static and dynamic. Static storage is performed in a circuit called a flip-flop. As the name implies, the circuit can flip-flop from one state to another. A flip can be a high and a flop could be a low. Dynamic storage is conducted by charging up a tiny capacitance in the bit circuit. A charge in the capacitance is a high and no charge is a low. Static storage is fairly stable and once the flip or flop has taken place the state will hold until forcibly changed. Dynamic storage is less certain as the capacitor high voltage won't hold and leaks off. The charge must be recharged, or as it is called "refreshed" faster than it can leak off so the voltage can't dissipate.

The static flip-flop

One flip-flop, that can store one bit (Fig. 8-3) consists of two identical amplifier circuits that are hooked together back-to-back. The circuits can be two vacuum tubes, two transistors, or even two logic gates (logic gates are covered in the previous chapter). The wiring of the two amplifiers, call them A and B, is such that while one of the circuits is turned on, the other is turned off. The two circuits also will hold that state as long as they are energized and are not disturbed. This is the way static memory holds a storage bit.

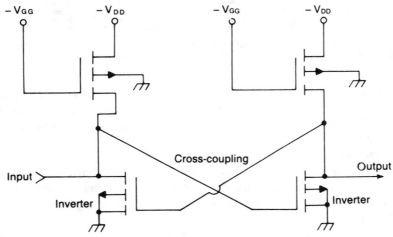

8-3 The static RAM circuit is a storage flip-flop because two FETs have their drains cross-coupled to opposite gates.

If A is turned on and B is turned off, the circuit pair is storing a high. Should A be turned off and B turned on the pair is storing a low. They will hold that state until a disturbing voltage state comes along. When a voltage state is applied properly, the circuit pair will flip-flop. For example if a low is applied to the side that is turned off, the pair will flip-flop, which changes the state of the bit that is being stored.

These flip-flop circuits can barely be seen under the microscope, so their actual circuits are of no practical interest for the servicer. The interest lies in the state that is being stored in the static bit holder. If these circuits won't hold highs and lows, the chip they are in must be discarded and a new one installed. The important thing to know about flip-flops is that they are able to store voltage states, and states can be flip-flopped and thus moved from bit holder to bit holder. They are also very stable and do not require any refreshing voltages as the dynamic bit holders do.

Dynamic bit holders

Static RAM requires a relatively large amount of chip space per bit holder. As a result not too many bits can be stored on a static RAM chip. Some popular static RAM chips are discussed later in this chapter to illustrate this point. Dynamic RAM, on the other hand can store enormous numbers of bit holders on a chip. As of this writing chips holding more than 256,000 bits are common in the marketplace for under $5 each (see Fig. 8-2). The popular *DRAMs* (dynamic read-only memories) is covered in this chapter too.

Dynamic RAM chips use microscopic IGFETs (insulated-gate field-effect transistors) wired together (Fig. 8-4). The original popular dynamic RAM chip that appeared in personal computers was the 4116. The 41 stands for dynamic and the 16 means there are 16K bit holders on the chip. Note they are bits, not bytes.

The next step upward in bit density was found in the 4164 chip. The 64 means there are 64K bits on the chip. Next the 41256 DRAM hit the marketplace. It has a bit density of 256K. The next chip that appeared was the 411024 chip. It has 1024K bits.

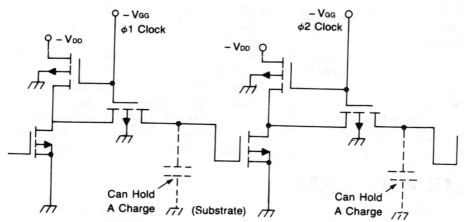

8-4 The dynamic RAM stages are able to store a logic state as capacitance charges. If the capacitance is charged the state is considered a high. When the capacitance is not charged, the state is a low.

The germ sized IGFETs can be used because of the insulated gate. An IGFET (Fig. 8-5) is made with a gate electrode that is connected to the body of the tiny transistor with a piece of glassy silicon dioxide. The gate electrode is thus insulated from the transistor and the glass acts as the dielectric of a minute capacitor to

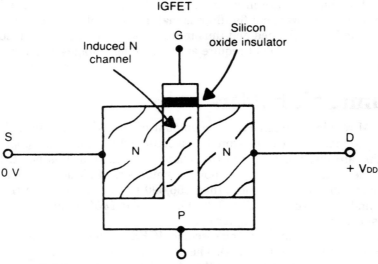

8-5 An IGFET is made with a silicon diode insulator between the body of the transistor and the gate electrode. Static electricity is able to pierce the insulator and kill the IGFET.

the chassis ground. This capacitor is subject to being charged. If it is charged it is wired to constitute a high. When it is not charged it is assigned the role of a low. The only trouble is that the charge will leak off unless it is refreshed.

The refreshing requires extra consideration but because the dynamic RAM can hold so many more memory bits than static RAM, the extra circuitry is very worthwhile.

Refreshing DRAMs is not that difficult. Each bit on a DRAM has its very own address. That means on a 64K dynamic RAM, there are 64K addresses. All that is needed to refresh a bit holder is to address it. There is more about this procedure in this chapter. The important point is that every bit holder has a gate capacitance where a high or low can be stored. The high or low will remain on that bit unless it is disturbed. The high can be changed to a low by forcibly removing the capacitance charge. A low can be made into a high by charging up the gate capacitance.

A 1K static RAM

One of the simplest static RAM chips you'll encounter in a personal computer is the 1K chip generically numbered, 2102L. It is organized as 1024 × 1 (Figs. 8-6 and 8-7). What that means is, there are 1024 individual bits in the RAM, each bit with its very own address. The operation is static and therefore requires no consideration as far as refreshing goes. Once a bit is installed at an address it will remain until disturbed.

If you look at the pin connections, there are 16 on the DIP. Pin 10 is where the +5 V power is applied and pin 9 connects to ground. The power energizes every single bit on the chip simultaneously.

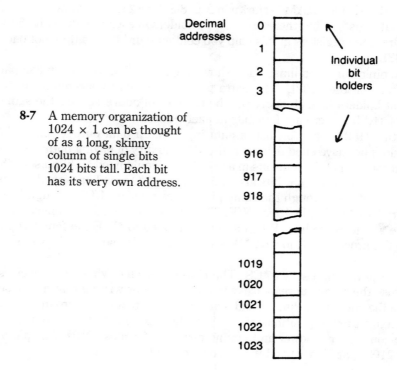

8-6 One of the simplest static RAM chips is the 16-pin 2102 with a 1024×1 organization.

8-7 A memory organization of 1024×1 can be thought of as a long, skinny column of single bits 1024 bits tall. Each bit has its very own address.

There are 10 address pins, A9 – A0. There are 1024 individual one bit registers in the chip, each with its own address. When the processor wants to read or write to one of the addresses, it sends a specific combination of ten bits over address lines A9 – A0. Ten address lines can form 1024 different combinations of highs and lows. The processor sends the combination to access only the one desired bit.

The time required to access one bit on this chip is 450 nanoseconds. What does that mean? A nanosecond is one billionth of a second. It is actually quite a long time as far as memory accessing goes. A fairly rapid accessing time found on more complex chips can be 250 or 150 nanoseconds. There will be a lot more about access times in the discussions of the memory and other chips.

Pin 13 is called *CE. With this pin the chip can be enabled with a low or placed into a three-state off condition with a high. Pin 3 is the read/write line. The processor can send a signal and the chip will let itself be read or will accept a bit if it is being written to.

The only pins left are the data in and data out at 11 and 12. These lines can be connected to places that can send data to the 2102L or receive data from it.

The chip is very straightforward and very useful in some applications. On occasion you will find one on a print board.

4K static RAM

The 2114L 4K static RAM is shown in Fig. 8-8. The 2114L is organized, with 1024 individual registers, but there are four-bit holders in each register (Fig. 8-9). When you address the registers in this chip you contact four bits at a time not one as with the 2102L.

The pin connection illustration shows the 2114L has 18 pins in comparison to the 16 pins on the 2102L. The extra pins are needed to accommodate the additional bit holders in each address. The number of addresses are the same (1024, which is 1K) but there are four bits at each address.

In the 2102L, each bit had a data input and a data output connection. The 2114L does not have enough pins to afford the luxury of having both a data in and a data out for each of the four bits in a register. It would need eight pins for that kind of design. Instead the four bits are each given an I/O pin. That way data can travel in both directions through the same pin. Those pins are I/O1 through I/O4 at pin numbers 14 – 11. At pin 10 is *WE. This is the write enable connection and acts just like a read/write line. When a high is applied to *WE the four I/O pins send data to the processor. A low on *WE allows the processor to write to the bit holders.

Pin 8 is the chip select *CS. The chip is selected when *CS receives a low. Otherwise the chip is unresponsive to any reading or writing that might be taking place in the computer. Pins 18 and 9 are the + 5 V power and ground connections. Incidentally, the pin positions of + 5 V at the top right and ground at bottom left are the conventional power and ground positions for most DIPs. The pin positions on the 2102L, at pins 10 and 9 is unconventional.

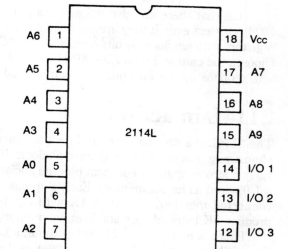

8-8 The common 2114L static RAM chip is found in an 18-pin package, organized as 1024 × 4.

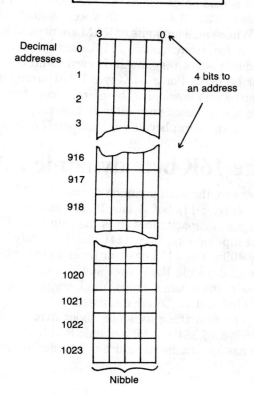

8-9 Each register has four bits and one address.

Note that there are also ten address pins on the 2114L. There are still only 1024 registers even if they are four bits each. The processor can address all those registers with ten address bits over A9 – A0. *CS is actually an 11th address bit. It chooses the chip and then A9 – A0 picks out the register. Once the register is chosen, it opens up. Its four bits can then be read or written to.

2114L in action

The 2114L is a very handy chip. It is a complete static memory. It can be wired to almost any processor and any normal clock. It was found as the main memory in early microcomputers. For example, the ancient VIC 20 had ten 2114L chips (Fig. 8-10) wired as its 5K memory. Each chip has 1K of four bits. When two chips are connected together, they form 1K with eight-bit registers. Five pairs of 2114Ls produce 5K bytes of very stable static memory.

There is no need for refreshing the bits because they are dc stable. The flip-flops will store bits. The voltage states will remain firm in the bits and not be destroyed as they are read.

Note in the schematic that each pair of 2114Ls are wired together. The I/O pins are connected to D7 – D0 of the system data bus. The address pins are all common except for the *CS pins. The *CS pins are connected as five pairs. When a chip select is made over one of the *CS lines a pair of chips are selected together. This makes two 2114Ls act as if they were a single chip with 1024 eight-bit registers.

When small amounts of RAM are needed in a computer, the 2114L is an excellent choice. However, two 2114Ls only provide 1K byte of RAM, which by today's standards is not very much. If even as little as 16K bytes are needed, 32 2114Ls must be used. For a 64K byte RAM arrangement, 128 chips are needed. This becomes very unwieldy. Therefore, except for special applications, the static RAM chips are not used very often in general-purpose computers. Dynamic RAM has become the norm because it lends itself to more bit density than the static.

The 16K byte dynamic RAM

Years ago, the most common dynamic RAM chip was the 4116. It is only a 16-pin DIP, (Fig. 8-11) but it has 16,384 individual dynamic bits, the ones that hold charges in capacitances. It is the same size DIP as the 2102L that only contains 1024 flip-flop bits. The 2114L chip is slightly larger than the 4116 but has less bits, only 4096. The 4116 has four times as many bits as the 2114L. That is the advantage of dynamic RAM over static. The 4116 also is one of the oldest and least dense of the dynamic chips. You'll see the newer densities on in this chapter, where the 4164 and 41256 are discussed.

The first thing to notice about dynamic chips is their bit organization. The 4116 is a 16,384 × 1 bit dynamic RAM. This means that every bit is an individual and has its own unique address. In order to construct byte-sized registers you must

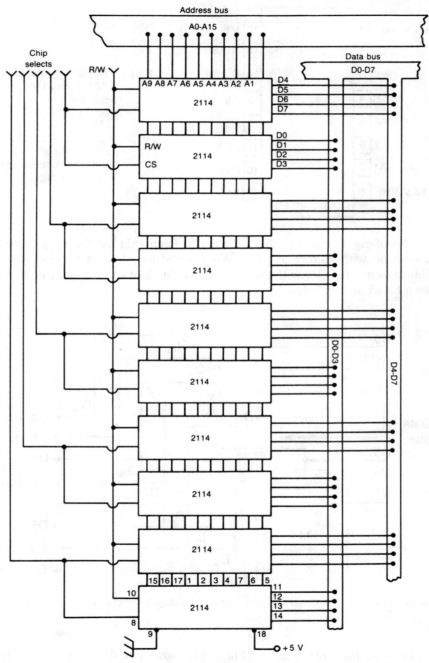

8-10 One of the simplest static RAM chips is the 16-pin 2102 with a 1024 × 1 organization.

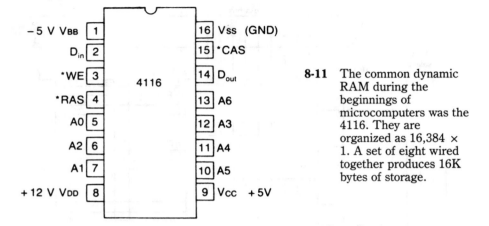

8-11 The common dynamic RAM during the beginnings of microcomputers was the 4116. They are organized as 16,384 × 1. A set of eight wired together produces 16K bytes of storage.

wire a set of eight chips together (Fig. 8-12). Each chip has the same number of bits, each bit with its own address. When wired together, each chip contributes one bit to form a register with eight bits. A set of eight 4116 chips (Fig. 8-13) produces a RAM of 16K bytes.

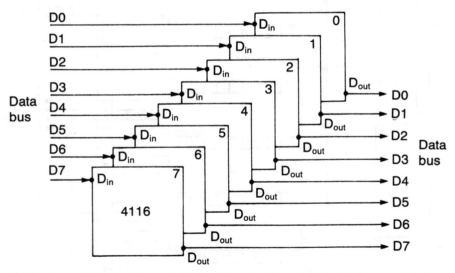

8-12 A set of 4116 chips are wired with each chip connected to its own data bus line.

The pin connection diagram (Fig. 8-11) shows one data in pin, D_{in}, and one date out pin, D_{out}. There are seven address pins, A6 – A0. Does that look right? Seven address lines can only form 128 different combinations of bits. To address 16,384 bits, 14 address lines are required. Yet there are only seven.

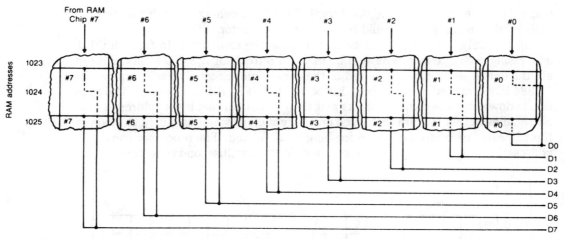

8-13   Each chip stores one type of bit. Chip 7 stores all the D7 bits, chip 6 all the D6 bits, etc.

The reason only seven address lines are needed is because the lines are multiplexed. The dictionary defines multiplex as "relating to a system of transmitting several messages simultaneously on the same circuit." This is what is happening here within a few billionths of a second. The seven address lines are connected to the output of a multiplex chip, covered in the last chapter. The input of the multiplex chip is connected to 14 address lines, A13 – A0. The multiplexer separates the incoming address bit into two sections. One comprises lines A13 – A7 and the second section to lines A6 – A0. The multiplexer then feeds the lines in two batches to address pins of the RAM chips, one batch at a time. That way A13 – A7 performs its addressing chores and then A6 – A0 does its addressing. The fourteen bits addresses one bit on each chip, which means a byte-sized register has been contacted.

The set of eight chips are all numbered and attached to the data bus. In Fig. 8-13, on chip number 7 are all the bit number 7s for all the registers. Chip number 7 is connected to data bus line D7. The same type of hookup is made for every chip down to chip number 0. Chip number 0 contains all the bit number 0s for all the registers. Chip number 0 is connected to data bus line D0.

4116 matrix

A 4116 has 16,384 bit circuits. Each bit is based around a tiny capacitance. Therefore, a dynamic chip is an array of capacitors. Each capacitor is charged or not. If it is charged and thus contains a high the preservation of the high is in jeopardy as it continually tries to leak off. It will leak off unless it is recharged at least once every two milliseconds. A millisecond is a thousandth of a second. This is relatively a long period of time if it is compared to a microsecond, which is a millionth of a second. However, there are 16,384 individual locations on a chip and with eight chips there are more than 128,000 bits that need refreshing. If each bit required individual refreshing, time could become a critical factor.

Fortunately, a lot of bits can be recharged at the same time. In fact, only 128 addressing recharge moves have to be made to refresh all 128,000+ bits. First of all, the entire set can be addressed at the same time. Secondly each chip has its 16,384 bits arranged in a matrix of 128 × 128 bits (Fig. 8-14). There are 128 rows of bits down and 128 columns of bits across. It works out that if you address a row, all 128 bits on that row are recharged on all eight chips simultaneously. As soon as the 128 rows are addressed the refreshing is completed. The processor can easily address 128 rows in its spare moments within the 2 millisecond time period.

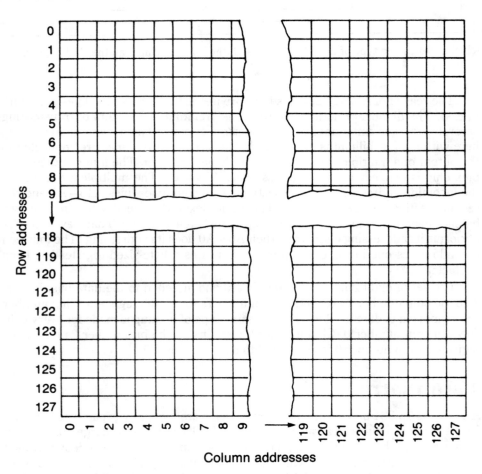

8-14   The 4116 memory matrix on the substrate is laid out with 128 rows and 128 columns.

Most computers provide some sort of circuit to conduct the refreshing. On one processor the Z80, there is a special register that does nothing but refresh the dynamic RAM. As mentioned, the refreshing operation is nothing more than an addressing sequence.

The addressing of dynamic RAM consists of row addressing and column addressing. The address lines are in two sections. There are seven lines for row addressing and seven lines for column addressing. Note that seven lines are able to form 128 different patterns of bits. The seven row bits can address one out of the 128 row addresses. The seven column bits are able to address one out of the 128 column addresses.

Once the exact row address is energized and the exact column address is energized, a single bit is crosshatched in the matrix. Each same bit on all eight chips are energized at the same time. The processor is then able to read or write to that formed byte register.

Access times

It was mentioned that the static RAM chip, the 2102L had an access time of about 450 nanoseconds. The dynamic chips usually operate at a much faster time (Fig. 8-2) such as 250 nanoseconds, or even as quickly as 60 nanoseconds. That operation must be put into perspective.

Every computer operates to the beat of a clock circuit. An example of clock frequency could be one megahertz. This means there are one million clock beats to a second or one beat to a microsecond. Because there are 1000 nanoseconds in a microsecond we can work with that figure. If a clock is oscillating at one megahertz, the processor will complete one cycle in one microsecond or 1000 nanoseconds. Figure 8-15 shows one processor cycle of 1000 nanoseconds.

The cycle consists of the clock beating once. That means, in 1000 nanoseconds, the clock signal will start off at 0 V, jump up to +5 V, stay at +5 V for about 500 nanoseconds, drop down to 0 V, hold there for another 500 nanoseconds, and then prepare for the next cycle. Actually the voltage can't change from 0 V to +5 V instantly. It takes the voltage about 25 nanoseconds to make the change. It also takes the voltage about 25 nanoseconds to drop from +5 V back down to 0 V.

If you graph this voltage change with volts as the vertical line and time in nanoseconds as the horizontal line, the resulting wave shape is a square wave. The square wave has names for the different parts of the wave. The 25 nanoseconds voltage-up line is called the *rising edge*. The 25 nanosceonds drop line is called the *falling edge*. The flat top high voltage is the high duration. The flat bottom low voltage is the low duration. The processor could use just one wave shape to conduct its business or it could use two wave shapes. When it uses two, there is one wave shape to trigger off the addressing system, called $\phi1$, and a second wave shape to handle the movement of data bits, called $\phi2$.

These square waves that are produced by the clock drive the processor. As the $\phi1$ rising edge enters the processor, it triggers the addressing bits. They begin leaving the processor out of the address pins. The rising edge also triggers the

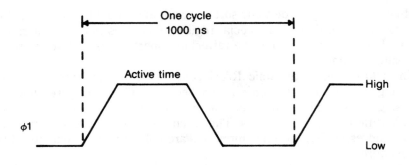

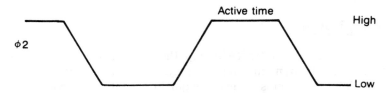

8-15 This is a dual-phase clock found in some old eight-bit processor systems. The 6800 and the 6502 used this clock.

read/write circuit. It sends out the read/write bit also called write enable or WE (Fig. 8-16). For instance, it sends out a high to set up a read operation or a low to start a write operation.

The rising edge also triggers other timing signals that might be needed. For instance, the 4116 chip needs timing signals to let it know what address bits are arriving from the multiplexer. For example, a signal called row address strobe, RAS, signals the entry circuits in the 4116 that the seven row address bits are arriving. The row bits are accepted and sent to the row address circuits in the chip.

Next, a signal called column address strobe, CAS, signals the entry circuits that the seven-column address bits are now arriving. The 4116 turns off the row clock circuits and turns on the column clock circuits. The column bits are accepted and sent to the column address circuits in the chip.

As a result of the rising edge of the clock signal the set of 4116 chips are addressed and the chosen register activated. This is the first part of the memory access. This could take about 200 nanoseconds. The addressed register is then ready to be read or written to. If it is read, a copy of its bit contents will be placed on the data bus. Should the processor be writing to the register, the processor will put bits on the data bus. They will be ready to travel to the register and be stored. Either operation takes time.

The $\phi 2$ square wave, is to handle the data chores. The $\phi 2$ is staggered with respect to the $\phi 1$. The $\phi 2$ is low when $\phi 1$ is high and high when the $\phi 1$ is low. The

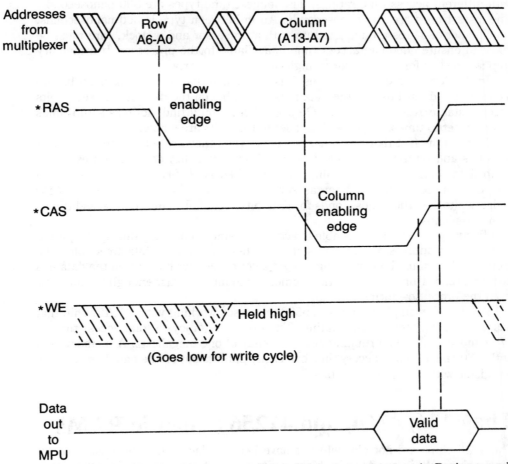

8-16 The 4116 chips operate with the processor when these signals power it. During a read cycle, the row addresses arrive first from the multiplexer. The *RAS then goes low and strobes the row addresses into the row address decoder in the chip. Then the column addresses arrive. At the same time the *CAS signal goes low and strobes the column addresses into the column address decoder. The addressed row and column intersect and open up a single bit on each of the chips in a set of eight. All the while, the *WE stays high, which allows the contents of the addressed bit to leave the chip and be read by the processor.

rise time of $\phi 2$ triggers the processor to place data on the bus. It takes the processor about 100 nanoseconds to put the data on the bus and have it ready for movement. Once the data is on the bus the falling edge of $\phi 2$ will strobe the data into the processor during a read or into the addressed memory register during a write.

The access time of the 4116 is measured from the time the address is stable on the address bus to the time that the data is stable on the data bus. The 4116s come with different access time ratings. The longest time types are 300 nanoseconds. The fastest ones are 150 nanoseconds. An in between type is 200 nanoseconds. When a set of 4116s are matched up with a processor and a clock, care must be taken to ensure adequate access time is available to the processor. If a memory chip is too slow for a processor it might not work properly.

In the definition of access times, it is mentioned that the address must be stable on the address bus and the data must be stable on the data bus. A set of bits become stable after a *setup time*. On spec sheets you'll find, address setup times and data setup times. At the end of a setup time bits are stable.

Besides the fact that bits must be stable when they are setup, they also must be held stable on the buses a short period of time after they do their addressing or go to data registers. This stability time is called *hold time*. Hold time is much shorter than setup time. Whereas setup time might be 300 nanoseconds for address bits and 100 nanoseconds for data bits, data hold times can be as little as 10 nanoseconds.

To sum up, a processor is able to access a memory chip only during the period of time when address bus bits are stable to when the data bus bits are stable. The memory chips must be fast enough to get a set of register bits out on the data bus during a read. During a write, the memory chip must be fast enough to store bits from the processor during a write.

An actual example would be a 6502 processor working with a RAM chip that has a 300 nanosecond access rating. The processor enjoys a total access time of 575 nanoseconds when running at a frequency of one megahertz. A memory chip with a 300 nanosecond access time can easily put bits out on the data bus or fill up a register with processor data bits.

The 4116, 4164, and 41256 dynamic RAMs

The 4116 chips are not obsolete but have been replaced, for the most part, by denser chips. While the 4116 is able to contain 16,384 capacitance circuits to store bits, the 4164 is able to contain 65,536 bits. This is a fourfold increase in the number of bits on the same size chip. This advance is very valuable. A set of 4164s is able to provide 64K of usable RAM.

The 4164 is constructed like the 4116 at about the same cost. The density is increased by improving the bit matrix (Fig. 8-17). The 4116 has a matrix of 128 bit rows by 128 bit columns, $128 \times 128 = 16,384$. The 4164 is built with a matrix of 256 rows by 256 columns, $256 \times 256 = 65,536$. It is said that the 4164 is upward compatible with the 4116. This means you can almost plug a 4164 chip in to replace a 4116. It is not quite that simple but almost as the further discussions will show.

The next step up in density is the 41256. Whereas the 4164 has 65,536 bit holders, the 41256 has 262,144 bit holders, a fourfold density increase over the 4164. The density is again achieved by increasing the matrix. A 41256 chip has a matrix that is 512 rows by 512 columns, $512 \times 512 = 262,144$.

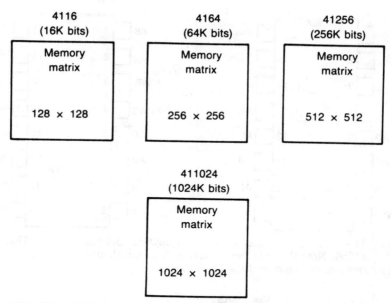

8-17 The 4164 has a matrix density of 256 × 256 in comparison to the 128 × 128 of the 4116. The 41256 has an even more dense 512 × 512 matrix. The 1 megabyte chip can have 1024 × 1024.

The 41256 again is considered upward compatible with the 4164. The three chips are quite alike in many ways (Figs. 8-18 and 8-19). They are each organized by 1. They are 16,384 × 1, 65,536 × 1 and 262,144 × 1. Each uses +5 V supplies, have one data input pin and one data output pin. They all need a *RAS signal, a *CAS signal and a write enable input. About the only pinout differences are the address lines. Because 4116s are only 16K they only need seven multiplexed address lines (A6 – A0) to acquire the required 14 address bits. The 4164 needs eight addressing lines (A7 – A0) to obtain its 16 bits. It takes 18 bits to address 256K so the 41256 needs multiplexed lines A8 – A0.

The amazing thing is that all three of these dynamic memory chip types are built into 16-pin DIPs. The 4116s (Fig. 8-11) are made with four power lines. There is pin 1 with VBB, pin 8 has VDD, pin 9 is VCC and pin 16 has VSS. VBB is – 5 V for a transistor base bias. VDD is + 12 V for an FET drain supply. VDD is the + 5 V conventional chip supply. VSS is the ground connection.

The designers of the 4164 eliminated the VBB and VCC connections at pin 1 and 9. These supply needs were derived and wired inside the chip. Pin 1 then became an unused pin (Fig. 8-18) and pin 9 was assigned to be the A7 address line. Otherwise the pinout remained the same as the 4116 DIP. Newer surface-mount packages though (Fig. 8-19) do have pin changes.

When the 41256 was made, all the DIP pins in use were untouched. All that was needed was a place for address pin A8. Because pin 1 was unused it was put to work. The insides of the chips, from a block diagram point of view remained quite

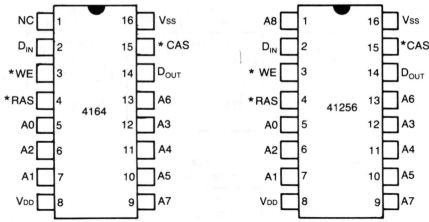

8-18   The 41256 is considered somewhat upward compatible to the 4164 and 41256. Note the only pin difference between them is pin 1. The 41256 requires one more address bit.

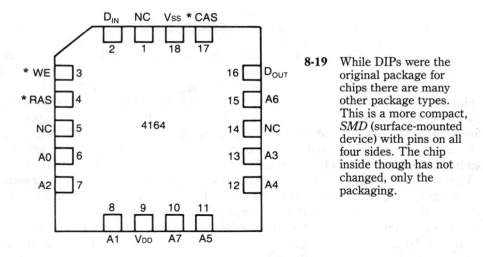

8-19   While DIPs were the original package for chips there are many other package types. This is a more compact, *SMD* (surface-mounted device) with pins on all four sides. The chip inside though has not changed, only the packaging.

the same also. The actual pattern the silicon is cast from though, has many changes. However, because they have been cast in a miniscule world they are not accessible. You can't fix troubles in that world where only bacteria traverse. When there is trouble there all we can do is change the chip. Look down on it.

Block-diagram servicing

Because we cannot get to the silicon circuits in the chip, we must consider a chip as a component with many leads sticking out. Every lead is a test point. On every leg (Fig. 8-20) there is some sort of voltage, pulse, or logic state indication. Chapter 9 goes into the details of testing these legs.

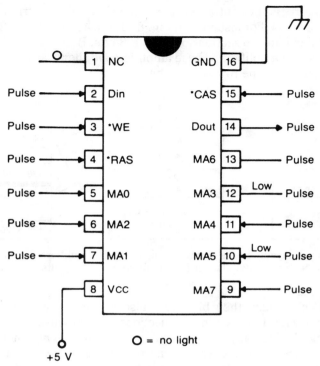

8-20   This top view of the 4164 pinout shows typical voltage states, and input and output directions.

The servicing approach is to try to figure out what chip is causing the trouble. All the theory that is needed for manual servicing is, to understand the workings of a chip from a block diagram view. The dynamic RAM chips appear in the following way (Fig. 8-12).

First of all, the DRAMs usually operate in a set, for example a set of eight. There might be a ninth chip in the group but it will be a parity controller and not one of the register participants. The eight chips that form the byte-sized registers are all working as one memory to form eight-bit registers, each register with an address. In a 16K set the address range from 0 to 16,383. Note there are 16,384 addresses but the first one is 0. This address of 0 is vital because binary numbers begin with 0.

In a 64K set, the addresses range from 0 to 65,535. A 256K set has addresses from 0 to 262,143. There are many forms of addressing, the above is only a general example.

The addresses mentioned are all in decimal numbers. These numbers are often coded into hexadecimal and/or binary. Table 6-2 shows the relationship of decimal, hexadecimal, and binary. It is also a chart to allow you to easily code decimal to hex or binary.

The bit matrix is the central portion of the chips. The matrix portion, is actually made in sections. For instance, in Fig. 8-21, the 4116 has the 128 × 128 memory array divided into two sections of 64 × 128 bits. Between the two sections is a group of 128 sense amplifiers. These amplifiers aid the arrays by sending refresh voltages to them from the row address bits.

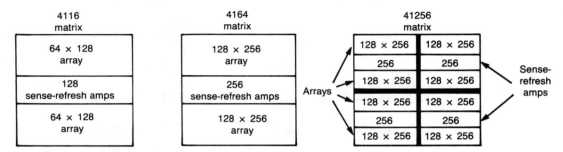

8-21   The matrix layouts in the dynamic chips require amplifiers for refreshing in addition to the bit holders. Note the 41256 layout is actually four 4164 layouts.

The 4164 chips have their bit matrix also divided in two. Each section has a 128 × 256 bit layout. Between the two sections are 256 sense amplifiers that aid in the refreshing. Incidentally, the refreshing of the 4164 chips need not be completed in 2 milliseconds. Newer designs permit the refreshing to take place in 4 milliseconds.

The 41256 chips have their bit matrix divided in four. Each of the four sections is a full 64K array that is divided into two sections like the 64K chip is. Therefore, the 41256 chip is actually four 64K chips squeezed into the one 16-pin DIP.

The 4116 and 4164 chips are almost exactly alike except the matrix in the 4116 is 128 × 128 bits while the 4164 has a matrix 256 × 256 bits. Each has a set of refresh amplifiers separating the two halves of the matrix.

The block diagram of the 4164 (Fig. 8-22) shows the address lines A7 – A0 entering the chip and connecting to the row address latch and the column address latch. Each of the address lines split into two lines, one for each latch. The row latch then connects to the row decoder and the column latch to the column decoder. The decoders connect to the actual rows and columns of bits.

There is one data input line to each chip in a set. Any data that enters is placed into a data latch. There are three input control lines. *WE connects to the data latch. If it is a low it opens up the data latch. *RAS connects to the row address latch. A low signals the latch that the rows are to be addressed. *CAS connects to the column address latch. A low signals the latch when the columns are to be addressed.

The address bits (shown in Fig. 8-23) during operation, are fed to the address latches from the external multiplexer chips seen in Fig. 8-24, eight bits at a time. First the row address bits are sent by the multiplexer and then the column address bits are sent. The multiplexer performs this bit feeding in sync with the signals

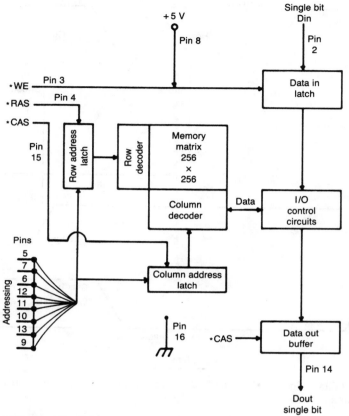

8-22 Inside the 4164 chip the eight row and eight column address bits take turns entering through the eight address pins. *RAS strobes the row address into its latch and *CAS strobes the column address into its latch. The memory matrix outputs a bit when a read operation takes place. The matrix takes in a bit during a write.

*RAS and *CAS. During *RAS the multiplexer feeds the row address bits and during *CAS it feeds the column address bits. That way all 16 address bits are injected into the eight 4164 address lines, eight bits at a time.

The array accepts the row addresses during *RAS, and then over the same lines, accepts the column addresses during *CAS. This multiplexing scheme uses only eight pins. The savings of eight pins is why the 4164 can be packages in a 16-pin DIP.

When both a row and a column have been addressed, the bit at the intersection of the row and column is energized. If there is a bit in the data latch it will charge up the capacitance if it is a high or leave the capacitance without a charge if it is a low.

When *WE is a high, the data latch is not turned on. If a bit is energized at that time a copy of the bit stored at that location leaves and enters the column decoder.

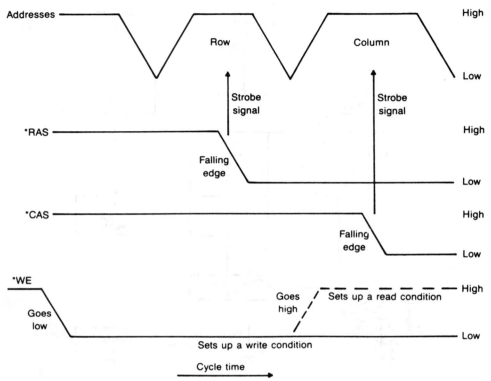

8-23 The falling edges of *RAS and *CAS signals are timed exactly to strobe the row and column addresses.

When a copy of the bit leaves the location, if it is a high, the bit voltage will fall somewhat. The refreshing voltage must then come along and recharge the bit.

The copy of the bit at the location enters the column decoder and continues on to the I/O section of the chip. From there the bit passes through the data out buffer and on to the data bus. A *CAS signal opens the buffer so the bit can pass through.

The above process is basically what happens in a DRAM when it is in operation. The 4116 and 4164 operate just about the same. The 41256 also operates that way except for the addressing. It is really four 64K chips in one package. The four chips are all addressed at the same time but only one bit from the four sections is located and energized. That one bit is then read from or written to.

Dynamic timing

The 4116, 4164, and 41256 are all timed about the same (Fig. 8-23). The timing is nothing more than making sure the address bits, the *WE signal, the *RAS signal, and the *CAS signal all arrive at the pins of the chips at the correct time. They

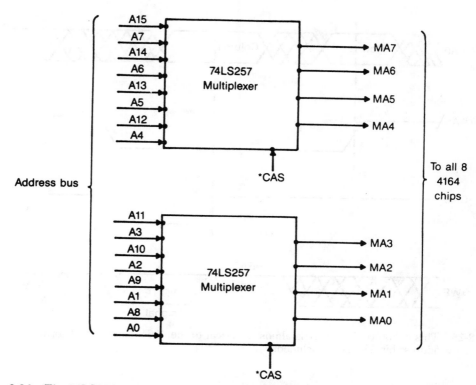

8-24 The 74LS257 type multiplexer chips are the ones used to separate the eight row address bits from the eight column address bits.

could be arriving from various chips over many different lines. The address bits originate in the processor but they must be multiplexed before the DRAMs get them. The *WE signal also originates at the processor but must travel over a copper trace line to get to the memory chip. The *RAS and *CAS signals are usually generated in some circuit and sent over to the DRAMs. The signals also have different arrangements for read operations and write operations. In general the DRAM signals will operate the chips when they arrive in the following manner.

The timing chart (Fig. 8-25) shows the address lines A8 – A0, to a 41256 set, appearing at the top left. The wave shape illustrates both highs and lows. The bottom of the waveform is 0 V. The top is + 5 V. The wave shape is shown with continuous highs and lows. This is to demonstrate that in all nine address lines there are an assortment of highs and lows.

As time elapses in nanoseconds, the wave shape that began with a crosshatch pattern changes to an open area called *row*. The crosshatch shows that, during the crosshatch time, there are no bits on the address lines. The lines are three-stating and are in a high impedance mode denoting no signal. As row appears, the pins A8 – A0 receive the row address bits. The bits are promptly put into the row address latch.

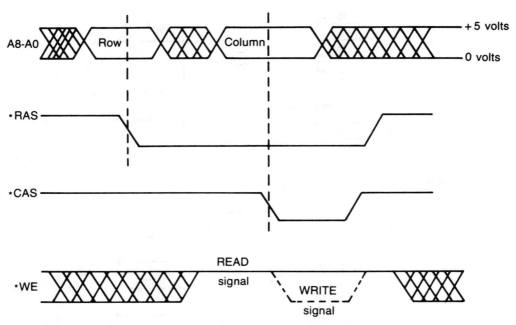

8-25   This 41256 timing chart is almost identical to the 4164 chart except for the additional address bit A8 that is included.

After the row address bits are latched, another short crosshatch area happens and then the column open area arrives. This shows that the column address bits are now entering pins A8 – A0. The column address bits are placed into the column address latch. After the column address bits enter the chip a final cross-hatch nonsignal mode takes place until the end of the cycle.

Meanwhile down at the ∗RAS pin, a high is being held. Then at the same time that the row addresses are entering the A8 – A0 pins, a low arrives. This is the ∗RAS signal. This low is the one that is operating the row address latch. It opens up the latch and lets the bits travel to the row decoder so the actual row addressing can take place.

At the ∗CAS pin a high is also being held. The high suddenly drops to a low at the same time the column addresses are entering A8 – A0. ∗CAS operates the column address latch. It opens up the latch and lets the bits travel to the column decoder so the actual column addressing can take place.

∗WE operates the data-in latch. If a write operation is in progress, ∗WE goes low and opens up the data latch so the bit from the processor can pass on to the matrix and be stored. Should a read operation be taking place, ∗WE goes high. This shuts off the data in latch. Then a copy of the addressed bit can leave through the output buffer and head over a data line to the processor. There is more about this vital read/write operating in other chapters.

Refresh timing

The one complication dynamic RAM has that static RAM avoids is refreshing. It has been mentioned a few times that every bit must be recharged periodically or it will lose its information as the charge decays below a certain voltage. The 4116 needs refreshing at least once every 2 milliseconds. The 4164 and 41256 only need refreshing every 4 milliseconds. Because the processor is working in nanoseconds, milliseconds are a lot slower and as a result much easier to handle.

In the 4116 all that is needed is to send *RAS and address bits over pins A6 – A0. Each of the 128 rows in each chip are strobed while *RAS is low. This refreshes all 16K bits. *CAS is held high during the refreshing, which keeps the output buffer shut off and there can be no output during the refresh operation.

In the 4164, the same type of refreshing takes place. Address bits are sent out over A7 – A0 and a low over the *RAS line occurs. Each of the 256 rows in each chip are strobed while *RAS is low. Again *CAS is held high during the refresh, which again keeps the output buffer closed and prevents unwanted output during the operation.

The 41256 can also be refreshed as shown in Fig. 8-26. Each chip contains four 64K matrix areas. All four matrixes are addressed at the same time with address lines A7 – A0. The additional line, A8 is used to choose among the four matrix sections. If address bits enter over A7 – A0 the four matrix sections on all the chips are addressed together. By strobing all 256 rows along with a low on the *RAS line it will refresh every bit in the memory set.

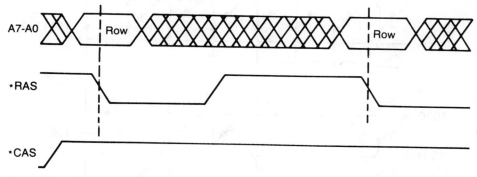

8-26 The refresh timing is timed to occur during off periods. That is, when the processor is not performing normal multiplexed addressing. A special *RAS signal triggers row addresses during those off periods. *CAS is held high and out of action while refreshing is going on.

This refreshing has absolutely nothing to do with the data processing that goes on in the computer. It is a separate operation. Therefore the refreshing is conducted separately. The refresh circuit only goes to work while the computer is busy with other jobs, not while RAM is being accessed.

Read-only memory chips

The first obvious difference between RAM and ROM is, the ROM cannot be written to. It has highs and lows burnt permanently into the bit holders. A ROM is addressed and controlled the same way a RAM is when a RAM is being read. It simply cannot be written to.

A typical ROM has neither flip-flop circuits like static RAM nor capacitance bit holders like dynamic RAM has. It contains a component such as a diode or transistor at each bit location (Figs. 8-27 and 8-28). There are memory matrixes

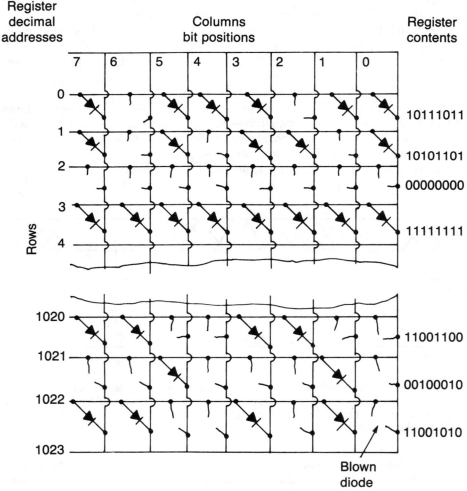

8-27 A ROM is a permanent storage place for operating system programs and others. A ROM is made with special components like diodes at bit positions. The diodes are wired to place a 1 in a bit holder when intact and a 0 when the diode is destroyed.

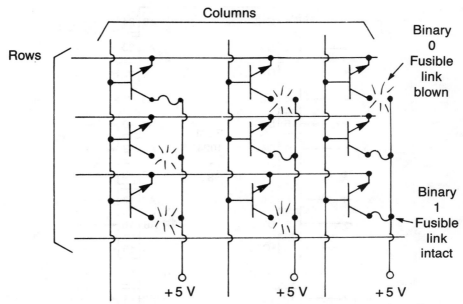

8-28 Instead of diodes, transistors like these NPN types with fusible links could be installed in bit holders.

with rows and columns. The microscopic components can be installed on every row to each column on the row. Many ROMs are made to have each row hold a byte. These ROMs are typically organized in bytes. For instance Fig. 8-29 has a 1024 × 8 organization. 4732 ROM has a 4096 × 8 organization. A 4764 ROM has an 8196 × 8 organization. A 47128 has a 16,384 × 8 organization and a 47256 is organized 32,768 × 8. The 4732 is a 4K ROM, the 4764 is an 8K ROM, the 47128 has 16K bytes and the 47256 is the 32K byte chip of the group.

The first two numerals 47 denotes the fact that these chips are ROMs. The second two numerals gives the number of thousands of bits, not bytes. The 2708 has 8K bits. The 4732 with its 4K bytes totals 32K bits because there are eight bits to a byte. The 47256 with 32K bytes contain 256K bit holders.

Each byte has an address in the digital world. If a ROM location is read before the chip is programmed, the data that would come out of the location would be HHHHHHHH. The ROM starts out as a chip with all Hs in the bit holders. When a row is addressed, it is energized. Each diode or transistor will conduct from the row line to each of the eight columns. The conduction causes a high to emerge from each bit. The columns are connected to the data bus lines, D7 – D0 and the eight highs emerge and go to the processor as HHHHHHHH.

Obviously, a chip full of highs is not very useful. The chip is then programmed. Some ROMs have operating programs installed. Others contain tables and language interpretation programs. Still others can hold character patterns. Whatever the useful contents might be, it must be installed.

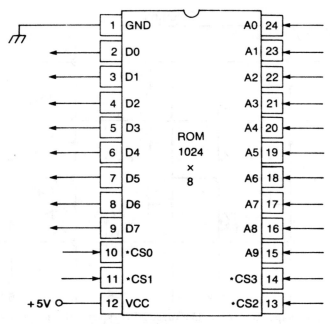

8-29 This ROM is organized in a 1024 × 8 format. Note there are four chip select pins, 10 input address pins, and eight data output pins.

To install a program it must first be written in binary machine language. Machine language is a list of bytes. Each byte contains an assortment of highs and lows. Once the program is written it is then burned into the ROM chip bit holders. The ROM starts life with a matrix full of Hs. All that is needed is to install the Ls of the program. Since the Hs are read from the ROM as a result of making a diode or transistor in the bit holder conduct, to install a low into a bit holder the component must be prevented from conducting. If the bit holders that are conducting are being read as Hs, a nonconducting holder will read L.

A special destruction voltage, much higher than normal is then applied to all the bit holders that are to read Ls. The voltage blows the diode or transistor apart. It can no longer conduct. After this destructive force has been applied, the machine language is permanently installed into the matrix. When the processor reads the ROM it will receive the byte of data that has been burnt into the location.

While this procedure is one way a ROM is programmed, during actual manufacturing nothing so slow can be used. When a ROM is designed, the program is installed in large printed circuit patterns. The junctions between the rows and the columns are drawn with a diode or transistor when an H is to be in a bit and left empty if an L is to be there. Once the pattern contains the program, it is reduced photographically and used to mass-produce the ROM.

ROM pin connections

The 4732 and 4764 ROMs (Fig. 8-30) are found in 24-pin DIPs. The 47128 and 47256 (Fig. 8-31) have 28 pins on their packages. The reason why the larger chips need the extra pins is for addressing. The 4732 only has 4K addresses. The 4764 has 8K addresses. 4K addresses need 12 address lines and use address bus bits A11–A0. 8K addresses require 13 address lines and use bits A12–A0.

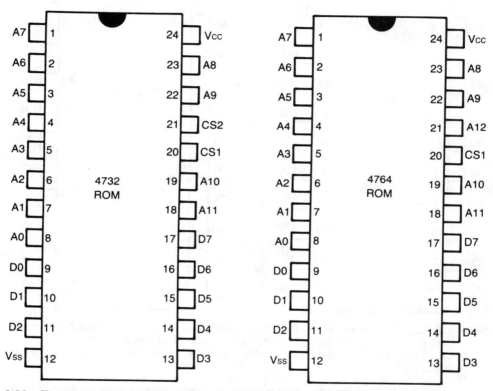

8-30 The 4732 and 4764 ROMs are packaged in 24-pin DIPs. Both have eight data pins. The 4732 has two chip selects and 12 address register selects. The 4764 only has one chip select, because it needs an extra pin for its 13 address register selects.

The larger chips need more address lines to locate the additional locations. The 47128 has 14 address pins, A13–A0, to locate the 16K register rows. The 47256 requires 15 address pins, A14–A0, for its 32K locations.

The first two numerals indicating that the chip is a ROM, need not be 47. The 47 is the designation for Texas Instruments ROMs. Other manufacturers use other numerals. For instance, IBM uses 92 in their PC.

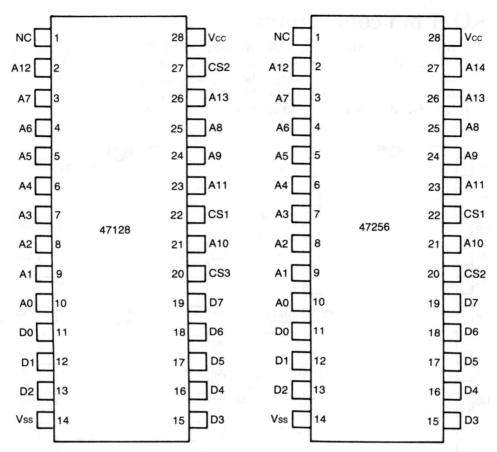

8-31 The larger 47128 and 47256 ROMs come in 28-pin DIPs. There are still only eight data pins. The 47128 has three chip selects and 14 address register selects. The 47256 only has two chip selects to allow an extra pin for the 15th address register select bit.

In addition to the 12 addressing pins on the 4764, there are eight data output pins, one stemming from each bit position on the registers. All of the same number bits in each register are connected together and are wired to one output pin, shown in Fig. 8-32. For example all bit position 7s are connected together and wired to pin D7. That way when one row is addressed and energized, all the rows stay off except the one addressed. That one row and only that row's byte is output through the output data pins to the processor.

If you examine the view of the 4732, the 12 address pins and the eight data out pins take care of 20 of the 24 pins on the DIP. The mandatory +5 V and ground use two more pins. That leaves two more pins to be accounted for.

They are connected to the address bus, too. They are the chip selects, CS's 1 and 2. Now these chips are made to be mask programmed along with the register bits. A computer maker, when designing the wiring can make the chip selects turn

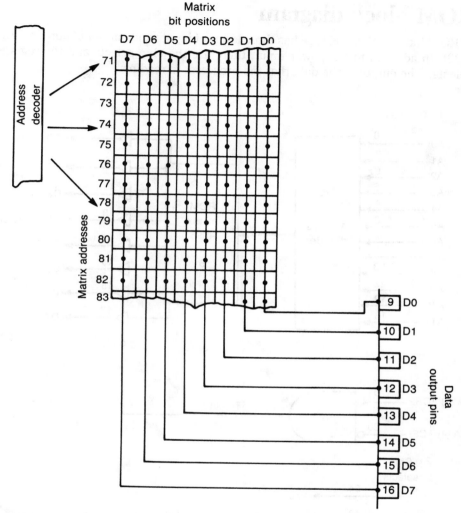

8-32 In a ROM with registers that are eight bits wide, all of the same number bit positions are wired together and to the data bus. During a read operation, only the register that is addressed will output a byte to the data bus.

on with either a low or a high. The option is open to set the selects in the way that is required for the design. When the designer lays out the print board and circuits, sometimes it is convenient to have a chip enabled with a low and other times with a high.

When a CS is enabled with a low, it then is given the title *CS. Should the chip select get turned on with a high then it is dubbed just plain CS. Therefore the CSs on this chip could end up as *CS1, CS1, *CS2, or CS2. If you ever see the same number ROMs with different CS designations, the above is the reason why.

ROM block diagram

A ROM like the 4732 4K type has three kinds of inputs and one set of outputs (Fig. 8-33). In addition to the power input, there are the chip selects and the register selects. The output is the data that the processor is reading.

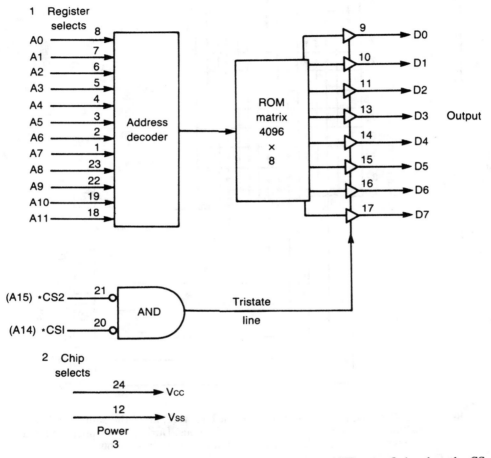

8-33 In the typical ROM, the chip-select pins connect to an AND gate. Only when the CS pins all enable the gate will the gate in turn enable the three-state buffers in the data bus lines. At that time, the register selects can be decoded and address one of the registers in the matrix. The contents of the addressed register can then exit the chip onto the data bus.

The chip selects and the register selects are all connected to the address bus. The chip selects could be connected to A15 and A14. The register selects can be attached to A11 – A0. The ROM has no need, in this case for the remaining lines such as A13 and A12. When the ROM is selected they do not enter into the activity.

Inside the ROM the two chip selects are connected to an AND gate. AND gates are discussed in detail in the previous chapter. The AND gate will turn on only when both of the CS pins are enabled. That is, when address pins A15 and A14 both contain the enabling bits to select this chip. Once the AND gate turns on, the chip is enabled. Note the AND gate connects to the ROMs output buffers. It turns the buffers on and off with the three-state controls of the buffers.

A11 – A0 pins are connected to the chips decoder circuits. The 12 bits provided by the pin inputs are processed by the decoder circuits. The decoder connects to the memory matrix and its gating circuits. The memory is organized as 4096 rows by eight bits each, 4096 × 8. The locations can be visualized as 4096 byte-sized registers stacked in a tall skinny pile with location 0 at the very top and location 4095 at the bottom. Actually the matrix is laid out physically like the dynamic RAM, but it is wired as a tall pile, like the static RAM, so we can consider it in that way.

The 12 address line bits chose one out of the 4K locations and energize that row. The turning on of the row causes a circuit to be closed from the chosen row to the eight columns (Fig. 8-32). The bits with working diodes (or transistors) conduct through to the columns. Highs are produced in those columns and continue on to the buffer stage. The bits without working diodes output 0 V or lows. The lows also continue on to the buffers.

The buffers are three-state types. They are nothing more than little amplifier stages. They perk up and match the highs and lows so they are fit to travel to the processor (that is, if the chip selects have turned on the AND gate). If the gate is off the buffers block off the bits and do not permit them to leave the chip.

This is needed because the address lines A11 – A0 are entering a lot of chips and are addressing a lot of bits at the same time. However, only the chosen chip is permitted to output bits over the data bus.

In general, that is how a ROM is read. The chip select chooses the chip, the register select chooses the register and the bits contained in the register are output to the data bus. Note that there are not any read/write lines. The chip can only be read. Should you write to it, the chip can't respond in any manner.

ROM timing

ROM chips have access time ratings like RAM chips. The access time is the time the ROM takes from the nanosecond it is addressed. It must complete its output operation in times like 300, 350, or 450 nanoseconds according to the rating of a particular chip.

There is only one cycle timing diagram, like Fig. 8-34, on the usual chip. There is only one type of operation, a read. The diagram begins as the address bits A11 – A0 hit the ROM pins. In a 350 nanosecond chip the operation has 350 nanoseconds from then to be completed.

About 230 nanoseconds after the A11 – A0 bits arrive, the two chips select bits complete the job of turning on the AND gate and having the AND gate turn on the output buffers. The chip then has 120 nanoseconds to get the bits onto the data bus. The register bits then speed out onto the data bus. The operation is complete.

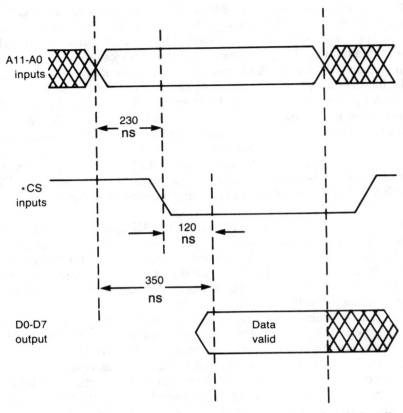

8-34 In a ROM there is one operation possible, a read. This timing diagram shows the address lines A11 – A0 from the processor entering the address pins of the ROM. 230 nanoseconds after the address pins enter the CS inputs enable, the AND gate and the data output buffers. The data bits leave the matrix and exit the chip 120 nanoseconds after the chip selecting.

In comparison to a lot of the other chip operations the ROM reading is relatively swift and simple.

SIMMs (single inline memory modules)

In many personal computers, memory chips are installed in sockets. Sockets have many advantages for test and replacement purposes, but sockets also, on occasion present a problem. Every time a computer is turned off at the end of the work day, allowed to cool overnight, and is then turned on the following morning, the sockets and the chips in the sockets pass through a heating, cooling, and then reheating cycle. The sockets and the chips will expand as they are heated, shrink as they are cooled, and then reheat once again. This happens daily. Every day the chips will creep ever so slightly out of the socket. Then one day a pin disconnects from a socket hole and the computer goes down.

The cure is very simple, press the chip back into the socket. However, a failure is a failure and is often a trying and expensive experience no matter how simple the actual repair turns out to be. Designers in an effort to eliminate this common chip, popping out of the circuit, trouble came up with SIMMs. They knew that they could just eliminate sockets and solder the chips directly to the print board. Unfortunately this approach just makes the chips very difficult to replace. They came up with SIMMs, the single inline memory modules.

A typical SIMM, as seen in Fig. 8-35, is a plug-in device. It is simply a little plug-in print board that goes into a connector socket on the motherboard. The memory chips, instead of being soldered on the motherboard, are soldered onto the SIMM board. The SIMM board is considered a module. The SIMM board is a very small one and is about the size of a 6-inch ruler. It usually contains nine DRAMs. There are eight DRAMs to supply the bytes of memory and a ninth DRAM that provides a set of parity bits for the memory. SIMMs, as seen on a price list, come in various byte capacities. The most common ones have memories of 256K, 512K, 1024K, and 2048K.

8-35 A typical SIMM is a collection of memory chips mounted on a thin print board. It is considered a module or one component. When one chip fails, the entire module is changed. The module conveniently plugs into the motherboard.

Computers that use SIMMs have SIMM connectors mounted on the motherboard. The SIMM plugs into the connectors and has a tab at each end of the module that snaps into place. To remove a SIMM, all you have to do is open the tabs and rock the SIMM gently out of the motherboard connector. The SIMMs are fairly rugged, but as with all print board components, remove it slowly and with care.

A SIMM is much easier to remove and is also easier to diagnose as defective than an individual chip. You do not have to pin a trouble on an individual chip. You simply change the entire suspected SIMM. The actual chip on the SIMM that has conked out need never be found. That is unless you are a purist and you want to repair the SIMM by pinpointing the one defective chip, unsolder it and resolder a new replacement chip.

Of course, the price of a nine-pin SIMM is more than the price of a single chip. It usually works out though, during computer servicing, the repairer's time is the most costly part of the job. The SIMM then, when time is of the essence, is typically replaced in its entirety even though its cost is higher than an individual chip.

Erasable programmable ROMS

There is a second form of ROM that is often found in personal computers or their accessories. It is ROM that can be programmed, erased, and reprogrammed again. Instead of using diode or ordinary transistors in ROM bit positions, special *MOS-FETs* (metal-oxide-silicon field-effect transistors are used). It so happens that if you apply about 20 – 25 volts between the source and drain electrodes a phenomenon called avalanche injection takes place and causes the gate electrode to lose its ability and act like a blown open circuit. No conduction can take place and an L is installed in the affected bit position. If other bits are not exposed to the programming voltage it retains its conductability and will output an H when addressed.

While this quality provides an easy way to program a ROM the erasable ROM, EPROM, exhibits a second capability. If you expose the bare chip to ultraviolet light for about a half hour (Fig. 8-36) the avalanche injection effect subsides and the gate can conduct an H once again. In other words the exposure to light erases the program on the EPROM and it can be used over and over again. In normal read only operation the EPROM is used exactly like any other ROM.

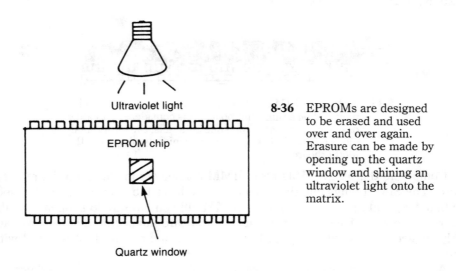

Ultraviolet light

EPROM chip

Quartz window

8-36   EPROMs are designed to be erased and used over and over again. Erasure can be made by opening up the quartz window and shining an ultraviolet light onto the matrix.

An EPROM has a little quartz window in the top of the package to shine the light through. The window should always be covered with some sort of opaque covering when in use. Normal room lighting usually has some ultraviolet light inherent in it. If the window is not covered, the room lights will, over time, erase the program. If the window is carefully covered the ROM will hold the program intact indefinitely.

9

Manual fault dictionary techniques

IN LARGE MULTIMILLION DOLLAR ELECTRONIC SYSTEMS TROUBLESHOOTING and repairs are attempted using *ATPG* (automatic test program generation). The word automatic implies the use of diagnostic programs that turn on and probe any faults that occur. In these programs are *fault dictionaries*. These table listings in the diagnostic software are consulted by the program when the program, as it is running, comes across a fault at a test node.

A *fault listing* in the dictionary is usually a *stuck-at* fault. That is, the program encounters a test point that is stuck-at a high or stuck-at a low. By being stuck-at, the test point has become permanently fixed at a high or at a low. This is an abnormal condition and indicates a fault is causing the stuck-at.

The program finds the stuck-at condition as it routinely tests pin after pin. If the test shows a pin is not stuck but operating normally then the program moves on to the next pin and the next. It keeps testing until it finds a stuck-at high or stuck-at low. When it does find a stuck-at, it stops testing and raises a flag indicating that a fault has been found.

The program then looks up the fault in the dictionary. In the dictionary listing is necessary information that will lead to the repair. The listing reveals the location of the test point, the type of stuck-at that has been found, whether the stuck-at is an input or output pin and any other information that will aid in further isolating the actual trouble and expediting the repair.

This ATPG system is very interesting and is needed for gigantic electronic installations. For personal computers though, you can perform a similar test manually. All you need is an MFD (manual fault dictionary) such as Tables 9-1 and 9-2. An MFD is simply a listing of the pins on a chip and the state of each pin while the computer is energized and on normal standby. That is the condition the computer should be in when you use the MFD.

Table 9-1. This is a manual fault dictionary for the Apple IIe. It lists all the chips on the motherboard, Fig. 5-6, and all the pins on each chip. Furthermore it shows what state should be on each pin when the computer is operating at standby. If a pin does not match the prescribed state, a Fault is indicated at that pin.

Manual Fault Dictionary + Pin Numbers

Chips (Left to Right Fig. 5-6)	1	2	3	4	5	6	7	8	9	10	11	12	13	14	15	16	17	18	19	20	21	22	23	24	25	26	27	28	29	30	31	32	33	34	35	36	37	38	39	40
LS 125	P	P	P	L	P	P	L	H	P	H	P	P	L	H																										
PLA	P	H	L	P	P	P	H	P	H	L	L	P	P						H																					
FF	L	L	L	P	H	P	H	L	P	L	L	P	P				P	P	P	H																				
Buffer	L	L	P	H	H	P	P	P	P	L	P	P	P		H	H	P	P	L	H																				
LS 245	P	P	P	P	P	P	P	P	P	P	P	P	P		P	P	P	P	P	H																				
LS 374	L	P	P	P	P	P	P	P	P	L	P	P	P		P	P	P	P	P	H																				
LS 244	L	P	P	P	P	P	P	L	L	L	P	P	P		P	P	L	P	L	H																				
Video ROM	P	P	P	L	P	L	P	P	L	L	P	H	P		P	L	P	L	P	P	L	L	P	P	H	P	P	P	P	P	P	P	P	P	P	P	P	P	P	P
Memory Manag	L	H	P	H	H	H	L	H	H	L	H	H	P	H	H	H	H	P	P	H	L	L	P	P	P	P	P	P	P	P	P	P	P	P	P	P	P	P	P	P
Micro-Processor	L	H	P	O	H	H	H	P	H	H	H	P	P	H	P	P	P	P	P	L	P	L	L	L	P	P	P	P	P	P	H	P	O	O	P	O	H	H	H	P
Shift Register	P	P	P	H	H	H	H	L	H	P	P	P	P	H	O	H	P	P	P	P	P	P	P	P	P	P	P	P	H	P	P	L	L	P	P	P	H	P	P	P
I/O	L	L	P	H	H	P	L	L	P	L	H	H	P	P	P	O	P	P	P		P	P	P	P	P	P	P	H	P											
LS10	L	L	P	L	P	L	L	L	L	H	H	H	P	P	H	P	P	P	P																					
Decoder	P	P	P	H	H	P	L	L	L	H	H	H	P	P	P	P	P	P	L																					
Demux	H	P	P	P	P	P	P	P	H	P	P	P	P	H	P	L	P	P	L	L	P	P	P	H	H	H	H	L	L											
All RAMs	H	H	P	P	P	P	L	L	L	P	P	P	P	H	H	P	P	P	P		P	P	P	P	P	P	P	H	L											
CD ROM	L	L	P	H	L	L	L	P	H	P	P	P	P	L	H	P	P	P	P	L	P	P	H	P	P	P	P	H	L											
S 202	H	H	P	H	H	H	H	L	H	P	H	P	L	H	H	H	H	P	P	P	P	H	P	P	H		P	H	H											
EF ROM	P	H	H	H	H	H	H	P	H	P	H	H	H	H	H	H	H	P	P	P	P	P	P	H																
LS 154	H	L	L	L	L	H	H	H	H	P	L	P	H	H	P	L	L	L	L	P	H	H																		
Keyboard ROM	P	P	P	L	L	L	L	H	P	P	P	P	H	H	P	P	P	L			L	H	H																	
LS 251	O	L	L	H	P	O	O	L	H	H	L	H	H	H	H	P	L	L	L																					
RC 741	P	L	P	P	P	P	H	P	P																															
NE 558	H	O	H	H	H	H	H	O	O	H	O	O	H		O	H																								
Decoder	P	P	P	L	L	L	L	L	L	L	H	H	H	H	L	L	L	L	L	L	L	L	L	L	L	L	L	L	H	H	H	L	P	P	P	P	P	P	P	P

Main Board

Logic probe indications
P = Pulse
H = High
L = Low
O = No Light

☐ = Readings made after "space bar" pressed

+ = Readings taken under normal stand-by conditions

Table 9-2. This is the manual fault dictionary for an IBM PC motherboard found in Fig. 5-5.
The chip indication U numbers are printed right on the board. Each pin on every chip can be tested one by one
with a logic probe while the board is energized. The readings should match the Dictionary listings or a fault is indicated.

IBM PC Model 5150

Manual Fault Dictionary + Pin Numbers

40 Hole DIP Socket

Main Board

Chips	1	2	3	4	5	6	7	8	9	10	11	12	13	14	15	16	17	18	19	20	21	22	23	24	25	26	27	28	29	30	31	32	33	34	35	36	37	38	39	40
U1	P	L	L	P	P	P	H	O	P	P	P	P	P	L	L	P	P	P	P	H	H	H	H	L	L	P	P	P	P	H	H	P	P	H	L	H	P	P	P	H
U2	L	P	H	P	P	P	P	P	P	P	P	P	L	O	P	P	P	L	P	L	L	P	H			P	P	H	P	H										
U3	L	P	P	P	P	P	P	P	P	P	P	P	L	H	P	P	P	L	L	L																				
U4	H	H	H	P	P	P	P	P	O	O	P	P	H	H	P	P	P	P	L	L																				
U5	H	L	H	P	P	P	L	P	O	O	P	P	P	O	P	P	P	P	P	H																				
U6	P	P	P	P	P	P	P	P	P	L	P	P	O	H	P	P	P	P	P	H																				
U7	P	P	P	P	P	P	P	P	O	L	P	P	P	P	P	P	P	P	P	H																				
U8	P	P	P	P	P	P	O	O	P	L	H	P	H	P	P	P	P	P	P	H																				
U9	P	P	P	P	P	H	P	P	H	L	P	P	P	O	P	P	P	P	P	H																				
U10	P	L	H	P	P	P	O	O	P	L	P	H	P	O	P	P	P	P	P	H																				
U11	P	H	P	P	P	H	H	P	P	L	H	P	P	O	L	H	H	H	L	H																				
U12	P	P	P	P	P	P	O	O	P	L	P	P	P	P	P	P	P	P	P	H																				
U13	P	P	P	P	P	P	H	P	H	L	P	H	L	P	P	P	P	P	P	H																				
U14	P	P	P	P	P	H	P	P	P	L	P	P	P	O	L	H	P	H	L	H																				
U15	P	P	P	P	P	P	P	P	P	L	P	P	P	P	P	P	P	P	P	H																				
U16	P	P	P	P	P	P	P	P	P	L	P	P	P	P	P	P	P	P	P	H																				
U17	P	P	P	P	P	H	H	H	H	L	H	P	P	P	P	P	P	P	P	H																				
U18	P	P	P	P	P	P	P	P	P	L	P	P	P	P	P	H	P	P	P	H																				
U19	P	P	P	P	H	H	L	P	P	L	P	P	P	P	P	P	P	P	P	H																				

RN1—Resistor Network
SW1—Switch (Disk Drive Select)
RN2—Resistor Network

Chips	1	2	3	4	5	6	7	8	9	10	11	12	13	14	15	16	17	18	19	20
U20																				
U21																				
U22								L	H	L	L	L	L	L	L	L	L	L	H	H
U23	H		L	H	H	L	L	L	L	L	L	L	H	L	L	L	L	H	H	H
U24	L	H	H	H	H	L	L	L	H	L	L	L	L	H	L	L	H	H	H	H
U25		L																		

SW2—Switch (RAM Select)

P = Pulse
H = High
L = Low

O = No Light
□ = Probe reads pulse (P) when any key is pressed

+ Readings taken under normal stand-by conditions

Table 9-2. Continued.

IBM PC Model 5150

Manual Fault Dictionary + Pin Numbers

Main Board

Annotations: 24 Hole DIP Socket — RN3—Resistor Network — (RAM Bank 0) — (RAM Bank 1) — (RAM Bank 2)

Chips	1	2	3	4	5	6	7	8	9	10	11	12	13	14	15	16	17	18	19	20	21	22	23	24	25	26	27	28	29	30	31	32	33	34	35	36	37	38	39	40
(Cont.)																																								
U26	H	H	L	H	H	P	H	L				P	P	L	L	H																								
U27	P	L	P	P	P	P	P	P				P	H	H	H																									
U28	P		L	P	P	P	L	P					L	H																										
U29	P	P	P	P	P	P	P	P	P	P	P	L	P	P	P	P	P	P	P	H	P	P	H	H																
U30	P	P	P	P	P	P	P	P	P	P	P	L	P	P	P	P	P	P	P	P	P	P	P	H																
U31	P	P	P	P	P	P	P	P	P	P	P	L	P	P	P	P	P	P	P	P	P	P	P	H																
U32	P	P	P	P	P	P	P	P	P	P	P	L	P	P	P	P	P	P	P	P	P	P	P	H																
U33	P	P	P	P	P	P	P	P	P	P	P	L	P	P	P	P	P	P	P	P	P	P	P	H																
U34	P	P	P	P	P	P	P	P	P	P	P	L	P	L	P	P	P	O	P	L	P	H	P	H																
U35	H	P	P	P	H	P	P	P	P	L	H	P	P	H	H	O	H	H	L	L	P	L	L	H	P	P														
U36	L	L	P	L	L	L	P	H	H	P	L	P	P	H	P	L	L							H	L	H	P	P	P	P	H	P	P	P	L	P	P	P	P	P
U37-U45	O	P	P	P	P	P	P	L	P	L	H	L	L	L	H	H							H	H			P	P	P	P	P	P	P	P	P	P				
U46	P	L	P	L	H	L	P	L	P	H	P	L	P	H	H	L	L									H		P	P	P	P	H	P	P	P	L				
U47	L	P	P	P	P	P	L	L	H	P	L	L	P	L	H	H	L															P	P	P	P	P				
U48	H	P	L	P	P	L	H	L	H	P	H	H	L	H	L	H																								
U49	L	L	P	P	H	L	L	L	H	L	H	H	H	H	H																									
U50	H	P	L	P	P	L	L	L	P	H	P	P	L	H	P											L	H													
U51	L	H	P	P	H	L	L	L	P	L	P	P	H	H	P	L																								
U52	L	P	L	L	P	L	L	H	H	L	H	P	P	H	P	H										H														
U53-U61	H	P	P	P	P	L	L	L	P	L	O	L	P	H																										
U62	O	P	H	P	P	P	H	L	P	P	P	P	P	P	P	H	H																							
U63	P	P	P	P	P	P	H	L	P	P	P	L	H	L	L																									
U64	P	P	P	P	P	P	L	P	I	I	I	P	P	I	I	H																								
U65	P	P	P	P	P	P	L	P	I	I	P	I	P	P	P																									
U66	P	P	P	P	P	P	L	P	P	P	P	P	P	H																										
U67	P	P	P	P	P	P	P	H	P	P	P	P	P	H																										
U68	O																																							
U69-U77	O	P							P	P	P	P	P	P	P	P	L				P																				

On each pin is a state. It could be a high, a low, a three-state condition, or a pulse. The idea is to test for the state and compare the results of the test with the MFD pin listing. The listing simply tells you what should be present. If the actual pin reading matches the MFD reading then the pin is probably o.k. Should the reading be incorrect, that is a fault clue and further thought and action can be taken.

Obtaining an MFD for your computer

You can buy or otherwise obtain service notes for some personal computers. The best place to try is the manufacturer of your machine. A second source of service notes are some of the electronic supply houses. There could be listing of states of pins in these notes or there might not be. However, the best MFD will be the one you produce yourself. It should not take more than an hour even if there are a couple hundred chips on your print boards. An extra bonus you will obtain is a comfortable familiarity with the inside of your machine.

The best time to make your MFD is before there is any inkling of trouble. That way you will know exactly what your machine pin readings should be when it is o.k. Then during servicing if you find an incorrect reading, you'll know for sure that it is actually a true clue.

In the computer service shop, where a technician will be spending time working on one computer after another and the computers are all the same makes and models, he or she will obtain or produce the handiest set of service notes ever. Figures 9-1, 9-2, and 9-3 are samples of professional type sketches you could draw for your personal computer.

Figure 9-1 is the top view of U3 in an IBM PC 5150. U3 is the processor, an 8088. The 8088 chip is contained in a 40-pin DIP. The top view is handy since it is an accurate representation of the actual 8088 in your machine. If you were taking readings of U3 using Table 9-1, after every probe touchdown, you must change your glance and relate the table listing to the actual pin on the chip. The pins and the table listings are tiny and a lot of checking back and forth is required to keep your mental gymnastics accurate.

If you have a top view such as Fig. 9-1, and you prop the sheet just above the chip, it is considerably easier and faster to run through all the probing and checking. With a bit of practice you are even able to see all the information on the top view with your peripheral vision as you simultaneously make your probe readings watching the tiny chip pins. With a little practice, using this peripheral vision technique you can save a lot of checking time especially on a large print board.

The information placed on Fig. 9-1 consists of the following. First of all there is the actual top view showing the chip notched keyway located between pins 1 and 40. The pins are numbered in a counterclockwise fashion with pin 20 at the bottom left and pin 21 at the bottom right. Alongside each pin, on the body of the chip is the name of the pin. Of particular interest are pins 9 – 16, which serve a dual multiplexed role. They act as address pins A7 – A0 and also data input-output pins D7 – D0. Vcc is at the upper right hand corner, pin 40, and gnd is at the bottom

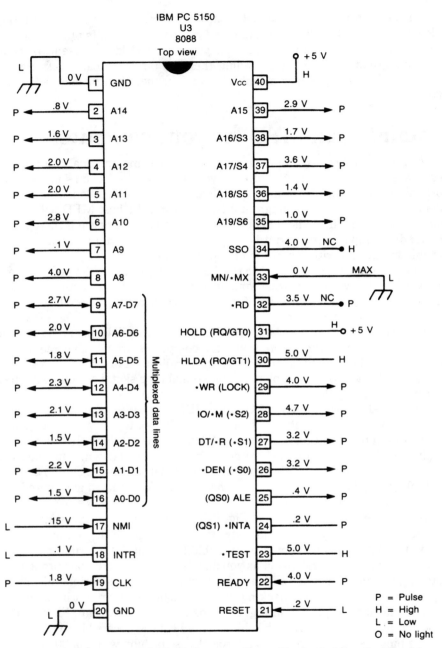

9-1 Although the manual fault dictionary will provide the information for chip-by-chip testing, the job will move faster and easier if you have a top view showing the actual pinout of a suspect chip. In addition, the pin names, pin logic states, and pin dc voltages in this closeup format, saves many service moves.

left, pin 20. There is a lot more detail on the workings of this popular 8088 processor in chapter 15.

Attached to every pin is an arrowed line. This shows the direction the logic states travel. The address pins and some others are outputs. A lot of the control pins are inputs. The data bus lines are both inputs and outputs since they have bits traveling in both directions.

On the very outside of the arrowed lines are the logic states that should be present on the processor while it is energized, has been initialized, and is waiting on stand-by. There are mostly pulses present on the pins, with some highs and lows.

Last there is a dc voltage, somewhere between 0 and +5 V on each pin. The technique for testing the pins varies somewhat with different technicians. Test the pins first for the logic state with either a logic probe or a voltmeter. If you find an incorrect state, then slow down and take an exact voltage measurement as you look for further clues to pinpoint the source of trouble.

Figure 9-2 is a top view of the Apple *II*e microprocessor, a 6502 chip, installed in a 40-pin DIP. The 6502 is an 8-bit processor. The 8088 has been referred to as 16-bit processor. They are both installed in 40-pin DIPs. However one obvious difference between the two processors are the address lines. The 6502 has 16 address lines, A15 – A0. It can directly address 64K of memory with those lines. The 8088 has 20 address lines, A19 – A0. With the 20 lines it can address a full megabyte of memory. There are many other internal circuit changes too. These are covered in chapters 14 and 15.

The Apple *II*e top view contains the same important servicing information the IBM PC view does. There are the pin numbers, the names of the pins, the direction arrows, the logic states and the dc voltages present on all the pins. Here again it is interesting to note that the voltages range between 0 and +5 V.

From a testing point of view, the simpler classic 8-bit 6502 and the more complex 16-bit 8088 are observed and acted upon by the tester in just about the same way. The MFD listings or the more detailed top views simply tell what logic states or dc voltages should be present and what directions the signals are traveling. The tester looks for a logic state or dc voltage that does not match up with what is shown to be normally present. Then when a fault is located, the direction of signal flow is determined. If an input is found at fault then the chip is probably good and the source of the trouble is in the circuits that feed the input. Should an output be at fault then the source of the trouble is probably located inside the chip under test. A chip that is indicated to be kaput must be replaced.

Variation on the packaging

The DIP has been the integrated circuit package of note for a long time. It however, is not really the best way, spacewise, to install the chip in a package. A chip is produced on a square piece of silicon and has connections on all four sides of the chip. There is more detail on this subject in chapter 11. At any rate, a DIP is shaped as a rectangle. This is so the legs the chip connections are attached to can be laid out

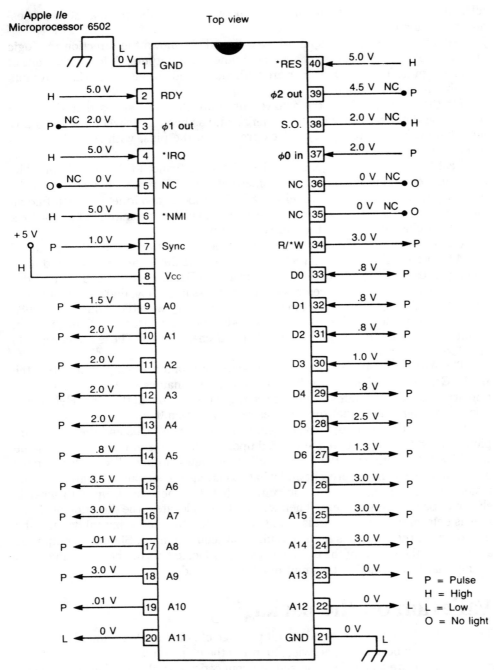

9-2 This is the pinout and test information for the Apple IIe.

neatly on the print board in-line and dual. This means the wires from the two sides of the chip connect directly to the sides of the DIP but the connections on the top and bottom of the chip must be extended to the longer sides of the DIP.

In the newer packages, known generally as *SMD* (surface mounted devices) the package is the same square shape as the chip and the wires from all four sides of the square connect directly to the package. This saves considerable space on a print board especially when there are a hundred or more chips on the board. The final board can be much smaller than one using the same chips but with the larger rectangular DIPs.

The new packaging also permits a high pin-count chip to appear in a smaller package. Figure 9-3 is a good example. It is the iAPX 186, which is a version of the 8086-8088 processor. It is mounted in a surface mount square package. It also comes with a chip socket so it can be easily removed and reinstalled.

The chip comes in a 68-pin square package. The square is laid out with the four sides each having 17 pins. The pin count starts, from a top view perspective, at the lower right-hand corner. The pins are counted from one to 17 on the bottom, right to left, opposite to the way the top view of the DIP is counted off. The pin count continues clockwise at pin 18 up to the top left-hand corner at pin 34. The count continues across the top from pin 35 to 51, then down the right side from pin 52 to 68. Aside from this change in shape, size, and the way the pins are counted, the chip is checked out in the same way. The chip is the same as the ones installed in DIPs, only the packaging has been changed.

Inputs and outputs

Discrete components like resistors, capacitors, coils, transistors, and vacuum tubes can be tested directly. They are large and individual. Integrated chips cannot be tested directly for resistance, capacitance, continuity, amplification, etc. They must be tested indirectly. The best test for a chip is to exercise it. If it does its job it's probably o.k. If it won't do its job it is considered defective.

In manufacturing plants and large electronic supply houses, there are chip testers. The chip testers are expensive and limited to a few chips. Each chip needs a program to be tested. There are a few chip testers around that will test most chips but they are hard to come by.

Another big test problem for chips is, they are very difficult to handle and most of the chips that need to be tested are in-circuit on a print board. If you try to exercise a chip on a board by itself, there are many other chips in its circuit that will interfere with the test. As you can see the problems are many.

Technicians find that the most expedient way to test a chip is to check its inputs and outputs. That is why there are the arrowheads on the 8088 and 6502 sketches (Figs. 9-1 and 9-2). The arrowheads show whether the pin is an input or an output.

The first input pin that should be tested on any suspect chip is the +5 V input. It powers all the circuits on the chip simultaneously. If the voltage is missing, the chip is probably good. The trouble is the missing voltage. The reason it is missing

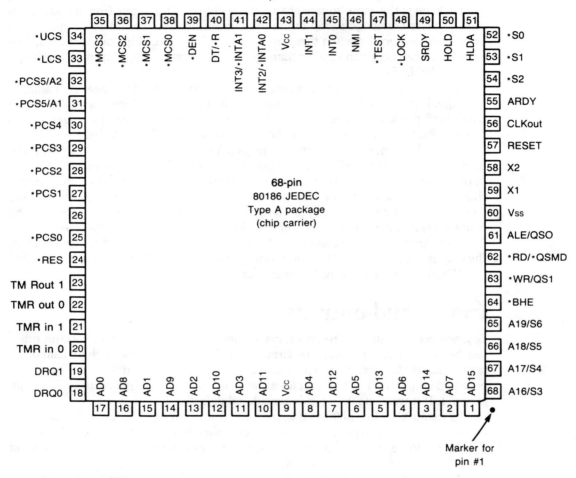

9-3 In addition to dual inline packages, be on the lookout for surface-mounted devices. This is the pinout of a chip-carrier package, one type of surface-mounted device.

must be investigated. The trouble will be in the power supply circuit. Trouble-shooting the power supply is discussed in chapter 25.

Some chips have more than one + voltage input. When there are a second or a third input, they all must be tested and deemed o.k. before further pin checking.

The voltmeter will give the most accurate check of the + volt input pins. The logic probe will also give a quick indication. It will light up the high LED when there is +5 volts on the pin.

The next pin to test is ground. The voltmeter will read 0 volts. However, the voltmeter will also read 0 volts if the ground connection is broken open. To check ground, the logic probe is more accurate. The logic probe will light its LOW LED when the ground connection is intact and the chip is energized. If the ground is broken the logic probe won't light. Should you encounter a suspect ground connection, disconnect the power and check the ground pin with a continuity tester or ohmmeter. The continuity tester will show a short when the ground is actually connected to the print board ground. An ohmmeter will read near zero ohms when the ground is intact and infinity if the ground connection is broken open.

Input considerations

Once the supply voltage is known to be correct, the other inputs can be tested. In various chips all sorts of inputs will be found. They could be address lines, data bus lines, interrupts, resets, or any number of control type connections. They all have one thing in common. Each input line at any instant (unless it is three-stating) is bringing to the chip one bit at a time. The bit can be a high, a low, or the line is in a three-state condition. The bit can be one that is held high, held low, or be an edge on a wave train. Your VOM and logic probe will tell you what is on the input pin being tested. It must match up with your MFD of the pin in order for the chip to be operating o.k.

According to which chip is being tested, the input bits could be coming from many places. The input bits are about to enter the chip to conduct the operation that is going on. The bit has not yet entered the chip environs when you become aware of its presence. Therefore, if the input test reveals an incorrect bit or no bit at all, the reason for the wrong bit is not due to problems with the chip you are testing. The bit has been made defective by something it encountered before it arrived at the test point.

In some rare cases, a short circuit just inside the chip at the pin under test could harm the state of the input bit. However this would be a very unusual instance. Since the likelihood of the chip itself harming one of its input bits is so rare, it can therefore be concluded that if an input bit is incorrect the reason for the trouble is in the path before the pin and not after the bit passes through the pin.

Output considerations

Once all the input pins are cleared of having input troubles, then the output pins can be tested. Here again the only signals that can appear on the pins of a good digital chip are logic states or a three-state condition. These bits and pulses are not approached with the same thoughts as the input bits. The input bits are entering the chip. The output bits have just been passed through the circuits in the chip and had all sorts of processing performed on them.

Whatever the processing though, the bits and pulses end up as bits and pulses, albeit, not the same as when they entered. If they went through NOT gates they were amplified and inverted. When they go through AND, OR, or other gates, two bits can end up as one. Bits and pulses that enter multiplexers or decoders, enter in one state, get gated, and exit in other states. The point is that the signals are predictably processed and have definite states that they must exit as. You recorded these output states when you produced your MFD before the computer ever developed trouble. The chip must output these predicted states or else the chip is not operating as it should.

The conclusion is, that when an output pin exhibits an incorrect logic state, in the great majority of cases, the chip is defective. The signal entered o.k. since the input pins read correct bits and pulses. The signal passed through the circuits on the chip and was processed. The signal then reached the output pins. When the signal is then incorrect, when it previously has been recorded as correct, the obvious conclusion is that some circuit inside the chip has become defective and cannot process the signal correctly anymore. The chip is bad.

There could be some rare cases where the output pin is in an external circuit that is shorted. When the bit arrives at the output pin it could then be shunted to ground or another circuit and cause the incorrect reading. However, this would be very unusual and not very likely. You would first have to change the indicated chip. If, on those rare occasions, the chip change does not cure the trouble and the pin showing the bad reading still reads bad, then you have run across one of these tough jobs. Just keep the remote possibility in the back of your mind even though you will probably never see it. If a chip output pin reads the wrong logic state, you can be 90% positive the chip itself has gone bad.

PEEK and POKE testing

When a computer is running a program it is following one instruction after another. The instructions are moving and processing data. At least 70% of the instructions in the program are moving data. If you want to test chips by exercising them, all you have to do is move data from place to place and observe whether or not the data was able to travel to a chosen destination and if the data arrived intact. If it did then the chips the data traveled through are o.k. Should the data fail to complete the trip there could be trouble along the way.

It really doesn't matter what language you use to move the data. If you are good with the assembly language of your machine you can use the two instructions STORE and LOAD. The store instructions have the processor write data bits to the addresses on the memory map. The load instructions have the processor read data bits out of the registers at the addresses on the memory map.

The idea though is make the moving of the data as simple and easy as possible. Assembly language is not the easiest method to use. A higher level language can do the same thing with a lot less program lines. For example, most personal computers can use BASIC. The PEEK and POKE instructions are identical to load and store. When you write a BASIC program line with PEEK it in turn calls out the machine language that reads a memory map location. If you write a program line with POKE it in turn causes the processor to write to a location.

When you move data a lot of computing energy is expended and a lot of the digital circuits are exercised. The processor is like a telephone exchange. The registers in RAM, ROM, I/O chips, video chips, audio chips, and so on are all subscribers to the exchange and each one has an address like a telephone number. Each one can be dialed up individually. In an 8-bit computer, the registers are mostly 8-bit types. When you move data to a register it passes through a lot of circuits and bus lines. By carefully choosing an address and just as carefully composing a byte of data you can do a lot of testing quickly.

Although this type of technique appears very useful, don't get too excited because it has one major drawback. It can't be used unless the processor and most of its support circuits are operating. If the computer is completely down it can't help you test itself. However, there are many troubles in chips, registers, and bus lines where the PEEKing and POKEing is handy.

To use PEEK and POKE properly, you must have the memory map and a schematic diagram of your print board. It would be useful to pencil in the addresses of the chips in the memory map on the schematic if the addresses are not already there. The memory map should have the addresses in decimal or hex or both. To PEEK or POKE in BASIC you must use decimal. If the map is in hex you'll have to convert the hex addresses to their decimal equivalents so BASIC will be able to use the addresses.

You must also be able to visualize what the bits in a register are when a decimal or hex number is used in an instruction. For instance suppose you want to test a register bit by bit. It could be a dynamic RAM register that is spread out over eight chips, one register bit to a RAM chip. As you test each bit, you are successfully testing the workings of each RAM chip. To test chip #7 of a set of 4164 chips, you'd write a high to #7 and lows to chips 6, 5, 4, 3, 2, 1, and 0. The byte of data that would do this would look like this, HLLLLLLL or in binary code, 10000000.

The decimal for binary 10000000 is 128. The POKE instruction to write HLLLLLLL would be an address like 2956 (or any address between 0-65535) plus the data coded to 128. The actual program line is POKE 2956, 128. This puts a high into address 2956 on RAM chip #7 and lows into addresses 2956 on all the rest of the RAM set. If you then PEEK 2956 and find the high arrived at #7 then the #7 RAM chip is probably o.k.

When you make the computer run this little BASIC test line, you are automatically testing a lot of chips and print board copper trace lines. First of all, you are exercising the keyboard and the keyboard I/O chip. The instruction must travel from your fingers through the keyboard, through the I/O chip onto the data bus to the processor. The processor then is exercised as it contacts the BASIC ROM and has the ROM run off the machine language program on the ROM that performs the POKE and PEEK. The RAM #7 chip is then tested.

All of the support chips in the address and data bus lines are also being checked. This includes gates and multiplexers. The video output chip must scan the video RAM and put the video RAM contents onto the TV display. Without going into every last operating detail, you can see that a lot of computer hardware gets tested besides the #7 chip.

If you have an understanding of the way the machine is computing then you can quickly tell which chips and circuits are operating o.k. The schematic diagram of your machine is drawn to reflect the way the binary signals travel through the circuits. Therefore if you can run the PEEK and POKE tests and consult the schematic diagram, also known as a logic diagram, you can quickly exonerate suspect circuits.

PEEK and POKE limitations

When you can use the PEEK and POKE tests you can check a lot of the computer. Unfortunately, the tests cannot be used in a lot of cases. That is when the Manual Fault Dictionary becomes invaluable. It can be used to troubleshoot in every instance.

The PEEK and POKE tests can only be used to check the arrangement between the processor and the registers in the memory map. Chapter 19 discusses the memory map in detail. The memory map is inside the digital world. It involves the processor and its array of registers that it is able to contact. The registers are the RAM, ROM, and I/O registers with addresses. Whatever circuits are included in the map (and can be addressed) can be PEEKed and POKEd. A circuit that is not mapped cannot be contacted directly with these instructions. If there are circuits or chips in the address, data, or control bus lines they might pass the address, data, or control bits. They can be tested to see if they successfully can pass the processor bits.

The clock circuits are not on the map and do not have addresses. They cannot be tested with the PEEK and POKE. The digital-to-analog and analog-to-digital chips without addresses cannot be tested. The PEEK and POKE instructions are only useful when a register with an address needs to be tested.

10
Using
diagnostic programs

THE PREVIOUS CHAPTER DISCUSSES THE MANUAL FAULT DICTIONARY
test technique. It must be resorted to when the computer is completely down. The
technique deals with taking a logic probe and other pieces of test equipment and
going right to the computer hardware, especially the pins on the chips. You then
proceed to look for problem clues by comparing the voltages that are actually
present to the voltages that are supposed to be present. Any deviations from the
prescribed norm are considered clues.

Diagnostics is different than the manual techniques. It can be used when the
computer is not completely down but is operating with problems. Diagnostics does
not require you to go directly to the hardware. When you use diagnostic problems
to pinpoint troubled circuits, you are dealing with the entire computer system, not
just the hardware. The hardware is only the bottom level of the system. There are
three distinct additional levels on top of the hardware in a computer system.

The four computer system levels

In a typical working computer, the overall system operates by using four stacked
subsystems such as Fig. 10-1. On the bottom is the computer hardware. The hardware is composed of silicon, copper, plastic and other materials with electricity
coursing through all the materials. The hardware is there. You can see it, touch it
and do hardware things with it.

The next level up is a set of software called *BIOS* (basic input-output system).
BIOS is a program and associated data that is used to start the computing. It handles all the computer inputs and outputs in addition to doing a lot of other jobs.
The BIOS program is typically burned into ROMs that are installed on the print
board. Because BIOS is in a chip, it could be considered hardware, but it really

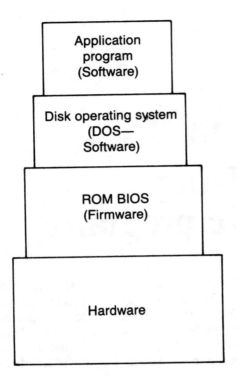

Levels of operation

Application program (Software)

Disk operating system (DOS— Software)

ROM BIOS (Firmware)

Hardware

10-1 Typically a computer works by means of four interlocking levels. At the very bottom is the hardware. On top of the hardware is *BIOS* (basic input-output system). Next up is the computer operating system, such as DOS. On the very top is the application program that is to be run.

isn't. Most of the BIOS could just as easily be installed in RAM from an external source like any other software. Usually though it is plugged into the motherboard in a ROM. Because it is in a ROM it is called *firmware* rather than software. Whatever its naming, it is a program that gets the computer started. It is the immediate system level on top of the bottom hardware level.

On top of the BIOS is another program that is considered the operating system. In different computers there are different operating systems. In the interest of compatibility, the number of operating systems has been kept low. For example, IBM and Microsoft got together years ago and agreed to use the same operating system. It is the well-known system called *DOS* (disk-operating system). Recently, as computers developed and DOS couldn't do the job on the more powerful machines, a newer system called *O/S 2* (operating system 2) was conceived. There will be many more operating systems born as time goes by. At any rate, the operating system is the third level, and it is on top of BIOS.

The operating system such as the popular DOS has the duty to run the disk drives. BIOS, in comparison, runs the input-output machinery of the computer. DOS takes over the disk drives among other things. Between the hardware that is sitting waiting for action, the BIOS taking over the I/O sections, and DOS running the disk drives, the computer becomes ready to work. What is its work? A computer has one main job. It runs application programs.

Once the three bottom levels are situated and running, then and only then, you can apply the fourth and top level of the computer system—the application program. When the application program is up and running, the computer is then fulfilling its duty.

From hardware to application

When you turn on a computer, the starter turns over the motor and a lot of events take place. If the computer is operating o.k., after a few seconds the computer will sign in. In early small computers, the computer could show a title describing the software that is going to do the job and a prompt such as "READY" or "OK," along with a blinking cursor. In larger, disk-equipped computers, along with a sign-in title, the name of the current disk that is available will appear. For example in an IBM type computer, when you turn on the computer, you could see the ROMBIOS name and version, the amount of memory available, and other things. Then you would hear the disks whirl, some pilot lights flash, and a single beep. After that, the sign-in information will disappear and the name of the disk, such as A or C will appear and remain on with a flashing cursor.

All you are seeing and hearing are indications that a lot is going on in the machine. There is a lot going on. The computer, starting with the hardware bottom level is going from level to level and arranging things so you can run your application program and get some work done. The following is a typical step-by-step description of how the computer steps up from the bottom level to the top.

1. In order to get running or *boot up* as it is called, there should be a disk with an operating system ready on line. For example, if you boot up with a hard disk, DOS should be installed on the hard disk. If you do not have a hard disk, then a disk containing DOS can be placed in a floppy disk drive such as drive A. Now you are ready and can turn on the power switch for the computer and its peripherals.

2. Typically, the power supplies have a self-test circuit in their makeup. They give themselves a test. They check out all the voltages and currents. When the test decides the electrical inputs and outputs are o.k., a supply sends a signal to the motherboard that it is ready to provide the correct voltages to run the hardware level of the computer.

3. A timer chip on the motherboard receives the power supply go-ahead signal. The timer chip turns off a processor protection reset signal that it generates upon computer turn on. The processor starts operating, and the hardware level begins its work.

4. The processor is set up to automatically access one memory location as it turns on. That is about the only move it can make independently. For all other moves, it must get instructions from above before it can do anything else. This start-up memory location contains a jump instruction. The jump

sends a signal to the ROMBIOS chip at the next level up. The signal turns on the BIOS, which acts as the brains of the processor.

5. The first thing the BIOS does is check a flag in memory. According to the status of the flag, the BIOS finds out if this start is a new cold start or has the computer been running and has simply been rebooted. If this is a cold start, the computer likes to run a diagnostic program to make sure all systems are go. Should this event be only a rebooting, most of the diagnostic program can be skipped, because it had already been run in full at the original cold start.

6. Assuming this is a cold start, the diagnostic is run. The diagnostic bytes are contained in the BIOS chip. There are many forms of diagnostics in different computers. The best known of these diagnostics is the IBM *POST* (power-on self-test). The POST is discussed in more detail in the next section of this chapter.

7. The POST tests all of the important circuits in the computer system and the complete memory is given a quick test. If all systems are go, the computer displays sign-on wording, some lights flash, a beep sounds, and after all that the current drive name, A, B, or what have you appears with a flashing cursor. Should the POST find some circuits not operating correctly, the POST will display error messages and sound various multiple beeps, as in Tables 10-1 and 10-2. The video and audio messages tell you what circuits are having trouble. The trouble must be fixed before the POST will allow the computer to be used.

**Table 10-1. If POST finds a fault, it will
signal you with beeps. The number of beeps is code
indicating what section of the computer is causing trouble.**

Audio error codes	Possible source of problem
No sound	Power supply
Continuous sound	Power supply
Continuous short beeps	Power supply
1 long & 1 short beep	Motherboard
1 long & 2 short beeps	Video generator adapter card
No display & 1 short beep	Display monitor
1 short beep & unit will not boot up	Disk adapter card or disk drive

8. Assuming all circuits are operating o.k., the BIOS continues to work after the POST has completed its tests. The BIOS begins testing any and all adapter cards that are installed in motherboard slots. BIOS is looking and testing for some other BIOS chips that might be on the cards. There is usually a video ROMBIOS present on the video adapter. There could be others on special cards. If the system BIOS discovers some companion BIOS chips, the system BIOS starts testing them. If they are installed correctly and are o.k., the system BIOS initializes them. These companion BIOS

**Table 10-2. In addition to beeps, the
POST could also display error codes indicating
what section of the computer is causing trouble.**

Typical device number error codes	Suspected device
20-29	Power supply
100-199	Motherboard
200-299	RAM
300-399	Keyboard
400-499	Monochrome display adapter
500-599	Color graphics adapter
600-699	Floppy drive or adapter
700-799	Math coprocessor
900-999	Parallel printer adapter

chips must mesh with the system BIOS properly. Their presence often changes the way the system BIOS operates in a designed positive manner. These additional BIOS chips usually give the computer system more capability and strength.

9. The next thing the BIOS does is to begin communication with the next level up, the DOS software system. It makes the first move by looking for drive A. If there is a DOS disk in drive A, BIOS will start reading the disk. BIOS loads the drives boot record program that is typically found on track 0, sector 1 and runs it. If there is no DOS disk in drive A, the sector can't be read. The BIOS then continues onto the hard disk.

10. BIOS looks for a boot record program on track 0, sector 1 of the hard disk. If it is there the sector is loaded and the program is run putting the hard disk into the system. The boot program then takes control of the system and BIOS steps into the background. BIOS is still active as a level but DOS, the next level up takes over the helm.

11. Now that DOS has taken over it starts loading its important control programs into memory. These programs have names like IBMBIO.COM, IBMDOS.COM. The program with the letters BIO stays in communication with the BIOS. It works with BIOS to run the entire system. The program with the letters DOS is used to communicate with the files in the DOS directory.

12. The program file IBMBIO.COM is now in control. It orders IBMDOS.COM to read one of the DOS programs called CONFIG.SYS. CONFIG.SYS is then used to configure the computer system. The configuration consists of loading device drivers and listed installable programs into memory.

13. Once the system is configured IBMBIO.COM tells IBMDOS.COM to load another program called COMMAND.COM. IBMBIO.COM then turns over control to COMMAND.COM.

14. COMMAND.COM in turn loads a program called AUTOEXEC.BAT. AUTOEXEC.BAT is run. The computer system is, at this point, fully operational and in software control. The DOS prompt appears with a flashing cursor. It is now ready to perform. The DOS prompt turns over control to you. All you have to do is install the fourth and top level, an application program, and go to work.

All of the events listed above happen in a twinkling. The computer proceeds step-by-step with each event triggered off by the event that occurred before it. As long as they take place as described, you are in business. Should one of the procedures not take place the computer has trouble. If you have an idea of the way the step-by-step start up is happening you will have some immediate rough diagnosis if troubles take place.

More about POST

The POST is a group of programs that are installed in the ROMBIOS along with all the other data the BIOS must contain. It consists of individual test routines for the processor, ROMs, support chips, RAM arrangement, and all the main peripherals configured in the system. POST goes to work automatically every time a cold start of the computer is made.

The tests are fast and not thorough. They simply exercise the components briefly to see if they are working. There is no in-depth study of circuits that is needed for serious troubleshooting. These types of tests are provided on other diagnostic disks to be used when hard-to-locate troubles are occurring. POST only tells the computer that chips are present and are operating. It does not tell the computer how well the chips are working. POST is little more than a go/no go type test.

When the computer system passes POST, a beep is heard and the drive name prompt appears with a cursor. Sometimes the computer won't POST. When this happens it means a serious problem exists. It also could mean that no diagnostic disk is going to be able to be used. The computer is down and out. You will probably have to resort to manual testing as described in the last chapter.

With lesser troubles, the computer will indeed POST but give you bad news. POST will supply you with multiple beeps or no beep at all. The display, instead of giving you a prompt and cursor will flash error code code numbers. Table 10-1 is a typical list of the error beeps a typical POST program might sound off with. Table 10-2 is a list of the error code numbers that might appear on the screen during a trouble period. The error codes indicate particular sections of the computer that POST discovered has trouble. For example, if POST finds a fault in the video adapter card it could make a computer sound off with one long and two short beeps. On the other hand, instead of or in addition to the audio error code, the POST might display a code number such as 526. When you get an audio or video error code you are directed to the circuit area where a trouble could be hidden.

If the code that was displayed was 500 instead of 526, that would indicate that device 5 is a good video display circuit area. The 5 is the device number for the

10-2 A typical menu to choose diagnostic tests can have these 12 listings.

```
<A> ALL TEST
<B> RUN ALL TEST MULTIPLE TIMES
<C> SET UP MODE
<D> SET DAY/TIME
<E> REBOOT
<F> MEMORY TEST
<G> FDC TEST (floppy disk)
<H> WDC TEST (hard disk)
<I > COLOR GRAPHIC CARD TEST
<J > RS232 PORT TEST
<K> PARALLEL PRINTER TEST
<L > KEYBOARD TEST
```

graphics adapter and the 00 means the adapter is good. On the other hand, the error code 526 shows that the device number 5 has a trouble categorized under the error 26. Typically, when a device number is followed by 00, that indicates a circuit without trouble that has passed the test. Any other number between 01 and 99 is an error code and means the device has flunked the test.

Most POST diagnostics count the memory as a side test. The count is displayed while the machine is starting up. If your computer has 640K in RAM, the count will display 640K if it is all working o.k. Should you have another section of extended memory installed in RAM, the amount of the extended memory will be displayed too.

There might or might not be error codes for RAM that is inoperative. You should note the amount of memory POST displays and compare it to what you know is in your machine. Any deviation could be trouble.

Also POST does not count expanded memory. Expanded memory is not extended memory as mentioned above. Extended memory is simply added RAM chips. For instance, conventional memory could be 640K. The 640K could be extended to 1 megabyte and be addressed directly by the processor. *EMS* (expanded memory) is different. It cannot be addressed directly by the processor. It can only be accessed through a special assigned 64K memory window. There will be more about the differences in extended and expanded memory in chapter 19.

There are many forms of POST in different computers. IBM originated the name *POST* and their particular tests. The audio and visual error codes for a specific IBM type computer is usually specific for that model. Tables 10-1 and 10-2 are simply general examples. Don't rely on those error codes for all makes and models. You must have the service manual for the computer you are working on to be sure that any error codes you might encounter are interpreted correctly.

Separate diagnostic programs

POST type diagnostics are usually installed in the BIOS chip of a computer. They are limited in what they can test. It simply verifies that components are present, accounted for, and are turning on o.k. There are much better diagnostics available. They are more on the order of an application program.

Once DOS turns the computer over to you, then you are able to use one or more of these separate diagnostics. One of the most common diagnostics comes on a separate DOS connected disk. On the disk are a number of important DOS files that you can boot the computer with. Among these boot files are COMMAND .COM and AUTOEXEC.BAT. When you place the disk in a floppy drive such as drive A, the computer will boot and access a file called DIAGNOST. If you watch carefully you'll see *diagnost* appear on the screen briefly and then the screen will display Fig. 10-2. Figure 10-2 is a menu of 12 diagnostic tests. These tests are much more extensive than POST. In this example disk the menu list is (A) through (L). Suppose you hit F on the keyboard and the following is displayed.

*Memory Test
1. On-board memory
2. Expansion memory
3. Exit

Next you press 1 on the keyboard. This tests the conventional memory in this case from 0 through 640K. A secondary menu appears. It looks like the following:

*Memory Test
A. Basic test
B. March test
C. Solid test
D. Ripple test
E. Check board test
F. Exit

You can then have the computer run tests and exercise all the memory in the 640K of ordinary RAM. The computer will display each test as it goes and render a pass or fail verdict. When you are finished with the 640K you can press F and exit that test section. The expansion test works in the same way. Suppose you have another 384K in RAM to provide you with 1 Mb of total RAM. The expansion test will check it out. Once you are finished testing, you hit the exit keys and find you are back in the main menu.

In this example test disk, the twelve circuit areas that can be tested are the following:

(A) All test—This is an overall test that checks all the system devices.

(B) Run all tests multiple times—This test is a loop that tests over and over again.

(C) Set-up mode—This is used to display *Set Up* on the screen and let you add, delete, or adjust all the system device descriptions as in Fig. 10-3.

System Configuration Setup
Time: 20:34:46
Date: Wed Feb 13, 1991

Diskette A:	5.25 Inch, 1.2 MB
Diskette B:	3.5 Inch, 1.44 MB
Hard disk 1:	Type 17

Cyl	977
Hds	5
Pre	300
LZ	977
Sec	17
Size	40

10-3 One important test that should be checked periodically is the system setup.

Hard disk 2:	Not installed
Base memory:	640 KB
Extended memory:	340 KB
Display:	VGA
Keyboard:	Installed
CPU speed:	Slow
Coprocessor:	Not installed

(D) Set day/time—This test checks the day/time clock and lets you correct if it is not the right time.

(E) Reboot—Pressing E causes a warm boot to take place.

(F) Memory test—This is the memory test described above.

(G) FDC test—This is the floppy disk or disks test. Remove the diagnostic disk for this test. Replace it with a blank or otherwise expendable disk. This test destroys all data on the test disk.

(H) WDC test—This is the hard disk test.

(I) Color graphics card test—This test puts the graphics card through its paces. For example, it puts designs and characters on the screen. They are made to blink, display many colors, check all the character sets, test the color 80 × 25 mode, the color 40 × 25 mode, the color 320 × 200 mode, the graphics 640 × 200 mode and the 80 × 20 four page.

(J) RS232 port test—For this test you must use a wrap plug that makes a loop between the output and input connection pins. The port then outputs a test signal that is immediately coupled right back to an input pin. The port checks itself in that way. It tests all the available baud rates. For example, one rate at a time from 110 to 9600.

(K)   Parallel printer test—This test puts lines of ASCII characters on the screen and then prints them out on a parallel printer. For the test to pass, the lines on the screen should be identical to the lines the printer puts out. If the lines do not match, the printer could have faults.

(L)   Keyboard test—A display of every keyboard character or sign appears on the screen. One by one hit each key. As each key is struck the character or sign on the key will disappear from the screen. Should a character or sign remain on the screen, that key is not working and requires attention.

Once the diagnostic is completed, you must do a hard reboot. Don't use the reboot provided in the test group. The testing has changed the contents of memory around. Either turn the computer off and then back on for normal operation or press the Reset button on the front panel of the computer if there is one.

Diagnostic on a hard disk

In many versions of DOS that are placed on a hard disk, DIAGNOST could be one of the DOS files. The diagnostic could be identical to the separate-disk version except it is not a pure application program that sits on top of DOS. As one of the DOS files, it must be accessed in the same way as any other command.

For example, if you want to use the diagnostic imbedded in DOS on a hard disk, you must bring up DOS and then command DOS to run DIAGNOST. Once the DIAGNOST menu comes up you can use it in the same way as the application program on the separate disk.

Diagnostic results

If you examine the dozen diagnostic tests on the typical program just discussed, aside from the memory test (F), the rest of the actual tests (G), (H), (I), (J), (K), and (L), are made on peripheral circuits. That is the area where the diagnostics are the strongest. Usually when a peripheral stops operating, the rest of the computer is still working. The diagnostic helps you answer the question, "Is the trouble being caused by the peripheral or the computer output circuit?" Actually, if you had a known good spare peripheral, for instance a printer, and substituted it for the one that stopped working, the test would be superior. If the replacement printer started working you would know the suspect device is indeed bad. Should the spare also refuse to work, then the computer output circuit is pointed out as the troublemaker. Unfortunately you do not always have a known good spare to perform the replacement test. The diagnostic program then becomes a good alternative tester.

What about the rest of the computer circuits? Will the diagnostic test them as well as the peripherals? Examine the diagnostic test ability of the software approach.

Processor problems

Fortunately, processors are very reliable. Most of the bad ones are removed during manufacturing quality control. The processors that make it into the field are the best ones that are made. However, they are electronic devices and as such are still subject to breakdown. The best test, of course, is to try a known good replacement. This is not always practical so some diagnostic tests are available.

A processor diagnostic must be written specifically for the processor and is applied through a special test machine. The test consists of putting the processor through its paces and outputting the results of the work the processor performs through its output pins to the tester. In the tester is a list of the predicted results the processor should be outputting. The work is compared to the predicted results. If they match, the processor passes the test. When the results do not match, the processor is thought to be in trouble and should be replaced.

ROM problems

When the computer signs in at start up, the printing on the display is coming from the ROM. The processor is reading the ROM and displaying the reading material. The sign in characters are usually contained in the beginning addresses of the ROM. The rest of the ROM contains many more programs. ROM chips have a lot of memory addresses. Each address typically represents a byte. In the byte there are bits. The bits are permanent burned-in residents of each address. If you counted the number of high bits and low bits, you would have a permanent census number. The number will not change unless some misfortune befalls a bit that erases its high or low value.

Such erasures can take place due to heat, humidity and even aging. When the ROM loses some bits and starts making the computer act in strange ways, it can be tested easily, if you have a diagnostic to test with.

A test program can check every bit in every register. The test consists of reading each byte individually and running each bit through a RAM type 16-bit shift register. The shift register exclusive ors each incoming bit from the ROM under test with it 6th, 8th, 11th, and 15th register bit. As each bit is passed through the register, the value in the register changes.

The register produces a new binary number pattern every time a bit is run through the 16 bits. The 16 bits are equivalent to four hex numbers. After every ROM bit goes through, the shift register ends up with four hex numbers. These resultant numbers are called a 4-digit *CRC* (cyclic redundancy check—the technical name for this ROM test). This test is actually a checksum error test that expert programmers use to check the accuracy of the transmission of a program from computer to computer. We troubleshooters use it to read and test the ROM.

After the entire ROM has been tested bit by bit, the shift register is left with a hex value. Each ROM will have its own special value according to the makeup of the burnt-in bits. For example, in one ROM, this test produces the hex value 9505. If the test is run and produces a printout of 9505, you know the ROM is o.k. Should the number ever change, you'll know the ROM is defective and install a new one. When the number is wrong, chances are a short or open has occurred in one or more of the ROM permanent registers. This test is supposed to be accurate 99% of the time.

Some ROM diagnostic programs that are specific for a computer contain the CRC numbers for the ROMs. In those cases, the test could be run and the resultant CRC number of a ROM will be compared to the prescribed number during the test. The diagnostic then, instead of reporting a CRC hex number will simply pronounce the ROM good or bad.

RAM problems

As mentioned earlier, start-up diagnostics, such as POST, check out all the RAM addresses every time the computer is booted up. A defective RAM chip is among the group of frequent troubles. There are usually many RAM chips in a computer. The test is made so you do not have to worry that you will get into the middle of a lengthy program execution and find it won't work because of defective RAM locations. It is common to have some registers in a RAM set become defective and if it wasn't checked out would fool you and appear to be o.k. The tipoff of trouble wouldn't occur until some errors produce weird results or a program suddenly crashes. This would be too late and can be very expensive.

RAM in computers could be made of *DRAMs* (dynamic RAMs) or *SRAMs* (static RAMs), as in Fig. 10-4. Typically, static RAM chips have 4-bit or 8-bit registers tied together on a single chip. In contrast, dynamic RAM chips have 1-bit registers. SRAMs, due to this multiple-bit layout, can have complete 8-bit registers on a single chip or on two 4-bit chips tied together. DRAMs, on the other hand require eight chips tied together to create an 8-bit register. When the RAM system uses a ninth bit in a register for parity checking, the DRAMs need nine chips to layout registers. These different layout schemes can cause complications during testing. This is because when you address SRAM you could be addressing only one or two chips. If you address a DRAM location you are contacting eight or nine chips.

Fortunately, even though static and dynamic RAMs have these basic bit and address differences, they will both respond to the diagnostic testing. A good diagnostic will pick out a defective static or dynamic chip. Less effective diagnostics will usually pick out a bad static chip since the entire register is on one chip. The tests will not always pick out the actual dynamic chip when it can't read and write to a register because the register is spread out over eight or nine chips.

When a dynamic chip fails, to determine the actual chip in a group of eight or nine, the test must pinpoint the bit number in the register that is not working. For example, during a breakdown, if bit #2 is defective, the test must show that. Since all bits #2 are on the same chip the #2 DRAM in the set is indicated as bad and can be replaced to cure the trouble.

When the diagnostic simply pinpoints the address number of the bad register,

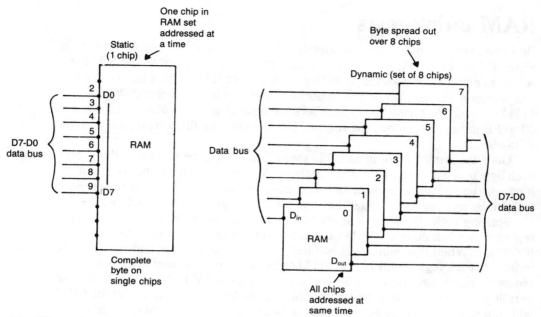

10-4 The testing of static or dynamic memory chips could require different tests because the locations are laid out in entirely different ways. Static byte locations could have all eight bits on one chip. Dynamic byte locations could have the bits distributed over eight chips.

other techniques, such as Fig. 10-5, must be used to isolate the bad chip. One way was mentioned earlier, the BASIC program's PEEK-and-POKE testing. Another way, if the chips are in sockets and no soldering is involved, is to swap the chips around and keep examining the test byte results. The latest method is to use SIMMs as mentioned earlier. The SIMM is the group of nine DRAMs that are changed en masse. The actual bad chip is not bothered with.

10-5 In some computers with dynamic memory, once a defective address is pinpointed, it might be necessary to swap chips around to find the defective bit.

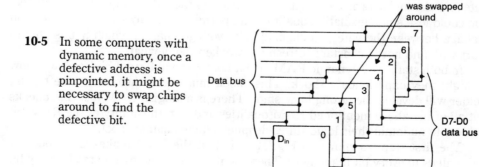

RAM quick tests

On some personal computers, the operating ROM will conduct a quick checkout of all the RAM. The ROM will first of all make the processor count all the RAM registers. The processor does this by filling every byte of RAM with a binary number. The value of the number is not important, any number between 00000000 and 11111111 will do. These binary numbers are equivalent to 0 – 255 in decimal and 00 to FF in hex. Of course, the register bits are actually filled with high and low voltages.

Once the numbers are installed in every RAM byte, the processor then reads each byte to see if the number is really there. As it reads each number successfully it counts the register as present and accounted for. As long as the quantity of registers are correct the ROM could then test for the rough quality of each register.

Starting with 00000000, it starts filling each register with that number. If the registers can handle that number the processor is made to fill each register with 00000001. When that number is handled o.k. the next number and the next are written to each register till 1111111111 has been written successfully. Once all the binary numbers have been written and read to every RAM location, the ROM will permit you to conduct your computing. Should the test not be successful the ROM will shut down the computer and print the fact that there is a RAM error and most tests will also tell you which RAM chip has failed. A RAM chip replacement of the indicated chip is then needed before computing can resume.

Longer RAM tests

The actual bit in a RAM bit holder is a high or low voltage. In static RAM, (Fig. 8-3) the voltage is contained in a cross-coupled double device that has one side conducting and the other side cutoff. When they flip-flop their conditions they change to the other state. As these circuits age their conduction abilities weaken somewhat and the bit holder becomes unstable. The instability can produce errors during computing.

A dynamic RAM stores a logic state (Fig. 8-4) as high voltage in a capacitance between the gate and the channel of an IGFET. The glassy insulation between the gate and channel acts as a capacitor dielectric. As the RAM chip ages, the dielectric could lose some insulation qualities and permit some tiny amounts of electron leakage between the gate and channel. The voltage charge, which is unstable to start with and needs constant refreshing, weakens somewhat.

In both static and dynamic RAM, as bit holders switch from high to low or low to high, they experience a shock. This shock must be withstood or else the bit holder will develop the wrong logic state. There is a longish RAM test that checks out all of the above mentioned RAM qualities and also the ability of the RAM bit holders to maintain their logic states despite voltage change shocks.

The first step (as shown in Fig. 10-6) is that the ROM makes the processor write all 0s to every bit in memory. Then the processor, one-by-one reads every bit in turn. When the processor reads a 0 in a bit it immediately writes a 1 to replace

RAM bit positions

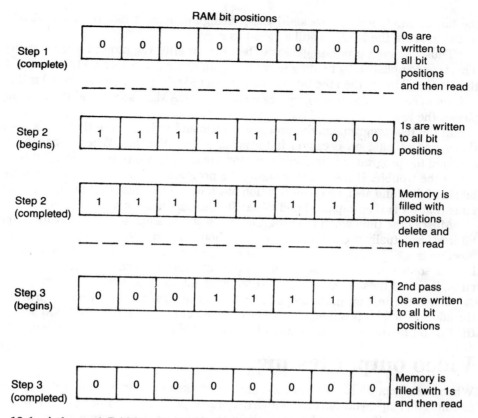

Step 1 (complete)

| 0 | 0 | 0 | 0 | 0 | 0 | 0 | 0 |

0s are written to all bit positions and then read

Step 2 (begins)

| 1 | 1 | 1 | 1 | 1 | 1 | 0 | 0 |

1s are written to all bit positions

Step 2 (completed)

| 1 | 1 | 1 | 1 | 1 | 1 | 1 | 1 |

Memory is filled with positions delete and then read

Step 3 (begins)

| 0 | 0 | 0 | 1 | 1 | 1 | 1 | 1 |

2nd pass 0s are written to all bit positions

Step 3 (completed)

| 0 | 0 | 0 | 0 | 0 | 0 | 0 | 0 |

Memory is filled with 1s and then read

10-6 A thorough RAM test could entail making sure that bits do not lose their charge during reading and writing.

that 0 it found. The processor then continues bit-by-bit through the entire RAM set installing 1s for each 0.

So far, the processor when successful to this juncture in the test has proved that every bit can store a 0. Each one of these 0s can be read. Each one of these 0s can also be replaced by a 1. This proves that the entire RAM is able to transfer logic states between the processor and itself. Should a bit have failed to travel successfully between the processor and RAM, the program would have instantly stopped at that bit. The program would then have identified that defective bit and printed the bad chip number.

The test so far is like the quick RAM test in that it found a bit that doesn't work and identified what chip the bad bit resides on. Actually the test shows a bit failing to hold its high charges as the next bit in line was being charged with a high. The shock from the target bit being charged killed the charge in the bit before the target bit. The test is checking the bit before the target bit. It is tested for stability as the target bit is charged with the 1. The test then, up to that point has checked the stability of the bit in front of a target bit. What about the bit after the target bit? It will get rocked by the changing charges too. It should also be tested to prove the RAM is still as good as ever.

Thus, the next program goal is to test the bit after the target bit for stability. This is accomplished by reading every bit again to see if the 1's are still present. If the 1's are all intact then the bits are all considered o.k. As a final touch, a 0 is then written to each 1. The testing proves good stable RAM locations and the memory passes the test.

In the test program, as the processor reads and writes to the thousands upon thousands of bits, on occasion it turns up a defective bit. When a bad bit is detected the program will immediately stop the testing of bits and print the discovery of the trouble. If the RAM is static, the program will print the address of the bit that failed and also which bit position has failed. The static RAM chip that contains that bit is then replaced and hopefully the computer is repaired.

Most of the time when the program prints out an address and bit position, the bit itself is actually the defect. Sometimes though the program will err and the bit position is o.k. A trouble could be in the bit input circuit, one of the address or data lines or some other out-of-the-ordinary line that happens to be conducted to the circuits. Some of these troubles are covered in chapters 18 and 19.

When the test program picks out a bad bit in dynamic RAM and it provides the address and bit position, then you can figure out what chip in the RAM set has the bad bit by the bit position. Each RAM chip holds all of the same bit positions.

Video output testing

When the computer is operating o.k. and you'd like to check out your video output circuits and chips, you can do it with a diagnostic program. In order to write such a program yourself you must know all about the registers in the output circuit and/or chip. A video output chip operates in a number of modes. You must program each mode and then get the chip to perform the graphics of that mode on the screen. If all the modes display properly then the chip is considered o.k. Should one or more of the modes not perform then there is some sort of defect in the circuits in the chip that operate that particular mode. In chapter 22, actual chips are covered in some detail.

Typically, a video chip will be able to display modes in alphanumerics, semigraphics, and graphics. For example, a chip can have two alphanumeric modes, five semigraphic modes, and eight graphics. Each mode has a particular set of bits, that when input to the chip will turn on one of the modes.

When you write a video diagnostic program, and choose a mode to test, you must get those bits into the correct inputs to set up the mode to be tested. Once you produce the mode you then have the program display a pattern on the screen. For instance, in one alphanumeric mode you might want to see a complete set of upper- and lowercase characters. The program you write would print these characters for you on the screen. The second alphanumeric mode is the inverted image of the first, that is the background color of a character switches places with the character color. To test that mode, you'd again print the set of numbers and characters on the screen. This time though they would appear inverted.

The other modes also are called by input bits to the chip registers and then the mode is proved by causing a graphic to be displayed. For example, you could input bits to put the chip into a mode that produces 256 × 192 graphic picture elements. Then a little graphic program could display a funny face. With the 256 × 192 graphic, 24 funny faces would be produced. This is in contrast to 2 funny faces that would be drawn if the graphic was only a 64 × 64 array.

To detect trouble the funny faces are examined for color and size. As long as they are identical the chip mode is working o.k. If the funny faces are not uniform in color, size, or if they are missing, then that mode could be defective.

There are many different types of video output chips. To run off a test on one, the important thing to know is how they work and then write a program to exercise it. According to the results of the exercise you find out which modes are working and which ones are not. The program can be in any language the computer can use for graphics.

Testing audio chips

Different computers produce audio in different ways. Some of them do not have a special audio chip but create audio frequencies by means of digital-to-analog circuits as the TRS-80 ColorComputer does. The Commodore 64 contains a special audio chip that produces audio output frequencies and even accepts some audio inputs to mix with the computer-made audio. Audio chips are discussed in chapter 22.

The way to test the audio is to write a program that produces audio signals and then note whether the signal can be heard from the computer's speaker system, either in the computer itself or part of the TV display.

In a computer that does not have an audio chip, the sound must be produced by developing a set of digital bits that the digital-to-analog circuit can convert to an analog sine wave, or other audio wave. Some of these D/A circuits can use a set of eight bits. These bits are arranged so a clock circuit will step through a binary count from 00000000 to 11111111 and back. The constantly changing byte count is applied to the D/A circuit. The circuit converts the bits from the digital voltages to a sine wave. If the sine wave is changing from a low of zero volts to a high of +5 V, 00000000 becomes zero volts and the 11111111 becomes +5 V. The binary numbers in between become the voltages that run between zero and +5 V. When the sine wave is then applied to an audio circuit, the voltage is amplified and applied to a speaker. The sine wave sounds like a wail.

In computers that use an audio chip, the test method is different. The test method is quite like the video test method. In the audio chip are a number of registers. Each register has a particular job to do. Each register has an address and I/Os to a data bus. A program must be written to exercise the registers in the chip. The program is simple. All you need to do is get the registers to produce some test tones.

For instance the chip in the C64 and C128 has a set of registers to produce a sound. One of the registers is a volume control. A second register is able to set up a sustain/release audio pattern. A third register will set up a frequency range. A fourth register can set different waveforms. If you POKE those registers with the proper bits, a test tone will sound off if the registers are o.k.

Once the tone comes on and proves the registers are good, you then POKE a fifth register and turn off the note. This shuts off the volume control. A little BASIC direct register exercise that can be used on the COMMODORE 64 is the following.

> POKE 42296,15 turns on the volume
> POKE 54278,248 sets the sustain/release
> POKE 54273,17 sets up a high frequency
> POKE 54276,17 sets a waveform

At that point a note will sound off from the speaker of an audio system that the COMMODORE 64 is attached to. The 64 does not have a speaker of its own. Once the note sounds the last step of the exercise is to turn off the volume control register that was turned on in the first POKE line. This is performed with:

> POKE 54296,0

While the POKEing is convenient and fast the bits can be sent to the register in any language that the computer will respond to. The idea in all these tests are to simply exercise the chip registers to determine if they are responding normally to addressing and data moving.

I/O testing

The I/O trouble symptoms are easy to recognize. The affected peripheral stops working. For example, the keyboard might become inoperative. Pressing keys has no noticeable effect yet the computer signs in as usual. Perhaps the printer will stop printing or a mouse won't perform its usual duties in a space game. In these cases the first diagnostic task is to determine whether the peripheral itself is in trouble or maybe the I/O circuits in the computer are not operating properly.

The best test move is to try a known good peripheral in place of the ailing one. If the replacement device starts operating normally while the suspect one was not, then 99% of the time the old peripheral contains the trouble. Should the known good replacement also refuse to work then chances are good the computer I/O circuits have the trouble.

Diagnostic tests are useful to check out I/O circuits and peripherals, but not as valuable as you might think. If a peripheral stops operating and you do not have a spare known good replacement, you can try a diagnostic test. However, if either the I/O circuit or the peripheral is completely shot, the diagnostic test won't work either, accomplishing no diagnostic goal of isolating the source of the trouble.

On the other hand, if the peripheral is performing, but it is not up to its usual standards, a diagnostic test might indicate whether the trouble is in the peripheral or the I/O circuits. For example, suppose your printer is printing but is switching the size of the characters from double size to single and back, producing a wild looking sheet of hard copy. Is the crazy printing being caused by the computer or the printer?

The printer could be receiving serial data from an RS-232 port. The first thing you'd do is run a diagnostic test on the RS-232 port. If the port is outputting and inputting properly, chances are the port is o.k. Should the port not be passing data correctly the port will be deemed defective.

One diagnostic test requires the computer to output data, short the output line to the input with a wrap plug, and then input the data it had must outputted right back into the computer. The test itself is simply running a wave train out and then reading the input and status lines to see if the wave train is coming back in as it went out. If it is the RS-232 port is o.k. If there is an error in the wave train that reenters the port, then the port circuit is defective. A message is then printed on the TV display: RS-232 PORT IS DEFECTIVE!. Should the wave train check out with no detectable errors, the message on the display will read, RS-232 PORT IS OK.

If the port is defective, it must be repaired as discussed in chapter 20. When the port is exonerated the printer becomes the prime suspect. A diagnostic test can be run on the printer. The printer diagnostic test is simple. A complete character set is output from the RS-232 port to the printer. The printer should then produce the character set. If it does then the printer is probably o.k. Should the printer not produce a correct set of characters and the computer is outputting a good set, then it is indicated that the printer is defective and needs repairs.

Computer self testing

Most personal computers are equipped with a post type self-test program along with its operating system program, usually contained in a ROM on the main board. The Commodore 64 has a test that sets the addressing range of RAM every time the machine is turned on. If the RAM becomes set according to the design plan then the computer signs on with its READY message.

The HEATH H-89A has a test routine that you can key into the machine. In the memory test part you can write a number into each byte of RAM and then go back and read the number at each location and make sure it is correct. If a wrong number is found in a memory register the address where the error is found and the actual incorrect contents of the register is displayed on the screen.

The Apple *II*e has a self test that can be run by pressing keys CONTROL, SOLID APPLE, and RESET. The test will be displayed by the screen turning white, then black, then white, then black and will display KERNAL OK, as long as the computer is working properly. Should some defect be present though, and the defect does not shut down the machine, an error message will be displayed giving some indication of what the trouble might be. If the defect is shutting down the computer, of course, there will be no indicating display.

Diagnostic adapter cards

Diagnostics are also found on adapter cards. For example, there are cards that plug into slots in 8086/286/386 systems. These cards are independent and do not need DOS to operate in conjunction with them. They will operate in place of DOS. They communicate directly with the ROMBIOS of most of these systems.

They plug into the 8/16 bit slots. These cards can be left in the computer and will perform the POST duties. Different cards will also do other jobs related to diagnostics. As time goes by, there will no doubt be many types of adapter cards that will provide more and more diagnostic support. As computers become more and more complex and troubles become harder to pin down, diagnostic cards will become important.

Other available diagnostics

Getting the sick computer to try and figure out what is wrong with itself is an entire category of program writing. Besides the diagnostics, built into ROMs, bundled in disks with your machine, available advanced disks also by your manufacturer, there is a plethora of other diagnostics from independent program writing companies.

First of all, and not to be ignored, are diagnostics in the public domain that are yours for the asking. The way to learn of the diagnostics freely available is to sign on to one of the bulletin boards that supports your machine. The board joins together many interested users of your machine. They will know what diagnostics are around and how you can get hold of them.

Although there are plenty of free diagnostics there are also some that are practically free. These are called *user supported* or *shareware* and you can get a disk for about $5.00 and give it a try. If you are pleased, you can then contribute some money to the author of the program and/or to the bulletin board that put you in touch with the author. There is a lot of friendly help out there. These bulletin board groups can also give you good troubleshooting and other valuable information for the asking.

In addition to the free or nearly free diagnostics that are available, there is some very good programs around you can buy. They are advanced diagnostics, comparable to the best a manufacturer can provide. You can get specific programs that will test memory, run all sorts of tests on floppy and hard drives, ones that will put video boards through its paces, etc.

An even more extensive type of diagnostics are programs that come with their very own computer. The test computer has plug-in processors and other components. The system is actually a dedicated computer tester. It can be used when the subject computer has failed and cannot test itself. This computer tester system can be used while ordinary diagnostics cannot. As you can imagine, these sophisticated test systems are quite expensive. They are used mostly in large computer repair centers where defective motherboards are repaired by the hundreds.

11
The latest chip-changing techniques and desoldering equipment

ONCE YOU PINPOINT A DEFECTIVE CHIP, NOT IN A SOCKET BUT SOLDERED to the print board, you know it must be replaced. It must be desoldered and a new replacement chip resoldered in its place. As you gaze at the miniature component with all the little legs sticking out and neatly soldered to the board, it is obvious that this chip replacement job is going to be a chore.

When the defective chip was originally soldered to the print board in the factory along with all the other chips on the board, the job was typically performed with hardly a human finger touching anything. The board was conceived at one end of an automated assembly line and was born at the other end, handled mostly by robotic machines. The resulting board is layed out precisely and pleasing to the eye. All of the solder connections are perfectly made with just the right amount of heat and solder. Unfortunately, human hands must perform the chip replacement. It is not an easy job, and in order for the replacement to be made successfully, expert techniques and modern soldering equipment must be used.

A close look at a print board reveals it is a laminated plastic board with foil (usually copper) bonded to both sides. A screen pattern is used to apply an etching solution, and all of the copper except the designed wiring is then washed away. Chips are typically mounted on the board in one of two ways. These most popular methods are *through-hole* and *surface mounted*. The through-hole mountings, as the name implies, has holes in the board for the legs of the chips to protrude through. The chips are mounted on one side of the board, the legs stick through to the other side and are soldered to the copper foil on that side. Figure 11-1 shows a typical through-hole chip called a *DIP* (dual inline package).

The other common method has the boards using surface-mounted devices known as *SMD*s. They do not use holes. Instead of holes, solder pads as shown in Fig. 11-2, are used. The SMDs have specially shaped legs that sit on the solder

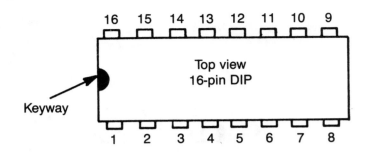

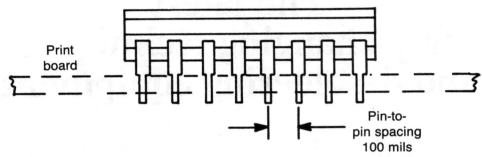

11-1   A chip in a dual inline package is a through-hole type that has its legs poked through holes in the print board. Each pin is soldered to the copper foil connection on the bottom of the board.

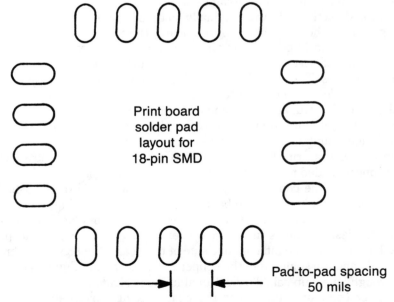

11-2   A chip packaged in a surface-mounted device has its feet standing on solder pads on the top side of the board, instead of poked through holes.

pads as in Figs. 11-3, 11-4, and 11-5. A bit of applied heat to the legs and pads connects the chips solidly. Many boards with solder pads and SMDs are made with chips mounted on both sides of the board. During a chip changing job, you are likely to encounter either a bad DIP-mounted as a through-hole or a defunct SMD

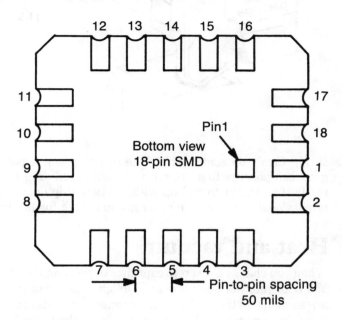

11-3 The bottom side of an SMD has the feet that match up and are soldered to the pads on the top side of the board.

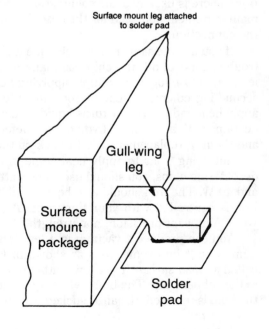

11-4 This SMD foot configuration is called the *gull wing*. It solders easily to the solder pad on the board.

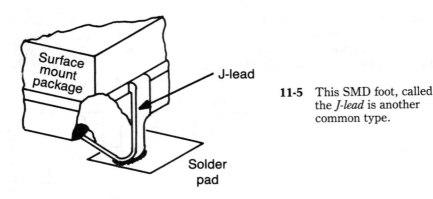

11-5   This SMD foot, called the *J-lead* is another common type.

sitting firmly on solder pads. The bad chip will usually be surrounded by many good components that are not to be disturbed. You have to change the chip correctly if you want to end up with the new chip operating properly. You must use professional techniques in order not to induce further troubles.

Heat and vacuum

When you change a discrete capacitor or resistor, the operation is relatively simple. You take your hot soldering iron, touch it to one of the solder connections, wait a few seconds till the solder on the connection melts, unwrap the lead, and remove it from the connection. The same is done to the second lead, and the component is free. There is usually some solder still sticking harmlessly to the connection. The main ingredient you used for the desoldering job was heat applied from the iron to the connection.

If you use the same rough technique to desolder a chip, you will run smack into trouble. First of all, the chip has many more than two leads. Secondly, the chip leads are close together. Simply applying heat will not do the job. You must use a second ingredient, a vacuum. You cannot leave solder on the connections. As you apply heat and the solder turns liquid, you must suck all the solder off all the connections with a vacuum. If you do, the defective chip will pull easily off the board and the new replacement will fit back on the board easily.

Soldering irons to apply heat come in many sizes and configurations. When desoldering chips, you should use a low wattage iron, for instance, one between 20 and 40 W. The iron should also be a pencil-grip type, not a pistol grip. The pencil iron is controlled with your fingertips. A pistol grip with your entire hand and wrist. You want precision, not strength.

You can produce a vacuum in a few convenient ways. The simplest type vacuum is built into some irons as shown in Fig. 11-6. This heat-vacuum device is called a *solder sucker*. It is a low wattage iron with a hole through its tip that leads to the rubber bulb. The bulb, when squeezed, will pump air out of the hole. When the bulb is released, the air is sucked back into the bulb. If the tip is against molten

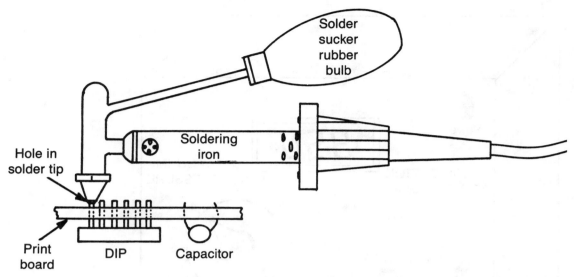

11-6 When desoldering a DIP, good technique dictates that a vacuum must be used to suck all the solder off the connections. A solder sucker like this one can do the job.

solder, the solder will be sucked into the bulb. The vacuum suction does the solder removal job during desoldering.

The solder sucker is very useful and will remove solder during a desoldering job. It is fine for use every now and then. Professionals find a solder sucker iron slow and unwieldy. In a modern repair shop, where a vacuum is needed all day long, there will be vacuum devices that cost hundreds of dollars. Examine the way these heat-vacuum machines do the job.

Replacing a through-hole chip

If you watched a technician remove a DIP from a print board at a solder workstation, he or she would proceed in this manner. On the workbench you'd see a desoldering machine such as Fig. 11-7. There would be one or more receptacles that holds pencil grip low-wattage irons. The irons have hollow, heated tips. The machine has a vacuum pump running constantly that keeps a continuous suction pulling air in through the hollow tip.

The technician applies the tip to a connection. The tip is hot enough to melt the solder on the connection and has suction at the tip to pull all the molten solder into the vacuum chamber. Once in the vacuum chamber, the melted solder is driven into a collection chamber where the solder can harden and safely become a solid once again.

The technician will touch the tip to connection after connection. The joint is heated quickly so the solder melts within three seconds. To ensure a smooth operation at each joint, a good system keeps the tip at a constant temperature. A heat

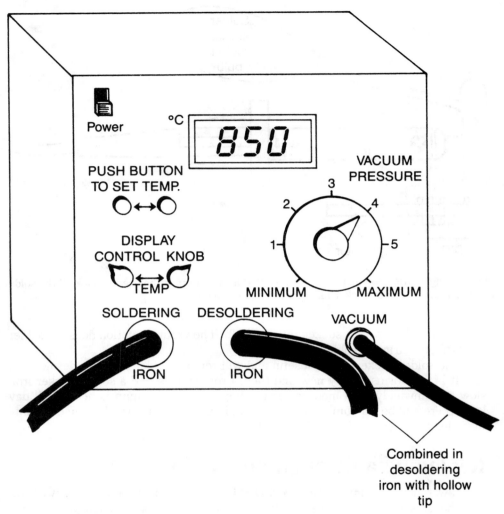

Power

°C

850

PUSH BUTTON
TO SET TEMP.

O↔O

DISPLAY
CONTROL KNOB

TEMP

VACUUM
PRESSURE

3

2   4

1   5

MINIMUM   MAXIMUM

SOLDERING   DESOLDERING   VACUUM

IRON   IRON

Combined in
desoldering
iron with hollow
tip

11-7 Desoldering machines come in many varieties. They are designed to provide correct heating and vacuuming of molten solder.

sensor is installed at the tip that acts as a thermostat that turns the current to the tip off and on. With a constant tip temperature the technician moves carefully from lead to lead heating and sucking solder continually.

The technician will also shake each lead a bit during desoldering. Leads that move are free. The vacuum then pulls air through its hole that cools the joint and prevents the heat from being absorbed into the body of the chip and possibly causing damage.

Although it would be nice to have the use of a desoldering machine just described, the job can still be done at a much slower rate with inexpensive hand tools. With a low wattage iron equipped with a solder sucker, you can heat and vacuum the solder out of each hole. Just place the print board into a comfortable angle with a bright light shining on the bottom of the board focused on the chip to be operated on. The bulb is then squeezed and the hole in the tip of the iron is placed over the first plated through pin. You can see the solder melt. When the solder has turned liquid, release the bulb. The solder at that pin is immediately sucked into the iron and into the bulb. Remove the iron and eject the solder by squeezing the bulb again.

If you are lucky, you will have freed the pin. If the pin is still attached, repeat the process and keep repeating until the pin is free. Once the pin can be wiggled and proves to be free, go to the next pin and free it. Proceed from pin to pin until they are all free. Remove the defective chip. Place the new replacement chip into the open holes. Should one or more of the holes still be clogged with solder, either suck it clean with the iron or just heat the solder and poke the excess out with a toothpick.

The resoldering, in comparison to the desoldering, is relatively easy. Put the new replacement into the holes, making sure the keyway is correct, (they will fit backwards but won't work), put solder sucker aside and use a regular iron of 30 W or less. The solder sucker is only used for desoldering, not resoldering. Apply a tiny bit of solder at each pin. Be careful that the solder doesn't drip or short across the tiny pins. The technique requires sure hands and patience. The desoldering can be tedious, especially the repeated squeezing and releasing of the rubber bulb.

The job isn't too trying with the low count pin DIPs, but as the count goes up (from 20 pins to 30, to 40, to 50, and so on), the tediousness and time-consuming nature of the job increases. It might be a good idea, after you pinpoint a dead DIP with a lot of pins soldered onto the print board, to decide to take the board to a large service shop and let them do the replacement.

Replacing surface-mounted devices

When you open an ailing computer and find it is full of SMDs, and then find a bad one, you have a replacement job on your hands. Since an SMD is soldered to only one side of the print board, you cannot get to the pins from the other side. Furthermore, there could be more SMDs on the other side of the board, making replacement complications multiplied many fold. What can you do?

Start by examining the way SMDs are installed in the first place. Typically a board is first constructed with all the solder pads installed. The pads are known to the technicians in the manufacturing plants as *footprints*. There are footprints for every SMD pin on the board. The pads are purposely made slightly larger than the foot on every pin. There is usually about 10 to 15 mil-inch clearance around every pin. The pins are spaced 50 mils from center to center. The pins have feet such as the gull wing or J-lead, mentioned earlier.

Each footprint is given a layer of solder paste. The paste during manufacturing is usually installed in quantity through a stencil or screen. Often a print board needs to be recycled and have one or more chips replaced. In those cases the solder paste is applied to footprints one at a time with a hand syringe. When you replace solder paste during a chip replacement you can do the same job with a hand syringe.

Whatever, the paste is applied liberally onto the footprints with great care taken so the paste does not run off the pad. The paste serves a double purpose. First of all it aids the smooth flow of solder. Secondly, the paste on the footprint lets the pin foot sink into and stick to the pad. The paste holds the chip in place rather well and the chip won't slide off the pad and onto the bare board during soldering.

Once the paste has been properly applied, the surface-mount device can be placed onto its footprints. In production the devices are installed by robotic pick-and-place machines at rapid speeds. If the board is being recycled and only one or a few chips are being changed, they are carefully placed by a technician by hand. The paste works well. When it is properly applied it will make up for chips that are installed slightly out of place. The paste will tend to make the chip self-align during the next step.

Once the paste and the SMDs are in place it is time to heat the solder pads so the solder will turn into a liquid and flow, connecting the wired up solder pads to the chip leg. When the solder cools and hardens, the chips are firmly installed. The solder should flow up the outside of the leg making a good solid connection.

The heating is conducted in an oven-type machine as seen in Fig. 11-8. The entire board is heated at the same time and all the solder on the board becomes molten and flows simultaneously. In production this is fine as all the chips are connected at the same time. During recycling though, it is not necessary to heat the entire board since most of the chips are already well connected. In manufacturing

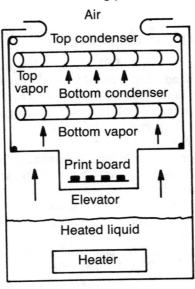

SMD soldering process

11-8   During manufacturing, SMDs can be soldered onto their footprints all in one batch with the use of a special oven. The board full of chips is lowered into hot vapors in the oven on a timed elevator. As soon as the solder flows, the elevator rises and the board is removed and cools down.

plants they could have specially sized conduction soldering irons that will heat up all the pins on one chip at the same time. That way individual chips can be installed. These same special irons could also have a set of tongs to grasp the chip. This is handy for desoldering. That way they could heat all the pins at the same time and then lift the desoldered chip up and away with the tongs.

At any rate, getting back to the soldering of a full SMD board, in the oven is an elevator. In order to heat the board the elevator is able to descend into the heated oven environment at a carefully calculated rate of speed, pass through two layers of special vapors, and then arrive at the bottom of the elevator shaft. The temperature in the bottom vapor is about 215 degrees Celsius. At the bottom a timer keeps the board still for between 10 – 30 seconds. The solder flows. The board is then raised back up to the top vapor layer where the molten solder becomes a solid once again. The legs are now securely connected to the footprints. The finished board is then removed from the oven area.

After the process the board is given a thorough cleaning to remove all of the solder flux that remains. The cleaning is performed with cleaning solvents that will take off all the residue and provide the components with good clearance between all connections. Now that you know how SMDs are installed in the factory, both a board at a time or individually, see what can be done to take them off and then reinstall them on your bench.

The solder sucker and other vacuum soldering machines aided in the removal of DIPs. They are not much help with the desoldering of SMDs. The tools needed for SMDs are lengths of solder braid, quantities of rosin, a fine-tipped low-wattage iron and a fine solder pick or small, sharp pocket-knife edges. Lastly, plenty of patience.

When the time arrives to desolder an SMD, position it in a bright light, flat on the bench top. Take a length of solder braid or solder wick and put generous amounts of rosin on the piece. Carefully place the solder braid across the pins on one of the four sides of the chip to be removed as in Fig. 11-9. Take the heated iron and place it against the braid. The braid will heat up and in turn the solder on the pins under the braid will become molten.

With the aid of the rosin, the braid starts soaking up the molten solder by capillary action. Rub the braid a bit on the pins to soak up as much of the solder as possible. When the braid becomes full of solder remove it from the pins. Snip off the section of the braid that is soaked with solder and continue with a new section of braid.

Work round and round the SMD carefully. You don't want to cause any heat problems or short excess solder across connections. Also, you do not want to ruin any solder pads or other print board wiring or components. Also, you don't want to kill the SMD in case it isn't defective after all. When you have soaked off as much solder as possible, you can stop using the solder braid.

Even with most of the solder removed, the SMD pins will still be sticking to the pads. However, they are now easily removed. With your fine-tipped iron and the solder pick heat each pin and pry it off the pad as the solder flows. Take your time and make sure each is free before starting on the next one. After awhile you'll

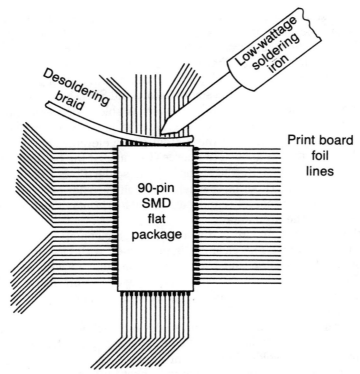

11-9 The key to successful desoldering of SMDs is to sop up most of the solder with desoldering braid or wick. The solder is absorbed into the braid by capillary action.

have freed all the pins. The SMD can be lifted off. Before lifting though, make a note of the position of the keyway and pin locations.

To install the replacement SMD, the process is much easier. It is a good idea if you apply tiny dots of solder paste with a hand syringe onto the footprints as the factory technicians do. Then place the new chip into place pin for pin. Take your iron and solder one of the pins at or near a corner. Then do the other four corners. This tacks the chip down solidly. Finally with great care, solder all the pins into place. If you didn't accidentally cause any shorts, opens, or damage, the SMD replacement should be complete.

Latest professional SMD techniques

The manual techniques needed to desolder and then resolder SMDs to pads on a print board, just described, are rough and ready. They will work though, when performed by an experienced technician with good hand-to-eye coordination. They are also slow, ticklish, and dangerous because SMDs by their very nature are built with tiny spaces between legs and miniscule leads from the legs to the microscopic circuits on the chip. They are more subject to thermal shock from overheating than DIPs.

There are many different shapes of soldering tips to fit the different pin layouts in SMDs. With these handy tips, many pins can be grasped and heated at the same time. These tips get very hot and can provide continuous heat. As a result, when these multiple-pin soldering tips are applied to a group of SMD pins, the heat travels to the circuits too quickly and can often cause damage. The damage to a bad chip being desoldered and to be discarded is not a problem, but damage to the new replacement chip is serious. Also damage to nearby good components in closely spaced circuit boards is also serious.

The answer to this heat-shock problem is to use a heat source that does not provide continuous heat. A foot switch that the technician can use to heat the soldering tip is the answer. For example, the soldering iron when not being applied to SMD pins is not energized and is cool. When it is time to heat pins and melt solder, the technician carefully places the tip onto the pins to be heated. As the technician watches the tip against the pin and the solder that is binding the pin to the print board, he or she presses the foot switch. The tip then gets hot. As the solder melts, and the pin is freed, the technician takes his foot off the switch. The tip immediately cools down.

In that way, a hot tip is not applied until the technician is in complete control. Only the amount of heat that is needed to melt the solder is gradually applied to the pins. There is no sudden heat shock into the circuits. Then, when the solder melts, the heat is removed as the foot switch is released. The pins rapidly cool down.

As mentioned, there is a large assortment of soldering tips for these SMD foot-switch controlled machines. These tips are custom designed for the different types of SMD designs. The tips not only can heat many pins at the same time, they are also made to be able to grab the pins and apply small amounts of pressure. That way, these tips can grab a group of pins while the tip is still cold. Then when the technician steps down on the foot pedal, the tip gradually heats up. The tips are made of a material that will not stick to the pins.

As the solder melts and the technician releases the foot switch, the cooling tip can still hold the pins in place. This makes sure that the pins remain on their respective board pads and do not slide off the pads and cause all sorts of problems.

If you are interested in repairing many SMD loaded print boards on a daily basis as in a large service shop, these professional soldering workstations are a must. This presentation is only an overview of what is available. Desoldering and resoldering integrated chip packages to a print board is tricky business and demands technique and good equipment.

Board swapping

As described, testing print boards and then replacing defective micro-components in the field can be a very difficult if not impossible job except for the most expert, lavishly equipped technicians. As a result, most boards that fail in the field are usually swapped if a replacement board is readily available. For example, in a factory service department, the technicians are separated into two groups. Number one is the field service people. They are equipped with the latest in electronic service tools. In addition they are given a stock of known good print boards for the computers they will be servicing in the course of their day. Some of the boards are cards with a few chips while others can be motherboards with a hundred or more chips of all sizes and package types.

The second group of technicians are the bench people. These persons are the elite; they are the ones with the best troubleshooting and repair skills. Among them are some super elite. These are the ones who are print-board artisans. They usually are the people who are able to desolder quickly and then resolder large pin count chips in DIP and SMD packages. About all they do all day is replace difficult chips.

When a computer system breaks down a field technician is dispatched. The technician arrives at a computer site and analyzes the trouble. He or she is usually able to isolate the seat of the trouble to a single print board. Once a print board is identified as containing the defect, without further ado, the technician removes the suspect board and replaces it with a known good board. If the trouble was indeed in the suspect board, the computer starts working again. The technician leaves and goes on to the next service call.

That evening, upon return to the shop, the technician places the inoperative board into the factory servicing line. Later on, a bench technician checks out the board with the special factory servicing equipment. The bad chip is pinpointed. If the technician is good enough, he or she will go ahead and install a new chip. If the job is too much, the job goes to one of the technicians with the artisan skills. The technician changes the chip, the board is thoroughly tested for quality and reliability and is then given to the parts department as a known good replacement.

As you can imagine, this complete procedure is very expensive and time consuming. However, computer downtime can mean a disaster for a user. With this arrangement, a computer system that breaks down is back up and running in the least amount of time.

Board swapping, with a shop backup, is the main way bad chips are located and replaced. You can go this route if you must get a computer up and running at once. Whether time is of the essence or not, if you pinpoint a large pin count chip as the culprit and it is not in a socket, having the factory service operation do the chip replacement is probably the best way to go.

If you can determine which board has the bad chip during a bout of trouble, you can probably eliminate the need for a field technician. You could remove the board, take it to a factory service outlet and work something out with them. They might repair your board while you wait or perhaps service it overnight. They could give you an allowance for your defective board and make some sort of swap with you. Most computer dealers and the factory-type services they use are usually cooperative and want your system back on line as soon as possible. With a bit of tact and some electronic skill, you can usually get them to help you without undue expense.

Static electricity considerations

ESD (electrostatic discharge) is a main worry when chips are replaced. As Fig. 11-10 shows, there is a sensitive glassy insulator between the gate lead of an IGFET and the substrate. This insulator is the weak link in the FET. It will blow if it receives a shot of ESD. In chips, especially DRAMs, there are thousands upon thousands of these FETs equipped with these glass insulators. You *must* take precautions to defend these chips from static electricity.

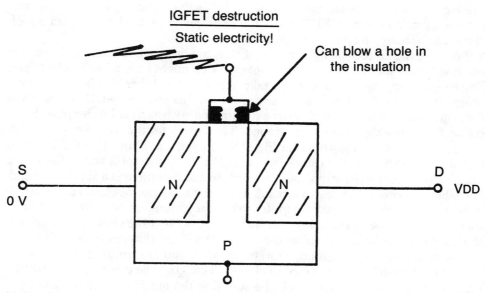

11-10 On a chip can be thousands upon thousands of these IGFETs. Each one has a microscopic piece of glassy insulation between the gate electrode and the channel. If one is shorted through by static electricity, the entire chip could be ruined.

A few years ago, the DRAM chips (like the 4K types), only had a few thousand FETs on the substrate. The spacing between leads of these FETs were about five microns wide. Today, on about the same size chips there are more than a million FETs on the 1 megabit DRAMs. The lead spacing has been reduced to less than one micron. As a result, the metallization between the FETs has also become vulnerable to electric shocks. It so happens that the smaller the sizes of features of the FETs on the chips, the more sensitive these chips are to ESD. Great care must be taken during chip replacement jobs. The handling techniques have been delineated by manufacturers. You must follow their instructions or you will cause yourself a lot of trouble.

Your body at all times, contains at least 100 or 200 V of static electricity potential. On a wet, humid day, there will be a minimum of about 100 V. On a dry day, the potential increases as you move around and brush your clothes against furniture, walls, the floor, and even the dry air itself, you can build up your personal static charge to a thousand volts or more. As you walk across a thick carpet, on a cold, dry day with low humidity and throw a spark at a doorknob, that shock could easily be measured in thousands of volts. If a spark like this is passed through a chip during handling, odds of that chip surviving the ESD are not very good.

While a chip is residing on a print board, soldered securely in the circuit, it is fairly safe. Its pins are connected securely to the chassis ground and other secure circuits. It is energized as designed and there is very little chance of some ESD gaining access to the insulated gates of the FETs. The glassy gate insulators and the metallization between FETs though, are placed in peril when handled out-of-circuit. Especially on dry, low-humidity days.

A professional technician is aware of the chip destruction static charges that could suddenly kill the new replacement chip that might have taken weeks to get. Before unpackaging the new chip, take measures to lower the inherent static charge in your body, down to as close to zero volts as you can get. Zero volts is at earth ground. Connect yourself to an earth ground such as a cold water pipe. Next, connect your workbench to earth ground. Then reach for the wrist strap.

The wrist strap, illustrated in Fig. 11-11, comes in a kit. The RCA type is called their Antistatic Kit (Stock No. 162351); it consists of a static dissipative mat, a lightweight wrist strap, and coil cord. In addition there is a six-foot grounding cable that connects to earth ground. The wrist strap can be connected to either wrist although some technicians prefer to put the grounding bracelet on the hand they hold the probe or soldering iron with. They say that the closer the strap is to the hand that works on the chips, the less ESD will get through to the chips.

Because you will be grounded to earth while you are working, you must be careful not to touch any open electrical lines. That could be dangerous. To further ensure that your grounding is safe, be sure that the outside of the wrist strap is insulated. In addition, there must be a resistor, such as 1 mΩ connected in series with the ground line at the wrist strap connection. That way, if you should cross a live electric line, the resistor will get zapped and not you.

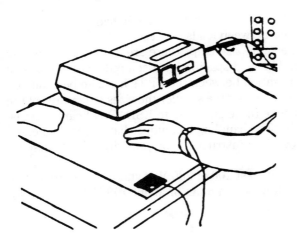

11-11 When handling FET components, everything that comes in contact with the chip must be grounded. An antistatic kit that has grounded wrist straps, ground connections for the service bench, will usually do the job.

There are a few more safety rules that will protect both you and the equipment you are working on:

- Never insert or remove a device from circuits unless the power to the circuits is off and the plug of the circuit is pulled out of electrical outlets.
- During the handling of chips, keep the chip in the conductive foam pad it came in. This keeps all the pins of the chips shorted together, which is the safest way for them to be, out-of-circuit.
- The chip must only be handled by the hand that is grounded with the bracelet grounding arrangement.
- All tools that contact the chip must be grounded at the time of contact. This includes chip pullers, chip inserters, pliers, screwdrivers, etc.

The soldering iron must have its tip grounded. The iron should have its plug pulled during the time the solder is heated or any time the iron touches the pins of the chip. This eliminates the possibility of the arc from the power company damaging the chip.

12
Block diagram of a typical personal computer

WHEN YOU THINK OF A COMPUTER SYSTEM IN BLOCK FORM, THINK OF THE middle block as you. Your very own personal computer is an extension of your brain. You connect up to the computer by placing your fingertips on a keyboard and focusing your eyes on the TV display screen. You input your thoughts to the computer through the keyboard. The computer outputs to your eyes after it processes your inputs.

What does this handy brain extension do? Nothing you couldn't eventually do without it. What is the computer's value? It processes your thinking fast! In seconds, it can output the answer to a problem that would take you years to work out with paper and pencil.

When you need the aid of your computer and hook into its system, you must convert your thinking to a step-by-step program in the mathematical, computer language of ones, zeros, and pulses. Of course, you can also buy ready-made programs that are designed to do your bidding. Either way, the job you want done is converted to what the computer can understand as you type letters, numbers, and symbols. The computer can then be commanded to run the program. After the program is processed, the computer then converts the ones, zeros, and pulses back to letters, numbers, symbols, or graphics. This output is then displayed on the TV screen. You read the output and receive the solutions to your problems. In this way, you are part of a closed-circuit computer system.

When you look at the vast array of available computers, 8-bit, 16-bit, 32-bit and higher, with processing speeds of 1, 6 – 12, 20, or 33 MhzH(and higher), with memories of 64, 128, 512, 640K, 1, or 8 Mb (and higher), with floppy disk drives, hard drives, monochrome and color displays with ever higher resolutions, with larger and larger processors and their hordes of support chips, and so on, your head swims. However, no matter the computer system, large or small, a computer is a computer; and they all work and fail in about the same way. The basic computer in all units, no matter what the special needs and equipment required, remains the same. Figure 12-1 is a block diagram that, in general, describes all of today's computers. The computer forms a digital world when it possesses input and output circuits to communicate with your world, a microprocessor to manipulate the ones, zeros, and pulses, and a memory to store the ones and zeros.

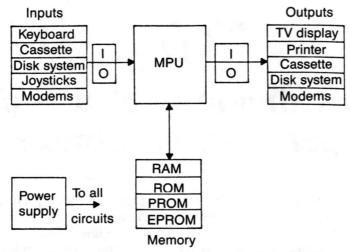

12-1   All personal computers are essentially the same. They consist of various input and output devices that connect to the internal digital circuits through I/O chips. The internal digital circuits are based around a microprocessor unit, sets of RAM, and another set of ROMs. All circuits are energized by a power supply.

A simple computer block diagram

A processor by itself can be a computer. A piece of electronic gear without a processor is not a computer. It follows that the processor is the most important part of the computer. It sits in the center of the action and performs. A processor connects to the rest of the computer through three bus lines. They are the address bus, the data bus, and the assorted control lines that can be called the control bus.

The MPU connects to the registers of the memory map (Fig. 12-2). The memory map is like a telephone directory (Fig. 12-3) that lists the addresses of the registers in numerical order. All of the registers do not have to be in the computer, but the memory map lists the numbers whether they contain physical locations or are empty.

If you think of the memory map as row after row of registers, the address bus connects to every register and can contact each register. Each register contains eight bit holders. Each bit holder is numbered from 0 to 7. All of the same number bit holders are connected to the data bus lines D0 – D7.

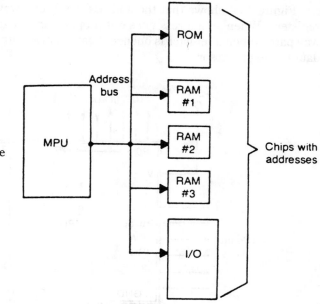

12-2 The MPU connects to all the circuits with addresses. They are the ROM, RAM, and I/O chips.

Memory Map

Decimal address	Hex address	Resident of address
0 to 1023	0000 to 03FF	Housekeeper
1024 to 1535	0400 to 05FF	Video RAM
1536 to 16383	0600 to 3FFF	RAM
16384 to 32767	4000 to 7FFF	Expansion RAM
32768 to 40959	8000 to 9FFF	Expansion ROM
40960 to 49151	A000 to BFFF	Operating ROM
49152 to 65279	C000 to FEFF	Cartridge ROM
65280 to 65535	FF00 to FFFF	I/O devices

12-3 An 8-bit processor is able to address 64K registers. The addresses are listed in decimal, hex, or both.

Figure 12-4 shows that the address bus is one way from the processor to the registers. When an address goes out it opens up a register. The data bus is a two way path. When a register is opened it can receive data from the processor or send data to the processor.

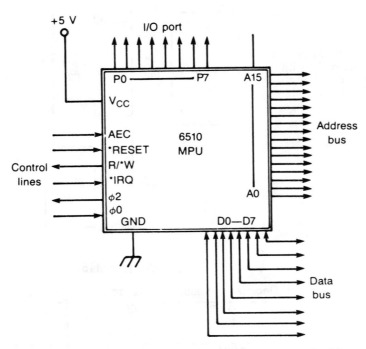

12-4   The lines that connect to the MPU are the one-way address bus, the two-way data bus, and the group of control lines.

The control lines are a potpourri of connections that perform a number of jobs. The bus lines are discussed in more detail in the next few chapters.

Registers in the memory map can be in RAM, ROM, I/O chips or others. Any chips that can be addressed by the processor are said to be memory mapped. The RAM is used to warehouse bytes and bits. Most of the activity that takes place in the computer is the transferring of highs and lows back and forth between the processor and RAM. ROM is used to store the operating system and language interpreters for the computer. The ROM is constantly read to get the instructions to run the programs.

The registers in the I/O chips are used to interface with the peripherals the computer needs to work with. For instance, one set of I/O registers can be assigned to bring the bits you generate on the keyboard to the processor. Another set of I/O registers can be used to output bits the computer produces, to a printer. Other I/O registers can input the results of an analog-to-digital converter. Still more I/O registers input and output to and from the cassette and disk drives.

The video output system and the audio output circuits might or might not be memory mapped. When they are the registers in these type chips are used to output to the TV display and an audio system.

That is all there is to the overview of a simple computer. In general, a key strike you make on a keyboard will travel the following path and encounter these chips and registers. Suppose you hit a key. The keyboard is a group of on-off switches. For instance, there could be 64 switches arranged in an 8 × 8 switch matrix (Fig. 12-5). When you strike the key you close one switch. That switch generates its own set of bits.

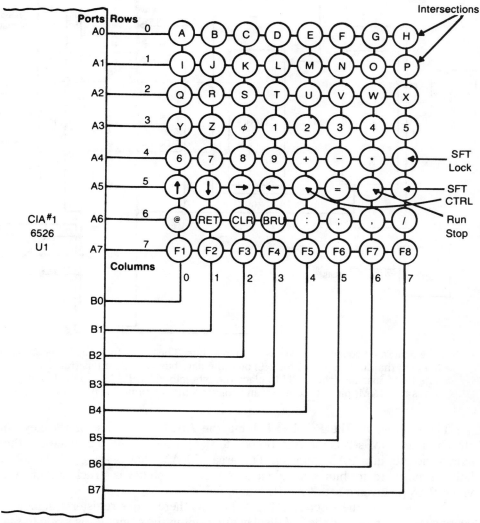

12-5 In an 8 × 8 keyboard matrix, there are eight rows and eight columns that produce 64 intersections. When a key is pressed, an intersection is shorted, and the character at that key is generated.

The bits are connected to a register in an I/O chip, like a PIA (Fig. 12-6). The register transfers the bits to the data bus. The data bus takes the bits to the processor. The processor in turn uses the bits to form an address on a ROM.

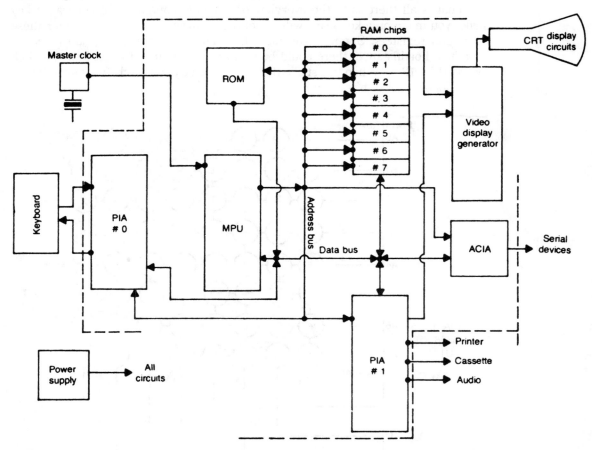

12-6 The generated coded character is a group of bits. These bits from the keyboard are connected to an I/O chip that in turn places the bits onto the data bus. The data bus transfers the bits to the MPU. The ROM instructs the MPU to place the bits into video RAM. The video display generator then scans the RAM, picks up the bits and converts them to images on the CRT display.

The address on the ROM is holding the ASCII code bits for the key you struck. The ROM sends the ASCII code to the processor and the processor then stores the bits in a RAM register. The area of RAM that is assigned the job of holding the character bits is called video RAM. As each key is struck, a register in video RAM is given a set of ASCII bits to hold.

As mentioned, the video RAM is laid out so there is one register assigned for every character space on the TV display. A circuit in the computer is made to scan the video RAM sixty times a second. The scanning picks up the ASCII bits in the video RAM and sends them to the video output circuits. They in turn produce a character pattern. The pattern is a group of highs and lows from a character ROM. A high lights a dot on the screen while a low extinguishes a dot of light. The pattern is sent to the TV display and the display is updated sixty times a second. The contents of video RAM is therefore always on exhibit in the TV picture.

The character you struck has to follow a complicated maze until it is stored in the video RAM and displayed on the TV screen. The bits that were generated from the keyboard strike have been transferred, coded, stored, scanned, decoded, recoded, and finally displayed.

Additional outputs

In addition to printing the keyboard symbols on the TV screen, the computer has many other outputs. The processor can send those same video RAM bytes to another I/O chip. This chip can then send the RAM bytes to a printer. The printer, which is a computer in its own right, takes the bytes and produces hard copy.

The output of the I/O chip can be sent to a digital-to-analog converter. The converter can then output to a cassette. The processor can send bytes directly over the data bus to an audio output chip without storing the bytes in video RAM.

In general, that is the way your computer can take key strikes, joystick inputs, cassette and disk drive inputs, and other forms of signals from the outside world into the digital world, process them, and then output the signals to the outside world once again. The outputs go to TV displays, line printers, cassettes, disks, loudspeakers, and other devices that require control.

When you look down at the print board after you familiarize yourself with the location of the chips, you should be able to visualize the block diagram of the board. This means you can physically see where the keyboard and other inputs are entering the computer. You should also see the I/O chips, the address and data bus lines, the set of RAM and ROM chips, the video output chips and any others in the digital world. These chips and buses will have a lot of meaning to you if you are familiar with the devices in the block diagram of your machine.

The block diagram shown in this chapter is typical of the inexpensive, single board, 8-bit processor, personal computers that are being sold. These computers are exemplified by the Apple II, Radio Shack Color Computer, the Commodore 64 types, the small Atari, and so forth. The section that follows, exhibits the so-called 16-bit computer. When IBM came out with their PC, they set a standard. Practically all of the other computer makers came out with some sort of compatible machine. The block diagram of the next section and the devices in the blocks are the kind of electronics you will find in these more expensive personal computers.

The IBM and its clones

The IBM PC (Fig. 12-7) is the standard. The clones all copy the PC's general layout to a more or less degree. They all have a boxlike housing that contains their main electronics and the disk drives. On top of the electronics housing sits the monitor and in front of the housing lies the keyboard.

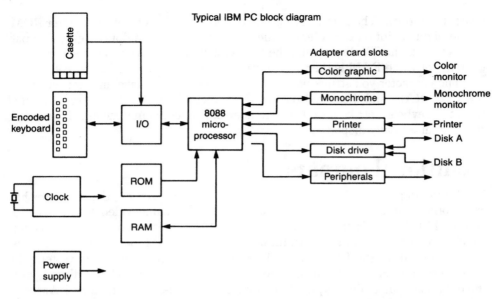

12-7 The typical IBM PC board layout consists of an encoded keyboard, the usual I/O, MPU, RAM chips, and ROM chips. In addition, there are the 62-pin slots wired in parallel that provide convenient connections to all the rest of the required circuit boards.

The keyboard is detachable and is a computer in its own right. It is a fully encoded keyboard. In the keyboard housing are computer circuits including a processor and a character ROM. When you press a key, the circuits in the keyboard do not simply form some bits that designate a particular key as in a nonencoded keyboard. The key strike causes the encoded circuits to generate the ASCII code for the key.

The big advantage that the encoded keyboard has over the nonencoded type is the number of keys. In the nonencoded keyboard the number of keys are somewhat restricted to 64. The keyboard works with an I/O chip that has two registers, one connected to the keyboard rows and the other to the keyboard columns. This forms a matrix of 8 × 8, totaling 64 possible keys.

An encoded keyboard is on its own and does not need to work in conjunction with the main computer circuits. As a result, it can have as many keys as it wants. In the IBM PC there are 83 keys that can generate all 128 ASCII characters and a grand total of 256 symbols and graphic shapes.

The keyboard feeds its ASCII output to the main housing. Inside the main housing is the large print board, a metal shield that contains the power supply and the disk drive or drives. The large print board has about 100 chips mounted on it and the IBM machine has five slots each with 62 connections. The slots are all wired in parallel so that any appropriate 62-pin print board will plug into any slot. The internal programming chooses a particular print board even if they are all wired in parallel. These cards add the peripherals to the computer. For example, there is a disk controller card that connects the disk drives to the main computer board. Then there is a monochrome adapter and parallel printer card. It adds the TV monitor and a parallel printer to the main board. A third card is a color/graphics adapter. It adds the ability to use a color monitor and graphics in color.

In addition to these cards there are many more made by many different manufacturers. The 62-pin slots provide the basic computer with many types of expansions. A modem can be plugged into a slot, additional external disk drives, voice recognition systems, additional memory, additional printers, and any peripheral with a properly designed card.

As a result of this layout, the IBM PC and its clone systems consist of separate encoded keyboards, a large main board and five expansion slots. The system is best described with separate diagrams, one for the keyboard and one for the main board. Let's examine some typical diagrams of the system.

The encoded keyboard

The typical encoded keyboard for these personal computers has five connections on the output plug (Fig. 12-8). Two of them are +5 V and ground. The other three are the interface between the keyboard and the main board. In the IBM PC a special keyboard processor, an 8048 chip is used. The 8048 is an 8-bit processor and contains 2K bytes of ROM. In the ROM is a special character code called a scan code.

The processor uses what is known as rowscanning on the keyboard matrix. Each key is physically connected to one of the row-column intersections. There are 96 intersections in the matrix. When you strike a key you cause one of the intersections to short-circuit.

Meanwhile the 8048 processor is scanning the rows for key strikes by outputting a high to each of the columns, one at a time. It scans the matrix once every 5 milliseconds, which is much faster than the best typist in the world. The 8048 receives a high from each row as long as a key has not been pressed. These highs are stored in a special scanning buffer register in the 8048.

When a key is struck and the intersection shorted, the high is changed to a low. The 8048 knows which column has been scanned at that time. It also receives a low from the row that was shorted. The knowledge of the column and the row pinpoints the intersection that was shorted. The 8048 immediately goes to its character ROM and generates a scan code for the intersection. It then outputs the scan code bits to the keyboard interface plug. The data goes into the main board circuits to the 8088 processor in the machine where it is then further processed.

If you look inside the keyboard, you'll find a print board with the row-column matrix and a bunch of electronic components such as chips and some discrete items. It happens to be a relatively simple circuit arrangement.

Figure 12-8 shows the keyboard logic layout. The chip is the 8048 processor. The chip has internal clock circuits, except for the crystal of the clock. The crystal is connected across X1 and X2. A couple of tiny bypass capacitors are also attached to those pins. The clock signal is generated, runs the processor and is also

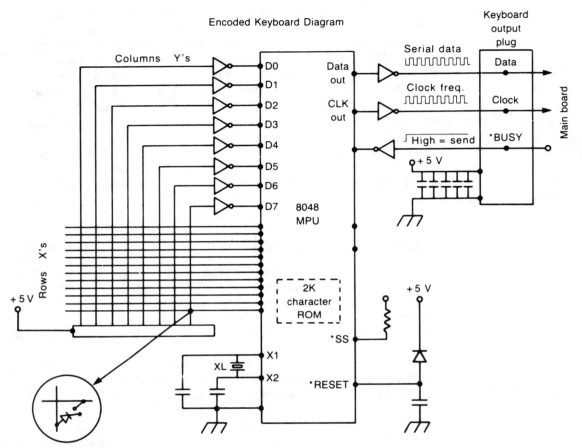

12-8 An encoded keyboard has its own microprocessor chip that contains a ROM character generator. It outputs actual ASCII bits rather than some code bits that must be converted as a nonencoded keyboard does.

output from the clock output pin to the main board. The clock output syncs the keyboard with the main board because they are essentially separate entities.

The matrix has rows and columns. The rows are labeled x's and the columns are the y's. Note there are 12 rows and eight columns. The rows, the x's, are held high with +5 V through a pullup resistor. The columns all have inverter amplifiers in their lines to couple the outputs to the buffer register. The rows are constantly scanned by the 8048 internal circuits. As long as a key is not struck the columns output highs into the buffer register of the 8048. As long as the register reads all highs nothing is output from the keyboard assembly.

As soon as a key is struck, the output where the key is located, changes its output to a low. The buffer register contents changes. The 8048 senses which row it had just scanned at that instant. The intersection is located. The 8048 goes to its internal character ROM and outputs a set of bits for the key strike. The set of bits leaves the 8048 and is input to the main board in a serial form.

Note the data output line and the clock output line both have a NOT gate in series pointing to the main board. The gate inverts the output and amplifies it so it is strong enough to drive the main board input circuits.

The third line is called BUSY, and it is a return line from the main board to the keyboard. It also has an inverter in its line. The BUSY signal lets the 8048 know when it is o.k. to send data or when not to send data, in case the main board is busy and can't take the data at that time. If the BUSY signal is high, the data can be sent. A low on the BUSY line stops the data from going to the main board.

The diagram shows a ground pin, some other power +5 V pins and a reset pin. The encoded keyboard is a small circuit. The only complex circuitry is inside the 8048 processor.

Debouncing problems

There is a troubleshooting phenomena that occurs whenever you strike a key. As you press the key and the bottom of the key closes onto the matrix metal connection, you create a tiny oscillator circuit for a few milliseconds. The high that is on the matrix point falls to a low, but when it hits zero volts, it bounces back up. It doesn't go all the way back to +5 V but it does rise most of the way there. It can't hold and falls again. It hits bottom again and bounces up again but not quite as high. It keeps doing that like a rubber ball until it finally stops and holds the zero volts.

When you let the key loose and go to the next one, the matrix point is pulled back up to the +5 V once again. The voltage hits +5 V and bounces back down. It repeats the bouncing only upside-down until it stabilizes once again at +5 V.

A complete key strike then happens like the following. You hit a key, the short makes the +5 V on the matrix point drop to 0 V. The voltage bounces a few milliseconds and then stabilizes at zero volts. Then there is a stable period of zero volts that stores the output in the buffer. After the subtle period you release the key and the matrix point voltage rises to +5 V. It bounces a few more milliseconds and then stabilizes once again at +5 V.

This could be a serious condition if not considered. In nonencoded keyboards a resistor and capacitor are wired as an RC filter. It smooths out the oscillations and kills the bouncing effect. In encoded keyboards (like the IBM and its clones) a short delay of a few milliseconds is used before the key strike is encoded. The delay is a programmed loop that is inserted to shut off the key action during the bouncing. Aptly it is called debouncing. The 8048 performs the debouncing by generating a delay and an interrupt during the time the keyboard voltage is bouncing.

The main board input

The keyboard outputs a serial data signal to the IBM type PCs and a clock signal. The main board (Fig. 12-9) sends a busy signal to the keyboard to let it know when it can send keyboard bits to the main board. The keyboard bits are sent serially, the least significant bit first and the most significant bit last. Each bit is 1/10th of a millisecond wide.

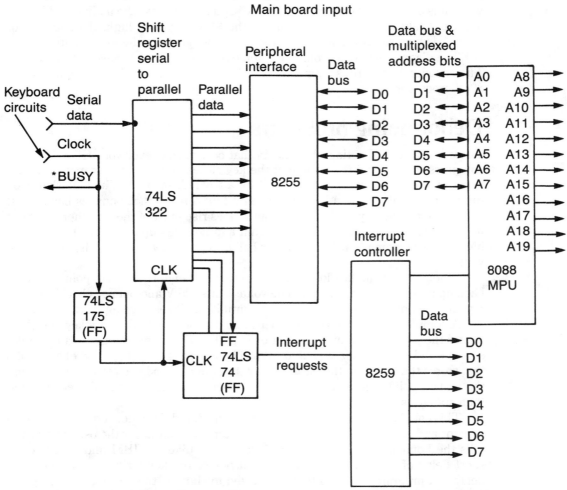

12-9 The three connections to the main board from the keyboard, are inputs of serial data, clock pulses, and an output control signal back to the keyboard called *BUSY. The serial data is converted to parallel and placed on the data bus. The clock pulses are transferred to a flip-flop, which is in the sync circuits.

The code is sent to a serial-to-parallel 74LS322 register. The serial code is changed from a serial format to parallel. The 74LS322 output is sent to a dual-D flip-flop, the 74LS74.

The clock signal is transferred from the 74LS175 to the serial/parallel register and the 74LS74 at the same time to get the main board in sync with the keyboard inputs. At this point in time, your keyboard strike has generated a scan code and a clock signal. The two signals were transferred from the keyboard assembly to the input chips of the main board. One input chip, the 74LS322, changed the serial input to parallel and a second input chip, the 74LS175 got the entire system synced to handle the incoming bits.

Each of the chips sends an output signal to the 74LS74 flip-flop. After the signals are input, and the clock causes the FF to change states, the FF generates a special signal called an interrupt. The interrupt bit is transferred to an 8259 chip. The 8259 is a programmable interrupt controller. It, in turn, generates its own output, the interrupt bit that the main processor, the 8088, can use.

Meanwhile back at the 74LS322, the shift register, parallel bits are output onto one of the ports of the 8255 I/O chips. The parallel bits then pass through the port chip and are let out onto the system data bus. Once on the bus the bits are read by the 8088 processor and stored in video RAM. From RAM the bits can be coded for display or for printing on paper.

The rest of the main board contains 36 chips to handle RAM, support chips to produce clock signals, a set of chips to handle the ROM chores and the I/O chips to adapt the computer to all the peripherals. The next nine chapters go into details on all these subsystems.

13
Clocks

THE COMPUTER CLOCK IS THE PACEMAKER OF THE PROCESSOR. IT RUNS AT an assigned frequency and this frequency can be likened to the cadence of a drill instructor. All of the marching through the circuits the highs and lows do, is done in step with the clock.

The clock consists of a crystal-controlled oscillator circuit. In some personal computers the clock circuit is configured out of a group of chips and discrete components. In other computers the clock circuit is contained in the processor chip itself. However, the crystal cannot be contained in the chip but is an external device that is connected to a pair of processor pins. The processor pins that hold the crystal are usually called X1 and X2, as shown in Fig. 12-8.

The clock is set to run at a particular fixed frequency. Different manufacturers cut their crystals to ring at a prescribed frequency to suit their machine. Just as a motor is made to rotate at some desired rpm and keep equipment operating, clocks are designed to run at a needed megahertz frequency and keep the computer processing data. The continuous output wave shape from the clock drives the highs and lows from place to place in the digital circuits.

The crystal oscillator is an analog circuit and produces a continuous sine-wave output. The sine wave won't work in a digital circuit because it is continuous. It goes from high to low in a gradual way. The sine wave must be converted to a square wave. The square wave goes from high to low in practically no time at all. The highs and lows are clearly defined.

Therefore, the sine wave (Fig. 13-1) is pumped into a digital converter circuit where the gradual movement from high to low and back is converted into square wave digital pulses. The square wave has those clearly defined highs and lows plus sharp rising edges and falling edges. The sharp edges can be used to trigger off all sorts of circuits.

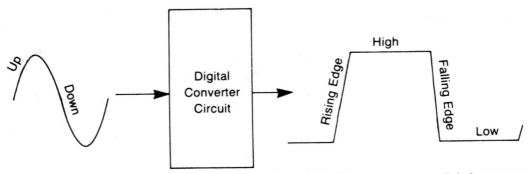

13-1 The crystal oscillator produces an analog sine wave that is pumped into a digital converter circuit where it is converted to a square wave. The smooth up-and-down motion of the sine wave is changed to a square wave with a rising edge, a high, a falling edge, and a low.

In different computers, different clock frequencies are used. In small inexpensive computers, a typical basic running frequency is about 1 megahertz. In larger computers the running frequency could be higher, running at 25 MHz and above. The faster the running frequency, the faster the data will be processed. The clock does not have to run at the computer's frequency. The computer's frequency is derived from the clock frequency.

For example, a common crystal used in small personal computers, is cut to oscillate at 14.31818 MHz (Fig. 13-2). This is the master frequency. That number has been picked because the color TV frequency is 3.579545 MHz and 14.31818/ 3.579545 = 4. This color oscillator frequency has been preordained by your color TV. If you want to use your personal computer with your color TV as the display, the color oscillator frequency makes it compatible.

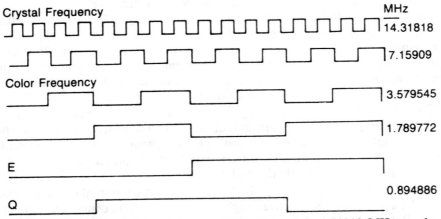

13-2 A square wave with master crystal frequency of 14.31818 MHz can be divided into many lower frequencies, including the 3.579545 TV color frequency.

The rest of the frequencies in the computer are not so restricted. They can be within wide parameters. The 14.31818 MHz can be divided by 16 to produce the running frequency around 1 MHz. To be exact the 14.31818/6 = 0.89 MHz, but that is close enough to 1 MHz to be used without any complications. The other frequencies used by the computer are also satisfactory. It is not necessary to round them off.

In some computers the clock oscillator circuit can be made up of discrete components. The oscillator circuit can consist of a crystal cut to run at 12.288 MHz and some serial and parallel resistors and capacitors (Fig. 13-3). The oscillator will start running when voltage is impressed on the sides of the crystal. The components are there to stabilize the frequency.

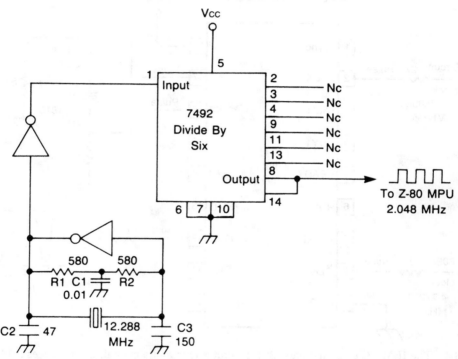

13-3   The old Z-80 processor clock had a master frequency of 12.288 MHz. The two NOT gates are able to convert the sine wave to a square wave.

Across the crystal is a NOT gate. When the circuit is turned on, the NOT gate will receive the sine wave that is generated and turn on and off at the peaks of the sine wave. The NOT gate in turn outputs to a second NOT gate. The second gate acts as a NOT switch. It will go off and on as the first NOT gates the highs and lows to it. The output of the second NOT gate is a square wave. The two NOT gates are an efficient square-wave generator.

Once the 12.288 MHz square wave is produced it is fed into a 7492 chip. The chip is a 4-bit counter. Inside the chip the frequency is divided by six. The output of the counter is a square wave with a 2.048 MHz frequency. This is fed to a Z-80 processor and is the driving force of the 8-bit system.

In newer 16-bit systems like the IBM PC family (Fig. 13-4), the clock components are usually either in the processor itself or in a clock generator chip such as the 8284. When the clock circuits are in the processor, you'll find two pins named X1 and X2, where the crystal is connected. When a clock generator chip is used, the chip often produces all the frequencies needed and distributes them to the rest of the machine.

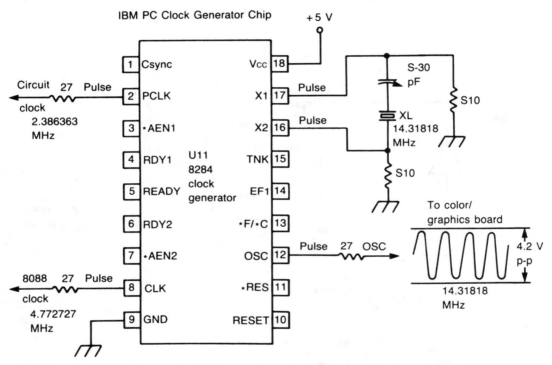

13-4 The IBM PC clock uses an 8284 generator chip and a crystal that produces a 14.31818 MHz master frequency. The chip then processes the master into three output frequencies.

The 8284 clock generator in the IBM PC, has a crystal connected across two pins. The crystal is the same one used in a lot of 8-bit computers, cut at 14.31818 MHz. When power is turned on, voltage is impressed on the crystal and it starts to oscillate. This is the master frequency. The clock generator internally divides the master by 3. This produces the system operating frequency of 4.772727 MHz.

The 4.772727 MHz is sent to the processor, an 8088, and also to all the 62-pin expansion slots. The master frequency is also divided by 6 in the 8284 producing a frequency of 2.386363 MHz. This signal is sent to a 74LS175 quad FF that in turn divides that frequency by 2. This produces a 1.1931817 MHz frequency that drives the 8253 programmable interrupt timer chip.

The clock generator chip has one other output, the master frequency, 14.31818 MHz. It is sent to the color graphics board. The master can be divided in the sync circuits to produce the horizontal and vertical sweep sync signals to place the horizontal and vertical sweep in the TV display under computer control. The master frequency is also made available to the expansion slot circuits in case some special card is plugged into a slot and needs the 14.31818 MHz frequency to operate.

Timing

All timing in a computer starts with the beating of the clock. The sine wave from the clock oscillator is changed to a square wave and becomes the driving force of the machine. All the frequencies are derived from the original master frequency. The clock can be running at 14 or 100 MHz. All clocks operate in the same way, the higher the frequency the faster the data is processed.

Most processors use the clock in one of two ways. One way (as in Figs. 13-5, 13-6, and 13-7) is to take the square wave and use it as it is. There is one wave train and it is used to handle both addressing and data movement. The second way a processor uses the clock is to split the square wave into two phases, both with the same frequency, and use one phase for addressing and the other phase for the transfer of data (as shown in Fig. 13-8). In 8-bit processors the single-phase is found in the Z-80 and 8085. A dual-phase clock is found in the 6800 and 6502 processor families. Sixteen-bit processors usually use single phase clocking.

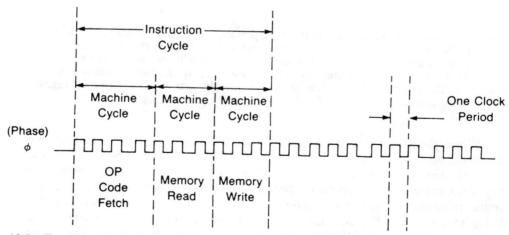

13-5 The Z-80 processor uses one continuous wave train called ϕ (phase). Each individual high and low is called one clock period. An instruction cycle is composed of 12 clock periods. The instruction cycle is divided into three machine cycles. They are the code fetch, the memory read and the memory write.

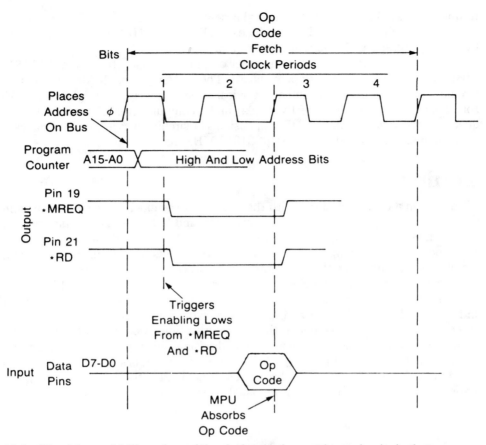

13-6 The rising and falling edges of the clock periods can trigger circuits in the processor. In the Z-80, the first rising edge of the op code fetch triggers the program counter to place its address bits onto the address bus. The first falling edge causes *MREQ and *RD to send bits to the memory to produce a read, which places the stored op code onto the data bus. The third rising edge strobes the data into the instruction register of the processor and turns of *MREQ and *RD.

When the family of support chips that aid a processor to computer are designed, one of the most important considerations is timing. The RAM, ROM, and I/O chips must be fast enough to allow the processor to access them. The accessing consists of the processor first addressing a register on a chip and then transferring data either to the register or receiving data from the register. The chip being accessed must be fast enough to permit the processor to either read or write to its registers. The operation takes place in one or more clock cycles. The cycles are fast and the addressed chip must make sure the addressing and data transferring takes place within the cycles. In addition, the operation must have spare time before and after the addressing and data transferring so the addresses and data are stabilized.

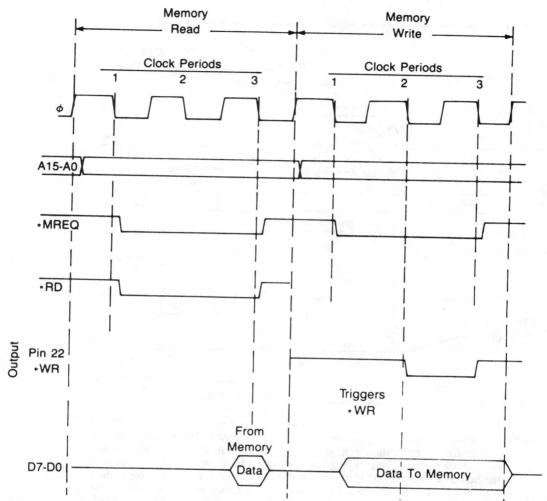

13-7 The memory read operation is quite like the fetch. The first rising edge places the address bits on its bus and the first falling edge sends *MREQ and *RD on their way. The third falling edge strobes the released data into the processor. The memory write operation does not use *RD but switches to *WR. The fall of the second write clock strobes data from the processor into the memory location.

These timings are measured in billionths of seconds or nanoseconds. Typical operation timings are a slow 350 nanoseconds or a quick 150 nanoseconds. You've seen those timings referred to on RAM chips. These timings are the access times.

A dual-phase clock

A common dual clock is found in the 6502 and 6800 family of 8-bit processors (Fig. 13-8). The master frequency in a computer that will generate a color TV display is,

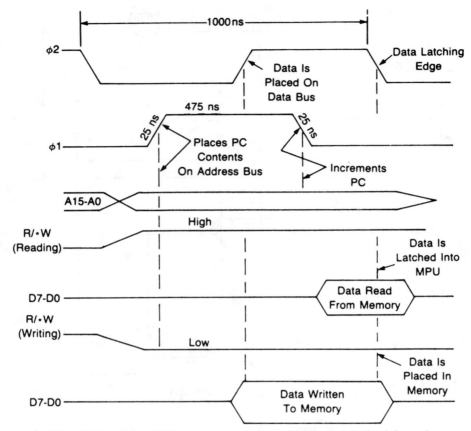

13-8 The 6800 and the 6502 processors use two φs (phases) derived from the one master frequency of the clock. φ1 and φ2 are both in a typical 1000 nanosecond clock period. The two phase periods can address and send data out over the bus. For example, φ1 can perform the addressing and φ2 can take in data during a read or send data during a write. The rising edge of φ1 places the address bits on the bus and sends out the correct read-write line bit. The falling edge of φ1 then increments the program counter in preparation for the next operation. Meanwhile, the rising edge of φ2 places data on the data bus. The falling edge of φ2 completes the cycle by strobing the data into the processor during a read or into the memory location during a write.

as mentioned, 14.31818 MHz. Divided by 16, the processor uses an approximate 1 MHz clock, that is precisely 0.89 MHz. This is close enough to 1 to be considered a 1 MHz system. The 1 MHz can be thought of as having one cycle take place in 1000 nanoseconds.

After the master is divided, the approximate 1 MHz square wave is passed through a phase splitting circuit (such as in Fig. 13-9) and outputs two 1 MHz identical signals except one of them leads the other. The first one out is called φ1 and the second signal is called φ2. Each is assigned a separate job. Since φ1 leads φ2 each job will take place alone and not interfere with each other.

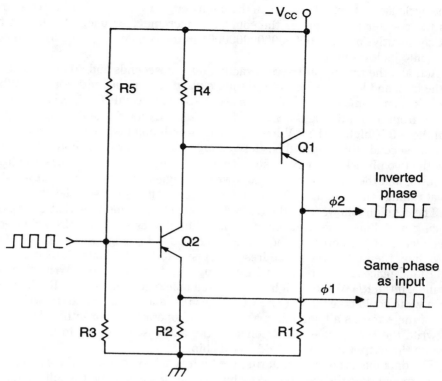

13-9 One clock signal can be split into two φs in a phase-splitting circuit. One wave train enters the network at the base of a PNP amplifier. The signal is then sent out of the collector to the base of a second PNP amplifier. Two signals are then output from the two PNP emitters. The time delay in the second PNP provides the phase change. The two outputs provide two out-of-phase signals with the same frequency. They are φ1 and φ2.

Each one is sent to separate circuits in the processor and there rising edges and falling edges will trigger the circuits they are input to. The φ1 signal is sent to the circuits that control the addressing output pins. The φ2 signal is sent to the circuits that control the data input and output pins. The Read/Write pin circuit decides whether the data is going to be sent out on the data bus or received from the data bus.

In the processor is a 16-bit register called the program counter. The program counter's 16 bits are connected to the 16 address pins. There will be more about the counter in the next chapter. φ1 operates the program counter. As the φ1 signal has a rising edge, the counter is triggered to place its contents on the address bus. This initiates the addressing. At the beginning of a program address LLLLLLLLLLLLLLLL is placed on the address bus. The memory register with that address is activated. The address in binary is 0000000000000000. This address is usually the first address in RAM.

Because the time required to execute a full cycle is 1000 nanoseconds, the high of the cycle lasts about 500 ns. Then the falling edge arrives. The falling edge triggers the counter too. It forces the counter to increment by one. This places the next consecutive address 0000000000000001 in the counter register. $\phi1$ then continues into its low duration.

Actually the timings are never exactly 500 nanoseconds and 500 nanoseconds for the high and low durations of the square wave. The rising edge and the falling edge take some time to occur. There is about 25 nanoseconds for the rising edge to change from 0 to +5 V and another 25 nanoseconds for the falling edge to drop from the +5 V high to the 0 V low. From an overall point of view though the 500-500 nanoseconds thinking will be close enough for any servicing chore. If you ever view the two phases on an expensive scope you will see the two phases, the highs and lows, and the way the highs and lows are staggered in time. If you ever need actual timings they are available on manufacturers spec sheets of the chip.

The $\phi2$ high follows after the $\phi1$ high. At about the same time that $\phi1$ is experiencing its falling edge and incrementing the address counter, $\phi2$s rising edge takes place. $\phi1$ has activated the address. The $\phi2$ rising edge with the help of the R/*W line, then connects the addressed register to the data bus. A read or write could take place in accordance with the logic state on the Read/Write line. For instance, if the R/*W line is high, a read could take place. Should the R/*W line be low, a write could take place. (The * indicates that a low will enable the write. The lack of the * means a high will enable the read operation.) For either the read or the write the rising edge of $\phi2$ connects the addressed register to the data bus through the output pins of the addressed chip.

The data bus is connected during the high of $\phi2$. Also during the $\phi2$ high, the data drifts out onto the data bus. $\phi2$'s high comes to an end and the falling edge of $\phi2$ occurs. The falling edge latches the data into the processor during a read or into the memory or I/O register if the operation is a write.

If the operation is a read, the processor takes the data into its input register and begins processing it. Should the operation be a write the data is either stored in memory or passed into the I/O chip for processing to the outside world. The next cycle begins immediately after the fall of $\phi2$ and the next location is addressed by the next $\phi1$ cycle.

$\phi1$ deals with the internal workings of the processor. It drives the program counter to place the desired address onto the address bus and then makes the processor increment the program counter by one. It doesn't do much else. $\phi2$, on the other hand, acts outside the processor. In addition to placing data on the data bus and latching data into a data destination, it performs other timings jobs on chips outside the processor.

The dual-phase clock is useful in that one phase can be used for addressing and the other phase for data movement. A single-phase clock must perform both duties with one steady wave train.

A single-phase clock

In processors like those in the Z-80 and the 8086 family, a steady wave train enters and is used directly to conduct the addressing and the data movement. Typically each full square wave, beginning at a low, rising to a high, and returning to the same place in the next low, is called a clock period (Fig. 13-5). The clock simultaneously makes the program counter output an address and move data. The clock signal is split into separate inputs to the address circuits and the data fetch and execute circuits.

A clock period is not a cycle. There are a lot of clock periods in a cycle. Since there is only one wave train it is usually named ϕ (Phase). On the first rising edge of ϕ the address circuits receive an input and the program counter in the processor places its contents onto the system address bus. A register in the memory map is addressed by the counter's bits.

In memory, a program is stored. Typically, the storage consists of first an instruction and then the data to be processed in accordance with the instruction. ϕ will run the program to match the memory instruction-data arrangement. An instruction fetch is called a machine cycle. Memory reads and writes are also called machine cycles. Typically, a machine cycle can be completed in three to six clock periods.

In Fig. 13-5, a ϕ wave train is shown performing one instruction cycle. The first four clocks, a machine cycle, conducts the instruction op code fetch. The next three clocks, another machine cycle, performs a memory read. The next three clocks, still another machine cycle, performs a memory write.

The wave train is built to run steady and apply the clocks to their appropriate circuits in the processor. The op code fetch clocks go to the circuits that will be working on the op codes as they arrive. The op code fetch is always a read operation since it is obtaining the instruction from memory. The memory read clocks are applied to the read circuits and the write clocks to the write circuits. All three machine cycles occur every time.

In order to trigger the activity in a read or write circuit, there are read and write lines. Their logic state tells the processor which way to conduct data over the two-way data bus.

Op code fetch in a Z-80

During the op code fetch period in Fig. 13-6, the processor carefully counts the incoming clock periods. The first four periods are all entered at the same time to a half dozen or so circuits. The first rising edge of the first clock triggers the program counter to address the first register in RAM that is holding the program bytes.

The falling edge of the same clock triggers off a signal called *MREQ. This is the memory request signal. A low leaves the *MREQ pin and enables the memory chips. The same falling edge also triggers an individual signal called *RD, which is the read line.

A sample of the op code enters the data bus as a result of these signals activating and opening up the memory location. The data becomes stable on the bus during the second clock period. As the rising edge of the third period arrives, the processor is able to absorb the contents of the data bus. The same rising edge also extinguishes the *MREQ and *RD signals.

The first four clock periods then, are there expressly to fetch op codes. They do the job easily by triggering circuits on and off as the edges of the periods rise and fall. Once the op code reaches the processor, the circuits are set-up to follow the instruction on processing the data that will follow.

Data movement in a Z-80

Once the first full machine cycle (made up of the first four clocks) is completed and an instruction is fetched, the next machine cycle (Fig. 13-7) consisting of three clock periods arrives. This machine cycle could be four or five clocks long, but we'll use three for our example. These clocks are arriving at breakneck speed, two clocks to a millionth of a second.

These three clocks are readers. They cause a fetch operation very similar to the op code fetch except they are fetching data and not an instruction. The timing diagram shows the similarities and the differences. Upon the rise of the first clocks in both the op code and data fetches, the address of the register holding the instruction or the data is placed on the address bus. As the first clocks fall, the signal *MREQ is made to output a low. At the same time *RD is also made to output an enabling low. The op code or the data moves out onto the data bus at that time.

The main difference between the op code fetch and the data read is when the bits are strobed into the processor from the data bus. If you look at the timing chart, the data is shown at the bottom. There is a straight line that means the data bus is in a disabled three-state condition. The straight line turns into an op code container in the op code chart and a data container in the read chart. The containers have highs and lows. This represents the highs and lows of the op code or the data that get into the eight data bus lines, D7 – D0.

Under the op code clocks, the instruction bits are strobed into the processor during the rise of the third clock. Under the memory read clocks the data is strobed into the processor during the fall of the third clock.

Immediately following the data read machine cycle are the clocks that can drive the data write machine cycle. Like the data read operation the data write operation typically uses three clocks, but often it uses more than three. The write operation is, of course, the act of sending data from the processor to the memory, unlike the read that sends data from the memory to the processor. The clock periods though are quite alike.

ϕ drives in the three clocks are needed to perform the write operation. Upon the rise of the write's first clock, the 16 address bits are placed onto the address bus exactly like the op code fetch and the data read did. As the first clock has its falling edge, a low is output from *MREQ. *RD remains high and inactive since this is a write operation and *RD is not needed.

With the address bus and the *MREQ turned on, the memory location opens up and is ready to receive data from the processor. The processor meanwhile lets the data bleed out onto the data bus. The data then becomes very stable on the bus. Then during the fall of the second write clock a low from the *WR write pin is output. This low strobes the data in the bus into the memory chips and specifically into the addressed location.

That is the way the clock periods are used in single-phase clocks to fetch instructions, read data, and write data. The crystal starts vibrating at its resonant frequency as voltage is impressed onto its crystalline structure. This vibration is a sine-wave voltage, converted to a square-wave voltage and adjusted in circuits to have a low of zero volts and a high of + 5 V. A prescribed number of clocks become the op-code fetch machine cycle, the data read cycle and the write cycle.

There are also a lot of other basic duties the clock is made to perform. It must energize the reading and writing to I/O chips, the refreshing of dynamic memory, the fabrication of the composite TV display signal, production of audio tones, and other things.

Processor background

There are four families of 8-bit processors although they actually come from only two ancestors. The 8080 was the first popular processor and was introduced in the early 1970s by Intel. Two of the Intel designers left and formed a company called Zilog. They introduced the Z-80. Both the 8080 and the Z-80 are single-phase processors.

About a year after, Intel brought out the 8080 and Motorola came out with the 6800. Some of their people left, formed Commodore and introduced the 6502. The 6800 and the 6502 are both dual-phase processors. All of the above processors went on to develop all sorts of families with improved characteristics.

The 16-bit processors followed immediately after the 8-bit types became popular. The generic numbers of the processors resemble their predecessors although the processors themselves are very different.

The 8080 8-bit family entered the 16-bit field with the 8086 family of processors. The Z-80 people introduced the Z-8000. The 6800 had the 68000 join its ranks. In the next chapter, 8-bit processors are covered. The chapters after that go into the popular 16-bit and 32-bit processors.

14

Those older 8-bit processors

IN THE EARLY 1980s, 8-BIT PROCESSORS WERE THE RAGE. THERE WERE the Tandy computer models based on the Z-80 processor; the Apple II's; Commodore's VIC 20, 64, and 128 that used the 6502; the Tandy Color Computer's 1, 2, and 3 that had a 6809 as microprocessor; and others. There were thousands of software packages written for these machines, all sorts of hardware peripherals, magazines focused on specific computers, and so on. There were millions and millions of these 8-bit wonders sold.

In recent years though, the IBM and its compatibles and the Macintosh machines have gradually taken over. Manufacturers have lost interest in the 8-bit computers. You can still find them for sale but there isn't much support for them anymore. However, there are still millions of them out in computerland being actively used. There are many hardcore 8-bit advocates who belong to specific computer clubs who use their machines daily.

The 8-bit computers, if your needs are personal and not too stringent, can be bought for absolutely bargain prices and do a good job. For example, a CoCo 3 (Tandy Color Computer 3) is very handy for some word processing. It performs as an excellent video generator to troubleshoot and set up color TVs and computer monitors.

There are hordes of Apple IIs in schools, homes, and businesses; there are millions of Commodore 64s and 128s all over the world; and so on. The 8-bit demand is down, but it is not out. It is still necessary for a computer literate to be very aware of and understand as much as possible about 8-bit processors. The 16-bit, 32-bit, and higher processors are based on the original 8-bit. The higher-bit processors work in the same way as the 8-bit only more so.

The two types of 8-bit processors

As mentioned, there are only two types of 8-bit machines that made it to the mass market. Number one type lists as its members the Z-80 and 8085. Number one differs mostly from the second type by one characteristic. These processors use a single-phase clock as discussed in the previous chapter. The other 8-bit type also has two members, the 6502 and the 6800. These processors use a dual-phase clock. Otherwise, all of the 8-bit processors, in general, work on the same principles. They all are installed in 40-pin DIPs. They are not interchangeable because the pin assignments are not anywhere identical and the internal components in the circuits do not match up. In general though, they are quite alike. If you learn how one of the four processors does its job, you will know how all four of them work.

The 8-bit computer and bytes

The 8-bit processor is so called because it is made to process data in 8-bit widths. The data enters and exits the processor through its D7 – D0 pins. The pins are connected to the D7 – D0 data bus lines. The data bus lines are connected to all the registers in the memory map. The byte-sized registers have bit positions D7 – D0 and are also connected to the same data bus lines.

The D7 – D0 bits, which are in reality low and high voltages, are coded in binary math as 0s and 1s. A D7 – D0 byte can be arranged in one of 256 bit combinations. Each bit combination can be code for a decimal number between 0 and 255. 0 in a register is 00000000 and 255 is 11111111, with all the other consecutive combinations, decimal numbers in between.

The processor is able to work on a byte and do the following thirteen things to it as shown in Fig. 14-1. It can add, subtract, multiply and divide a byte with another byte. It can AND, OR, and EOR a byte with another byte. It can shift or rotate a byte to the right or the left in a register. It can increment or decrement the bits in a byte. It can clear any byte to a value of zero. It can complement each bit to its opposite state.

That is about all the processor can do with a byte. The rest of its activity has to do with transferring bytes back and forth to and from the registers in the memory map. While this does not seem to be a lot of important performances, it is. These things are what computing is all about. See how the processor actually performs these manipulations.

Arithmetic logic unit

The *ALU* is the part of the computer that does most of the above work. It is basically composed of three byte-sized registers. There are two input registers and one output, something like a large logic gate. Between the registers are a group of electronic circuits that take care of the jobs that occur between the two input sets of flip-flops and the one output register.

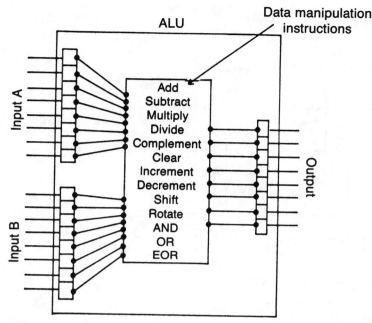

14-1 The *ALU* (arithmetic logic unit) is a set of circuits in all processors. There are two input registers and one output.

The ALU is quite the same electronically as any calculator. In fact you can use your computer as an ordinary calculator, if you so desire. However, the real power of computers has to do with the running of programs. Instead of simply responding to punching buttons on the calculator, the ALU in the computer is able to go to work automatically on instructions and data stored in memory. Once the program is in memory the computer runs it from beginning to end at blinding speed.

The processor is able to go to a program in memory, fetch the bytes of instructions and data, one at a time, and bring the data bytes to the ALU. The data bytes are then fed to the two input registers of the ALU. If the instruction is an add, the two binary bytes are added together by the electronic circuits and then placed in the ALU output register.

If the instruction is an AND, the binary data is placed in the input registers and ANDed. The results are then placed in the output register. The ALU can also shift the bits in the registers, complement the bits, clear the register to a binary zero, increment or decrement a register. The results are placed in the output register.

The ALU is connected (as shown in Fig. 14-2) to another 8-bit register called the *CCR* (condition code register). The CCR contains eight individual flip-flop circuits (Fig. 14-3). They all do individual jobs. These bits are called *flags*. According to the results of the ALU manipulations, one or more of these flags might be

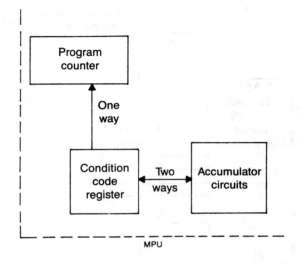

14-2 The ALU is part of the accumulator. It connects to the *CCR* (condition code register).

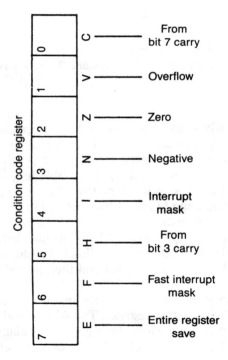

14-3 In the 8-bit processor, the CCR is a collection of individual flip-flops, each able to hold a bit called a *flag*.

thrown. Throwing a flag means changing the state of the flip-flop from low to high or vice versa. When a flag is thrown it in turn changes states in other processor registers. There will be more about these flag bits later in this chapter.

Besides the above jobs the ALU is able to distinguish between positive and negative numbers. When a number is positive the ALU operates in one way. Should the number be negative it performs in a different way. The ALU must also be careful when it handles the number zero. It cannot divide by zero since it has no way of knowing what infinity is. A division by zero causes a computer error to occur.

Accumulator

The ALU is buried deep in the internals of the processor chip. Between it and the pin connections are many circuits and other registers. The ALU itself is completely inaccessible to test equipment probes.

In order for data bits to get to the ALU, they must enter the chip pins and pass through a lot of circuitry (Fig. 14-4). In the 8-bit processor, the circuits and registers the data passes through are able to handle eight parallel bits. The circuits are multiplexers, storage registers, and other arithmetic and logic circuits. All of these circuits and the ALU itself is loosely called the accumulator. A programmer thinks of the accumulator as one 8-bit storage register that can perform arithmetic, logic, and the other bit manipulations described. A technician thinks of the accumulator as one 8-bit register that is connected to the data pins D7 – D0.

A logic diagram of the accumulator is shown in Fig. 14-5. Over the data bus lines from memory come two types of data. One is the op codes and the second is the data to be worked on in accordance to the op-code instruction. The op code only travels from memory to the processor. The op codes enter the processor and are sent to an instruction register and decoder. From there the op code is inserted into the accumulator from one side.

The data that is worked on comes to the accumulator and after it is processed leaves the accumulator to go back to the memory. This two-way data movement takes place on the other side of the accumulator. Sometimes the instruction deals with addressing and not data. In those cases the accumulator outputs to addressing circuits, which are discussed later in this chapter.

The accumulator
and the instruction register

Inside the processor is an internal data bus that is connected to pins D7 – D0 and then to the system data bus that runs around the print board to all the registers in the memory map. The data bus, both the processor internal section and the print board external part, is two directional. All of the important registers in the processor are connected to the data bus. This gives all the internal registers two way contact with the registers in the memory map except the instruction register. The *IR* (instruction register) only requires a data bus input. It does not need an output line to the data bus. It only needs to receive op codes. Op codes only travel from RAM to ROM to the instruction register.

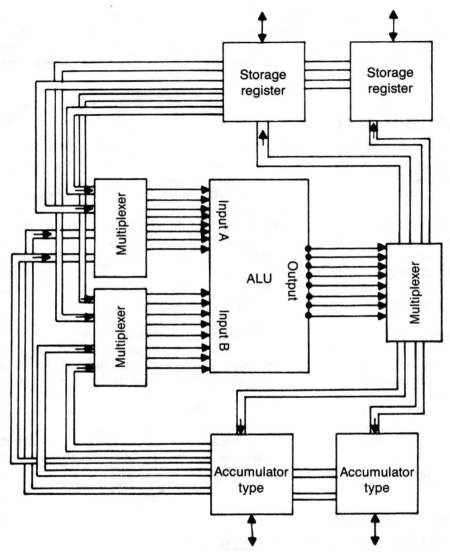

14-4   The accumulator is a group of circuits with its centerpiece being the ALU.

During the op-code fetch, the instruction bits are stored in the instruction register and are then decoded by the circuits of the IR. The output of the IR is then injected into the accumulator. In the accumulator, the bits of the op code readies the accumulator circuits for the data processing. The IR then shuts its entrances so no data can enter the IR. The IR is only interested in incoming op codes. The data known as *operands* (that will be moved over the data bus as the next addressing takes place) are not permitted into the IR.

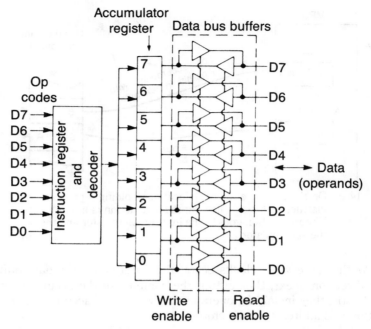

14-5 The accumulator register receives op code bits by way of the instruction-decoder network. The accumulator receives and transmits data bits through the data bus buffers.

The accumulator and the data bus

In a program, after an instruction byte, there are the operand data bytes (Fig. 14-6). Referring back to the single-phase clock (Fig. 13-5) the first four clocks of ϕ fetched the op code over the data bus and placed the bits into the IR. If the op code is a read type then the next three clocks are placed into action. Their driving energy causes the addressed location to place its operand byte onto the data bus. The byte travels the bus to pins D7 – D0 of the processor.

The operand encounters two pathways inside the processor. One goes to the IR, but the IR is closed. The operand can't take that route. The second pathway is a set of three-state buffers that are turned on. The operand passes quickly through the buffers and receives some amplifying. The operand then arrives at the accumulator register. The accumulator then receives and processes the operand according to the nature of the op-code instruction.

When the operation is a write type, a similar event takes place, with the operand moving in the other direction. The write op code will arrive at the IR in the same way and by the same four clock periods as the read operation did. The three clocks after the op code fetch the read clocks. They do not do anything during a write operation but just pulse past. The last three clocks in the series are the ones that power the write operation.

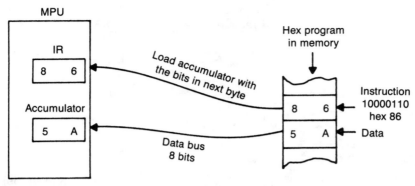

14-6 On the right are memory locations holding a program. Hex 86 is an instruction byte. Following the instruction is hex 5A (a byte of data). The instruction goes to the instruction register and the data is sent to the accumulator.

As the three write clocks occur, they first cause the data buffers to reverse their direction. Next, they output the contents of the accumulator onto the data bus. Lastly, they install the operand that was in the accumulator into the memory location it is addressed to be stored at.

The program counter

Eight-bit computers have program counters (such as Fig. 14-7) with 16 register bits. The program counter deals in addresses. The register is given its name because it is built to start counting at 0 in decimal and continue unabated as long as the clock is pulsing. Sixteen register bits are able to form 65,536 different bit combinations. Therefore the program counter can form binary addresses from 0000000000000000 to 1111111111111111, which is coded in decimal as 0 to 65,535. This is considered 64K addresses. It is said that an 8-bit processor can address 64K of memory and I/O locations. A typical 8-bit processor memory map will list the occupied addresses of the 65,536 locations the program counter is able to dial up.

The program counter register is connected to the 16 address pins, A15 – A0. These pins are connected to the 16 address bus lines, A15 – A0. The register is built to begin outputting 16 lows and then count in sequence one bit at a time until it outputs 16 highs. The program counter is also subject to about a half dozen instructions that can make the counter stop its normal sequencing and branch or jump to a different address out of sequence. These instructions trigger another processor register to accomplish this end. This change of address is covered later in this chapter.

The addressing out of the address pins, A15 – A0, and the data moving through the data pins, D7 – D0, are two separate but coordinated activities. In a single phase processor the addressing is triggered at the beginning of each machine cycle and the data read or write signal is triggered later in the cycle. A

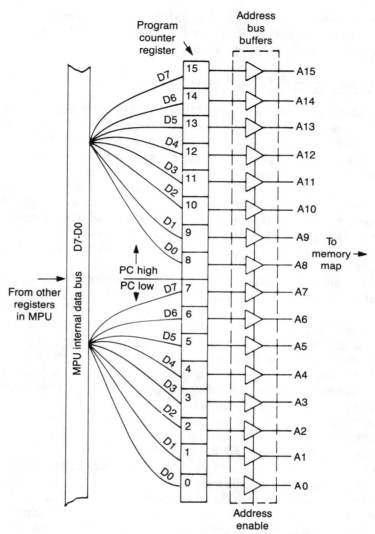

14-7 An 8-bit processor has 16 address bits in its program counter register. The 16 bits can form 65,536 different combinations of bits. The program counter is built to automatically output the 16 bits to the address bus and then increment itself by one. Other MPU registers are able to stop the automatic incrementing, alter the bit combination, and force a change of address.

dual-phase processor has the addressing accomplished by one of the phases, $\phi1$, and the data movement is made with the other phase, $\phi2$. The timings are critical.

In the dual-phase processors all the addressing consists of is the $\phi1$ rising edge placing the addresses onto the address bus, A15 – A0. The falling edge of the same pulse then increments the program counter by one bit. The addressed location is thus opened up during the high of $\phi1$. $\phi1$ then continues to keep addressing location after location unless some instruction comes along and changes the bit pattern output and causes a change of address.

Processor address changing

A computer is made to run programs. It can also perform just like a calculator, that is responding to button pushing, but that is not computing. Computing consists of placing a program into RAM and/or ROM. In the 8-bit computer, a program is simply a set of eight bits placed in row after row of memory locations that can be addressed. The bits, of course, are code for the program lines.

The program counter is built to start addressing the first program line and then automatically keep addressing line after line. Upon each addressing, a line of the program is sent to the data pins of the processor. The program counter will keep addressing until there are not any more locations full of program line bits. That is, it will keep addressing unless it receives an instruction to stop or to change the addressing sequence.

This is not at all unusual, in fact there are rarely any programs that can be run off and not experience any change of addresses. Practically every program has many lines that contain instructions to change the address. The address changing is made with the help of some other processor registers. These other registers force the program counter to suddenly stop the sequencing and place a newly calculated address onto the address bus. The sudden changes do not upset anything, the address bus can instantly output any address no matter how far away from the normal sequencing the address change might be. The only requirement is that the address is occupied in the computer.

As mentioned there are about a half dozen instructions that will cause a change of address. If one of these op codes finds its way over the data bus to the instruction register, the following action will take place.

Normally, when instructions arrive at the IR and the bits are one of the data processing op codes, the IR sends them directly to the accumulator. However, when the instruction is one of the change of address op codes, the IR could bypass the accumulator and send the bits to the program counter circuits. There the counter has the bits added or subtracted from its register bits or the register contents could simply be changed altogether. The altered states of the program counter are then placed on the address bus and a change of address takes place. The change of addresses have names like Jump, Branch, Call, Return, or Halt.

Jump and Branch address changes

The Jump and Branch instructions are somewhat alike. (In some computers they are exactly alike.) There can be differences in their operation in the following manner. For example, when a Jump op code arrives at the instruction counter the program counter can be stopped from automatically sequencing. As the register diagram (Fig. 14-8) shows, three 8-bit memory locations can hold an op code Jump instruction and two trailer lines of code. The trailers contain the address the pro-

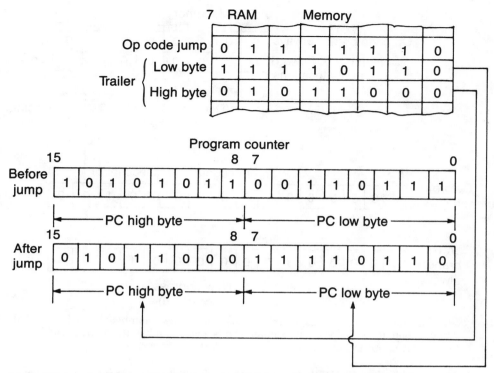

14-8 When a Jump op code arrives at the *IR* (instruction register) the following two bytes are a new address. These trailers are then sent to the program counter to replace the normal address sequencing and form a change of address.

gram must jump to at that stage. There are 16 bits in the two trailers and they will be interpreted by the IR and decoder as the 16 bits of a new address.

The Jump instruction causes the processor to take the 16 bits in the trailer and place the bits into the program counter. The counter outputs the bits onto the address bus and the location is activated. That is how the counter can Jump to a new address.

The Branch Always instruction changes the sequencing and the address in a different way. Figure 14-9 shows that the branch instruction also has a byte or bytes trailing after the instruction byte but the trailer is not a new address. It is a + or − number that is to be added or subtracted from the current address in the sequence, plus 2. When the branch op code arrives at the IR, the next byte or bytes plus 2 is added or subtracted to the existing contents of the counter register. The resultant set of 16 bits is then placed on the address bus and the new location accessed.

There are usually a group of branch instructions in a processor instruction set. The Branch Always just mentioned is only one of them. The rest of the branch instructions have conditions attached to them. The Branch Always instruction as the name implies, has no strings attached. When the byte containing the code bits of

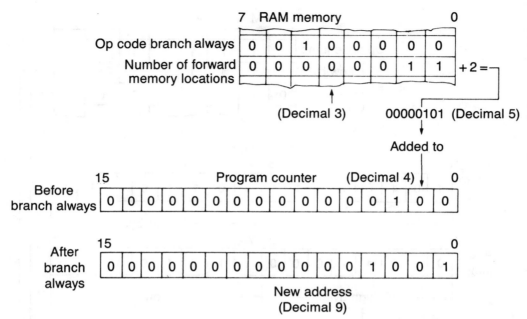

14-9   When a Branch Always op code arrives, it is followed by a number that will be added, plus 2 to the contents of the program counter. If it is a plus number, the address will be changed forward. A minus number will change the address backward.

Branch Always arrives at the IR, the IR forces the trailer byte or bytes into the counter and the address gets changed. With the rest of the branch instructions, the IR first checks with the flip-flops in the condition code register to see if any of the flags are thrown. If the flag that applies to that particular branch instruction is not thrown, then the counter is allowed to continue its sequencing and no change of address takes place. When a flag is thrown the trailer is permitted to enter the counter and change the address. There will be more about the CCR register in the next section.

The Call and Return change of address instructions deal in subroutines. A subroutine is a separate little program installed way off in memory somewhere that is to perform a special job. For instance, most processors can't really multiply. They can perform multiplication by repeated addition. For small multiplication problems, repeated addition works fine. However, if there is going to be a lot of extensive mathematics, it is a good idea to simply write a multiplication program and install it deep in memory. Then when it becomes time in the main program to perform some multiplication, you can Call the little subroutine, do the multiplication, and then Return from the subroutine back to the main program.

The Call op code changes the counter output in the same way that the Jump op code does. Then the counter sequences through the subroutine multiplying your number. Once the operation is complete the last op code in the routine is encountered. It is the Return op code. This changes the counter address bits back to the main program address. The program then continues on where it had left off before it was called upon to multiply.

Another op code that controls the counter output is the Halt instruction. The Halt stops the counter from incrementing. A Halt op code is often used as a form of Stop in the middle of programs. This is different than an End op code that usually signifies the very end of a program run.

The condition code register

The CCR is a register that has independent bits. Each bit is either on or off and the output of each bit acts as a control switch for a particular circuit. The bits have very little to do with each other. The bits are called flags.

In the 8-bit processor there are eight bits in the CCR. All the bits might not be used in some of the processors. The CCR (Fig. 14-2) is typically connected between the accumulator circuits and the program counter. There are two-way lines between the accumulator and the CCR. There is only a one-way line between the CCR and the program counter. The accumulator and the CCR must send bits back and forth to each other. The CCR only outputs bits to the program counter. The CCR has no need for the program counter to send bits back to it.

As a program is run, the accumulator and the CCR keep up a steady communication with each other. The two of them check every program byte that is fetched, to see if the byte is an op code that might want the counter to conduct a change of address. A flag can be set with a high or cleared with a low. Most op codes contain bits that require one or more of the flags to be set or cleared. The flag in turn can cause all sorts of changes in the accumulator and the program counter.

Typical names of the flags are carry, overflow, zero, negative, interrupt, half-carry, fast interrupt, and save. These flags are the off-on switches for some of the most important functions of the processor. A good machine language programmer must watch every program byte he conceives and note which flags are set and cleared as the program is run. One wrong flag could cause a program to crash.

Carry

The carry flag, known as the C flag, works with the 8-bit accumulator. It becomes the ninth bit of the accumulator (Fig. 14-10). In many computations, the binary number becomes larger than eight bits. The C flag will then step in and catch the bit. Other times the accumulator will act as a shift register. During a shift right the bit that was in bit position 0 will fall out. The C flag can act as an extra bit to hold the fallout. If there is a shift left the bit in bit position 7 could fall out. Here again the C flag can hold that bit. These shift operations are called names like shift right, shift left, rotate right, and rotate left. The C flag is used to store any loose bits that come out of the accumulator register ends.

When a flag is thrown it enters into the operation of an instruction. As the processor performs according to an instruction, it checks and notes the condition of the flags. For instance, the carry flag is normally clear until it is needed. Then if an addition uses the C bit it becomes set with a 1. The processor during the addition will check the C bit and if a 1 is in there it will use the 1 in the addition operation.

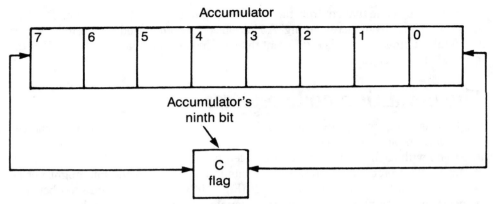

14-10   The carry flag in the CCR can act as a ninth bit holder for the 8-bit accumulator register. It can store the extra bit that might occur during adding, shifting and rotating.

Negative

The N flag (Fig. 14-11) is called negative. The accumulator register is capable of containing a negative number. It uses bit 7 to designate the sign of the number. When bit 7 is an L or 0, bits 6 – 0 hold a positive binary number with a decimal value between 0 and 127. When bit 7 is an H or 1, then the accumulator holds a negative binary number with a value between – 128 and – 1.

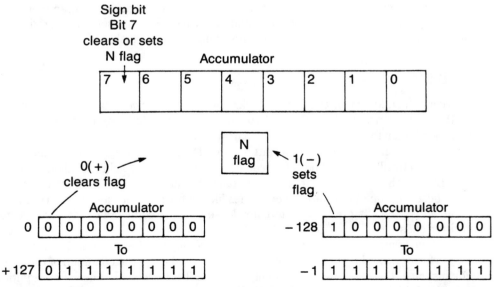

14-11   The negative flag holds the status of the sign bit, bit seven, of the accumulator. A 0 in the N flag means the sign is 0 or + . A 1 in the N flag shows bit seven is a 1 or – .

There are 256 bit combinations possible in the 8-bit accumulator. If the numbers are unsigned the bit combinations are code for decimal values between 0 and 255. When the numbers are signed the same bit combinations become code for decimal values between – 128 and + 127. Tables 14-1 and 14-2 show how the bits are coded for signed and unsigned numbers.

Table 14-1. Conversion table for byte-size signed numbers.

Decimal	Binary	Hex
0	00000000	0 0
+1	00000001	0 1
↕ (Same as unsigned numbers in Table 14-2.) ↕	↕	↕
+126	01111110	7 E
+127	01111111	7 F
–128	10000000	8 0
–127	10000001	8 1
–126	10000010	8 2
–125	10000011	8 3
–124	10000100	8 4
–123	10000101	8 5
–122	10000110	8 6
–121	10000111	8 7
–120	10001000	8 8
–119	10001001	8 9
–118	10001010	8 A
–117	10001011	8 B
–116	10001100	8 C
–115	10001101	8 D
–114	10001110	8 E
–113	10001111	8 F
–112	10010000	9 0
–111	10010001	9 1
–110	10010010	9 2
–109	10010011	9 3
–108	10010100	9 4
–107	10010101	9 5
–106	10010110	9 6
–105	10010111	9 7
–104	10011000	9 8
–103	10011001	9 9
–102	10011010	9 A
–101	10011011	9 B
–100	10011100	9 C
–99	10011101	9 D
–98	10011110	9 E
–97	10011111	9 F
–96	10100000	A 0
–95	10100001	A 1
–94	10100010	A 2
–93	10100011	A 3
–92	10100100	A 4
–91	10100101	A 5

Decimal	Binary	Hex
–84	10101100	A C
–83	10101101	A D
–82	10101110	A E
–81	10101111	A F
–80	10110000	B 0
–79	10110001	B 1
–78	10110010	B 2
–77	10110011	B 3
–76	10110100	B 4
–75	10110101	B 5
–74	10110110	B 6
–73	10110111	B 7
–72	10111000	B 8
–71	10111001	B 9
–70	10111010	B A
–69	10111011	B B
–68	10111100	B C
–67	10111101	B D
–66	10111110	B E
–65	10111111	B F
–64	11000000	C 0
–63	11000001	C 1
–62	11000010	C 2
–61	11000011	C 3
–60	11000100	C 4
–59	11000101	C 5
–58	11000110	C 6
–57	11000111	C 7
–56	11001000	C 8
–55	11001001	C 9
–54	11001010	C A
–53	11001011	C B
–52	11001100	C C
–51	11001101	C D
–50	11001110	C E
–49	11001111	C F
–48	11010000	D 0
–47	11010001	D 1
–46	11010010	D 2
–45	11010011	D 3
–44	11010100	D 4
–43	11010101	D 5
–42	11010110	D 6
–41	11010111	D 7
–40	11011000	D 8
–39	11011001	D 9

Table 14-1. Continued.

Decimal	Binary	Hex		Decimal	Binary	Hex	
−90	10100110	A	6	−38	11011010	D	A
−89	10100111	A	7	−37	11011011	D	B
−88	10101000	A	8	−36	11011100	D	C
−87	10101001	A	9	−35	11011101	D	D
−86	10101010	A	A	−34	11011110	D	E
−85	10101011	A	B	−33	11011111	D	F
−32	11100000	E	0	−16	11110000	F	0
−31	11100001	E	1	−15	11110001	F	1
−30	11100010	E	2	−14	11110010	F	2
−29	11100011	E	3	−13	11110011	F	3
−28	11100100	E	4	−12	11110100	F	4
−27	11100101	E	5	−11	11110101	F	5
−26	11100110	E	6	−10	11110110	F	6
−25	11100111	E	7	−9	11110111	F	7
−24	11101000	E	8	−8	11111000	F	8
−23	11101001	E	9	−7	11111001	F	9
−22	11101010	E	A	−6	11111010	F	A
−21	11101011	E	B	−5	11111011	F	B
−20	11101100	E	C	−4	11111100	F	C
−19	11101101	E	D	−3	11111101	F	D
−18	11101110	E	E	−2	11111110	F	E
−17	11101111	E	F	−1	11111111	F	F

Table 14-2. Conversion table for byte-size unsigned numbers.

Decimal	Binary		Hex		Decimal	Binary		Hex	
0	0000	0000	0	0	51	0011	0011	3	3
1	0000	0001	0	1	52	0011	0100	3	4
2	0000	0010	0	2	53	0011	0101	3	5
3	0000	0011	0	3	54	0011	0110	3	6
4	0000	0100	0	4	55	0011	0111	3	7
5	0000	0101	0	5	56	0011	1000	3	8
6	0000	0110	0	6	57	0011	1001	3	9
7	0000	0111	0	7	58	0011	1010	3	A
8	0000	1000	0	8	59	0011	1011	3	B
9	0000	1001	0	9	60	0011	1100	3	C
10	0000	1010	0	A	61	0011	1101	3	D
11	0000	1011	0	B	62	0011	1110	3	E
12	0000	1100	0	C	63	0011	1111	3	F
13	0000	1101	0	D					
14	0000	1110	0	E	64	0100	0000	4	0
15	0000	1111	0	F	65	0100	0001	4	1
					66	0100	0010	4	2
16	0001	0000	1	0	67	0100	0011	4	3
17	0001	0001	1	1	68	0100	0100	4	4
18	0001	0010	1	2	69	0100	0101	4	5
19	0001	0011	1	3	70	0100	0110	4	6
20	0001	0100	1	4	71	0100	0111	4	7
21	0001	0101	1	5	72	0100	1000	4	8
22	0001	0110	1	6	73	0100	1001	4	9

Table 14-2. Continued.

Decimal	Binary		Hex		Decimal	Binary		Hex	
23	0001	0111	1	7	74	0100	1010	4	A
24	0001	1000	1	8	75	0100	1011	4	B
25	0001	1001	1	9	76	0100	1100	4	C
26	0001	1010	1	A	77	0100	1101	4	D
27	0001	1011	1	B	78	0100	1110	4	E
28	0001	1100	1	C	79	0100	1111	4	F
29	0001	1101	1	D					
30	0001	1110	1	E	80	0101	0000	5	0
31	0001	1111	1	F	81	0101	0001	5	1
					82	0101	0010	5	2
32	0010	0000	2	0	83	0101	0011	5	3
33	0010	0001	2	1	84	0101	0100	5	4
34	0010	0010	2	2	85	0101	0101	5	5
35	0010	0011	2	3	86	0101	0110	5	6
36	0010	0100	2	4	87	0101	0111	5	7
37	0010	0101	2	5	88	0101	1000	5	8
38	0010	0110	2	6	89	0101	1001	5	9
39	0010	0111	2	7	90	0101	1010	5	A
40	0010	1000	2	8	91	0101	1011	5	B
41	0010	1001	2	9	92	0101	1100	5	C
42	0010	1010	2	A	93	0101	1101	5	D
43	0010	1011	2	B	94	0101	1110	5	E
44	0010	1100	2	C	95	0101	1111	5	F
45	0010	1101	2	D					
46	0010	1110	2	E	96	0110	0000	6	0
47	0010	1111	2	F	97	0110	0001	6	1
					98	0110	0010	6	2
48	0011	0000	3	0	99	0110	0011	6	3
49	0011	0001	3	1	100	0110	0100	6	4
50	0011	0010	3	2	101	0110	0101	6	5
102	0110	0110	6	6	155	1001	1011	9	B
103	0110	0111	6	7	156	1001	1100	9	C
104	0110	1000	6	8	157	1001	1101	9	D
105	0110	1001	6	9	158	1001	1110	9	E
106	0110	1010	6	A	159	1001	1111	9	F
107	0110	1011	6	B					
108	0110	1100	6	C	160	1010	0000	A	0
109	0110	1101	6	D	161	1010	0001	A	1
110	0110	1110	6	E	162	1010	0010	A	2
111	0110	1111	6	F	163	1010	0011	A	3
					164	1010	0100	A	4
112	0111	0000	7	0	165	1010	0101	A	5
113	0111	0001	7	1	166	1010	0110	A	6
114	0111	0010	7	2	167	1010	0111	A	7
115	0111	0011	7	3	168	1010	1000	A	8
116	0111	0100	7	4	169	1010	1001	A	9
117	0111	0101	7	5	170	1010	1010	A	A
118	0111	0110	7	6	171	1010	1011	A	B
119	0111	0111	7	7	172	1010	1100	A	C
120	0111	1000	7	8	173	1010	1101	A	D
121	0111	1001	7	9	174	1010	1110	A	E
122	0111	1010	7	A	175	1010	1111	A	F
123	0111	1011	7	B					
124	0111	1100	7	C	176	1011	0000	B	0
125	0111	1101	7	D	177	1011	0001	B	1
126	0111	1110	7	E	178	1011	0010	B	2
127	0111	1111	7	F	179	1011	0011	B	3

Table 14-2. Continued.

Decimal	Binary		Hex		Decimal	Binary		Hex	
					180	1011	0100	B	4
128	1000	0000	8	0	181	1011	0101	B	5
129	1000	0001	8	1	182	1011	0110	B	6
130	1000	0010	8	2	183	1011	0111	B	7
131	1000	0011	8	3	184	1011	1000	B	8
132	1000	0100	8	4	185	1011	1001	B	9
133	1000	0101	8	5	186	1011	1010	B	A
134	1000	0110	8	6	187	1011	1011	B	B
135	1000	0111	8	7	188	1011	1100	B	C
136	1000	1000	8	8	189	1011	1101	B	D
137	1000	1001	8	9	190	1011	1110	B	E
138	1000	1010	8	A	191	1011	1111	B	F
139	1000	1011	8	B					
140	1000	1100	8	C	192	1100	0000	C	0
141	1000	1101	8	D	193	1100	0001	C	1
142	1000	1110	8	E	194	1100	0010	C	2
143	1000	1111	8	F	195	1100	0011	C	3
					196	1100	0100	C	4
144	1001	0000	9	0	197	1100	0101	C	5
145	1001	0001	9	1	198	1100	0110	C	6
146	1001	0010	9	2	199	1100	0111	C	7
147	1001	0011	9	3	200	1100	1000	C	8
148	1001	0100	9	4	201	1100	1001	C	9
149	1001	0101	9	5	202	1100	1010	C	A
150	1001	0110	9	6	203	1100	1011	C	B
151	1001	0111	9	7	204	1100	1100	C	C
152	1001	1000	9	8	205	1100	1101	C	D
153	1001	1001	9	9	206	1100	1110	C	E
154	1001	1010	9	A	207	1100	1111	C	F
208	1101	0000	D	0	232	1110	1000	E	8
209	1101	0001	D	1	233	1110	1001	E	9
210	1101	0010	D	2	234	1110	1010	E	A
211	1101	0011	D	3	235	1110	1011	E	B
212	1101	0100	D	4	236	1110	1100	E	C
213	1101	0101	D	5	237	1110	1101	E	D
214	1101	0110	D	6	238	1110	1110	E	E
215	1101	0111	D	7	239	1110	1111	E	F
216	1101	1000	D	8					
217	1101	1001	D	9	240	1111	0000	F	0
218	1101	1010	D	A	241	1111	0001	F	1
219	1101	1011	D	B	242	1111	0010	F	2
220	1101	1100	D	C	243	1111	0011	F	3
221	1101	1101	D	D	244	1111	0100	F	4
222	1101	1110	D	E	245	1111	0101	F	5
223	1101	1111	D	F	246	1111	0110	F	6
					247	1111	0111	F	7
224	1110	0000	E	0	248	1111	1000	F	8
225	1110	0001	E	1	249	1111	1001	F	9
226	1110	0010	E	2	250	1111	1010	F	A
227	1110	0011	E	3	251	1111	1011	F	B
228	1110	0100	E	4	252	1111	1100	F	C
229	1110	0101	E	5	253	1111	1101	F	D
230	1110	0110	E	6	254	1111	1110	F	E
231	1110	0111	E	7	255	1111	1111	F	F

When signed numbers are used, the most significant bit, bit 7 is occupied indicating the sign. That only leaves bits 6 – 0 to hold the binary code for the decimal. The seven bits, 6 – 0, can only code 128 bit combinations. That means the bits can only code the decimal numbers from 0 to + 127. That would be the combinations in order from 00000000 to 01111111.

The next combination after + 127 is 10000000. In the signed number scheme of things, it is recognized as – 128. The next binary group in line is 10000001. This now becomes – 127. As a count continues, the accumulator cycles to 11111111. That is considered the signed decimal number of – 1. Therefore, the signed numbers decimal count, as the accumulator is incremented from 00000000 to 11111111, goes from 0 to + 127 then from – 128 down to – 1.

The N flag signals when the sign changes. The N flag is cleared as long as bit 7 of the accumulator is positive and showing a 0. Should bit 7 of the accumulator go negative by getting set to a 1, the N flag in turn also gets set and becomes an H or a 1. This signals the ALU and the program counter that bit 7 of the accumulator is set and contains a negative number. They take the flag setting and compute accordingly.

Overflow

Another flag is V, the overflow (Fig. 14-12). What kind of overflow does it indicate? The V flag gets set when there is an overflow from bit 6 to bit 7 and the sign gets changed. The V flag always gets thrown when there is an overflow from 6 to 7 whether signed numbers are being used or not. If the flag is thrown while unsigned numbers are being computed, the flag can be ignored in the computations, although the programmer must take into consideration that the flag was thrown, and not let that event interfere with the operation.

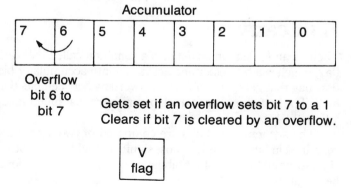

14-12 The overflow flag holds the status of any overflow from bit six of the accumulator to bit seven. An overflow could change the sign of bit seven. If there is no overflow then the flag is 0. An overflow causes the flag to get set at 1.

The V flag then is the lookout for potential overflows from bit 6 to bit 7. The V flag monitors the overflow. Should a 1 get shifted from bit 6 to bit 7, and the state in bit 7 get cleared to a 0, then the V flag also clears to a 0. This overflow occurs when the result of an operation places a number larger than the – 128 to + 127 in the 7-bit range.

Zero

The Z flag is a simple one. The Z flag (Fig. 14-13) gets set to a 1 whenever the accumulator register reaches a state of 00000000. If the accumulator has any other set of bits the Z flag is clear. The Z flag is handy during a countdown. The program can be written to have a countdown to zero and bring the program to a halt when the accumulator becomes 00000000.

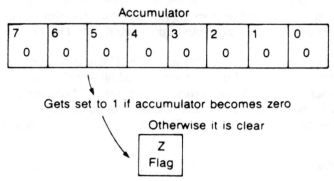

14-13 The zero flag holds the status of the accumulator. The accumulator is either in a state of all 0s or not. When the accumulator contains any value other than zero the flag remains clear at 0. If the accumulator becomes all zeros, then the flag is set at 1.

The Z flag is connected to the program counter. As the end arrives and the accumulator becomes zero, the Z flag is thrown and program counting is halted. The Z flag has many uses and is used often in programming.

Half carry

There is an H flag which denotes a condition called half-carry. It is not like the carry flag, which is a bit holder and acts as a ninth accumulator bit. It is more like the overflow flag that gets thrown when an overflow between bits 6 and 7 changes the state of bit 7. The half-carry keeps track of any carry that might take place between bits 3 and 4 (Fig. 14-14).

The accumulator 8 bits are composed of two separate 4-bit nibbles. The nibble contained in bits 7 – 4 is the most significant nibble and the one in bits 3 – 0 is the least significant nibble. The 4-bit nibble, of course, is the code for a single decimal digit or a hex digit.

When the accumulator is performing arithmetic, such as addition, it is actually adding one nibble to the other. If there is a binary carry from bit 3 to bit 4, the carry is taking place from the LS (least significant) nibble to the MS (most significant) nibble. This is a special carry unlike the carries that take place inside the nibbles. In certain cases, the carry must be taken into consideration during a program run.

The H flag monitors the nibble-to-nibble carry, which is called half-carry because it takes place in the halfway bits of the accumulator. When a half-carry takes place, the

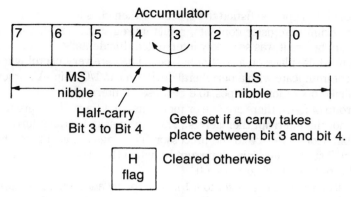

14-14 The half-carry flag watches for any carry that might occur between bits three and four of the accumulator. It is a form of overflow flag. The byte contains two nibbles. The line between the two nibbles is between bits three and four. Sometimes it is necessary to know whether there was a nibble overflow. If there was none the flag remains clear at 0. Should the half-carry happen, the flag is set at 1.

H flag is thrown and will then hold a 1. If no half-carry takes place during an addition op code execution, then H flag is cleared and holds a 0. The H flag normally remains clear until a half-carry sets it.

Interrupts

One of the most important abilities of a computer is an interrupt. During the running of a program, the I/O and other chips that are connected to the processor, are able to send bits to the processor that interrupts the program and makes the processor pay attention to the interrupt. When an interrupt bit suddenly arrives at the processor the following happens. The processor will finish the machine cycle it was in the middle of and stop to handle the interrupt.

The typical first step the processor does in handling the interrupt, is to store the contents of its registers in a safe place in memory called the stack. If the processor stores the register contents, then when the interrupt has been serviced it can restore the registers to the states they were in and continue the program where it had left off after being interrupted.

Once the processor has the essential register states safely in the stack, it goes into a predetermined interrupt routine. The interrupt makes the processor place a special interrupt address on the program counter. The address, usually on a ROM, is of a vector. The word vector in this context means two byte address. In other words the processor goes to an address in ROM where an address is stored. The processor then reads that vector address and places it into the program counter.

The vector address is the start byte of a special program that will service the interrupt as it is run. The processor then sequences through the service program and takes care of the interrupt.

Once the interrupt is satisfied the processor then goes into memory to the stack. It retrieves its original register contents, refills its registers, and continues on with its main program before it was so rudely interrupted. Incidentally, most interrupts are not unusual. They take place on a continual basis. They are very useful when the processor has to communicate with a peripheral device via an I/O chip. All processor/peripheral handshake operations are possible because of interrupts.

In a group of flags, there are one or more interrupt flags. They are the I flags. The I flags are not the interrupt themselves. They are masks for the interrupts. The interrupts are bits from a device to the processor. The flags act as a mask for the bits. A mask flag will stop an incoming interrupt bit when the mask is set with a 1. It lets the interrupt bit past while cleared to a 0.

The reason the mask gets set to a 1 is to stop any additional interrupts from interrupting an interrupt in progress. The processor can only handle one interrupt at a time. Any other interrupts that try to gain the attention of the processor are masked off.

The I bit will mask off most interrupts when it is set. However, there is one type of interrupt called *nonmaskable*. When one of these special interrupts comes along it is sent to its own special pin on the processor. It will cause an interrupt whether the I bit is set or not. The *nonmaskable interrupt* happens only when the computer has an emergency. For instance, if the computer senses an impending power failure it could generate a nonmaskable interrupt. This interrupt will override all I masks that might be set.

The flags and the branch op codes

The CCR register that acts as the flag holder, does a lot of its work with incoming op codes that perform address branching. Except for Branch Always, the unconditional branch instruction, the conditional branches use the flags to determine the condition of whether to branch to an address or not. When Branch Always arrives at the processor, the processor goes right ahead, adds the op code trailer to the program counter and places the new branch address on the address bus. When one of the other conditional branches arrives at the processor, the processor checks the flags to see if conditions are correct to execute the branch.

For instance, the instruction, Branch if the accumulator is zero, could arrive at the instruction register. When the accumulator is 00000000, the Z flag gets set. Should the accumulator be any other binary value but zero, then the Z flag is cleared.

The processor checks the Z flag. If the accumulator is zero, the Z flag will be set and the processor will go ahead and execute the branch. The operand trailers will be added to the program counter and the new address is accessed. Should the Z flag be cleared though, that means the accumulator is not zero. The branch op code and its trailing operands will be ignored and the program counter will simply address the next program line instead.

The flag connection in the condition code register is wired into the processor between the accumulator and the program counter. The instructions, as they are executed, set and clear the flags almost with every op code byte. The assembly or machine-language programmer must be on his toes and be aware of every flag move that takes place as a program is run. Flag control is a vital ingredient in good programming technique.

When you are writing code in high-level languages, the flags are taken care of automatically by the compiler or interpreter ROM that converts your high-level code to machine language. However, during factory type troubleshooting there are a lot of diagnostic tests and programs that are entered in machine language and flag attention is required.

Stack pointer

As mentioned, a section of RAM is assigned the job of acting as a stack. The stack's job is to store the processor's register contents while the processor is forced to stop in the middle of a program and service an interrupt. Stacks can be made up of hundreds of consecutive bytes. Each stack byte has an address in the memory map.

The starting address of the consecutive stack bytes in the most important one to the processor. The rest of the stack can be addressed by incrementing or decrementing the address counting. However, this can only be accomplished if the processor knows the starting stack address. To keep the address on hand the processor has a 16-bit register called the stack pointer (Fig. 14-15).

All the word pointer means is address. The address bits in the 16-bit stack pointer point at the first byte of the stack. The stack can be anywhere on a 64K memory map so 16 bits are needed to store the address. Each location is an 8-bit register. During an interrupt all of the registers in the processor, except the stack pointer, can have their contents stored in the stack. The 8-bit processor registers store their contents easily in one stack byte. The 16-bit processor registers use two stack bytes to store their contents. The stack pointer doesn't need to have its contents stored. Its job is to only point out the starting stack address.

The stack pointer is wired in parallel with the program counter. It can place 16 bits on the address bus the same way the program counter can. The address on the address bus then becomes the one the stack pointer register contains. It was mentioned that the stack points to the beginning address of the stack. Go through the routine the processor goes through in storing its register contents during an interrupt.

In the typical dual-phase 8-bit processor (Fig. 14-16) there could be nine 8-bit programming register segments. Note the program counter, the index register, and the stack pointer are all 16-bit registers. They are in actuality two 8-bit registers hooked together. There is a high part of the register that contains the MS bits and a low part containing the LS bits. This example processor has:

- Two accumulators, A and B.
- The program counter high and low bytes.
- The stack pointer high and low bytes.
- The index register high and low bytes.
- The condition code register eight individual bits.

During a program run, as op code and operand bytes are fetched and executed, these registers at any one point in time have contents that are conducting the program.

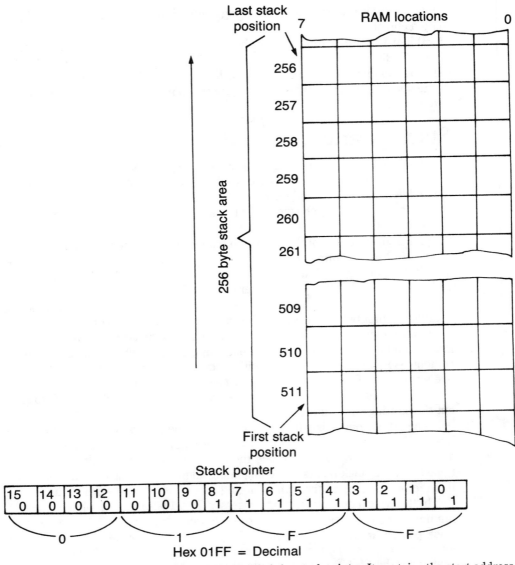

14-15 8-bit processors have a 16-bit register called the *stack pointer*. It contains the start address of a RAM area that is assigned to store all the contents of the registers in the processor when there is an interrupt. This stack of register contents is contained at RAM decimal addresses 256-511. The first stack byte is at 511 and is counted backwards to 256.

When interrupt bits are sent to the processor from a device, and the interrupt bits are not masked, the processor is alerted to take a break in the program run and service the interrupt. The interrupt routine will need the registers in the processor to conduct the interrupt servicing program. At the end of the current machine cycle the processor begins servicing the interrupt.

To preserve the register contents, the processor puts the stack pointer's address bits on the address bus. This activates the first stack byte. The processor then proceeds to write to the stack bytes. First it places the CCR bits on the data bus and stores the bits in the first stack byte. Then the stack pointer is decremented and the contents of Accumulator B is written to that address. The stack pointer is decremented again and the contents of Accumulator A is written to that address.

Suppose the first stack address was decimal 511. The CCR bits are stored there. B accumulator is then placed in 510. A accumulator goes in 509, index high in 508, index low in 507, program counter high in 506, and program counter low in 505. As mentioned, the stack pointer is not stored because it is the storage address-or and is needed in the processor at all times.

The CCR was the first byte stored and is at the highest address number in the stack, decimal 511. The program counter low was the last byte stored and is at the lowest address number in the stack, decimal 505. The stack pointer at this time contains the last address stored, 505, which holds the Program counter low contents.

After the interrupt has been serviced, the processor is ready to go back to the original program it was running. It wants to read the stack back into its registers. The stack pointer has the last address, 505, coded in its 16 bits. These bits are placed on the address bits and the program counter low byte is read back into its register. The last one in the stack is the first one out of the stack. Then as the processor keeps reading, the stack pointer is incremented to 506 and the program counter high bits are returned to their register. The stack pointer then keeps on incrementing until it retrieves all seven bytes back to their original assigned processor registers.

While this stacking and unstacking seems a long tedious job, the processor could care less. It is operating in billionths of a second. During a program run, the register bits keep getting stacked and retrieved many, many times. During the stacking and retrieving the stack pointer operates as if it were the program counter.

Index register

The index register is also wired in parallel with the program counter and performs addressing chores. Indexing is an old technique that dates back to computers that were in existence in the 1940s and 50s. Indexing is an alternative way to addressing, besides automatic sequencing, jumping, and branching.

In 8-bit computers, the index register has 16 bits. It is the same size as the program counter and the stack pointer. The index register conducts addressing in the following way.

During a program run, when an op code arrives and orders some address indexing, the program counter lets the index register take over the addressing chore. Address bits will then be calculated in the index register and these bits will be placed on the address bus and reading or writing to memory locations can take place.

The indexing op code has a trailer operand. This operand is added to the contents of the index register. The contents of the 16-bit register plus the operand form a 16-bit address. At this address is the data needed for the program. The index register places this address on the address bus and the location is accessed.

Not all processors have index registers. When the processor doesn't have an index register other types of addressing must take place. While indexing is not a must, it is a handy addressing means, especially when the program needs to look up a lot of values in lookup tables.

The instruction register

The IR is loosely thought of as both the input register and the instruction decoder, even though they have separate circuits. The input register is connected directly to the data pins and the system data bus. The input register, as its name implies, is an input-only register, even though the data pins are two way. There are other connections to the data pins that output but not from the IR input register.

In memory, the program lineup consists of an op code and then operands. The IR input register is the place where the op codes go. The operands go to input buffer circuits connected to the processor's internal data bus that both receives inputs and sends outputs.

The IR and the I/O buffers are all three-state circuits. They must have the three-state qualities so they tell the difference between the op codes and the operands and not let op-code instructions go to the I/O buffers or operands to the instruction input register. Examine the way program lines enter the processor.

In the memory, the program bytes are meticulously installed. The op-code instruction byte comes first, and then the operand that the instruction is concerned with comes trailing along. The programs in RAM or ROM are both installed in the same way. The processor accesses both of them in the same way and takes a copy of the register bytes one at a time.

As the processor reads program line after program line, the three entrances are turned off and on in accordance to the program. The three entrances that all use the eight data pins are the IR input register, the input operand buffer, and the output data buffer. During the time op code instruction is read, the IR entrance is on. Then as the op code finishes and the operand trailer is read the IR entrance is three-stated, the eight input buffers are turned on, and the eight output buffers are three-stated. Should the instruction have been a write, then the input buffers are three-stated and the output buffers are enabled.

The IR only deals in op code instructions. The op codes (Table 14-3) are all listed in the instruction set for the processor. The processor works when its op codes are input to its IR from the program in memory. The operands are simply data that needs to be worked on by the processor as the instruction dictates. The op codes tell the accumulator and other registers what sort of work the data is to be subjected to.

Table 14-3. The 6800 instruction set.

1 LOAD ACCUMULATOR A

86	IMMEDIATE
96	DIRECT
B6	EXTENDED
A6	INDEXED

2 LOAD ACCUMULATOR B

C6	IMMEDIATE
D6	DIRECT
F6	EXTENDED
E6	INDEXED

Flags affected, N. Z. Flag cleared, V.

3 LOAD STACK POINTER

8E	IMMEDIATE
9E	DIRECT
BE	EXTENDED
AE	INDEXED

Flags affected, N. Z. Flag cleared, V.

4 LOAD INDEX REGISTER

CE	IMMEDIATE
DE	DIRECT
FE	EXTENDED
EE	INDEXED

Flags affected, N. Z. Flag cleared, V.

5 STORE ACCUMULATOR A

97	DIRECT
B7	EXTENDED
A7	INDEXED

6 STORE ACCUMULATOR B

D7	DIRECT
F7	EXTENDED
E7	INDEXED

Flags affected, N. Z. Flag cleared, V.

7 STORE STACK POINTER

9F	DIRECT
BF	EXTENDED
AF	INDEXED

Flags affected, N. Z. Flag cleared, V.

8 STORE INDEX REGISTER

DF	DIRECT
FF	EXTENDED
EF	INDEXED

Flags affected, N. Z. Flag cleared, V.

9 PUSH DATA onto STACK

36	(Push accumulator A onto stack)
37	(Push accumulator b onto stack)

No flags are affected by these instructions.

10 PULL DATA from STACK

32	(Load the A accumulator from stack)
33	(load the B accumulator from stack)

No flags are affected by these instructions

11 TRANSFER from ACCUMULATOR A to ACCUMULATOR B

16

12 TRANSFER from ACCUMULATOR B to ACCUMULATOR A

17

Flags affected, N. Z. Flag cleared, V.

13 TRANSFER from INDEX REGISTER to STACK POINTER

35

14 TRANSFER from STACK POINTER to INDEX REGISTER

30

No flags are affected by these instructions.

15 TRANSFER from ACCUMULATOR A to CONDITION CODE REGISTER

06

16 TRANSFER from CONDITION CODE REGISTER to ACCUMULATOR A

07

Table 14-3. Continued.

Flags are affected when accumulator A transfers contents into CCR. Whatever was in the accumulator register bits 0-5 will be in bits 0-5 of the CCR.

17 INCREMENT

4C	ACCUMULATOR A
5C	ACCUMULATOR B
7C	EXTENDED ADDRESS
6C	INDEXED ADDRESS

Flags affected are N, Z, V.

18 INCREMENT STACK POINTER

31

No flags affected

19 INCREMENT INDEX REGISTER

08

The Z flag is set if all 16 bits are cleared.

20 DECREMENT

4A	ACCUMULATOR A
5A	ACCUMULATOR B
7A	EXTENDED ADDRESS
6A	INDEXED ADDRESS

Flags affected are N, Z, V.

21 DECREMENT STACK POINTER
34

No flags are affected.

22 DECREMENT INDEX REGISTER
09

The Z flag can be affected.

23 CLEAR

4F	ACCUMULATOR A
5F	ACCUMULATOR B
7F	EXTENDED ADDRESS
6F	INDEXED ADDRESS

The Z flag is set. The N, V, and C flags are cleared.

24 CLEAR 2'S COMPLEMENT OVERFLOW BIT

0A

The V flag is cleared.

25 CLEAR CARRY

0C

The C flag is cleared.

26 CLEAR INTERRUPT MASK

0E

The I flag is cleared.

27 SET 2'S COMPLEMENT OVERFLOW BIT

0B

The V flag is set to 1.

28 SET INTERRUPT MASK

0F

The I flag is set to 1.

29 SET CARRY

0D

The C flag is set to 1.

30 TEST N or Z

4D	ACCUMULATOR A
5D	ACCUMULATOR B
7D	EXTENDED ADDRESS
6D	INDEXED ADDRESS

Flags affected, N, Z. The V flag is cleared.

31 LOGICAL SHIFT RIGHT

44	ACCUMULATOR A
54	ACCUMULATOR B
74	EXTENDED ADDRESS
64	INDEXED ADDRESS

Flags that can be affected, Z, V, C. The N flag is cleared.

32 ROTATE LEFT

49	ACCUMULATOR A
59	ACCUMULATOR B
79	EXTENDED ADDRESS
69	INDEXED ADDRESS

Flags that can be affected, N, Z, C, V.

Table 14-3. Continued.

33 ROTATE RIGHT

46	ACCUMULATOR A
56	ACCUMULATOR B
76	EXTENDED ADDRESS
66	INDEXED ADDRESS

Flags that can be affected, N, Z, C, V.

34 ARITHMETIC SHIFT RIGHT

47	ACCUMULATOR A
57	ACCUMULATOR B
77	EXTENDED ADDRESS
67	INDEXED ADDRESS

Flags that can be affected, N, Z, V, C.

35 ARITHMETIC SHIFT LEFT

48	ACCUMULATOR A
58	ACCUMULATOR B
78	EXTENDED ADDRESS
68	INDEXED ADDRESS

Flags that can be affected, N, Z, V, C.

36 COMPLEMENT

43	ACCUMULATOR A
53	ACCUMULATOR B
73	EXTENDED ADDRESS
63	INDEXED ADDRESS

Flags that can be affected, N, Z. C is set to 1.
V is cleared.

37 NEGATE

40	ACCUMULATOR A
50	ACCUMULATOR B
70	EXTENDED ADDRESS
60	INDEXED ADDRESS

Flags that can be affected, N, Z, V, C.

38 ADD ACCUMULATOR A TO ACCUMULATOR B

1B

Flags that can be affected, N, Z, V, C, H.

39 SUBTRACT ACCUMULATORS

10

Flags that can be affected, N, Z, V, C.

40 ADD WITH CARRY IN ACCUMULATOR A

89	IMMEDIATE
99	DIRECT
B9	EXTENDED
A9	INDEXED

Flags affected are, N, Z, V, C, H.

41 ADD WITH CARRY IN ACCUMULATOR B

C9	IMMEDIATE
D9	DIRECT
F9	EXTENDED
E9	INDEXED

Flags affected are, N, Z, V, C.

42 ADD WITHOUT CARRY IN ACCUMULATOR A

8B	IMMEDIATE
9B	DIRECT
BB	EXTENDED
AB	INDEXED

Flags affected are, N, Z, V, C, H.

43 ADD WITHOUT CARRY IN ACCUMULATOR B

CB	IMMEDIATE
DB	DIRECT
FB	EXTENDED
EB	INDEXED

Flags affected are, N, Z, V, C. H.

44 SUBTRACT WITH CARRY IN ACCUMULATOR A

82	IMMEDIATE
92	DIRECT
B2	EXTENDED
A2	INDEXED

Flags that can be affected are, N, Z, V. C.

45 SUBTRACT WITH CARRY IN ACCUMULATOR B

C2	IMMEDIATE
D2	DIRECT
F2	EXTENDED
E2	INDEXED

Flags that can be affected are, N, Z, V, C.

Table 14-3. Continued.

46 SUBTRACT (memory byte from ACCUMULATOR A)

    80   IMMEDIATE
    90   DIRECT
    B0   EXTENDED
    A0   INDEXED

    Flags that can be affected, N, Z, V, C.

47 SUBTRACT (memory byte from ACCUMULATOR B)

    C0   IMMEDIATE
    D0   DIRECT
    F0   EXTENDED
    E0   INDEXED

    Flags that can be affected, N, Z, V, C.

48 DECIMAL ADJUST the A ACCUMULATOR

    Flags that can be affected are N. Z. C.

49 LOGICAL AND ACCUMULATOR A

    84   IMMEDIATE
    94   DIRECT
    B4   EXTENDED
    A4   INDEXED

    Flags that can be affected, N, Z. The V flag is cleared.

50 LOGICAL AND ACCUMULATOR B

    C4   IMMEDIATE
    D4   DIRECT
    F4   EXTENDED
    E4   INDEXED

    Flags that can be affected, N, Z. The V is cleared.

51 INCLUSIVE OR (Logical OR) ACCUMULATOR A

    8A   IMMEDIATE
    9A   DIRECT
    BA   EXTENDED
    AA   INDEXED

    Flags that can be affected, N, Z. The V flag is cleared.

52 INCLUSIVE OR (LOGICAL OR) ACCUMULATOR B

    CA   IMMEDIATE
    DA   DIRECT
    FA   EXTENDED
    EA   INDEXED

    Flags that can be affected, N, Z. The V flag is cleared.

53 EXCLUSIVE OR ACCUMULATOR A

    88   IMMEDIATE
    98   DIRECT
    B8   EXTENDED
    A8   INDEXED

    Flags that can be affected, N, Z. The V flag is cleared.

54 EXCLUSIVE OR ACCUMULATOR B

    C8   IMMEDIATE
    D8   DIRECT
    F8   EXTENDED
    E8   INDEX

    Flags that can be affected, N, Z. The V flag is cleared.

55 BRANCH ALWAYS

    20   Unconditional

56 BRANCH to SUBROUTINE

    8D   Unconditional

57 RETURN from SUBROUTINE

    39

58 BRANCH if CARRY SET

    25   Conditional, C is set to 1.

59 BRANCH if CARRY CLEAR

    24   Conditional, C is cleared to 0.

60 BRANCH if OVERFLOW SET

    29   Conditional, V is set to 1.

61 BRANCH if OVERFLOW CLEAR

    28   Conditional, V is cleared to 0.

62 BRANCH if ZERO SET

    27   Conditional, Z is set to 1.

63 BRANCH if ZERO CLEAR

    26   Conditional, Z is cleared to 0.

Table 14-3. Continued.

64 BRANCH if NEGATIVE SET

    28   Conditional, N is set to 1.

65 BRANCH if NEGATIVE CLEAR

    2A   Conditional, N is cleared to 0.

66 BRANCH if HIGHER

    22   Conditional, C or Z is cleared to 0.

67 BRANCH if LOWER or SAME

    23   Conditional, C or Z is set to 1.

68 BRANCH is LESS THAN ZERO
    2D   Conditional, N is set to 1 and V is
                cleared to 0, or N is cleared to 0 and V
                is set to 1.

69 BRANCH if LESS THAN or EQUAL TO ZERO

    2F   Conditional, Z is set to 1, N is set to 1
                and V is cleared to 0, or, Z is set to 1,
                N is cleared to 0 and V is set to 1.

70 BRANCH if GREATER THAN ZERO

    2E   Conditional, z is cleared to 0, N is set to
                1 and V is set to 1. Or Z is cleared to 0.
                N is cleared to 0 and V is cleared to 0.

71 BRANCH if GREATER THAN or EQUAL TO ZERO

    2C   Conditional, N and V are set to 1, or, N
                and V are cleared to 0.

72 JUMP

    7E   EXTENDED ADDRESS
    6E   INDEXED ADDRESS

73 JUMP to SUBROUTINE

    DB   EXTENDED ADDRESS
    AD   INDEXED ADDRESS

74 RETURN from SUBROUTINE
    39

75 NO OPERATION
    01

76 COMPARE ACCUMULATORS
    11

    Flags that could be affected, N, Z, V, C.

77 COMPARE ACCUMULATOR A

    81   IMMEDIATE
    91   DIRECT
    B1   EXTENDED
    A1   INDEXED

    Flags that could be affected, N, Z, V, C.

78 COMPARE ACCUMULATOR B

    C1   IMMEDIATE
    D1   DIRECT
    F1   EXTENDED
    E1   INDEXED

    Flags that could be affected, N, Z, V, C.

79 COMPARE INDEX REGISTER

    8C   IMMEDIATE
    9C   DIRECT
    BC   EXTENDED
    AC   INDEXED

    Flags that could be affected, N, Z, V.

80 RETURN from INTERRUPT

    3B

81 SOFTWARE INTERRUPT

    3F

    The I flag is set to 1.

82 WAIT for INTERRUPT

    3F

    The I flag can be affected.

Op codes in an 8-bit processor are usually one byte in size. In eight bits there are 256 combinations. This means an 8-bit processor is able to easily process 256 different instructions. However, there is really no need at this time to have that many different codes. A total near 75 is more than enough to do an adequate job of computing. Actually there is a lot of repetition in the codes. They cover a lot of the same jobs just using different registers and addressing modes. There are only about two dozen different basic jobs the computer does. The instruction set consists of a lot of variation of the same jobs.

An instruction set

The 75 or so instructions a processor is built to respond to come in three general types. The most used instruction type deals with moving op codes and operands to and from the processor and the residents of the memory map. You'll find these instructions with names like Load, Store, Move, and Transfer. There are many registers in the processor and the memory map. Each separate movement of bytes between them requires a special op code. Therefore, there are a lot of these instructions in the Set. These instructions take up at least 75% of the bytes you'll find in a program.

The second type of instructions are those that process the operands in the accumulator circuits. They do the arithmetic, logic, and register bit manipulations such as shift, increment, clear, and complement. They are the calculator instructions the processor responds to.

The third type of instruction has little to do with the processing data. They deal with the addressing mechanism of the processor. They are the ones that are called Jump, Branch, Call, Return, and Halt. They and the automatic incrementing of the program counter keep the processor accessing the correct locations in the memory map.

These instructions can number around 75. This leaves about 175 possible opcode spaces that could be installed in future 8-bit processors. No doubt as time goes by and additional computing needs arise, many more variations of the original 75 will be created as well as many new ones with capabilities as yet unknown. The instruction set table (Table 14-3) lists typical instructions. They were taken from a processor like the 6800.

Testing a processor

All of the preceding discussion of an 8-bit processor is the way a technician must view a processor. In order to intelligently figure out what is wrong with such a device you must have a good idea of how the thing is working and what it is doing. Down at the chip pin level, when you make tests, you are working with the machine language of the processor.

If you know the inputs, the outputs, and the special control and power supply pin operations, you can test and come to some logical conclusions of where a trouble might be. If the inputs are o.k., but some output pins read incorrectly, chances are good the processor is defective. Should the inputs be incorrect, odds are that the processor itself is o.k., but some input circuit external to the processor is sending the wrong voltage level or pulse.

There are all sorts of diagrams and charts that accompany a processor. Some of them are good service aids while others are primarily needed for machine language programming. The diagram that shows the bit sizes of the processor registers (like Fig. 14-16) is of limited use for troubleshooting and repair. It is helpful if you are going to write a machine-language diagnostic but aside from that, it won't reveal the quality of your processor.

14-16 This is a programmer's block diagram of the registers in an 8-bit processor. It shows a programmer the registers that are available. Note that the only electronic information is the register bit sizes.

The block diagram of the computer (such as Fig. 14-17) and the block diagram of its processor internals provides a lot of troubleshooting information. The chip manufacturer's pin location drawing is quite valuable. It gives you an actual top view of the chip with all the names of the pins. The only problem that happens on occasion is when a computer assembler does not use the processor in a conventional way. He could leave some pins unused, others with odd but workable duties, and make other changes. You could find an output pin with a wrong state and conclude the processor is defective only to find the pin is unused and tied to ground or +5 V to keep it from interfering with the operation.

The best piece of service information is the computer's schematic diagram, complete with service notes and parts list. Then the only difficulty becomes relating the schematic symbols to the actual hardware.

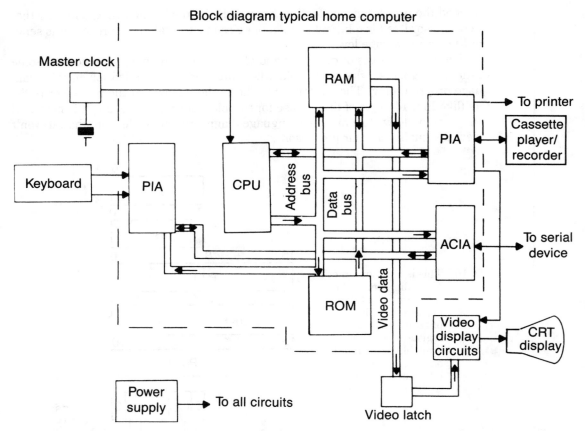

14-17 A specific block diagram in service notes that shows the general signal processing layout gives the troubleshooter a quick overview of the computer.

As you look down on the main print board you could see a hundred or more chips laid out neatly on the board. The processor is typically in a large DIP or SMD. Most 8-bit processors are in 40-pin or larger packages. It is usually easy to find them even with a lot of chips on the board. It is also often mounted in a socket. If you suspect the processor and it is in a socket and you have a known good spare, the first test would be direct replacement. Aside from that you must test the processor for logic states and pulses. Go through a typical checkout with a logic probe.

A processor like the 6502 found in many 8-bit computers has 40 pins. They are numbered 1 – 40. There is no concern with the special numbering that takes place with items like data and address buses starting with zero. The physical chip has pins 1 and 40 on either side of the keyway that could be a notch or a paint dot on a DIP or an index dot and index corner on an SMD. The 6502 pins are counted counterclockwise.

The schematic drawing does not show the physical chip pin layout. The schematic shows the pins in a convenient position so the connecting lines can be drawn as short as possible. That is where the relating comes in. When you look at an actual chip package and then look at the schematic drawing of the same package, they bear no physical relationship to each other. You must look at the schematic for the electronic signal flow information and then find the actual pin on the chip.

On our example processor (Fig. 14-18) pin 1 is at the upper left-hand corner, pin 20 at the bottom left-hand, pin 21 at the bottom right and pin 40 at the top right. These numbers on the schematic (Fig. 14-19) can be anywhere on the processor rectangle symbol. You must relate the schematic to the physical processor.

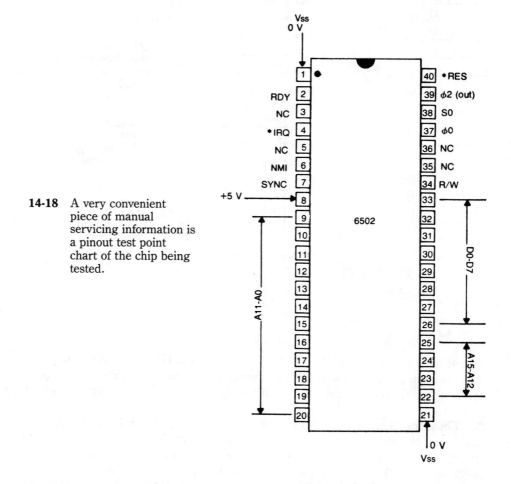

14-18 A very convenient piece of manual servicing information is a pinout test point chart of the chip being tested.

In order to use a logic probe the computer must be energized. It doesn't matter whether the display is coming on or not. Using the logic probe is old fashioned tried and true digital circuit testing. It always provides some service information unlike diagnostic program testing that only can be used when the computer is still able to function somewhat. See Table 14-4.

The first test is always power. There is supposed to be +5 V applied to pin 8. If you were using a VOM the pin input, if o.k., should read +5 V. The logic probe

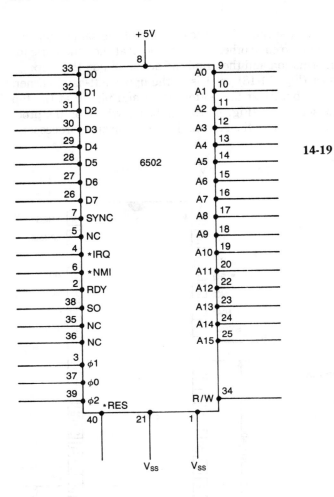

14-19 This is the schematic diagram of the 6502 processor shown in Fig. 14-18. Note this is not a physical pinout. The pins are not in numerical order. To use the schematic diagram and take a voltage reading, you must relate the diagram to the actual chip, not quite as convenient as the actual pinout.

should have its LED glow HIGH. If the +5 V or the HIGH is not at the pin then the power supply becomes the prime suspect. If the supply is o.k., then the processor itself could have developed a fault to ground and is shorting the +5 V to ground.

These processors are MOS chips. They contain IGFETs with drains and sources. The source connections, Vss, are connected to the computer ground. These are two Vss connections on this processor. They are hooked together and the pins 1 and 21 are grounded. They should read 0 V on the VOM and the logic probe should have its LOW LED lit upon application. If there is any voltage there, then the ground connection has come off and must be reconnected.

Once the power has been determined to be present and correct, then the rest of the pins can be tested, preferably with the logic probe first. Twenty four of the pins can be disposed of in seconds. They are the eight data bus pins, D7 – D0, and the 16 address pins, A15 – A0. The data pins are numbers 26 through 33. They should all make the logic probe light its PULSE LED. What you are reading is the clock

Table 14-4. A logic service chart like this one for the chip under test is another approach. A good chip that is energized should show these highs, lows, and pulses. Any deviation from the norm could indicate a problem area.

Pin Number		High (1)	Low (0)	Pulse
V ss			✓	
RDY	2	✓		
NC	3			
*IRQ	4	✓		✓
NC	5			
NMI	6	✓		
SYNC	7		✓	
+5 V	8	✓	✓	✓
A0	9			✓
A1	10			✓
A2	11			✓
A3	12			✓
A4	13			✓
A5	14			✓
A6	15			✓
A7	16			✓
A8	17			✓
A9	18			✓
A10	19			✓
A11	20			✓
Vss	21		✓	✓
A12	22			✓
A13	23			✓
A14	24			✓
A15	25			✓
D7	26			✓
D6	27			✓
D5	28			✓
D4	29			✓
D3	30			✓
D2	31			✓
D1	32			✓
D0	33			✓
R/W	34			✓
NC	35			
NC	36			
φ0	37			
SO	38	✓		✓
φ2	39			✓
*RES	40	✓		✓

signal being applied to the data bus. The clock is like the motor of the data bus. The data bus is idling, waiting for some logic states to travel between the processor and the memory map.

Actually, during this idling a lot is still going on. The TV display is being fed a continual composite TV signal. Some circuit in the computer is constantly scanning the video RAM and updating the display so it won't disappear on you. The processor could be involved in this updating or another chip like the video output could be doing the video RAM update reading.

If the processor is not involved with the updating and is truly idling, then VOM tests of the data pins will show a three-state 1.2 to 2.5 V reading. If the processor is doing the updating then the data pins will not be three-stating and will show some logic and not the high impedance state. The VIC 20 and Commodore 64, both use the video output chip to update the video RAM. Their processors (both a 6502 type) have the data bus idling and the VOM shows three-stating. The TRS-80 Color Computer on the other hand uses the processor to help out in updating the video display by scanning video RAM and does not show three-stating on the data pins. All of them though show the data pins pulsing on a continual basis. Incidentally the presence of the pulses means that the clock is running and is probably o.k.

The 16 address pins are numbers 9 through 25, except for 21, which is one of the VSS pins. They also should show PULSE on every pin while the processor is idling. You can quickly touch down on all the pins with the logic probe and detect the pulses. The pulses should be present on every pin. If a pulse is missing, that is a valid clue. All the address pins, and as a matter of fact the data pins too, must have a pulse while idling. If one or more of the pulses are gone, chances are good the processor has given up the ghost.

Should all the pulses be gone, not just a few, then you must test the clock circuits with the logic probe. If the clock is pulsing and inputting a good signal into the processor, and the pulses are not exiting the address and data pins, then the processor becomes the prime suspect. Should the clock not be pulsing, then of course, the clock is the reason there are no pulses at the processor output.

There is always the possibility, when the clock input pulses are o.k., but pulses are not reading at the address and data pins, that the bus line that connects to the pin without the pulse, has developed some type of fault and is shorting the pulse to ground. This is easily determined. Disconnect the one bus line from the processor. If the pulse returns upon the disconnection, then the bus line has the fault. Should the pulse still be missing, then the processor is almost certainly defective. The clock is inputting a good pulse but somewhere in the multitude of circuits in the processor the pulse is lost. Only a new processor will cure the condition.

The three power and 24 bus lines take up 27 pins. That leaves about 13 pins to handle the various control lines. If there are any pins left over they are designated NC (no connection) on the schematic. Some computers use some control lines and other computers use other control lines. The NC lines are usually connected to either +5 V or are grounded. This keeps them from interfering with the processor operation. Even though the schematic of the computer shows them as NC they could still be connected internally to vital circuit positions. The processor spec sheet shows which unused pins are to be connected to +5 V and which ones to ground.

The control line R/W, the read-write line is always used. It is the traffic cop for the data bus and its setting determines the direction the data bits will flow on the data bus. In this processor the line is called R/*W. This is pronounced in a technician's mind as "read, not write." What that means is the data bus will permit the processor to read data from the memory when the line is held high or at 1. The *W or "not write" indicates that the processor can write data to memory when the line is held low or at a 0 state.

When you test the R/W line while the processor is idling, the logic probe will read a pulse. This means the clock is applying a pulse to the pin. The VOM could read three-state or a logic state according to different type computers. In this particular processor the two readings were PULSE and a three-state voltage around +2 V.

The asterisk in front of W (*W) gave the W the "not" part of "not write." The same "not" notation is placed on all the pins in the computer. In the processor the power pins come from the supply and the address-data bus pins are all pulse driven, so there is no reason to notate any of them with an asterisk. The control lines, however, control various aspects by being held high or being held low. When a line is held high and is off, then is forced low and thus enabled, the line receives an asterisk. This is a schematic symbol that means the line is off when high and on when low.

The lack of an asterisk denotes the line is held low and will be turned on with the application of a high. If you find a line that is supposed to be held high and it is low, that could be a clue. Should you touch down on a pin and it is held low instead of its noted condition, which is being held high, that could be a clue. If a pin is reading wrong you might have pinpointed the trouble. There is one problem though. Every now and then you will encounter a pin that does not follow the above logic. That is why I said you might have found the trouble. In some instances a pin with an asterisk will be held low and one without an asterisk be held high. What can you do about it? Just be on the lookout for these exceptions. That is part of troubleshooting.

The *RES pin is a reset input pin. It is held high. The reset circuit will be activated when a low arrives on this pin. It is used to initialize the processor registers when the computer is turned on. In other computers it is used to reinitialize the processor registers after a reset interrupt.

*IRQ and *NMI are two more input lines. They are the interrupts. *IRQ is called interrupt request. It is held high until an interrupt arrives. As long as the mask flag is not set the interrupt request will make the processor service the interrupt. *NMI is called a nonmaskable interrupt. It is held high. When a low arrives on this pin the interrupt will happen whether the mask flag is set or not.

That is the way the processor receives inputs and sends outputs. There are all sorts of specialized control inputs the processor might receive, or outputs the processor might send to control some circuit. The 8-bit computer though is relatively simple in these respects. As you examine some of the 16-bit processors in the next chapter, there will be some more complicated addressing, data moving, and controlling.

The best test of a processor is to try a new one, although this is often very inconvenient or even impossible. Then pin testing becomes a valuable technique. In order to test the pins in a way that will yield troubleshooting information results, you should have some idea of how the processor operates and what voltages and/or pulses should be on the pins while the process is idling. As you take the logic probe and VOM readings, the condition of the processor will be revealed. You should, after testing a few, get the feel of whether a pin is receiving the correct input or if it is outputting the right voltage or pulse. That way as you encounter a troubled pin, you'll recognize its condition and be able to make some sense out of what is happening. Once you understand the fault, the repair will quickly follow.

15

The original
16-bit processors

WHILE MILLIONS OF COMPUTERS WITH 8-BIT PROCESSORS WERE SELLING during the early 1980's, IBM introduced the original PC, Apple brought forth the first Macintosh, and Commodore the Amiga. These were the first commercial 16-bit machines and were priced much higher than their 8-bit predecessors. The IBM PC appeared with Intel's 8088 and 8086, and the Macintosh and Amiga used a Motorola 68000. There were a number of other 16-bit processors that also surfaced around that time period, such as the Zilog Z8001 and Z8002, Texas Instruments 9900, National Semiconductors 16000 and others. The 8088-8086 and 68000 held sway and persisted.

These two types of 16-bit processors were followed by advanced models from the same manufacturers that were upwardly compatible. This means that each new processor model could use most of the software that had been written for the earlier models. For instance, the Intel 80286, an advanced new model of the 8088-8086, was able not only to use the software that was written for itself, but could also run the software that had been prepared for the earlier 8088-8086 processors. This fact is a main reason the 80286 and further models have been so successful. These more advanced and newer processors are discussed in the next two chapters. Examine the differences and advantages of the 16-bit processors over the 8-bit types.

General classifications

In general terms, computers are generally classified as 8-bit, 16-bit, 32-bit, or higher. The bit numbers are derived from the number of wires found in the data bus. The data bus winds its way from the processor to all the locations on the memory map. As discussed, the data bus is the pathway the instructions and data, in the programs and stored in memory, take to travel to and from the processor, as a program is run. An 8-bit machine only has eight wires in its data bus, a 16-bit computer can have 16 wires. With the 16 wires, the 16-bit computer is able to transport two bytes at a time instead of one byte as an 8-bit computer is limited to. Just as an 8-bit piece of data is called a byte, a 16-bit data collection is called a word. Figure 15-1 shows two bytes of data, a word, being transferred from the processor to a location on the memory map.

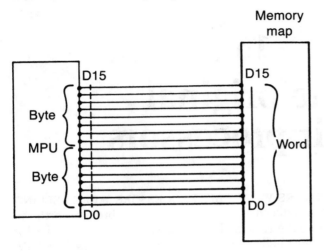

15-1   The 16-bit data bus is able to transfer a word at a time. A word is composed of two bytes.

16-bit memory

In a 16-bit computer, compared to an 8-bit, memory locations have twice as many bit positions. There are many memory schemes that can be used to fill the memory locations, but they are usually dynamic types. For example, a set of 64K bit chips can be used (Fig. 15-2). The chips are organized as 64K × 1 each. If you use 16 such chips with a 16 line data bus, the MPU can address one location, one bit position on each chip, at one time.

In the 8-bit computer, the same type of dynamic memory can be used. Only in the eight line data bus are eight bit positions on eight memory chips addressed at one time. The 16-bit MPU, therefore, addresses twice as many bits at the same time as the 8-bit MPU. This automatically doubles the rate of operations possible in the 16-bit type.

Addressing

There are a lot of 16-bit MPUs on the market, which transport 16 bits at a time over a 16-bit data bus. However, the address bus size of many of them do not follow the same pattern. The 8-bit computer typically has eight data lines in the data bus and 16 address lines in the address bus. It should follow, then, that a 16-bit computer should have twice as many address lines as the 8-bit. This means a 16-bit MPU should have 32 address lines.

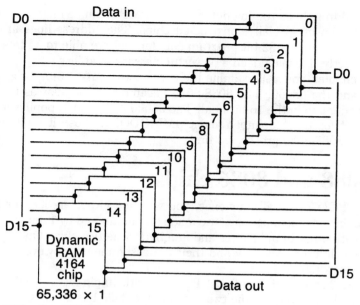

15-2 One 16-bit memory layout could have sixteen 4164 dynamic memory chips attached to the 16 lines in the data bus.

Thirty-two address lines gives the MPU an almost inconceivable ability to directly address a memory map. Examine the address line numbers.

In an 8-bit computer there are 16 address lines. This enables the MPU to directly access 64K individual locations. There are addressing schemes that use a special addressing chip to place additional address lines into a computer. If the lines are increased from 16 the number of addresses the MPU can contact doubles with each additional line.

Address Lines	8-Bit Locations
16	64K
17	128K
18	256K
19	512K
20	1024K
21	2058K
22	4096K
23	8192K
24	16 Mbytes
.	
.	
.	
32	4 gigabytes (billions)

The 16 address lines coming out of the 8-bit MPU can be increased in number with the addition of specially-constructed chips. The address lines in the 16-bit MPU can come out of a 32-bit program counter and are able to address 4 billion locations directly. This is indeed a powerful increase in ability.

In this chapter, you will examine the two most popular 16-bit processors, the 8088-8086 and the 68000. The 8088-8086 became very popular as the IBM PC took over leadership in the 16-bit field. The 68000 is second in popularity because Apple used it for the Macintosh and COMMODORE chose it for their Amiga. Examine the 8088-8086 processors first.

The 8088 and 8086 chips

In the IBM PC/XT and all its clones, you will find either an 8088 or 8086 type chip. The chips, for the most part, are made and numbered by Intel, but you could find them with other brand names and numbers. The two chips have some differences in their internal circuitry and their pin assignments, however they use the exact same instruction set.

Figure 15-3 shows the two chips. They are both 40-pin DIPs like the 8-bit processors. If you look closely at the two pinouts, the 8086 has 16 data pins. They are pins 2 – 16 and 39. These 16 pins are used by both the address bus and the data bus. On the other hand, the 8088 only uses eight data pins, 9 – 16. This makes the 8088 appear at first glance, to be an 8-bit processor while the 8086 looks like a 16-bit processor. The 8088 is just as much a 16-bit processor as the 8086. The 8088 has a slight handicap. It must make two passes to access a 16-bit data register in memory, eight bits at a time. The 8086 can access 16-bits with a single pass.

Aside from the difference in the layout of the data pins, the 8088 and 8086 are similar in most other ways. They both output the same address, data, and control signals to transfer data back and forth between themselves and the residents of the memory map.

They both have 20 address lines, A0 – A19. This allows the 8088-8086 to directly address 1,048,576 memory map bytes. This is called 1 Mb. These are 8-bit registers in the 1 Mb map. The map can also be considered in terms of 2 byte registers, called words. The 8088-8086 therefore is said to be able to directly address 524,288 memory map words.

The 8088-8086 is equipped with fourteen 16-bit registers, shown in Fig. 15-4. Note there are no registers larger than 16-bits. This makes the register set resemble an 8-bit processor. In many respects there are 8-bit processors that can perform as well as the 8088-8086. However, the 8088-8086 has 20 address lines and can address 1 Mb, but an 8-bit processor only has 16 address lines and can only address 64K. This is one of the advantages the 8088-8086 has, among other things, over an 8-bit processor and is considered a 16-bit processor.

In order to fully utilize the 1 Mb address space the 8088-8086 is given an instruction set with 135 instructions. These instructions are designed to perform operations on data of many sizes. It can work on single bit data, 8-bit bytes, 16-bit words, and 32-bit double words. Most of the instructions though, operate only on

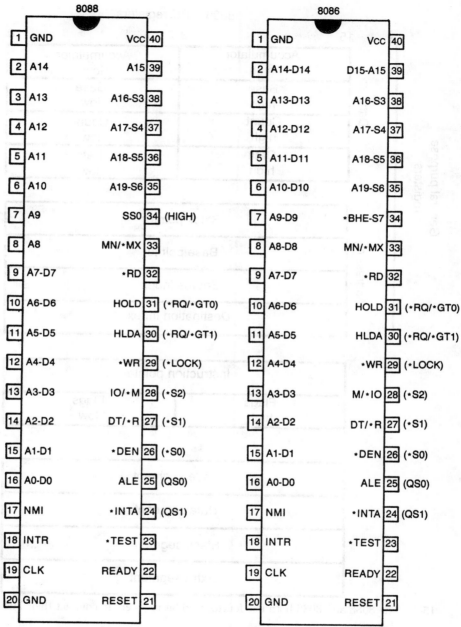

	8088		
1	GND	Vcc	40
2	A14	A15	39
3	A13	A16-S3	38
4	A12	A17-S4	37
5	A11	A18-S5	36
6	A10	A19-S6	35
7	A9	SS0	34 (HIGH)
8	A8	MN/•MX	33
9	A7-D7	•RD	32
10	A6-D6	HOLD	31 (•RQ/•GT0)
11	A5-D5	HLDA	30 (•RQ/•GT1)
12	A4-D4	•WR	29 (•LOCK)
13	A3-D3	IO/•M	28 (•S2)
14	A2-D2	DT/•R	27 (•S1)
15	A1-D1	•DEN	26 (•S0)
16	A0-D0	ALE	25 (QS0)
17	NMI	•INTA	24 (QS1)
18	INTR	•TEST	23
19	CLK	READY	22
20	GND	RESET	21

	8086		
1	GND	Vcc	40
2	A14-D14	D15-A15	39
3	A13-D13	A16-S3	38
4	A12-D12	A17-S4	37
5	A11-D11	A18-S5	36
6	A10-D10	A19-S6	35
7	A9-D9	•BHE-S7	34
8	A8-D8	MN/•MX	33
9	A7-D7	•RD	32
10	A6-D6	HOLD	31 (•RQ/•GT0)
11	A5-D5	HLDA	30 (•RQ/•GT1)
12	A4-D4	•WR	29 (•LOCK)
13	A3-D3	M/•IO	28 (•S2)
14	A2-D2	DT/•R	27 (•S1)
15	A1-D1	•DEN	26 (•S0)
16	A0-D0	ALE	25 (QS0)
17	NMI	•INTA	24 (QS1)
18	INTR	•TEST	23
19	CLK	READY	22
20	GND	RESET	21

Note pins 33 on both chips, MN/•MX, minimum and maximum mode controls.
In minimum mode the pin functions inside chip area are active. In maximum
mode the functions in parentheses outside chip area take over their pins.

15-3   The 8088 and 8086 chips are able to be installed in 40-pin DIPs because they use some of the same pins in a multiplex scheme to output both address and data bits.

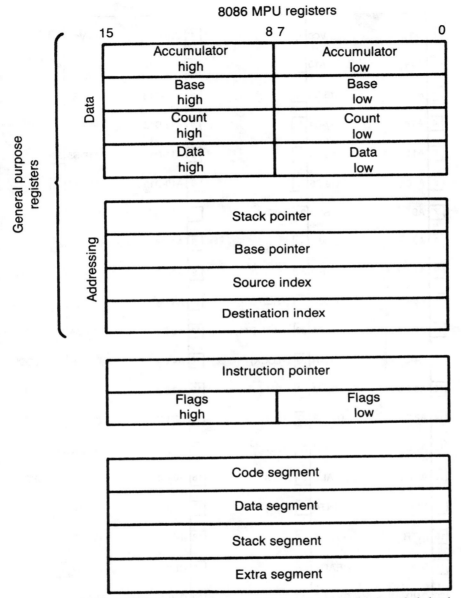

8086 MPU registers

15-4 The 8088 and 8086 both use fourteen 16-bit registers to conduct their business.

8-bit and 16-bit data. The single bit and 32-bit operations are available but few in number.

The 8088-8086 is said to be *register oriented*. This means the processor and its instructions tend to use the internal registers to manipulate data as much as possible rather than transferring data back and forth to memory. This saves all sorts of time. To implement this specialized activity, eight of the fourteen internal 16-bit registers are general purpose. The processor can use them in many ways including making them act as RAM.

The 8088-8086 clock speed can be made to run between 4 and 8 MHz. The 8-bit processors ran around 1 or 2 MHz. The 8088-8086 is considerably faster. For example, in a processor running at 5 MHz, a short instruction such as register to register transfer would take 400 nanoseconds to execute. A long instruction like a signed 16-bit by 16-bit division takes 42 microseconds to run off. In a processor with 1 MHz speed, these instructions would take many times longer to complete an instruction cycle.

The fourteen registers

There are three sections to the fourteen registers. There are the accumulator data handling group, the pointers and indexes, and the segment registers. Figure 15-4 shows the programmer's diagram. The accumulator group, the pointers and indexes make up the group of general purpose registers. The four accumulator types are divided even further. Each 16-bit register comprises of useful 8-bit registers, with high and low bytes.

The eight 8-bit or four 16-bit accumulator type registers, however you want to describe them, are primarily data handlers. The other four general purpose registers, the pointers and the indexers, are primarliy addressers.

The data handlers are named accumulator, base, count, and data. Each 16-bit register has two 8-bit sections called high and low. They are somewhat interchangeable according to the instruction being executed. Some instructions specify a particular register, while other instructions are able to be more flexible.

The four other general purpose registers also can be used for specific purposes. The stack pointer can be used to provide the 16 most significant bits of the address of the stack. The four least significant bits for the stack address is provided by the stack segment register, which we will get to shortly. The base pointer, source index, and destination index can be used to provide 16 bits of 20-bit addresses when the 8088-8086 addresses the 1 Mb memory map. Sometimes just the base pointer is used. Other times the source index or destination index could be added to the base pointer to produce a final address. Still other times the base pointer and indexes could be used with the data segment register to generate an address. The 8088-8086 addressing ability is quite versatile. Don't forget these eight 16-bit registers, besides doing assigned duties are also general purpose. They are all capable of performing general operations between all eight registers. Data can be transferred, added, subtracted, shifted, rotated, incremented, decremented, etc., between them.

The four segment registers, code, data, stack, and extra are not really thought of as general purpose, although there are some instructions that can change the contents of the registers. These registers are there primarily to aid in the addressing of the 1 Mb address space. These registers are used to store 16-bit segment addresses. Examine the way the 8088-8086 is able to get 20 address bits out of the 16-bit registers.

Generating a 20-bit address

Figure 15-5 shows a segment register 16 bits wide in the center of the illustration. It could be any of the four segment registers, code, data, stack or extra. The segment register has its 16 bits in address positions 19 – 4. Address positions 3 – 0 are appended zeros. If you add an address to the segment that is offset from the segment address position by four bits, you will have a 20-bit address. The offset could come from any of the other registers in the processor. With the proper selection of bits all 1,048,576 bytes in the map can be addressed.

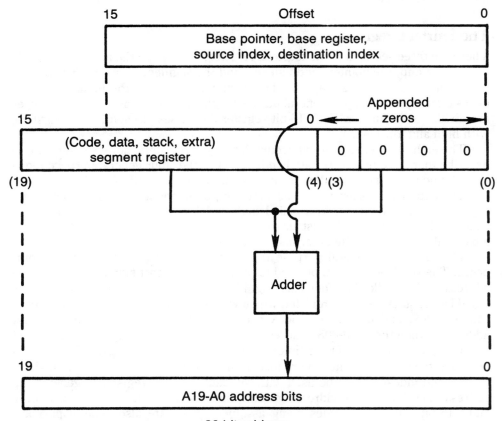

15-5   A 20-bit address can be derived from 16-bit registers. For example, place a segment register into bit positions 19 – 4. Then append four zeros to bit positions 3 – 0. Finally add and offset to the created 20-bit register.

Table 15-1 shows the addressing modes that can be used in the 8088-8086. The modes are immediate, register, base index, index, base, indirect, direct, and relative. The mode is attained by adding together the indicated registers and obtaining a 20-bit result.

**Table 15-1. Data can be located in the
8088-8086 memory by use of these eight addressing modes.**

Addressing Mode	Data Location
Immediate	In the instruction itself
Register	In designated register
Register Indirect	In memory addressed by offset in register
Direct	In memory addressed by offset in instruction
Index	In memory addressed by adding index register to displacement in Instruction
Base	In memory addressed by adding base register to displacement in Instruction
Base-Index	In memory addressed by adding base register plus index register plus displacement
Relative	In memory addressed by adding displacement to a segment register

Actual addressing is performed by machine language programmers. Combining all these values to produce these 20-bit addresses can get very complex. The technician will usually not have to do very much in this area but you never know what you might have to do when working on these machines.

One of the features of this ability to add 16-bit registers together to produce 20-bit addresses is the allocation of separate memory areas for the program code, the needed data, and the stack. In the 8-bit computer all of the code, data, and stack registers had to be in the same 64K section of RAM. With separate 16-bit segment registers, a separate 64K RAM area can be allocated for code, data, and stack. In addition there is the extra segment register that can be used if needed. Figure 15-6 shows the way the segment registers can allocate separate map areas for these purpose. An adept programmer makes good use of the qualities that are not found on the 8-bit computer.

The addressing modes

Referring back to Table 15-1 the different addressing modes are shown. In immediate addressing the instruction itself contains an 8-bit or 16-bit piece of data that needs work. According to the instruction being executed, the byte or word of data could be stored into a processor or a memory location. The data also could be sent to the ALU and be added, subtracted, ANDed or ORed. The immediate designation means that the data does not have to be read separately from memory. It is read at the same time that the instruction is. Immediate is the only mode that does not use segment addresses, pointers, indexes, and so forth.

When the Register addressing mode is employed, the instruction op code contains the name of the processor register whose contents need work. The processor

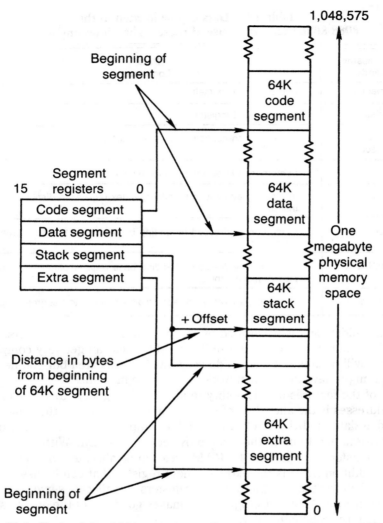

15-6 Each of the 16-bit segment registers can set up its own 64K memory area in the 1Mb physical memory space.

then quickly accesses the register and performs the dictates of the instruction on the contents. The instruction could simply be, move the specified register contents to another register. The processor will then execute the instruction.

The reason for all these addressing modes is to give the processor many different ways it can access storage areas and obtain operands to work on. The Immediate mode is the simplest. The processor doesn't have to address anything. The operand is contained in the instruction line with the op code. The Register mode is also simple. The operand to be worked on is already in an 8088-8086 internal register. The op code specifies the register and the processor goes to work on it. These two modes are the only simple ones. The rest of them get tricky.

The first tricky one is called indirect register addressing. The trick is to generate a 20-bit address. In this address is an operand the processor needs for the program being run. The typical way the address is generated is to take the contents of the data segment register and add it to the contents of one of the following registers, the base, base pointer, source index or destination index. The results of this addition is the 20-bit address where the needed operand resides. The operand is then brought to the processor and used in the program.

The contents of the base, *BP* (base pointer), *SI* (source index), and *DI* (destination index) registers are called *EA* (effective address). Effective addresses when added to segment registers produce actual 20-bit addresses to be accessed.

A variation on the indirect addressing is direct addressing. Here again a 20-bit address must be generated with the aid of a segment register. However, the bits needed to supplement the segment register are not in another processor register. These address bits are contained in the instruction along with the op code. This arrangement is something like immediate addressing. The difference is, in immediate addressing, the actual operand is in with the op code. With direct addressing, the address bits to be added to the segment register are in with the op code.

Once these bits are added with the segment register, a 20-bit address is generated and the location accessed. The operand in the location is read and the processor uses it in the program.

The next type of addressing mode is the index. This brings into play another kind of address bits. In the preceding modes, address bits were found in the segment registers, in the base, base pointer, and index registers. They were also found in with the op codes. There are also other address bits that are found in with the op codes. These bits are called a displacement. They can be added to the other involved registers to form other addressing modes.

A good example is the index addressing mode. When a displacement arrives with an op code, it can be added to one of the Index registers. Together they form an EA. The effective address is then added to a segment register to form the 20-bit address. The address is then accessed and the desired operand is retrieved. Note that if there is no displacement, the mode is an indirect register type. The two modes are almost identical, except for the displacement.

The modes become more complex. The next one is base addressing. This is somewhat like indirect register addressing but one step further. In indirect, the contents of the base, base pointer or index registers are EAs. They are added to a segment register to form the 20-bit address. If you add a displacement to the EAs in indirect, you will have performed Base addressing. The 20-bit address formed with the indirect EA, displacement, and segment register, contains the needed operand.

Taking the addition one step further and Base Index addressing occurs. To obtain a base index EA, you must add together the contents of the base register, to an Index register, plus an optional displacement. Once you have the base index EA, the EA is then added to the contents of a segment register. The result is the 20-bit address where the needed operand is stored. It can then be obtained and used by the processor.

The last mode is called relative addressing. It is a simple one but very important. It permits programmers to enjoy position-independent programs. All that is needed is to add a displacement to a segment register to form the 20-bit address. This is the mode that works to aid the processor to perform Jumps and Calls.

The many different ways the 8088-8086 is able to obtain operands is one of the great strengths the processor is endowed with. The operands are stashed all over. They are found contained in program lines along with the op code in the internal processor registers, in RAM and ROM. When the operands are accompanying the op code and when they are in processor registers the Immediate and Register addressing modes fetch them without further ado.

When the operands are stashed around in the 1 Mb memory map, then the other addressing modes must be used to gather them up. The other modes, indirect, direct, index, base address, base index, and relative are all various schemes to generate the 20-bit address to access the location containing the desired operand.

The schemes consist of adding together combinations of segments, pointers, displacements and indexes. To find instructions in memory the instruction pointer is added to the code segment register contents. To locate stack bytes the stack pointer is added to the stack segment register. To obtain data bytes in memory the base register is added to the base pointer, an index, and a displacement when required. The result is added to the data segment contents. The extra segment register can also be used in the same way. Adding a base register to an index plus a displacement to the extra segment register will also locate data.

Getting the various addressing modes under your hat is not easy. However, if you want to be able to write machine language programs for the 8088-8086, the addressing techniques must be learned. It is important for the technician to know about them. The more you understand the workings of the processor in a computer you are working on, the easier it will be to do your job.

The 8088-8086 instruction set

In the addressing mode section you learned about the way operands are located and brought to the processor to be worked on. Mention was made that operands might be installed along with op codes, that addresses are installed with op codes, and that displacements also can accompany op codes. It is now time to look closer at the way op codes travel along with these other bit set types. Figure 15-7 illustrates different sized instructions. The sizes vary from one to six bytes long.

The number of bytes in an instruction is dependent on what entities are contained in the instruction. The bytes can consist of the op code, the addressing mode, displacement bits, address bits and data.

The 8088-8086 had been given 8-bit op codes. The first byte in the total instruction length is the op code. The op code defines the operation that is to be performed. For example, MOVE, ADD, JUMP, etc. The second byte (when there is a second byte), specifies the addressing mode in the two MOD bits and the three R/M bits.

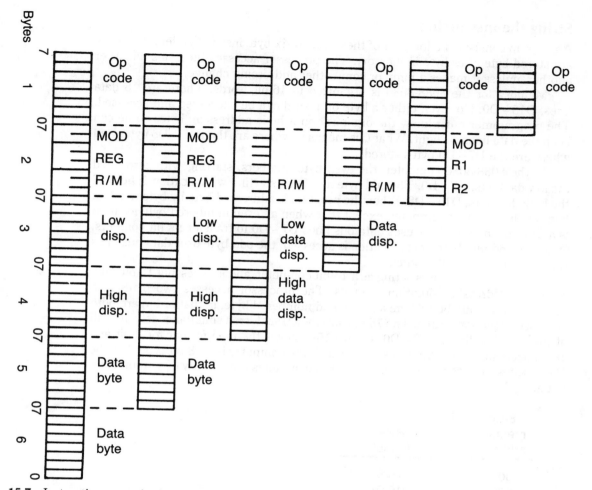

15-7 Instructions come in sizes from one byte to six bytes. The op code of the instruction is always in first position.

When the addressing mode specifies that a displacement is to be in the instruction length, one or two bytes are assigned to hold the displacement. In the three byte instruction the third byte will hold the displacement bits. In the four, five or six byte instructions, two bytes can be assigned to hold the displacement. The displacement is then used by the processor as needed to generate the 20-bit address that contains data for the program.

The op code and addressing mode could specify one or two bytes of immediate data. When that happens the data will be found after or instead of the displacement byte or bytes. Figure 15-7 shows the example arrangements of op codes, addressing modes, displacements, and data in one to six byte instruction lengths.

String the instructions

A program consists of a long list of these one to six byte instruction lengths. They are stored byte after byte in memory. The processor accesses the bytes one after another, unless it makes a jump or some other addressing change.

Memory for the 8088-8086 is organized in 16-bit words. There are 16 data lines, D15 – D0. However, either a byte or a word can be addressed and accessed. The programmer must know the organization if he is addressing bytes so he can keep the data lines straight. What this means is, where are the D15 – D8 bytes and where are the D7 – D0 bytes stored?

In the 8088-8086 computer, the even byte numbers, starting with zero, hold the low data bits, D7 – D0. The odd byte numbers, starting with location 1, hold all the high data bits, D15 – D8. When the program is addressed byte by byte the data bus acts like an 8-bit computer, except that when an even numbered byte location is accessed, the even byte uses data bus lines D7 – D0 to transfer its bit contents. When an odd numbered byte location is accessed, the odd byte uses data bus lines D15 – D8 to transfer its contents.

When the processor is acting as a 16-bit computer, and is accessing 16 bits at a time, the addressing situation changes. The processor accesses two bytes at a time. One even numbered byte and one odd numbered byte, in that order, are both accessed at the same time. The 16 bits are then transferred simultaneously over all of the data bus lines, D15 – D0. Figure 15-8 shows the map format for 8-bit and 16-bit accesses. The 8-bit access works as if the computer is an 8-bit type. For the 16-bit access, the computer changes hats and assumes the identity of a 16-bit computer.

8-Bit memory address	Byte format
0000	D7-D0
0001	D15-D8
0002	D7-D0
0003	D15-D8
0004	D7-D0
0005	D15-D8

16-Bit memory address	Word format
0000	D7-D0, D15-D8
0002	D7-D0, D15-D8
0004	D7-D0, D15-D8

15-8 The even-byte addresses starting with zero hold the lower bits of a word, D7 – D0, and the odd addresses contain the higher bits, D15 – D8.

The 135 instructions

Intel breaks down the 135 instructions into seven categories. The categories are called, data transfer, arithmetic, logic, control transfer, string manipulation, interrupt, and processor control.

The instructions make use of all the registers in the 8088-8086. You have read about the general purpose and segment registers, there was no mention of the 16-bit status flag register. No discussion of the instruction set would be complete without the flag register. As programs are run and instructions are processed, the flag register is deeply involved. As an instruction is executed, chances are good that one or more of the flags in the register will have its state changed.

There are nine bits of the 16-bit flag register that are in action in the 8086. As time goes by and newer versions of the 8086 are produced, more bits in the register could be assigned jobs. Meanwhile there are the following one single bit registers installed in the 16-bit space.

Figure 15-9 illustrates the 16-bit status flag register. The nine flags in use are:

Bit 0	C	the carry flag
2	P	the parity flag
4	A	the auxiliary carry flag
6	Z	the zero flag
7	S	the sign flag
8	T	the trap flag
9	I	the interrupt enable flag
10	D	the direction flag
11	Q	the overflow flag

Bits 1, 3, 5, 12, 13, 14, and 15 are unused. They represent excess capacity that will eventually be filled.

If you'll notice the names of some of the flags are similar to the names of the flags in the 8-bit 6800 processor discussed earlier. They perform similar jobs in the 8088-8086. They are especially active as arithmetic and logic instructions are executed. There will be more information on the flags and their activity as we go through the instructions and see what they do and what registers they use.

Data transfer

Intel further breaks down the data transfer category into six subcategories. Their mnemonics used to write machine language programs are MOV (move), PUSH (push), POP (pop), XCHG (exchange), IN (input from) and OUT (output to).

There are seven kinds of MOV instructions. These type of instructions in 8-bit processors were called load and store. In the 8088-8086 they are all lumped together as MOV. There are some load and store instructions that supplement the MOV instructions. They will be covered later in this section. According to the bit structure of the instruction bytes, the direction of the data movement is specified. In Fig. 15-10 the seven bit structures are shown. As you can see, the moves can go either way. For instance, the fourth instruction specifies a data movement from memory to accumulator. The fifth instruction, using the same pathway but in the

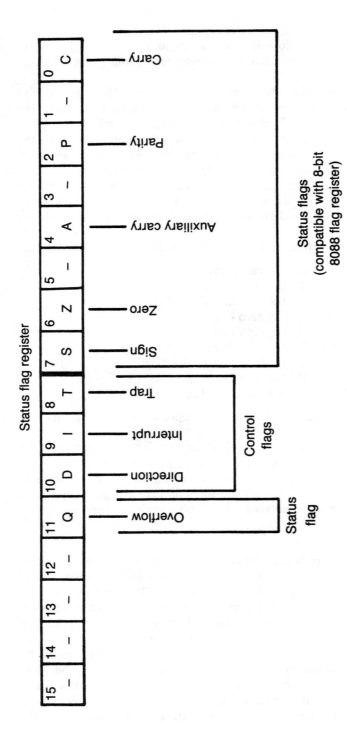

15-9 The 16-bit status flag register holds six status flag bits and three control bits.

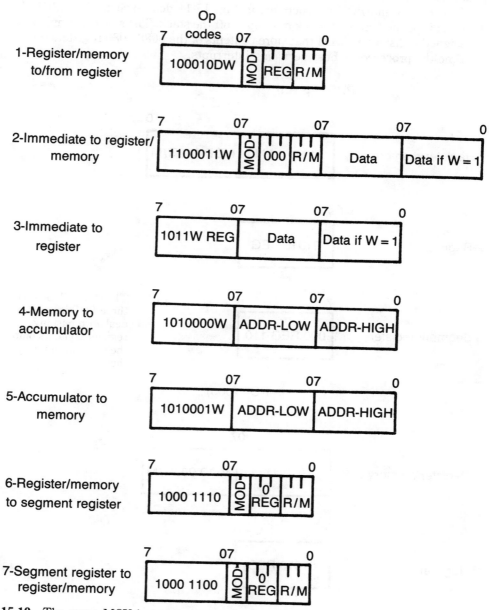

15-10 The seven MOV instructions are constructed as two, three, and four byte structures.

other direction, specifies accumulator to memory. According to the instruction either an 8-bit or 16-bit piece of data can be moved.

The PUSH and POP instructions, in Fig. 15-11 deal exclusively with 16-bit data that is pushed onto the stack or popped off the stack. The stack is simply a set of assigned registers in RAM that store contents of the 8088-8086 registers during the time the processor is busy servicing interrupts.

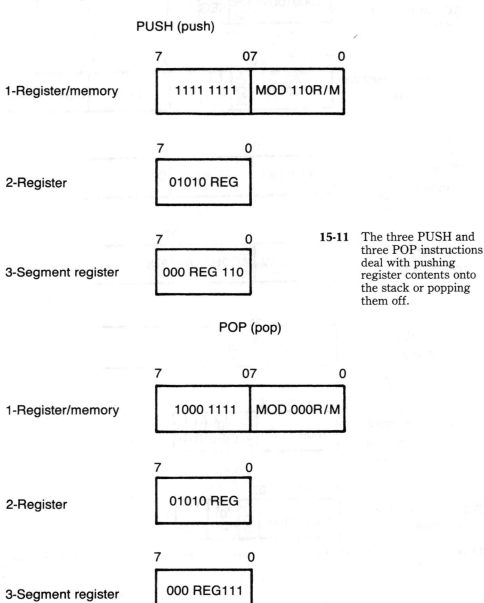

PUSH (push)

1-Register/memory   1111 1111   MOD 110R/M

2-Register   01010 REG

3-Segment register   000 REG 110

15-11 The three PUSH and three POP instructions deal with pushing register contents onto the stack or popping them off.

POP (pop)

1-Register/memory   1000 1111   MOD 000R/M

2-Register   01010 REG

3-Segment register   000 REG111

The XCHG instructions shown in Fig. 15-12 handles either 8-bit or 16-bit data. The instruction causes data in two registers to be swapped with each other. The registers affected can be either in memory or in the processor. The exchange instruction causes swaps between two processor registers or between a processor register and a memory location. It does not swap data between two memory locations.

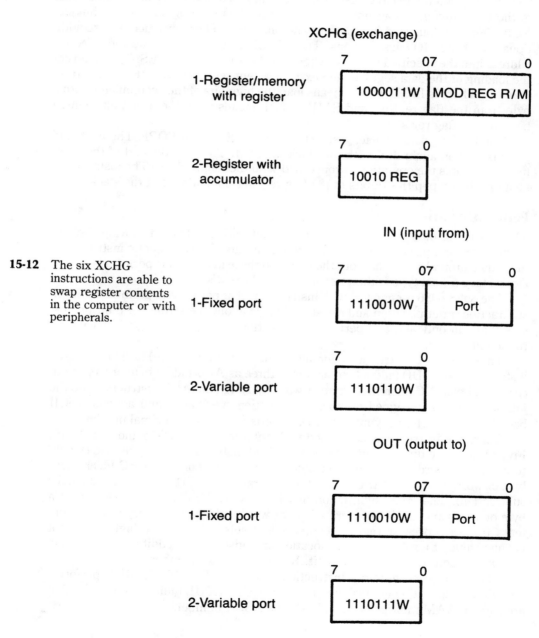

15-12 The six XCHG instructions are able to swap register contents in the computer or with peripherals.

The IN (input) instruction and the OUT (output) instructions, also in Fig. 15-12, deal with transferring data to and from the accumulator register and peripheral devices. As their name suggests, they are I/O instructions that transfer data.

There are eight instructions in Fig. 15-13 that are not in any of the above groups. XLAT is said to translate a byte to the low bits of the accumulator register. This description relates to transferring the contents of a register in a lookup table to the low bytes in the accumulator. This is a valuable programming technique. Next, there are four load instructions and one store. These instructions are additional to all the MOV instructions. There is LEA. This means load the effective address into the specified register. After that there is LDS and LES. They instruct the loading of the data segment and extra segment registers with 16-bit data from memory. There is LAHF which means load the high bits of the accumulator with a byte from the flag register and SAHF, which means store the accumulator high bits into the flag register.

The last two data transfer instructions are PUSHF and POPF. The push and pop instruction again deal with the stack in RAM. The F at the end of the mnemonic indicates the operation is concerned with the flag register. The instructions mean push and pop the 16-bits of the flag register onto and off of the stack.

Performing arithmetic

The preceding data transfer instructions dealt with the task of moving 8-bit or 16-bit data from place to place in the digital circuits. The arithmetic instructions, move data around somewhat, but the main job these instructions perform is simply elementary school type 'rithmetic, one of the three R's.

The 8088-8086 is endowed with instructions that permit it to perform addition, subtraction, multiplication and division. This is a long step from the 8-bit processors that can only add and performs subtraction, multiplication, and division by roundabout means.

There are ten instructions for addition, seen in Fig. 15-14. Three of the instructions are ADD (add a byte or word), three as ADC (add a byte or word with carry) and two INC (increment byte or word by 1). All the ADD instructions do the job on signed or unsigned numbers. Instruction AAA adds and adjusts ASCII back to the correct binary numbers. DAA adds and adjusts decimal numbers.

There are instructions concerned with subtract in Fig. 15-15 and Fig. 15-16. Five of them are direct counterparts of the add instructions. They are SUB (subtract byte or word), SBB (subtract byte or word with borrow), DEC (decrement byte or word by 1), ASS (ASCII adjust for subtraction) and DAS (decimal adjust for subtraction). The other subtraction instructions are NEG (change the sign of a byte or word) and CMP (compare a byte or word, subtracts memory location contents from a processor register contents and sets a flag accordingly, does not change value of involved memory location or register). The addition and subtraction instructions do their job on 8-bit, 16-bit, and larger numbers.

There are three multiply instructions shown in Fig. 15-17. MUL performs straight multiplication on unsigned bytes or words. IMUL multiplies integers that are signed. AAM multiplies and adjusts the ASCII number.

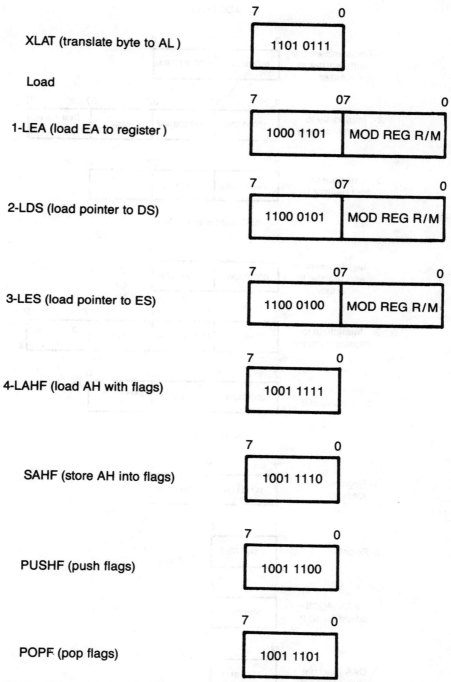

XLAT (translate byte to AL)

Load

1-LEA (load EA to register)

2-LDS (load pointer to DS)

3-LES (load pointer to ES)

4-LAHF (load AH with flags)

SAHF (store AH into flags)

PUSHF (push flags)

POPF (pop flags)

15-13   These eight instructions move data but are not in any of the previous categories. They are one- and two-byte types.

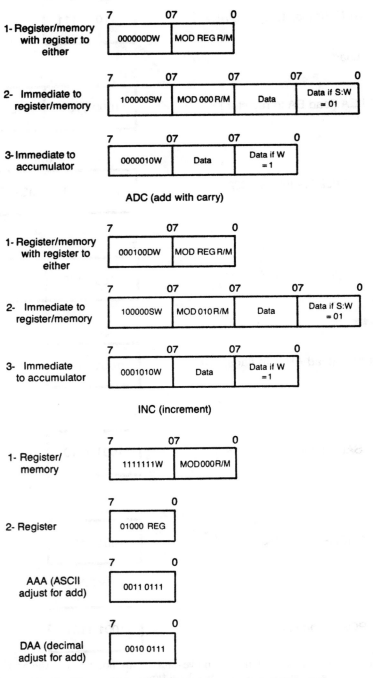

15-14 These 10 instructions perform most of the adding.

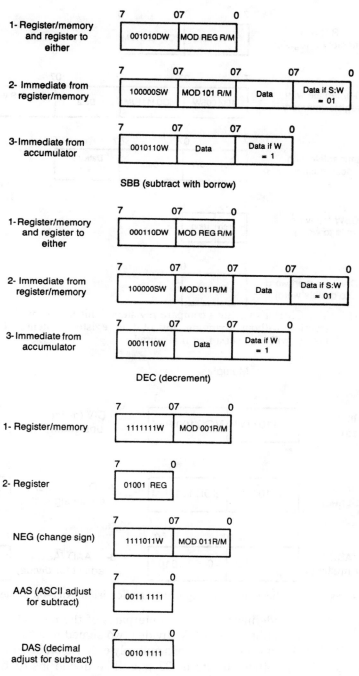

15-15 There are 11 subtract-type instructions.

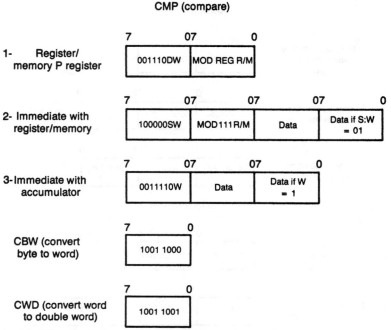

CMP (compare)

1- Register/
memory P register

| 001110DW | MOD REG R/M |

2- Immediate with
register/memory

| 100000SW | MOD 111 R/M | Data | Data if S:W = 01 |

3- Immediate with
accumulator

| 0011110W | Data | Data if W = 1 |

CBW (convert
byte to word)

| 1001 1000 |

CWD (convert word
to double word)

| 1001 1001 |

15-16 The CMP instructions compare registers. This is a form of subtraction without changing any of the register contents. The results will only set a flag if required.

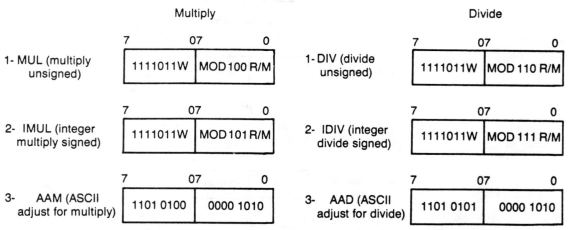

Multiply

1- MUL (multiply
unsigned)

| 1111011W | MOD 100 R/M |

2- IMUL (integer
multiply signed)

| 1111011W | MOD 101 R/M |

3- AAM (ASCII
adjust for multiply)

| 1101 0100 | 0000 1010 |

Divide

1- DIV (divide
unsigned)

| 1111011W | MOD 110 R/M |

2- IDIV (integer
divide signed)

| 1111011W | MOD 111 R/M |

3- AAD (ASCII
adjust for divide)

| 1101 0101 | 0000 1010 |

15-17 This processor is able to form multiplication and division. An 8-bit processor cannot do this directly.

There are three divide instructions, counterparts of the multiply types. DIV divides two unsigned numbers and IDIV divides two signed numbers. AAD does the job on ASCII. The multiply instructions multiply either 8-bit or 16-bit numbers with the results being either 16 bits or 32 bits. The divide instructions divide 16-bit or 32-bit numbers and the results are either 16 bits or 8 bits.

All of the arithmetic instructions affect the individual bits in the flag register. Figure 15-9 shows the bit positions and functions of the nine flags. As the instructions are executed, flags get set and reset according to the instruction. Some of the flags such as carry, zero, interrupt enable, and overflow act somewhat like the flags in the 8-bit processors. Other bits, the direction flag, single step and parity are new in the 8088-8086. If you are going to do machine language programming you must learn the job each does from the table. They are an important part of programming. The 8088-8086 makes a lot of decisions according to which flags are set and which ones are cleared.

The logicals

In addition to being able to do arithmetic, the Arithmetic Logic Unit in the 8088-8086 is able to perform tricks of logic. The logicals, as Intel calls them, consist of the usual ANDing, ORing, NOTing, XORing, and an instruction called EST. Besides those the shifting and rotating that an accumulator register is able to do, round out the rest of the logicals.

Figure 15-18 lists the AND, OR, NOT, and XOR logic instructions. All the instructions are able to perform logic on bytes or words. All the logic instructions are quite the same as the AND, OR, and XOR, shift and rotate instructions in an 8-bit processor except that 16-bit pieces of data can also receive treatment. There is only one NOT instruction and three each for logic operations, AND, OR and XOR (exclusive or). There are three shift operations and four rotates as listed in Fig. 15-19.

The TESTing operation is also like an 8-bit processor's TEST but using 16-bit data. The instruction is used to determine what will happen to the flags when two 16-bit registers are ANDed together. The flags will change when TEST is executed but the two registers being ANDed do not have their contents altered. All the TEST instruction does is set or reset flags. The programmer finds this instruction valuable during his efforts to keep control of the many flag changes that go on as arithmetic and logic instructions are executed.

Control transfer

The control transfer instructions could also be called change of address instructions. They deal with addressing. The program counter circuits are built to start their addressing at address zero and automatically increment by one at each succeeding address move. A control transfer instruction, stops the automatic incrementing and causes an entirely different memory location to be addressed, not in the arithmetical order.

There are three kinds of control transfer instructions. First there are 16 conditional JUMP type instructions. These instructions are shown in Fig. 15-20. They take a reading of the flag register, and according to the state of the flags, can either ignore the flags or cause a change of address to take place. Then at the change of address site in memory, the processor continues on with its automatic incremental addressing. All these conditional jumps are made in relation to whatever the contents of the instruction pointer is at that instant. The jump is restricted to a range of -128 to $+127$ bytes.

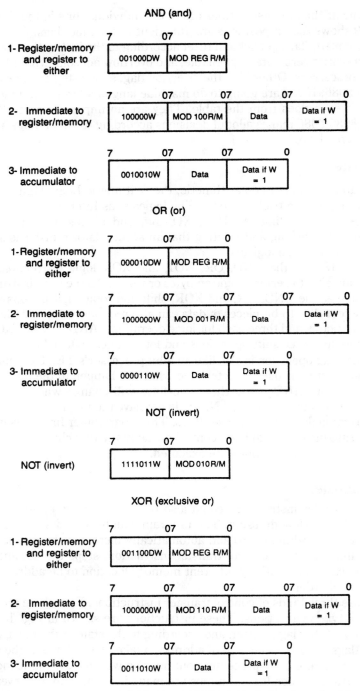

15-18 The AND, OR, NOT, and XOR logic is conducted with these instructions.

TEST (AND function to flags, no result)

1- Register/memory
and register

7	07	0
1000010W	MOD REG R/M	

2- Immediate data
and register/memory

7	07	07	07	0
1111011W	MOD 000 R/M	Data	Data if W = 1	

3- Immediate data
and accumulator

7	07	07	0
1010100W	Data	Data if W = 1	

SHIFT

1- SHL/SAL (shift
logical/arithmetic left)

7	07	0
110100VW	MOD 100 R/M	

2- SHR (shift
logical right)

7	07	0
110100VW	MOD 101 R/M	

3- SAR (shift
arithmetic right)

7	07	0
110100VW	MOD 111 R/M	

ROTATE

1- ROL (rotate left)

7	07	0
110100VW	MOD 000 R/M	

2- ROR (rotate right)
carry flag left)

7	07	0
110100VW	MOD 001 R/M	

3-RCL (rotate through

7	07	0
110100VW	MOD 010 R/M	

4- RCR (rotate through
carry right)

7	07	0
110100VW	MOD 011 R/M	

15-19 TEST, SHIFT, and ROTATE is accomplished with these byte arrangements.

Conditional Jumps and Loops

	7 07 0	
1-JE/JZ (jump on equal/zero)	0111 0100	Displacement
2-JL/JNGE (jump on less/not greater or equal)	0111 1100	"
3-JLE/JNG (jump on less or equal/not greater)	0111 1110	"
4-JB/JNAE (jump on below/not above or equal)	0111 0010	"
5-JBE/JNE (jump on below or equal/not above)	0111 0110	"
6-JP/JPE (jump on parity/parity even)	0111 1010	"
7-JO (jump on overflow)	0111 0000	"
8-JS (jump on sign)	0111 1000	"
9-JNE/JNZ (jump on not equal/not zero)	0111 0101	"
10-JNL/JGE (jump on not less/greater or equal)	0111 1101	"
11-JNLE/JG (jump on not less or equal/greater)	0111 1111	"
12-JNB/JAE (jump on not below/above or equal)	0111 0011	"
13-JNBE/JA (jump on not below or equal above)	0111 0111	"
14-JNP/JPO (jump on not par/par odd)	0111 1011	"
15-JNO (jump on not overflow)	0111 0001	"
16-JNS (jump on not sign)	0111 1001	"
1-LOOP (loop CX times, count not zero)	0111 0010	"
2-LOOPE/LOOPZ (loop while zero(equal))	0111 0001	"
3-LOOPNE/LOOPNZ (loop while not zero(equal))	0111 0000	"
JCXZ (jump on CX zero)	0111 0011	"

15-20   These instructions will cause a change of address or put a program into a loop if the proper conditions occur as the program is run. They are unconditional.

A JUMP instruction will contain a displacement or might address registers for their contents to be placed into the code segment register or the instruction pointer. The use of these new address bits forms a new address where the processor jumps to.

An example of the JUMP type instruction is JO (jump on overflow). The overflow flag is bit 11 in the flag register. As JO is run it notes the state of bit 11. If bit 11 is set to a 1, the instruction will make the processor JUMP to the new address that is specified. Should bit 11 be cleared to 0, the processor will simply increment the addressing register and ignore the JO instruction. Programmers say that this ability gives the processor decision making qualities. It can decide to jump or not according to its flag register.

These listed JUMP instructions in Fig. 15-20 are said to be conditional. That is, they will make the jump or not according to the condition of the flag register. There is one more JUMP group of instructions that are unconditional. They are found in Fig. 15-21. When their specific bits arrive at the processor, the processor will execute a jump no matter what the state of the flag register bits. There are two more unconditional transfer instructions that also change addresses no matter the state of flag bits in Fig. 15-22.

They are CALL and RETURN. These instructions are valuable to cause a jump to a subroutine stashed away in memory someplace and then after the subroutine is run the processor can return to the main program. For example, suppose you needed to compute the log of numbers in a program time and time again. All that is needed is to install a log conversion subroutine program somewhere in memory. When the subroutine is needed to compute a log, it is CALLed. After the log is computed, a RETURN instruction is executed, the processor returns to the instruction just after the CALL instruction.

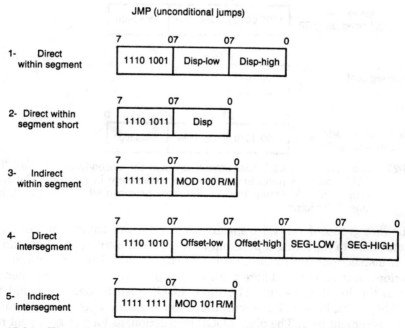

15-21 These instructions will cause a change of address no matter what the conditions are. They are unconditional.

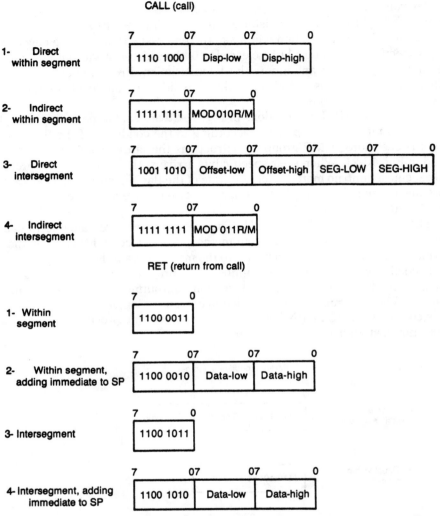

15-22   The CALL and RET instructions are like the unconditional jumps. The CALL causes a jump to a subroutine somewhere in memory. The RET returns the addressing back to the main program where the CALL had caused the jump.

The last group of control transfer instructions are called iteration controls. Iteration refers to repeating a program area over and over again. Accordingly the iteration instructions are in the LOOP family. A LOOP keeps running the same instructions over and over. There are three loop instructions and another special JUMP in the iteration group. The three LOOP instructions are found in Fig. 15-20. They work hand-in-hand with the count register. They all make the count register decrement by 1. The plain LOOP instruction, as long as the count register is not zero makes the processor loop back to an instruction within the range of

– 128 to +127 bytes. This makes the count register decrement by 1 after every loop and keep count of the process.

The LOOPE/LOOPZ will execute its loop after it checks both the zero flag bit and the count register. The loop will be executed only when they are zero. The other loop instruction, LOOPNE/LOOPNZ acts in the opposite way. It will cause a loop to be executed when the count register and Z flag are not equal to zero. These instructions let the processor get into loops and then to get out of loops when the count register reaches zero or when other zero-non-zero conditions occur.

The last jump instruction JCXZ in Fig. 15-20 also deals with the count register. It causes the processor to execute a jump to a new address when the count register is equal to zero. It is different than the other JUMP instructions. The other jumps are made with reference to the flags. JCXZ depends on the count register.

String manipulation

A string to a programmer is usually a sequence of characters. Strings are written from left to right and are connected. The analogy to a computer string is a string of beads. The beads are usually characters.The group of characters ABCDEF is a string. Numbers can be in strings but when they are they're considered to be characters.

The 8088-8086 only has six string op codes (Fig. 15-23). There are only a few jobs that are needed on strings. One job required is called concatenation. This is the process of adding one string section to another to form a total string. Another required job is called pattern matching. This is the process of comparing and scanning strings with each other to find substrings in the total string that have specific relationships with each other.

A third job is to change strings around after pattern matching to get desired strings. These jobs are essential when handling characters and numbers in many applications.

The string instructions in the 8088-8086 provide the abilities of moving, comparing, and scanning strings of binary bits. Other instructions can load and store strings to and from the accumulator register. The string instructions simply handle binary bits. The instructions will do the jobs whether the bits represent the six bit per character *BCD* (binary-coded decimal) set, the seven bit per character ASCII set, the eight bit per character *EBCDIC* (extended binary-coded decimal interchange code) set, or any alphanumeric or numerical arrangement of binary bits.

The instruction group includes MOVS (move string). All the string instructions use the source index and data segment registers for addresses. They can also use a combination of the source index, data segment, and the destination index and extra segment registers. The MOVS instruction uses these registers to move strings from one section of memory to another.

The MOVS instruction is only able to move one 8-bit or one 16-bit of data at a time. After one move the source index and destination index will be incremented or decremented by 1 or 2 according to the nature of the MOVS op code that is used.

String Manipulation

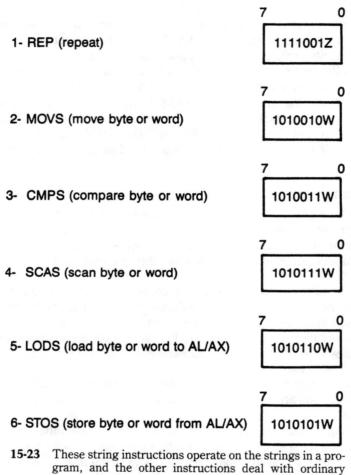

1- REP (repeat)

```
7          0
1111001Z
```

2- MOVS (move byte or word)

```
7          0
1010010W
```

3- CMPS (compare byte or word)

```
7          0
1010011W
```

4- SCAS (scan byte or word)

```
7          0
1010111W
```

5- LODS (load byte or word to AL/AX)

```
7          0
1010110W
```

6- STOS (store byte or word from AL/AX)

```
7          0
1010101W
```

15-23   These string instructions operate on the strings in a program, and the other instructions deal with ordinary data.

If a number of bytes or words are to be used, another string instruction, REP (repeat) is employed. The repeat op code is placed in memory in the address preceding the MOVS instruction. When REP is utilized, the MOVS instruction will keep repeating itself for the number of times that is specified in the count register. This repeat instruction saves the programmer from having to write a MOVS instruction over and over again.

The CMPS (compare string) instruction will compare two strings byte by byte or word for word. The source index and destination index registers are automatically incremented or decremented during this operation. The repeat instruction can be placed in front of the compare in the same way REP is used for the MOVS instruction. When REP is used the compare instruction will keep repeating itself as long as the strings match perfectly bit for bit. The processor will stop the operation as soon as the strings do not match. The operation will also stop when the counter register decrements down to zero.

The SCAS (scan string) works like the compare except when the repeat instruction is used the processor will keep comparing until a byte or word match is found. When the repeat instruction is used, the processor will stop comparing when the counter register decrements to zero, just like the CMPS instruction.

The last two instructions LODS (load accumulator with string) and STOS (store string from accumulator) are straightforward. The load instruction places a string into the accumulator. The store instruction sends a string in the accumulator to a memory location. The repeat instruction is rarely used with the load and store.

The interrupts

There are three different types of interrupts in the 8088-8086. No matter which interrupt is activated the processor starts off with the same procedure. It pushes the contents of the instruction pointer, the code segment register and the flags onto the stack. The processor then goes to the first 1K of memory where new instruction pointers and new code segment register contents are stored. The processor will then choose contents according to what interrupt occurred. These new contents are placed into the instruction pointer and code segment register. They form an address where the interrupt service routine is stored.

The INT (interrupt) instructions shown in Fig. 15-24, are used to get the interrupt service programs stored in memory to start running. There are 256 possible interrupt programs stored in memory. These subroutines are used to help peripheral devices communicate with the processor. The INT instructions is two bytes long. The first byte is the interrupt op code. The second byte, according to its bit structure, specifies which of the 256 subroutines should be run to service the interrupt.

In the first 1K of memory, hex addresses 000 – 3FF, is an interrupt vector table that contains the vectors to be placed into the instruction pointer and code segment

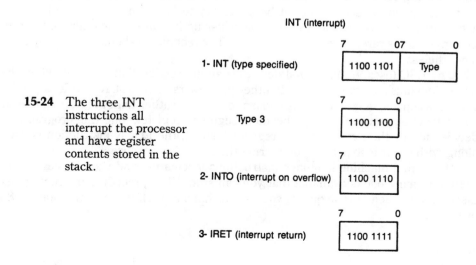

15-24 The three INT instructions all interrupt the processor and have register contents stored in the stack.

register. With the correct vectors installed in the *IP* (instruction pointer) and *CS* (code segment), the processor is then able to address the service subroutine and get it running, once the original contents of the IP, the CS and flags have been pushed onto the stack.

Once the interrupt service subroutine has been run, the processor is ready to return to the main program it had been running before the interrupt from the peripheral had arrived. Accordingly there is an instruction to get the processor back to the main program. It is called IRET (interrupt return).

This instruction is always placed at the end of all interrupt service routines. It is a one byte instruction. As the last instruction in an interrupt service routine, the first thing it does is pop the original contents of the flag register, the instruciton pointer and the code segment register, off the stack and back into their original registers in the processor. Then the IRET instruction returns the processor to the next instruction in the main program, after the one that was last executed when the interrupt occurred.

The other interrupt is called INTO (interrupt on overflow). This is one byte instruction that allows the processor to interrupt itself. The interrupt will be executed if an overflow occurs. It has a four byte interrupt vector starting at hex address 010. This interrupt is a time saver. The same procedure could also be accomplished by a jump instruction with a lot of bytes. One byte runs faster than five or six.

Processor control

The last category of instructions deal with controlling the processor. Most of these are single byte instructions that set and clear some of the flag register bits. There is a CLC (clear carry), STC (set carry), CLI (clear interrupt), and others that are in Fig. 15-25.

The last four instructions are used for external synchronization. If it is desirable to bring HLT (halt) to operations until an interrupt or reset can take place, that instruction is used. Should it be necessary to WAIT unit pin 23, *TEST, is active, then that instruction is used. These instructions are in the realm of the programmer and is rarely used by technicians. The technician should know they exist nevertheless.

The ESC (escape to external device) is an instruction that is useful when the 8088-8086 must operate along with other processors. The LOCK (bus lock prefix) is used when a special register is chosen to be used rather than the normal one. If an instruction normally uses the data segment register, but the programmer decides to use the extra segment register instead, the LOCK instruction is used along with other instructions to override the normal procedure.

If you find machine language instructions fascinating and want to learn more there are many books available that you can study. The preceding instruction set discussion is needed to acquaint you as a technician with the way the 8088-8086 operates.

Processor Control

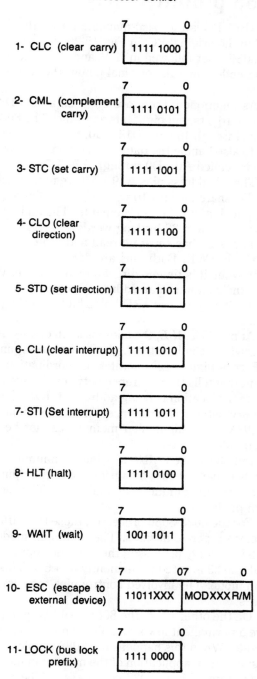

1- CLC (clear carry)

7 0

`1111 1000`

2- CML (complement carry)

7 0

`1111 0101`

3- STC (set carry)

7 0

`1111 1001`

4- CLO (clear direction)

7 0

`1111 1100`

5- STD (set direction)

7 0

`1111 1101`

15-25 These eleven instructions control the processor in special ways during a program run.

6- CLI (clear interrupt)

7 0

`1111 1010`

7- STI (Set interrupt)

7 0

`1111 1011`

8- HLT (halt)

7 0

`1111 0100`

9- WAIT (wait)

7 0

`1001 1011`

10- ESC (escape to external device)

7 0 7 0

`11011XXX` `MODXXXR/M`

11- LOCK (bus lock prefix)

7 0

`1111 0000`

8088 pinout

The IBM PC is the base machine for all the PC-type machines that follow. The 8088 in the original PC, in Fig. 15-26 is used as the pinout example. All the 8088s and 8086s that followed in IBM and clone machines operate along the same lines. If you understand the original pinout the rest will be easy even if there are differences.

As mentioned, there are eight data pins D7 – D0 that do multiplex duty and transfer 16 bits, but eight bits at a time. The 8086 improves on this by transferring 16 bits through 16 pins, D15 – D0. Both the 8088 and 8086 use some of the address pins to also handle the data ins and outs. The 8088 shares pins with A0 – A7. The pins are called A0 – D0 through A7 – D7.

The 20 address pins A19 – A0 are numbered 35 – 39 and 2 – 16. The data pins D7 – D0 share pins 9 – 16 with A7 – A0. These pins transfer both address bits and data pins but at different moments. The address and data pins handle 8-bit bytes, 16-bit words and 32-bit long words.

The 8088 has separate read and write output pins. Pin 32 is called *RD and pin *29 is *WR. Both pins are dormant when they are held high. They become active when it is time to direct a read or write. When *RD goes low, the processor reads the contents of an addressed memory location. *WR stays high at that time. When *WR goes low *RD holds high and the processor can write data to a location.

At pin 25 is *ALE*, the address latch enable. ALE is disabled low and starts enabling when it is brought high. The address pins do not output address bits until ALE goes high. ALE operates in coordination with pin 28, IO/*M. IO/*M is the circuit that tells the difference between the system memory and I/O devices. When a memory location is being addressed, IO/*M goes low. The address bits travel to memory without interference. At that moment, I/O devices cannot be addressed. If IO/*M goes high, then memory cannot be addressed. Only I/O circuits will accept address bits.

Pin 33 is called MN/*MX for minimum/maximum mode. Note the various pin initials in parentheses alongside the regular pin initials. These letters in parentheses are the maximum mode indicators. The regular initials show the 8088's minimum mode.

For the 8088-8086 processor, these two different modes are used to handle two different types of designs. The minimum mode is used in a computer where the 8088 is the only processor, there are no coprocessors. When the minimum mode is used, pin 33 is wired permanently to +5 V. This holds the pin high and in the minimum mode. The involved control pins then assume the name that is not in parentheses.

On the other hand, the 8088 could have pin 33 tied to zero volts or ground and have a permanent low state. The pin names in parentheses are then the ones that operate. When this happens the 8088 is able to coexist with other processors. The most common application of the maximum mode is in the IBM PC where the 8088 is wired up with an 8087 coprocessor. The 8087 works along with the 8088 and speeds things up during number crunching. The minimum and maximum modes

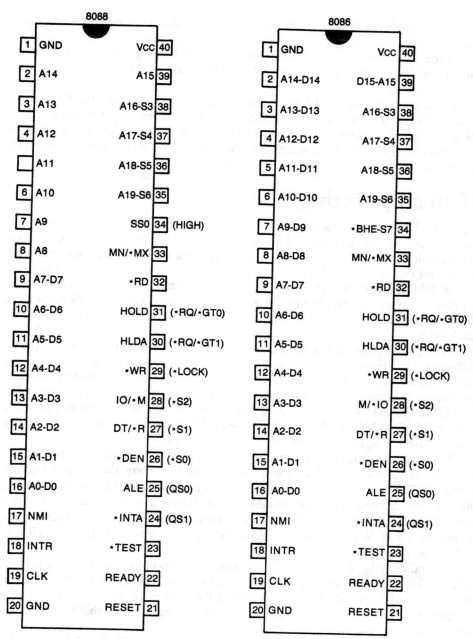

8088

Pin	Left	Right	Pin	
1	GND	VCC	40	
2	A14	A15	39	
3	A13	A16-S3	38	
4	A12	A17-S4	37	
	A11	A18-S5	36	
6	A10	A19-S6	35	
7	A9	SS0	34	(HIGH)
8	A8	MN/•MX	33	
9	A7-D7	•RD	32	
10	A6-D6	HOLD	31	(•RQ/•GT0)
11	A5-D5	HLDA	30	(•RQ/•GT1)
12	A4-D4	•WR	29	(•LOCK)
13	A3-D3	IO/•M	28	(•S2)
14	A2-D2	DT/•R	27	(•S1)
15	A1-D1	•DEN	26	(•S0)
16	A0-D0	ALE	25	(QS0)
17	NMI	•INTA	24	(QS1)
18	INTR	•TEST	23	
19	CLK	READY	22	
20	GND	RESET	21	

8086

Pin	Left	Right	Pin	
1	GND	VCC	40	
2	A14-D14	D15-A15	39	
3	A13-D13	A16-S3	38	
4	A12-D12	A17-S4	37	
5	A11-D11	A18-S5	36	
6	A10-D10	A19-S6	35	
7	A9-D9	•BHE-S7	34	
8	A8-D8	MN/•MX	33	
9	A7-D7	•RD	32	
10	A6-D6	HOLD	31	(•RQ/•GT0)
11	A5-D5	HLDA	30	(•RQ/•GT1)
12	A4-D4	•WR	29	(•LOCK)
13	A3-D3	M/•IO	28	(•S2)
14	A2-D2	DT/•R	27	(•S1)
15	A1-D1	•DEN	26	(•S0)
16	A0-D0	ALE	25	(QS0)
17	NMI	•INTA	24	(QS1)
18	INTR	•TEST	23	
19	CLK	READY	22	
20	GND	RESET	21	

Note pins 33 on both chips, MN/•MX, minimum and maximum mode controls. In minimum mode the pin functions inside chip area are active. In maximum mode the functions in parentheses outside chip area take over their pins.

15-26 It is a good idea to understand the function of every pin, what typical voltages and logic states are present, and whether a pin is an input or output. During testing, the knowledge will help you pick out wrong values.

each have a number of special circuits in the 8088 that they use on an exclusive basis.

In the maximum mode, the 8088 could work with a large number of coprocessors. Typical uses are coprocessors that have specialties such as mathematics and I/O applications.

These two different modes the 8088-8086 can operate in were the forerunners of the different modes in the 80286 and 80386 processors. The various modes in these 16-bit and 32-bit processors is one of the main reasons they are so versatile and powerful. The 80286 is discussed in chapter 16. The 80386 also gets coverage in chapter 16.

8086 chip timing

Figure 15-27 shows a block diagram of a small minimum mode 8086 single processor computer. All of the operations the processor conducts are driven by the beat of the clock. This small computer uses an 8284 clock generator chip with an external crystal cut to run at 14.31818 MHz, a commonly used frequency. The clock chip is able to divide up the crystal frequency and output an approximate 5 MHz operating frequency. The timing diagram in Fig. 15-28 shows the clock output as a single phase driving frequency. One bus cycle of the processor consists of four clock cycles.

Pin 33, MN/*MX, of the 8086 is connected to +5 V making the 8086 operate in the minimum mode on a permanent basis. With the minimum mode in place, the 8086 then needs the following connections to conduct a read operation shown in the timing diagram, Fig. 15-28. First of all there are the address and data pins, A19 – A16 and A15 – A0, D15 – D0. Next there is ALE, the address enable latch, M/*IO and *RD. Also needed and shown with the A19 – A16 bits in the timing diagram is *BHE, the bus high enable.

The first low of the processor cycle applies the A19 – A0 bits to the address bus. The signal *BHE is ANDed with A0. A0 and *BHE are able to form four different AND output patterns. This permits A0 and *BHE to choose from among the following entities. There is available, the high byte of a word, the low byte of a word, the entire word or none of the word at an addressed location. Whatever the access choice of bits, the clock applies the correct address bit to the A19 – A0 address output circuits.

The falling edge of the first clock period also triggers a high from ALE. This fulfills the next step in getting the processor to access a memory location. Also at the same instant, the M/*IO is made high if the read is going to be made from a memory location. Should the read be one from a peripheral, the M/*IO pin is forced low.

Once all these accessing prerequisites have occurred, the processor makes the *RD pin output a low during the second low of the processor cycle. The *WR pin, at that time, is held high and thus inactive during the read cycle. When all these clock events have taken place, then and only then, the addressed location is ready to let a copy of its contents out on the system data bus. The data does not leave the location until *RD goes low.

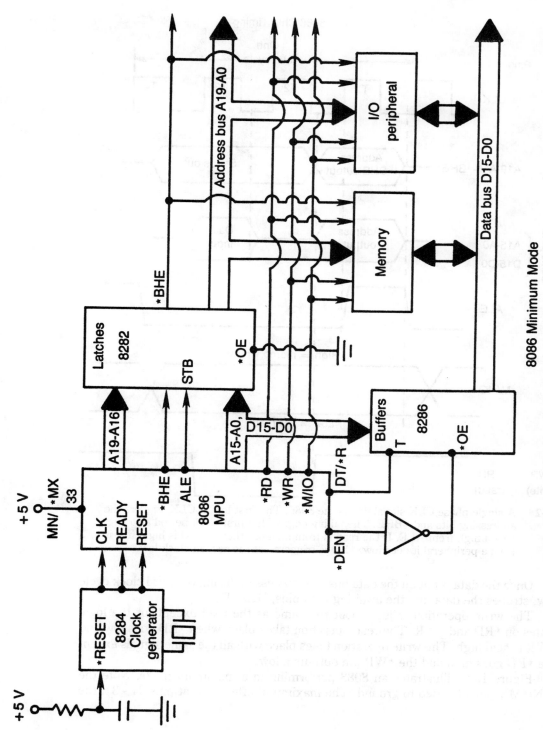

8086 Minimum Mode

15-27 A typical 8086-based computer system can be wired in this manner.

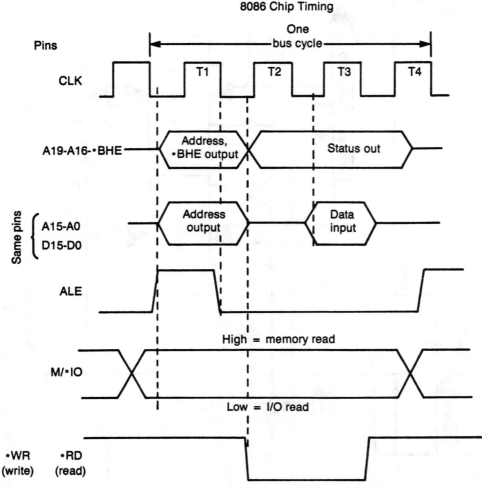

15-28 A single phase CLK signal drives the 8086. The first low of CLK triggers the addressing bits and *BHE. The falling edge of the first clock period also triggers a high from ALE. If the read is from memory then M/*IO is high, if it is from a peripheral it goes low. *RD is triggered at the second clock low.

Once the data is out on the data bus, the processor, during the third clock cycle low, strobes the data into the awaiting data pins, D15 – D0.

The write operation is just about the same as the read except for the logic states on *RD and *WR. The read operation takes place when *RD goes low and *WR is held high. The write operation takes place with all the same signals except the *RD goes high and the *WR pin outputs a low.

Figure 15-29 illustrates an 8088 performing in a maximum mode. Note the MN/*MX pin 33 is tied to ground. The maximum differs in that pins 24 – 31, the

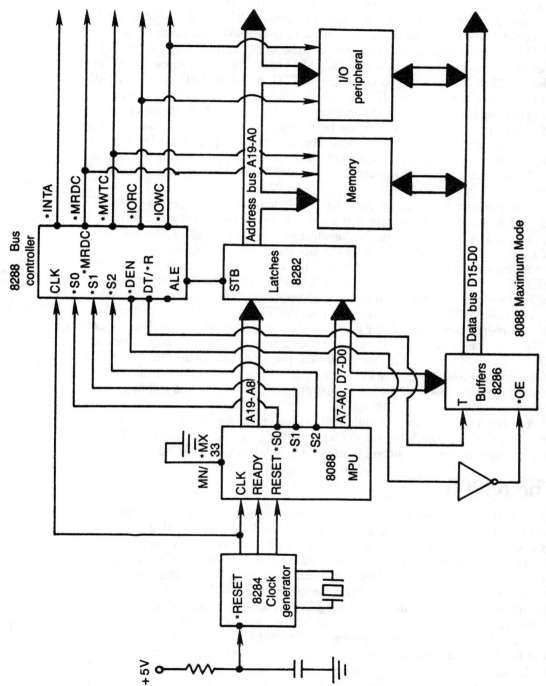

15-29 This is a typical 8088 computer system operating in a maximum mode. Note pin 33 the MN/*MX is tied to ground.

memory and peripheral signals are shut down. Another chip, an 8288 bus controller is added to the circuitry and connected to pins 26, 27, and 28, S0, S1, and S2 that become status outputs when the processor goes into a maximum mode.

The bus controller chip in turn decodes the status outputs and generates the required signals to control the memory and I/O addresses. These new signals are called, *MRDC, memory read control, *MWTC, memory write control, IORC, input output read control and IOWC, input output write control.

In the two block diagrams, the address bus and data bus lines appropriately go to the memory data holders and the peripherals that also deal in data. In the address lines are inserted a pair of chips. This design is an application developed at Intel. These chips in the address lines are latches. They are needed in the address lines because of ALE. ALE works with A0 to direct the address bits, as mentioned earlier.

Note in the timing diagram that ALE is only high for a short period of time. In this 5 MHz system, ALE is active only about 100 ns. Many memory and peripheral devices need more time than that to be addressed. A peripheral could need 400 or 500 ns to be addressed. That's where the latches come into play. When an address in this circuit is generated, it is latched. This keeps the address at memory or a peripheral long enough to be addressed and be able to transfer data back and forth. The address will then hold until the next address and ALE comes out of the 8088.

The 8088-8086 processors are very popular. There are millions upon millions of them around the world residing in personal computers from IBM and clone manufacturers. They will remain in style for a long time to come. Manufacturers are still churning out the machines based around these processors despite all the new processors that are also appearing on the scene. The 8088-8086 has become the standard for most IBM compatible computers. As a technician you will be encountering them often.

Another 16-bit processor family that is also important and sets a standard in the Apple world, is the Motorola 68000. It is the processor of choice that Apple placed in the original Macintosh. Commodore installed it in their Amiga.

The 68000

The 68000 is packaged in a larger DIP than the 8086 and 8088. Figure 15-30 shows the 68000 has 64 pins in comparison to the 40 pins on the 8088-8086 packages. One of the reasons for the increase in pins on the 68000 package is an increase in the number of address pins. Inside the 68000, the addressing registers use 24 bits to conduct the addressing. With 24 address bits in use, the 68000 is able to directly address 16 megabytes. In contrast the 8088 only has 20 address bits and is restricted to addressing 1 megabyte. The four additional address bits in the 68000 permits a 16 fold increase in addressing ability. The 68000's addressing is also conducted without any segmenting. The 8088, as you'll recall, needed segment manipulating in order to get the 20 correct bits out on the address bus.

Actually, the 68000 chip has addressing registers with 32 bits. However, only A23 – A0 is used. The other eight address bits, A31 – A24, are used in other members of the 68000 family of processors, for instance the 68020. If these additional

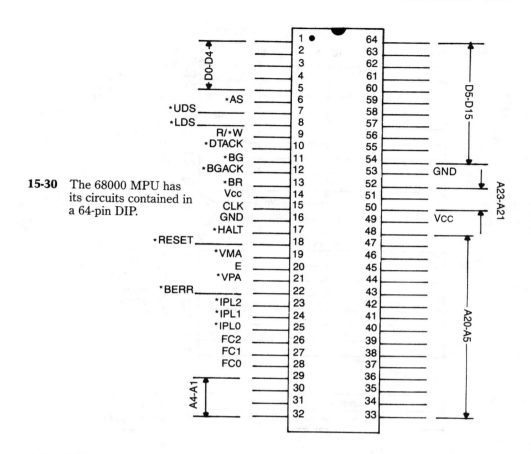

15-30 The 68000 MPU has its circuits contained in a 64-pin DIP.

address bits are used, the package must be larger and provide more pins for addressing. When all 32 address bits are used, the processor is able to address 4 gigabytes (billions) of direct memory. This large capability is impressive as far as direct memory addressing goes.

Figure 15-30 is the pinout of the 64 pin 68000 in this discussion. As the pins are examined one by one, Vcc is found at both pins 14 and 49. Ground connects to both pins 16 and 53. The 16 data pins, D15 – D0, are arranged clockwise, starting with pin 5, going to pin 1, crossing the top of the package and continuing through pins 64 to 54. The address pins are arranged counterclockwise at pins 29 – 48 and 50 – 52. Note the address pins are labeled A1 – A23. A0 is conspicuously missing. A0 is encoded internally and is controlled with two external pins. These A0 involved pins will be covered shortly.

The 16 data pins are the link to eight 32-bit data registers on the chip. These 32-bit registers, shown in Fig. 15-31, can be accessed in a few different ways. Since they are 32-bits wide the 68000 can use them to handle 8-bit bytes, 16-bit words or 32-bit long words. Their register addresses are D7 – D0.

The 68000 has seven address-type registers. These are also 32 bits and can be used in a general purpose fashion. They are not quite as versatile as the data regis-

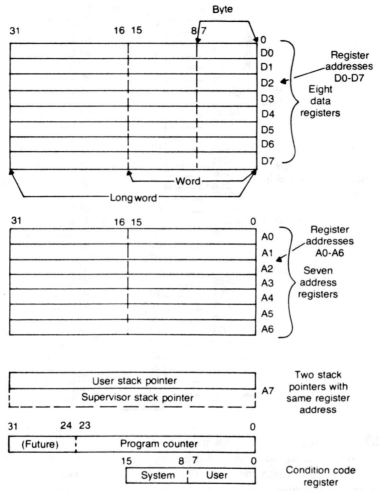

15-31   The 68000 has 32-bit data registers, address registers, stack pointers, and program counter. The CCR has 16 bits.

ters. They can only be accessed by 16-bit words and 32-bit long words. They do not respond as single byte registers. Their register addresses are A0 – A6.

The A7 register address is the stack pointer. There are two stack pointers, but they share the same address since they do not both operate at the same time. The 68000 operates in one of two states, a user state and a supervisor state. The two stack pointers are a user pointer and a supervisor pointer.

The program counter is also a 32-bit register as mentioned earlier. However, in the 68000, the highest eight bits are not connected to external pins. They have been designed into the configuration for the future. When they are put into use, the 68000 will be able to address 4 billion byte-sized locations. This chip is able to address 16,777,216 byte-sized locations with the 24 lower address bits.

It was mentioned that only 23 of the 24 address bits, A1 – A23, exited through pins to the address bus. A0 is not pinned directly. This complication is there so the address can choose either a byte transfer or a word transfer from the 16-bit memory locations. Figure 15-32 shows the memory locations are arranged in 16-bit sizes. However, each 16-bit location has a high byte and a low byte. The bytes are the numbers on the memory map not the 16-bit locations. All the high bytes are the even numbers. All the lower bytes are the odd numbers on the map.

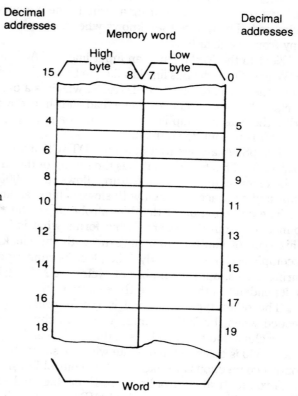

15-32 The memory words each have two addresses. The high byte is always an even address, and the low byte an odd address.

The 16-bit location can be accessed in three ways. The high byte, bits 15 – 8, can be retrieved by itself. The low byte, bits 7 – 0, can be retrieved by itself. The complete word, bits 15 – 0, can be accessed in its entirely.

On the chip pinout, A0 is missing. In its place, there are two pins, *UDS pin 7 and *LDS pin 8. They are called *Upper Data Strobe* and *Lower Data Strobe*. They produce outputs when A0 is gated internally with the instruction size as the program is run. They can produce three forms of data transfers between the MPU and memory.

When the 68000 accesses bytes and there are two bytes to a 16-bit location, the 68000 is addressing 16 megabytes of individual locations. If the 68000 is addressing words, and there is only one word to a 16-bit location, the addressing is thought of as eight *megawords*. Eight megawords of locations have the same number of bits as 16 megabytes.

The actual accessing is accomplished with the aid of the two control lines *UDS and *LDS. When *UDS goes low, the bits that travel in the data bus lines D15 – D8 are transferred. If *LDS goes low, the data bus lines D7 – D0 carry the low order bits between the MPU and memory. Should both *UDS and *LDS go low, then the entire word length of 16 bits traverses the full data bus.

There is a routine R/*W line coming out of pin 9. It operates by sending a high during a read and a low during a write to the memory or I/O device the MPU has addressed. The device then knows whether to place copy on the data bus or gate copy from the data bus.

Next to the R/*W pin is an input line *DTACK at pin 10. It operates with the R/*W line. Once the bus line has data in transit, it sends a low to pin 10 of the MPU. When the low is received at *DTACK, which is a data acknowledgment, the MPU reacts. It latches the data during a read and shuts down the bus. If the operation is a write, the external chip is sending a message that the data is received. The MPU knows it is to shut down the bus.

The 68000 always waits for the *DTACK input signal before it completes the operations. This feature matches the timing of the MPU operation with the timing of the external device. This feature allows the 68000 to speed up access with fast chips and slow access down with slower chips, an amazing ability.

The combination of the data strobe lines, the *R/*W line and the *DTACK connection from the external chip forms what is known as *asynchronous control*. This type of control is not in sync with the clock. The transferring of data is accomplished independently. The clock is running and the operation takes place during cycles, but the number of cycles the MPU takes to complete the operation is dependent on the speed of the external chip.

The other type of control is *synchronous*. Asynchronous control is usually needed when the MPU is interfaced with chips that are not in the 68000 family. Those chips that are members of the family can be synced in with the clock cycles. The 68000 is designed to operate with the same chips the 6800 used. Synchronous control connections are like the 6800 control lines.

Two identical control lines are E, enable, and *VMA, valid memory address. There is a third sync signal called *VPA at pin 21. The E pin 20, outputs a $\phi2$ type signal to the chips the MPU is in contact with. The E signal syncs all chips into the same sync frequency. It is derived from the CLK input at pin 15. E is $1/10$ the frequency of the CLK signal.

*VPA is a signal from the external chips that tells the MPU that a chip in sync is being addressed. It is the counterpart of the *DTACK. *DTACK notifies the MPU that an asynchronous chip is transferring data. *VPA tells the MPU that a synchronous chip is transferring data. When the MPU receives a *VPA low, it responds with a *VMA signal.

The rest of the pins on the chip perform their own jobs. *AS on pin 6 is an address strobe. It announces to all the chips that a valid address is on the address bus. FC2, FC1, and FC0 on pins 26, 27, and 28 work together to set up the operating state of the MPU. The three functions can arrange eight different functions.

*IPL2, *IPL1, and *IPL0 at pins 23, 24, and 25 are interrupt lines. *BG, *BGACK, and *BR at pins 11, 12, and 13 are used by other microprocessors to gain control over the bus lines. *BERR, *HALT and *RESET are other controls and state indicators. *HALF and *RESET can be useful to the technician if you want to reset or halt the operation of the MPU.

During voltage or logic probe testing of the pins, a good idea of the operation can be obtained. The pins with asterisks are usually held high and the pins without are held low. The asterisk pins are enabled with a low and the others are enabled with a high. The bus lines should all show activity. Vcc and ground, of course, must have the correct supply voltages in order to operate.

PIAs and 16-bit operation

The same PIAs that are used with the 6800 can be connected directly to the 68000 data bus. It is a synchronous chip and connects to the address bus and control lines. The PIA also connects to the outside world peripherals without any undue complications. The PIA circuits to the outside world are discussed later.

The 6821 PIAs that the 68000 uses are the same ones that the 6800 use. The 6800 has an eight-line data bus and the 68000 has a 16-line data bus. How is the difference in bus line numbers handled by the PIAs?

Two PIAs are used for the 68000 where one was used for the 6800. Two PIAs wired in parallel are connected to the data bus. Eight data pins on one PIA are attached to data lines D15 – D8 and eight data pins on the other PIA are attached to bus lines D7 – D0 (Fig. 15-33).

The 68000 is designed to transfer 16 bits at a time and the two parallel PIAs are able to each transfer eight of the 16.

The PIAs are typically interfaced to the 68000 in the following way. They are installed in the memory map near the top between hex FEF800 and FEFFFF. Each PIA needs four addresses.

Registers	PIA #1	PIA #2
PDRA/DDRAs	FEFF00	FEFF01
CRAs	FEFF02	FEFF03
PDRB/DDRBs	FEFF04	FEFF05
CRBs	FEFF06	FEFF07

Using 8-bit PIAs with
16-bit data bus

Note that each 24 address bits are described with six hex characters. Each address is able to output eight bits of data. It takes two addresses of data to fill the 16-bit data bus.

When the MPU accesses locations FEFF00 and FEFF01, it can transfer data over the 16-bit data bus to and from both Peripheral Data Registers A in the two PIAs. If the MPU accesses locations FEFF04 and FEFF05, it can transfer data between itself and the PDRB registers in the two PIAs. As far as the MPU is concerned, the two PIAs look like one large PIA with a 16-bit data bus and 16-bit internal registers.

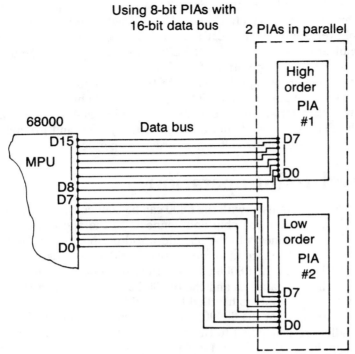

15-33   The 68000 is able to interface directly with a lot of the 8-bit chips that were originally designed for use with the old 8-bit 6800. This is a 68000-PIA hookup.

To dial up the PIAs, 23 bits are used: A23 – A1 (Fig. 15-34). The PIAs are wired in parallel. Bits A1 and A2 of the address are connected to the internal register pins of the PIAs. A1 and A2 are connected to both RS0s and RS1s of the PIAs. When one of the four registers in a PIA is selected, the same register in the parallel PIA is also selected at the same time.

In this addressing scheme, the chip selects (*CS2, CS1, and CS0) on each PIA are also connected together, A2, A4, and A5 address lines select the PIAs when they are high. They enter a decoder that enables *CS2 when A3, A4, and A5 are high. The CS1s receive a low from the address bus. The CS0s are wired to VMA.

The R/*W lines decide if the PIAs are to be read from or written to. E syncs the PIAs in step with the clock. *RESET is there in case the PIA must be started over after a problem.

The 68000 must learn if the peripheral has been satisfactorily addressed by having *VPA turned on. *VPA needs a low to turn on. *VPA has two inputs, one from the address strobe, *AS, and the other form a multiple NAND gate.

*AS goes low at the beginning of the cycle. This low into one of the *VPA gates inputs is the enabling pulse. The low enters a NOT circle and becomes a high.

The other *VPA gate input comes from a multiple NAND gate that has 13 address bits as its inputs. When all thirteen address bits enter with the correct

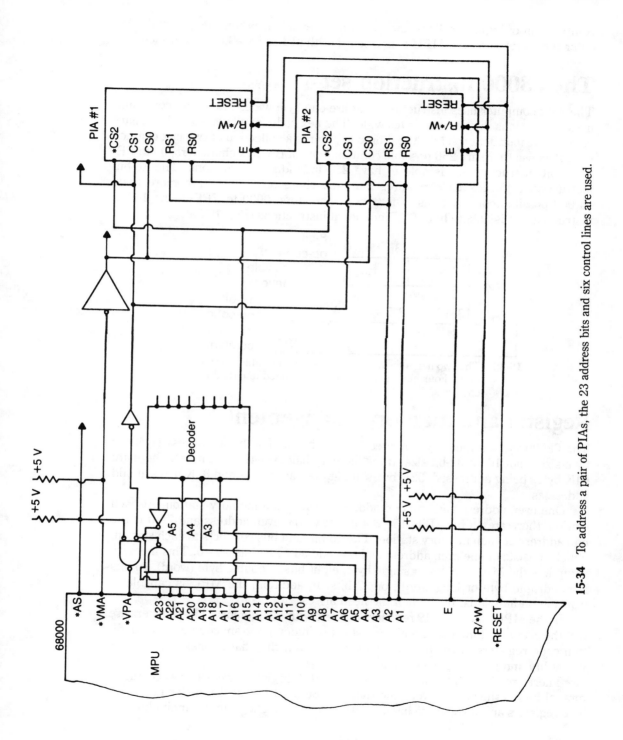

15-34 To address a pair of PIAs, the 23 address bits and six control lines are used.

combination of highs and lows, the gate will be enabled. When the gate and *AS enter the *VPA gate, the MPU is notified that the PIAs have been addressed.

The 68000 instruction set

The 8-bit computer uses instructions that are one byte wide. The 16-bit computer uses instructions that are two bytes wide. The hex code for a byte is two hex characters. The instruction set for the 8-bit computer is a collection of two hex characters. Because there are 256 possible combinations of two hex characters, 00 to FF, the 8-bit instruction set is able to have 256 individual instructions. The 16-bit instruction set's hex code requires four hex characters. There are more than 64,000 possible combinations of four hex characters, 0000 to FFFF. The 16-bit instruction set is able to have 64K individual instructions (Fig. 15-35).

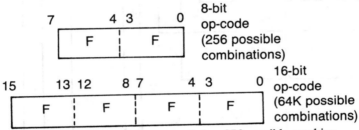

15-35   The two hex number op code has 256 possible combinations. Four hex numbers can be arranged in 64K different ways.

Register and memory arrangement

The 68000 faces a memory arranged in 8-bit bytes. The basic address layout is byte-sized, not 16- or 32-bit size. If the memory bank is 64K, that means there are 64K bytes being addressed. 32K bytes are at even addresses and 32K bytes at odd addresses.

One even address and one odd address makes up a memory station. At each station, there are 16 bits. Bits 15 – 8 are always the even address and 7 – 0 is the odd address at each memory station. The 16-bit data bus connects to each station, which consists of one even address and one odd address, bits 15 – 0. This memory setup lets the MPU address a single byte, eight bits, a double byte (word), 16 bits (a quadruple byte or long word), or 32 bits. In addition, the MPU is capable of working on individual bits, when the need arises.

In the MPU, there are 19 registers to work with the memory. The registers are like the accumulators, index registers, stack pointers, program counter, and condition code registers in the 8-bit computer. However, they have considerably more versatility and general purpose qualities.

There are eight 32-bit data registers. The data registers are used as accumulators, although they are so versatile they can be used for most register purposes. The registers are designed to handle data of any size. They can use individual bit, bytes, words, and long words. They are 32 bits wide. Bits 7 – 0 can be accessed as bytes, bits 15 – 0 as words, and all 32 bits can be accessed for a long word transfer or manipulation. The eight data registers have register addresses. These addresses are not included in the memory map. They are MPU internal addresses, D0 through D7.

In the MPU, there is a condition code register. All the data registers affect the condition code bits. This is mentioned because other registers in the MPU do not affect the CCR bits, an important 68000 feature.

The data registers are all identical. Each one is able to handle bytes in bits 7 – 0. Two bytes or a word is worked on in bits 15 – 0. Long words are manipulated in the full 32-bit register.

There are seven 32-bit address registers. They are a lot like the data registers except for a few details. First of all, an address register cannot access bytes directly. It can deal with words and long words easily enough, but individual bytes cannot be accessed. In Fig. 15-31, you see the data registers with dotted lines at the byte and word separations. The address registers are only separated at the word marker between bits 16 and 15.

The address register does not affect the flags in the CCR as the data registers do. This is a carefully thought-out feature that makes life easier for the programmer. For the technician, it is only a feature to be aware of during maintenance or repair.

In the 8-bit processor, most of the registers affect the flags. They are changing states constantly during a program run. A large percentage of the flags that change are not needed in the program run. In fact, the flag changing is often a nuisance and extra instructions must be used to nullify their effects.

Flags are very important to the data processing. Flags can be a nuisance during addressing. The 68000 is designed therefore to throw flags during data register processing and to have the flags left alone when the address registers are in action.

The seven address registers are given the MPU addresses A0 through A6. The registers are able to handle 16 and 32-bit wide pieces of data.

The stack pointer, which is a form of address register, has the address A7. A7 is really the address for two stack pointers. The two pointers are never used in the same operating state, so they can both share the same address. The two states are called the *user* and the *supervisor*. The user state is the normal way the computer operates. The supervisor state is a special state needed in certain instances.

The program counter in the 68000 is 32 bits wide. It can address up to 4 billion individual byte addresses directly. However, the 32-bit address is not needed at this time in the 68000. It is used in the 68020.

There are only 23 bits used directly; the 24th bit is controlled by *UDS and *LDS circuits. The total of 24 bits allows addressing up to 16 million bytes. The bytes are divided in two, with 8 million even and 8 million odd bytes. Each even and odd byte adds up to a 16-bit word. The program counter can address 8 million 16-bit words. Each word address usually starts off with an even number. The program counter can address 4 million long word addresses. Each long word starts off with an even number but skips every other number.

The 68000 is built to operate quickly on word and long word addresses that start with even numbers. In those instances where the 68000 must start with an odd address, the operation runs more slowly because two operations must be made to access the address. Every effort is usually made to start word and long word accesses with even addresses. When single bytes are accessed, the addressing can be odd or even.

The condition code register (also called the status register) is a 16-bit register (Fig. 15-36). It is the only 16-bit register in the group. The 16 bits are divided between two groups of eight. The upper bits are reserved for the system's work and lower bits are for the user.

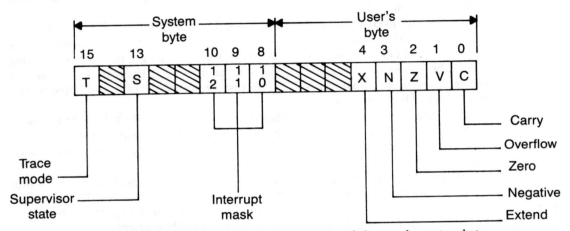

15-36 The 16-bit CCR register is divided into a user's byte and a system byte.

The lower bits contain five flags that can be set or cleared by the actions of the data registers. Four of the registers are the same as the 6800. Bit 0 is C for carry, bit 1 is V for overflow, bit 2 is Z for zero, and bit 3 is N for negative. In addition, bit 4 is X for extend.

The X bit is a helpmate to C. In the 68000 the C bit performs two jobs. It is used both as an arithmetic carry and for program control. During the execution of some branch instructions, the bit is tested. According to its state and the dictates of the instruction, the program may or may not branch.

The X bit takes over the arithmetic carry operation. The C bit is used as a test for the branch operations. This gives the programmer some simplification and more control.

The system byte has several bits. Bits 8, 9, and 10 are an interrupt mask. Bit 13 shows the operating state of the MPU. If the bit is 1, the MPU is in the supervisor state. When the bit is 0, the user state is in effect.

Bit 15 is of great use to the sophisticated technician. When bit 15 is set, the computer is in a trace mode. The 68000 has built-in tracing circuits.

You can install a user written trace service routine. When it is necessary to debug a problem, the trace mode can be set with bit 15. The 68000 then runs through a program one step at a time. As each step is run, the 68000 is in the supervisor state. With bit 15 set and the 68000 in the supervisor state, the program counter develops a specific vector address. The vector sends the 68000 to a special trace service program. The service program can be used to trace the contents of the memory map, registers, flag settings, and so forth. This trace mode is valuable to the programmer for debugging software and to the technician when you check out hardware.

68000 addressing modes

In the vast memory map of the 68000, there can be storage areas of data, or *operands* in many places. The operands can be in the form of bytes, words, and long words, in odd or even addresses. It could be in a table of numbers or stored as individual operands. In order to locate operands, it is useful to have many ways to address them. The 68000 has 14 addressing modes that fall under only six categories.

This discussion covers the six general addressing modes; the six are called inherent, register, immediate, absolute, indirect, and relative. They are similar to the addressing modes of the 6800, with the addition of the indirect mode.

You'll notice that in the discussion of the op codes and operands in the 6800, we used hex numbers in the instruction set rather than mnemonics. Mnemonics are needed when assembly language is used to describe the hex code numbers. Assembly language is the realm of the programmer. Technicians usually do not need assembly language to work on the hardware; you'll probably prefer using the hex codes. In fact, binary is ideal for tests, but most microcomputers cannot accept binary directly. Therefore, you'll end up coding your tiny binary test programs into hex, and installing the hex into the machines.

With only 256 possible byte-sized op codes, byte-sized data bus and memory locations, and only a few MPU registers, hex can be used without undue hardship. However, in 16-bit computers with a possible 64,000 word-sized op codes of four hex characters each, 16-bit data buses and memory locations, and multiple 32-bit MPU registers, hex numbers are very unwieldy. The mnemonics of the instruction set with its appropriate addressing mode is easier to use. In this discussion, we will use mnemonics rather than the hex numbers. The resulting assembly language has to be installed in the computer with an assembler. The assembler will take care of the massive job of generating the hex/binary version of the op code the computer uses.

Inherent

The *inherent addressing* mode is an automatic one. The location of the operand is implied in the mnemonic. For example, there is an op code called jump. The mnemonic is JMP. When executed, the jump instruction always loads the program counter with the jump address. The program counter is always implied as the register where the address is destined to be loaded. The program counter is called the *destination* register of the jump load instruction. The program counter, although never mentioned by name, is inherent in the instruction JMP (Table 15-2).

Table 15-2. Inherent addressing mode.

Mnemonic	Some implied instructions	Implied register
BRA	Branch always	Program counter
JMP	Jump	Program counter
JSR	Jump to subroutine	Program counter stack pointer
MOVE CCR	Move condition codes	Condition code register
RTE	Return from exception	Program counter stack pointer condition code register

Register

The next addressing mode is like inherent, except the name of the destination is mentioned. It is called *register addressing*. In the MPU, the registers all have their own MPU addresses. These addresses are not located on the memory map, only inside the MPU.

There is a general instruction in the 68000 called *MOVE*. It is a powerful instruction that is described in detail later in this chapter. One of the MOVE instructions can move data from one MPU register to another. For instance, the assembly language instruction MOVE D7, D6 will move the contents of data register D7 to register D6 (Fig. 15-37).

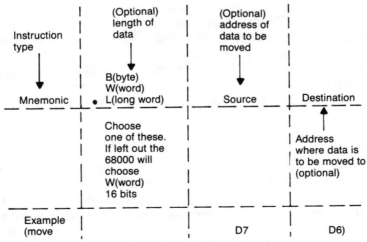

15-37 One line of the 16-bit assembly language format can accommodate both the source and destination address codes.

This is a register addressing mode. The register D7 is called the *source* address. It is specified with 16 bits. The register D6 is the destination address. It is also specified with its own 16 bits. The instruction moves the data contents from source to destination.

The instruction MOVE is also specified with 16 bits. The 16 bits in the instruction contains both the exact nature of the operation and the type of addressing mode.

Absolute

The next mode is called *absolute addressing.* This can be compared to the direct and extended modes used in the 6800. The operand address is specified directly and absolutely found after the instruction. For example, the mnemonic MOVE can be followed with the source and destination addresses, $FF23, D4. This says to move the contents of hex FF23 to data register D4.

Immediate

The next addressing mode is almost exactly the same as the 6800 Immediate addressing mode. It is also called *immediate.* It works like this. Suppose an instruction line to be executed is MOVE #9, D1. The MPU interprets the symbol # as the Immediate mode of addressing. This means the number immediately following the symbol is the operand. The location of the operand is the memory location in the program immediately following the location of the binary bits that specify the # symbol. The MPU, according to the instruction, moves the 9 from the program location to data register D1.

Indirect

The next category is *indirect.* In this case, the addressing after the mnemonic is not the address of the operand. It is the address of an address where the operand is found.

With this addressing mode, the indirect address is enclosed in parentheses. The address in the parentheses is the address of the address of the operand. An example is an instruction like MOVE (A3), D4. The contents of register A3 is 200. The contents of address 200 in the memory map is 32F. Here is what happens when the instruction MOVE (A3), D4 is executed (Fig. 15-38).

The MPU goes to its address register A3 as a source address. The MPU sees the parentheses and knows that the contents of A3 is not the operand, but is instead the address of the operand. It finds the address 200 there. The MPU then knows that the 200 is its source address. It goes to 200 and finds the number 32F there. That is the operand.

Once the source address is located indirectly, the MPU moves the contents 32F into the destination address, data register D4.

This indirect addressing mode has a number of variations. While they are essential to the programmer, as a technician, you can get by with only a brief overview of the variations. If you ever get into a particular situation where you must use this addressing mode, you can learn the variation in detail at that time.

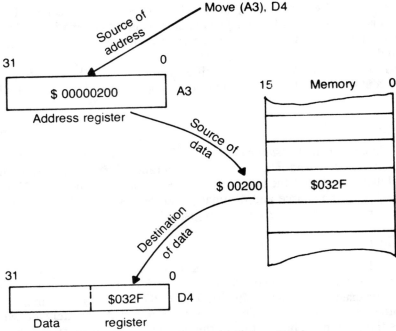

15-38 The parentheses around A3 tells the assembly language programmer that the source address contains an address of the data that is needed.

Indirect addressing with predecrement or *postincrement* is one pair of variations. Predecrement means that the address register is decremented before its contents are used as the effective address. Postincrement means that the address register is incremented after the contents are used as the address.

For instance, to keep predecrementing address register A3, the assembly code −(A3) is used. To keep postincrementing the address register A3, the code (A3)+ is used. Preincrementing and postdecrementing is especially valuable when the program has to loop through a program section that is numbered in sequence. It automatically performs the MOVE operation on all the addresses in order. It works on bytes, words, and long words.

There are a number of other variations the indirect address mode uses. Most of them become very complex, and are not needed by the technician except in isolated cases. If you are curious, you can study 68000 assembly language for more details.

Relative

The last general category of addressing is *relative addressing* modes. Like the 6800, the relative addressing mode refers to the program counter. There are two variations of the technique. One simply adds an offset to the value of the program counter. The second adds an offset plus another value found in one of the address or data registers.

The addressing mode changes the address in the program counter to one above or below the address of the current instruction being run. The main difference between the relative mode and the others is that there is no destination operand in the instruction. The source address is specified, but the destination location for the data in the source location is not given.

There is no destination for the data. The source operand is the beginning of a program to be run. The offset from the program counter is the address of a piece of position-independent code relative to the main program being run. Position-independent code can be a subroutine in RAM or a program in ROM. The nice part of position-independent code is the location of the code can be anywhere that is convenient on the memory map. It can be used with any combination of other programs. This might not appear significant to the new technician, but a programmer finds the position-independent capability of relative addressing very convenient.

68000 instruction mnemonics

The 16-bit instruction set programs are best written in assembly language. Because the instructions are defined in 16 bits and 16 bits have 64K possible combinations, there can really be more than 64,000 individual hex op codes. Each code specifies an operation, the size of the data to be handled, plus the addressing mode to locate the operands in storage.

The layout of the assembly language in bits is in full 16-bit words. The instruction format starts off with the mnemonic and the size of the data to be handled. Not all the instructions handle data, but those that do receive a B, W, or L for byte, word, or long word after the mnemonic. This part of the instruction line is contained in the first 16 bits of the line. A period (.) is placed between the mnemonic and the data length initial. If no length is specified, the 68000 assumes a 16-bit word is in the works.

The next set of 16 bits provide the data source. If the data source is in the immediate addressing mode, the bits are the data itself. Otherwise, the bits are the source address of the data. The remaining sets of 16 bits on the line are the destination addresses of the data. There is a comma (,) between the source and destination addresses of the data.

The op code and modes are specified in one word. The operands, immediate mode, source address, and destination address are either one or two words each. An assembly language line can occupy one to ten words in memory. A one-word line could be one of the inherent addressing mode instructions. A five-word line could have two word source and destination addresses.

When you write an instruction, you must first find the mnemonic to do the job. Next, figure out the data size. These are contained in the first part of the line. Decide on one of the 14 addressing modes that will locate the operands. Then work out the address of the operand to be moved. Lastly, decide where the results of the operation should be located. A second addressing mode is decided on in many operations. When data is moved, however, any mode can be used. These decisions are contained in the list part of the line.

The op codes in the 68000 are defined in 16 bits. This is deliberate. One of the benefits is that instructions can always be started on even-byte addresses. The 68000 works fastest with 16-bit quantities. The 16-bit even-odd unit is the basic unit of the computer. The fact that it can operate on 8-bit units is only a special feature.

The 68000 has 56 mnemonics (Table 15-3). This is less than the 6800, which uses 72. However, the mnemonics are only code for part of the general instruction. The 16 bits that specify the operation also contain information on data size, addressing mode, and other tidbits. There are three data sizes and 14 possible addressing modes. Each mnemonic is multiplied by the factors that apply to them. One instruction mnemonic can produce one of many binary bit possibilities.

Table 15-3. 68000 assembly language mnemonics.

	Mnemonic	Meaning
#1	MOVE	Move
	MOVEM	Move multiple registers
	MOVEP	Move peripheral data
#2	EXG	Exchange registers
	SWAP	Swap dta register values
#3	LEA	Load effective address
	PEA	Push effective address
#4	ADD	Add
	ABCE	Add decimal with extend
	SUB	Subtract
	SBCD, NBCP	Subtract decimal with extend
	MULS	Signed multiply
	MULU	Unsigned multiply
	DIVS	Signed divide
	DIVU	Unsigned divide
	CMP	Compare
	CLR	CLear operand
	NEG	Negate
	TST, TAS	Test, test and set operand
	EXT	Sign extend
#5	AND	Logical AND
	OR	Logical OR
	EXCLUSIVE OR	Exclusive OR
	NOT	One's complement
#6	ASR	Arithmetic shift right
	ASL	Arithmetic shift left
	LSR	Logical shift right
	LSL	Logical shift left
	ROR	Rotate right without extend
	ROL	Rotate left without extend
	ROXR	Rotate right with extend
	ROXL	Rotate left with extend
#7	BTST	Bit test
	BSET	Bit test and set

Table 15-3. Continued.

	Mnemonic	Meaning
	BCLR	Bit test and clear
	BCHG	Bit test and change
#8	Unconditional	
	BRA	Branch always
	BSR	Branch to subroutine
	JMP	Jump
	JSR	Jumpt to subroutine
	Conditional	SCC set conditionally
	ALL BRANCH	BCC branch conditionally
	Conditionals, 14	DBCC decrement & branch
	Conditions	
#9	RTR	Return & restore condition code
	RTS	REturn from subroutine
#10	TRAP	Trap
	TRAPV	Trap on overflow
#11	Privileged	
	STOP	Stop
	RESET	Reset external devices
	RTE	Return from exception
#12	LINK	Link stack
	UNLK	Unlink
	CHK	Check register against bounds
	NOP	No operation

Data movement instructions

The most amazing mnemonic is MOVE, with its variations (Table 15-3, mnemonic #1). The 68000 has streamlined its data movement mnemonics into MOVE. There are no LOAD, STORE, stack pointer PUSH and PULL, or I/O instructions. They are all variations of MOVE. In addition, moving data in the 68000 is much freer of restrictions than in older MPUs. Binary data can be moved from almost any place in the environs of the digital circuits to anywhere else in the digital circuits.

MOVE comes in three general versions. One is *MOVE* itself, which replaces the LOAD and STORE instructions used in 8-bit computers. Second is *MOVEM*. MOVEM is a change of mnemonic for the stack pointer instructions of PUSH, PULL, and POP used on smaller MPUs. *MOVEP* is a mnemonic reserved for use on peripheral I/O type chips in the memory map.

The straight MOVE mnemonic has tremendous power when coupled with the many addressing modes. It can copy bytes, words, or long words between most any registers in the MPU or memory map. The data contents of registers can be copied not only between MPU registers and memory, but also from a memory location directly to another memory location. There are ten addressing modes that locate the source address and seven modes that find the destination address.

MOVEM is used to save MPU registers when a subroutine must be called or an interrupt must be serviced by the MPU. During the change from sequential addressing to the subroutine or interrupt, the MPU register contents have to be saved. The MOVEM instruction transfers any or all of the 16 address and data registers to a stack place in memory. The register contents can be saved there safely until the MPU is ready to resume the main program after the subroutine or interrupt is over.

MOVEP is needed in a new way. There are no similar instructions in the 8-bit computer. The MOVEP instruction is needed to make the 16-bit computer compatible in certain ways with the earlier 8-bit types.

Because the 8-bit MPU has had such a wide and popular acceptance, there are many 8-bit peripherals that have been developed, perfected, and are readily available. The designers of the 68000 figured that, if these 8-bit devices could be easily used by the 68000, many uses for the 68000 would be immediately available. The move peripheral or MOVEP instruction was created to allow the 8-bit peripherals to be used by the 68000.

It is shown how two 8-bit PIAs were connected in parallel to the 16-bit data bus, one PIA to lines D15 – D8 and the other one to D7 – D0. In the memory map where the PIAs are addressed, all D15 – D8 bits are at an even address and D7 – D0 bits are an odd address.

Suppose you want to use one of the PIAs, the one connected to data bus lines D15 – D8. In order to load memory in preparation of the use, the data in the 32-bit registers in the MPU must be all placed into even addresses. Otherwise, the data bus will not be able to transfer data from memory to the peripheral over the correct data lines.

The MOVEP instruction lets you take the data in an MPU 32-bit register, break it up into four-byte pieces and transfer it to four even addresses in memory. The even addresses are connected to data lines D15 – D8 which are also connected to the desired PIA of the parallel pair.

Besides the MOVE type instructions there are a pair of mnemonics that swap data inside the MPU from one register to another (Table 15-3, mnemonic #2). The exchanges can be made between any of the address and data registers. One of the instructions is called *EXG*, which exchanges entire registers. The second is called *SWAP*, which is able to swap only the high order or low order 16 bits.

Effective addresses

Another pair of instructions, *LEA* and *PEA*, deal with *effective addresses* (Table 15-3, mnemonic #3). The effective address is the final computed address where the MPU finds or stores the actual data or operand it uses. The effective address can be simple or difficult to find. When the immediate addressing mode is used, the EA is simple. The operand is found in the memory location immediately following the location in the program the instruction came from.

The EA is hard to figure out when the indirect addressing mode is used. The EA is found by first going to an address specified by the program line. The contents of that address is itself an address. The MPU then goes to that second address. That is the residence of the operand. That address is the effective address.

LEA loads the effective address into an address register rather than the contents of the effective address. PEA pushes the effective address onto the stack rather than the contents of the address. These two instructions are valuable to programmers writing machine language programs. They are interesting to technicians.

The various data movement instructions are used about 70 percent of the time a program is being run. The other types of instructions have to split up the remaining program time.

Computation instructions

While moving data around from place to place in the digital world of the computer takes up most of the program line, the actual computing is accomplished with the arithmetic and logic instructions.

The 68000 is able to do the arithmetic operations listed on Table 15-2, mnemonic #4. It can add (ADD), subtract (SUB), multiply (MULS, MULU), divide (DIVS, DIVU), and compare (CMP) a pair of operands. It can also clear (CLR), negate (NEG), test (TST), and sign extend (EXT). The instructions are quite like the 6800 comparable instructions and the accompanying table shows the differences.

The logic instructions are AND, OR, Exclusive OR, and NOT. They are written with source and destination addresses that are logically combined. If you want to logically affect a register with a constant, you can use ANDI, ORI, and XORI (Table 15-2, mnemonic #5). This is the immediate mode. The constant can be installed in the program line as the source operand. An important use of the I mode is to set or clear individual flag bits in the condition code register.

The 68000 has instructions for arithmetic shift right (ASR), arithmetic shift left (ASL), logic shift right (LSR), and logic shift left (LSL) (Table 15-2, mnemonic #6). The ASR mnemonic causes the least significant bit to be placed in the X and C flag positions. The MS bit remains intact and a copy of the MOS bit is installed next to the MS bit.

The other three shift operations install the bit that is pushed out of the shifted register into the X or C flag position. The empty bit in the register, due to the shift, is filled with a 0.

The rotate instructions are rotate right (ROR) and rotate left (ROL). Rotation shifts the bits around so the end bit that loses its place in the register is installed in the other end. In addition, the bit is copied into the C flag. If you want a copy of that rotating bit in the X flag too, *ROXR* or *ROXL* is used instead of ROR or ROL.

In the 68000, the programmer has strong bit-testing capabilities. Specifically, it does this for him. First the test instruction can target a bit in a memory location or MPU register. Next, it is able to place a copy of the target bit into the Z flag. Finally, the instruction can make a decision on the test result and perform an operation.

For example, a single bit is often the off-on switch of a machine. With control of the bit, the MPU can tell if the machine is off or on and take appropriate action.

The programmer writes the appropriate action into the program. The decision to take the action is determined by the bit tests.

The mnemonics for the tests are bit test (BTST), bit set (BSET), bit test and clear (BCLR), and bit test and change (BCHG) (Table 15-3, mnemonic #7). With these tests, individual bits can be tested to see if they are high or low. Then, according to their logical state, they can be set, cleared, or both (toggled). This provides control over the devices or programs the bit will affect.

Address manipulation

The data movement instructions get the data into the right registers at the right time so it can be processed. The computation instructions process the data. The program runs smoothly, since the MPU is built to automatically start at the first address in the program and run the program lines in sequence. However, the sequential processing of address locations is not enough to accomplish satisfactory results. The time comes in programs when the next address in the row will not do the job. The MPU must branch or jump to some other location in the memory map for the next instruction (Table 15-3, mnemonic #8).

Branch and jump instructions look the same at first glance. They are not. One important difference is the type of code that each will produce. When a branch instruction is written, position-independent code is produced. Jump instructions result in transferring program control to absolute addresses. a second difference between them is the word *if*. Branch instructions will perform if one of the flags is set or cleared in a specified way. Branch instructions will not perform if the designated flag is not affected. This makes branch instructions conditional. Except for branch always and branch to subroutine, they will only work if certain flag conditions are met. Jump instructions are unconditional. They always perform as written. They can use any of the addressing modes to locate the destination address in the program line.

Both types of instructions fit into the same instruction category: program address manipulators. All they do is change the program run from executing automatically address by sequential address to some other specified arrangement.

Branch instructions do this by adding an offset to the program counter. The offset is a signed 8- or 16-bit number that is in the program followed by the branch instruction. When the MPU receives the instruction, it checks the flags to see if the flag condition is met. If the flag condition is not met, the MPU ignores the offset and proceeds to the next instruction. However, when the flag condition is met, the MPU adds the offset to the program counter. The resultant PC value becomes the next location to be addressed. The automatic sequential addressing is altered.

Because the offset is signed, it is either a + number or a − number. A + offset makes the branch advance in a forward way. A − number causes a backward branch. If the offset is an 8-bit number, the offset is restricted to the 256 combinations of the byte. The sign bit causes the 256 possibilities to be from − 128 to + 127. The branch can be up to 128 addresses backward or 127 addresses forward.

When the offset is a 16-bit signed number, the range of addresses the branch can locate is − 32,768 to + 32,767.

The offset added to the program counter is said to produce an address *relative to* the value in the program counter. The effective address can be made anywhere in the memory map according to the PC value. The offset is absolute but not the effective address. This is position-independent code that is so convenient for the programmer.

The jump instruction has absolute addresses and is unconditional. The address for the jump is contained in the instruction line. When the MPU receives the jump instruction, it changes the program counter to the address following the instruction. The new absolute address goes out on the address bus and the normal sequential addressing is jumped to the new memory location.

The branch-jump address manipulation instructions are shown in two tables. One table shows the unconditional instructions and the other the flag conditional instructions. There are only four unconditional instructions. Branch always and jump are both unconditional. They differ only in the way they affect the program counter. Branch uses an offset added to the PC and jump changes the PC entirely. This limits the branch instructions to $-32,768$ and $+32,767$. Jump has no numerical limit and can address the entire memory map.

Branch to subroutine and jump to subroutine are also both unconditional. The branch instruction has the same limiting offset, while the jump instruction is not so encumbered.

The change of address to a subroutine needs another instruction once the subroutine is run. This is a return instruction, which changes the address back to the main program. There are two return instructions, RTS and RTR (Table 15-3, mnemonic #9). They are *Return from Subroutine* and *Return and Restore condition.*

When you branch or jump to a subroutine, the call saves the return address on the stack. When the subroutine has been completed, RTS could be the last instruction in the routine. This instruction restores the stacked value back into the program counter. The program counter places the value onto the address bus and the MPU starts processing the main program again.

Often it is necessary to save the value of the flags in the MPU too. In those cases, RTR will be the last subroutine instruction. It will restore all the flag states that were stored in the stack, at the beginning of the subroutine, back into the condition code register.

Other 68000 instructions

The 68000 has two general modes. One is called the user mode and the other is the supervisor. All the instructions discussed so far operate in the user mode. The 68000 spends most of its time in the user mode. The user mode is considered the lower level of operation and the Supervisor the higher level. Bit 13 of the condition code register controls which mode the 68000 will operate in.

The supervisor mode is a protection level. It sets up electronic walls around the operating system and its resources so defects in a user program can't cause troubles. Switching from mode to mode is handled in the following way.

If the computer is in the supervisor mode and needs to run a User program, the operating system changes the state of bit 13 in the CCR. The system goes into the User mode and begins program execution.

The program runs and stays out of the supervisor level unless a TRAP instruction occurs (Table 15-3, mnemonic #10). There are 16 TRAP instructions, and all are triggered if a troublesome User program happening occurs. Some of these happenings are an attempt to divide by zero, an attempt to execute an illegal instruction or a bad address. The MPU is forced to save the contents of the PC and CCR on the supervisor stack.

The MPU then goes to a vector table where it gets an address that is loaded into the program counter. The address is the start of a special routine to service the TRAP. Each type of TRAP has its own service routine that corrects the problem and returns the program counter back to the original program.

The 68000 has a few privileged instructions which can be used only when the 68000 is in the supervisor mode—most of them would cause trouble in the user mode (Table 15-3, mnemonic #11). The first such instruction is STOP. The instruction stops execution but also loads the CCR with a 16-bit value. The change in the CCR bits would throw off the program operation in the user mode.

Another privileged instruction is RESET. This instruction resets the entire computing environment except for the MPU itself. This must be done in the supervisor mode.

RTE is a privilege instruction, *return from exception*. What constitutes an exception? Any eventuality that stops the MPU from running its normal instructions. For example, traps are exceptions. Interrupts are exceptions. At the end of the exception the RTE takes the values of the program counter and condition code register from the stack and restores them to their registers in the MPU.

MOVE USP means access the user stack pointer. During activity in the supervisor mode the supervisor stack pointer that shares register address A7 is used. There are periods when the user stack pointer register must be initialized for activity. MOVE USP will access the user stack pointer.

The instructions MOVE AND, OR, and XOR, when used to move a 16-bit value to the CCR or combine a value with the CCR, become privilege instructions. This is because the high order bits in the CCR, the S/U bit 13, the trace mode bit 15, and the three interrupt bits 8, 9, and 10, all must be under the control of the operating system and not the user program.

You'll find it helpful to understand how the application of instruction bits into the data pin of the MPU forces the MPU to perform tasks such as data movement, data processing, and addressing changes. During sophisticated maintenance and servicing, you'll be called upon to test voltages, logic states, and oscilloscope patterns, and you must be able to detect incorrect readings. You can't do that unless you know what the correct readings were in the first place.

Quite often, you are required to write little test programs to see if the MPU and memory map is responding to various instructions. These programs are usually written in machine or assembly language. This requires some expertise in working with the instruction set of the computer.

16

The newer multibit processors

THE INTEL FAMILY OF PROCESSORS, IS USED IN ABOUT 40% OF ALL THE microcomputers in the world. Besides the fact that they are viable machines, giant computer maker IBM decided to use them in their microcomputers. IBM then set the standard for the PC line of computers. The PCs and their clones all sell and work well. The magic words are IBM-compatible.

In chapter 15 the 8088-8086 processors are covered. In this chapter, the 80286 and 80386 are discussed. What happened to the 80186? Examine this interim processor that appeared between the 8088-8086 and the 80286 before you cover the rest. These circuits are similar to those found in the 80286.

A look at the 80186

The 80186 does not look like an 8086. The 8086 chip is contained in a 40-pin DIP. The 80186 package, in contrast, has 68 pins. The chip is packaged as a square device in a surface mount socket as shown in Fig. 16-1. The 80186 chip contains a complete 8086 processor. The 8086 on the 80186 chip is complete and uses the same instruction set. The 80186 is a superset of the 8088-8086 instruction set. The 80186 has ten more instruction types. These additional instructions are used to handle the additional circuits the 80186 chip has on board.

The 80186 is upwardly compatible to the 8086 and the 8088. Whatever software can be run on the 8088-8086 can also be run on the 80186 without any changes necessary. If the 80186 is so similar to the 8086, what is the reason for the additional 28 pins?

The 80186 chip has a number of circuits that were not on the 8086. These circuits were in additional chips that were installed along with the 8086 in the PCs

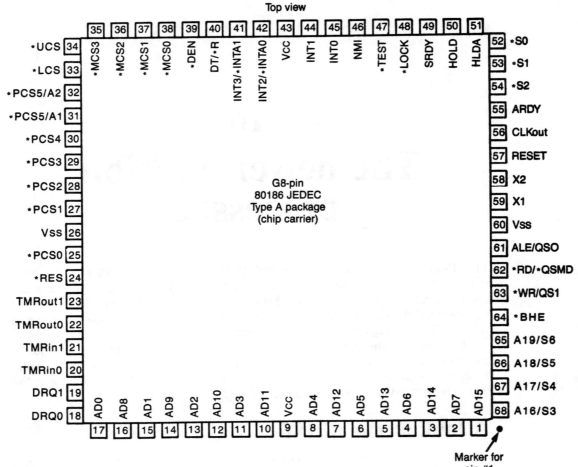

TRS-80 2000
U76
iAPX 186 (8086-2)
Top view

16-1   The 80186 does not physically resemble an 8086. It is packaged as a 68-pin square-surface-mounted device. The package is called a chip carrier. Note that the pins are arranged around all four sides of the package, not only on two sides like the DIP.

and clones. The 80186 is therefore a collection of 15 to 20 individual chips. The 8086 processor is only one of the group of chips.

The 80186 block diagram in Fig. 16-2 displays the different integrated circuits the chip contains. Besides the 8086 circuits, there is a clock generator, a programmable interrupt controller, programmable timers, a bus interface unit, chip select unit, and a programmable *DMA* (direct-memory controller).

The clock generator needs an external crystal to run. The clock comes in two versions, 8 and 6 MHz. When the 80186 is ordered the purchaser has the option to buy either one. The 6 MHz version is considered cost effective.

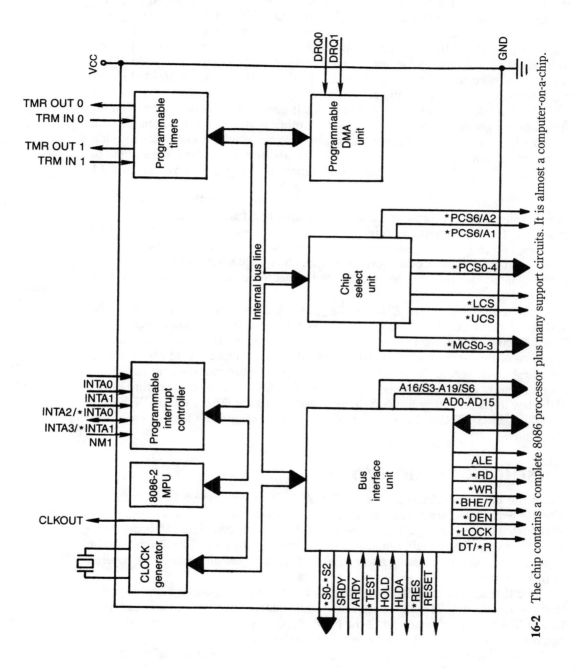

16-2 The chip contains a complete 8086 processor plus many support circuits. It is almost a computer-on-a-chip.

The 8086 MPU section is souped up in comparison to the conventional 8086. It has twice the throughput as the regular 8086. The 8086 unit is aided by a programmable interrupt controller. Some of the additional instructions are used to get these circuits in use. There are five types of interrupts that can be utilized.

There are three 16-bit programmable timers. Two of the timers are connected to external pins. They can be used to count events in the computer system. They can also be used to generate waveforms. The third timer is not connected externally and can be used internally for coding and time delay operations.

The bus interface unit is a bus controller. It generates the bus control signals. It can be programmed to shut down and let other systems in the computer take over the bus lines. The chip select unit is also programmable. It generates the chip select bits to address the memory and peripherals. It can also be programmed to be in a READY or WAIT state. It is able to supply, among other things, A0 and A1 bits.

The 80186 *DMA* (direct memory controller) is able to directly address 1 megabyte of memory. The programmable DMA unit has two separate independent channels. These channels can transfer data between memory and I/O, memory to memory, and I/O to I/O. The data can be 8-bit bytes or 16-bit words. They can be transferred from even or odd addresses. Each channel has a 20-bit wide source or destination pointer that can be incremented or decremented by one or two after a data transfer.

Despite the fact that the 80186 was a greatly improved version of the 8086, the 186 never really became too popular. It was used in a few machines such as the Tandy 2000, but it never took off. One of the reasons for its non-use was the appearance of the 80286 and IBM. IBM made the 286 its processor of choice for its popular PC/AT series. As usual, many other manufacturers tooled up and introduced all sorts of AT clones and peripherals. The 286 took the architecture of the 186 a few important steps forward. Intel formally calls the 80186, the iAPX186 and the 80286, the iAPX286. Let us refer to them as the 186 and 286 for the rest of this discussion.

First look at the 286

All of the members of the 8088-8086-186-286-386 family have a lot in common. The 8088 and 8086 are almost identical, except for a few design differences such as the 8088 having eight data pins and the 8086 with sixteen. The 186 is quite like the 8086 except for the additional support circuits on the chip. The 286 is like the 186 but takes microprocessing a few steps further. The 386 differences are covered in this chapter.

The thread that binds them all together is their instruction set and registers that support the set. The 286 contains the same instruction set as all the rest of the family. The 286 has a super set of the 8088, 8086, and 186. Any program that can run on the 8088-8086 will also run directly on the 286.

In fact, when you first turn on a 286 computer, it comes up as an 8086. It defaults to an 8086. It runs all 8086 software immediately as if it is an 8086. It will continue to operate as an 8086 unless stopped and given special 286 instructions.

There is only one major difference between the 286 in the 8086 mode and an actual 8086 machine. The 286 is much faster than the 8086. This speeds up processing to an astounding extent. Most of the time the increase in speed is a good feature. However, if you try running some game programs at the higher speed you won't be able to keep up with the activity.

Although the 286 is designed to run with faster clock speeds, that isn't the main reason for the processing speedup. The design of the 286 has the processor executing instructions with less clock cycles. For example, in Table 16-1, a MOV instruction in an 8086 takes 19 clocks to be fully executed. The same MOV instruction in a 286 is completed in 5 clocks. A MUL (multiply) instruction in an 8086 takes 140 clocks. The MUL in the 286 only requires 24 clocks. All of the instructions right down the line need less clocks to execute in the 286 in contrast to the 8086. The 8088 requires even more clock cycles than the 8086, but the difference is not that great. The MOV in the 8088 needs 23 clocks. The MUL takes 144 clocks. Not too much difference between the 8086 and 8088. There is quite a difference when the 286 is run.

Table 16-1. The 80286 has the same instruction set as the 8088-8086 but runs the instructions with less clocks. This makes the 286 much faster.

Instruction	Clocks		
	8088	8086	80286
MOV	23	19	5
MUL	144	140	24
DIV	171	167	25
ADD	31	23	5
SUB	31	23	5

Besides the mode the 286 defaults to, called the real address mode, it has a second mode called, the protected virtual address mode as seen in Fig. 16-3. The two modes are quite different. It's as if the 286 is two different processors on the same chip. In a way you could say the 286 is both an 8086 and a 286. The 286 has a complement of 150,000 transistors. The 8086 contains about 40,000. The 286 consists of the 40,000 8086 transistors plus another 110,000 that makes it two processors in one.

Note the two different modes deal expressly in addressing. They both execute code in much the same way except for addressing instructions. The addressing is where most of the differences lie. The real address mode addresses one megabyte of physical memory with 20 address bits, A20 – A0. The protected virtual address mode utilizes 24 address bits, A23 – A0 (Fig. 16-4). It can address 16 megabytes of physical memory.

The instruction pointer register (Fig. 16-5) in the 286 is 32 bits wide, consisting of a 16-bit selector register and a 16-bit offset register. With some manipulation and some external support chips, the 32-bit register is able to address a billion bytes of address space for one task. This is, for all present practical purposes, an unlimited amount of addressing space. The programmer can use addresses without worrying about running out of space.

Operating modes

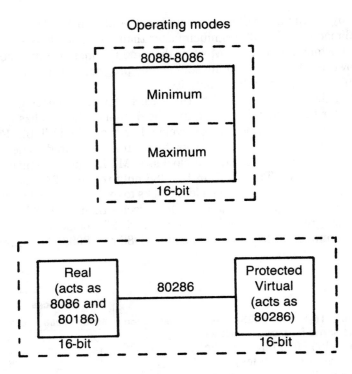

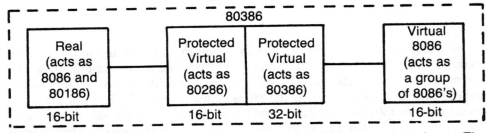

16-3   The 8088-8086 processors can run in two modes, minimum and maximum. The 80286 also has two general modes. In real mode it emulates an 8088-8086 or the 80188-80186. In its protected virtual address mode, the 286 is in its natural state and runs with all of its features. The 80386 is able to operate with four modes. In real mode it emulates the 8088-8086 and 80188-80186. Next, it has a protected virtual mode that emulates the 80286. Third, it has its own native protected virtual mode. Finally it has a special virtual 8086 mode. In that mode it can multitask, that is it can run a lot of 8086 programs at the same time.

In the name, protected virtual address mode, the word *virtual* conveys the following meaning. There are two kinds of address space. There is physical and virtual. Physical space describes addresses that are occupied by physical memory chips, for instance 4164s, the 64K DRAM. Virtual space describes the addresses that the processor is able to access whether there are physical occupants or not.

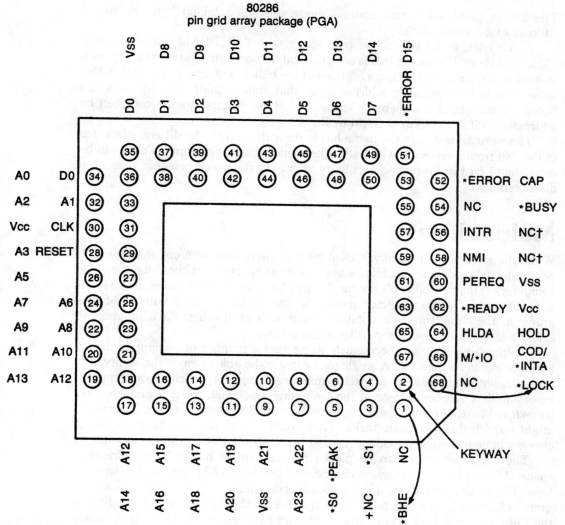

16-4 The 286 is packaged in a 68-pin *PGA* (pin-grid array). Note there are 24 address pins—A23 – A0. It can address 16 Mb of physical memory.

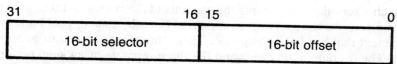

16-5 The instruction pointer register in the 286 is 32 bits wide. 32 bits can address a billion bytes.

The 286 in protected virtual address mode supplies a billion bytes of virtual address space for one task.

If you tried to fill the billion byte space with 64K DRAMs, it would take 131,072 of them. Obviously, this is not practical. However, if you use memory such as hard disks, you could fill large sections of the billion byte space. The 286 in this mode is able to manipulate addressing so that storage addresses on disks can become residents of the memory space. This type of data storage can then be addressed as if it is a form of RAM or ROM.

The word *protection* in the name has to do with keeping the different features of the 286 from interfering with each other and crashing programs. There will be more detail on the Protection capability as multitasking and privilege levels are discussed next.

Multitasking

While the 8086 mode typically is used by a single person with one machine, the 286 protected mode has capabilities to make it useful as a member of a network of computers. This capability allows the 286 machine to act as if it is a mini and not a microcomputer. In the protected mode, the 286 is able to run a number of programs at the same time without interfering with each other. Each program is called a *task* and the process is called multitasking.

Multitasking does not necessarily mean that a number of computers linked together has to be the case. A single user can also be able to enjoy the ability. For example, with multitasking, a businessman preparing a report can have the processor handle a number of tasks at the same time. Each task will act completely on its own and have its own register contents and virtual addressing space. The report might require three separate tasks. They could be editing text, have a spelling checker in operation, and loading the text into a spooler for temporary storage.

The three programs can be placed into the single billion byte addressing space. The application programs can be installed into RAM, onto disks, or even tape. The three applications are completely independent of each other. Each program believes it has its own billion byte space, even though they are all residing in the same gigabyte area. They have no contact between them. There is so much memory that they can remain completely apart.

Even though the application programs are unaware of each other, they all share the operating system that is running the show. The *OS* (operating system) is also in the gigabyte memory space apart from the application programs.

As the user types his report the text editor is in charge and uses the general purpose registers to work with the editor program. When a word is misspelled, the spelling checker takes over, stores the contents of the registers, takes over the registers, and corrects the spelling error. At that time the spooler could take over and store the text that had been composed. These three tasks appear to go on simultaneously. The overall job proceeds and the three separate tasks keep performing.

Multitasking is defined in the following way. During multitasking operations, at any given instant in time, one task is running. That task is called the *current task*. At that instant, the current task has control of the general purpose 286 registers and is using the virtual memory space where its application programs are installed. The current task is also using the operating system programs.

Typically, the billion byte addressing space is arranged so that half the billion addresses are used for application programs, and the other half for operating system programs as in Fig. 16-6. Suppose there are three application programs and the operating system program in the memory space. The three application programs are in separate sections of their half-billion byte space. The operating system program is in the other half-billion space. The three applications are completely isolated from each other but they all share in using the operating system.

The operating system's half of the virtual space is called the *global region*. The application program's half is called the *local region*. In the local area there can be many tasks. However, only one task can be active at one time. It is the current task.

Multitasking is the ability of the 286 to be able to operate a number of tasks one at a time. The 286 is also able to switch from task to task at breathtaking

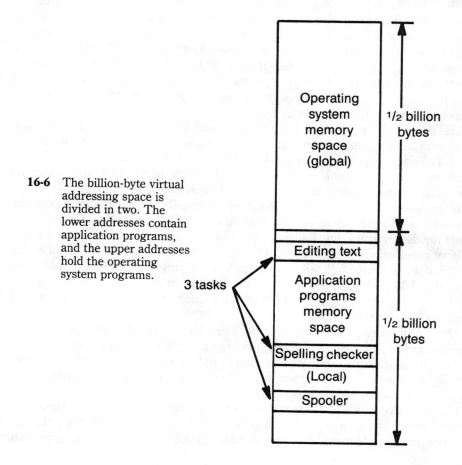

16-6 The billion-byte virtual addressing space is divided in two. The lower addresses contain application programs, and the upper addresses hold the operating system programs.

speed; so fast that the tasks appear to be running simultaneously. The switching is easy to perform. You can switch from one task to another with a special JMP or CALL instruction.

Privilege levels

The last section that discussed multitasking used the protected virtual address mode of the 286. The billion byte addressing space the 286 is able to access has been described. It was shown how a number of tasks can be installed, completely independent of each other in the virtual address space. Besides being independent, each task is given another capability called *protection*. The protection is afforded by means of privilege levels.

The protection given to each task is accomplished by arranging the code and data in memory at different privilege levels. The 286 is able to set up four privilege levels. What sort of privileges are given to the different levels?

At the lowest level, the 286 stops the program that is running from executing certain instructions that might cause troubles in the program run. At the lowest level the 286 conducts the users application programs. The application program might have in its repertoire some I/O instructions to peripheral devices. These instructions could possibly cause the program to crash, because the I/O activity is geared to operate at slower frequencies. These I/O instructions should be run at a different level, not at the lowest level. If the level specified for the I/O instructions is not the lowest one, the 286 will not permit the instructions to be executed in the lowest privilege level. The program run is thus protected from running these dangerous instructions by the privilege levels.

The 286 has four privilege levels. The lowest one, as mentioned, is the one that application programs are run at. The levels are numbered 0, 1, 2, and 3 as in Fig. 16-7. The least privileged or the lowest level is 3. 2 is more privileged, 1 even more, and 0 the most privileged. 3 is reserved for the user's application program running. 2, 1, and 0 usually handle the operating systems'.

When a programmer writes his program he usually divides the total program into modules. He then assigns each module a privilege level. The 286 will then watch over the program run. The more privileged levels running the operating system have practically no restrictions. The low level that is running the application program does not have full reign. The application program will be stopped from performing I/O instructions directly, from reading or writing to addresses that have been assigned a higher level, and from contacting the operating system except under special conditions.

These four levels of privilege give the 286 a lot of value that is appreciated by the programmer. As a technician the privilege levels are only of passing interest. The four levels need not be used in many applications. You can use one level. When only one level is used it must be the highest level so all instructions will be able to be executed and none restricted.

The privilege levels also keep a watchful eye on the tasks. If an attempt is made to switch tasks, but the switch is to be from one level to another, the 286 might not permit it. Uncontrolled task switching could easily crash a program run.

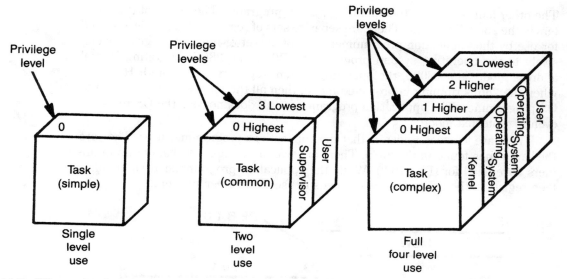

16-7 When a simple task is being run, it can be set to operate at the 0-privilege level. When the task is not simple but common, it can be set to operate with two privilege levels of protection. Should a complex task be operating, all four protection levels can be brought into play.

The 286 will allow a task switch to a level with the same privilege level or lower. If the switch is to a higher level the 296 will stop it.

To switch from one level to another, instructions similar to a task switch are used. These are variations of the same JMP and CALL instructions. These instructions can be executed directly as long as the destination address is allowed according to the rule of privilege levels.

When a level switch is not permitted since the destination is on a high level, caution is required. It probably means there is a fault in the program as written. However, there are ways to gain entry to higher privilege levels. The way to do it is through CALL gates which are in the programmers province. If you want to be able to program the 286 in machine language there are a number of good books on the market or you can purchase Intel's programming manual.

To summarize the last section, the 286 acts as two separate processors. It is a complete 8086 while in its real address mode, but performs two and a half times faster than an actual 8086 at the same clock frequency. It is also a 286 in its protected virtual address mode. As a 286 is able to perform multitasking with each task protected with four privilege levels. It is important for you as a technician to know about the special capabilities of this chip that is so advanced. Take a look at its registers and internal bus lines.

The programmer's registers

It was mentioned in the last section that the billion byte memory space is divided in half. One half is used to store the code and data to run application programs.

The other half is used by the operating system programs. The layout of the registers in the 286 follows suit. There are separate sets of registers. One set is assigned for use by the application programmer. The other set of registers is given exclusively to the operating system programmer. When the 286 is operating in real address mode as an 8086, the operating system registers are ignored. However, when the 286 is running in protected mode, then all the registers are used by the OS programmer. The application programmer still does not use the OS registers even in protected mode.

There are fourteen registers that the applications programmer uses. They are the same ones found in the 8086. There are five more registers that OS programmers have need for (Fig. 16-8). While the application programmer uses his fourteen registers, the OS programmer needs to use all nineteen of them.

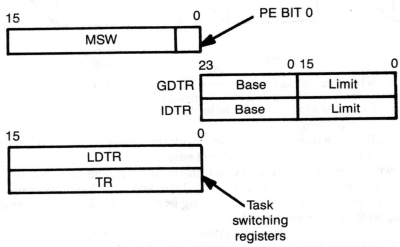

16-8   In addition to the 14 application registers, the operating system programmer needs five more registers.

The OS programmer with his five system registers sets up the machine for the applications to be run. The OS registers handle the multitasking and billion byte memory space that is available in protected mode. The first step the OS registers need is to be set up so the machine is put into protected mode. Remember, the 286 comes on either from a cold start or after a reset, in the real mode. It will stay in real mode and operate as a super fast 8086 unless the protected mode is activated.

The first step to get into protected mode is to initialize the *GDTR* (global descriptor table register) and the interrupt descriptor table register (IDTR), shown in Fig. 16-8. The next step is to initialize the machine status word register (MSW). In the MSW is the protection enable bit (PE). The computer goes directly into protected mode when this bit is set.

With the computer in the protected mode the 286 begins running a task. If the task is all that is desired, the machine is off and running. If you want the 286 to run some other tasks too, then you operate the last two registers so you can affect task switching. You initialize the task register (TR) and the *LDTR* (local descriptor table register).

For most task executions, that's it. The actual details of the contents needed in these registers can be found in the 286 programming book. The 286 is arranged for protected mode operation. Once set, these registers need not, in most cases, be touched again. The fourteen application registers though, are not as easy to handle.

Note that the fourteen application registers have the same layout as the fourteen in an actual 8086. There are eight general purpose registers that do accumulator type duty. They are there mainly to store and manipulate the operands for the arithmetic and logic work. They are all 16-bit types. For the most part they are interchangeable. they are capable of handling either 8-bit or 16-bit pieces of data.

Five of the general purpose registers are able to store both address and data bits. As in Fig. 16-9, they are the BX, SI, DI, BP, and SP. When they perform addressing chores, the BX register usually will be given an address offset to hold that will point to a segment of data. A segment is a group of registers in the memory space that can hold either a collection of data or a collection of addresses. These segments are then called data segments or address segments. The two Index registers, source index, SI or destination index, DI, are also used to hold an offset that points to a particular data segment in memory.

The stack pointer register, SP, and the base pointer, BP are usually holding address offsets (displacements), that point to the top of a stack in memory.

Whenever these registers are not needed to hold an address offset, they can be used to hold data, both logic and arithmetic, that is to be processed by the 286. As a rule though, the following usually applies. The BX, SP, and BP registers are assigned to do addressing duties, such as holding address offsets. The AX, DX, CX, and both index registers, SI and DI, are used for logic and arithmetic data holding.

16-9 Typically three general-purpose registers are used to hold data bits. The other five can contain both data and address bits.

15		0
AX	Data bits	
CX	Data bits	
DX	Data bits	
BX	Data & address bits	
SI	Data & address bits	
DI	Data & address bits	
BP	Data & address bits	
SP	Data & address bits	

Segment registers

The general purpose registers are eight of the fourteen application registers. Next in line are four segment registers. As mentioned, a segment is a group of addresses in memory that contain either a batch of data or addresses. One segment in the 286 can be as large as 64K bytes. The 16 bits in a segment register are able to address that many bytes.

There are four segment registers, code, CS, stack, SS, data, DS, and extra, ES, just like the ones in the 8086. Any address calculation that takes place in the 286 involves one of these segment registers. To put it another way, all of the code and data in memory is positioned relative to a segment address.

These segment pointer registers give the 286 a quality called relocatability. This is a valuable programming feature. What this means is, complete segments can be moved around in memory and get change of addresses easily. The new address is then easily applied by simply changing the segment register's base address. This is known as *position independence*.

This position independence of memory segments is available in both real or protected modes. The segmentation though is especially needed in protected mode. For multitasking with protection levels, segments must be used. Without segmenting the code and data in memory, there would be no distinct separation between the code and data and they would mix at certain times causing the program being run to crash. There would also be no distinction between physical memory and memory areas occupied by other storage means, such as disks. The virtual billion byte memory area would be a treacherous place for accessing activity.

The instruction pointer

The instruction pointer acts somewhat like a program counter found in other processors. It will hold a 16-bit address offset that points to the instruction in a code segment that is to be executed. After the instruction is fetched and executed the IP is incremented to the next instruction address in sequence. The incrementation could be one or more bytes according to how many bytes there were in memory for the instruction.

The IP will keep on incrementing automatically unless an instruction such as a jump, call, or interrupt instruction is the one executed. Then the IP obeys the instruction and changes its address accordingly or takes the correct action. A jump simply causes a change of address but a call or interrupt causes further activity. During the execution of a call or interrupt the IP bits are pushed onto the stack. Then the change of address is placed into the IP. That way the stacked IP contents can be used to return the IP to its original sequencing once the call or interrupt is taken care of.

Flag register

The 286 has a 16-bit flag register. These individual bits, each an independent register of its own, consist of six flags that affect logic and arithmetic activities, and five control flags, as shown in Fig. 16-10.

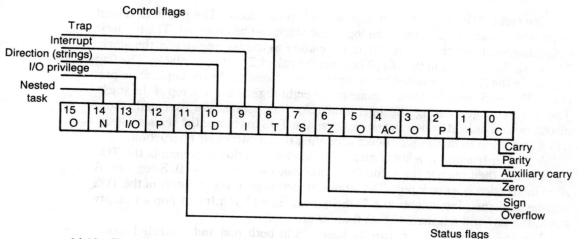

16-10 The flag register of the 286 has six status-flag bits and five control-flag bits.

The carry, parity, auxiliary carry, zero, sign, and overflow flag are used to let the 286 know what happened as a result of the last logic or arithmetic operation. According to the results of the operation, a conditional branch decision is made.

The control flags are also affected by logic and arithmetic calculations. These controls consist of allowing single stepping of instructions for test purposes, permitting an interrupt to take place, giving the privilege level to execute I/O activities, determines whether a task is a nested type, and provides string instruction information on whether to increment or decrement through memory.

About the 80287 coprocessor

Near the 286 in a computer, you will probably find a socket for an 80287 companion processor for the 286; the socket might or might not be filled. The 287 coprocessor is made to be a part of the 286 but installed into a different package. They are wired together and act as one unit. They are programmed as one even though they are two.

The 287 is a numeric processor. It is an upgrade of the 8087 that is used as a coprocessor with the 8086. There is also an 80387 that is used with the 80386. These coprocessors are specifically designed to give the 8086, 286, and 386 additional accuracy when calculating large numbers.

There are eight general purpose registers in the 287 that act like the general purpose registers in the 286. The only thing is, the 287 registers are 80 bits wide. They can handle very large numeric values without having to round them off as the 286 must do by itself. These registers can perform register to register, memory to register, and register to memory arithmetic operations.

These registers only handle arithmetic. They do not perform any address calculations. All addressing is performed in the 286. The 287 holds only operations for arithmetic. Its 80-bit register width simply provides more accuracy.

The eight 80-bit registers act as a form of special stack. The registers cannot be addressed individually. Only the top of the stack can be accessed. The numeric instructions contact the 287 registers in relation to the top register in the stack. There is a flag register in the 287. There is a bit called *TOS* (top of stack). The flag register in the 287 is controlled by the operating system, not by the application program. The TOS could indicate any one of the eight registers as the top of the stack. The TOS changes during the operations. As instructions are executed, those instructions that load or pop the stack cause the TOS to change the register designated as the top to move up or down according to the particular instruction.

A load instruction is a stack push. The load instruction decrements the TOS by one, and then pushes the value to be processed into the new TOS register. A store instruction is a stack pop. The store instruction pops the contents of the TOS register and then increments the TOS by one. Should you try to pop an empty stack, the 287 will tell the 286 that there is an error.

The 287 operates along with its host 286 in both real and protected mode. There are two bits in the machine status word register (MSW) in the 286 that deal with the 287. If you recall bit 0 of the MSW determined whether the machine should be in real or protected mode. When the PE bit is set, protected mode is enabled. Otherwise, the real mode is in charge. The next highest bit in that same MSW register is called math present (MP). The bit following that is Emulate Math (EM). These two bits arrange things for the 287 whether it is in its socket or not.

In real mode these bits are clear and are not included in the 287 activity. The 287 operates alone or in conjunction with the 286 as an 8086/8087 combination. In protected mode however, the operating system tests for the presence of the 287 in its socket. If the 287 is present then the math present bit is to be set. This enables the processors to operate as a 286/287 pair. This improves numeric performance.

If the 287 is not in its designated socket, the operating system notes the condition. In that event, the emulate math bit is set and the math present bit is left in a clear state. When the EM bit is set, the 286 knows it must act on its own without help of the 287. The 286 then emulates the action of a 286/287 pair as best as it can. It uses software as a substitute for the 287 hardware. This is usually quite satisfactory. Incidentally, do not set both the MP and EM bits at the same time. This combination is used only in certain test procedures that went on during the manufacturing of the 286.

The physical 80286

As mentioned, the 286 is a 68-pin chip. It is not packaged in a DIP. Figure 16-4 shows the pinout in a pin grid array package, PGA. The address and data lines all have their very own pins, unlike the 8088-8086 packages that multiplex the various address and data lines with pin sharing.

The PGA packaging lays the pin structure out in a square. There is an outside row of pins and an inside row. This arrangement complicates pin testing. Care and patience is required to adequately test the pins one at a time. Fortunately, the PGA package is typically held in a 68-pin socket. If necessary, the chip can be tested by direct substitution with a known good 286. This is always the best test of the chip.

Figure 16-11 is the schematic drawing of a 286. This is drawn to show the signal flow of the 286. The pin locations in the schematic bear no physical resemblance to the PGA package layout. During testing, when you are using the schematic you must relate the schematic to the actual chip to find desired pins.

There are 24 address lines, A23 – A0 at pins 7 – 28 and 32 – 34. The 16 data lines D15 – D0 are found at pins 51 – 36.

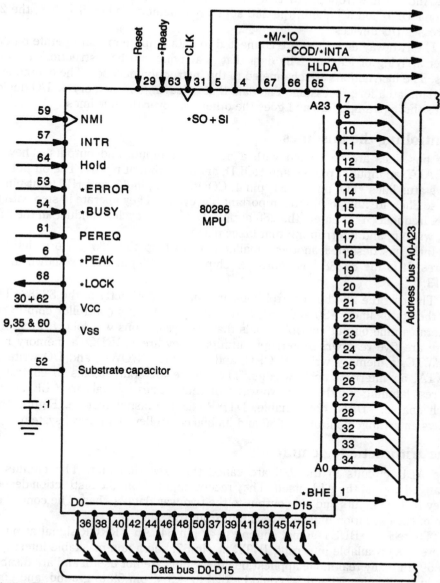

16-11 The schematic drawing of the 286 shows the signals and flow direction of the inputs and outputs.

Figure 16-12 is the block diagram of the 286 chip. Using both the schematic and the block diagram, you can see the 24 address lines emerging from the address latches and amplifiers. Also emerging with the address lines from the same circuits, out of pin 1 is *BHE, bus high enable, that is often hooked up with address line A0. Between A0 and *BHE they can select the high byte of a word, the low byte, the whole word or none of the word, in a memory location or from a peripheral. Another line from pin 67 that comes out of the same circuit is M/*IO, memory or I/O. When it is high, the 286 addresses memory. When it is low, the 286 addresses I/O devices.

The two-way data lines are connected to data amplifiers that operate on data either arriving or leaving. The data that is arriving can be instructions or operands. The instructions are channeled to the instruction decoder. The operands go to a data latch for processing. The data that is leaving for memory or I/O devices leaves through amplifiers and goes the other way over the bus lines.

Controlling the bus lines

The bus lines are controlled with a number of inputs and outputs. They are *READY, an input at pin 63, and HOLD, another input at pin 64. The outputs are two status lines *SO, pin 5, *S1, pin 4, COD/INTA, pin 66, and HLDA at pin 65. These lines are able to run the important bus cycles. They operate in step with the CLK frequency that enters the 286 at pin 31. The bus cycles conduct all the reading, writing, and interrupting that takes place.

Intel has designed another smaller chip to help the 286 perform its cycle chores. It is the 82288 bus controller chip. It is a 20-pin DIP as shown in Fig. 16-13.

Three of the 286 bus control lines are connected directly to the 82288. They are the status lines, *S0 and *S1, and *M/*I/O. The bus controller chip in turn generates nine output control signals that the system bus will follow. First of all there are five read/write/interrupt outputs. They are *MRDC, a memory read, *MWTC, a memory write, *I/ORC, and I/O read, *I/OWC, and I/O write and *INTA, an interrupt acknowledge. Then there are four signals to control the address latching and the data two-way amplifiers. These signals are ALE, address latch enable, *DEN, data enable, DT/*R, data transmit/receive. Figure 16-14 shows an arrangement of the 286 and its bus controller in a typical system.

The arithmetic logic unit

The ALU circuits in the 286 are called the execution unit. The circuits are arranged around the ALU itself. They receive inputs from the instruction decoder. They receive inputs and also output to the two-way data latches. The control section of the execution unit receives input from the pins.

There is a *BUSY signal coming in at pin 54. An ERROR signal at pin 53. There is an available interrupt, INTR at pin 57, and a non-maskable interrupt at pin 59. In many real mode applications these pins are not useful and are disabled. For instance, pins 53 and 54 could be tied to +5 V, pin 59 to ground, and pin 57 just left disconnected. They do come in handy in protected mode.

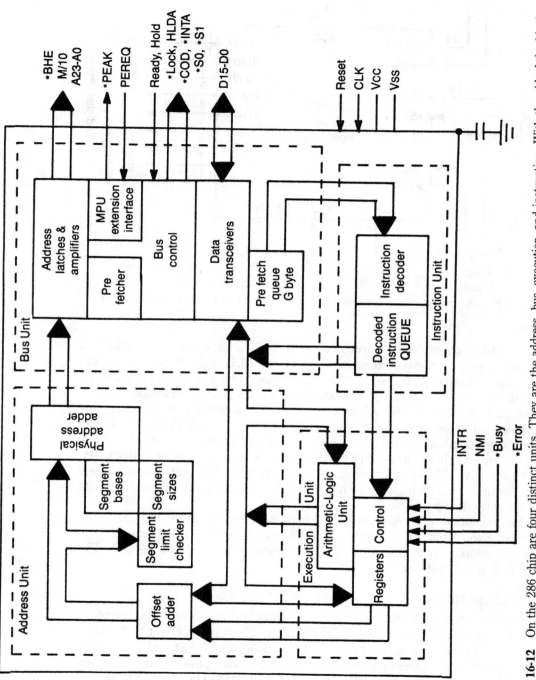

16-12 On the 286 chip are four distinct units. They are the address, bus, execution, and instruction. With the aid of the block diagram and the schematic drawing, the general operation can be observed.

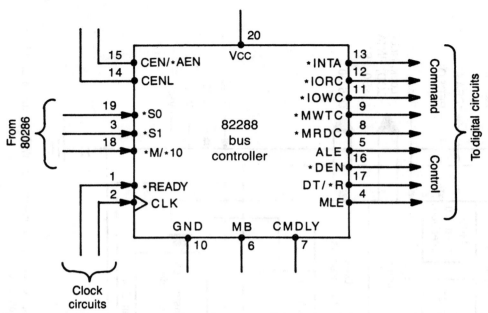

16-13 A companion bus-controller chip can condition a lot of the command and control lines.

The ALU is contained in a circuit enclave called the execution unit. In the unit there are a group of registers that operate with the ALU to do the arithmetic and logic processing that is the heart of the computing. The bus control circuits are called the bus unit and is also a separate circuit enclave as the execution unit is.

There is a third enclave of circuits called the instruction unit. It receives instruction op codes from the bus unit. The instruction unit then decodes the instructions and sends the decoded instructions to the execution unit. The execution unit with its all-important ALU is the center of the computation activity.

Once the ALU finishes processing the data from the bus unit, it immediately sends the finished data back to the bus unit. The bus unit can then send the data back out onto the system bus.

The execution unit not only processes data but it deals in calculating addresses also. After it has done its part in the addressing calculations, the unit sends the address information to the fourth enclave type unit of the 286. The fourth unit is called the address unit.

The address unit

The registers around the ALU connect to address unit registers called the offset adder. As its name suggests, the offset registers calculate the offset that will be used in the final addressing of the memory locations. The offset registers in turn connect to both the segment address base registers and the physical address adder. Between these registers the effective address is calculated. The finished address is then coupled out of the addressing unit back to the bus unit and into the address

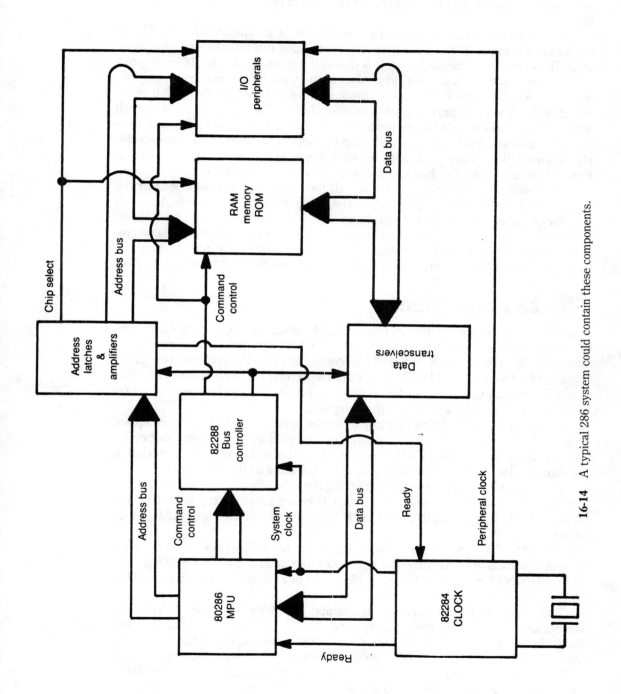

16-14 A typical 286 system could contain these components.

latches. They are readied for their trip on the system bus and then output onto the bus.

This brings up an important feature of the 286. It is called *pipelining*. This is not a new technique. It has been used in mini and mainframe computers for many years. It is new in microcomputers. It is one of the reasons why the 286 is so powerful. It was not used in smaller processors such as the 8-bit types.

Note that there are four separate circuit enclaves on the 286 that are all wired together. Each enclave performs its particular duties. The separate steps of each program line are conducted in the units. The bus unit controls the cycles that drive the addresses and fetches data to and from memory. The instruction unit decodes the op codes. The addressing unit calculates the effective addresses. The execution unit processes all the data and helps in the address calculation.

Pipelining is the technique of having all four units conduct their jobs at the same time. In an 8-bit processor, each of the above steps also take place, but each step is conducted one at a time. In the larger 286 all four units conduct their operations, in their private enclaves, at the same time. The reason, of course, is to save time. Pipelining is one of the reasons why the 286, even in real mode when it is emulating an 8086, performs the 8086 jobs many times faster than an actual 8086.

The 286 bus cycles

The 286, as a processor, generates five distinct types of bus cycles. They are memory read, memory write, I/O read, I/O write, and interrupt acknowledge. As discussed earlier, the 286 uses an 82288 bus controller chip. It injects the two status signals, ∗S0/∗S1, and the M/∗IO into the status decoder of the controller chip. The controller in turn can generate five command outputs. These five outputs represent the five types of bus cycles in the computer.

Figure 16-15 is the timing diagram of a read cycle in the 286. The top square wave depicts the beating of the clock. Note the designations for the previous cycle, the read cycle and the next cycle. Because of pipelining there is some overlap of the signals, since all four units of the 286 are operating at the same time.

The first step in the read cycle is putting the effective address out on the system bus. This happens as the previous cycle is near its end. At the same time the signals, M/∗IO, and COD/∗INTA are made valid. The 24 address bits, A23 – A0 go out on the bus lines.

The ∗READY signal is turned on to signal the end of the previous cycle, then the status signals are activated. For a memory data read the signals ∗S0, ∗S1, M/∗IO, COD/∗INTA must be 1010, see Table 16-2. For a memory instruction read the signals must be 1011.

The bus controller decodes the signals and generates ALE and ∗MRDC, the address latch enable and the memory read signal. ALE goes active at the next clock edge after the bus controller has decoded the status signals. ALE turns on its latches and makes them hold the pipelined address for the rest of the cycle.

DEN, the data enable, and DTR, the data transmit/receive, set up the direction of signal flow from memory to processor. ∗MRDC then goes low and enables

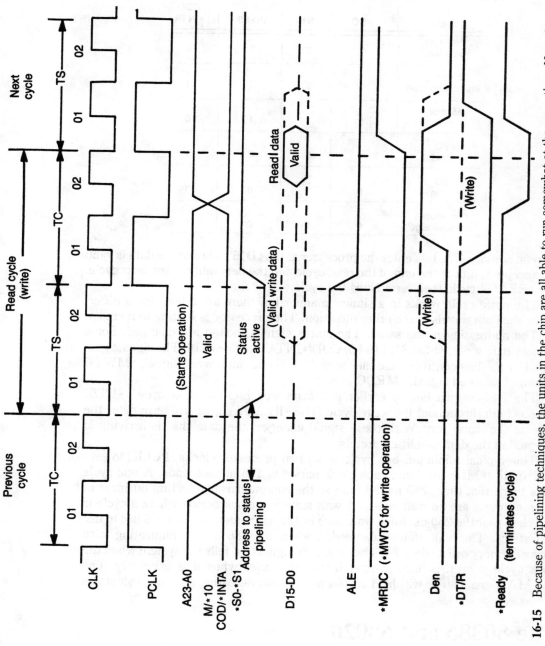

16-15 Because of pipelining techniques, the units in the chip are all able to run somewhat at the same time. Note the overlaps of signals in the previous cycle, the current read cycle, and the next cycle.

Table 16-2. The four signals ∗SO, ∗SI, M/∗IO and COD/∗INTA will attain these states during the various bus cycles.

Bus cycle	∗SO	∗S1	M/∗10	COD ∗INTA
Memory data read	1	0	1	0
Memory instruction read	1	0	1	1
Memory data write	0	1	1	0
I/O read	1	0	0	1
I/O write	0	1	0	1
Interrupt acknowledge	0	0	0	0

the read activity. The bits enter the processor at pins D15 – D0 and the data is valid and accepted right at the end of the read cycle and the beginning of the next cycle. The ∗READY cycle then terminates the cycle.

The write cycle works in a similar manner but there are a few signal differences, the data travels in the other direction. The processor is writing to memory.

The addressing is the same. The status signals though are changed. For a memory data write, ∗SO/∗S1, M/∗IO, COD/∗INTA must be 0110. The signals generated by the bus controller are the same ALE signal but a write signal, ∗MWTC instead of the read signal, ∗MRDC.

The DEN signal begins earlier and lasts well into the next cycle. ∗DT/R remains high throughout the write cycle. The ∗READY signal still terminates the cycle in the same way. With these signal changes, the data that is arriving is accepted in the data amplifier circuits.

This typical minimum bus cycle takes two processor clocks, PCLK, to execute. In an 8 MHz machine, each clock period is 125 nanoseconds. A bus cycle takes twice that time, 250 ns. As long as the computer is conducting business at this rate, there are no wait states. A wait state is a clock period where a cycle is stretched past the 250 ns. Each wait state is 125 ns. Sometimes the 286 has to use wait states. The wait states are needed when the 286 is communicating with slower memory or I/O devices. The ∗READY signal that tells the system when the clock cycle is over, is used to stretch the bus cycles when it is necessary. The ∗READY signal can be withheld as long as necessary creating as many wait states as needed.

The 80386 and 68020

When the 8-bit processors such as the 8085, Z80, 6800 and 6502 emerged in the late 70s and early 80s, they gave birth to a new species of inexpensive computers.

These single board microcomputers had never existed before. They sold by the millions. Computer people, electronic technicians, experimenters, hobbyists, and just plain people snapped them up. They were fascinated and felt they were on to something unbelievable. They were, they had a helpmate for their brains.

There wasn't much software around in those days. It didn't matter too much. These computer pioneers were mainly interested in writing their own programs anyway. Today there is a hard core of millions of these people who spend untold hours on their Apple IIs, COMMODORE VIC 20, 64s, and 128s, CoCo 1s, 2s, and 3s, and others. The manuscript for this book was typed on a ten year old modified CoCo 1.

Then along came the 16-bit processors such as the 8088-8086 and the 68000, they gave birth to the IBM PC compatibles, the Macintosh, and the Amiga. While many of the 8-bit aficionados switched to the more advanced designs, the more important result was the advanced uses the new machines could undertake. They could be used for more serious jobs in education, business, and research. However, writing software for them was a prodigious task. Their success was astounding and immediate. They were a lot more expensive than the 8-bit types. The higher prices reduced sales to the average person. The machines made great inroads into the serious business-type applications. These 16-bit machines almost had the same capacity and power as the minicomputers that have been used in large business applications for years.

The next obvious step was the construction of 32-bit computers. The 80186 and 80286 were interim steps. The 80386 and the 68020 were true 32-bit processors. They can do the work a mini performs. They come close to matching the power of a mainframe. Their use in complex business situations is valuable beyond measure. The way the 80386 and 68020 is constructed and works is discussed in the rest of this chapter. Start with the Intel 386.

The compatibility

When Intel designed the 8088-8086 it looked forward to the future. Intel appreciated the factor of compatibility. They realized that a lot of software and hardware would be designed around their processors. They built the 8088-8086 with an instruction set that could be expanded in future processors of the same family. The 8088-8086 was established as a standard. It was to be a sub-set of future super-sets.

The instruction set was cast into the chip. The set is a group of microinstructions built into a ROM-like structure on the 8086 chip. Portions of this microcode is run off according to an instruction that enters the 8086 instruction decoder from memory.

After the 8086, Intel came out with the 80186. The 186 contained a complete 8086 instruction set, a complete set of registers and other pertinent silicon cast circuits. In addition the 186 chip contained a lot of support circuitry. It was billed as a computer-on-a-chip. The additional support circuitry required the 186 instruction set to have ten more instructions than its predecessor the 8086, shown in Table 16-3.

Table 16-3. The 80186 has the same instruction set as the 8086 plus ten more instructions to operate the additional support circuits.

	Mnemonic	Operation
Data transfer	PUSH A	PUSH ON STACK (All registers)
	POP A	POP OFF STACK (All Registers)
String manipulation	INS	Input Bytes or Word String
	OUTS	Output Bytes or Word String
	REPE/REPZ	Repeat while Equal Zero
	REPNE/REPNZ	Repeat while Note Equal Not Zero
	ENTER	Format Stack to Procedure Entry
	LEAVE	Restore Stack for Procedure Exit
	BOUND	Detects Value Outside Prescribed Range
	NOP	No Operation

After the 186 came the 286. The 286 was not to be a computer-on-a-chip. It's important advancement was the protected mode. However, it maintained compatibility by having the real mode. The real mode is nothing more than an 8086 processor installed on the chip. All of the instruction set from the 8086 and 80186 is in the 286 plus some more instructions to handle the different modes the 286 is able to run at. The 286 has a super-set of the 8086 instruction set. The additional instructions are in Table 16-4. All of the thousands of programs the 8086 is rich in can also be run on the 286. The 286 though runs the programs much faster and more efficiently.

Table 16-4. The 80286 also has the same 8086 instruction set plus these additional instructions for its special circuits.

	Mnemonic	Operation
Processor control	LMSW	Load Machine Status Word
	SMSW	Store Machine Status Word

The 386, with its 32-bit architecture, is even more so (Table 16-5). It covers all of the features of the 8086, the 286 and then adds on a lot of new goodies. It has three general modes. One of the three modes has two sub-modes. The first obvious mode is a real mode. This is the mode that completely emulates the 8086. In this mode the 386 acts as if it is a 8086. Like the 286, the 386 defaults to the real mode. As it comes on in the real mode it acts like a superfast 8086. It runs 8086 software at very fast speeds. It is so fast that some 8086 applications, such as graphics have to be slowed somewhat in order to make any sense of the displays.

The name *real mode* is so called because an 8086 is not able to directly address virtual memory. Virtual memory space, besides using RAM and ROM as ad-

Table 16-5. The 80386 follows the same 8086 compatibility and has these additional instructions for its special circuits.

	Mnemonic	Operation
Data transfer	MOV/ZX	Move Byte or Word, DWord with Zero Extension
	MOV/SX	Move Byte or Word, DWord, Sign Extended
	CWD	Convert Word or DWord
	CWDE	Convert Word to DWord Extended
	CDQ	Convert DWord to QWord
	LFS	Load Pointer into F Segment Register
	LGS	Load Pointer into G Segment Register
	LSS	Load Pointer into S Segment Register
	PUSH FD	PUSH E Flags onto Stack
	POP FD	POP E Flags off Stack
Shift/ rotate	SHLD	Double Shift Left
	SHRD	Double Shift Right
Bit manipulation	BT	Bit Test
	BTS	Bit Test and Set
	BTR	Bit Test and Reset
	BTC	Bit Test and Complement
	BSF	Bit Scan Forward
	BSR	Bit Scan Reverse
	IBTS	Insert Bit String
	XBTS	Exact Bit String
	SETCC	Set Byte Equal to Condition Code
Protection model	SGDT	Store Global Descriptor Table
	SIDT	Store Interrupt Descriptor Table
	STR	Store Task Register
	SLDT	Store Local Descriptor Table
	LGDT	Load Global Descriptor Table
	LIDT	Load Interrupt Descriptor Table
	LTR	Load Task Register
	LLDT	Load Local Descriptor Table
	ARPL	Adjust Requested Privilege Level
	LAR	Load Access Rights
	LSL	Load Segment Limit
	VERR	Verify Segment for Reading
	VERW	VErify Segment for Writing
	LMSW	Load Machine Status Word
	SMSW	Store Machine Status Word

dresses, is also able to use disks and other storage mediums. The 8086 can't perform the virtual memory tricks. It can only access its own physical memory.

Once the 386 is up and running, it can then be placed into the protected mode by software instructing it to do so. In protected mode, the 386 is able to operate in one of two sub-modes. The first sub-mode is a 16-bit form that emulates the 286. The 386, in effect contains a complete 286 processor, in addition to the 8086.

The 386 can also be instructed to operate in a 32-bit form. This is the true 386 operating type. This is the mode that all the 32-bit software that is written, will operate in.

Figure 16-3 illustrates the modes that ensure upward compatibility between the 8086, 80286, and 80386. The real mode has the 386 acting as an 8086. The 16-bit protected mode makes the 386 into a 286. The 32-bit section of the protected mode lets the 386 be itself, a full featured 386. Then there is one more mode the 386 can get into.

This is a separate mode that is called virtual 8086. This is an 8086 mode but it is different than the real mode. The real mode has the 386 acting the part of an ordinary 8086 except for the fact that it runs the 8086 application programs many times faster than an actual 8086 processor. In the real mode, as it emulates an 8086 the 386 is limited to running one program or task at a time. The real mode does not allow the 386 to perform multitasking. Because the real mode can run only one task at a time, it does not need any protection from interference with other tasks. About all the 386 in real mode is a very fast 8086 with 1 Mb of physical memory space.

In the virtual 8086 mode, the 386 sheds these restrictions. In the virtual 8086 mode the 386 is able to provide protection and is also able to run a number of 8086 application programs at the same time. Each 8086 task is assigned its own 1 Mb memory space and runs as if it is the only task in operation. It is not aware of any other 8086 tasks that might be in operation at the same time. They all have their very own operating systems like DOS and perform under the overall protection of the master operating system provided to run the virtual 8086 mode. Besides running a number of 8086 programs in virtual 8086 mode, the 386 is able, at the same time, to run tasks in the 286 and 386 protected modes.

The three modes are distinguished from each other by their operating systems, the way the memory is addressed, and the amount of memory that each mode or sub-mode is able to use. The real mode only needs an operating system such as one of the DOS (disk operating system) types. The protected modes need more complex operating systems. The development of these systems is expensive and requires a lot of time to produce. The protected 286 mode is able to use OS/2, which is a single user multitasking operating system that will run 286 programs. OS/2 can only run the 286 mode of the 386. The 386 part of the mode requires more complex operating systems.

The 386 architecture

The 386 is a CMOS chip. It incorporates the low power needs of a CMOS and the high performance of an HMOS. There are about 250,000 transistors on the chip. The physical features of each transistor have been scaled down to a tiny measurement of 1.5 microns.

The chip comes in a 132-pin ceramic pin-grid-array, PGA. The 386 has three rows of pins as shown in Fig. 16-16. The illustration shows address pins A31 – A2. A1 and A0 are connected internally at the 32-bit address register and emerge in combination with other signals.

A close look at the pinout shows a number of the same pins that were also on the 286 and 8086. Examples are reset, error, busy, ready, and so on. Another interesting pin arrangement is the large number of Vcc and Vss power connections.

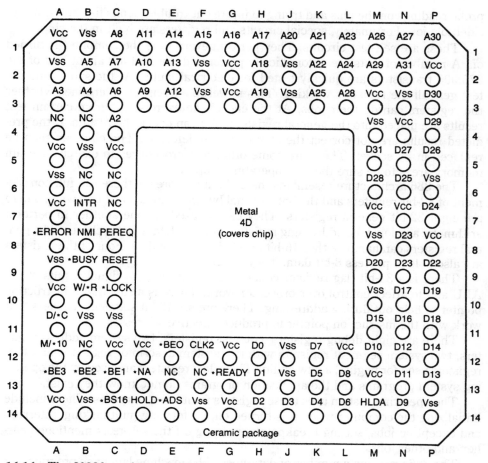

16-16 The 80386 can be packaged in a three-pin row 132-pin PGA. The pins are designated with both numbers and letters to aid in identification.

There are a lot of different circuit areas on the chip and it was not possible to service them all with power from a single Vcc and Vss pair.

There are so many pins in the three rows that numbering them from 1 through 132 would be cumbersome. Intel arranged a row-column identification system. The top and bottom pin labels are arranged along a set of letters, A-P, leaving out I and O. The sides of the square are numbered 1-14. To identify a pin, you must read it out of the grid. For instance, the *READY pin is found in row 13 at column G. In other words, *READY is found at the intersection of 13-G.

Chip registers

The 132 pins are connected to the chip in the center of the package under the metal lid. The pins are typically plugged into a socket. Running voltage or logic probe readings on the pins and trying to figure out troubles looks like and is a considerable job. Fortunately, special circuits and registers are built in the chip.

These are self-test circuits. They perform every time the computer is turned on. A number of tests are automatically performed. First of all, about half of the 275,000 transistors are quickly tested for electrical faults. At the same time the test gets all the registers working. This powerup exercising determines whether the registers can do their jobs. At the end of the exercise program certain test results are placed into the general registers. You can check the results. If the predicted results are not correct the chip could be defective. The chip can then be replaced in its socket. There are some other test procedures to exercise certain memory areas to be sure they are operating properly.

The 386 architecture resembles the 286 but is more so, there is a full complement of 32-bit registers and the 386 internal bus lines are also 32-bits wide. There are eight 32-bit general registers. They can be used for one another to perform arithmetic and logic, be addressing registers, and do data register chores. The general registers can handle either 16-bit or 32 bit pieces of data. Four of the registers are also able to process 8-bit data. They appear in Fig. 16-17.

There is a 32-bit flag register containing typical flags to signal results of the ALU and to affect control over processor work. There is also a 32-bit instruction pointer to help out during addressing. There are six 16-bit segment registers that work with the instruction pointer to produce effective addresses.

There are eight debug registers, two test registers, two system address registers, two system segment registers with two system descriptor registers, and four registers used for paging, a new ability. These last registers are used by the operating system programs and the application programs do not know they exist.

The operating system uses these registers for its own purposes. These include initializing the computer when it is turned on, performing multitasking, interrupt and exception jobs, setting breakpoints, running off the self-tests mentioned earlier, and other jobs.

The 386 works on a number of datatypes. The machine language programmer is very interested in what datatypes the 386 can work on. They are called 8-, 16-, and 32-bit integers and ordinals, packed and unpacked decimals, near and far pointers and strings. The strings can be bits, bytes, words, and double words. For detailed explanations of these datatypes look them up in a programming manual.

These are the datatypes that the instruction set of the 386 are able to work on. The 386 instruction set is the largest of the three sets in the family. The 386 set includes the smaller 286 set and the even smaller 8086 set.

The 386 features pipelining as the 286 does, Fig. 16-18 shows the different units the 386 is arranged in. There is the bus unit, instruction prefetcher unit, the instruction decoder, the execution unit, the segment unit and the new paging unit. All of these units are able to work, more or less, independent of each other and therefore are all able to do their jobs while the other units are busy doing their jobs. For instance, the bus unit can be moving data from place to place while at the same time the prefetch unit places the next four bytes of code into the prefetch queue. This is parallel operation rather than series operation where each unit must wait in line and take its turn operating. Pipelining speeds up the system.

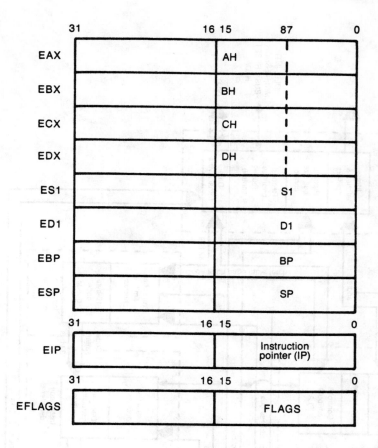

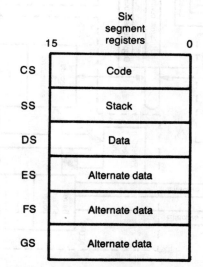

16-17 The registers in the 386 are both 32-bit and 16-bit types.

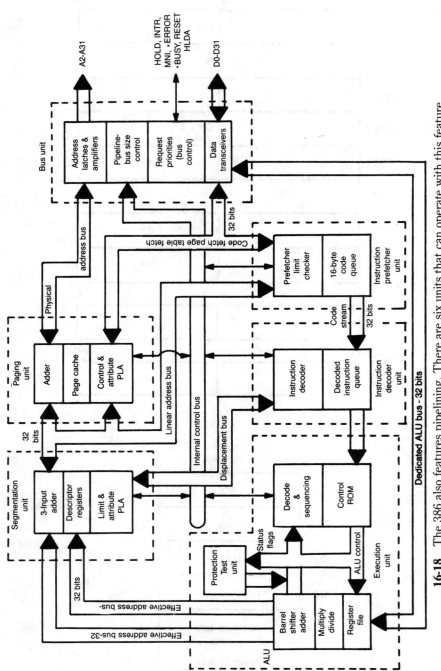

16-18 The 386 also features pipelining. There are six units that can operate with this feature.

These units that enable pipelining in the 386 are connected together with bus lines, that are 32 bits wide. In addition to allowing several instructions to be run at the same time, the various stages of the instruction sequence also overlap each other. While one instruction is being executed the next one can be decoded, and still another one can be read out of memory. However, the simultaneous execution of a number of instructions can only be performed when the program is being run one instruction after another from one memory address after another numerically. Should an instruction like an indirect jump come along, the pipelining feature has to be abandoned and the instructions that are not in numerical order must be run one at a time. Once the processor goes back to its sequential fetching of instructions the pipelining advantage can be used once again.

The eight general-purpose registers are all 32-bit types. They can handle 32-bit pieces of data without having to divide up the four bytes. When 16-bit pieces are received by these registers, when the 286 or 8086 modes are used the registers can be accessed as if they are 16-bit types. The 16-bit pieces are installed in the lower end bits of the 32-bit registers. They appear to the 286 and 8086 modes as 16-bit registers.If 8-bit data is being processed, only the top four registers as shown in Fig. 16-17 are able to handle the 8-bits. They are processed in the lower bits of the 32-bit registers. Even though the 16-bit and 8-bit data pieces are installed into 32-bit registers, the registers adopt the size and act as if they are the size of the data widths. They even throw flags according to the size they adopt. For instance, if there is a need for a Carry while handling 8 bits, the carry flag will be activated.

Mode operations

When the 386 was designed, upward compatibility with the 286 and 8086 was one of the most important design goals. As mentioned earlier, the 386 is able to adopt three different modes with one of the modes having two sub-sections.

There are two separate modes for the 8086 emulation, the real mode and the virtual 8086 mode. They both run 8086 programs. They both use the common operating system known as *DOS* (disk operating system). The real mode acts as if the processor is an 8086. The processor uses 20 address lines and addresses 1 megabyte of physical memory. It cannot address disks or other such storage memory in a virtual memory fashion. The real mode simply acts as if it is a very fast 8086, even faster than the way the 286 emulates the 8086. There are computers with a 386 processor that do not do anything but act as if it is a superfast 8086. The other 386 features are never used, and in some machines there are not even any circuits that can access the full power of the 386.

The virtual 8086 mode is more versatile than the real mode. It is a protected mode, and requires an operating program other than ordinary DOS to get going. There are a number of special DOS programs that can activate the virtual mode.

Once activated, the 8086 virtual mode is able to run, at the same time, a number of 8086 DOS based programs. This feature is valuable for many applications, especially when a number of computers are hooked together in a network. In virtual 8086 mode, each 8086 application task operates as if it were using its very own 8086 processor and its own 1 megabyte address space.

The 386 that is providing this 8086 multiple environment is working with a 4 gigabyte physical address space. Each 8086 task can be installed somewhere in the 4 gigabyte area. When it is time for that task to be addressed, the 386 maps the task to the first megabyte so the address numbers are correct. The 386 is able to do this trick with the paging unit that is discussed in this chapter.

When the 386 is in virtual 8086 mode, it is in a protected state. All the interrupts are vectored through special descriptor tables that control the interrupts outside of the 8086 application program. The 386 also traps privileged instructions and keeps control over the I/O ports.

Addressing in the virtual mode is quite like the real mode. 20-bit addresses are constructed in the same way as all the other 8086 addressing that goes on in an actual 8086 and 286. The address consists of two parts. There is the segment formed in the segment register and the offset. The segment register is shifted to the left by four bits and then the 16-bit offset is added to it.

The 386 also has its own protected virtual modes for 16-bit 286 and 32-bit 386 operations. For these modes the technology ran ahead of the available software to run parts of these modes. The DOS operating system does not activate these modes. It is only useful in the 8086 modes.

There isn't too much trouble when the 386 emulates a 286. There is an operating system called OS/2. It is designed to be used by a single user desiring multitasking. It works on both the 286 and 386 processors to free up a protected virtual addressing mode. However, OS/2 only activates a protected 286 mode. In a 286 based machine this is fine. OS/2 allows the turn on the 286 protected virtual mode with its multitasking and privilege levels. When run in a 386 based machine, OS/2 only does the same thing. It activates the emulated 286 protected virtual mode. It does not permit the operation of the 386 virtual mode. OS/2 in the 386 makes the processor act like a fast 286, not a 386.

In both the 286 and 386 it allows each processor to address 16 megabytes of physical memory and 1 gigabyte of virtual address space. This expanded memory is available because the 286 and 386 conduct segmentation in a different way than the 8086. The virtual address is installed into the segment unit. This unit converts it into an actual address number in memory that is in the 64K segment in use at that time. This is the actual physical memory address.

The virtual address that was constructed and applied to the segment registers is the result of a 16-bit offset and a 16-bit selector. The 16-bit offset is used for the 286 protected mode. Should an address be calculated for the 386 protected mode, then a 32-bit offset is used as in Fig. 16-19.

The 16-bit selector is a pointer to a segment descriptor table. For the 386 mode, the value found in the table by the selector is added to the 32-bit offset. This produces a 32-bit physical address. 32 bits are able to locate 4 gigabytes of address space. There is more detail on this procedure in the next section.

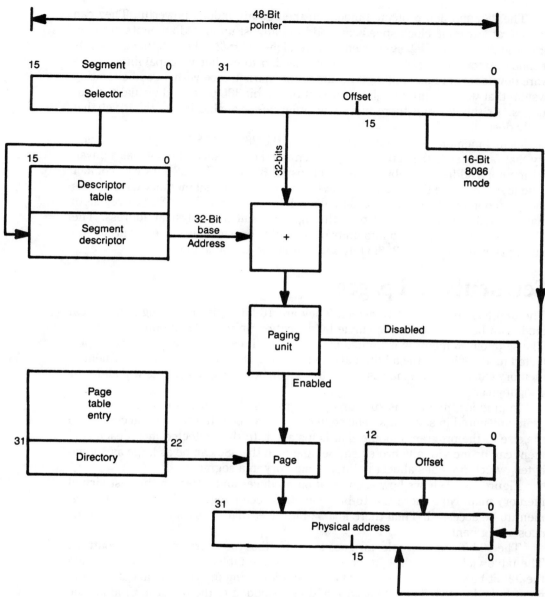

16-19 The 386 generates 32-bit addresses that can locate data in 4 gigabytes of physical address space. It uses the features of segmenting and paging.

The value in the descriptor table is 16-bits wide and 14 of the bits are used to locate a physical address. This addition of bits results in an address that is 14 bits from the descriptor table and 32 bits from the offset. The resulting 46 bits can produce a virtual address space of 64 terabytes.

The 286 and 386 protected modes in the 386 are indeed powerful. They can operate at awesome clock speeds and address almost unlimited amounts of memory. The 286 is very well supported with versions of OS/2. The 386 though has its technology too far ahead of the software needed to exploit its capabilities. Software developers are scrambling to come to the marketplace with a good operating system that will free up the full features of the 32-bit 386 protected virtual address modes. At this writing there are some programs available but nothing yet that really does the job.

Virtual memory is a result of the action of the 286 and 386 that provides memory that far exceeds the actual physical memory. For instance, the 386 has a physical memory addressing ability based on using 32 bits. The 32 bits can contact 4 gigabytes or more than 4 billion 8-bit locations. The virtual memory uses 46 bits and can contact 64 terabytes or 64 trillion 8-bit locations. The 386 has registers that the addressing bits must pass through to result in a physical address. The address space is divided up into units of segments or pages. Both segmenting and paging is available in the 386. Only segmenting is available in the 286.

Segments and pages

The 386 has six segment registers. They are 16-bit registers. A segment in real mode can be any size from a single byte location up to a 64K group of locations. The segment in memory is limited by the 16 bits it can use as an address. In protected mode, with all the additional descriptor register bits available, a segment in memory can still be as small as one byte but can be as large as 32 bits will allow, or 4 gigabytes.

In practice, memory is split up into segments. The various modules of a program are stored in segments. The segments can all be different sizes according to the size of the program module that is installed. In the protected mode each segment can be individually protected. Segments in the 386 can be as large as 4 gigabytes, which provides almost unlimited memory in a segment.

Figure 16-19 shows how segmentation produces an address in the vast virtual memory map. Note there is a 16-bit segment selector register. It chooses the segment to be accessed. Then there is a 32-bit offset that chooses the address in the chosen segment.

The 16-bit segment selector goes to a table that the operating system controls. The table yields an eight-byte descriptor from the table. The eight bytes contain the 32-bit base address and other pertinent addressing information about the segment to be located. The 32-bit base address is added to the offset to produce the actual address in virtual memory.

If there is no paging, this virtual address is also the physical address. When paging is used, this virtual address is passed into the paging unit. A page consists of small 4K groups of memory. The technique keeps the memory organized like a book. The entire memory, if considered as a book, is composed of uniform 4K byte pages.

The paging unit produces a 32-bit physical address. The highest ten bits come from a page directory table. This gives the page table address of the desired location. The next highest ten bits are added to the page table ten bits to produce the page number. The lowest 12 bits are then added to the page number to produce a 32-bit address that points to the physical address.

In the 386 segmentation and paging are individual systems. Segmentation can be used alone or with paging. Paging can also be used by itself or along with segmentation. The decision is made by the programmer.

The two systems are memory management options. Segmentation provides means to conduct data sharing, to use protection and perform multiple tasks. Paging deals with physical memory management. When both are used together, the segmentation system produces a 32-bit virtual address for the paging system. The paging unit converts the 32 bits into the actual physical address that goes out over the address bus.

The Motorola 68020 32-bit processor

The 68020 is the 32-bit upgrade of the Motorola 68000 discussed in this book. The 68000 contained address registers that had 32 bits. However, only 24 of the 32 bits were brought out to pins in its package. The 24 pins were able to address 16 megabytes of address space. In the 68020 the unused eight bits of the 68000 are placed into action. All of the bits are output from the 68020 package and as a result, the 68020 is able to address the full 4 gigabytes. The addressing capability is flat. All the complex addition of segments and offsets that the Intel family of processors uses to address memory is not needed in the Motorola group of processors. The 68000 and its upgrade the 68020 directly conduct addressing according to the bits in the addressing registers.

Figure 16-20 is a block diagram of the 68020 processor. It is a full 32-bit machine with separate 32-bit address and data buses. It is upward compatible with the 68000. It does have some more addressing modes that help it handle higher level languages that are used with it in addition to machine languages.

The 68020 is an HCMOS and has over 200,000 transistors cast on its chip. It operates with a 16 MHz frequency. The chip circuits are separated into a number of units. They are the sequencer and control unit, the execution unit, the bus controller unit, and the instruction prefetch and decode unit. The sequencer and control section is in the middle of the action. It connects to all the other units. It is the manager of the chip. It exerts control over the execution unit, the chip's registers, and internal bus lines.

The 32-bit external address bus is connected to the execution unit. The execution unit as the name implies performs all the calculations that the instructions and data require. The program counter is in the execution unit. In the program counter circuits all the instruction addresses are calculated. There is also a data section in the execution unit. The data section processes all the data in an ALU and its associated registers.

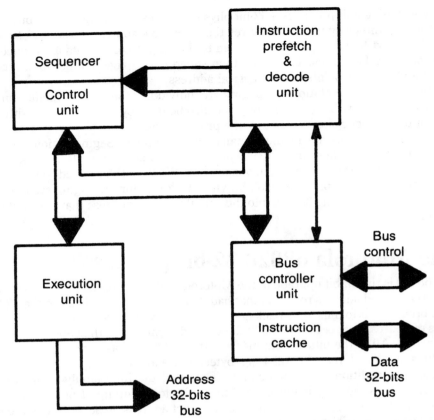

16-20 The 68020 is divided into four sections. They generate 32-bit address and data signals.

The bus controller handles the accessing of memory. It also contains an instruction cache. What is a *cache*?

It is a set aside portion of easily read memory. For example, the 80386 based computer can have a cache, a section of separate memory, installed between the main physical memory and the 386 internals. The cache is arranged so that it will store instructions or data that will be used constantly in a program run. That way, every time the MPU needs some of this often used data, it checks the cache memory first before accessing main memory. If this needed data is in the cache, the MPU obtains it quickly and doesn't have to spend extra time accessing main memory. The cache usually consists of a small amount of memory.

The 68020 features an instruction cache on board in the bus controller unit. The bus controller itself is the source of all the control lines that go out to and come in from the computer. These control lines were covered in the earlier 68000 discussion. They are just about the same lines except they are operating with a 32-bit 68020 instead of the 16-bit 68000. The instruction cache is connected to the 32-bit external data bus lines.

The instruction prefetch and decode unit works with the execution unit. It fetches and decodes instructions from memory. The prefetch section is a group of registers that fetch three instruction words at a time and then decode them. That way the MPU doesn't have to fetch instructions and decode them one at a time. As the instructions are needed by the MPU they are already in the MPU circuits and decoded. There is a lot of time saved as the fetching and decoding takes place at the same time as the previous instruction is being executed.

The instruction addressing for the prefetch is computed in a different circuit than the data addressing. That way, the instruction and data addressing can be worked out at the same time. If the instruction is installed in the instruction cache and the data is residing in the main memory, the instruction and the data can both be fetched at the same time.

Cache registers

The instruction cache is able to contain 256 bytes of instructions at one time. With these bytes filled with needed instructions, the MPU can obtain a large percentage of instructions without having to go outside of its package. This saves a great deal of time as the number of bus cycles for instruction fetches are drastically reduced. As mentioned, only instructions are stored in the cache. There is no data there.

The cache has two important registers, in Fig. 16-21. There is the cache control register, the CACR, and the cache address register, CAAR. They are 32-bit registers. The CACR only uses bits 0-3. The rest of the bits are always clear and set with lows. Bits 0-3 can be set. The operating system can cause the CACR to do one of four jobs. The cache can be cleared by setting bit 3, clear an entry, freeze the cache or enable the cache, in that order.

The CAAR can have a 32-bit address installed to locate a routine that will control the cache. The CAAR is activated when bit 3 of the CACR is set and clears the cache.

The cache can be disabled by an external signal. The pin *CDIS when enabled will shut down the cache. A signal into *CDIS will override any settings of bits in the cache and disable the cache.

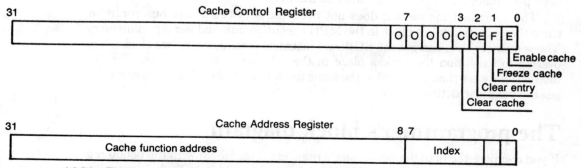

16-21   The important cache registers are the 32-bit control and address registers.

Instruction overlapping

When the bus controller unit and the sequencer unit are operating they could both be working on different instructions at the same time. In Fig. 16-22 such an activity is illustrated. At the top of the timing sketch are nine clocks. Beneath the clocks is a bus movement depicting a prefetch, a write, and the next instruction.

Beneath these entities is the activity of the bus controller and sequencer lined up with the timing of the clock. In this example it is shown how a Move instruction and a SUBtract instruction are operated on and overlap each other in the same time frame.

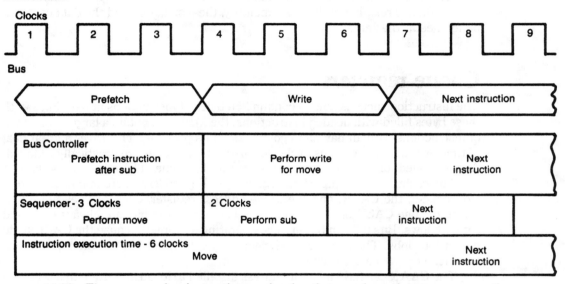

16-22   The processor has instruction overlapping that speeds up the program execution.

The move instruction takes six clocks to perform. The sequencer gets the move executing in three clocks. The bus controller then takes over and performs the Move in the following three clocks. Meanwhile, after the third clock, the sequencer has finished with Move and is ready to do the next instruction that has been prefetched. This is the SUBtract instruction.

The SUBtract instruction does not need the services of the bus controller since the operation takes place in the MPU execution unit and not out in memory. The sequencer thus can get the SUBtract instruction executed in two clocks. The overlap in execution time takes place in the 4th, 5th and 6th clocks. The two instructions were then executed at the same time. In fact, the 6th clock was used to get the next instruction started.

The programmer's block diagram

If you compare the 68020 programmer's registers (Fig. 16-23) with the 68000 registers you'll see a lot of similarity. They both have eight 32-bit general purpose data

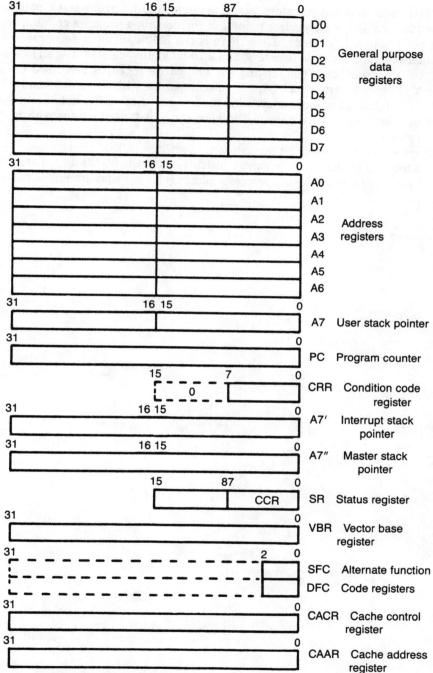

16-23   The 68020 has eight general-purpose data registers and seven address registers just like the 68000.

registers, seven address registers, stack pointers (the interrupt stack pointer is almost identical to the supervisor pointer in the 68000), a program counter, and a 16-bit condition code register. Then there is the 32-bit vector base register, two 3-bit alternate function code registers, and a 16-bit status register. The all new registers are a master stack pointer and the two cache registers discussed earlier. These MPU registers make the 68020 code compatible with the 68000 family. The 68020 though has a few more addressing modes and some additional instructions. These new instructions are designed to have the 68020 work easier with higher level languages.

Chapter 15 discusses using the instruction set in a 68000. There are only two more addressing modes and a few more instructions in the 68020. If you are interested in programming the 68020 processor please refer to its programming manual.

17
General description of the 80486

IF YOU PLACE THE 80486 NEXT TO ITS PREDECESSOR, THE 80386, AS IN FIG. 17-1, the first noticeable difference is, there are more pins. If you take the time to count pins on actual chips, you'll find the 486 has 36 more pins. Although the 386 is complex enough with 132, the 486 adds to the complication with a grand total of 168. Actually the 486 has 39 more pins to do its job, but three pins that perform 386 chores are not needed anymore and are removed. Table 17-1 is a list of the new 486 pins and the jobs they are there to do.

The 486, on the inside, is equipped with about 1.2 million transistors in comparison to the 386, which only sports about 250,000 transistors. Yet the 486, as far as the processor itself goes, is really just an enhanced 386. The reason for all the extra transistors is, the 486 has on board a number of circuits shown in Fig. 17-2, that usually are built onto individual chips.

First of all, an improved 80387 coprocessor circuit is fully installed onto the 486 substrate. Next, 8K bytes of static RAM is mounted in the 486 as a memory cache. Third, a cache controller is integrated with these other circuit groups on the chip. With all these extra circuits that normally are on their own chips, the 386 is transformed into a 486 with an extraordinary 1.2 million transistors to do the work.

The pin-out differences

Referring to Table 17-1, the new pins, the first three additional pins are nonlogic types. There are: a ground, dc power, and a pin that is not connected. It is always a good idea to have as many grounded pins as possible. This reduces interference from little unwanted electron movements that often occur in hard-working, fast-acting circuits. There are seven pins on the 486 that are assigned to grounding purposes. The tiny currents are grounded and do not cause logic errors. In the same

455

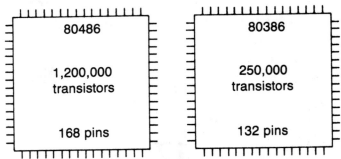

17-1 The most noticeable differences between the 486 and the 386, from a servicing point of view, are—the 486 chip is larger, has more pins, and has more than four times as many transistors.

Table 17-1. The 486 has 39 new pins that are not found on the 386. Three pins that were used to connect a discrete coprocessor to the 386 are eliminated in the 486. Another pin used in 386 pipelining is also not on the 486. The 486 though does have 129 pins that are identical to those found on the 386.

Type	Category	New Pins* Number of Pins
Grounds	nonlogic	7 pins
dc power	nonlogic	4 pins
Not connected	nonlogic	8 pins
80387 coprocessor	new circuit	2 pins
Cache controller	new circuit	6 pins
Parity path	new features	5 pins
Burst transfers	new features	2 pins
Bus operation	new features	3 pins
8-bit interface	new features	1 pin
AT emulation	new features	1 pin
	Total	39 pins

* There is no pipeline operation, which eliminates one pin. The 80387 coprocessor is built in, which eliminates 3 pins.

way, it is always good to have redundant dc voltage power connections. Four pins are given dc power duty.

Eight pins are emerging from the package without any apparent connections. These pins are very important. They might or might not actually be connected to some circuit inside the 486 chip. Whether they are or are not, they represent places for future models of the 486 to use as improvements and additional features are conceived.

The next group of eight pins deals with connecting the new coprocessor and cache controller on the 486 chip to the rest of the computer. Two pins connect the new version of the 80387 coprocessor to the print board as in Fig. 17-3. These two pins allow the 486 to delete three pins that the 386 uses to hook up to the 80387 coprocessor that is a separate expensive chip on a 386 motherboard.

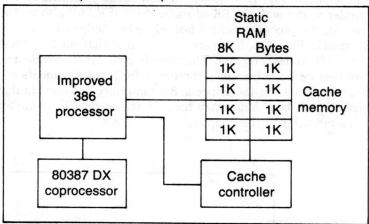

80486 processor chip

17-2 In addition to a completely improved 386 processor, the 486 chip also has on board an 80387DX coprocessor and a cache controller with an 8K static RAM cache memory.

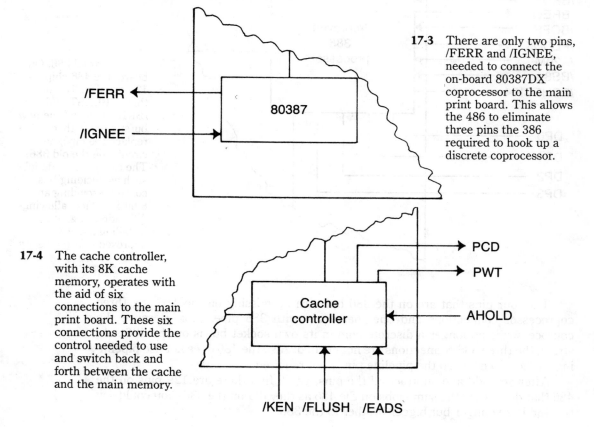

17-3 There are only two pins, /FERR and /IGNEE, needed to connect the on-board 80387DX coprocessor to the main print board. This allows the 486 to eliminate three pins the 386 required to hook up a discrete coprocessor.

17-4 The cache controller, with its 8K cache memory, operates with the aid of six connections to the main print board. These six connections provide the control needed to use and switch back and forth between the cache and the main memory.

Six pins, shown in Fig. 17-4, attach the new cache controller on the 486. The cache controller works with the 8K of static RAM (SRAM) also on the 486 substrate, to provide the processor with a fast, close by, memory cache.

Finally, seen in Fig. 17-5, there are 12 more pins that connect additional new features in the 486 to the computer. There are five pins that provide a special parity path, two pins for burst transfers, three pins for bus assignments and bus control, one pin that allows the 486 a special 8-bit interface and one pin that provides an additional address bus, A20, when the 486 acts as an AT. These features are discussed in more detail in this chapter.

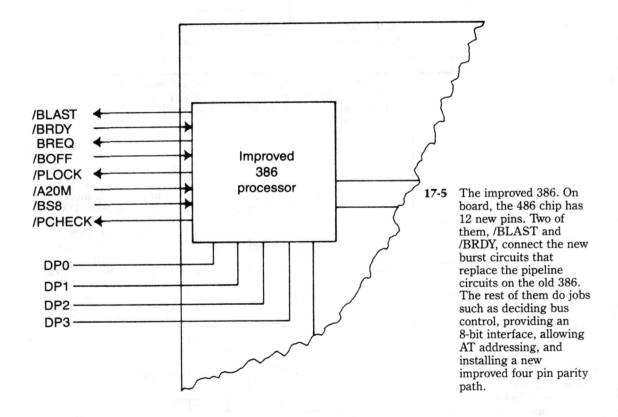

17-5 The improved 386. On board, the 486 chip has 12 new pins. Two of them, /BLAST and /BRDY, connect the new burst circuits that replace the pipeline circuits on the old 386. The rest of them do jobs such as deciding bus control, providing an 8-bit interface, allowing AT addressing, and installing a new improved four pin parity path.

The four pins that are on the 386 but turn up missing on the 486 are, three coprocessor connections and one that deals with 386 pipelining. Because the coprocessor is no longer a discrete chip in its own socket but is on the 486 substrate, the three 386 connections are not needed. Also the 486 does not use pipelining as the 386 does, so the pipeline pin is not required.

After you add and subtract all the pins, you'll find there are 129 pins on the 486 that do exactly the same jobs on the 486 as they did on the 386. You could say the 486 is a younger but bigger brother to the 386.

What the new pins do

The two coprocessor pins are called /FERR and /IGNEE (Fig. 17-3). /FERR is the floating-point error output pin. It is used to generate an interrupt. This interrupt is numbered 13 in the AT scheme of things. It is quite like the error pin on a discrete 80387 coprocessor in a 386 machine.

/IGNNE is the ignore numeric processor error. At the present time, it is not used but it is connected. It can be activated if consideration is given to it in programs being run. The pin has some special use that has not yet been given to the world at the time of this writing.

The cache control pins (Fig. 17-4) start off with /KEN, the cache enable. Despite being called an enabler, /KEN actually is a disabler. It is used to disable particular sections of memory that cannot be used as a cache. A cache is a section of memory close by the processor that handles the memory chores that are most often used. Because the cache memory is physically so close to the processor, the amount of time it takes logic to travel back and forth between the processor and the cache is much shorter. The 8K of SRAM on the 486 chip acts as the cache.

During AT-type duty, the area of memory above 640K up to 1 Mb should not be used as a cache. This is because this section of the memory map contains I/O and other data that came from peripheral devices. If you try to use this memory as a cache the program could crash. /KEN is used to disable this memory area so the processor can't accidentally use that section of memory as a cache and cause trouble.

The AHOLD pin, address hold, is an input from a device to the 486. The /EADS pin, external address strobe is also an input from an outside device. The two inputs can inject an address to the 486. The processor then checks its internal cache to see if that address is in the cache. If the address is in the cache, the processor invalidates the data that is associated with the address.

The pin named PWT is called, page write through. PCD is another associated pin, page cache-disable. They are output pins. They can output the state of bits in certain internal registers. They perform a job somewhat like /KEN does. /KEN is an input that allows hardware to disable memory areas above 640K. PWT and PCD output the caching control information that software has performed on memory sections.

/FLUSH is an input pin that tells the 486 that its cache has become completely invalid. This prevents the 486 from going to its cache when the contents are invalid. If it did, serious problems can occur.

It so happens that when the 486 switches from one of its available memory systems to another, its entire cache becomes invalid. The 486 must be aware of this fact. /FLUSH provides the information.

The new five parity path pins, (Fig. 17-5) are called, /PCHECK and DP3 – DP0. /PCHECK, the parity checker, is an output pin that sends out a parity error signal when it occurs. It operates as an AT memory parity check. Sometimes the pin will output a parity error signal that is false. When that happens the rest of the computer must be able to ignore false parity signals. During design, the computer system must be equipped to tell the difference between valid and false signals.

DP3 – DP0, the data path parity pins are I/O in nature. They are newly designed to perform a faster memory interface when compared to the parity operation of the 386.

/BLAST, the burst last pin deals in the transfer of data by means of the technique called *burst*. This method is used in the 486 and replaces the pipelining procedure that the 386 transfers data with. There is more about burst techniques in this chapter. /BLAST is an output signal that tells the computer that the burst transfer of data has been completed. /BLAST operates in conjunction with /BRDY.

/BRDY, the burst ready input pin tells the 486 that the last complete cycle is over and the computer is now ready to receive data during the next clock cycle. That is, the computer is deemed ready unless the /BLAST signal is output.

There are three new bus assignment and control pins. There is a BREQ, the bus request output pin the bus request signal comes out of to the computer. This signal tells the system that the 486 wants the address and data bus lines for its own use.

Next there is /BOFF, the back off pin that receives an input from the system that tells the 486 the computer wants the bus lines. The 486 is to back off and give the computer the bus even if the 486 is in the middle of a cycle.

The third new bus control signal is /PLOCK, pseudolock. There is another 386 type pin called /LOCK on the 486. /LOCK is not new because it is identical to the 386 /LOCK pin. /LOCK tells the rest of the computer that the 486 is not going to relinquish the bus lines until it finishes with the operation it is working on.

/PLOCK is not quite that firm with its output signal. It is only a pseudosignal. It asks the interrupting device to please wait for the bus lines until it finishes transferring its data. The computer might or might not wait depending on where the bus request is coming from.

Another new pin is called /BS8, the bus size 8 bits input signal. In the 286 and 386 this pin was not present and its function was performed by other circuits. In the 486 this pin allows the 32-bit processor to handle transfer requests from 8-bit devices.

The final new logic pin is also an input called, /A20M. This pin permits the 486 to have addressing compatibility with the 8086 processor and all of its software. When the computer wants the 486 to act the part of an 8086 it forces this pin low. This eliminates A20 and the remaining lower address pins A19 – A0 then can only address 1 megabyte. This maintains the 8086 addressing compatibility.

Pipelining versus burst

In the previous chapter, the 80386 is discussed. One of the features of the 386 is a supposed memory access strength called pipelining. Pipelining is an ability whereby a group of units in the processor are able to work more or less independently of each other. Therefore they are all able to do their jobs simultaneously while other units are busy doing their jobs. This is in contrast (in earlier processors) to having units waiting in line to do their jobs. That is, they can't go to work until the unit before them in line finishes its job. Pipelining, as a result, gets work done faster. Pipelining is an important feature of both the 286 and the 386. Pipelining can be thought of as a parallel operation rather than series operation where each unit must wait in line and take its turn operating. Pipelining is designed to speed up the computing.

As it worked out in practice, pipelining did not completely fulfill its expectations. Pipelining memory access presents the address of the next line of code while the previous piece of code is still being worked on. That way the memory could be addressed beforehand and be ready to transfer data at the completion of the previous operation, saving addressing time.

As it turned out, the addresses mixed in somewhat with the data movement and both reads and writes were left waiting. There was a lot of mixed up unneeded activity that in the end worked out o.k. but not much time was saved. The unnecessary work took place in the instruction-prefetcher unit. The instruction prefetcher was actually acting somewhat like a memory cache close to the processor unit. The Intel designers decided to get rid of this awkward 386 design when they conceived the 486. They got rid of the pipeline system, including the prefetcher. They replaced the prefetcher with an actual SRAM cache.

This design move changed the 386 to a 486. Because the pipelining system was gone, the designers replaced it with a burst mode. Burst techniques are not new. They have been used in mainframes for many years. The burst operates on the theory that most of the time expended in accessing memory is the opening of a specific address. As soon as that first address is opened, all the data in and around that address is readily and quickly available. Properly handled, the first addressing opens up the path to a lot of data. It is not necessary to re-address any of the other addresses in the immediate vicinity. The data in those surrounding addresses can be transferred without further addressing. A good example of this technique is the access of video RAM. The entire video RAM section can be accessed by addressing the first byte. Burst is a data-block transfer ability.

The trick to engineering the burst mode in the 486 is to lay out the main memory of the computer, 64 bits wide, as in Fig. 17-6. That way one address can open up the full 64 bits. When compared to the pipelining in the 386, the burst transfer in the 486 is twice as fast. In the 386 the pipeline requires two clocks per transfer. In the 486, the same amount of data can be transferred in one clock.

If you compare the way pipelining accesses four sequential 16-bit words with the way burst accesses the same four words, the speed advantage of burst over pipelining becomes clear. Table 17-2 shows the clock steps.

In the 386, the memory is arranged in 16-bit words. As the clock ticks, the following happens. On the first clock, the processor addresses the first word. The second clock sends the word to the MPU. The third clock addresses the second word. The fourth clock sends the second word to the MPU. The fifth clock addresses the third word. The sixth clock sends the third word to the MPU. The seventh clock addresses the fourth word. The eighth clock sends the word to the MPU. That completes the accessing of the four words comprised of 64 bits. There is nothing special. This is routine accessing of four 16-bit words in a memory layout that is 16 bits wide.

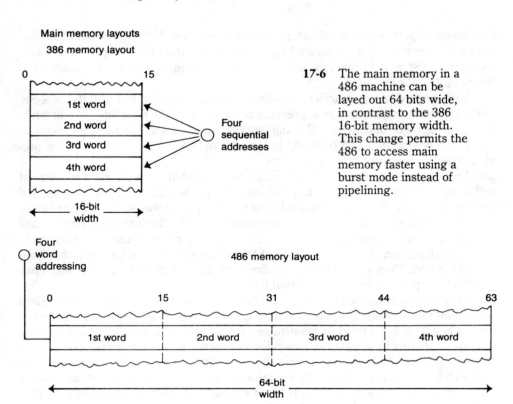

Main memory layouts

386 memory layout

17-6 The main memory in a 486 machine can be layed out 64 bits wide, in contrast to the 386 16-bit memory width. This change permits the 486 to access main memory faster using a burst mode instead of pipelining.

486 memory layout

Table 17-2. A comparison of the action that takes place in the 386 and the 486 as the clock ticks shows the 486 can do the same job in less clocks.

Clock	386 Pipelining	486 Burst
1	Addresses 1st word	Addresses 1st word
2	1st word sent to MPU	No action
3	Addresses 2nd word	1st word sent to MPU
4	2nd word sent to MPU	2nd word sent to MPU
5	Addresses 3rd word	3rd word sent to MPU
6	3rd word sent to MPU	4th word sent to MPU
7	Addresses 4th word	
8	4th word sent to MPU	

In comparison, the 486 with a 64-bit wide memory layout can access the same four 16-bit words in six clocks instead of eight. The 486 accesses the four 16-bit words in the following way.

At the first clock, the 486, in the same manner as the 386 addresses its 16-bit locations, addresses the 64-bit memory location. The second clock is expended as the memory is not ready. Then the third clock finds the memory ready and sends the first word to the 486. Also during the third clock the burst is turned on. The fourth clock sends the second word to the MPU. The fifth clock sends the third word to the MPU. The sixth clock transfers the fourth 16-bit word of the 64-bit wide location. As you can see, once the burst is on, the 16-bit words automatically transfer to the 486 as each clock cycle ticks away. The addressing only has to be performed once at the first clock of the group.

Wait states

Wait states in microcomputers were not much of a consideration until the 80286 processor became popular a few years ago. Because a wait state is measured in clock cycles and is a period wherein a clock ticks but the computer does not do anything but wait, the wait state deals in performance. The ideal computing system would be one that has no wait states. Any wait state during computing is a waste of time, except for some occasional special purpose waiting.

As discussed in chapter 8, one of the parameters of memory chips is their access time. For example, a 6 MHz 80286 processor would need memory chips that could operate fast enough to complete a 167-nanosecond access. (1000 nanoseconds/6 MHz = 167 nanoseconds.) Each 167-nanosecond time period is equal to a state. If the access is completed in 167 nanoseconds, then there is no waiting. The 6 MHz clock is said to be operating in a zero-wait state, as in Table 17-3.

Table 17-3. A zero-wait state has the clock ticking and performing a job during each clock. If a second clock takes place with no action, you have a one-wait state situation. Should a third inactive clock occur, that is defined as a two-wait state.

Given: clock cycle—167 nanoseconds, 6 MHz clock

Wait States	Clocks	Nanoseconds
Zero	1	167
One	2	334
Two	3	501
Three	4	663

(1000 nanoseconds/6 MHz = 167 nanoseconds)

Should the access take place in two clocks, or 334 ns, in this 6 MHz system, then the action took place with one-wait state. If the computing step took three clocks or 501 nanoseconds, that represents a two-wait-state activity. As the clock frequency increases, wait states become shorter and shorter. A 16 MHz clock would have wait states of 62.5 nanoseconds. A 35 MHz clock has wait states of 28.5 nanoseconds. At any rate, wait states are usually a waste of time. The goal of software and hardware designers is to run programs with zero-wait states or as few wait states as possible.

Parity testing

As in all AT systems, there are extra memory chips in the 486 system to check for parity errors. In the earlier AT systems such as the computers based on the 286 and 386, discussed in the previous two chapters, the parity bits for each address are encompassed in with the bytes that hold data. The entire address width is checked for parity along with the reading of the data. A parity checkbit is then generated and noted by the computer. Should the parity checkbit reveal an error, steps have to be taken to correct the situation.

In the 386, the parity checkbit was noted after the data was transferred. This took up some time. In the 486, the new four pin parity path is installed. The parity checkbit does not have to travel after the data has been moved. It travels over its own path at the same time the data is moving. At the same time the data on the data bus is determined to be valid, the parity bits have also been given the go-ahead. This saves time.

As mentioned in this chapter, in addition to the parity path pins, DP3 – DP0, there is a parity check output pin, /PCHECK, that can signal the computer when there is a parity error. On occasion, there are false parity signals output over /PCHECK due to the circuits the 486 is working in at that moment. It is then up to the computer to figure out if the parity signal error is real or a false alarm. This ability to discern the difference between real and false alarms must be designed into the computer system circuitry.

Advantages of the 486 computer

The 386 can do everything the 486 is designed for. The 486 simply does it faster. First of all, the 486 has replaced pipelining with burst accessing. That eliminates a lot of addressing. Instead of having to individually address every byte or word of data, the 486 is able to easily transfer 32 bits of data in one clock cycle. The burst appears to be about twice as fast as the 16-bit data transfer ability of the pipelined type transfer.

Second, the 486 has installed on board an 8K cache of memory along with the cache controller. The cache is loaded with constantly used data. The processor then can look first in the cache for wanted data. If the data is in the cache, the processor can then access this nearby, much used, data again and again instead of having to go to main memory as in the earlier processors. This easy, close by data access saves a lot of computing time. The SRAM cache memory provides data in about 25 nanoseconds while the slower DRAM main memory can take up to 100 nanoseconds to respond. In addition it so happens when the processor must continually address main memory, access after access, a large number of wait states take place. In contrast, when the processor accesses the cache, the wait states are reduced to a great degree.

Third, the 486 also has on board, a model of an 80387DX coprocessor chip. In earlier processors like the 386 and 286, the coprocessors were installed, as options, in sockets near the processor. These discrete coprocessors often were never installed because many applications have no use for them.

The coprocessors find their niche in applications that require floating point intensive work. The coprocessors speed numeric type applications up to a large degree. The on-board coprocessor of the 486 chip really speeds things up. When compared to the socketed coprocessors, one benchmark test showed a 25 MHz 486 machine performing about 11 *MIPS* (million instructions per second), compared to a 33 MHz 386 computer doing 8 MIPS.

Other advantages are in the 486 instruction set. It is just about the same as the 386, but the instructions have been pruned somewhat to look like the more-efficient *RISC*-type code (restricted instruction set code) that has become popular.

Besides all of the above, just the fact that it is a later model and the internal circuits have been reworked, there is a more efficient parity path and other minor new features, makes the 486 an improvement over the 386 and its predecessors. The most important feature, that is not new but has been carried over from the 386 is, the 486 is still compatible with the 386, 286, 8086, and all of the variations in the family.

Servicing the 486 system

Although there are design improvements in the 486 processor, troubleshooting and repairing a 486 computer is quite like repairing a 386 or 286. They are all in the AT family. The 486 is still nothing but an enhanced 386 with some chips that were external and discrete to the 386 installed onto the 486 substrate. From the servicers point of view, the 486, with all of its sophisticated complexity is still serviced as just a single chip. When it conks out, it can be easily tested by direct substitution, or a chip tester that can handle it, or it can be done with diagnostics when it is operating somewhat.

The 486 complete system still comes packaged in the usual desktop or tower cases. They come apart in the same way the 286 and 386 unbolt and can be tested in sections as described in chapter 3. The step-by-step servicing procedures are performed with the same routine test equipment and using the same techniques as its predecessors undergo.

For the programmer and user, especially in floating-point intensive applications, the 486 is an exciting new development. For the servicer though, the 486 system is a newer AT model, quite the same as the older ones. The electronics and mechanical servicing examinations do not change. The power supply, chips, transistors, resistors, capacitors, and so on, all receive voltage and move current in the same old way. When a component fails, it must be pinpointed, replaced, or repaired with the same tried-and-true service techniques. The good old reliable measures includes understanding, from a technician's point of view, how the 486 works, as this chapter describes.

18
Repairing
bus lines and slots

BETWEEN THE PROCESSOR AND THE RESIDENTS OF THE MEMORY MAP ARE the address, data, and control line wires. These buses carry the address, data, and control bits. The bits though are not always the right voltage, the correct amounts of current, traveling at the right times, maintaining logic states for a long enough period and there are other troublesome problems. In the instances where the bits are not traveling over the copper tracings in the right way, they are made to pass through circuits that will change their condition to the desired one. These circuits are usually in chips and require testing when the computer develops troubles.

For example, the 8086 processor transfers data to and from the memory map. One of the important control signals is the *ALE* (address latch enable). If you look back at the timing diagram (Fig. 15-28) the ALE signal is only active high for one clock, (T1) about 100 nanoseconds, then it goes inactive low.

If a RAM chip has an access time that is considerably longer than 100 ns, the ALE signal will not be active long enough to let the processor access the chip. Typical access times for RAMs are 150 or 250 nanoseconds. There could be a problem here.

To ensure the fact that there will be no access troubles, latch chips such as the 8282 in Fig. 18-1, are installed in the address lines. Latch chips receive all the address lines and the ALE signal. The ALE signal turns on the latches so they will receive the address bits and in turn put them out on the address bus. That way when the ALE signal goes inactive, the address bits are in the latch and the address bus. They stay there until the next ALE signal, which doesn't happen until the next processor accessing cycle. Then the next address is latched and placed on the address bus. The 100 nanoseconds ALE signal under these circumstances presents no problem.

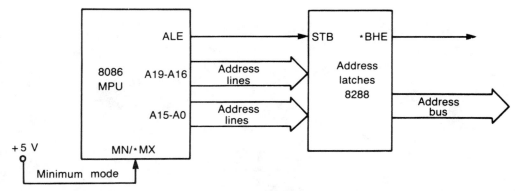

18-1 Latch chips like this one are installed in the address bus lines to cure access problems that might occur between the processor and the memory locations. This case cures an ALE signal timing mismatch.

In other cases the address or data bit currents are not strong enough to drive through the bus lines and become installed in the destination registers. When this situation is apparent, buffers are installed in the bus lines. A buffer YES gate or a buffer NOT gate are amplifiers. They will amplify the currents so they will be strong enough to activate the destination registers.

Another problem develops when address bits are attempting to contact dynamic RAM chips. DRAMs typically have eight address pins to handle 16 address bits from the processor. A RAM location is addressed by first finding a row location with eight bits and then finding a column location with the other eight bits. The processor sends all 16 at the same time. To interface the 16 address bits to the eight RAM address pins a pair of multiplex chips can be used. They separate the bits correctly and apply them to the RAM chips in the right order.

When bus-line trouble strikes

The bus lines of the computer link up all the chips in the memory map to the processor. When trouble strikes in this area the commonest symptom is a screenful of garbage. When this trouble occurs diagnostic software is useless. Diagnosis must be done through direct replacement of suspect chips and the use of test equipment that will show the condition of the test points on all the involved chips and connections. Up to this point in the book, the various chips of the computer have been discussed and the typical logic states and pulses that are found on the pins of the chips have been discussed. It is now time to examine actual troubleshooting techniques.

With the common garbage symptom, the involved chips are the processor, RAM, ROM, I/O, and the chips in the bus lines that connect them. The first step is to look for any chips in the suspect group that are in DIP or SMD sockets. If you have known good replacements, you should change the socketed chips one at a time, trying the computer after each change. Should the computer start operating again, you are lucky, the repair is complete. If the chip changing yields no results, the old chips are probably o.k.

Be sure to exercise the necessary MOS chip handling techniques so you do not accidentally shock good chips with static electricity during the replacements. Any chip electrocution will introduce a new trouble and complicate the repair. If the chip replacement is performed properly, chances are good that the trouble will be gone. A large percentage of garbage troubles are due to defective circuits on one of the socketed chips.

The visual test

When the trouble persists after a careful chip replacement test, the next suspects are the bus lines that connect all the digital chips. The print board copper trace lines, the DIP pin-hold areas, the Surface Mount Device pad layouts and all the rest of the print board environment is subject to short circuiting and breaks. A short or open can cause the symptoms.

In the factory, shorted and open print board troubles are a fact of life. However, sophisticated quality control measures pinpoint most of these conditions quickly and they are rarely overlooked and make it out of the factory.

On those occasions when a defective print board does slip through, the faults can often be detected with your eyes, a bright light and a magnifier. Sometimes a miniscule piece of solder might elude detection because it is on a spot that is not causing trouble. Then after the computer is shipped, the solder will move to a spot where it does short something out. For instance, it could get across some parallel bus lines or ground. The first test is visual. Look for the trouble. On occasion you'll find a loose piece of solder that is easily removed. Incidentally, all of these tests should be performed with the computer off and disconnected from electricity.

When the visual test proves fruitless, the next thing to test is the continuity of the bus lines to ground. All the bus lines should read the same way to ground, a high resistance. In some computers the resistance might not be too high, but they should all read about the same resistance to ground. If one or more of these lines is not the same as the others, this is a valid clue that you could be close to a shorted line. If you do locate a difference in a line, check it out. This includes the pins of all the chips the line is connected to.

Another test checks out the way the print board ground planes (when they are present) are installed to the bottom of a board. The ground plane acts as a shield, as well as being a handy place to attach to chassis ground. In lots of computers, the ground plane covers all the board bottom including the bottom wiring, connections and components. The ground plane, which is nothing more than a slice of thin metal, could be slightly askew or tightened against a connection or component lead. If it is possible, without undue desoldering and unwiring, remove the ground plane and trim any excess leads that might show. Reinstall the ground plane in a way that you feel comfortable that it is not touching energized spots. As the name indicates, the ground plane is the main grounding source for the print board.

Energy testing

The preceding tests are quick checks that you should make with the computer unplugged. Often the trouble is found with these tests. More often though the trouble is not found so easily. However, the quick checks must be made to eliminate obvious possibilities as causing the trouble.

Place the print board into a comfortable testing position so you can make logic state and pulse tests without being off balance. One slip of the probe while the computer is on could cause additional troubles. The first place to test is the pins of the processor, whatever it is, 8-bit or 16-bit. The processor could be a high pin-count DIP or a complex SMD. The DIPs pins are counted from a top view. Pin 1 is on the left side of the keyway. The count goes counterclockwise. There are two lines of pins.

SMDs have pins arranged all the way around the package. There are a number of different packages. There could be an index corner and/or an index dot. The index corner could mean that pin 1 starts there or that pin 1 is nearby. The index dot, when it is present, is found next to pin 1. The pin count is typically counterclockwise. Don't be confused by the different packaging and pin counting, the chips inside the packages are still the same.

It is very helpful if you have the service notes for the computer. In the notes will be a schematic diagram and pinouts of the computer with accompanying tables showing what logic states and pulses should be present. The idea then is to energize the machine, start taking logic probe and VOM readings and compare the readings to the ones the service notes say should be present. If they are present, all well and good. If you find a missing or wrong reading, you could have a valid clue.

Typical buses

Once the socketed and other main chips are checked and exonerated, the next circuits to suspect are the bus lines (Fig. 18-2). They contain the copper traces, a number of small discrete components like resistors, capacitors and coils, and small chips. The small chips are the buffers, latches, multiplexers, and perhaps some others.

Data bus lines connect the processor to all the registers in the memory map. Most data bus lines need buffer circuits to boost the amounts of current present in the logic states. The buffers are in series with the lines. A logic state must pass through a buffer as it travels over the copper foil pathway.

Besides amplifying the current, the buffers match up the different type chips that are communicating with each other. In the computer there are TTLs, NMOS, PMOS, etc., chips. The buffers match up their characteristics so they will operate together in an efficient way.

Another useful characteristic of buffers is their possible three-state capabilities. They can be turned off and on like traffic lights. They can be made to pass states at the correct times.

Buffers can be YES or NOT gates according to the need. Two buffers can be wired together in a head-to-toe configuration and placed in series with a bus line.

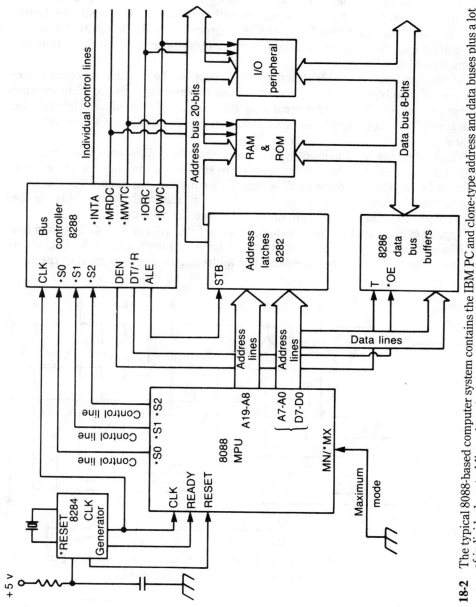

18-2 The typical 8088-based computer system contains the IBM PC and clone-type address and data buses plus a lot of individual control lines, loosely referred to as the control bus.

When data is moving from the processor to the memory map, the buffer pointing in that direction can be turned on and the other one turned off. Then when the memory map is sending data to the processor, the other buffer can be turned on and the original one turned off. The amplifier circuit in the buffer processes the state from a source register that passes through it. The state then exits the buffer in an amplified and matched form, and then proceeds to its destination register. The traffic direction can be controlled by read-write and other lines that are assigned to help out.

The address bus resembles the data bus except for the fact that it is only a one-way bus. The address bits can travel only from the processor to the memory map and not return. Any buffers that are installed in series with the address lines do the same type of job, but there is no head-to-toe wiring, there is just a single buffer in the line.

The buffers are used to amplify and match the bits to different type chips. The three-state capability of the buffers are able to shut down the address bus when it might be in the way and must be disabled. This condition happens when the processor is transferring data between itself and some external device. Most of the time though, the address lines are on and can transfer data at will.

Typical circuits that use buffers are shown in Figs. 18-3 and 18-4. The data bus line has the pair of buffers in series with the lines and uses some NAND gates to change the traffic direction of the bus. The address bus line is on most of the time

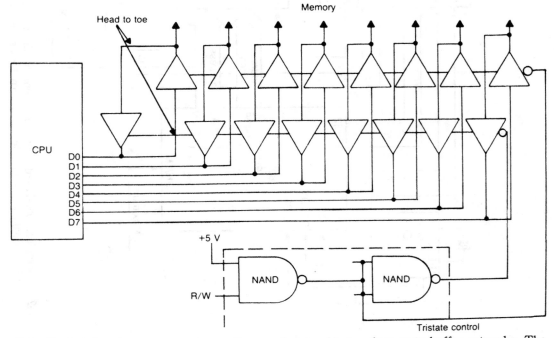

18-3   Typical data bus components are the so-called head-to-toe three-state buffer networks. The buffer in line with the signal flow is able to be turned on at the same time the buffer not in line is turned off.

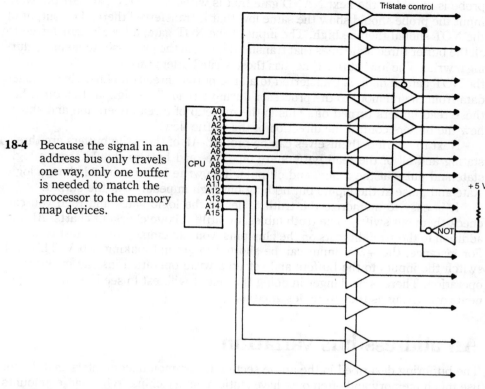

Tristate control

+5 V

NOT

CPU A0 A1 A2 A3 A4 A5 A6 A7 A8 A9 A10 A11 A12 A13 A14 A15

18-4 Because the signal in an address bus only travels one way, only one buffer is needed to match the processor to the memory map devices.

and does not need to change direction. It only requires a NOT gate connected to its buffer's three-state controls. With the aid of the NOT gate, the processor can turn the address bus off and on.

Bus checkout

Because short and open circuit conditions are common in bus lines they must be checked and cleared as troublemakers in the beginning stages of a repair. They can be quickly tested with the aid of a logic probe and the computer schematic. Some schematics are incomplete, so the use of chip manufacturers spec sheets are a good adjunct to the schematic. The information you want from the service notes are the physical location of the pins you want to take your readings at and the type of voltage or pulse that should be on those pins.

The actual test examines the logic state on each bus pin that takes place in a bit transfer. For example, in the data bus just discussed (Fig. 18-3) the read-write NAND input could be high-pulse when the computer is probed. If it is, then that input is o.k. Next the +5 V NAND input should be high due to the +5 V. The probe will show the high without a pulse when that input is o.k.

The next touchdown is at the output of the NAND gate. With two input highs, the output should be a low according to the NAND truth table. If it is, then the probe is moved to the next NAND gate that is wired as a NOT gate. At the NOT input the probe should show the same low that is transferred there. The output of the NOT should then be high. The input of the NOT gate, a low, is transferred to all the buffer three-state lines that transfer data from the processor to memory during a write. The low, at this time, has those write buffers turned off. The output of the NOT gate, a high, is transferred to all the buffer three-state lines that transfer data from the memory to the processor during a read. The high, at this time, has those read buffers turned on. This is the makeup of a read operation and shows how the buffers control the direction of the traffic flow.

Next the buffers themselves can be probed. All of the write buffers are three-stating and all of the read buffers are on. The read buffers should show a logic state and pulse at the inputs and outputs. The write buffers should show a logic state and pulse at the inputs but nothing but high impedance at the output.

It is easy to memorize the truth tables of the logic gates and then you can check them out swiftly. The truth tables are little voltage checkout charts. Also in addition to the straight tests on the chip pins, you can employ simple test controls. For instance, the +5 V input can be shorted to ground making it 0 V. This will switch the inputs to the buffers and set up a write operation instead of this read operation. There is no danger in doing this and it will test to see if all the components are acting as they were designed to.

An address bus variation

The buffering described in the above section is common in computers that do not use much memory and often only have static memory chips. When large amounts of dynamic memory are being used, the situation becomes unwieldy and larger chips that can replace the groups of buffers are available. In addition these chips can handle tasks such as producing the clock frequency, refreshing the DRAMs, latching signals and multiplexing the address lines for various uses.

One such large chip is the 6883 called *SAM* (synchronous address multiplexer), a member of the 6800 processor family, and a 40-pin DIP. SAM (Fig. 18-5) has 16 input address lines (Fig. 18-6). The processor output address lines are connected directly to those pins.

Besides the 16 address lines from the processor, the R/W line is connected at the SAM pin 15. SAM outputs eight address lines MA7 – MA0 from pins 35 – 28. The 16 input lines are output eight at a time to the DRAMs. This multiplexing action permits the eight input address lines on the DRAMs to first address the rows and then address the columns. SAM also outputs a ∗RAS, row address strobe and a ∗CAS, column address strobe, that syncs the DRAMs to the multiplexed address bits that go from SAM to the DRAMs. Besides normal addressing, the ∗RAS signal can sync the row addresses to perform refreshing in between normal access timings. ∗RAS is from pin 12 and ∗CAS from pin 11. SAM also sends a ∗WE, write enable signal from pin 10 to the DRAM chips to act as an R/W line.

Out of pins 25, 26, and 27, SAM sends three chip select signals that are derived inside SAM from the address bits. These three signals can form eight dif-

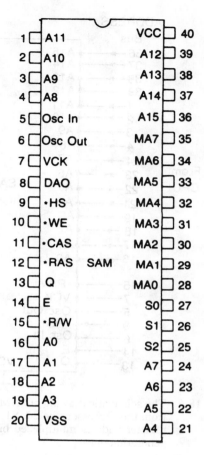

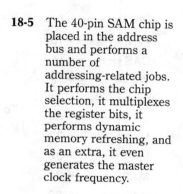

18-5 The 40-pin SAM chip is placed in the address bus and performs a number of addressing-related jobs. It performs the chip selection, it multiplexes the register bits, it performs dynamic memory refreshing, and as an extra, it even generates the master clock frequency.

ferent bit patterns. These bits are placed into a decoder chip (shown in Fig. 18-7) that produces the eight individual outputs. The eight outputs are able to select one out of eight desired chips or circuits.

The crystal oscillator is installed across pins 5 and 6. The crystal frequency is made into a square wave inside SAM. Then SAM outputs the system clock signal from pins 14 and 13 called E and Q. These are the $\phi 1$ and $\phi 2$ signals a dual-phase 6800 type processor needs to work with.

The *HS, DA0 and VCK signals are the horizontal sync and other sync signals that connect with a video display output chip. These signals ensure that the video display will be in perfect sync with the processor operation. The TV picture will be fixed at its prescribed location with the correct video and color.

Note that SAM is very involved with the address bus but has no connections to the data bus. SAM is the controller for the dynamic RAM addressing and the data bus has no place here. SAM has two main jobs: doing all the addressing for the computer and generating all the system timing.

SAM is controlled by an internal 16-bit register (Fig. 18-8). In order to perform its job SAM's register bits must be cleared or set according to plan. Yet there are

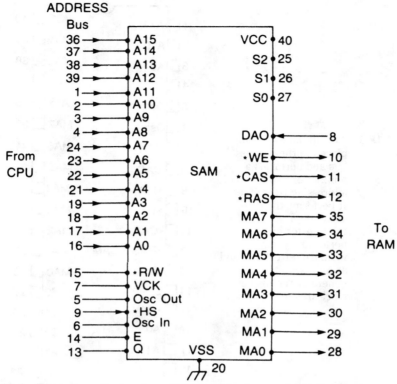

18-6 The schematic drawing of SAM shows the entry of 16 address lines from the processor, the S0, S1, and S2 chip-select bits, the output-register address multiplexed bits, the control lines, and the clock generation lines.

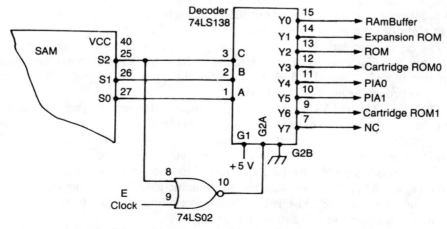

18-7 SAM outputs S0, S1, and S2 to a decoder that uses the three chip select signals to produce eight chip selects.

Hex address To clear	Hex address To set	SAM 16-Bit control register	
FFDE	FFDF	0	To choose map type (1 bit)
FFDC	FFDD	1	To choose memory size (2 bits) 4K or 16K
FFDA	FFD8	0	
FFDB	FFD9	1	To choose MPU clock rate (2 bits)
FFD6	FFD7	0	
FFD4	FFD5	0	Page switch (1 bit)
FFD2	FFD3	6	
FFD0	FFD1	5	
FFCE	FFCF	4	Offset to address video RAM by (7 bits) multiplexer
FFCC	FFCD	3	
FFCA	FFCE	2	
FFCB	FFCQ	1	
FFC6	FFCT	0	
FFC4	FFC5	2	To choose VDG mode (3 bits)
FFC2	FFC3	1	
FFC0	FFC1	0	

18-8 SAM has one 16-bit register. Each register bit has two addresses. When you write to each two addresses, you can clear a bit with one address or set the bit with the other address.

no data bus connections whereby the processor can write bits and produce the correct register bit pattern. In order to install the control bits into the SAM register an addressing scheme must be used without regard for data bus transfers.

SAMs registers are built so that each register bit has two addresses, one odd and one even. This gives SAM 32 addresses on the memory map, two for each register. If you write to the even number, the register bit will clear. When you address an odd number, the bit will be set. It doesn't matter what data you put into the write instruction line. Simply write to the address. The data will never leave the data bus.

The clearing or setting of a register bit decides the job that SAM will perform. The register has its bits configured in the following way. There are three bits to choose a video display mode, seven bits to position video RAM on the memory map, one bit page switch, two bits for clock rate selection, two bits to select a memory size and one bit to choose a map type.

Table 18-1. When SAM becomes suspected of causing troubles, you can check its operation with this service checkout chart.

Pin Number		High (1)	Sam Service Checkout Chart Logic Probe Low (0)	Pulse
Vcc	40	✓		
GND	20		✓	
A15	36	✓		✓
	37			✓
	38	✓		✓
	39			✓
	1			✓
	2	✓		✓
	3	✓		✓
	4	✓		✓
	24	✓		✓
	23	✓		✓
	22			✓
	21	✓		✓
	19			✓
	18			✓
	17			✓
A0	16			✓
OSC IN	6			
OSC OUT	5			
•R/W	15	✓		✓
E	14			✓
Q	13			✓
S2	2		✓	✓
S1	26	✓		✓
S0	27		✓	✓
MA7	35			✓
MA6	34			✓
MA5	33		✓	✓
MA4	32		✓	✓
MA3	31			✓
MA2	30			✓
MA1	29			✓
MA0	28			✓
•CAS	11			✓
•RAS	12			✓
•WE	10	✓	→	✓
•HS	9	✓	→	✓
DA0	8	✓	✓	✓
VCK	7			✓

(Rows 1 through 16 correspond to the 16 Address Lines A0-A15)

Quick checking the SAM chip

SAM is really the addressing mechanism for the computer. The processor sends the 16 address bits to SAM and the 40-pin chip takes it from there. Since SAM is the addressor, most of its pins will be pulsing as address pins do.

The logic probe shows pulses so it is a better SAM tester than the voltmeter. The first pins to test, of course, are the +5 V and ground connections, pins 40 and 20. Neither pin should have a pulse, +5 V should glow a HIGH and ground a LOW.

The OSC IN and OSC OUT are the other two pins that do not show pulses. In fact, they will not light the logic probe LEDs at all. They are the connections to the crystal oscillator. The crystal is producing a sine wave. Analog sine waves do not produce any effect on a digital probe. You can't tell if the oscillator is running by touching down in the crystal circuit with a digital probe.

You can tell if the oscillator is running by touching down on any of the other pins. They should all be pulsing. As long as they are, the oscillator is running because it is the original source of all the pulses in the machine.

The address lines, besides showing a pulse could show highs, lows, or no logic at all. The highs and lows could be an address the processor is idling at. When there are highs on some pins and no logic on others, the lack of a low means low too.

The R/W line will often show a high but it could also show a low. E and Q will show a pulse without any logic. The Select pins will each have either a high or low according to the chip it selects during its idling period.

The output address lines, MA7 – MA0, and the rest of the control lines, while all will be pulsing, might or might not have any logic indications. The important test is the PULSE indication. It must be present or the computer is not operating. It must be present on all the PULSE designated pins. Even if a single required pulse is missing, that is a sign of trouble. A good quick check, after the +5 V and ground test, is to touch down rapidly on all pins except OSC IN and OSC OUT. Look for a PULSE on each pin. Odds are good that if all the pulses are present the chip is good. Should an input pulse be missing there could be a problem in that input line and probably not in the SAM chip. If an output pulse is gone, you probably have discovered a defective SAM chip.

Expansion slots

In the early single-board, 8-bit computers, on the side or rear of the case were slots. Into these slots a cartridge could be inserted. Typically, a cartridge contained a ROM chip. On the ROM was a program. The program could be a word processor, a spreadsheet, a filing system, a game, or what have you. These cartridge programs compared to the programs of today were very simple. The cartridges were the forerunner of todays card boards that plug into a motherboard. However, the cartridge connectors, not much more than an overgrown plug, did provide a way to tap into the computer's insides and expand their usefulness.

A second vital use of the cartridge connectors was to a person who wanted to access the computer innards for electronic repair or experimentation. Practically every signal in the small computers could be found on the connector pins. This convenient test entrance to the computer could be used, without taking the case apart to, signal inject, signal trace, take voltage and scope readings, place the logic probe into, plug in diagnostic programs, plus other useful test techniques.

These connectors became a most important and powerful means to expand the capability of the main print board. The Apple people recognized this fact early. Apple installed seven such connectors, called slots, on their Apple IIe models. The

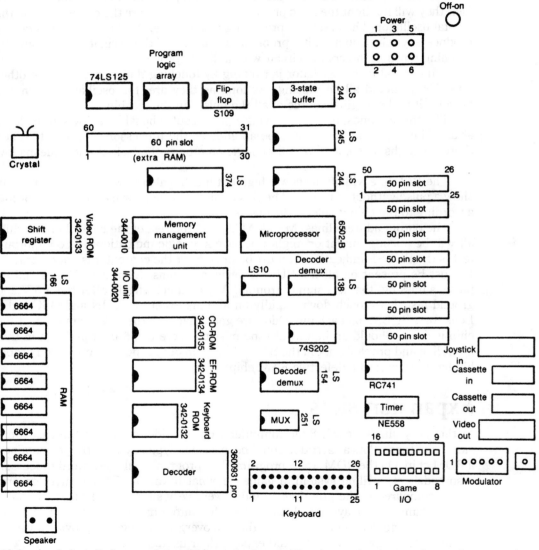

18-9 Apple installed seven slots on this motherboard. The pins on the slots can be used as test points for the address, data, and control buses.

slots were mounted directly onto the main board, as shown in Fig. 18-9. These type boards became known as motherboards. Seven more additional circuits on print boards could be plugged into the slots. Apple came out with a line of these boards that are now known as cards.

Smaller manufacturers recognized opportunity and began creating all sorts of cards that plugged into the slots. These new circuit cards greatly expanded the usability of the Apple. Even though the Apple IIe was using an 8-bit processor, the 6502, these seven slots made the IIe series of computers very popular.

Then IBM came out with their Personal Computer, and that coined the term *PC*. It had five slots as shown in Fig. 18-10. The PC is really a bare bones computer that depends on the slots for its features. The slots are connected to the processor, memory, and other circuits in the digital world by the bus lines. The slots extend the address, data, and control bus lines to the circuits on the cards. The cards can be the interface to peripherals. In the early 8-bit computers, these

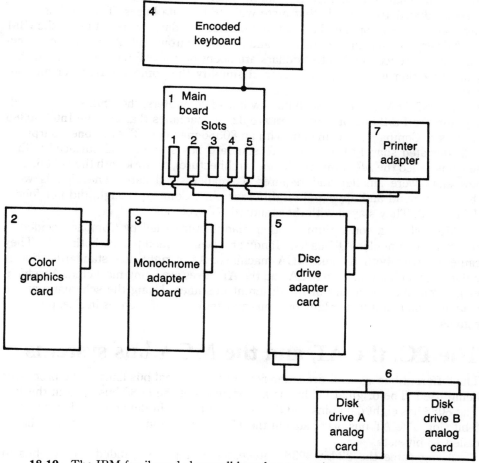

18-10   The IBM family and clones all have bus-test points available at the slots.

peripheral interface circuits were complete on the main board. For example, on early 8-bit machines, such as the C64 or CoCo, there were video circuits, on the main board. They provided video directly to the CRT monitor. However, in the PC family the video circuits are put on cards and are plugged into a slot. The computer sends a digital input to the card, the card converts the digital signal to video. The card then sends the video to the CRT monitor. The PC uses one card to provide monochrome video to a monochrome monitor and a second card to transmit color video to a color monitor.

Figure 18-11 is the layout of an 8-bit expansion slot in an IBM or IBM PC compatible. The same sort of slot is found in the PC/XT. Standardization in these compatible machines is the name of the game. The cards are mass produced and there is a large demand for cards that use the standard. The PC/XT standard has an 8-bit data bus that the 8088-8086 processors can use.

When the PC/AT came out it had an 80286 processor. A 16-bit card standard was used. Smaller manufacturers immediately jumped on the bandwagon and mass produced 16-bit cards that mate with 16-bit data buses. The AT bus cards have become very popular. The fact that precise standards were set made the IBM PC/AT very popular in the business and school environment. A very large following is in existence and a lot of dollars are spent on the AT bus. It appeared that standardization was going to reign and simplify the computer field for all concerned.

In 1987, IBM came out with its new line of computers, the PS/2 series. Standing atop the PS/2 line of computers are 32-bit machines that use the Intel 80386 processor. Compaq also came out with an 80386 machine. To everyone's surprise, IBM deviated sharply from their AT standard bus systems and surfaced with a new bus called the *MCA* (micro channel architecture), to work with the 80386. The new slots were smaller and required a smaller sized card. The signals were changed around and appeared on different pins. Compaq though, did not follow IBM's lead. They stayed with the standard AT type bus.

Meanwhile, a consortium of other manufacturers led by Compaq decided to stay with the popular AT bus too. Tandy and Dell decided to play both ends. They came out with both AT and MCA machines. As of right now standardization is muddled, and both the new MCA and the AT buses are being marketed. As a technician you must be aware of the different bus lines. Using the schematic of the machine you might be working on, you can handle the differences in size, pins, and signals.

The PC, the AT, and the MCA bus systems

The different bus systems are extensions of the internal bus lines in the processor being used. The original PC bus is an extension of the 8088 bus used in the PC. The 8088 has eight data pins and the 8088 slot has eight data pins and is called an 8-bit slot. The AT bus originates in the 16-bit 80286 and accordingly has what is called 16-bit slots.

Along came the 32-bit 80386 processor. Compaq expanded the AT bus to 32-bits to accommodate the internal bus lines of the 80386. This made the

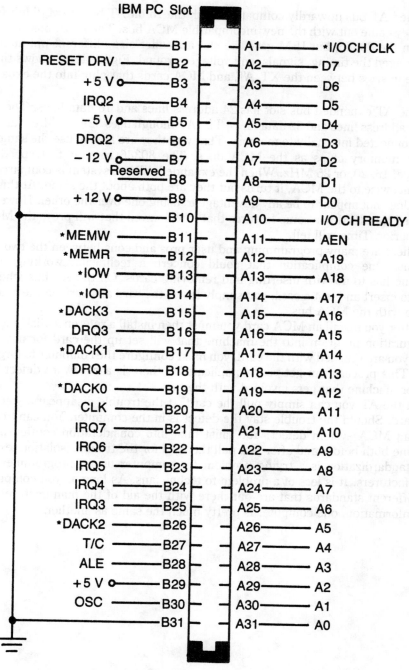

IBM PC Slot

	B1 · A1	*I/O CH CLK
RESET DRV	B2 · A2	D7
+5 V	B3 · A3	D6
IRQ2	B4 · A4	D5
−5 V	B5 · A5	D4
DRQ2	B6 · A6	D3
−12 V	B7 · A7	D2
Reserved	B8 · A8	D1
+12 V	B9 · A9	D0
	B10 · A10	I/O CH READY
*MEMW	B11 · A11	AEN
*MEMR	B12 · A12	A19
*IOW	B13 · A13	A18
*IOR	B14 · A14	A17
*DACK3	B15 · A15	A16
DRQ3	B16 · A16	A15
*DACK1	B17 · A17	A14
DRQ1	B18 · A18	A13
*DACK0	B19 · A19	A12
CLK	B20 · A20	A11
IRQ7	B21 · A21	A10
IRQ6	B22 · A22	A9
IRQ5	B23 · A23	A8
IRQ4	B24 · A24	A7
IRQ3	B25 · A25	A6
*DACK2	B26 · A26	A5
T/C	B27 · A27	A4
ALE	B28 · A28	A3
+5 V	B29 · A29	A2
OSC	B30 · A30	A1
	B31 · A31	A0

18-11 A PC type slot layout can be used as a test point chart in the same way a chip pinout chart is used. All of these circuit lines are easily accessed with test probes.

expanded AT bus upwardly compatible with the 16-bit AT bus. IBM didn't follow suit. they came out with the new incompatible MCA bus. The MCA bus also originates in the 80386, but IBM gave the slot a smaller size, different pin numbers, and changed the timing, signals, and voltages around. Figure 18-12 shows the difference in sizes between the XT, AT, and MCA cards that plug into the expansion slots.

The AT expanded bus slot has 24 address lines and 16 data lines. The MCA has 32 address lines and 32 data lines. The AT though uses 32-bit address and data lines connected internally to memory. That way they are able to use the same type of fast memory chips as the MCA does. The 80386 runs at fast speeds, for instance, 16, 20, or 25 MHz. When the expanded AT bus system is compared performancewise to the MCA, it turns out they are both about the same. At this time there does not appear to be any advantage to using one over the other. However, it is hinted that IBM has some features that it will unveil that will prove the MCA to be superior. Time will tell.

There are many programming and user pros and cons between the two 32-bit systems. One complication that could concern a technician working on the machine has to do with inserting and removing cards. On the AT bus when you want to insert and test a card, you simply insert the card and turn on the machine. Not so with the MCA bus.

After you install an MCA card you must then install a reference disk and put a configuration program into the machine that will set up the card for use. Then when you are finished with the card, you must configure the computer to forget the card. This process can get very complicated if there is a hardware defect in the card or machine that gets involved with the bus.

In the AT you can simply pull the card. If the trouble disappears, you had a bad card. Should the trouble stay the defect is in the computer. You can't do that with an MCA system defect. You must take into consideration configuring the machine both before and after you pull the card for the trouble isolation test.

Standardization is a trying problem for computer users, programmers, and manufacturers. It is less of a problem to technicians. As long as you comprehend the different standards that are out there with the aid of the manufacturer's service information, one computer is pretty much the same as another.

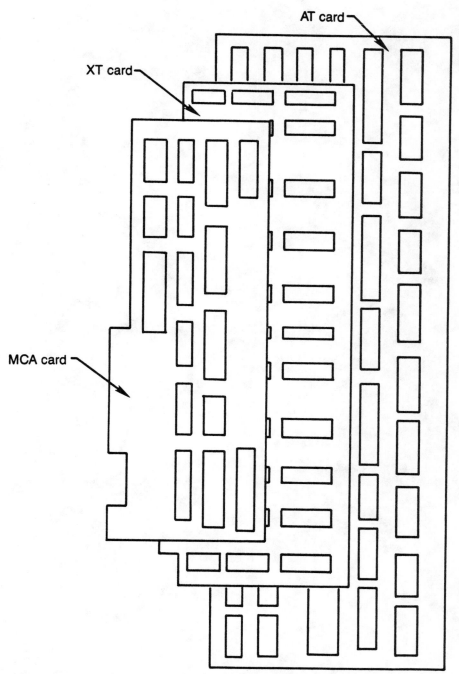

18-12 Note the difference between the XT, AT, and MCA adapter card sizes. The smaller the card, the less chips it can contain and the harder it is to probe with test equipment.

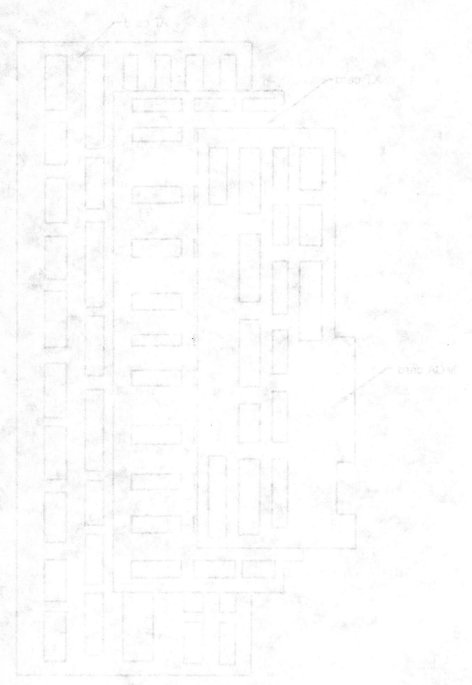

19
Memory map residents

ONE ANALOGY THAT IS USED TO DESCRIBE THE COMPUTER MEMORY MAP is that the microprocessor plays the role of a telephone exchange and the addresses in the memory are the individual telephones. Each map address has its own telephone number. When someone at the exchange must contact an address, it dials the specific address number. Once the address is contacted, a message can be sent to or received from that memory location. There are all types of processors. They are known as 8-bit, 16-bit, 32-bit, or what have you. The more extensive the processor, the more addresses it is able to handle. The number of addresses a processor can call upon is dependent on how many address lines it possesses. If a processor only has one address line it can only contact two addresses. One address when it outputs a high (H or 1, whatever you want to call it) and one address when it outputs a low (L or 0). Incidentally, an address line can only output bits. It is not capable of receiving input bits. It is a one-way line.

If a processor only has two address lines, it is only able to address four locations. The two address lines are able to form four combinations of bits to output. They are HH, HL, LH, and LL (11, 10, 01, and 00). As the number of address lines on a processor increases, the number of addresses it can contact increases. For every additional address line, the number of addresses the processor is capable of directly addressing doubles. As you can see, millions and billions of addresses become accessible with not that many address lines.

For example, a typical 8-bit processor has 16 address lines. This permits it to output 65,536 (64K) individual combinations of bits and access that many separate locations. The 8088-8086 processors add on four more lines for a total of 20 address lines, allowing it to form 1,048,576 (1M) bit combinations. As more and more address lines are added on, the total locations the processor can call upon keeps doubling with each line and locations numbering in many billions become available.

Each location is typically composed of eight bit holders and can handle a byte of data. There could be some special locations that can only store a nibble or just a single bit. There could be some other locations that can handle two bytes (or as it is called a *word*) of data. Still other locations are built to accommodate four bytes. Four bytes is known as a *double word*.

Each memory location is accessed by means of a bit decoder. The right combination of Hs and Ls input to the bit decoder opens up the location while all the rest of the locations on the map remain closed. All the locations are wired in parallel and held in an off position. When a set of address bits are output by the processor, the bits contact every decoder at every location at the same time. One location out of all of them will be unlocked by the bits. Only the location that is decoded will turn on.

Meanwhile, the processor could load the data bits being worked on into the lines of the data bus. The data bus also connects to every location. The data bus does not connect to the decoder of the location, it connects directly to the individual bit holders. For example, data bus line 0 connects to all the bit holders designated 0. The data bus line 1 connects to bit holder 1, etc.

The location that is unlocked by the action of the decoder circuit lets the data bus bits into the bit holders to be stored. That is what happens when the R/W line is in the write position. Should the R/W line be in the read position, then the bits could be traveling over the data bus the other way, from the bit holders to the processor. The data bus lines are two-way lines, unlike the address bus lines (which are one-way), from the processor out to the residents of the memory map.

Different map layouts

A memory map is simply a directory showing the address of all the locations and the name of the functions that take up residence at those locations. As you can imagine, an 8-bit computer with only 64K of memory will have a small map. As memory sizes increase, the map becomes larger and more complicated. For example, in the old Commodore 64, the map is simply and easily read and understood. As you expand your computer system and perhaps start using an AT-type machine with a 286 processor and one megabyte of memory, the map becomes more complicated.

A memory map such as Table 19-1 appears confusing at first. The numbering system is in hexadecimal instead of ordinary decimal. To convert the hexadecimal back to decimal, you could use Tables 6-1 and 6-2. If you have a computer handy and it is equipped with the BASIC language, it will also convert the hexadecimal to decimal and vice versa. If you are going to need to do a lot of converting back and forth, then you must become very familiar with the conversion process. Most of the time the aid of Tables 6-1 and 6-2 and some of the copy accompanying the tables will see you through.

The memory map is important to the programmer, but it is also valuable for troubleshooting. The paper map describes actual hardware and can be used as service notes. It is the hardware that breaks down. If you comprehend the relation-

Table 19-1. A typical AT 1 Mb memory map numbered in hexadecimal.

First megabyte hex addresses																	
	0	1	2	3	4	5	6	7	8	9	A	B	C	D	E	F	
000000																	
010000																	
020000																	
030000																	
040000																	
050000																	
060000																	
080000																	
090000																	1024k
0A0000	V	V	V	V	V	V	V	V	V	V	V	V	V	V	V	V	
0B0000	V	V	V	V	V	V	V	V	V	V	V	V	V	V	V	V	128K
0C0000	A	A	A	A	A	A	A	A	A	A	A	A	A	A	A	A	
0D0000	A	A	A	A	A	A	A	A	A	A	A	A	A	A	A	A	
0E0000	R	R	R	R	R	R	R	R	R	R	R	R	R	R	R	R	
0F0000	R	R	R	R	R	R	B	B	B	B	B	B	B	B	R	R	64K

V—video RAM
A—adapter boards: ROM and RAM
R—motherboard
B—IBM cassette basic
Empty spaces are user's memory.

ship between the map and the hardware, fixing computers becomes that much easier.

A memory map is a memory map. As mentioned, it can be simple or extensive according to the hardware memory system it is describing. The addresses can be numbered in decimal or hexadecimal according to the design engineer who wrote the map. Whatever the numbering system, the chips and bus lines remain the same.

The processor is not usually part of the map. The map describes RAM, ROM, I/O locations, memory management chips, and other chips or hardware that require numbering to be addressed and contacted. The processor, like its telephone exchange comparison, has the job of dialing up the residents of the map. The map residents do not ordinarily call the processor. The processor is in control as far as the addressing goes. There are other control lines that do alert the processor, such as interrupts, but those special lines do not call the processor with addresses. They have lines connected directly to processor pins. The map is a special area that finds the processor reading and writing data bits to and from addresses on the map.

The memory map designers spend a lot of time laying out a map for a computer. If you understand what their thinking procedure consists of as they design a map, that knowledge will prove to be valuable when you troubleshoot, repair, or upgrade a computer. A simple map design is not too difficult to comprehend. A more complicated map design uses essentially the same thinking patterns as a simple one. A simple memory map that would operate in a computer system is designed in the following text.

The different bit jobs

Using a 16-bit address line as an example (as in Fig. 19-1) there is a set of bits named A15 through A0. A15 is the most significant bit and A0 is the least significant. The higher type bits are usually used to select a chip in the memory map. The lower significant bits are normally used to select a register on that chip.

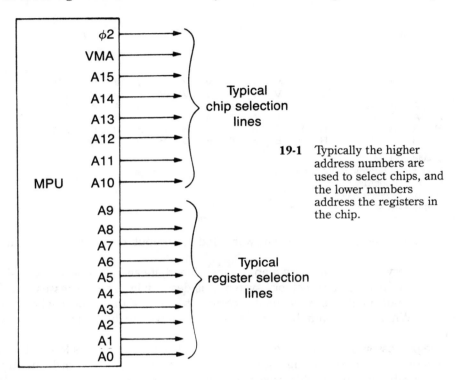

19-1 Typically the higher address numbers are used to select chips, and the lower numbers address the registers in the chip.

If you look at a typical memory map chip, it could have one off-on pin called CS or *CS. CS stands for chip select (Fig. 19-2). The CS pin is usually held low when it is off and will be enabled with a high. *CS is held high and will be enabled with a low. There could be other enabling pins on the chip, but the CSs are typically connected to address bits while the other enabling pins like $\phi 2$, valid memory address, and so on connect to control lines. Don't use that last statement as a hard and fast rule because different designers make all sorts of changes.

Once a chip is selected by the higher bits, the lower bits will select one of the registers. Different chips will have different numbers of registers. If a chip only has two registers, only one address bit need be assigned the register selection duty. If the bit is a high it will select one register and if it is a low it will select the other register.

Should a chip have four registers then two address bits can choose among them. If the chip has 1K registers then ten bits are needed. When the chip has 32K registers there are 15 address bits needed to choose among them.

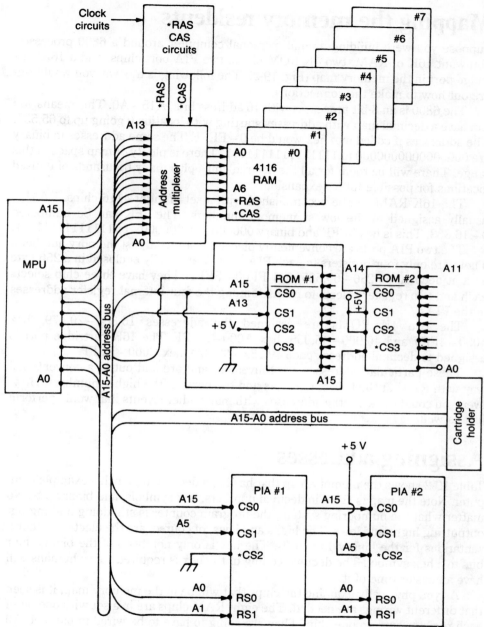

19-2 A typical address system reveals CS and *CS connections on ROM and PIA chips that select the chips with the higher address bits. On the PIAs are RS connections that select the registers with the lower address bits. The RAM chips are addressed through an address multiplexer with both high and low address bits. The cartridge holder or slot has all the address bits connected to it. All of these chips and the slot are residents of the memory map.

Mapping the memory residents

Suppose you were building a small personal computer around a 6800 processor. You want 16K of RAM, two 4K ROM chips, two PIA port chips, and a 16K cartridge port in the memory map (Fig. 19-2). The following is the way you would figure out how to make the connections.

The 6800 is an 8-bit processor with 16 address bits, A15 – A0. This means you can have a decimal map with addresses starting with location 0 going up to 65,535. The addresses if coded into hex would be 0 – FFFF. The same addresses in binary are 0000000000000000 to 1111111111111111. There is plenty of map space in this range. There will be room for all the desired chips plus many thousands of unused locations for possible future expansion.

The 16K RAM can be accomplished with a set of eight 4116 chips. RAM is usually assigned to the lowest memory numbers. The 16K can be numbered 0 – 16,383. This is hex 3FFF and binary 0000000000000000 – 0011111111111111.

The two PIA ports are conveniently placed up at the largest memory numbers. There are only four registers in each PIA so they are easily enclosed in a 256 byte area at decimal 65,280 – 65,535, hex FF00 – FFFF. They have three chip selects each and two register selects to choose among the four internal register addresses in the PIAs.

The two 4K ROMs are assigned the addresses 16,384 – 20,479, hex 4000 – 4FFF and 40,960 – 45,055, hex A000 – AFFF. The 16K cartridge port is assigned to decimal address space 49,152 – 65,279, hex C000 – FFFF.

These particular addresses are convenient and are laid out in a conventional way with RAM at the lowest numbers and the ports at the higher numbers. However, you could work out the addresses with many other layouts that would perform just as well.

Assigning addresses

Table 19-2 shows the memory map that has been decided on for this example computer. Note the map is listed in decimal numbers, hex symbols, and binary bits. No matter what the numbering system, the program counter is still doing nothing but outputting highs and lows. The highs and lows, of course, are the electronic representations for the binary 1s and 0s. The hex is only notations of the binary, four bits to a hex symbol. The decimal coding of the hex is required so we humans will have an easier time of it.

As you physically examine the chips that will be in the memory map, it is seen that different wirings are needed. The eight RAM chips are in a set with one bit of each register byte on one chip. They are going to have to be wired in parallel. All the bits 7s are on RAM chip #7, all bit 6s are on RAM chip #6 and so on. In order to address one register the processor is going to have to address all eight chips at the same time. Therefore, all eight chips will have to have the same addresses as if they were one chip. Only the data bus connections will be different and the data bus is not a concern in the memory map.

Table 19-2. A convenient 64K memory map in decimal, binary, and hex.

Chips	Decimal	Binary	Hex
RAM	0 to 16383	0000000000000000 0011111111111111	0000 3FFF
ROM 1	16384 to 20479	0100000000000000 0100111111111111	4000 4FFF
ROM 2	40960 to 45055	1010000000000000 1010111111111111	A000 AFFF
Cart- ridge	49152 to 65279	1100000000000000 1111111011111111	C000 FEFF
PIA 2	65280 to 65283	1111111100000000 1111111100000011	FF00 FF03
PIA 1	65312 to 65315	1111111100100000 1111111100100011	FF20 FF23

The registers on the RAM set are also accessed in a row-column multiplexed arrangement. The chip selects turn on multiplex chips and the register bits input to the multiplexer. The multiplexers in turn input the correct bits into the RAM address input pins.

The two 4K ROMs contain their byte-size registers. The registers are not disturbed between the ROMs as they are in the DRAMs. When one ROM chip is selected a full byte can be accessed. Therefore, each ROM is wired on its own and has its own private address. The ROM is addressed by having chip select bits to choose the chip and then register select bits to find the desired register.

The PIAs have four addresses each that access their register sets. The higher PIA address bits are assigned to the chip selects. The lower bits are given the job of choosing one register out of the four addresses.

The wiring of the cartridge port does not need any particular figuring. The cartridge port is simply an extension of every available address, data and control line that is available in the machine. The cartridge port is also a source of +5 V, ground and any other special wiring the design calls for. The cartridge port is made so any and all sorts of expansion is possible. All that is needed is to wire the 40 pins of the cartridge port to all available lines. There is no need to worry about special chip or register selects.

When the address wiring begins, the first step is to assign the register to address bits for all the chips. The first chips of concern are the RAM set. The 4116 RAMs have 16K byte locations. To address 16K locations is going to require the use of 14 address lines. RAM registers are going to need A13 – A0. A13 – A0 are going to go to all eight chips simultaneously. X out all of those bits on layout Table 19-3.

The actual solder connections are going to the multiplexer chips. A13 – A7 are going to address the rows in the chips while A6 – A0 will be addressing the columns. Therefore, A13 – A0 will be tied to the correct multiplexer connections to get the register addressing done.

Each of the ROMs contain 4K byte registers. To address 4K requires the use of 12 address lines. A11 – A0 are going to be used to address the 4096 registers in each ROM. You can X out the A11 – A0 bits for each ROM on Table 19-3. The A11 – A0 address bus connections are to be wired to ROM pins A11 – A0.

On the PIAs are two pins called RS1 and RS0. They are register select 1 and register select 0. If address bits A1 and A0 are connected to RS1 and RS0 then the processor can choose one out of four registers in the PIA set.

Addressing the registers is the easy part of the layout. The same lower address bits are connected to all the registers on all the chips. When bits go out over the address bus they access only one register because only one register is enabled. All the rest of the registers ignore the presence of the bits because they remain closed in a high impedance state. Only one register location is opened. The higher number bits as they perform the chip selects ensure that only one register in the memory map will be accessed.

Figuring the chip selects

In this example computer memory map, there are only four chip selects that have to be figured. On the map are found four chips that have chip selects that are wired directly to the address bits. They are the two ROMs and the two PIAs. The eight RAM chips are addressed through the multiplexers. The multiplexers receive all the necessary address bits and then strobe them into the actual RAM chips. The cartridge port has no chip selects because all of the address bits connect directly to the port connections.

To have the processor select one of the ROMs or one of the PIAs the following scheme is used. The selects are figured by starting with the select of the chip that has the highest number address. You'll find this avoids accidentally addressing more than one chip at a time and having a faulty map.

Table 19-3 is a chip select wiring guide. The address bus lines are listed across the top. The chips these lines connect to are listed on the left. Where the rows and columns intersect is found the chip pin that the bus line connects to. On the right are the address ranges the chips occupy on the map. Note that some of the chip pins are CS and others are *CS. A CS pin is turned on with a 1 and a *CS is turned on with a 0. A chip will only turn on when all of its chip select pins are turned on. If even one pin is off, the chip will not be selected.

Table 19-3. The address wiring for these hex addresses.

Chip Connections	Address Wiring A15-A0																Hex Addresses	
	15	14	13	12	11	10 9 8 7 6	5	4 3	2	1	0		FROM	TO
PIA 1	CS0						CS1			RS1	RS2		FF20	FF23
PIA 2	CS0						*CS2			RS1	RS0		FF00	FF03
ROM 1	CS0		CS1	X	X	X X X X X	X	X X	X	X	X		A000	AFFF
ROM 2	*CS3	CS0		X	X	X X X X X	X	X X	X	X	X		4000	4FFF
RAM Multiplexers			X	X	X	X X X X X	X	X X	X	X	X		0000	3FFF

PIA #1 has three chip selects pins, CS0, CS1, and *CS2. In order to select PIA #1, CS0 must be a 1, CS1 a 1 and *CS2 a 0. CS0 is then tied to A15. CS1 is connected to A5. *CS2 is wired permanently to ground. Lets see what we have.

With CS0 connected to A15, CS0 will be turned on when a 1 arrives over A15. There are no connections to A14 – A6. It won't matter what bits arrive over those address lines. CS1 is connected to A5. CS1 will turn on if a 1 arrives over A5. Again there are no connections over A4 – A2. The register selects are wired to A1 and A0. With this arrangement, if the address 1111111100100000 is sent out over the bus, the first register in the PIA will be contacted. The first address is at hex FF20, which is the code for the address bit combination.

The third chip select, *CS2, is not needed for the addressing chore. *CS2 can be tied to ground, which is a logic 0. This will keep *CS2 on all the time and it will not interfere with the PIA #1 addressing. The other three registers in the chip can be contacted by varying the registers bits A1 and A0 but keeping the chip select bits the same. The four binary addresses for the PIA and their accompanying hex codes look like the following:

$$1111111100100000 \quad FF20$$
$$1111111100100001 \quad FF21$$
$$1111111100100010 \quad FF22$$
$$1111111100100011 \quad FF23$$

This is the initial wiring of the map. If there are no other chips to be selected FF20-FF23 will dial up the four registers.

In order to install PIA #2 at FF00 – FF03, a complication must be considered. The complication could cause both PIAs to be selected at the same time, which is disaster. CS0 is connected in the same way to A15. With this address CS1 is not needed. CS1 is therefore connected permanently to + 5 V. CS1 must be wired so it is on all the time so it won't interfere with the PIA selection. + 5 V is a logic 1 that will turn CS1 on and keep it on.

The problem surfaces at this point. With CS0 connected to A15 both PIAs will turn on at the same time when a 1 arrives at the two CS0s over A15. Therefore *CS2, instead of being connected to ground is instead connected to A5. With *CS2 connected to A5, when a 1 arrives over A5 as it addresses the other PIA #1, PIA # 2's A5 will turn off. *CS2 can only turn on if a 0 is coming over A5. A low does arrive when PIA #2 is addressed. PIA #2's first register is addressed when 1111111100000000 comes over the address bus. Note there is a 0 in bit position 5 coming over A5.

These few connections are all that are needed to properly address the two PIAs. The full 16 address lines are not needed by the PIAs. The only voltages needed to enable the PIAs are the three input chip selects and two bits for the register selects. The unconnected bits can be highs or lows. The PIAs have no connections to them at all. Even though the processor does send out the correct address on all 16 lines the five connected ones perform the chip and register selection.

Wiring the ROMs is accomplished much like the PIAs. The important difference is the 4096 register addresses in the ROM in comparison to only four in each PIA. These example ROMs have four chip selects, three enabled with 1s and one with a 0. However, the ROMs have 12 register select pins. They are shown as pins A11 – A0. They present no problem and are simply connected to address bus lines A11 – A0.

This leaves address lines A15 – A12 to conduct the chip selection. The first register in ROM #1 is located A000 and its last register is at AFFF. The registers are all addressed by the 12 least significant bits with the binary ranging from 000000000000 to 111111111111 which in hex is 000 to FFF. The chip selection must take place by placing the bits 1010 into A15 – A12, which in hex is the symbol A.

There are four chip select pins on the ROM, CS0, CS1, CS2, and *CS3. Only two pins are needed so the two 1's in 1010 can enable the chip. CS0 and CS1 are connected to A15 and A13 so 1010 will enable the chip. CS2 and *CS3 are connected to + 5 V and ground respectively to get them out of the way and to keep them turned on all the time the computer is energized.

ROM #2 can then be wired. Except for the register contents it is the same chip as ROM #1. It must be wired up in a way that it will not be enabled at the same time ROM #1 is. To do this ROM #2 is assigned hex addresses 4000 – 4FFF. The 12 register addresses are exactly the same but the four chip select bits are different. ROM #1 is selected with hex A. ROM #2 will be selected with hex 4, plus a special connection.

In binary 4 is 0100. This nibble can ride over lines A15 – A12 into the chip selects by connecting A14 of the bus to CS0. Since the other three bits are 0s, they do not have to be connected to get the 0s into the chip select pins.

To get them out of the way, CS1 and CS2 are connected to +5 V. *CS3 could be connected to ground to keep it enabled but good practice has *CS3 connected to A15. That way when other addresses are on the bus an incidental high on A14 won't turn on the chip. The A15 connection would have to receive a low at the same time the incidental high enters A14 in order for the chip to be enabled.

RAM addressing

Once the PIAs and ROMs are tied to their respective addresses then the set of DRAMs could be attached. The 16K locations on the chips need 14 address bits to contact all 65,536 registers spread over the eight chips. Each register needs seven row bits and seven address bits to locate the eight bits in the register, one bit on a chip. First the 128 rows on each chip are addressed and then the 128 columns are addressed.

The row address numbers and the column address numbers are both 0-127. It takes seven address bits to locate one out of 128 locations. There are seven address pins on the 4116s all wired in parallel. The seven connections receive the row bits first, then when the row bits are latched in the chips, the column bits arrive and they are latched. This multiplexing continues as the addressing goes on.

The DRAM chips need two strobe pulses to conduct the multiplex addressing. One pulse is called *RAS, the row address strobe, while the other one is *CAS the column address strobe. As the strobe signals go low they enable the rows or the columns to accept the addresses.

At every intersection of each row and column is a bit holder. As they are energized by the row column addressing they either give up a copy of their contents during a read or receive a bit from the data bus during a write. The R/W line from the processor controls the direction of the data bit.

The two sets of seven address bits leave the processor over A13 – A0. The address bus connects to the multiplexer stage. The stage could consist of two 74LS257 chips. In that case the bits would be input in a staggered format. The two multiplexers then output to pins A6 – A0 of the DRAMs. They can then output address bits, A6 – A0 during the low of *RAS and then output A13 – A7 during the low of *CAS.

In actual practice, all 16 of the address bits A15 – A0 are wired to the inputs of the multiplexers even though there is no need for the two highest bits, A15 and A14. This is because computers should be prepared for future expansion. With this method, 4164 chips could replace the 4116 chips and the memory upgraded from 16K to 64K. The 4164 is almost pin-for-pin identical to the 4116.

Suppose you wanted to increase the amount of RAM in this example memory map? How would you assign the additional registers in a 4164 correct addresses? It is relatively easy. The 4116 RAM chips have 16K registers. The registers have been assigned to address numbers in decimal 0 to 16,383. These addresses are dialed up with the 14 address bit combinations between 00000000000000 and 11111111111111.

The 4164 RAM chips have 64K registers. The registers can be contacted by addressing numbers in decimal 0 to 65,583. These addresses are dialed up with the 16 address bit combinations between 0000000000000000 to 1111111111111111. The 4164 has 256 rows and 256 columns. The rows can be addressed over A7 – A0 and the columns through A15 – A8. Actual wiring conversion instructions come with a 4164 set of chips in a kit.

The complication in our example map is, the ROMs, cartridge holder and PIAs are in the upper half of the map numbers. There are 64K registers on the 4164 that take up the entire map. What should be done about the addresses with both RAM and other residents? There would be an addressing conflict.

One answer to the conflict is to disable all RAM addresses above 32,767. The map is open up to this 32K point and the RAM will fit in from 0 to 32,767 fine. The RAM addresses from 32,768 to 65,535 are to be disabled. The disabling can consist of only allowing *CAS to be active when 0 – 32,767 are being addressed. During any addressing above 32,767 the *CAS signal is shut off. This won't bother the ROM and PIA addressing since they do not use *CAS in their addressing arrangement.

If you want to make use of the 32,768 – 65,535 RAM addresses, you could set up what is known as a banking system. This would be a circuit that would, upon command, reenable the *CAS signal and the simultaneous disabling of the ROM and PIA chip selects, when the upper RAM addresses are to be used. The circuits simply turn off and turn on different addressing pulses as needed.

Data bus involvement

Wiring the data bus in comparison to the address bus requires practically no figuring. All the recipients of the data bus are in parallel. In our example computer (Fig. 19-3) the processor has pins D7 – D0. The data bus lines D7 – D0. The ROMs, PIAs and cartridge holder have connections D7 – D0. The set of eight RAM chips have one data bus line to each chip. Chip #7 has connection D7. Chip #0 has connection D0 and all the chips in between have their respective D pins too.

All data bus lines connect to all their respective pins. If static RAM chips happen to be in a computer, they will also have the D7 – D0 type pins exactly the same way a ROM layout would.

As long as a chip in the memory map has eight data pins the D7 – D0 wiring arrangement is the norm. Some chips have less than eight pins. For instance a RAM chip could have nibble registers instead of byte sized. The pins would then be named D3 – D0. If two chips were being used to hold a byte then one of the D3 – D0 pin sets would be connected to data bus lines D7 – D4 and the other D3 – D0 pins to bus lines D3 – D0.

Some computers could use just one RAM chip with a nibble register. In that case the D3 – D0 pins would go to bus lines D3 – D0. The D7 – D4 bus lines would

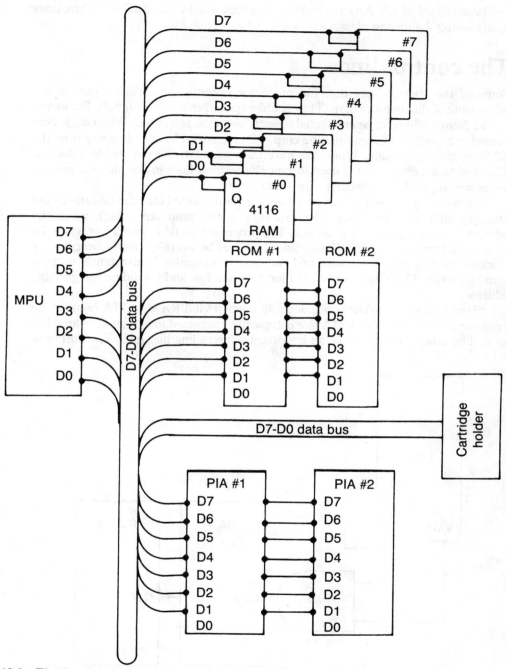

19-3 The data bus does not require careful calculation of the connections. The D7 – D0 lines from the processor simply connect to the D7 – D0 lines of all the addresses chips and connectors.

not be attached at all. Any inadvertent bits that would travel D7 – D0 bus lines would simply be meaningless.

The control lines

Some of the control lines that the processor outputs could take a part in the addressing of the memory map. They act like special chip select signals. For example $\phi 2$ from a 6800 can be connected directly to a chip select pin. When $\phi 2$ is connected to a positive CS pin then the chip will be enabled by the pin every time the $\phi 2$ wave train goes high. When the wave train goes low the pin will be disabled. This additional chip select is used to sync the address lines to any chip the processor is writing to. It is a clocked chip select.

Another way an address can be enabled is with a signal that can be called valid memory address (Fig. 19-4). The processor could send out a high when the address it is putting out is a good one. The processor would output a low when the address is a wrong one. An address can sometimes be worthless as the processor is working on data in its registers and the program counter inadvertently outputs some garbage. The VMA pin would then output a low and invalidate the garbage address.

Should an invalid address accidentally reach a vital RAM or PIA register the program could crash. The VMA line is typically connected to one input of an AND gate. The other input could be an important address line like A15. The output of

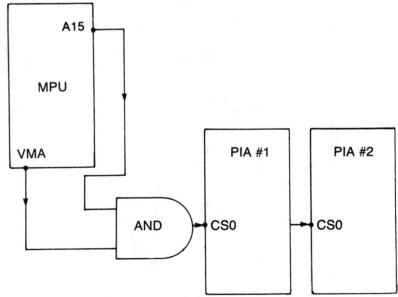

19-4 In order to install a *VMA* (valid memory address) control line into the address bus, an AND gate can be used. That way the bus line so connected will only get through when VMA is on.

the AND gate could then be connected to a CS pin. If the address is valid then VMA would be high and the AND gate will output A15, whatever it is. Should the address be invalid then VMA will be low and the AND gate will output a low. This will cut off CS and the invalid address will cause no trouble.

Other memory maps you will encounter

Although the preceding sections of this chapter get you started on understanding memory maps, you are not likely to meet very many 8-bit computers any more except for the Apple II series. The great majority of personal computers in use today are 16-bit or higher. There is a good number of Macintosh and Amiga machines around that use the 68000 family of processors. However, the great majority of computers in use are IBM or IBM compatible machines. They use the 8086-8088, 80286, and 80386 processors. There are also some of the 80186 machines around. In addition, the 80486 is becoming popular. If you are familiar with the memory maps that are typically used with these processors, you will benefit as you meet these machines when they fail. Go over some of the typical memory map layouts this family of computers use.

The first 640K

The original PC and its upgrade XT compatible have 20 address lines, A19 – A0. Twenty address lines are able to form one megabyte worth of bit combinations. This means the 8086-8088 processors are able to contact 1M individual byte sized locations on the map. Table 19-1 shows a typical IBM type map. The numbers in hex run from 00000 to FFFFF which in decimal is 0 – 1,048,576. The map is laid out in 16 sections of 64K each.

The first ten 64K sections are usually reserved for you the user. In this 640K memory area, conventional programs and the data that goes with or results from the programs can find storage space. In hex this area is numbered 00000 – 9FFFF, which in decimal is 0 – 655,360.

The remaining 384K

The next 128K, from hex A0000 – BFFFF (655,361 – 786,432 decimal) is usually earmarked to be used for video RAM. The video RAM memory space is the place where text and graphics are stored that are to appear on the display. The video RAM is memory that is constantly scanned by the processor and/or the video output circuits. These circuits take the results of the scanning, turns the bits that are obtained into video and send the video onto the display monitor, either monochrome or color. This memory space can be said to contain, in digital code, the images you will see on the screen. In the 8-bit computer, the video RAM only held a thousand or two bytes of digital code to be displayed. This 16-bit video RAM has 128K of storage compared to the 1K or 2K the 8-bit machine can only hold. This additional video RAM space enables the computer to display much higher resolution pictures than the smaller machines. Actually, there are many video systems that do not use all of the 128K reserved video space. In those instances the leftover memory locations can often be used by other active programs such as DOS to store programs and data.

The next 128K from hex C0000 – DFFFF (786,433 – 917,504 decimal), is reserved for the programs found in ROM chips some of the adapter cards possess that get plugged into the slots. Besides providing a place for the ROMs this 128K section also gives addresses to the hard disk controller cards, the various communications cards, expanded memory cards, graphics cards and lots of other boards or cards that might be plugged into the slots.

The last two 64K areas from hex E0000-FFFFF (decimal 917,505 – 1,048,576) is used for the bottom layer of operating system contained in the basic input-output system, the BIOS chip. The BIOS chip holds the operating system that gets the computer started up when you first turn it on. The programs that are in the BIOS chip must always be present whether the computer is off or on. This is unlike other operating systems such as DOS or OS/2 that are transmitted from a disk to volatile RAM memory. The BIOS is the bottom layer of the operating systems. Once BIOS gets the machine up and running, then the others like DOS can be installed into RAM to do their jobs.

In the BIOS chip is found the POST diagnostic that is run every time the machine is booted and rebooted. These programs on the BIOS chip thus test and get the machine to load an operating system from a floppy or hard disk.

Cassette complication

The IBM and all the compatibles follow the above layout just about the same. There is one complication in the last section of the F0000 – FFFFF area that dates back to the early days of the first PCs that came out in 1981. In those days it was common to use a cassette machine to record computer programs and data on cassette tapes as an alternative procedure to the disk drive. Built into the BIOS ROM were programs to allow the IBM PC to use a cassette instead of a disk drive. The programs occupied the final area of address section F0000 – FFFFF. These programs controlled the loading and saving of programs to and from the cassette. They were counterparts to the programs that load and save information to and from the disk drive.

In the back of the PC was a cassette port to accommodate the cassette. However, the use of the cassette on a PC disappeared as time went by. Disk drives became the norm. When the XTs and all the compatibles arrived on the scene, they were made with no cassette port. Yet this cassette program remained burned into the system ROM and kept using the memory map areas at the end of the memory space. It is known as cassette BASIC.

This BASIC interpreter program that is not needed to run cassette operation anymore, is still required for other reasons. The disk program that you use to write and run BASIC code requires the presence of cassette BASIC at those old designated locations, as an overlay to avoid the duplication of that software code on the disk. As a result, in order to run the BASIC interpreter with IBM PC DOS requires that it can find cassette BASIC in memory and will not work without it.

In IBM compatibles, there is no cassette BASIC in memory. Therefore, in order to run a BASIC interpreter another version of BASIC called GWBASIC (graphics workstation BASIC) that is specific for the IBM compatible you are operating on must be used. The GWBASIC will have a substitute code sequence to replace the IBM PC BASIC and permit the compatible machine to appear to operate in the exact same way the IBM equivalent machine does.

Beyond the 1 megabyte boundary

The memory map just discussed is the one that is used with 8086-8088 processors in a PC or XT system. It is also the one that is used for some 286 and 386 processor based systems. When the 1Mb memory map is the only one used with a 286 or 386 processor, these processors are not being utilized to their full extent. The 286 and 386 as discussed earlier have multiple modes and are the basis for an AT and other advanced systems. One of the modes has the 286 and 386 processors acting just like the 8086. It is called the real mode. When the processor is in the 8086 mode, it uses the 1Mb memory map. It acts as if it is an 8086 except it can run considerably faster. Some manufacturers build a computer, install a 286, and only give it circuits to act like a fast 8086. In those cases, the 286 simply uses the 1Mb memory map and ignores its other superior modes. The computer in effect then is a PC or XT that is very fast. There are a lot of these type machines around.

In a true AT system, the memory map is extended. The 286 has its other modes freed. The 286 has four more address lines than the 20 lines the 8086 puts out. With four more lines, a total of 24 address lines, the processor can produce 16 megabytes of bit combinations. The memory past 1Mb is called extended memory. There is 15Mb of extended memory that is added on to the 1Mb of conventional memory. Table 19-4 illustrates the map with the 1Mb of conventional memory plus the 15Mb extended memory. The 8086 mode, of the 286 addresses only the 1Mb with 20 of the 24 address lines. The native mode of the 286 known as the protected mode, addresses the entire 16Mb map with its 24 address lines.

In the 8086 1Mb memory, it is mentioned that the first 640K was used as general program and data memory. The remaining 384K was reserved for video RAM, the various adapter cards, the ROM BIOS, and IBM cassette BASIC or alternatives. In the 16Mb memory map used with the 286, most of the 15Mb extended memory is used as general memory, except for the very last 128K.

The last 128K is reserved like the 384K in the first 1Mb. This causes a total of 512K to be reserved, the original 384K plus this additional 128K. This 128K reserved section is given an exact replica of the data in the last two sections of the 1Mb memory, that is, the ROM BIOS and the cassette BASIC or its alternative. This replica at the very end of memory, is known as *shadow memory*.

The 128K of shadow memory is required by the 286 and 386 processors. It is used when these larger processors are in their protected modes and must switch back and forth between protected modes and real modes. When in real mode, the

**Table 19-4. A memory map that shows the 15Mb of
extended memory after the conventional 16Mb of memory.**

	Last megabyte in 16 Mb map																
	0	1	2	3	4	5	6	7	8	9	A	B	C	D	E	F	
F00000																	
F10000																	
F20000																	
F30000																	
F40000																	
F50000																	
F60000																	
F70000																	
F80000																	
F90000																	
FA0000																	
FB0000																	
FC0000																	
FD0000																	
FE0000	R	R	R	R	R	R	R	R	R	R	R	R	R	R	R		
FF0000	R	R	R	R	R	R	B	B	B	B	B	B	B	B	R	R	128K

R—motherboard
B—IBM cassette basic

"Shadow" of first megabyte map contents

286 is only able to access the first 1 Mb of its 16 Mb memory map. As mentioned, it simply acts like a souped up 8086. However, when in its protected mode, the 286 is able to access all 16 Mb, use a larger instruction set, and perform in a superior manner.

The 286 is upwardly compatible to the 8086. It is capable of running all 8086 software in its real mode. About the only complication is the faster clock pace, which could cause a game program to look like a speeded up movie. Other than that the speed up is usually beneficial. On the other hand an 8086 processor cannot use any software that is expressly written for the 286 protected mode.

Expanded memory

There is often confusion between the extended memory just discussed and another memory scheme called expanded memory. Extended memory is the range between the original 1Mb that can be accessed with 20 address lines and the end of a 16Mb range that needs 24 address lines for accessing. On the other hand, expanded memory cannot be accessed directly as extended memory can. It can only be accessed by means of a 64K memory segment called a window. The window is usually installed as a segment in the first 1Mb somewhere above the video RAM area at a place that is usually not used otherwise.

The window looks out to a special memory adapter card that contains a number of 64K segments. The card will have circuits that allow it to access a 64K segment in the first 1Mb. Then as the 64K segment fills up the data, that segment is switched back to the memory card and a fresh 64K segment is switched into the 1Mb memory area at the same address as the one that was switched out. This segment switching can go on and on as long as there are empty 64K segments on the memory card.

This expanded memory was devised to give users with only a 1Mb or even a 16Mb memory map more memory. Expanded memory is not as handy as extended memory. It is not usually used in 386 systems. The 386 has 32 address lines and can access directly up to 4 gigabytes (4 billion) individual locations. 4Gb memory maps are said to provide unlimited memory. The 4Gb map has the first 1Mb mapped for its Real Mode that gives it compatibility with the 8086 in the same way the 286 is upwardly compatible. The rest of the 4Gb map is then used as extended memory and supplies all the memory most users would ever need.

20

The digital-to-digital
I/O circuits

THE WORLD IS USUALLY THOUGHT OF AS ANALOG WHILE THE COMPUTER'S world is considered digital. There is a lot of information in our world that is analog, but there is also a lot of digital items too. For example, when we enter data into our computer via the keyboard we are automatically converting the movement of our fingers onto the off-on switches of the keys. The off-on switches generate digital data. The keyboard inputs the digital data into the digital computer circuits without further conversion activity (Fig. 20-1).

In addition, after the computer finishes processing the data it could send the resulting digital bits to a printer or another computer. The bits then are utilized by the printer (to produce hard copy) or by the next computer in line for further processing. From the keyboard strike to the digital output the entire process was conducted in digital form with no analog work taking place.

The digital-to-digital interfacing is simpler than having to convert analog to digital and then converting back from digital to analog as a lot of computing must do. However, digital interfacing is not that simple and circuits still must be used to perform the I/O interfacing. First of all, serial and parallel data movement must be considered. Often a digital input is in serial form (as in Fig. 20-2) and must be converted to parallel for the computer to work on it. An output could be parallel (as Fig. 20-3 shows) and must be converted back to serial for use in some device like a modem.

Another problem is synchronization between the devices that are interfaced. The clock speeds and other circuits could make the synchronization difficult. The digital-to-digital interface must sync the devices into step with each other.

There could be voltage level differences between the interface devices. The interface circuits must take these different voltages and make them mesh. Other differences that complicate the data transferring are current outputs instead of

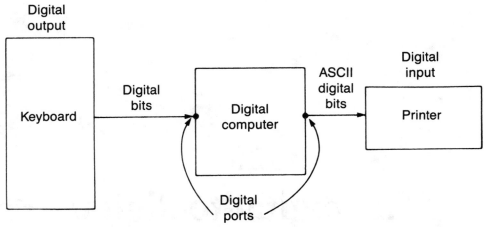

20-1   A keyboard input and a printer output is a good example of a digital-to-digital I/O system. The keyboard inputs digital signals to the computer through a digital input port. The computer (after processing the data) outputs a digital signal through a digital output port.

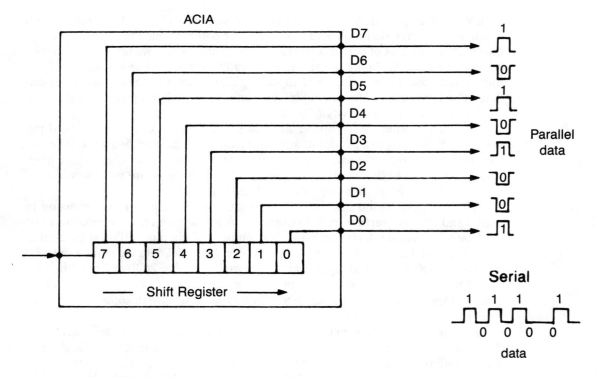

20-2   When digital signals are in a serial form, they must be converted to parallel for use in the computer. This is accomplished with a shift register. The incoming data enters the register at bit 7, shifts over bit by bit until it fills the register. Then all bits are output simultaneously to the data bus.

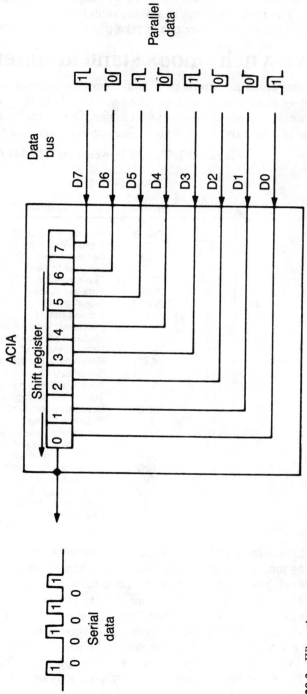

20-3 When the computer must output serial bytes, the parallel bytes are input to a shift register a byte at a time. The register then shifts the bytes a bit at a time out of bit 0.

voltage, different word lengths, special control signals, different data formats, and so on. The interface must be able to match the transmitters and receivers or else the transfer will be faulty or not take place at all.

An asynchronous standard interface

Personal computers must be able to communicate with outside world devices. Fortunately some standards have been set and there is a large array of devices that will work with standard interface circuits. One of the most common interface standards is called the RS-232-C (Reference Standard #232 Revision C) (Table 20-1).

Table 20-1. The 25 conventional RS-232-C signals.

Pin#	Symbol	Description
1	PGND	Protective ground
2	TD	Transmitted data
3	RD	Received data
4	RTS	Request to send
5	CTS	Clear to send
6	DSR	Data set ready
7	SGND	Signal ground
8	CD	Carried detect
9	- -	(Reserved for data set test)
10	- -	(Reserved for data set test)
11	- -	Unassigned
12	RLSD	Received line signal detector
13	SCTS	Secondary clear to send
14	STD	Secondary transmitted data
15	TT	Transmitter timing
16	SRD	Secondary received data
17	RT	Receiver timing
18	SUN	Secondary Unassigned
19	SRTS	Secondary request to send
20	DTR	Data terminal ready
21	SQD	Signal quality detector
22	RI	Ring indicator
23	DRS	Data rate selector
24	TT	Transmitter timing
25	- -	Unassigned

RS-232 ports, in different computers can have as many as 25 pin connections or as few as four according to the number of characteristics it must match and adjust. Let's see how the connections manage their interfacing duties.

The first job these circuits must do is arrange two different sync types of circuits to work with each other. This is called asynchronous communication. An asynchronous digital signal of this type is composed of data bytes. Eight bits at a time are transmitted from one side to be received on the other side. The data is able to go both ways, from computer to peripheral or back.

The bytes are traveling in an asynchronous manner, which means there is no set timing. The bytes simply move from transmitter to receiver with no regularly spaced pattern. A good example of this lack of pattern is the rate you type data into your keyboard. You can type fast, slow, or pause awhile. There is no clock reference pulse to your input.

Because there is no clocking to indicate the start and stop point where each byte starts and stops, start and stop bits (such as those in Fig. 20-4) must be framed around the data byte so the devices know where to start and stop. The start bits are installed at the beginning of each byte. Typically, the data line containing the bytes is held high. As a byte is output the line is brought low. The time of the start signal is the same way as any other of the bits. Therefore, the start bit is one low bit.

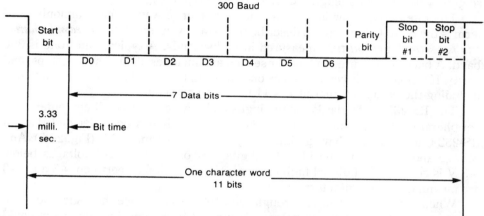

20-4 Asynchronous bytes do not operate with the system clock. They must be controlled with stop, start and parity bits.

After the start bit the byte of data follows. At the end of the byte the line is brought high again and held for two bits. These two bits are the stop bits and are both highs. With one start bit, eight data bits and two stop bits these asynchronous signals are called "characters" and are 11 bits long.

When a transmitter sends characters out over wires to receivers, the length of the wiring could be across the room, over a telephone or through space. There is a possibility of a bit here and there that could get lost. This could mess up a lot of data. To ensure accuracy and be able to detect errors, in the data byte a "parity" bit could be included. The parity bit is often placed in the significant bit position immediately before the stop bits.

There are two types of parity, odd and even. We'll discuss odd parity and the even parity will become evident. The odd parity bit is calculated for each character by the transmitter. If the number of 1s in the byte are an odd number such as 1, 3, 5, or 7, the parity will be made a 0. Should the number of 1s in the byte be an even number such as 0, 2, 4, or 6 then the parity bit will be made a 1. That way the total number of 1s in the byte, including the parity bit, will always be an odd number.

In the receiver is a parity detection circuit. It tests every byte to make sure it has an odd number of 1s. If a byte is found with an even number of 1s then an error is detected and appropriate measures can be taken to correct it. Should the system use even parity, the parity detection circuit will check every incoming byte for an even number of 1s. As long as every byte has an even number of 1s all is well. If a byte with an odd number of 1s should come along then an error is detected and must be coped with.

The system is very useful but not perfect. If two bits are lost instead of one, then the parity circuit won't detect the loss. Only if one bit is lost will the error be detected and an error message produced. There are more complex ways to detect errors but for routine personal computer work this odd or even parity detection is deemed satisfactory.

Asynchronous data transmission works well with short bursts of data. It is not so good with long data lengths without the clock pulsings.

The rate of data flow is measured in a number of ways. The commonly used term is the *baud*. Other ways to describe the data flow is *data bits per second, characters per second*, and *bit time* measured in milliseconds. A typical baud rate is 300 baud. A baud is measured in bits per second and includes all bits, starts, stops, and parity. If a character is considered as one start bit, two stop bits and eight data bits including the parity bit, that places 11 bits in a character.

The RS-232-C standards for the highs and lows are set so all computers and peripheral devices are able to be hooked together. It has been decided that an RS-232-C interface will have digital voltage levels of + 3 and − 3 V (Fig. 20-5). Any voltage above + 3 V is considered a digital low or binary 0. All voltages below − 3 V is considered a digital high or binary 1. The voltages between + 3 and − 3 are meaningless in digital terms.

When a wave train passes through the RS-232-C interface the logic levels can be set at any range above and below + 3 and − 3 V. A typical arrangement could have + 12 V as lows and − 12 V as highs. The wave train will then be converted by the input circuits that feed the interface to these voltage levels for the passage through the port. Once the voltages exit the port they enter other circuits that convert the voltages for their purposes. The important factor that standardizes the

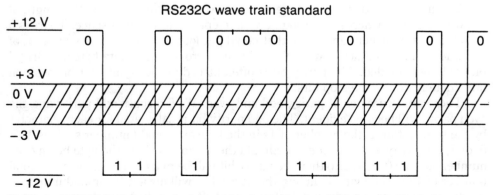

20-5   An RS-232-C wave train is designed to have all voltages above + 3 V considered a 0 and all voltages below − 3 V considered a 1. Any voltage between + 3 and − 3 V is indeterminate.

port is the converting of the lows and highs to voltages above $+3$ V and below -3 V for the wave trains passage through the port.

Standard RS-232-C signal arrangements

Table 20-1 shows commonly used pin assignments for the RS-232-C 25-pin arrangement. While the 25 separate signal spaces are in the standard, in most applications all of them are not used. Most applications require, at the most a dozen of the available signals to interface a computer to a peripheral like a serial printer or a modem.

Pins 1 and 7 are grounds. Pin 2 is called TD for transmitted data. It is an output pin from the computer to a peripheral. It is a one-way data transmission line. Serial data could be coming out of one PIA output pin (Fig. 20-6). The serial string is then injected into ($-$) input of an op amp acting as a comparator chip. The ($+$) input of the op amp is held at $+1.5$ V. The op amp is connected across $+12$ and -12 V.

If the input signal at ($-$) is $+5$ V and higher than the $+1.5$ V on ($+$), then the op amp output will be -12 V which is a logic 1. Should the input signal at ($-$) be 0 V and lower than ($+$), the op amp output will be $+12$ V, which is a logic 0. As the output wave train moves along, the op amp output will switch from -12 to $+12$ V. This representation of 1s and 0s passes though the port to the peripheral.

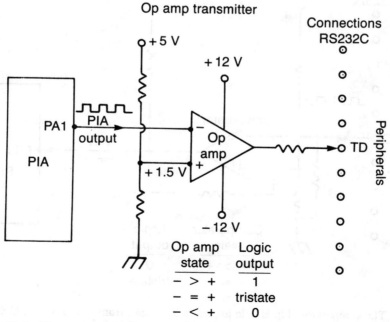

20-6 The op amp is able to switch its output from $+12$ to -12 V as highs and lows are input at the ($-$) connection from the PIA.

Pin 3, of Table 20-1, is RD called received data. A similar interface circuit can be used (Fig. 20-7). The peripheral sends a signal to the RS-232-C RD pin. The pin is connected to the anode of a small diode. The cathode of the diode goes to (−) of a comparator. (+) of the comparator is held at +2 V. If the signal exceeds +2.5 V the diode will conduct and the comparator will conduct and its output goes to 0 V which is a logic 0. When the signal is less than 2.5 V the comparator will not conduct and the +5 V on its output will remain. This is a logic 1. As the signal from the peripheral switches logic the comparator output will also switch logic and input the signal to a PIA input pin.

Pin 8, of Table 20-1, is CD for carrier detect. It operates exactly like RD except it sends an interrupt signal to a PIA interrupt pin (Fig. 20-8). It signals the PIA that the peripheral is ready and able to send data. It is simply a status input line.

The above signals are the most used and can conduct a one-way or two-way communication arrangement between a computer and peripheral. However, it is limited and cannot conduct complex communication tasks such as handshaking. In order to perform a handshaking operation, other signals must supplement the ones just covered. For instance, at pin 6 is DSR the data set ready. It informs the peripheral that the computer has data ready to be sent. Then through pin 20 the peripheral can send a return signal, a DTR, which lets the computer know it is ready to receive any data the computer might be ready to send.

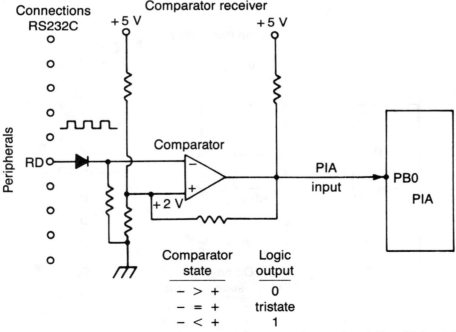

20-7   The comparator chip is able to switch its output from +5 to 0 V as highs and lows are input at the (−) connection from the diode.

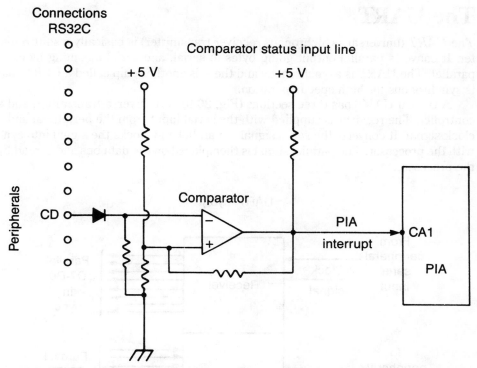

20-8 The input from a peripheral at the CD connection acts just like the previous RD connection except it is an interrupt rather than an RD control line.

Pin 5 is *CTS* (clear to send) signal. This is a pin that receives a signal from a peripheral like a modem, to a register in the I/O chip, that the modem is either ready or not ready to transmit a signal over a telephone line. Pin 4 is *RTS* (request-to-send) signal. This is a pin that sends a signal to a modem from the I/O chip that lets the processor control the action of the modem. The rest of the RS-232-C pins are all used in complex interface circuits.

The I/O interface chips

In personal computers you are liable to encounter circuits like the op amp or other simple chips with a few registers or a large circuit structure on its own print board. Whatever the complexity of the arrangement they all must be connected to the processor and its bus environment.

The I/O activity usually takes place in either serial or parallel form. When the data transferring through a port is serial the chips used are the UART or ACIA. When the data is moving through parallel ports then chips like the PIA and CIA are needed. Let's examine their I/O activity. If you have an idea of what is happening when their pins are tested with a logic probe the results will have more meaning.

The UART

The *UART* (universal asynchronous receiver transmitter) is basically a shift register. It converts parallel output going bytes to serial, and serial incoming bytes to parallel. The UART is asynchronous and there is another chip called a USRT that is synchronous for high speed operation.

A typical UART has three sections (Fig. 20-9), a receiver, a transmitter, and a controller. The receiver is supplied with the serial input from the peripheral and a clock signal. It converts the serial signal to parallel and clocks the signal into sync with the processor. The parallel signal is then placed on the data bus and is read by the processor.

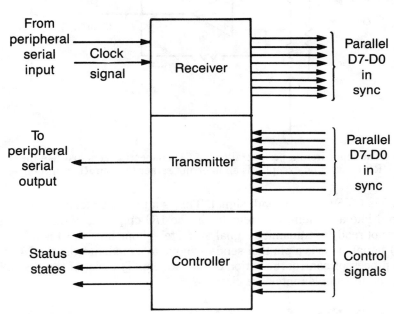

20-9 A *UART* (universal asynchronous receiver-transmitter) consists of a receiver that has serial inputs from a peripheral, a transmitter that sends serial signals to a peripheral, and a controller that sends status signals to a peripheral.

The transmitter is supplied with a parallel signal from the processor and data bus. It converts the parallel to serial and outputs the signal to the port for the peripheral. The controller receives control information from the processor and makes sure the operation is going properly. Then it supplies status and control information so the peripheral is properly interfaced.

The UART handles the start, stop, and parity bits so the asynchronous operation can take place smoothly. During the transmission from computer to peripheral the UART installs the start, stop, and parity bits around the inside the data bits. When the UART receives characters from the peripheral it removes the stop and start bits and checks the parity. The UART is used mostly with modems and on some occasions works with serial printer inputs.

An ACIA

An ACIA is quite like a UART. The DIP shown in Fig. 20-10, is a 24-pin *ACIA* (*asynchronous communication interface adapter*). It is installed in the memory map and receives four address bus lines, three chip selects, and one register select. There are two pairs of registers in the ACIA. One register select pin can choose one of the two register pairs.

The chips selects, CS0, CS1, and *CS2 need two highs and one low to be chosen. At pin 14 is a clock signal E, for enable, that receives a $\phi2$ clock signal. This clocks data to and from the ACIA input or output buffers.

The register select at pin 11 chooses either the transmit and receiver registers with a high or the control and status registers with a low. The R/*W line chooses between transmit and receive registers or control and status registers (Fig. 20-11). The correct mixing of highs and lows into the pin 11 register select and the pin 13 R/W lines, from the processor, will choose one of the four registers in the ACIA to be accessed and either read or written to.

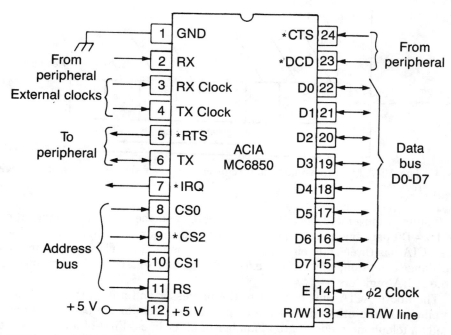

20-10   An ACIA is like a UART in that it also conducts serial input and output communications with a peripheral.

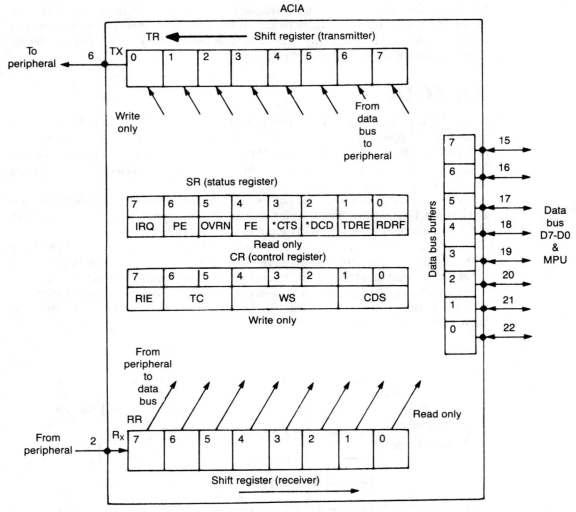

20-11 The ACIA has a transmitter shift register, a receiver shift register, a status register, and a control register.

The data movement between the processor and the ACIA is conducted over the D7–D0 data bus lines. They connect to this example ACIA at pins 15–22. The ACIA has three-state circuits at each pin connection. They remain in a high impedance condition, which is off, except during a processor read operation of one of the ACIA registers.

The above ACIA pins connect to the processor and are on the inside of the computer. On the other side of the chip, that connects to the peripheral device, usually a telephone modem, are a number of other lines. First of all there are the data lines, one for transmitting data from the ACIA to the modem, TX and a second for the ACIA to receive data from the modem, RX (Fig. 20-12).

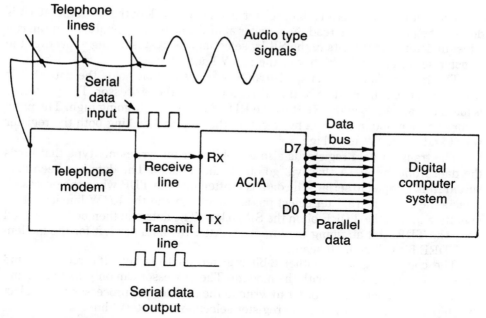

20-12 The main job the ACIA performs is as a connection to a telephone modem. The modem is a device that takes serial digital outputs from the ACIA and converts the bits to audio signals that are transmitted over the telephone. The modem also receives audio signals, converts them to digital bits, then inputs them to the receiver in the ACIA.

Before transmitting data the ACIA will add the start bit to the data and then add the stop and parity bits from the control register bits 2, 3, and 4. With this bit information installed the modem will be able to use the data and send it on over the telephone.

When the ACIA receives data from the modem it will strip start, stop, and parity bits from the character word and use the parity bit to check the number of 1s in the data. Then it will convert the serial data to parallel and output the data over the data bus.

There are two external clock inputs, one for a receiving operation and one for a transmit operation. There are CTS (clear to send), RTS (request to send) and data carrier detect (DCD) pins that operate in the same way as their counterparts in the UART.

The ACIA four registers consist of two that are "read only" and two "write only." This means that the processor cannot write to the read register nor read from the write registers. This makes it difficult to test these registers because you cannot write test bits to one of the registers and then read it to see if the bits arrived and were stored safely.

The read only registers are the status register (SR) and the receiver data register (RDR). The write only registers are the transmit data register (TDR) and the control register (CR).

The status register is an 8-bit register that keeps track of the work the ACIA is doing. The processor can read the register at any time to check status. You can run a test to determine the bits in the SR by selecting the chip, sending a low over the register select line and a high over the R/*W line.

The receive data register is also an 8-bit register that holds the data that is transferred from the modem to the ACIA for use by the processor. The processor is alerted that data is in the RDR by the RDRF bit in the SR going high. The processor can then obtain the data by selecting the chip and making both the register select and the R/*W lines high.

The transmit data register is also an 8-bit register write-only type that holds the data from the ACIA that will go out to the modem. The data has been converted from parallel to serial. The data is written into the TDR when the processor selects the chip, the register select pin is made high and the R/*W line low. This operation makes the TDRE bit in the SR go low. The data will then be transmitted upon the TDRE bit attaining the low state. After the data has left for the modem the TDRE bit will go high again.

The control register, another 8-bit register, controls both the receiving and transmitting of serial data with the modem. The processor can only write to it and cannot read its contents. In order to write to the register the processor must select the chip, and sends lows over the register select and the R/*W line.

The CR has bits to control the action of the transmitter and divide ratios in both the receiver and transmitter. The CR is also able to select the word length it will use, the number of stop bits and the type of parity, odd or even.

The parallel I/O interfaces

The serial interfaces are important when data must be transferred over any distance, even 30 feet across an office. It is less complicated to connect one wire that transfers a single file of bits than to attach eight wires to carry a parallel byte. However, if the distance the wires have to go is short, then it is practical to use eight wires and transfer a byte at a time instead of a bit. Some peripheral devices have both a serial and parallal plug to handle any eventuality. A typical device with bold interface plugs is a printer. It can be driven through a single serial wire or eight parallel wires.

Comparator chips, UARTs, and ACIAs conduct the serial operation. Parallel input-output chips perform parallel transfers. Typical parallel chips are called PIAs, CIAs, PPIs, PIOs, and PDCs. Aside from small designer's differences they all do about the same jobs. First of all they must latch the bytes so the computer and peripheral, operating at different speeds, can obtain the data.

There must be two latches, A and B, one for data that is moving from the peripheral to the processor (Fig. 20-13) and one for data moving the other way (Fig. 20-14). For example, when the peripheral sends a byte of data over eight lines to the computer, the data is latched in a PIA register. It will stay there until the processor is ready to use it. When the processor is ready, it will read the byte. After that the peripheral will send the next byte to be latched.

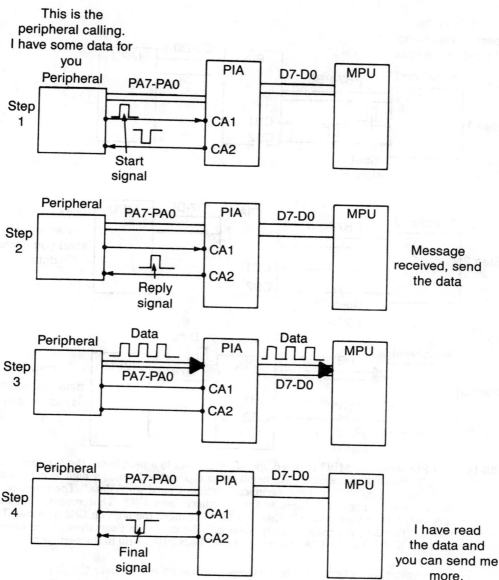

20-13 In a PIA, when data is moved from a peripheral to the I/O chip and then to the MPU, the A registers are used. The data is moved into PIA pins PA7–PA0. Control lines CA1 and CA2 can conduct a handshake operation between the peripheral and the processor using the PIA as the go between. The start of the operation has the peripheral send a high to CA1 that tells the processor, "This is the peripheral calling. I have some data for you." The processor then sends back a high via CA2 that means, "Message received. Send the data." The peripheral then sends the data over PA7–PA0 lines to the PIA then over D7–D0 to the MPU. Once the data arrives the processor changes CA2 to a low, which is the statement, "I have read the data and you can send me more."

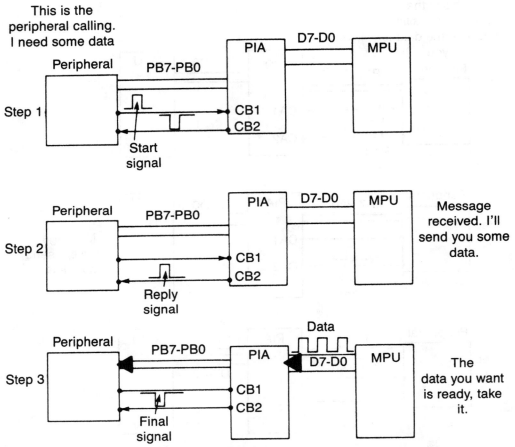

20-14 In a PIA when the MPU is called upon to send data to a peripheral, the B registers are used. A handshake operation will begin when a peripheral sends a high to control line CB1. This means, "This is the peripheral calling. I need some data." The processor in turns causes a high to be sent to the peripheral over CB2. That means, "Message received. I'll send some data." Then the MPU changes the high on CB2 to a low. This states, "The data you want is ready. Take it." The data then flows through the internal data bus D7 – D0 to the PIA and then out over lines PB7 – PB0 to the peripheral.

For data going the other way, the processor will send a byte over the data bus to the I/O chip. The byte will be latched. When the peripheral is ready it will send a signal to the I/O and the processor will let the data out of the latch. The byte will leave the computer and travel over the eight wires to the peripheral. After that the processor will send the next byte to the latch in the I/O.

In addition to the latches themselves the status of the latches must be known so the processor can conduct the data transfers. When the peripheral sends a byte to the input latch, the processor must know the validity of the byte. A signal from a status bit in the I/O chip must be sent to the processor that indicates the validity of the byte.

When the processor sends a byte to the output latch, the processor must know whether the latch is full or empty. A second status bit or an interrupt must let the processor know whether the latch is full and the processor must wait or it is empty and the byte can be sent. Then there must be other status bits to tell the peripheral whether its input latch is full or empty.

Therefore, a parallel I/O chip must have a latch for the processor to read the bytes from the peripheral, another latch for the processor to use when it writes to the peripheral, a register to hold status bits and interrupt bits. All of these registers are connected to the internal data bus and can be addressed by the processor.

If a computer is single purpose and connects to the 8-bit peripheral, then the I/O chip would only need one set of eight output pins. However, personal computers have many applications and connect to all sorts of peripherals. An I/O chip must have at least two or three sets of parallel port output pins. Each port will have its own latch and status-interrupt register. There will only be one latch connected to the internal data bus though. The single data bus latch is multiplexed to the port registers.

The registers in the I/O chip are all addressable and thus are programmable. The fact that the chips can be programmed gives them many abilities. One important programmable feature is that each output port line can be individually programmed in direction. By writing highs or lows to a port register bit, that bit can be made into a single input or output port. It is possible to make some of the lines inputs while at the same time other lines in the same byte are made into outputs. This gives the ports both serial and parallel transfer abilities with either input or output signals.

Other useful qualities that can be programmed into the I/O chip are the ability to make the logic used either positive or negative, the generating of interrupts and the generation of pulses. Various I/O chips have an assortment of special registers according to their design. For example, a set of registers that act as a time clock is found in some. Others will have shift registers and besides performing the parallel data transferring, can perform serial transferring too. They are indeed amazing chips. They are used with 16-bit processors as well as 8-bit. They are simply mounted in parallel (as the two PIAs are in Fig. 20-15) when more data input lines are needed or more data output lines have to be used.

Peripheral interface adapter

The 6821 PIA (in Fig. 20-16) is a 40-pin DIP that represents a typical parallel I/O chip. It has eight pins D0 – D7 that connect to the internal data bus and the processor. The processor can contact peripherals through these eight pins. The chip has three chip select lines, CS0, CS1, *CS2. These are connected to high address lines such as A15 – A12. There are four addresses for the PIA on the memory map and there are two register select pins RS0 and RS1 that choose among the four register addresses. An E line at pin 25 from a ϕ2 clock turns on the chip during the E pulse. Between the chip selects, the register selects, and the E pulse, one of the four registers can be accessed. During the access time data can be transferred over the

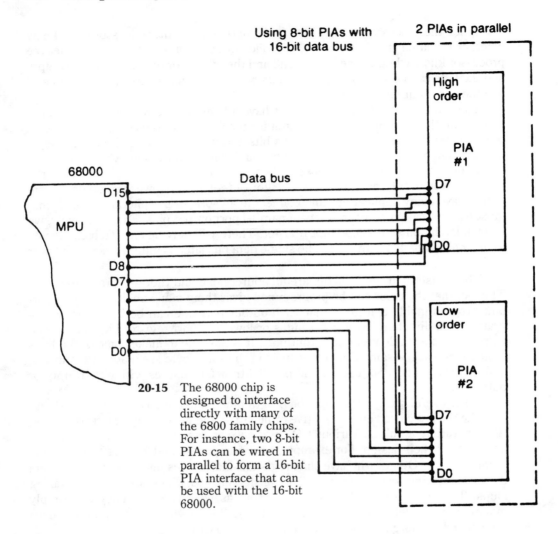

20-15 The 68000 chip is designed to interface directly with many of the 6800 family chips. For instance, two 8-bit PIAs can be wired in parallel to form a 16-bit PIA interface that can be used with the 16-bit 68000.

eight data bus lines. R/*W at pin 21 from the processor decides the direction of the data flow just as it does for RAM.

On the other side of the chip there are two eight bit ports that lead to peripherals. They are called PA7-PA0 and PB7-PB0 at pins 2-17. All of these pins can be programmed to be an input or an output. To be an output a 1 must be loaded into a data direction register, DDR, in the bit that corresponds with the pin. If the bit is to be an input a 0 is loaded into the DDR.

There is a reset line that is held high except when the registers must be reset. At that time a low is sent to the PIA and all the registers are restarted at 0. This causes all of the I/O lines to become inputs as the DDR receives all 0's.

There are four control lines, CA1, CA2, CB1 and CB2 besides two interrupt lines *IRQA and *IRQB. These will be discussed in the following section concerning the internals of the chip.

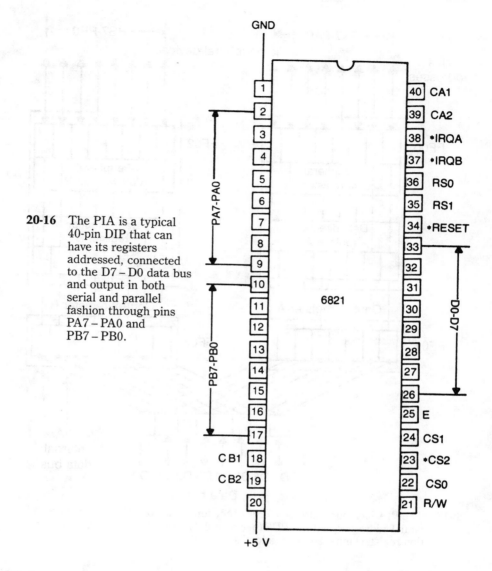

20-16 The PIA is a typical 40-pin DIP that can have its registers addressed, connected to the D7 – D0 data bus and output in both serial and parallel fashion through pins PA7 – PA0 and PB7 – PB0.

PIA register activity

The PIA has two sides A and B (Fig. 20-17). Each side has three registers, a peripheral data register, PDR, a data direction register, DDR and a control register, CR. The peripheral data registers are the interfaces between the PIA and the peripherals. Each PDR can hold a byte.

The data direction registers (Fig. 20-18) are only used to define each line from the peripheral data registers. When a 1 is placed in a DDR bit position, the corresponding PDR bit becomes an output. If a 0 is placed in a DDR bit the same PDR bit becomes an input.

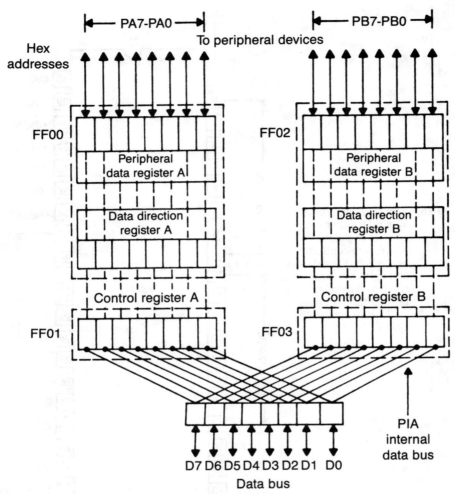

20-17   The PIA has four addresses for six registers. The control registers have individual addresses, but the *PDR* (peripheral data register) and *DDR* (data direction register) must share an address.

The control registers (Fig. 20-19) are needed to let the processor control the way the four control lines CA1, CA2, CB1, and CB2 will perform. The CR is also used to control the states of the interrupt lines, IRQA and IRQB, to the processor from the PIA.

The control register does another important job with its bit 2. It was mentioned that there are four addresses for the PIA, yet it can be seen that there are six registers. That is because the peripheral data register and the data direction register share one address. When the PIA is first turned on, bit 2 of the control register is a 0 and the data direction register is in charge of the address in question. The DDR is then programmed to control the direction of the PDR bits.

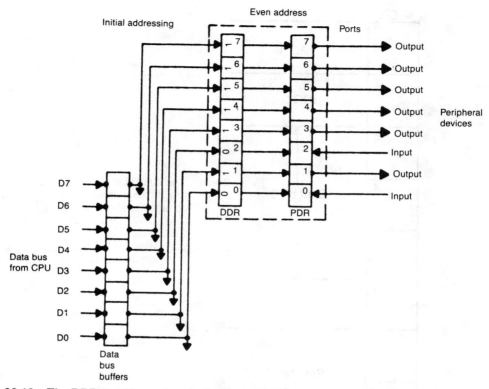

20-18 The DDR is addressed at the beginning of an operation to set up the input-output status of the PDR. Once that is done the DDR relinquishes the address to the PDR.

Once the direction of the PDR bits is determined the DDR has done its job and is not needed. Bit 2 of the CR is set to a 1. This switches the address circuit from the DDR to the PDR. The address will remain on the PDR as long as bit 2 stays at 1.

The control registers

The peripheral data registers and the data direction registers are not overly complicated. The PDRs and the data bus register D7 – D0 are connected together and act as a multiplexer to get the D7 – D0 to work through PA7 – PA0 and PB7 – PB0. So the processor can communicate with peripherals, the DDR simply sets up the direction that each data bit should flow.

The eight bits in the control register are not that simple to handle. The control register arranges for the automatic transferring of data and solves little difficulties in transferring that might arise. The eight bits in each CR are distributed as shown in Fig. 20-19.

Bits 0 and 1 are called CA1 or CB1 Control. These bits decide whether their *IRQ line to the processor should be pulled low and cause the processor to be

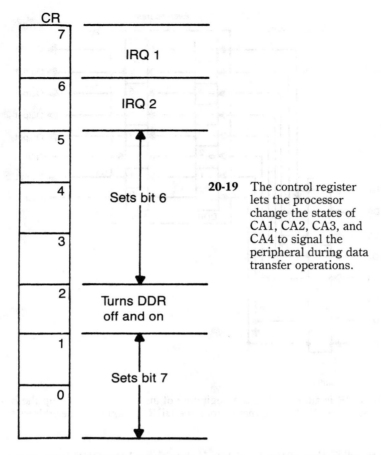

20-19 The control register lets the processor change the states of CA1, CA2, CA3, and CA4 to signal the peripheral during data transfer operations.

interrupted. It does this if the following set of events takes place. First the input line CA1 receives a 0. Next bit 1 of the CR is a 0. These two happenings set bit 7, the IRQ1 status flag to a 1. Then, if bit 0 is a 1 the *IRQ line will output a low and interrupt the processor.

A second way the *IRQ line will output the interruption low is the following. First the input line CA1 receives a 1. Next bit 1 of the CR is a 1. These two happenings set bit 7, the IRQ1 flag to a 1. Then if bit 0 is a 1 also, the *IRQ output pin will send off a low that interrupts the processor. Should bit 0 be a 0, in either of the above situations, the *IRQ pin will be held high and the interrupt will not occur.

Therefore, it can be seen that bit 0 of the CR is the IRQ1 mask bit. If bit 0 is a 0 then bit 7 IRQ1 is masked and even if bit 7 does become set to a 1 the output pin *IRQ will not go low and interrupt the processor. Only when the mask bit 0 is set to a 1 and bit 7 the IRQ1 bit gets set to a 1 will the *IRQ pin go low and produce the processor interruption.

Bit 2, called the DDR bit is the third register select pin in the PIA. There are two pins RS0 and RS1 that connect to the address bus lines such as A0 and A1. These two lines can address four registers. However, there are six registers in the

PIA. To cut the six registers down to four addresses, the data direction registers and the peripheral data registers are combined into two pairs, and each pair can be addressed with one address. The control registers each get their own address.

One processor address operation can then either locate a DDR-PDR pair or one CR. A third bit is needed to address one of the DDR-PDR registers. This is bit 2 in the CR. When it is necessary to address a DDR bit 2 is cleared to a 0. If a PDR is to be addressed bit 2 is set to a 1. Bit 2 can be set or cleared if the processor writes to the CR and installs the appropriate bit.

Bits 3, 4, and 5 control their respective CA2 or CB2 pins. The pins can become either inputs and cause the PIA to interrupt the processor or outputs and become port lines to peripherals. The operation the pins will perform is decided by the bits that are installed into the CR bits 3, 4, and 5.

Bit 5 controls the direction of the CA2 or CB2 pins. If bit 5 in one of the control registers is set to a 1, its respective pin will become an output and be able to send data to a peripheral. Should bit 5 become cleared to 0 then its line will become an input interrupt.

When bit 5 is 0 and its line CA2 is an input interrupt, then bits 3 and 4 decide how an interrupt is to be handled. Bits 3 and 4 work with any interrupt that might enter the CA2 or CB2 pins. If bit 4 is a 0 and a low-going interrupt enters a pin, the two entities cause bit 6 the IRQ2 to be set to a 1. Also, if bit 4 is a 1 and a high-going interrupt pulse enters a pin the two signals will cause bit 6 the IRQ2 to be set to a 1. Any other combinations of a CA2 or CB2 input and bit 4 will not affect IRQ2.

Bit 3 is the mask bit for this interrupt arrangement. If bit 3 is a 1, when bit 6 the IRQ2 is set to a 1, the *IRQ pin will output a low to the processor and interrupt the processor. Should bit 3, the mask bit, be cleared to a 0 though, even though bit 6 does get set to a 1, the *IRQ pin will be held high and not output an interrupt to the processor.

21

Digital-to-analog and analog-to-digital circuits

THERE ARE TWO TYPES OF COMPUTERS. FIRST OF ALL THERE IS THE widely known digital computer. Second there is the not so well-known analog computer. In your personal computer there are both digital and analog circuits but the computing that goes on is strictly of a digital nature.

Digital computing is simply the job of coding all problems into binary arithmetic and then this arithmetic is run through the digital world. In the digital world, the arithmetic is processed until resultant digits are produced. These end digits are then output to digital or analog devices so the results can be displayed or otherwise put to good use.

An analog computer, on the other hand, does not solve problems by manipulating digits. It is a device that sets up a mathematical analogy of a problem. It then solves the analogy and uses the answer as the solution of the original problem. A calculator is an example of a digital computer. A slide rule is an example of an analog computer. The calculator receives a digital input by having its buttons punched. It solves the problem in its processor circuit and then outputs a digital result on a display. A slide rule receives an analog input as two pieces of wood are moved so markings line up. It solves the problem by the relationship of the two pieces of wood. The output is found at another spot in this analog relationship of the wood strips.

Before electronic digital computers practically all of the jobs we performed were accomplished by analog means. Besides the analogy two pieces of wood can form, needles on meters, volume controls, scales, radio and TV signals, calculations involving physical volume, length, width, etc., were all made using analogies of a problem and then arriving at a solution by means of the analogy. Trying to solve problems by digital arithmetic had been the hard way to go.

Digital electronics has changed all that. The only problem with counting is that it is very slow if it is done mechanically. Digital electronic counting is accomplished in a few billionths of a second. The cumbersome counting process of solving problems is no problem for an electronic digital circuit. With digital electronics it is much faster in lots of cases than setting up an analogy and solving it. The digital approach takes the problem and first converts it into arithmetic. Next the arithmetic is converted into binary. Then the binary 1s and 0s are made into highs and lows. The highs and lows are fed into the digital world and are promptly processed. After processing the digital answers are then converted into a form that can be used. The conversion is either into a digital or analog form. Let's examine this process as inputs and outputs of the digital computer.

Digital computer analog inputs

The personal computer has been called upon to perform all sorts of jobs. Besides receiving digital inputs from devices like the keyboard, it must also receive analog inputs from items like the cassette, joysticks, speedometers, thermometers, and so on. The possibilities are unlimited. Information could come from many analog sources that have signals that vary from a top to a bottom with many positions in between. The information must be changed to a digital voltage that has a top level and bottom level and no in between. This is what changing an analog situation to a digital one is all about.

Because the computer processes electronic signals only, the first step in preparing the digital circuit inputs is to turn all the physical information into terms of voltages, currents, and frequencies. For example, a sound wave in the air, can be input to a microphone and move a coil in a circuit. Or a shaft can be attached to a potentiometer and the movement of the shaft can change the voltage output of a variable resistor in the device. Or a photonegative can be placed in a beam of light that is aimed at a photosensitive device. The changes brought about by the photo shadings vary an electronic circuit. All of these potential inputs for the computer can be made into electrical forms in similar ways. Once the analog information has been changed into analog voltages or currents, it can then be entered into an analog-to-digital converter circuit (Fig. 21-1).

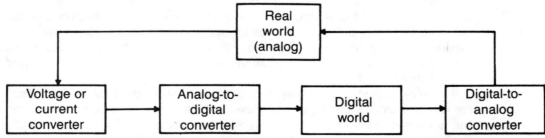

21-1   In the analog section of the world, problems arise. To solve the problems by electronic digital means, the problem information must be converted to voltage, current, or other electronic entities. Next the voltage, etc., must be converted from analog electricity to digital. Then the digital world can process the problem. Once a digital solution has been found it must be converted back to analog for use in the real world.

Once the physical analog inputs are changed to electronic analog inputs, they must be then changed to digital electronic inputs. Actual analog-to-digital circuits are discussed later in this chapter. After the analog becomes digital it can then be injected into the digital world. In the digital world the signals are processed and then output so the computer can continue on with the next information that needs processing. The digital output is then changed back to analog, first electronic analog and then physical analog.

At first glance, this procedure of first changing analog to digital, computing the digital, and then changing the digital back to analog looks like a lot of trouble. It is trouble to set the system up but once the system is in operation it works at such blazing speeds and can process utterly amazing amounts of data, that until something better comes along, there is no other practical way to do the job.

A/D and D/A converters

The *A/D* (analog-to-digital) converter is a *D/A* (digital-to-analog) converter with one more circuit attached. You'll examine a digital-to-analog circuit first and then add the circuit that then produces the analog-to-digital circuit. Most D/A circuits consist of a collection of electronic switches and resistors (as in Fig. 21-2). These switches and resistors convert a collection of individual digital high and low voltages into a continuous analog voltage. There is one switch for every bit involved in the conversion. The resistors act as voltage dividers and pullups.

A good example of a simple D/A converter is one that can convert a nibble to an electronic wave that will drive a siren. The bits are the digital input to the circuit, that will be converted into the varying electronic waveform. The waveform in turn will be injected into a siren.

In a parallel nibble, there are four bits that travel abreast over four data bus lines. The four data bus lines are connected to four inputs of the D/A converter. In order to produce a siren-like sound, the nibble bit sets must be varied so they will produce a steady change of pitch in the siren from a low pitch to a high and back. As the pitch goes from a low to a high the following 16 machine language program lines will do the job.

```
0000
0001
0010
0011
0100
0101
0110
0111
1000
1001
1010
1011
1100
```

1101
1110
1111

Four bits at a time are input at the four switches of the D/A converter. The switches are connected to the resistors. The resistor voltage dividers have a source of +5 V and are returned to 0 V or ground. Each nibble as it enters the D/A circuit, produces a slightly different voltage output. The effect of the resistors is to permit each input nibble to be converted to a voltage between +5 and 0 V. Examine what happens as the different combinations of bits in each nibble energize the D/A circuit.

The 0000 places each switch at ground or 0 V. The +5 V bus has no effect. The output of the four switches is 0 V. Then as each subsequent nibble enters the

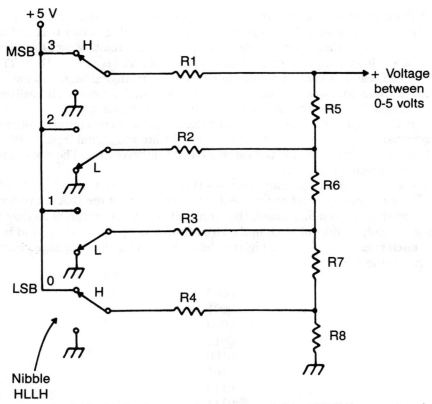

21-2 A nibble can be input to the switches of this 4-bit D/A converter. A closed switch is a high and an open switch is a low. The switches connect to a resistive voltage divider. Each one of the 16 possible switch settings produces a different output voltage between 0 and +5 V. The nibble is thus converted to an output voltage level.

switch circuit, the 1s start connecting the switches to the +5 V line. The output of the four switches varies according to the number of switches that get connected, the series resistors that the current passes through and the voltage divider. When the nibbles vary from 0000 to 1111 the output voltage will vary from just above 0 volts to just below +5 V. As the nibbles then vary back from 1111 to 0000 the voltage will vary from near +5 V back down to near 0 V. If the varying voltage is then input to an audio system, a siren-type sound will emanate. All sorts of sounds can be produced with this form of D/A converter.

This four-bit input is able to form 16 different sound tones and is aptly called a 4-bit D/A circuit. A 5-bit circuit could produce 32 different voltages. Six-bits can make 64 voltages, 7-bits 128 voltages and so on. This is the basic D/A technique. It is the way a few digital inputs can produce a large array of voltage outputs that when combined form an analog voltage.

Analog-to-digital conversions

The above conversion of digital bits into an analog voltage is very convenient when it is necessary to output an analog voltage from the digital world, as needed by devices like the cassette recorder and audio circuits. Getting analog voltages into the digital world in the form of bits, requires some additional circuitry.

The switch-resistor D/A circuit is also involved in A/D work. It is in the center of the A/D network as shown in Fig. 21-3. Surrounding the D/A converter is an input called a counter register and an output called a comparator. The counter is a register arrangement that starts counting at 0 and counts up to its potential. For instance, a nibble counter can count the four bits from decimal 0 to 15. A byte-sized counter can count from 0 to 255. A two-byte counter has a range of 0 to 65,535. The counter inputs its bit sets into the D/A inputs. The switches in the D/A respond as described and the voltage output of the D/A circuit changes gradually as the count goes on.

The D/A voltage output is input to the comparator circuit. The comparator has two inputs which result in one output. The D/A input is one input. A second input arrives from the analog circuit.

A comparator circuit (like Fig. 21-4) has one input designated as − and one as +. The − input is the reference input. The D/A voltage that has been generated by the counter and the D/A switch-resistor network, is the reference voltage. The + input is the place where an analog signal input can be injected. It is the signal that is to be converted from analog to digital.

Back in the counter, a clock input is keeping it counting continually. If it is a nibble counter it is outputting a steady 0000 through 1111 and then starting over at 0000. The D/A circuit is in turn continually outputting a steady voltage from 0 to +5 V and then starting over again at 0 V. If you graph the bit input set to the D/A converter to its voltage output, you'll draw the stair step waveform shown in Fig. 21-5. This steadily changing voltage is applied to the reference input of the comparator.

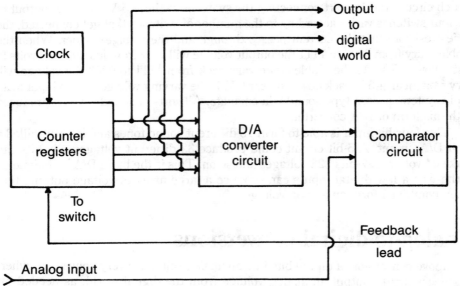

21-3   A D/A converter when set with these other circuits helps in A/D conversion. The counter sends a steady binary count to the switches in the D/A converter. The D/A in response outputs a constantly changing voltage to the comparator circuit. Also input to the comparator is the analog signal that is to be changed to digital. They are compared and an output logic state obtained. The logic state is fed back to the counter registers. The logic state operates a switch in the counter that outputs the correct digital signals to the digital world.

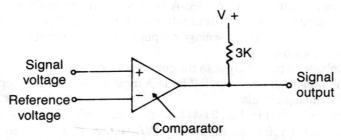

21-4   The comparator is a voltage controlled device that compares a signal voltage to a reference voltage and then outputs a voltage state.

As long as the reference voltage at input − , is more negative than the analog signal entering at input + , the comparator will not output any voltage. The comparator output is fed back to a special switch in the counter circuits. The switch operates a special output to the digital world. The output has four lines and will carry the current bits that are in the counter at that time. When the switch is thrown the current bits are output to the digital world. The switch is controlled by the output of the comparator.

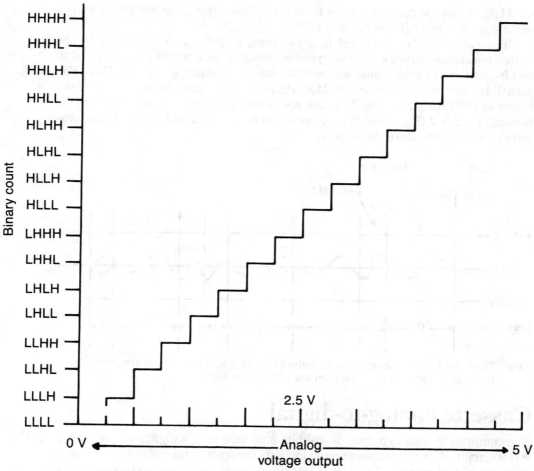

21-5 The input to the reference voltage pin of the comparator is coming from D/A and if graphed, looks like a stair step.

The comparator will output a switch voltage when the reference at input −, goes more positive than the analog voltage at input +. That is the way the analog input makes a set of digital bits exit the counter and enter the digital world. It is the digital representation of the analog input. See how these circuits work for a typical device like a cassette.

Cassette digital-to-analog

The cassette tape machine for a computer is nothing more than an audio tape device. It can only store audio frequencies from 0 to about 30,000 hertz. In order to store bits on the audio tape, the digital bits must be converted to audio tones. One conventional way this is done is the following. The computer is given some programs on ROM that codes every 1 to the two bits. Every 0 bit is made into the nibble 1100. When the cassette tape is to be loaded from the computer the 1s and 0s in the data will be coded to 10s and 1100s.

The coded bits are then fed in serial fashion to the D/A converter. In the switch-resistance network the two types of digital square waves are converted to two frequencies of analog sine waves. The sine waves emerge from the D/A. The digital 1s have become bursts of 2400 Hz sine waves and the 0s have become bursts of 1200 Hz sine waves. The sine waves vary between a top of +2.5 V and a bottom of −2.5 V (Fig. 21-6). These are audio frequencies and voltages. The cassette tape is able to store them easily.

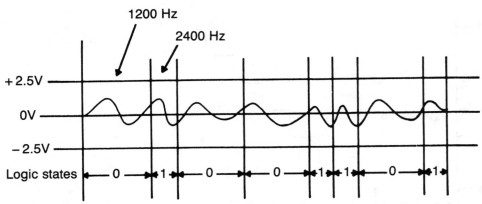

21-6   The binary 1s are converted to an audio 2400 Hz, and the binary 0s are made into 1200 Hz. A cassette tape can then store the audio signals.

Cassette analog-to-digital

The computer is able to output digital bits onto tape with a digital-to-analog converter circuit. When the cassette must input its contents to the computer it uses an analog-to-digital circuit. The tape contains magnetic bit representations in the form of 2400 Hz and 1200 Hz sine waves. These sine waves can be input directly to a comparator. They are bursts of audio pulses that are varying from a high of +2.5 V and a low of −2.5 V. The other comparator input is a reference voltage.

When the cassette inputs the sine wave bursts, the signal is made to pass through a "zero crossing detector" circuit. The signal is a sine wave that rises to a high of +2.5 V, falls through zero volts to a low of −2.5 V, and then rises through zero again, on and on.

The detector circuit (Fig. 21-7) is based around a diode with its cathode connected to the input line. During the positive excursion of the sine wave, the diode is reverse biased and will not conduct. The full plus voltage passes the diode connection and is more positive than the reference voltage. These inputs make the comparator output a low.

As the sine wave goes negative, the diode conducts and the input voltage drops below the reference voltage. These inputs make the comparator switch states and output a high.

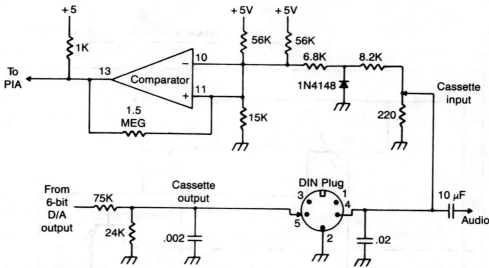

21-7 A zero crossing detector circuit feeding into a comparator converts the digital audio on a cassette tape into digital voltage of +5 and 0 V.

The diode circuit and the comparator is acting as an analog-to-digital converter. The 2400 Hz sine wave bursts are converted to a steady stream of square waves in a 10 configuration. The 1200 Hz sine wave bursts are converted to square waves laid out as 1100. The 10s are code for binary 1. The 1100s are code for binary 0. The square waves are decoded by some ROM software into normal highs and lows for storage in RAM.

Joystick interface

When you move the joystick shaft, you are changing the position of the shaft in space. The changing position can be converted to a varying voltage. This voltage can then be converted into digital bits and the movement displayed, in some convenient manner, on the screen.

In the joystick mechanism is a potentiometer circuit that is nothing but two resistors with wiping arms (like Fig. 21-8). There is +5 V attached to one resistor end and the other end is connected to ground. As you move the joystick, it causes a wiping arm to move over the resistor and vary the resistance the voltage must traverse. As a result of the variable resistance the output voltage of the circuit is varied from +5 V down to 0 V. This varying voltage is an analog voltage. It can have any one of an infinite number of different voltages between +5 V and 0.

Here again a comparator circuit is used. It has two inputs, one from a stair step counter as described earlier and the second from the joystick potentiometer. The stair step is continually counting bits and is producing a separate voltage from 0 to +5 V, step by step. Each bit set represents a different voltage level. The joystick output is a voltage that is constantly compared to the stair step voltage.

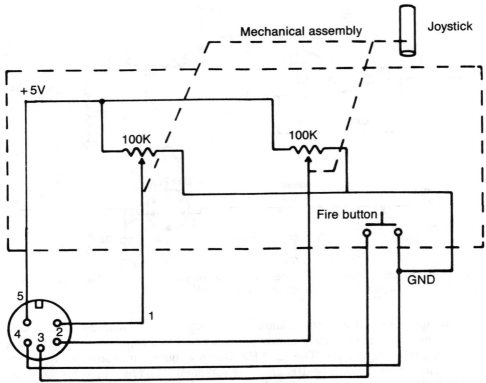

21-8 A joystick is a shaft connected to two potentiometers. As you move the shaft position, you are also changing a voltage in the potentiometer between 0 and +5 V.

As long as the stair step voltage is more negative than the joystick output, the comparator remains dormant and the feedback of its output to the counter switch is inactive. As soon as the stair step voltage inputs a value that is more positive than the joystick input, the comparator switches. This new comparator state is fed back to the counter switch. The counter switch is turned on and the set of bits that is in the counter register, at that moment, is output to the digital world.

The analog voltage level from the joystick is input to the comparator and the digital count at that instant, which is the digital representation of the joystick's analog voltage, is output. The analog is thus converted to digital.

22

Display monitor interfaces

THE TV DISPLAY MONITOR THAT YOU STARE AT AND HEAR NOISES FROM
are relatively new devices. A couple of decades ago, you would probably have been
staring at the output of a teletype machine. The only noise would have been the
clacking of the teletype as it printed the code from the memory. Today the teletype
is a relic as far as computers are concerned. The teletype has been replaced by
keyboards for inputs and TV display monitors for viewable outputs. For permanent hard copy, a printer is used.

With the advent of display monitors, new video circuits had to be installed in
the computer. These new circuits can be likened to a TV transmitter. These circuits have the job of continuously scanning the video RAM section and taking a
copy of the video RAM contents. These video circuits also have the job of generating a TV signal that can drive the TV monitor. After the video circuits take a copy
of the video RAM contents, they then mount the RAM data onto the TV signal
they generated. This TV signal containing the video RAM contents is then output
over a cable to the TV display monitor. The display monitor then processes the TV
signal loaded with RAM data and shows it on the brightly lit screen.

The display raster

When you look at a display, you see a bright light with darkened sections. For
instance, if text is on the screen, the text could be dark and the background lit.
The bright areas are produced by the monitor and is called a *raster*. The raster
shown in Fig. 22-1 is a carefully designed area of light. In older monitors, the raster was drawn on the screen with the same characteristics as a conventional home
TV. As time went by, these characteristics were found not to be ideal, and different
parameters were decided upon. These new parameters improved the ability of the

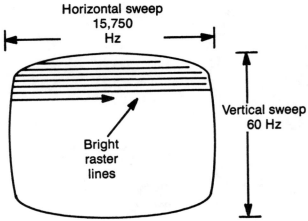

22-1   The *raster* is a carefully designed area of light on the monitor face. It is generated by the monitor and consists of a group of horizontal brightness lines.

raster to show computer pictures with better performance. These new characteristics are discussed in more detail in this and the next chapter.

The home TV raster is the one still used in a lot of computers in the field, and it is drawn on the screen in the following way, as shown in Fig. 22-1. Starting at the top left of the screen and scanned across like writing, 525 brightness lines are drawn one on top of the other till they fill the picture tube face. The lines are drawn at a rate of 15,750 per second. These lines are drawn from the left side to the right side of the screen. This movement is called *horizontal sweep*. This horizontal sweep is occurring at a frequency rate of 15,750 Hz.

The lines are made to fill the screen at a rate of 30 full frames per second. The lines are numbered. The even-numbered lines are drawn first, and the odd-numbered lines are drawn next. The even-numbered lines are the first field in a frame, and the odd-numbered lines are the second field. This is call *interlaced scanning*. Each field is drawn at a rate of 60 per second, resulting in a full frame rate of 30 per second. This scanning is taking place down and then retraced up on the screen. This activity is called *vertical sweep*. Each field is drawn at a frequency rate of 60 Hz.

The raster is a screenful of light. There are no dark areas at all in a raster. When the monitor is turned on, it generates the raster and keeps generating it till it is turned off. The TV signal from the computer is input to the monitor, is processed, and the resultant signal is further input to the picture tube where it is placed into the environs of the raster.

The TV signal

A typical TV signal that the video output circuits generate and send to the display monitor, must match up with the raster, if a correct display is to result. A monochrome signal that will work with the raster just discussed is shown in Fig. 6-29.

The horizontal axis represents time. The vertical axis shows peak-to-peak voltage. The total time shown is one field screenful of light, 1/60th of a second. Two of these fields would produce an interlaced frame that occurs every 1/30th of a second. The p-p (peak-to-peak) voltage shown is 0 – 2.75 V. The 2.75 V produces a brightly lit raster. As the voltage drops slowly to zero volts the screen darkens to shades of gray culminating in black. Note the white level and black level. In between these two levels are shades of gray.

In this example arrangement, each raster field consists of 264 horizontal scan lines drawn one beneath the other. The top of the screen at the left corner is shown as the corner of a square pulse. This is where the raster begins its sweeping. This corner is at zero volts and as a result is at a black level, no light. Even though there is no light, the horizontal sweep still goes on. The break in the top duration of the pulse simply shows that many, many pulses took place between the beginning of the break and the end of the break. The pulse with breaks represent many of the drawn lines during the horizontal sweep. As shown, each of these wide pulses designate one scan line from the left side to the right.

Note each scan line wide pulse is followed by a narrow down-going pulse. These narrow pulses between each wide scan duration, are horizontal sync pulses. They are occurring at the 15,750 Hz rate. They synchronize the incoming TV signal with the 15,750 Hz rate the raster is running at. The raster rate is free running. The sync pulses lock the free running raster into step with the TV signal.

The sync pulses are below the voltage black level. They are not to be seen. It is said that they are in the blacker than black voltage area. There are also some vertical sync pulses at the end of the signal line that are also in the blacker than black area. This keeps the horizontal and vertical pulses black during the retrace time. During retrace, the scan travels ends at the right side of the screen and is retraced back to the left side to begin the next line of light and when the screenful is finished, and the vertical sweep retraces back to the top of the screen.

The vertical sync pulses, are only found at the end of a screenful of video. Note the bottom of screen at the very end of the screenful of signal. The vertical sync rate occurs at a slow 60 Hz rate in comparison to the horizontal sweep pulses at a 15,750 rate. The vertical sync pulses lock the free-running 60 Hz vertical sweep frequency in step with the 60 Hz rate of the video signal.

All of the sync pulses have voltage levels that keep them in the black level. In order to produce visible video, the signal voltage must increase into the white level area. Note the video dot signals perched on the top of some of the scan line durations. They are dot switching signals. When a dot on the screen is to be lit, there is a quick high voltage spike that extends up into the white level. When a dot is supposed to be dark there is no spike, the scan duration just stays at the same level.

When the computer video output circuits generate such a TV signal with horizontal sync pulses, vertical sync pulses and video RAM data a steady stream of the signal is transmitted to the monitor. Once in the monitor, the different signal types are separated from one another and processed. The two sync signals lock the raster in step with the computer circuits and the video RAM data is converted to voltage spikes and displayed as dots of light. The display monitor receiver circuits are discussed in the next chapter. Meanwhile, examine the display transmitter that is in the computer.

Video demands

In the early days of computer video display, designers installed a number of components on the main print board that generated the TV-type signal just discussed in Fig. 6-29. The signal resembled those that were produced in commercial TV stations. The important difference was, the commercial TV transmitter sent the signal out over the airwaves contained in a carrier wave specific to the stations assigned frequency. The computer-generated TV signal was simply output from a video port without a carrier and connected to the display monitor. As a result, computer monitors, in those days, were simply TV sets with all the unneeded carrier tuning circuits deleted.

In fact, the computer generated signal was so like the local TV signals, that some computer manufacturers installed *rf* (radio frequency) amplifiers in their computers. These rf amplifiers produced a carrier wave, usually channels 3 or 4, packaged up the computer video, in the channel 3 or 4 carrier and connected the computer to an ordinary TV receiver. The TV set showed the computer display.

Using a TV set shows a satisfactory display for a lot of home uses. Using a simple monitor also is satisfactory in a lot of cases. However, these displays are crude and fall far short of being able to be used for serious business purposes. First of all, there is considerable flicker in a still TV picture. Second, fine detail in the picture cannot be seen satisfactorily. A person using a word processor or large spreadsheet all day, an engineer designing with a computer-aided program, or a multitude of other users and applications, cannot work with these crude displays. As a result, new computer video-transmitter circuits have been developed that can send signals to new high-resolution display monitors.

The commercial TV stations are locked into the old *FCC* (Federal Communications Commission) signal specifications called *NTSC* (National Television System Committee) or the European *PAL* (phase-alternation line) signals. These are old specs designed way back in 1938 that are still being used. They can't be changed because every TV receiver in the U.S. or Europe would have to be scrapped. The TVs would not be able to receive, through the airwaves, a changed signal.

Computer monitors suffer from no such restriction. A computer-generated video signal is not transmitted through the air. It is simply cabled directly to its monitor. The computer-monitor system is a closed circuit. Designers can use any system they want. There are now a number of special video-transmitter systems available. They all attempt to make improvements in the monitor display. The toughest improvement that is continuously being worked on is resolution.

Resolution

Like type, a letter on the TV display is composed of a number of points. In the TV display, these points are picture elements or they are called pixels. Each drawn line

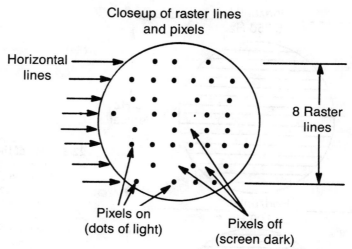

Closeup of raster lines
and pixels

Horizontal
lines

8 Raster
lines

Pixels on
(dots of light)

Pixels off
(screen dark)

22-2 Each line of the raster is intensity modulated by a number of picture element dots called *pixels*. The dots can be turned off and on by the video circuits in the computer.

is composed of a number of pixels, Fig. 22-2. These pixels are switched on and off by the state of the bit in video RAM that controls that pixel. In a computer that syncs with the display at 15,750 Hz horizontal and 60 Hz vertical, there could be 320 pixels on one drawn line. The pixels in the line will be off and on in accordance with its controlling RAM bit.

In a vertical column, since it is not as long as a line, there could be 200 pixels. With this arrangement, it is said that the display has a resolution of 320 × 200. This gives the display block 64,000 pixels of resolution. Resolution is a direct result of the number of pixels. The more pixels there are the better is the resolution. The better the resolution the sharper and crisper the picture will be.

In order to increase resolution, one of the things that can be done is increase the horizontal sync signal that comes out of the video generator, Fig. 22-3. Instead of using 15.75 kHz, sync signals of 21.8, 31.5, 35 kHz and even higher can be output from the video generator. The vertical frequency remains around 60 Hz. The vertical frequency from display to display can vary a bit, from about 40 to 75 Hz.

With the horizontal frequency increased and the vertical held about the same, the scanning produces a lot more horizontal lines for each cycle the vertical pulls the lines down from the top of the display. The increased number of lines in the picture fills in the spaces between lines. It becomes harder to discern the scanning lines, increasing the picture clarity. There are a lot more pixels in the picture too. Each additional line adds its pixel content to the pixel number.

A second way to improve resolution, has to do with picture bandwidth. The bandwidth is the measurement of the speed a pixel is made to turn off or on, Fig. 22-4. The faster a pixel is made to turn off and on, the more pixels can be placed on a line. The more pixels there are the better is the resolution, which is what this effort is all about. Graphics become sharper and sharper as the resolution in-

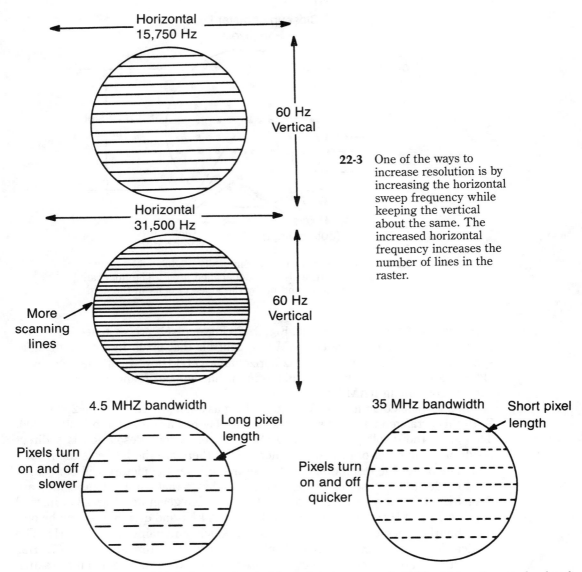

22-3 One of the ways to increase resolution is by increasing the horizontal sweep frequency while keeping the vertical about the same. The increased horizontal frequency increases the number of lines in the raster.

22-4 The picture bandwidth is the speed a pixel is made to turn on and off. The higher the speed or bandwidth, the shorter the pixel length and the better the resolution.

creases. In many applications such as *CAD* (computer-aided drafting), medical imaging, government defenses, and others resolution can be vitally important.

The ordinary TV set has a bandwidth of about 4.5 MHz. One set of horizontal lines is drawn at this rate. This means that 80 to 120 lines are drawn during the time one megahertz takes place. This is a relatively slow pace to turn pixels off and on. The resolution will be average. Not good enough for high-resolution needs.

In higher resolution displays, the bandwidth is picked up to about 35 MHz or higher. At these higher frequencies the pixels are switched at a quicker pace. Exceptional high-resolution pictures can be produced at these higher bandwidths.

Table 22-1 shows a list of some of the more popular display systems that are found in personal computers. These are the ones that are in the IBM created—CGA, EGA, and VGA—the Macintosh II system, and the NEC Multisync. There will be more about these systems in this chapter, and the next chapter.

The computer does its part to increase resolution by increasing the horizontal scanning frequency and increasing the bandwidth of its TV output. The increased horizontal frequency puts more lines on the screen. The increased bandwidth puts more pixels on a line. The larger the total number of pixels, the better is the resolution.

The idea is to fool the human eye. If the pixels are increased in number and

Table 22-1. These are some of the more popular display systems readily available.

Display Name	Resolution	Typical Display Characteristics		Horiz. Sweep	Verti. Sweep
		Bandwidth	Input		
CGA Color graphics adapter	320 × 200 4 of 16 colors	35 MHz	Digital	15.6 Hz	60 Hz
EGA Enhanced graphics adapter	640 × 350 16 of 64 colors	35 MHz	Digital	21.8 Hz	60 Hz
VGA video graphics array	320 × 350 256 of 256,000 colors	35 MHz	Analog	31.5 KHz	60 Hz
Macintosh II	16 Million		Analog	35 KHz	60 Hz
NEC Multisync	1024 × 768 and Lower	65 MHz	Analog Digital	Variable 15.75-35.5 KHz	60 Hz

each pixel made smaller, the eye can't see individual pixels. The eye sees one picture with fine detail. Just like a fine photo with many tiny points.

Digital and analog display systems

The differences between digital and analog signals are discussed in previous chapters. The TV signals that are generated in the computer, can also be digital or analog. If the signal is digital, there can be only a few different voltage levels. When the signal is analog in nature, there can be an infinite number of voltage levels.

The composite TV signal is analog. As the signal is output from the computer, the video section of the composite varies from voltage to voltage in a continuous manner. The varying voltage represents the brightness level of the signal. If the signal is a black and white one, then the voltage is varying from black to white with an infinite number of shades of gray in between.

Should the signal be color, then there are three signals. One signal for red, one for blue, and one for green. Each signal is like the black and white. The difference is the red signal varies from an intense red to a very pale red with shades of red in between. The companion blue and green signals perform in the same way.

In order to display a color picture, these three signals light up three colors of phosphor, each color individually. The three dots of phosphor are spaced closely on the screen in trios, as in Fig. 22-5. As these three colors are lit, the light generated

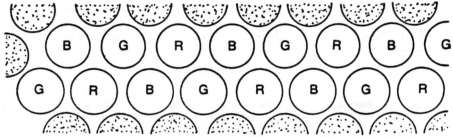

22-5　The color phosphor dots can be laid out on the glass faceplate in the triad patterns.

adds together. The dots are so close the human eye is only able to see the color addition observed as a single resultant color. Each dot trio on the TV screen is considered as one dot of light. A few of these dot triads can form a color pixel.

The continuous analog color signals are able to each form an almost infinite number of voltage levels. This gives the analog output the ability to produce an almost infinite number of colors. Even though the possibility of an infinite number of colors can be produced, the actual number of analog colors are limited to the ability of the video display circuits in the computer. The latest IBM VGA circuits can output up to 265,000 colors. The Macintosh II can produce more than 16 million colors.

Digital signal outputs, in comparison to analog, are very limited in the number of colors they can put out. There are three color signals that must add together to produce a color resultant for digital outputs too. In addition, the overall brightness signal, called I for intensity, is also added when the resultant color light is produced.

Each of these signals—R, G, B, and I (red, green, blue, and intensity) have their voltages fixed at their digital levels. The signals can be high or low (Table 22-2). Because there are four signals, each being able to go high or low, there are 16 possible total voltage levels that can be added together. Each total voltage level when applied to the TV screen produces a color. In the CGA video board, the digital output can produce a total of 16 colors.

To increase the total number of colors, some boards divide each color into two levels instead of just the one. In the EGA adapter, there are two sets of levels for each color, R1, R2, B1, B2, G1, G2, I1, and I2. This produces eight levels. With

**Table 22-2. With four digital signals—R, B, G, and I—
generated in the CGA adapter card with each color having a high
and low, these 16 different combinations of color levels can be generated.**

COLOR –	R	G	B	I
1	Low	Low	Low	Low
2	Low	Low	Low	High
3	Low	Low	High	Low
4	Low	Low	High	High
5	Low	High	Low	Low
6	Low	High	Low	High
7	Low	High	High	Low
8	Low	High	High	High
9	High	Low	Low	Low
10	High	Low	Low	High
11	High	Low	High	Low
12	High	Low	High	High
13	High	High	Low	Low
14	High	High	Low	High
15	High	High	High	Low
16	High	High	High	High

eight levels there are 64 possible combinations to add together giving a total of 64 possible colors.

Video adapter cards

The older video transmitter circuits were wired right on the main computer board, but for the most part, the newer circuits are wired onto a separate small card that plugs into one of the slots on a motherboard. The adapter card is a module. It plugs into the motherboard, as shown in Fig. 22-6, and the monitor plugs into the card. If a card is suspected of causing trouble it is easily replaced and thus tested by direct substitution. If you do not have a known good replacement, you can test it by plugging it into another computer. If it works in the other computer, the card is good. Should it not work in the second computer either, the card is probably defective.

Repairing defective cards is a major problem. The symptoms of no video or poor video are easy to diagnose. However, it is difficult if not impossible to obtain service notes, schematics and replacement components. The cards are considered throw-away items. Often however, you can trade it in on a new one. Should you have or can get the service notes and schematic you could give the repair a try. There is nothing mysterious on the cards and the fault can be found using ordinary service measures with a logic probe, VOM, and oscilloscope. The first step is to make sure the trouble is located on the card and not in the display monitor. Scope pictures will quickly determine that. Examine some of the common cards.

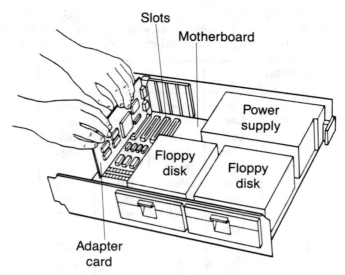

22-6 The adapter cards plug into the expansion slots on the motherboard.

A monochrome I/O card

The IBM PC has a separate adapter card (Fig. 22-7) that plugs into one of its I/O sockets and provides a port for a monochrome display. This modular approach makes it convenient for servicing. When the monochrome picture disappears you can try replacing the card.

On the card is a video output chip called 6845 CRT controller. It is the main actor in the conversion of digital bits from the computer to a monochrome TV picture to the TV monitor. There are dozens of other support chips including a 4K static RAM and an MK-36000 character ROM.

The RAM is a resident of the memory map. It is the video RAM. On the TV screen there is a block matrix of 80 × 25, which totals 2000 characters on display. Each character requires two bytes of RAM to operate. One byte contains the ASCII code for the character and the second contains control bits to accommodate features such as blinking of the character, high or normal intensity and normal or reverse video. With a total of 2,000 characters, each with two bytes, the RAM must be able to hold 4,000 bytes, which is the reason for the 4K size.

The address of the video RAM ranges from hex B0000 to B0F9F. The starting address of the RAM corresponds with the upper left-hand character block on the screen. The lower right-hand corner is the final RAM address.

The video RAM is constantly scanned byte by byte. The contents of each byte is then encoded and sent to the electron gun to turn the dots on and off. This keeps the TV display intact. To make sure the display doesn't start rolling or whip into a bunch of horizontal lines, the card manufactures the horizontal and vertical sync signals that lock the TV's scanning circuits into step with the computer.

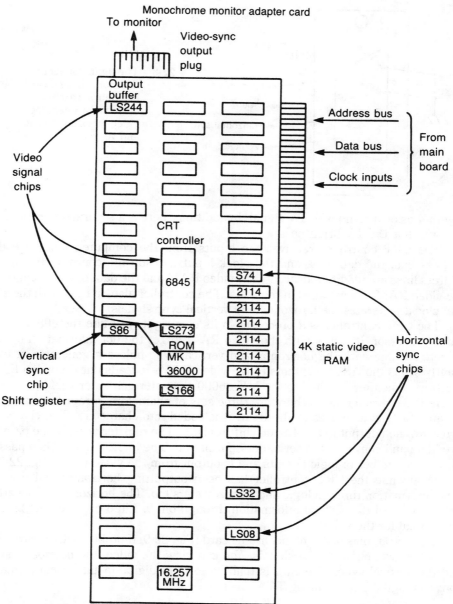

22-7 The monochrome adapter card receives computer inputs when it is plugged into an expansion slot. It can then process the digital signals and generate monochrome video and sync signals to drive a monochrome monitor.

If you look at the 9-pin connector the monochrome card uses to hook up with the TV (Fig. 22-8) you'll find there are four active pins, 6-intensity, 7-video, 8-horizontal sync and 9-vertical sync. Pins 1 and 2 are grounds and 3, 4, and 5 are unused. Note that the video and sync exit the card as separate entities and not

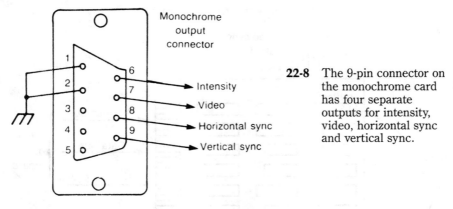

22-8 The 9-pin connector on the monochrome card has four separate outputs for intensity, video, horizontal sync and vertical sync.

together as on a composite TV signal. In addition, there is a separate intensity signal, which is the TV brightness.

The CRT controller receives the inputs from the computer. They are the address bus, the data bus, and the clock inputs. Inside the controller chip, the address lines are modified to access the video RAM and the data bits are sent on to the video RAM and installed in registers. The controller also, in time with the system clock, generates the horizontal and vertical sync signals.

The CRT controller is a processor in its own right, just like the 8088. It is a video processor. It works with the video RAM to get the dot information on the screen. In time with the horizontal and vertical sync pulses it generates, it constantly scans the ASCII contents of the video RAM. It reads out the video RAM registers, one after another, to the MK-36000 character-generator ROM.

In the character ROM there are three sets of characters in register matrixes. As an ASCII byte arrives at the ROM it is coded into characters. The character bytes are then output to a 74LS166 shift register. The register accepts the parallel byte data and converts it to serial dot information. The information is then passed through a number of logic circuits and is output from the video pin 7 (Fig. 22-9).

Meanwhile the CRT controller has been outputting horizontal and vertical sync information through logic and shift registers too. The horizontal information exits pin 8 and the vertical information through pin 9. Pin 6 provides the brightness signal for the video.

The output pins of the monochrome card (Fig. 22-9) if probed with an ordinary TV scope, will show all the signals. You can view the video, the horizontal sync and the vertical sync. The card is really a form of digital-to-analog converter. It converts digital bits to analog TV signals.

A color/graphics card

A color/graphics card has the same type of circuits as the monochrome card, plus color and graphics. Various cards that fit into the IBM PC from other manufacturers have all sorts of other features too. The card IBM provides contains the circuits shown in Fig. 22-10.

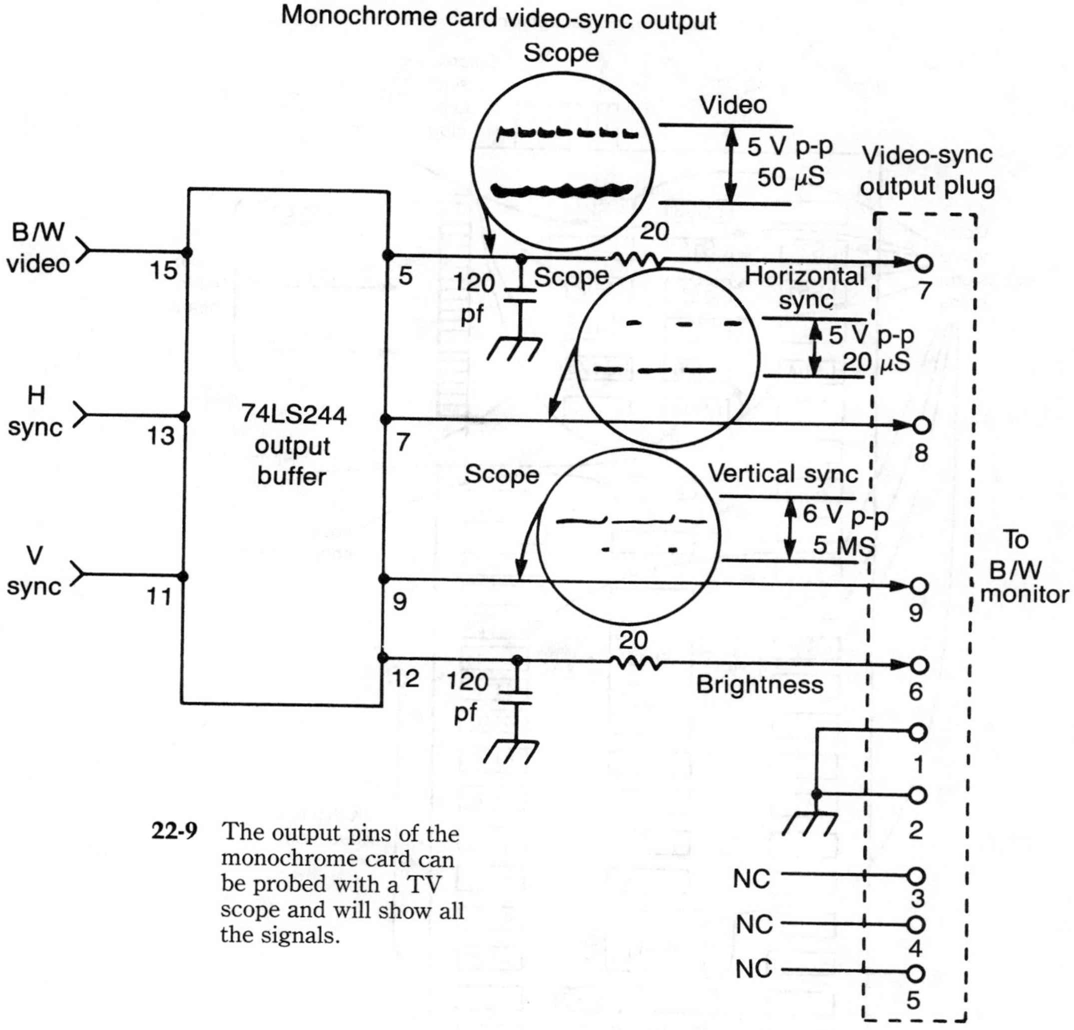

22-9 The output pins of the monochrome card can be probed with a TV scope and will show all the signals.

Another 6845 CRT video processor handles the input from the computer. The video RAM though, is dynamic rather than static and as a result operates in a slower manner. About the only obvious problem with the slower RAM is some blinking during scrolling. The RAM can hold 16K bytes. It is addressed with 14 address lines, A13 – A0. The starting address is B8000. The locations are accessed through four multiplex chips.

The dynamic RAM outputs its contents to an MK-36000 character ROM. The ROM outputs to a number of logic and shift register chips. The outputs are sent to the same type of 9-pin DIN (Deutsche Industrie Norm) connector.

Figure 22-11 shows that pins 3, 4, and 5 output the color TV signal red, green and blue. Pin 6 is the intensity or brightness signal. Pin 7 is unused. Pins 8 and 9

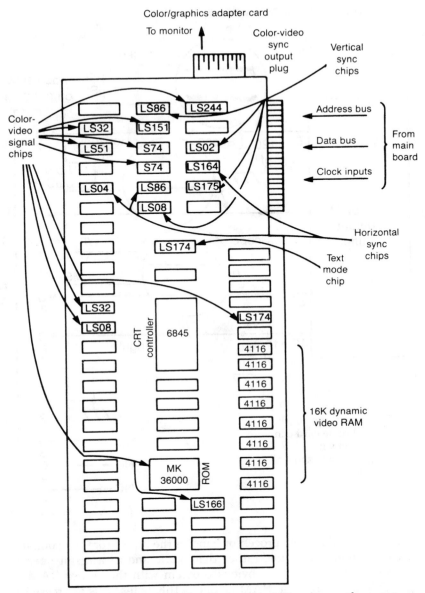

22-10 The color/graphics adapter card operates in a similar way as the monochrome card but with the addition of color.

are the horizontal and vertical sync. These signals are called the color direct. They plug into an IBM color monitor.

In addition to these signals for the monitor, the color/graphics card has two more optional output plugs. One is an RCA jack that provides a 1.5 V composite video signal. The three color outputs, the color burst, and clock signals are all

Color/graphics card video-sync output

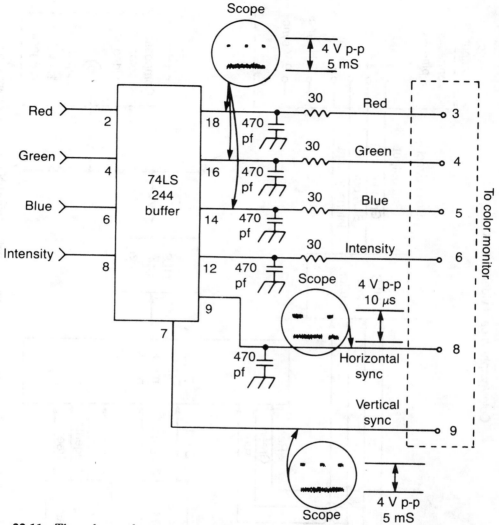

22-11 The color card outputs separate color and intensity signals. The TV scope will show pictures of the color, intensity, and sync signals.

combined in a 74LS151 multiplexer chip, fed to 74LS244 buffer and output to the RCA jack, as in Fig. 22-12.

A second optional output is on a 4-pin Berg strip. This is the same output as the RCA jack plus a tap into the +12 V power supply. This is handy if you want to connect the computer to a home TV. Another accessory, an rf modulator is needed. The rf modulator, which will output either channel 3 or 4 of the commercial broadcast band, can be plugged into this Berg strip. The rf modulator is an oscillator

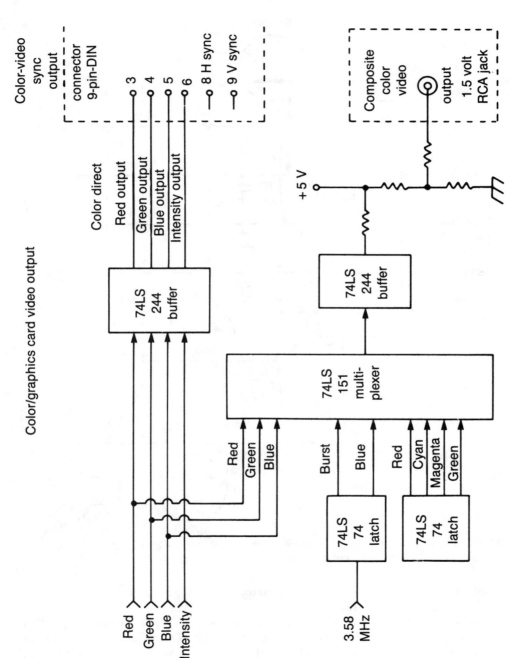

22-12 The color card, in addition to having separate color outputs through a 9-pin DIN plug, also outputs a composite color video through an RCA jack.

circuit running at channel 3 or 4. The strip provides a + 12 V supply for the oscillator and then a composite color TV signal that can be modulated. Attachment to the antenna terminals of any TV will then display the computer's video RAM contents.

Here again the ordinary TV service scope will take good pictures of the output signals of the card. The illustration (Fig. 22-11) shows the signals that will appear on the scope face when the pins are probed.

Video outputs

When the video becomes poor or disappears altogether from the monitor, the two main suspects are the monitor itself or the display adapter circuits. The best place to determine which half of the video system has conked out is the video output connector between the adapter card and the monitor. Each different video system has different connector pinouts.

In the IBM and compatible machines, there are monochrome and color displays that output both analog and digital video with a number of different horizontal and vertical sync frequencies with various resolutions. When you test for problems, you should know the characteristics of the video system you are examining. The information is in the adapter card manuals.

Monochrome

Monochrome adapter cards come in both analog and digital versions. One monochrome card is the *MDA* for (monochrome display adapter).

This display is digital and only shows text, as in Fig. 22-13. It has no graphics ability. The display is clear and has good resolution. It is relatively inexpensive and is an excellent choice for word processing and spreadsheets. However, this adapter has unusual characteristics. Its design is to expressly produce 80 characters on a line and 25 rows of text. It displays 350 raster lines on the screen which is a good number for text display. Each character is made up of a matrix of 7 dots across and 9 dots high. The characters are in a dot box 9 dots across and 14 dots high. The extra dots around the character are there to provide spaces between characters and room for ascending letters such as *t* or descending letters like *g*.

In a home TV, the vertical frequency is 60 Hz. In this adapter, the vertical frequency generated is different—it is 50 Hz. The conventional 15,750 Hz horizontal frequency is also different. It is a higher 18,432 Hz. These frequencies are the ones required to produce a text display by producing a raster with 350 lines.

Because graphics could not be generated in this card, a card was produced by another company, Hercules. This card called *HGC* (Hercules graphics controller) generates monochrome graphics when driven by appropriate software. It too produces 350 raster lines. On the lines are 750 dots across to be compatible with the MDA card. These cards connect to MDA monitors. The unconventional sync frequencies require a special monitor to accommodate the differences. The MDA connector uses a 6-pin DIN plug and has 4 signal lines as shown in Fig. 22-14. There is a TTL video, intensity, vertical sync and horizontal sync. The sync color signals are negative going.

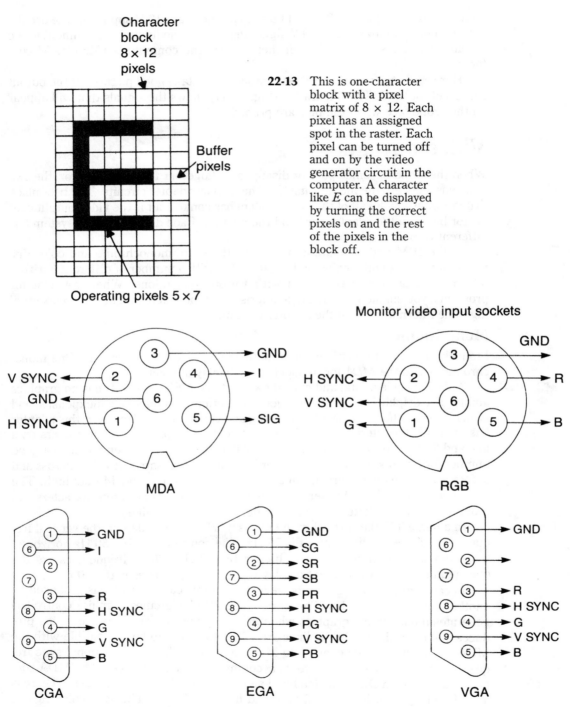

22-13 This is one-character block with a pixel matrix of 8 × 12. Each pixel has an assigned spot in the raster. Each pixel can be turned off and on by the video generator circuit in the computer. A character like *E* can be displayed by turning the correct pixels on and the rest of the pixels in the block off.

22-14 These are the typical input-plug configurations found on the various computer TV monitors.

While the monochrome cards were useful in many applications, there is also a need for color in the display. IBM released a color card about the same time, the *CGA* (color graphics adapter), discussed earlier. The CGA did not have unconventional frequencies, it has 60 Hz vertical and 15,750 Hz horizontal. The video is, like the MDA, of a digital nature. There is one unusual characteristic in the CGA signal generation.

In a home TV, the raster is formed by interlaced scanning. In the CGA, the raster is formed by progressive scanning. That is, the lines are scanned in order without regards for the odd and even numbers. The lines are drawn from 1 straight through to 240 from the top to the bottom of the screen.

The conventional sweep frequencies end up drawing only 240 lines. This forces the vertical scanning resolution to be 240. The number of card generated dots on a line is 640. There are still 80 columns of characters by 25 rows of characters. There is sometimes confusion between character resolution and card-generated dot resolution. To summarize, 80 × 25 characters is the character resolution. 640 × 200 is the dot resolution generated on the card. The CGA card produces 8 × 8 dots in a character box. (These numbers have nothing to do with the numbers of color phosphor dots on the monitor faceplate. The CRT phosphor dot-resolution ability is discussed as a separate item in the next chapter.) The CGA card is only able to generate two colors when in the 640 × 200 mode. It can produce four colors if it reduces the dot resolution to 320 × 200. It can choose from a palette of 16 colors that it is able to produce. These restrictions are due to the small amount of memory the CGA card possesses. When the card generates 640 × 200 it uses up so much of its memory that data for two colors is all it can store. When it reduces dot resolution to 320 × 200, memory is freed and four colors can be produced.

The CGA card outputs to an 8-pin DIN monitor plug shown in Fig. 22-14. There are six signal lines, one each for the primary colors red (R), green (G) and blue (B), and one for the brightness or luminance signal called I for intensity. In addition there is the vertical sync and horizontal sync both positive going voltages.

Other adapters

There are a number of other adapters that have come along since these early monochrome and color cards. There is the *RGB* (red-green-blue), *EGA* (enhanced-graphics adapter), *PGA* (professional graphics adapter), and *VGA* (video graphics array). Their characteristics are categorized in Table 22-3. In 1987, the VGA cards in both monochrome and polychrome became available. They have become very popular and have many advantages over the earlier types. VGA is an analog system and began life with a dot resolution of 640 × 480. It has been improved, can now be called *SVGA* (super video graphics array), and has card resolutions of 800 × 600 and 1024 × 768, with promises of even better numbers.

Color VGA has multiple display modes and can emulate most of the earlier display cards. Since it is analog in nature, it can display 256 colors from a palette of 256,000 colors in a 320 × 200 dot mode. VGA uses a horizontal frequency of 31,500 Hz and a variable vertical frequency that ranges from 60–70 Hz. The increased horizontal frequency can produce many more lines in a 60 Hz raster than

**Table 22-3. Typical characteristics of
the signals produced by the various video adapter cards.**

Video System	Adapter Card Resolution H × V		# of Colors	Raster Scan Rates		Analog Digital
	Horiz.	Vertical		Horiz.	Vertical	
MDA	720	350	2 shades of gray	18,432 Hz	50 Hz	Digital
HGA	720	348	4 shades of gray	18,432 Hz	50 Hz	Digital
RGB	640	480	Infinite variety all colors	15,734 Hz	60 Hz	Analog
CGA	300 640	200 200	4 of 16	15,750 Hz	60 Hz	Digital
EGA	640	200 350	16 of 64	21,800 Hz	60 Hz	Digital
PGC	720	480	256 of 4096	30,480 Hz	60-70 Hz	Analog
VGA	640	350 400 480	256 of 256,000	31,500 Hz	60-70 Hz	Analog
Super VGA	800 1024 1280	600 768 1024	256 of 256,000	35,200 Hz 37,800 Hz 48,000 Hz	56-72 Hz	Analog
Home TV	330	480	Infinite variety all colors	15,750 Hz	60 Hz	Analog

the lower frequencies. The more lines produced, the less the raster line structure can be seen.

The vertical frequency is also known as the *refresh rate*. Each vertical sync pulse occurs once during a raster scan, at the end. The sync pulse causes the scanning line to retrace from the bottom right of the screen back up to the top left, so it can begin the next raster display. It refreshes the light on the screen.

The refresh rate is important to reduce *flicker*. The human eye, can be fooled to think it is seeing a full raster of light if the scanning lines are happening fast enough. The critical number to the eye is 24. If the number of rasters per second drop below 24, the raster will have a noticeable flicker like an ancient black-and-white silent film. Above 24 rasters a second, and the flicker disappears. A refresh rate of 60 – 70 full rasters a second eliminates all traces of flicker. Add to that an increased number of lines per second and the eye thinks it is looking at a steady light without any scan lines. The video can then be installed in with the brightness to produce a clear, rock-steady display.

The VGA card outputs to a 15-pin D connector monitor plug with 8 signal lines as shown in Fig. 22-14. In addition to the usual R, G, B, vertical sync, and horizontal sync pins, there are some others. There is a self-test pin, and two monitor identification lines. The self-test line is grounded when the card is plugged in. When the cable is not connected to a computer, the video amplifiers in the monitor display a bright, white raster. This test proves the monitor can show a raster, which could in turn prove the raster maker is o.k. and if there is trouble it could be elsewhere, perhaps on the card. The monitor ID lines tells the card whether it is operating into a color or monochrome VGA monitor.

More about the VGA in depth

At this time, the VGA system has taken over the market and appears to be the dominant display system for the immediate future. The VGA is upwardly compatible with all the previous IBM video output systems. That is, it will run all the software that is around for the MCGA, CGA, EGA, Hercules graphics card and other such video outputs and monitors.

The VGA was originally developed for use in the IBM PS/2 machines. It did not appear on a card at first but was built right on the motherboard of the PS/2 models 50, 60 and 80. In the 25 and 30 models, a smaller version of the VGA named *MCGA* for (multi color graphics array) was used. There is a video connector on the rear panel of these machines that the monitor can plug into.

Shortly after it was introduced as a motherboard built in, the VGA appeared on cards. IBM introduced a Micro Channel card and called it the 8514 adapter. There is a top-of-the-line IBM 8514 color monitor the card was designed to operate into. Since then there are all sorts of VGA cards available from second sources. If you are going to buy an IBM or compatible, odds are you will end up with a VGA system.

Typical VGA modes

Table 22-4 shows the modes the VGA adapters will put out. For showing monochrome text, the card simply provides an 80 column by 25 row of character boxes. For color text it shows two displays, an 80 × 25 and a 40 × 25 set of character boxes. It is able to produce 16 distinct colors in this mode. In addition for both monochrome and color, the card can provide a 132 × 25 and also a 132 × 43 text character box matrix.

VGA can emulate the older CGA graphics card. It can produce a dot structure of 320 horizontal and 200 vertical with four colors. It also is able to show the higher resolution 640 × 200 dot matrix but only with two colors. However, the two dot matrixes are both double scanned and display 400 lines on the screen.

The VGA emulation of the Hercules monochrome graphics provides a dot resolution of 720 × 348. The VGA emulation of the EGA card gives resolutions that

**Table 22-4. A listing of the
many modes the VGA card can assume.**

Mode	Resolution	Colors
Monochrome text	80 columns × 25 rows	Off P on (monochrome)
Color text	80 columns × 25 rows 40 columns × 25 rows	16 16
132 column text	132 columns × 25 rows 132 columns × 43 rows	16 16
CGA graphics	320 × 200, double scanned 640 × 200, double scanned	4 2
Hercules graphics	720 × 348	Off & on (monochrome)
EGA graphics	320 × 200, double scanned 640 × 200, double scanned 640 × 350 640 × 350	16 16 64 Off & on (monochrome)
VGA graphics (included McGa)	320 × 200, double scanned 640 × 480 640 × 480	256 2 16
Extended graphics	800 × 600	16

range from 320 × 200 to 640 × 350 with the lower resolutions able to show 16 colors and the higher one 64 colors.

Then there are the native VGA modes, 320 × 200 up to 640 × 480, with the former having 256 available colors and the latter 16 colors. In addition, VGA cards are capable of some extended graphics. For example, a resolution of 800 × 400 can be had with 16 colors. There are others on different VGA cards. These extended graphics would require special software drivers and monitors such as the multifrequency monitors discussed in the next chapter. The individual documentation software with the extended graphics cards provide the ability to use these extended graphics.

There are a number of different size character boxes that appear with the different modes. They range from an 8 × 8 matrix to 9 × 16. The 8 × 8 boxes are usually found accompanying the 320 × 200 dot pixel resolutions and the 9 × 16 with the 720 × 350, with the other types in between.

The VGA main actors

There is a large chip called the VGA *IC* (integrated circuit). It is the main actor in the VGA card system. The first supporting role is played by the video RAM that is placed in 256K of memory chips on the card instead of in the main system memory.

Then there are the dot clock, a CRT controller, sequencer, graphics controller, attribute controller, and a *DAC* (digital-to-analog converter). Somewhere in the system there is usually a character ROM that contains the different character shapes that are to appear on the screen.

The VGA IC is in control and is the interface between the microprocessor and the video RAM. The processor cannot write directly to the video RAM. All data must pass through the VGA IC interface. This writing control is necessary to maintain the correct timing between the processor and the video RAM. If the timing goes awry, during the sweep retrace periods, hash could appear in the display.

The video RAM is layed out in four sections, each with 64K bytes. The starting address for these memory sections can be programmed to three different values. With this addressing flexibility, the VGA is able to be compatible with all of the other adapter cards it can emulate.

The dot clock is timed by two crystals. One crystal is cut to run at 25.175 MHz and the other at 28.322 MHz. The choice of clock is made when the desired mode is chosen by the ROM BIOS of the system. The BIOS places a 1 or 0 into a sequencer register. The low frequency produces timing for characters that are 8 bits wide and the higher frequency generates 9-bit wide characters.

The CRT controller does the following. One, the video RAM chips in the VGA are dynamic. They need constant refreshing. The CRT controller constantly addresses them, keeping their contents safe. Second, the addresses of the incoming video data are generated by the controller. Next are two timing functions. The attributes of cursor control and underlining must be timed correctly. Also the horizontal and vertical sync signals must be timed exactly. The CRT controller takes care of these functions.

The sequencer circuits produce the timing for the VGA cycles. The video RAM works according to the character clock to show the display. The display time in turn is used to control the reading of the data from the memory that contains character and attribute information for the text modes. For the text modes each character has two bytes, one for the character code and the second for the attributes that go with that character. These are attributes such as blinking, reversing of character and background lighting, etc. The sequencer performs the timing chores for these sections of video RAM. If the timing is off, the display will show a lot of interference.

While the sequencer handles the video RAM timing, the graphics controller handles the movement of the RAM data. During the time the processor is reading or writing to the video RAM the graphics controller connects the video RAM to the system data bus. Then when the cycle changes and the display information from the video RAM is to be output, the graphics controller connects the RAM to the attribute controller.

Once the data is output to the attribute controller, it is processed for final output to the digital-to-analog converter. There are a number of attributes that can be displayed. There is the blink bit, which turns dots on and off, there is the attribute of underlining, that shows characters with lines under them, then there are the colors that the characters should be displayed in.

The VGA always uses a color palette that is 8-bits wide. CGA emulation uses 4 bits. EGA emulation uses 6 bits. The color bit sections are used as a pointer to generate the desired color. In the digital-to-analog circuits there is a section of memory called a *look-up* table. There are 256 addresses in the table. When the pointer contacts a table entry, an 18-bit value is generated. This is sent to the digital-to-analog converter. The digital bits are converted to an analog signal. The 18 bits are actually three 6-bit values, each 6 bits assigned to a color—red, green, and blue. These color signals are then sent on to the monitor.

In addition to the color signals, the DAC generates a blanking signal to turn the raster off during the horizontal and vertical sync pulses, so they do not appear on the screen and cause interference. Each register in the look-up table can be accessed by the processor directly without using any other system in the computer. As a result the system ROM BIOS is able to exercise strong control over the video output.

The text characters are displayed by using a character generator in the VGA system. The character-generator memory can be loaded as RAM with as many as eight 256 character fonts or four 512 character sets. When a text mode is selected, one of the character fonts from a character ROM chip is loaded into the character generator. If the fonts in the character ROM are unsatisfactory, special user fonts can be loaded instead.

VGA registers

Most of the time the many registers in the VGA system, built in to the motherboard or on an adapter card, are set and reset by the system ROM BIOS. However, the registers can also be written to or read from by a user or troubleshooter. The registers are distributed in five categories. There are attribute registers, CRT controller registers, sequencer registers, graphics registers, and general-purpose registers.

Attribute registers

There are seven attribute registers. First there is the attribute-address register. This is a two-way read/write set of bit holders that are used to contain the pointers for a second attribute-data register and the palette registers. There are 16 palette registers that can be read or written to. Each palette register contains 6 bits that acts as a pointer into the digital-to-analog converter.

The next read/write color-select register contains data to change colors in the DAC output. The attribute mode-control register is used to choose between monochrome and color modes and also between text and graphics. BIOS usually sets the mode. The read/write overscan register is used to set the color for the border in some of the color modes. The color-plane enable register is used to turn on or turn off color bit planes in the video RAM.

Finally the horizontal PEL-planning register in the attribute registers is a read/write type. It is used to pan the picture to the left. This register determines the number of dots the picture will be moved. The movement can be up to eight dots at a time except in the 256 color mode, only three dots at a time.

CRT controller registers

In the CRT controller there are 26 registers that are needed to properly place the display on the face of the picture tube in the monitor. They are the CRTC address register that all the rest of the controller registers are counted off from. The horizontal-total register and the start and stop horizontal retrace registers determine the timing for the horizontal and vertical retrace periods. These registers contain the exact timing which is five less than the number of characters in one horizontal scan line plus the retrace period. The horizontal display enable end register contains the number of characters less one, on a scan line. The offset register contains the line width of the display.

The start and stop horizontal blanking registers determine the timing of the horizontal blanking during retrace. The vertical retrace start and end registers control the vertical retrace period, while the vertical total register holds the total number of horizontal scan lines in a display, less two.

The vertical display enable end register controls the end of the rastered display. The start and end vertical blanking registers control the end of the vertical blanking period. The CRT controller overflow register is used to hold any excess bits that might not fit into other registers. For example, the vertical retrace start or the vertical display end could have more bits than it can hold. This overflow register will hold them so the bits are not lost and the display can be placed on the phosphor screen correctly.

The start address high and the start address low registers start the raster after the vertical retrace period. The preset row scan register is set to display the first scan row after the vertical retrace period. The maximum scan register is the one that originates the 400 scan line display. In addition it determines the number of scan lines that each character is built on.

The cursor start and end and the cursor location high and low registers control the location of the cursor on the screen. The underline location register controls the location of underlined characters on the screen. The line-compare register is used to scroll the display. It is capable of just scrolling part of the display and leaving other parts holding still.

The mode-control register in the CRT controller does a number of jobs. It can be used to divide the vertical timing clock by two and double the vertical resolution of the CRT controller. In addition, it has a special bit to give the VGA card compatibility with the older CGA card. It can be used to turn on the horizontal or vertical retrace. Besides that it can be used to select byte, word and double word addressing.

Sequencer registers

The VGA system has six sequencer registers. The sequencer address register is used as the master addresser to the rest of the sequencer locations. This register must be used to access the other registers. The reset register can be set in one of two modes. They are synchronous and asynchronous. The synchronous mode, when set, causes the sequencer to shut down and clears all the bits in an orderly fashion. The asynchronous mode reset is more of an emergency measure and shuts the register down instantly. The shock of doing this could cause the loss of video RAM data. When the cause of the reset is eliminated, the sequencer can be set once again by setting both of the reset bits.

There is a clocking-mode register in the sequencer group. It can turn off the picture. This is useful when a lot of data must be loaded into the video RAM. The data can be put into RAM much faster if the screen is off and does not need constant refreshing. This allows the sequencer output register to be loaded with a byte, a word or a double word every single character clock. Another job the clocking mode can do is to set the sequencer to generate the 9 dots per character clock for those modes that require 9 dots instead of 8 dots.

There is a map-mask register that can be used along with a memory-mode register. This combination permits any of the video bit maps to be turned on and off so they can be written to by the processor. In addition the memory-mode register allows more than 64K of the video RAM to be accessed. This, in turn, opens the door to the rest of the 256K that is found in the VGA system. There is a character map select register that provides access to the various character maps that are being used.

Graphics registers

The graphics controller uses nine registers. The key register for the graphics is called the graphics-address register. In the same way the attribute, CRT controller and sequencer address registers are used, the graphics-address register also operates. It is the pointer to the other graphics registers.

The set/reset register is needed to work with the enable set/reset to select among the various memory maps that are being used. Then there is the read-map select register that lets the processor know which map to read. In addition there is a color-compare register that tells the processor about all of the dots on a memory map that have a particular designed color. Next is the data-rotate register. This register is able to manipulate the data in the video RAM. It is able to rotate the data from the processor to the VGA circuits to the right. It can also AND, OR, and Exclusive OR the data in the video RAM.

A graphics-mode register is there to load the shift registers properly so they can conduct the 256 color mode. In addition these registers set up the shift registers to handle the CGA compatibility. The scan lines are stored in two sections of the video RAM, one memory section for the odd number lines and the other for the even number lines. This register stores the video dot information in with the scan line data. This register also directs the processor to read either the color compare function results or the data in the selected memory map.

The graphics-mode register also performs other jobs. These are specific write operations from the processor to the VGA system. One write job is conducted by a miscellaneous register in the graphics-mode register area, that controls the size of the memory maps for the dot data that is written to the parts of video RAM that contains the character and attribute data for text modes. Another write job is to set a bit in this register and bits in the graphics-mode register so the video modes that store video dot data with odd and even scan lines are controlled. In addition, this register is needed to change modes between text and graphics.

A color don't-care register is associated with the color compare register, mentioned above, to select desired memory maps. A bit-mask register can hide any bit so it cannot be accessed by the processor.

General-purpose registers

The VGA system was designed by IBM with five general purpose registers. One original register, the feature-control register has some future IBM purpose. Then there are two read only input-status registers that store data on the VGA status. The data could tell about the status of the CRT interrupt which is a vertical retrace due signal, a switch sense bit which tells the processor whether a monochrome or polychrome monitor is being used, and whether or not a picture is being displayed.

A video subsystem enable register permits video and I/O decoding. A miscellaneous-output register has the job of selecting the polarity of the horizontal and vertical sync pulses. This is needed when different numbers of scan lines are used in the display.

The miscellaneous-output register also chooses the clock rates for the VGA operation. There is a choice of two clocks, one for the 640 horizontal dot display and the other for the 720 dot mode. Also a non-VGA clock can be set or reset by a bit in this register. In addition, the I/O addresses for the CGA compatibility and the monochrome monitor are chosen by this register. Finally, this register can turn the video RAM off and on.

The VGA system operates in a general way like its predecessors but more so. It is nothing more than the transmitter section of a closed circuit TV system with the monitor being the receiver section. The VGA is fed digital data that is code for video. The VGA generates a signal with horizontal and vertical sweep information. The video data from the keyboard or input through the disk drive is then loaded into the VGA generated signal and the whole works output to the receiver. The next chapter deals with the receiver section of the special closed-circuit TV display system.

Audio outputs

There are all sorts of audio outputs from personal computers. The systems can be simple or complex. The noises generated in a computer can vary from simple clicks through sirens, explosions, music, and even speech. The sounds are usually devised in software. In the last chapter the programming of sound circuit to produce a siren-like noise was explained. This circuit was one that produced the sound and then output it to a TV where it activated a speaker. The computer itself did not have a speaker. The IBM and some of its clones, though, have their own speaker and audio circuits (Fig. 22-15).

The audio circuit that will respond to the data in a program like BASIC, as well as the machine language, works through four chips. The speaker itself is driven by a 75477 relay driver chip. The relay driver amplifies incoming bit signals and the

IBM PC Type Audio System

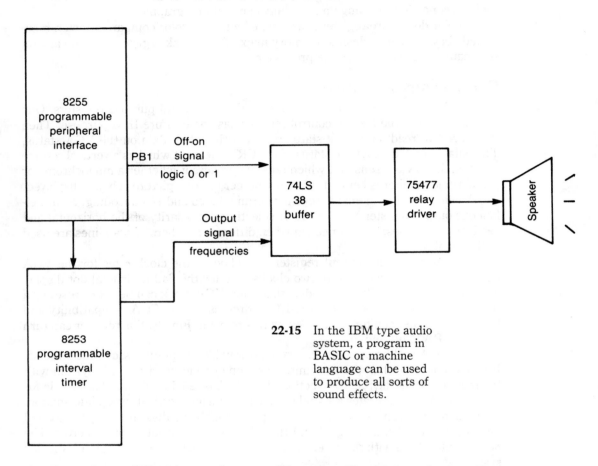

22-15 In the IBM type audio system, a program in BASIC or machine language can be used to produce all sorts of sound effects.

signals can be applied to the speaker cone. The cone will move in and out producing loud clicks. By controlling the frequency of the movement you can produce a wide range of sounds. BASIC can produce a range up to about 1000 Hz while machine language can produce sounds up to 3000 Hz.

There is a programmable peripheral interface chip, an 8255 that uses one of its output port pins (pin 1) as an off-on switch for the audio. That pin can output a high or a low if it is addressed at hex 0061. A high turns the speaker system on and a low turns it off. This is one of the software controls. This is called the speaker enable and the signal is connected to a pin on a 74LS38 NAND buffer.

Meanwhile, there is a signal from an 8253 Programmable Interval Timer that is also inputting a signal to the NAND buffer. This signal is also software controlled. When the two are both on, the buffer will output to the relay driver. The speaker will respond according to the buffer output. The audio frequencies will be a result of the off-on signal from the PPI and the output of the PIT. A third contributor to the final sound can be the clock signal that is also applied to the PIT.

Special audio chips

Some personal computers that are designed to produce wide ranges of audio will have special large chips that are designed to produce these sounds. One such chip (Fig. 22-16) is the *sound interface device*, known as SID. The chip is installed in the memory map in the same way that a ROM is. It is connected to the processor through the address, data, and control bus lines. The chip can be completely con-

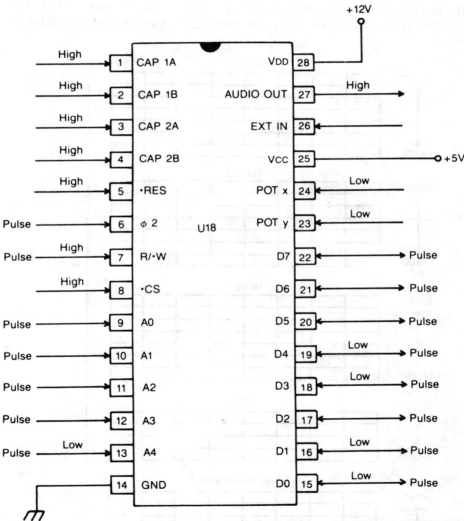

22-16 A specially designed sound chip like this *SID* (sound-interface device), needs only connections to the processor to produce sound effects. This test point pinout chart shows the signals present on a SID that is energized but not producing any sounds. These chips are found in many Commodore computer models.

trolled by software. It has 29 addressable byte-sized registers (shown in Fig. 22-17). The registers consist of 25 write-only and four read-only registers. Besides using machine language, the registers can be written to in BASIC with POKE statements or read with a PEEK function.

The SID chip registers are divided into five sets. There are three sets of voice registers, one set of registers for a filter and one odd-job set. The voice and filter registers are all write-only. The four odd-job registers are read-only. The registers are all byte sized.

The bits in the registers control the circuits that generate the audio output. The bits can be likened to push buttons on a control board to produce sound effects and other related functions. There are seven registers assigned to each of the three voices.

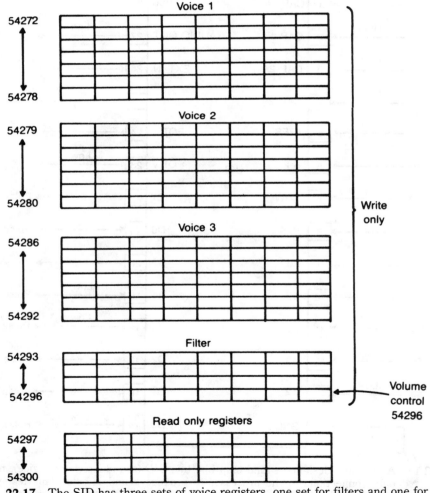

22-17 The SID has three sets of voice registers, one set for filters and one for read only purposes.

The first voice

Of the seven registers in Fig. 22-18, there are two to control the frequency. They are wired together and one controls the *frequency high* while the other controls *frequency low*. They form a 16-bit frequency register. Each voice contains a tone oscillator circuit. If you POKE a decimal number into the 16-bit register the SID chip will generate a musical note. In an SID user's guide, there is a table of numbers and what musical notes they will generate.

Two more registers are called *pulse-width high* and *pulse-width low*. These two registers are also wired together to form another 16-bit register. However, only 12 of the 16 bits are used. The four highest bits are unused. This 12-bit register is used to control the pulse width of the waveform generated in the tone oscillator. This permits the audio output frequency changes to be smooth as the tone varies.

The pulse can vary from a constant dc output at one extreme to a square wave with equal highs and lows at the other extreme. To produce a constant low, 000000000000 can be placed in the 12 bits. A constant dc high can be achieved with 000011111111 in the register. A square wave requires 010000000000. Other binary bit lineups will produce pulses in between the two exchanges.

The other three registers in the voice are one voice control register, one attack-decay register, and a sustain-release register. Examine their operation.

The voice-control register

The eight bits in this register (Fig. 22-19) make the tone oscillator do tricks. Bit 0 is called the gate bit. When the bit is a 1, an envelope generator on the chip is turned on. This begins the attack-decay/sustain cycle, seen in Fig. 22-20 and discussed in the next section. A 0 in this bit allows the release cycle to take over.

Bit 1 is the SYNC. When it is set to a 1, the tone oscillator in voice 1 is synchronized with the tone oscillator in voice 3. This produces harmonic sounds.

Bit 3 is the test bit. When it is set to a 1 it resets and locks the tone oscillator at zero. It also resets the noise waveform of the oscillator and the pulse waveform is placed at a steady dc level. This positioning is needed for program tests. It is also needed by the programmer so he may be able to synchronize the oscillator with sound external to SID.

Bit 4 when set to a 1 is the control that turns on the triangle waveform in the tone oscillator. The triangle waveform is the means by which SID is able to imitate a flute.

Bit 5 when set to a 1 is the sawtooth waveform the oscillator can produce. It can imitate a brass instrument. Bit 6 turns on the pulse waveform in the oscillator. Then the Pulse Width can be used as discussed before. These different waveshapes permit SID to emit all types of interesting sounds from a booming hollow sound to a squeaky peep.

Bit 7 is the noise output. Noise is a very important output. Besides being able to be adjusted to produce rumbling, hissing, explosions, windstorms, drums and cymbals, it can be used as a random number generator. Noise is truly random and if the pulses are converted to numbers, the numbers will be random.

Register	Name	Bit 7	Bit 6	Bit 5	Bit 4	Bit 3	Bit 2	Bit 1	Bit 0
Voice 1									
54272	Frequency low	7	6	5	4	3	2	1	0
54273	Frequency high	15	14	13	12	11	10	9	8
54274	Pulse width low	7	6	5	4	3	2	1	0
54275	Pulse width high	—	—	—	—	11	10	9	8
54276	Voice control	7 ⌇	6 ⊓⊔	5 ⟋	4 ⋀	3 Test	2 Ring mod	1 Sync	0 Gate
54277	Attack-decay	3	2	1 (Attack)	0	3	2	1 (Decay)	0
54278	Sustain-release	3	2	1 (Sustain)	0	3	2	1 (Release)	0
Voice 2									
54279									

22-18 In voice 1 of SID, these registers produce sound signals.

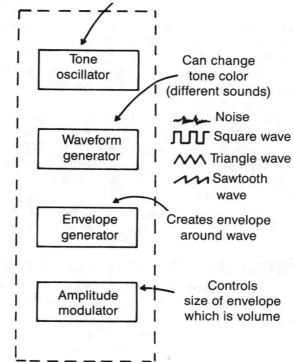

Can change frequencies
(pitch of voice)

22-19 The registers act as an audio control panel for these circuits—a tone oscillator, a waveform generator, an envelope generator, and an amplitude generator.

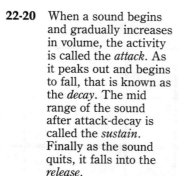

22-20 When a sound begins and gradually increases in volume, the activity is called the *attack*. As it peaks out and begins to fall, that is known as the *decay*. The mid range of the sound after attack-decay is called the *sustain*. Finally as the sound quits, it falls into the *release*.

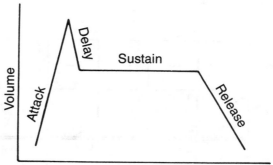

The envelope registers

The attack-decay register and the sustain release register control the envelope generator circuits on SID. In audio work, when a sound begins and rises in volume, the event is called the attack rate of volume. When the volume rises to its peak and then falls in volume, this movement is called the decay. There is an 8-bit register in the voice that controls the envelope generator to cause the attack and the decay. The four highest bits are the attack bits. The four lowest bits are the decay bits.

If the decay does not fall to zero volume but maintains some mid range for a while, that mid range is called the sustain. Sustain is a volume level. When the sound finally quits, it falls to dead silence, no volume. The rate at which the volume falls to nothing is called the release. Figure 22-20 illustrates the attack-decay/sustain-release concept.

There is a companion register to the attack-decay register called the sustain-release register. The higher four bits are used for the sustain control and the lower four bits control the release.

The two other voices and their seven registers are essentially identical to the first voice. When an expert programmer goes to work with a SID chip, he can produce some truly amazing sound effects. The SID is often used in arcade machines.

When the voices are operated, the first step is to select the frequency you want to produce. Next, there is the choice of the wave shape. Third, you must pick out the effect that is needed. This is done with the SYNC and Ring Mod bits. The envelope rates are decided after that. The decision of when to turn on the sound or turn it off is last. The voices can be used as solos or as a choir.

Filters and mode/volume registers

Of the 29 addressable registers, the voices use up 21. There are four more write-only registers (Fig. 22-21). Three of them are filters. Two of them set the frequency range the SID chip will produce. The available range is 30 Hz to 12 kHz. The two filter registers are called FC LOW and FC HIGH. They are combined to form a 16-bit register. They set the cutoff points of 30 Hz on the low side and 12 kHz on the high side. Only 11 bits are needed to do the job so bits 3 – 7 of the FC LOW byte remain unused.

Filter

54293	—	—	—	—	2	1	0		FC low
54294	10	9	8	7	6	5	4	3	FC high
54295	3	2 (Resonance)	1	0	External in filter	3 Filter 3	2 Filter 2	1 Filter 1	Resonance filter
54296	Voice 3 off-on switch	High pass	Band pass	Low pass	Volume 3	Volume 2	Volume 1	Volume 0	Mode volume

22-21 The filter sets up the cutoff range of the audio between 30 Hz and 12 kHz.

Writing bits to the filter tunes it and the filter will resonate at a particular frequency. This gives the tuned frequency a sharper sound as the sounds in that range are emphasized.

The third filter is called RES/FILT. The four higher bits are able to tune to one particular frequency. The four lower bits act as a switch to route the sounds of the different voices and any audio input to the SID. Bit 0 routes voice 1 either through the filter with a 1, or around the filter, directly to the audio output pin with a 0. Bits 1 and 2 perform the same job for the other two voices. Bit 3 routes any external audio input to SID either through a filter or bypasses the audio around the filter.

The last write-only register is called MODE/VOLUME. The register is separated into two nibbles. The higher nibble, bits 7-4, can be programmed for the filter's mode of operation. Bit 4 is the LP bit. When bit 4 is set to a 1 the low-pass mode of the filter is used. All frequencies below 30 Hz are passed as is. The frequencies above 30 Hz are attenuated. This produces hearty sounds.

Bit 5 is called BP for bandpass outputs. The passband for the audio output is between 30 Hz and 12 kHz. When bit 5 is set to a 1, the frequencies in the passband are allowed through and the frequencies above and below the band are attenuated. This mode produces normal sound with no harmonic content.

Bit 6 is the high-pass output, HP. All the frequencies that are above 12 kHz are passed as is. All the frequencies below 12 kHz are attenuated when the bit is set to a 1. The sound in this mode is tinny. Bit 7 is the off-on switch for the third voice. When it is set to a 1, the third voice is disconnected from the circuit.

The lower nibble of the register is the volume part. Bits 3 – 0 are able to choose between 16 levels of volume that will emanate from the audio output. If you write 0000 to these bits, the volume will be cut off. A bit set of 1111 produces maximum volume. The bit levels in between produce varying levels of volume.

The preceding 25 registers were all programmable, that is, you can write bits to any of them either with BASIC POKEs or with machine language. This ability is very useful during troubleshooting. The chip can be exercised in detail with a simple little diagnostic program. The last four registers in the SID chip are read-only. These registers are not like a ROM. A ROM has permanent program lines burnt into its registers. These SID registers do not have permanent bits. They are ordinary RAM registers. They are fed data from the SID and record the progress of operations. When they are read, they report results.

The pot registers

There are two registers where the positions of the two POTs, x and y, are stored (Fig. 22-22). The input to the register for POT x is pin 24. As the potentiometer is varied a dc voltage is varied. The voltage enters an analog-to-digital circuit that changes the voltage from a single dc value to a relative binary number between 00000000 and 11111111. The zeros represent minimum resistance and the ones maximum resistance of the pot settings.

Read only

	7	6	5	4	3	2	1	0	
54297	7	6	5	4	3	2	1	0	Pot x
54298	7	6	5	4	3	2	1	0	Pot y
54299	7	6	5	4	3	2	1	0	OSC3 random
54300	7	6	5	4	3	2	1	0	Envelope 3

22-22   All of the registers mentioned above are write only. These four are read only.

The binary values are stored in POT register x. The value that can be read out of the register is always the current pot setting that is updated every 512 $\phi2$ clocks when the SID is working with a 6502 processor. POT y works in exactly the same way except the input to SID is pin 23.

OSC 3/random register

Computers need some sort of random number generator as one of their staple items. When a computer has an SID chip, it can use this register to generate random binary numbers. Noise is a true random sound. If a noise waveform is generated in the third voice by setting the noise bit to a 1, this read-only register will record the constantly changing noise as constantly changing binary bits. This register stores the upper eight bits of the third voice tone oscillator. These bits are thus the result of the changing noise waveform that the oscillator generates. The random binary numbers can then be read by the processor and used in programs as random numbers.

Besides being a random number generator, this register can also be used for many timing or sequencing purposes. Because this register is constantly changing and recording the upper eight bits of the third voice, different waveforms will produce different types of changing number sets. If bit 5 of the control register is set, then the oscillator will go into generating a sawtooth in the third voice.

This read-only register will then have its bits changing in a regular pattern starting 00000000, going to 11111111 and then repeating the count over and over again. Should bit 4 of the control register become set to 1, the triangle waveform will drive the bits in the OSC 3/RANDOM register. The register will then count in a slightly different manner. It will begin the same way by counting from 00000000 to 11111111. Then instead of starting over at 00000000 and continuing to increment, it will instead count backwards to 11111110, 11111101, etc., until it reaches 00000000 again. At that time it will start incrementing again.

The register can produce a set of changing bits that designate a square wave, too. A square wave goes from high to low and back and so on. The register codes this in bits by going from 11111111 directly to 00000000 in response to a high that goes to low. Just as the square wave has no gradations between the high and low, the register, in turn, does not record any binary numbers that represent in between states either.

This register acts as a modulation generator. The binary bit patterns that can be generated by changing around the input waveforms, can be used in a program to produce all kinds of interesting sound effects. The speaker will emanate sirens, moaning, groaning, and many other familiar sounds. The OSC 3/RANDOM register operates in a smooth manner with the pulse-width registers, the filters, and the oscillator.

The ENV 3 register

The final read-only register is the ENV for envelope. This register records for the processor the output of the third voice envelope generator when it is running. The bit patterns produced in this register can then be added to the other registers for additional sound effects.

Quick testing the SID chip

You can test the SID chip if the computer is operating o.k. except for sound trouble. Each register has an address. If you set up a voice, turn it on and hear a tone, chances are good that the chip is fine. If the voice won't sound off then trouble is indicated.

To set up a voice (as seen in Fig. 22-23) first you turn on the volume as high as

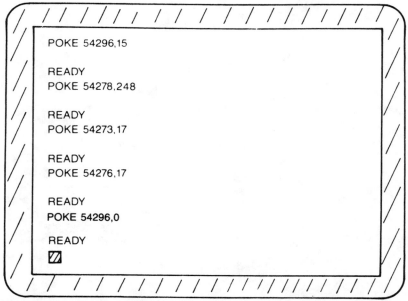

```
POKE 54296,15

READY
POKE 54278,248

READY
POKE 54273,17

READY
POKE 54276,17

READY
POKE 54296,0

READY
```

22-23 This Commodore SID chip can be tested quickly with this little BASIC POKE test. Test produces a tone from voice 1 and then turns it off.

possible. If you are testing in BASIC and the volume control is at decimal address 54296, you can POKE 54296 with a decimal 15. Decimal 15 sends its binary code 00001111 to the volume control. The control is set loud.

Next you set the attack-decay/sustain-release register. The address could be 54278 and the decimal bit data pattern, is 248. Next you can set a register for a high frequency range. The POKE is 54273,17. A fourth POKE 54276,17 sets bit 5 so the sawtooth waveform will be heard.

As soon as you set the sawtooth, a good loud and clear note should be heard from the speaker if the voice is good. If it does not sound off then the SID could be in trouble.

To turn off the note POKE 54296,0 the volume control again. The decimal 0, 00000000 in binary will clear the register and turn off the note. For a complete checkout, use the same test steps but change the register addresses for the other voices.

23
Video-display repair techniques

THE VIDEO DISPLAY SYSTEMS DISCUSSED IN THE PREVIOUS CHAPTER ARE forms of closed-circuit TV transmitters. Their job is to take the results of the digital computing that takes place in the digital world and place them onto the raster that is generated in the TV display monitor. The monitor is the TV receiver.

In the previous chapter, you saw that the transmitter circuits generated signals that had various horizontal and sync frequencies and video. The video could be made as monochrome, color, and with digital or analog natures. The transmitter then passed the completed signal onto the monitor for display.

When microcomputers first arrived on the scene in the 1970s, the generated signals and monitors were little more than abbreviated TV receivers. The generated signal was a replica of the signal developed at commercial TV stations. The computers sold in the U.S. used the NTSC signal. The European computers used the PAL signal. Today, the computer-generated signal takes many forms. As discussed, in addition to the NTSC and PAL composite monochrome or color signals, there is RGB, MDA, CGA, EGA, VGA, and others. As the generated signals were improved with many changes and enhancements, the original computer TV monitors would not work very well with new video output circuits. As a result, new kinds of TV monitors had to be designed and manufactured.

Today, besides the original monochrome and color monitors that display NTSC and PAL signals, there are many other monitors. They are built to be compatible with the new video adapter cards and are often sold with the cards as a system. The common types that have become popular are mentioned in the previous chapter. As examples, in this chapter you will cover the original monitor types first and then discuss some of the other monitors.

Adapter-card resolution

The most important reason computer video adapter card circuits and the monitors had to be improved, is an exploding demand for better and better picture resolution. In the previous chapter, the newer adapter cards were shown to produce improved resolution. From the viewpoint of the adapter circuits, resolution is defined as the number of light dots horizontally versus the number of dots vertically. For example, a typical high resolution generated on a card could be 640 × 480. The light dots (commonly known as *pixels*, which is a contraction of the words *picture* and *elements*), could come in many matrixes. A low resolution could be broadcast TV 330 × 480. A very high resolution could be 1024 × 1024, known as 1K × 1K. Even higher resolutions could be 2K × 2K or 4K × 4K. These are pixel resolutions that are generated on the adapter card. The adapter card resolution is only restricted by the circuits on the card. The ability of the monitor to display the generated resolution is another story.

The circuit card resolution is determined by three characteristics shown in Table 23-1. One is the number of pixels it can generate. Two is the vertical sweep frequency, or as it is called, the refresh rate. If the refresh rate is too slow, the human eye will see flicker. The higher the rate, the less flicker. The third characteristic is the horizontal frequency and type of scanning. If the horizontal frequency is increased, more horizontal lines will be scanned, the line structure will not be seen. In addition if progressive scanning, one line after another without regard for line numbers, is used instead of interlaced scanning, odd-numbered lines then even-numbered lines, the picture will have improved resolution.

Aside from these characteristics, the card cannot do any more to improve resolution. Further improvements have to come from the display monitor.

Table 23-1. The viewable resolution of the display is dependent on the adapter card and the TV monitor both contributing these good characteristics.

Generated by Adapter Cards	Generated by Monitor
Defined as, # of horizontal dots versus # of vertical dots	Defined as, result of electron beam spot size impinging on phosphor dot size
1—# of pixels generated 2—Vertical frequency (refresh rate) 3—Horiz. frequency (# of lines, type of scanning)	1—Dot pitch 2—Focus ability of CRT 3—Improved bandwidth ability

Monitor resolution

With the transmitter card sending signals with high pixel matrixes, higher than conventional refresh rates, and higher horizontal frequencies, the monitor must take these resolution enhancers and add some of its own. The monitor can display high resolution, fine-detailed pictures by improving three of its characteristics. First of all there is dot pitch. In a color display, there are three types of phosphor—red, green and blue—deposited on the inside of the faceplate. In some color CRTs, the phosphors are deposited as dots and in other CRTs as stripes. The phosphors are arranged in *triads*. There are three electron beams, one each for red, green, and blue. The beams are aimed at their respective color phosphors. When the beams hit the phosphor targets, the phosphors light and the three color lights add together. Your eye sees the resultant color that is developed.

The dot pitch is the distance between the color dot triads, center to center. The closer together the triads are placed, the better the total picture will appear to your eye. As a result, color CRT manufacturers attempt to make the dot pitch as tiny as possible. Typical dot pitches in high resolution CRTs are measured as 0.41 millimeters, 0.31 millimeters, 0.21 millimeters, and so on. Tiny dot pitches are vital to producing high resolution. No matter how good a video card might generate a high-resolution pixel matrix, if the dot pitch of the CRT is too large, the display will not show high resolution.

It works out that if there are many tiny triads lighting up one card developed pixel, the resolution will be excellent. The fine detail in the display will show up nicely like a color photo. On the other hand, should the card pixel be smaller than a single triad, the resolution of the picture will be poor. The display will have an annoying grainy appearance like a newspaper picture.

A second factor that could make or break the resolution of the color display is the focusing ability of the CRT. The focusing consists of making the electrons in the three beams focus onto the phosphor dots or stripes. The beams are produced in the electron guns and are fired at the phosphor to light the colors up. The electron beams can be thought of as light beams. They must be focused like a light beam is. That is, brought to a point onto their phosphor targets. If they are not, and impact the phosphor defocused, the light that is generated will consist of large spots. The spot size must be as small as possible. Picture resolution is dependent on small focused spots. The tinier the spots, the better the resolution. Focusing is dependent on the focusing electrodes in the CRT. The better the CRT the better the focus and the resolution will be.

The third item that is needed for improved resolution is improved bandwidth. As discussed in the beginning of the last chapter, the bandwidth determines how fast a pixel can turn on and off. The faster the bandwidth the better the resolution will be.

In a home TV, the bandwidth of the video is a maximum of 4.5 MHz. Actually the average TV has a bandwidth much lower than that, somewhere in the vicinity of 3 MHz. Some home videos that you might rent to run on a VCR only deliver 2 MHz. That is why a lot of the videos do not show good detail in the picture.

A *MHz* or *megahertz* is a million cycles per second. 4.5 MHz means the picture can go from black to bright light or bright to black in $1/4{,}500{,}000$ of a second. This is relatively quick for a light change and will produce good detail to the raster as it is scanned. In a home TV receiver, the circuits must be able to pass and process the fast changing video detail that is in the moving picture.

When the bandwidth of the receiver is increased, as in a computer monitor, the detail in the picture is able to change from light to dark much faster than in the home TV. Bandwidths of 35 MHz and higher are common. These bandwidths will produce pictures with ultra high detail. The circuits in the monitor must be able to pass these high frequencies without being degraded. This is not an easy task for the video amplifiers and they must be souped up to do the job. These monitors can be expensive.

The computer monitor therefore does not originate the resolution of the display. The adapter card or other video circuits in the computer does that. The monitor just has to be able to handle the resolution and display it without degrading it.

Computer display monitors

When monitors were originally made to display computer outputs, circuitwise they were abbreviated home TV receivers. Technicians had an easy time repairing them. The video generating and transmitter circuits in the computer simply produced a composite TV signal, monochrome or color, and cabled the signal into awaiting video and sync circuits in the monitor. The displays were simple still pictures of text or graphics. Any movement that occurred in the display was performed by changing data in the video RAM and not the showing of moving video pictures. There were no true motion pictures shown. The display is only a window that shows the digital contents of the video RAM. Video RAM sections consisted of 1K, 2K, or other such small numbers of RAM bytes. Text was displayed by filling video RAM bytes, on a one to one basis with the character blocks in the display, with character codes. These video RAM bytes were scanned 60 times a second and the scanning updated the display. Graphics were produced by coding each bit in each byte with a 0 if the bit was supposed to turn its dot of light off or a 1 if the bit was to turn the light on. The video output from the computer was a composite TV signal containing the information bytes or bits that were residing in the video RAM. Characteristics such as high resolution was not too much of a consideration.

As the demand for higher and higher abilities to display fine detail came about, the video interface circuits were gradually improved. These early monitors could not display the high-resolution pictures the computer put out, so new improved monitors were developed and are still being developed. The rest of this chapter discusses the repair techniques of the insides of the monitors and how the monitors evolved.

Original monochrome monitors

As mentioned, original monochrome monitor (Fig. 23-1) is a window that can reveal the contents of the video RAM as in Fig. 23-2. The video is cabled to the monitor. The original signals were composite TV as shown in Fig. 23-3. You can view the signal (Fig. 23-4) as it passes through the cable from the computer port to the monitor input pins, with an ordinary TV repair oscilloscope (set at the horizon-

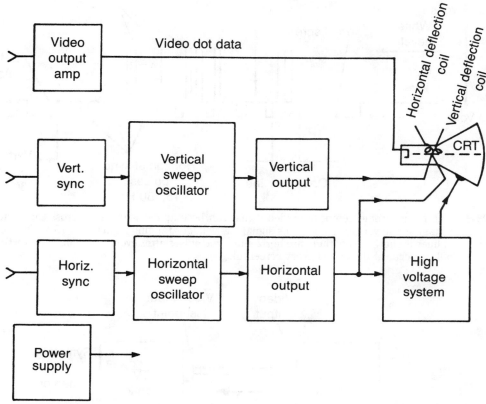

23-1 A monochrome computer monitor produces a picture by having the high voltage attract the electron beam to land on and light up the single color phosphor, the video output modulating the beam with video dot data, the horizontal deflection coil scanning the beam from side to side and the vertical deflection coil pulling the beam down and up.

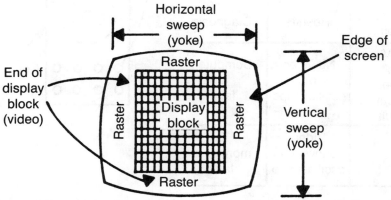

23-2 The monitor picture is simply a window showing the contents of video RAM.

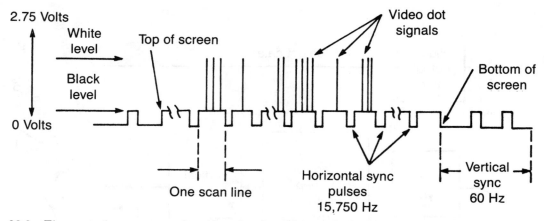

23-3 The monochrome composite video signal can be graphed with time across the bottom and voltage in the vertical plane. This signal has voltages ranging from 0 to 2.75 V. One screenful of lines is shown. Note there are horizontal sync pulses after every scan line. The vertical sync pulses occur at the end of every screenful.

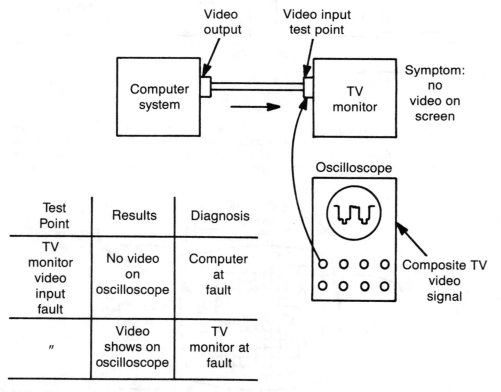

23-4 When the monitor is not displaying, the video input can be quickly checked with an ordinary TV service scope.

tal rate), at the output of the computer or the input of the monitor. If the monitor is not showing the display and the signal is being input to the monitor o.k. as the scope picture will testify, there is probably something wrong with the monitor. Should the signal not be coming out of the computer, odds are the monitor is o.k. and the computer is causing the trouble.

Video amplifier in the monitor

Once it is verified that the signal is getting into the monitor, it is applied directly to a video amplifier section (Fig. 23-5). The computer monitor output signal is usually quite weak. Typically it can have a peak-to-peak voltage about 1 or 1.5 V. In order to get the signal input to the CRT, the 1.5 V must be amplified to about 20 V p-p.

In this circuit, the signal first passes through one transistor amplifier, then through an IC buffer that conditions the signal, through two more transistors until it is at the 20 V p-p level. The signal is then injected into the cathode of the single gun monochrome picture tube. The composite video enters the CRT in serial form. The signal is placed into action so that each line gets its pixel switching instructions at precisely the right time.

As an example, an 8-bit computer could produce a display that consists of 512 character blocks, 32 across and 16 down. In video RAM there are 512 bytes reserved. Byte 0 corresponds with the upper left-hand corner character block, and byte 511 is at the bottom right-hand corner, and all other blocks are in between.

Each byte in RAM contains a set of ASCII bits. The video display generator chip codes the ASCII bits into a video keyboard character that can be displayed in the correct block on the TV screen. The video is installed in the composite TV signal. The video is coupled to the monitor from the computer through a piece of 72 Ω coaxial cable. The connections of the cable are test points where you can view the composite signal on the oscilloscope.

Once inside the monitor, the signal gets amplified from stage to stage until it has enough voltage to drive the cathode of the CRT. You can trace the signal with an oscilloscope from the coax input all the way to the CRT, as in Fig. 23-5. Starting at the coax input, a good video amp section will show ever increasing peak-to-peak voltage video signals as you touch down stage after stage. When the video circuits have troubles, you can detect where the trouble is occurring as you signal trace. Should the signal suddenly not appear at the next test point, you have just passed over the circuit containing the trouble.

Once you have pinpointed the troubled circuit, each component in the circuit becomes a suspect and can be tested with voltage and resistance checks.

Sync circuits

In addition to the video, the composite signal contains horizontal and vertical sync signals, shown in Fig. 23-3. These signals, in this example, are 15.75 kHz for horizontal and 60 Hz for vertical. These signals are placed into the composite signal so they trigger the scanning of the lines. The horizontal sync pulse is placed at the end of each line of light. It triggers the horizontal oscillator to pulse, which causes

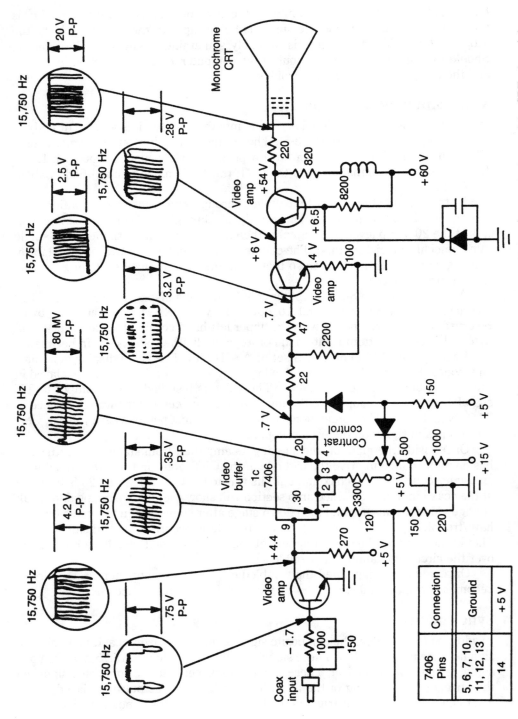

23-5 A typical monochrome video amplifier circuit in the monitor processes the 0.75 V p-p signal to the input of the CRT where it becomes 20 V p-p. The TV scope is capable of tracing the signal from the input to the output at the cathode of the CRT. Voltages and resistance can be tested with a VOM.

7406 Pins	Connection	
	Ground	+ 5 V
5, 6, 7, 10, 11, 12, 13		
14		

the line being drawn to halt at the right side of the screen, retrace, and begin the next line at the left side of the screen.

The vertical sync pulse is placed at the end of every complete raster scan. It triggers the vertical oscillator to pulse. This makes the vertical sweep stop at the bottom of the picture, retrace, and begin the next vertical scan at the top of the picture. The two sync pulses are vital to keep the display block and all the little character blocks in place on the TV screen. The display is then the window into video RAM.

In this example arrangement, each raster frame consists of 264 horizontal scan lines that are drawn one beneath the other. Out of the 264 available lines, only 192 are lit up to display the RAM window, 72 lines at the top and bottom are blacked out to form a border. Also the beginning of each scan line and the end is blacked out to form the side borders of the display block.

Figure 23-3 shows a typical composite monochrome signal a computer can generate. The signal could vary from zero to 2.75 V peak to peak. Each level of voltage causes a change in the brightness of the picture as the level enters the cathode of the CRT. At zero volts, the picture is cut off and the pixels or light dots at the spot are black. At 2.75 V, the picture dots concerned are at their brightest, and if it is a black and white CRT they are at their whitest.

As the picture is scanned the pixels that are to be lit get the higher voltage, while the dots that are to remain black remain at the low zero volts. The illustration depicts the voltages for one raster scan. Each square wave duration is at the zero volt level. These durations are the scan lines. Perched on top of the scan lines are the pixel or dot switching signals. When a pixel is to be lit, there is a quick high spike shown as a line extending up to the white level. Should a pixel be off, there is no spike, the scan line voltage just remains at the black level. The horizontal sync pulses are between each scan line. The sync pulses extend down into the blacker-than-black voltage region, below zero volts. This keeps the raster blacked out during the horizontal retrace.

Once a raster is scanned, line by line, from the top of the screen to the bottom of the screen, then the vertical sync pulses are activated. They retrace the raster back up to the top of the screen. Note the vertical sync pulses are really durations of the square wave. They are also in the blacker-than-black region. This keeps the raster blacked out during the vertical retrace.

The computer video circuits are constantly at work scanning the video RAM, raster after raster. This keeps a steady stream of video entering the monitor. In this way the display stays put and is constantly updated as the display changes during computer activity.

You can see many troubles in the computer's logic circuits as the symptoms show up in the 192 lines of the display block. The commonest computer logic trouble is known as garbage. The symptom is evidenced by the display filling up the little blocks with meaningless characters, symbols, numbers, and random blackouts. The entire 512 blocks can fill with garbage, or only sections will show the nonsense. A variation of garbage is the appearance of a blank display area. Whichever version appears, the symptom indicates troubles in the digital logic areas of the computer. This includes all the sections that use binary and the video display generator.

If the display block itself should disappear and only the raster remains then the entire composite signal is not getting through. This trouble is likely to be located in the video amplifier section of the monitor. The signal is probably getting to the transistors, but not past them. The test is easy with the oscilloscope. Look for the signal at the circuit input and output. If the signal is at the input but not at the output, then the amplifier is defective.

Should the signal be present at the circuit output, trace it to the cathode of the CRT. A defective electron gun in the CRT could possibly kill the video. A new CRT would be needed in that case.

This loss of signal can be blamed on the computer circuits if the oscilloscope shows the signal is not at the input. Trace back through the input circuits.

In addition to the video-fed cathode, the electron gun has these inputs; + 15 V filaments, a control grid, screen grid, and focus grid. These elements make up the electron gun of the CRT in Fig. 23-6. If the filaments open up, the CRT screen will go dark. Dead filaments are obvious to the troubleshooter.

When the other grids short together or open up, the picture will be black, have fixed brightness with or without video, lose focus, or display other CRT troubles. The best test of the electron gun in the CRT is to try a new CRT.

In order to produce a raster from the cathode ray, some external forces must grab ahold of the cathode ray as it passes through the neck of the CRT. These forces are electromagnetic from a yoke around the neck and electrostatic high voltage around the bell of the CRT, shown in Fig. 23-7. Go through the circuits that sweep the cathode ray and produce the scan lines of the raster.

Vertical oscillator

The vertical oscillator is the originator of a 60 Hz sweep frequency (Fig. 23-8). This frequency is used to draw the cathode ray down and up. As the lines are scanned, the vertical frequency causes them to start at the top of the screen and then be drawn one after and beneath the other. A single frame is made up of 264 lines. Each frame appears 60 times a second.

In this sample circuit, the vertical oscillator is based around a unijunction transistor. It is built to run free at 50 Hz, not 60 Hz. A sync pulse from the computer is going to force it to perform at 60 Hz. The 60 Hz pulse comes from the MPU circuit and is applied to the gate of the oscillator through a .01 μF capacitor and a diode.

After the 60 Hz pulse is generated, it continues on to a voltage follower PNP. The follower feeds some signal back to the oscillator through a 20K vertical linearity pot. This gives the circuit some control over the linearity of the 60 Hz sawtooth waveform.

When trouble strikes in the vertical oscillator, the vertical sweep will collapse into a bright horizontal line across the screen if the oscillator stops running. This

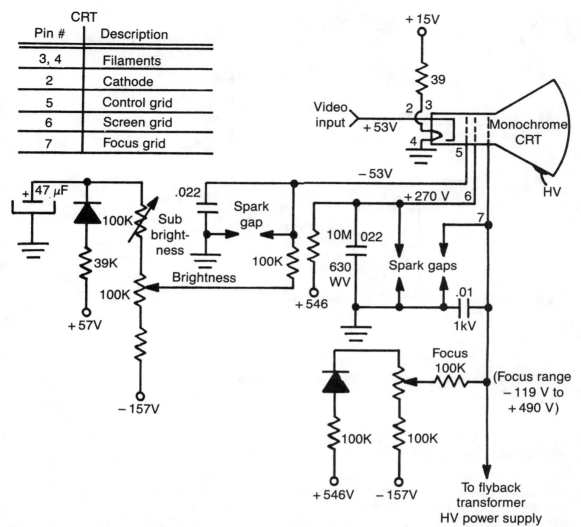

23-6 The monochrome CRT has video inserted at the cathode. The rest of the electron gun elements need voltages too. The control grid has the brightness control, the screen grid is given +270 V attraction for the electrons and the focus grid has the focus control circuit.

could happen if the sync pulse from the computer does not arrive, if one of the oscillator transistors dies, or if any of the related components quit.

If the picture happens to develop vertical jittering, the capacitors between the two transistors could have shorted or changed value. Should the vertical sweep be insufficient, the resistors around the vertical size pot or the pot resistive element itself could have failed.

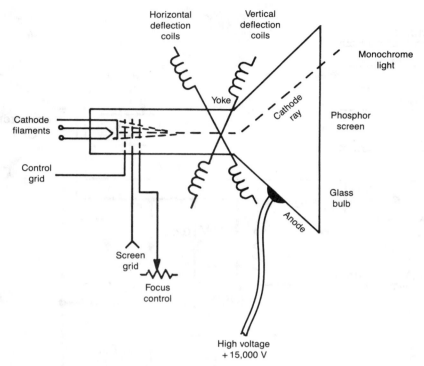

23-7 The remaining elements to drive the CRT are the deflection coils and the high voltage anode.

Vertical output

The vertical output circuit is based around a half-dozen bipolar transistors. They do the job of amplifying the vertical sawtooth generated by the oscillator into a large enough signal that it will be able to be used by the yoke circuit. The circuit outputs its signal through a capacitor between a pair of output transistors tied together emitters.

The vertical windings in the yoke take the sawtooth wave shape and deflects the cathode ray down and up the CRT face at the 60 Hz rate. When the vertical output circuit fails, the picture could have a bright white line exactly like the symptom the oscillator can cause.

The vertical output can also exhibit a decrease in vertical sweep like the oscillator might. However, the vertical output circuit can also produce too much vertical sweep during trouble times. When there is too much vertical sweep, the picture is likely to fold over on the bottom with a whitish haze appearing.

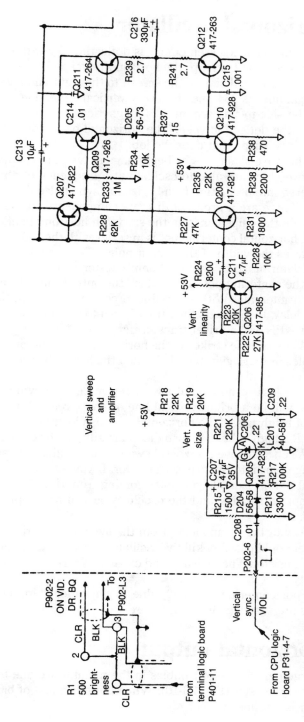

23-8 The vertical sweep circuits can originate in a unijunction transistor that acts as a free-running 50 Hz oscillator. It needs vertical sync from the computer to lock it in step with the incoming signal.

Horizontal oscillator

While the vertical sweep circuit is deflecting the cathode ray from the top of the screen and then back up, the horizontal sweep circuit is drawing the cathode ray from the left-hand side of the screen to the right and back (Fig. 23-9). The rate of the scan lines is 264 lines for every vertical deflection cycle.

The side-to-side scanning is magnetically performed by the horizontal windings of the deflection yoke. The horizontal oscillator is the originator of the sawtooth wave shape that does the job.

The wave shape has its beginnings in two timing chips that are like flip-flops. The two chips are able to oscillate at a frequency of about 15,750 Hz. They are triggered into oscillation by a horizontal sync pulse that comes from the MPU circuits. There are a group of discrete components that are in the oscillator circuit that help the chips generate the sawtooth horizontal deflection frequency.

A horizontal centering pot is in series with the $+6$ V supply line. Adjusting the pot varies the width of the output pulse. The actual frequency the timers pulse is at, is determined by the 3900 ohm resistor and the .0047 μF capacitor in parallel with the centering pot. They cause the output pulse from pin 3 to have 20 microsecond intervals. With the pulse forced to have a specified width and specified time delay, the pulse is then transferred to the horizontal output circuit through a driver NPN and a driver transformer.

When trouble strikes in the horizontal oscillator circuit, there are two common troubles in these chip-based circuits: the loss of horizontal sweep, and no horizontal centering ability.

The loss of horizontal sweep resembles the symptom of no vertical sweep. There will be a bright vertical line on the screen. A variation of this symptom is loss of brightness. The horizontal sweep is lost; however, the trouble often causes the CRT high voltage to also die. This kills the brightness.

When you have horizontal sweep, the oscilloscope shows an output from the timing chips into the driver transistor. If you lose sweep, the oscilloscope will still reveal the horizontal sync pulse coming from the MPU circuits, but the oscillator will not be running and the oscilloscope will not display any wave shapes in the oscillator.

Any of the components from the sync input to the output of the driver transformer could possibly kill the oscillator. Especially vulnerable are the diode, chips, and transistor. The resistors and capacitors rarely die since the supply voltages are so tiny.

Poor centering is usually due to the timer chip, although the series components are suspects during a failure.

Horizontal output

A large percentage of troubles in the monitor are due to failure of the horizontal output transistor (Fig. 23-10). When there is a loss of brightness, this power transistor is a prime suspect.

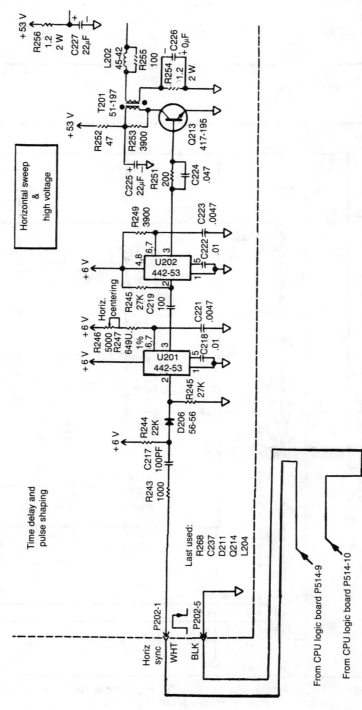

23-9 The horizontal oscillator originates in two IC timing chips. They are triggered into signal lock step by sync pulses from the computer.

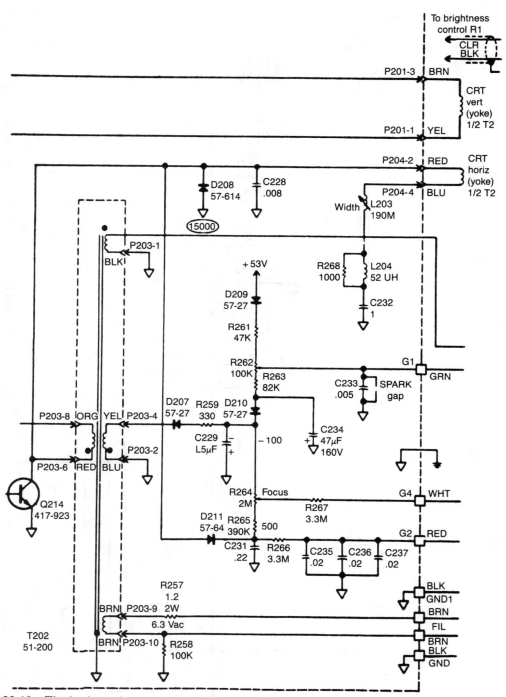

23-10 The horizontal output is also the originator of the high voltage the CRT needs. A flyback transformer produces about 15,000 V.

The well-shaped horizontal pulse generated in the oscillator is transferred into the horizontal output transistor through the driver transformer. The transistor is a switch that controls the flow of current through the horizontal output transformer known as the flyback. The flyback connects to the horizontal windings of the deflection yoke around the CRT neck. The windings in turn deflects the cathode ray across the screen. The deflection scheme is tricky and works like the following.

When the transistor is forced to turn on, current flows to the +53 V supply. The current takes a path from ground through a 1 μF capacitor, a 52 microhenry choke, a 19 microhenry width coil, the horizontal deflection coils, and the primary windings of the flyback. During this passage of current, the yoke current increases in a linear fashion and deflects the cathode ray to the right side of the screen. Note, that the ray is being drawn all the way to the edge of the screen, not the end of the display window that the video RAM uses to show its contents.

When the ray reaches the right side, the output transistor switches off. This sudden turn-off transfers the energy that was stored in the yokes to the .006 μF capacitor that is bypassing the yoke windings. This energy takes the form of a halfwave voltage pulse with an amplitude of 550 V. As the yoke drops to zero, the cathode ray is drawn to screen center. The capacitor is then able to discharge current back into the yoke. The current now going the other way is able to draw the cathode ray the rest of the distance to the left side of the screen.

As the capacitor discharges to zero, it joins with the yoke and primary of the flyback to form a resonant circuit that tries to ring. As it tries to oscillate, the energy that had been transferred to the yoke now draws the ray back to screen center. The damper diode then acts by dampening the impending oscillation and charging the capacitor for the first half of the scanning. As the output transistor switches on and off, it is able to control the cathode ray and cause it to scan the screen horizontally.

The two coils in series with the yoke are the *width* and *horizontal linearity* coils. The width control adjusts the total current through the yoke. The amount of current can spread or shrink the scan somewhat. The linearity coil is fixed and provides a certain amount of linearity correction to the scan lines.

The monitor is, in effect, a raster manufacturing plant. The raster in the monitor is almost identical to the raster developed in TV receivers. The vertical and horizontal sweep circuits, as they operate in unison, draw the scanning lines. The only contribution the computer makes are the triggering horizontal and vertical sync pulses that keep the raster in control by the MPU.

High voltage

In order for the cathode ray to arrive at the phosphor screen and the electrons to smack the phosphor hard enough to light it up, a dc high voltage of around 15,000 V must be on the bell. This attraction voltage is developed as a byproduct of the *flyback transformer*.

The flyback is so called because of the voltage pulse that is developed during the horizontal retrace. The retrace is the time between the end of one scan line and the beginning of the next scan line. That is the interval when the scan line has ended on the right side and is drawn back to the beginning on the left side. The brightness is blanked off during that time.

The primary of the flyback is coupled to three secondary windings. The top winding is where an ac version of the high voltage is developed. The flyback pulse developed in the collector of the transistor is stepped up to a 15 kV level. This ac HV is then rectified by an HV diode and applied to the bell of the CRT through the HV well in the side of the bell, seen in Fig. 23-11. The internal capacitance of the CRT bell is about 500 pF and acts as the filter for the HV. Once the 15 kV is installed in the bell as filtered dc, it can do its electron attraction job.

The bottom flyback winding has an output of 6.3 V at 450 milliamps. This is sufficient to light and heat the filaments in this CRT. The center winding is for a $-100\ V_{dc}$ supply. The winding produces the -100 V, and the diode and capacitor

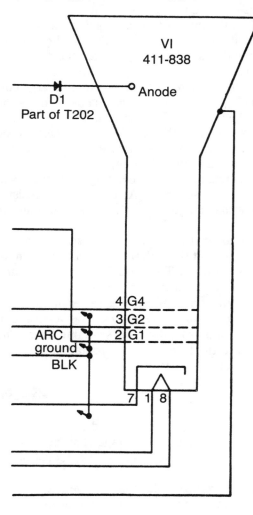

23-11   The CRT has a diode at the anode to rectify the 15,000 V ac to dc. The CRT internal capacitance filters the high dc voltage. The electron gun receives filament voltage. video, screen-grid voltage, and focus grid voltage.

rectifies and filters the voltage until the output is $-100\ V_{dc}$. Another flyback-related output is a tap into the output transistor collector line. This voltage is needed by the screen grid of the CRT as an acceleration voltage for the cathode ray.

The focus voltage for the CRT is taken from a tap between the -100 and the $+500$ voltages. The focus control and the series 390K resistor are a variable voltage divider to obtain a correct focus voltage. Still another voltage divider from $+53$ V, of a diode, a 47K resistor and a 100K potentiometer provide the control grid with an adjustable bias.

These assorted voltages provide the CRT with the following voltages and abilities. The $6.3\ V_{ac}$ heats the filaments. The cathode gets hot and emits a cathode ray. The ray passes through the control grid and has its intensity adjusted which adjusts CRT brightness levels. The electrons are then accelerated by the screen grid's $+500$ V. The focus grid then narrows the beam into a well focused condition. The ray then passes through the varying electromagnetic influence of the deflection yoke and is scanned across and back by the horizontal winding and down and up by the vertical windings. The 15 kV then attracts the electrons and makes them impinge on the phosphor screen to produce the raster.

When trouble strikes in the horizontal and HV circuits, the symptom is usually no brightness. Due to the complex interaction between all the circuits from the IC timers to the anode of the CRT, most of the components in these circuits could be suspects. Therefore, it would be a good idea to narrow the search area down before checking individual components. This can be done with a neon bulb, an HV probe, and a test horizontal output signal substitution. The neon bulb will light if the rf of the flyback is active.

The HV probe is used to check to see if the $15\ kV_{dc}$ is present on the CRT well. A signal substitute device is usually one of the standby pieces of test equipment in a TV repair shop. Once the circuit area is narrowed down a bit, the components in the suspect area can then be tested with normal analog measures.

Color monitors

Most monochrome monitors are relatively simple devices. All that is needed to drive it is a monochrome composite signal replete with pixel switching information and sync signals. You can purchase a decent monochrome monitor for under $100.

A color monitor is a much more complex device. The main reason for the complications is the need for a color picture tube instead of a monochrome type. A monochrome CRT, invented about 80 years ago, consists of a single electron gun, contained in a bulb and pointed at a single color phosphor screen. The electron gun fires negatively charged electrons at the highly positively charged phosphor screen and lights the phosphor. A focus electrode in the gun narrows the beam into a round shape. A deflection yoke sweeps the beam over the screen like writing, starting at the upper left-hand corner.

On the other hand, a color tube must show a wide range of colors, not just varying shades of one color. In order to show color, three different color phosphors, red, green, and blue, must be laid out on the screen. The colored phosphors are put down in dots or stripes. The dot or stripe layout must be precise and placed closely together.

For instance, three dots are placed together in a triad as mentioned earlier. They must be so close together, that when they are lit, the colors add together and fool the eye into thinking the three dots are only one colored dot. In addition to that the triads must be placed together to fool the eye that all the triads are one expanse of phosphor. The closer the dots are placed the clearer the eye will see the total picture.

The distance between the dots is called dot pitch. The distance between the dot triads is called tridot pitch. The tridot pitch is usually considered a benchmark measurement of the color tube. Good-quality tridot pitches range from a high of 0.32 millimeters to a low of 0.25 millimeters. The smaller the tridot pitch, the better is the resolution and fine detail in graphics displays show up satisfactorily.

While the monochrome CRT only requires a single electron gun to light up the single expanse of phosphor, a color CRT needs three guns, one for each color. There is a red gun, a green gun, and a blue gun, Fig. 23-12. These three guns produce three beams of electrons. Each beam is aimed at its corresponding phosphor on the screen. Each beam produces one of the three primary colors by lighting its own phosphor.

You might have heard of some color tubes that have a single gun. This is true but the gun is divided into three sections and each part fires a beam. There are still three beams to light up the phosphors even if they do originate in one cathode of a single gun.

There is one more item in a color tube. It is called, the shadow mask. The shadow mask is a thin metal plate perforated with one hole for each dot triad. When the three beams arrive at the mask, they must converge at the holes. That way, the three beams pass through the holes, diverge and hit the dot they are aimed at. The rest of the electrons are absorbed by the metal mask.

The reason for the shadow mask is to separate the three beams so they impinge only on their assigned phosphor dots. If the mask was not there, all of the electrons in all three beams would strike all three color phosphors on the screen. The mask shadows the electron beams from striking all the phosphors. Only the electrons that make it through the holes reach the phosphor.

Figure 23-13 shows a section of a shadow mask with round holes and the way the three beams reach their assigned phosphor dot targets. Figure 23-14 illustrates a shadow mask section with slotted apertures. This slotted arrangement is used when the three beams are to strike phosphor stripes rather than dots.

Like the monochrome CRT, the color picture tube has a deflection yoke around the neck of the bulb to grab ahold of the three beams electromagnetically and scan them over the screen in horizontal and vertical patterns. Unlike the monochrome CRT, the color CRT has more devices wrapped around the neck of the bulb. First of all there is a purity magnet.

Purity deals with making the three beams impinge only on their own phosphor and not on adjoining phosphors. When the beams are only striking their assigned phosphor, the purity of the colors is assured.

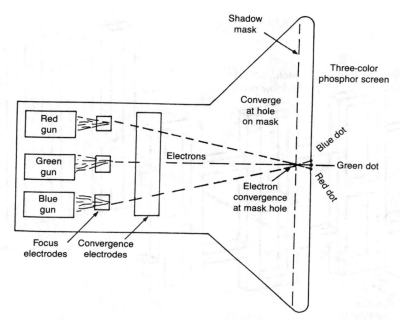

23-12 A color picture tube consists of a glass envelope, with a three-gun assembly at the neck end and three-color phosphor target at the face. A shadow mask in front of the phosphor has one hole for every three phosphor dots. The three electron beams converge at the mask and then separate to land on their assigned phosphor dots.

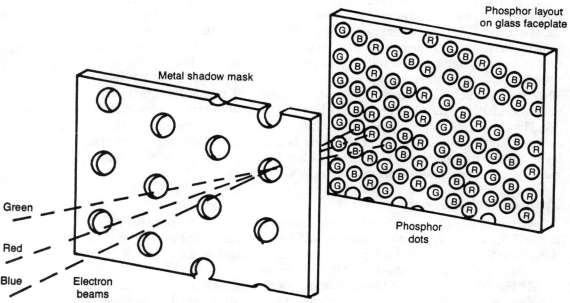

23-13 The three color beams converge at one shadow mask hole and then diverge to land on three phosphor dots.

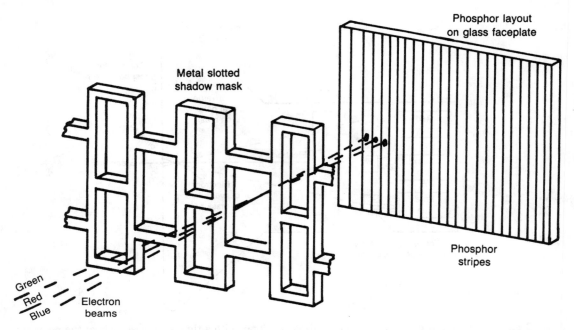

Phosphor layout
on glass faceplate

Metal slotted
shadow mask

Phosphor
stripes

Green
Red
Blue

Electron
beams

23-14 Some color CRTs use a shadow mask with rectangular slots instead of holes. That way color phosphor stripes can be used instead of dots.

Next, there are two sets of convergence magnets, static and dynamic. These magnets are used to make sure the three beams converge at the holes in the shadow mask. The static magnets when adjusted affect the center of the TV screen where there is little or no deflection taking place. The dynamic magnets are usually electromagnetic coils rather than permanent magnets like the purity and statics. The dynamic magnets affect all of the screen, top, bottom, and both sides. They can handle convergence problems no matter what the deflection angles might be. Later in the chapter, the way to make these adjustments is described.

The color CRT display is becoming vitally important as computers proliferate and new applications are discovered. There is a constant race going on between color monitor manufacturers to come up with better and better displays. As a technician you will encounter many color monitors.

Typical block diagram

A color monitor can be considered as an abbreviated color TV. To check out a monitor or TV, use an ordinary oscilloscope and begin at the output and work backwards into the TV toward the input. Start at the cathodes of the color CRT. The color signals are injected into the CRT at the cathode.

As Fig. 23-15 shows, the three color signals are displayed on the oscilloscope as video signals. The oscilloscope shows them to be all alike since the oscilloscope

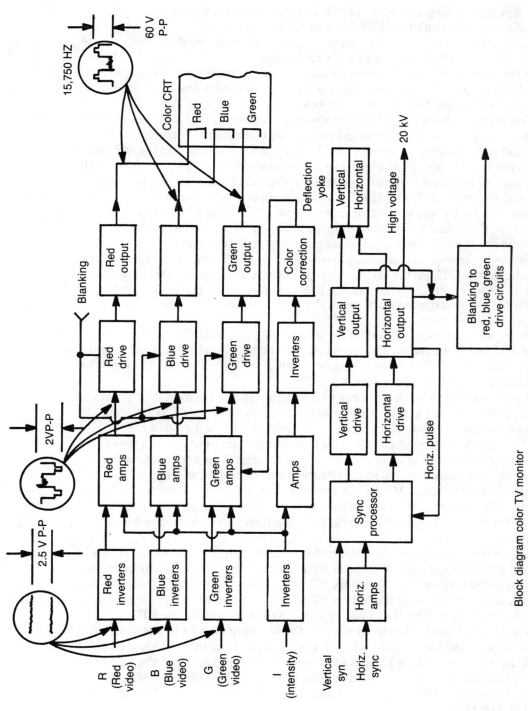

23-15 The color TV monitor has a complex video arrangement since it must process R, B, G, and I signals. However, each color video circuit is about the same as the one monochrome video circuit.

Block diagram color TV monitor

is not equipped to display colors. The three color signals in this example are each present and have a peak-to-peak voltage of 60 V.

Moving back over the three output stages, which are based around discrete full sized transistors, the p-p voltage for each signal is still showing 60 V. Moving still further back, over the three driver stages, with more discrete transistors, the p-p voltage drops. At these touchdown points the p-p comes down to a lowly 2 V. The drivers gave the 2 V a boost up to 60 V.

The next touchdown point is over the amp stages. The oscilloscope pictures are not as clear cut. In the amp stages each of the color amps are combined with a black and white brightness signal called I for intensity. For instance, the red video checks out at 1.4 V p-p. The I signal has a p-p voltage of 0.6 V. The I is mixed with the R and the resultant is the 2 V p-p read earlier. All three colors are mixed with the I in the same way. The I signal is coming from the computer too.

Now you have come to the four input stages, R, B, G, and I. The oscilloscope shows that the actual p-p voltage inputs are 2.5 V. They are fed to the inverter stages where they are inverted and amplified to 4 V. Incidentally, this example monitor uses conventional scanning frequencies of 15.75 kHz for horizontal and 60 Hz for vertical. These p-p oscilloscope readings you have been taking have been at the 15.75 kHz setting. If the monitor had been one with a higher horizontal frequency, the oscilloscope would be set at the higher frequency in order to be able to view the oscilloscope picture.

So far we have examined four of the monitors inputs, R, B, G, and I. The I was mixed with the R, B, and G, and the resultants connected to the three cathodes of the three CRT guns. There are two more inputs from the computer. They are the horizontal and vertical sync signals.

These two sync signals are sent to the inputs of the horizontal and vertical sweep circuits. These circuits do three jobs. One, they drive the deflection yoke. In the yoke are two separate coil sections. The yoke is wrapped around the neck of the CRT bulb. The three electron beams therefore stream right through the center of the yoke where the magnetic fields are developed. The horizontal yoke part sweeps the beams from left to right, retraces from right back to left, and then left to right again and again. Meanwhile the vertical yoke section sweeps the beams from the top of the picture to the bottom, retraces back to the top and then back to the bottom again and again. The result is a full screen sweep producing brightness full of logic.

The second job the sweep circuits do, actually only the horizontal sweep is involved in this one, is work with the horizontal output and the flyback transformer to produce the high voltage. A color CRT needs more high voltage than a monochrome. A color CRT could use at least 20,000 V_{dc} in order to attract the electrons from the three guns. The HV is placed into a well in the side of the CRT.

The third job these circuits perform is the blanking out of the picture brightness during the horizontal and vertical retraces. If the brightness was not blanked out at that time, the retrace lines would show as white lines and hurt the fidelity of the display. The horizontal blanking signal is derived from the horizontal output circuit. The vertical blanking signal from the vertical output circuit. They are combined into one line.

This presents no interference problem because the horizontal is at 15.75 kHz and the vertical is at 60 Hz. The signals are simply strong sync pulses that put the brightness voltage level into the blacker-than-black region as they add to the video input. The blanking signals are then put through a transistor amplifier and connected to the R, B, and G driver inputs where they mix with the three color videos and cause blanking during retrace time.

The sync signals themselves are needed to sync the free running horizontal and vertical oscillators into step with the computer signals. They enter a sync processor stage in an IC. The vertical enters directly while the horizontal is passed through a transistor amplifier first. In the IC are the free running oscillators. They are synced into step with the video signal movement. From there the vertical oscillator output is sent to a vertical drive and a vertical output circuit. They produce the vertical yoke sweep signals. The horizontal oscillator output is sent to a horizontal drive and a horizontal output circuit. This circuit produces the horizontal yoke sweep signal and also the 20 kV needed to attract electrons in the color CRT. These circuits are identical to those that drive color CRTs in TV receivers. These circuits can be traced with an ordinary TV oscillscope set to the frequency of the circuit under test, 15.75 kHz and 60 Hz.

The rest of the circuitry in the monitor is concerned with producing the supply voltages for the circuits just discussed. These power supplies in monitors are conventional and resemble supplies found in home TVs. A typical supply is shown in chapter 25.

Troubleshooting a color monitor

When computer troubles strike, the monitor quite often displays symptoms of the trouble. There are two types of problems. First, there are the problems that are caused by defects in the computer. Second are the TV problems that are happening because the monitor has a fault.

The isolation test is simple. If you are not sure whether the trouble is in the computer or monitor, try a different, known good monitor. If the replacement monitor has the same symptoms, chances are the suspect monitor is good and the trouble is originating in the computer. When the replacement monitor works, then the suspect monitor indeed contains the fault.

In the color monitor, troubles break down into a few categories shown in Table 23-2. They are all color TV type troubles. In order to troubleshoot these conditions you need the arsenal of test equipment that a TV repairman must have to service color TVs. For example, if there is no vertical sweep, just a white horizontal line, you need a signal generator that outputs a 60 Hz signal. The signal is injected into the vertical sweep circuit at various test points in an effort to restore the sweep with the test signal. When you are able to restore the sweep with the test signal you are near the source of the trouble.

The same sort of signal injection technique is needed to test a horizontal circuit trouble. Loss of horizontal sweep or even loss of raster can be tested with a 15.75 kHz signal. If you find a spot where the signal produces the return of the raster or the sweep, you are near the fault.

Table 23-2. Typical color-monitor problems, and suspects.

Dead set

Approach	Suspects
Check voltages with VOM	Low voltage supply High voltage supply (Chapter 25)

Shrunken picture

Approach	Suspects
Check voltages with VOM	Horiz. output Vertical output Low voltage supply High voltage supply

Picture out of sync

Approach	Suspects
Check horiz. & vertical sync from computer with oscilloscope	Computer sync Output circuits Monitor sync Input circuits

No Picture with Raster OK

Approach	Suspects
Check video from Computer test from monitor input, to video amplifiers to CRT cathode with oscilloscope	Video amplifiers CRT electron gun

Bright red or greenish-blue picture

Approach	Suspects
(Inject video signal) Check R video amplifier with with oscilloscope	R video Amplifiers

Bright blue or greenish-red picture

Approach	Suspects
(Inject video signal) Check B video amplifiers with VOM and oscilloscope	B video Amplifiers

Bright green or blueish-red picture

Approach	Suspects
(Inject video signal) Check G video amplifiers with VOM and oscilloscope	G video Amplifiers

Picture Too Dark or Too Bright

Approach	Suspects
Check I video amplifiers with VOM and oscilloscope	I video Amplifiers

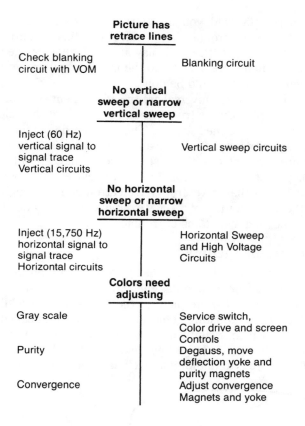

**Picture has
retrace lines**

Check blanking
circuit with VOM

Blanking circuit

**No vertical
sweep or narrow
vertical sweep**

Inject (60 Hz)
vertical signal to
signal trace
Vertical circuits

Vertical sweep circuits

**No horizontal
sweep or narrow
horizontal sweep**

Inject (15,750 Hz)
horizontal signal to
signal trace
Horizontal circuits

Horizontal Sweep
and High Voltage
Circuits

**Colors need
adjusting**

Gray scale

Service switch,
Color drive and screen
Controls

Purity

Degauss, move
deflection yoke and
purity magnets

Convergence

Adjust convergence
Magnets and yoke

Red, blue, and green picture losses or mixups can often be fixed with the aid of video-type injection signals. The signal is injected into various test points in the three color amplifier lines. The injected signal can alter or restore color losses. Then you must figure out what has failed, and why the injection signal is producing its results.

The troubleshooting table lists the common troubles that could befall the monitor, the test approach that should be taken to pinpoint the circuit, and the circuits that are indicated as prime suspects. For further troubleshooting and repair techniques consult some color TV repair books. When you are working on monitors, you are working on TVs.

Color monitor adjustments

The color monitor only has a few inside adjustments available. You'll need the service notes for the specific monitor for some of the adjustments. For instance the dc B+ voltage that the power supply puts out, is adjustable. In the IBM PC you must connect a voltmeter to a test point and adjust a control for exactly +115 V output.

To adjust the horizontal hold, you are instructed to connect a .1 microfarad capacitor from a test point to ground. The control is adjusted until the display floats around the picture. To produce a display an RGB color bar generator is advised. These type adjustments are specific to the monitor you are working on. The service notes spell out what should be done.

Less specific and more universal are the adjustments that are often required to produce a color display that is true. Around the neck of the color CRT bulb are a number of devices mentioned earlier. There is the deflection yoke, convergence magnets, and a purity magnet. There are also some potentiometer controls on the chassis that are associated with these devices. They are all adjustable in most monitors. They are the magnetic and resistive devices that control the path of the three electron beams that travel from the electron guns, through the shadow mask and land on the phosphor targets. Let's examine what they do. These adjustments can cure the following symptoms of trouble.

Poor monochrome picture

In a color monitor, when the three colors are perfectly adjusted, a perfect black and white picture can be attained as the three colors add together. If you are not getting a good black and white picture, the colors are not adding properly, as in Fig. 23-16. They need adjusting. This adjustment is often called the color temperature adjustment, which is confusing the first time you see the name. I call it gray scale tracking. What is needed is the mixing of the three primary colors on the screen to fool the eye into thinking a black and white picture is there.

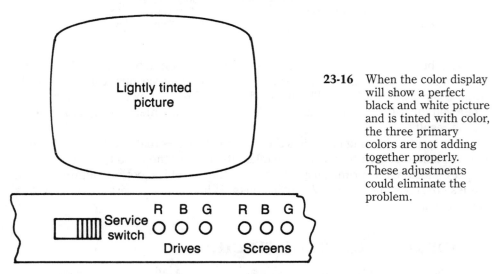

23-16   When the color display will show a perfect black and white picture and is tinted with color, the three primary colors are not adding together properly. These adjustments could eliminate the problem.

Lots of monitors follow color TV chassis design and provide what is called a service switch. When you flick the switch, the vertical sweep is killed leaving a horizontal line. The next step is to adjust the red, blue, and green drive controls. These controls make the lines bright or dim red, blue, and green. Adjust the three lines until they are superimposed on top of one another, and they produce a dim black and white picture. Reset the service switch and the full display will reappear. It should be a fairly good black and white display. If it is slightly off, readjust the blue and green drive controls until the black and white picture is true.

Poor purity

One serious drawback with the three-gun color CRT is that the three beams can be affected by the lines of force in the earth's magnetic field. It has been suggested that a color CRT should operate in a north-south position so it is not cutting the Earth's magnetic field.

Another problem in the same vein occurs when some of the metal in the monitor becomes magnetized. This too can affect the paths of the beams and produce distorted colors. The symptoms of the trouble that happens due to extraneous magnetic influence is color splotches in the display Fig. 23-17, especially around the perimeter of the CRT face. The splotches can be any color and can be caused by spurious magnetization or misadjusted CRT neck devices.

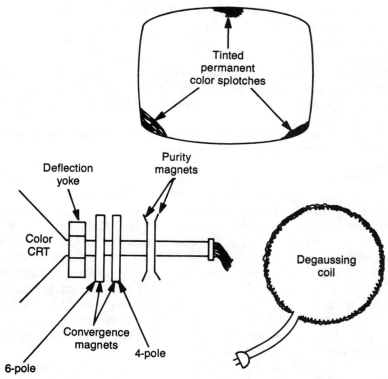

23-17   When the three beams do not land on their assigned phosphor, color splotches will be seen. The purity problem can be remedied with use of a degaussing coil, adjusting the purity magnets and moving the yoke.

The first step in curing poor picture purity is to demagnetize the magnetized spots. Technicians call it degaussing. Usually a color CRT will have a degaussing coil wound around the bulb near the faceplate. The degaussing coil is then automatically activated everytime the monitor is turned on. You can see the effect of the coil. The picture, especially around the perimeter, will show moving color rainbows for a few seconds at turn on. This demagnetizes the area.

Sometimes the built-in coil is not strong enough to do the job. Then you must use an external degaussing coil. It's easy; just energize and rotate the round coil from around the perimeter of the faceplate. You can do it with the set on or off, before, during, or after the repair. Just keep the coil away from the rear of the TV. You don't want to demagnetize the magnets in the monitor. Also keep the degausser away from your computer disks! It can erase your software when the degausser is energized.

If after degaussing, some color splotches still remain, analyze their screen position. Are they around the rim of the tube or near screen center?

Screen center impurities can be removed by adjusting the purity magnets. Follow this procedure. Turn the blue and green drive controls all the way down. This leaves a red picture. Adjust the red drive control so the red picture is vivid and the impurities stand out. Adjust the purity tabs that move the purity magnets until the splotches are gone and a uniform red picture is displayed.

When the color splotches are around the perimeter of the screen, the cure is to loosen and move the deflection yoke back and forth until the red picture is uniform. There could be a lot of interaction between the purity magnets and the yoke movement. You will probably have to go back and forth between the purity tabs and the yoke positioning until you obtain your uniform red field. If you care to, you could even degauss again.

Once you have a uniform red field you can perform the gray scale tracking procedure to restore a true black and white picture.

Color bleeding

The gray scale tracking adds the proper amounts of red, blue, and green lights to produce black and white. The purity adjustments adjust the trajectory of the three beams so they only land on their assigned phosphor. A third trouble is bleeding colors. In the picture, sometimes you will observe an extraneous color bleeding out of the edges of objects on the screen (Fig. 23-18). The bleeding is most noticeable during a black and white display. Red, blue, or green outlines will appear around figures. It looks almost like a TV ghost trouble but it is different. It is being caused by incorrect trajectories of the three beams. The beams could be landing on the correct color phosphors, but the three beams are not converging at the holes in the shadow mask at the spots showing the bleeding. The cure is to make them converge and the bleeding will disappear.

To see where the bleeding is occurring you should connect a dot-bar generator to the monitor and display either a dot or bar pattern. The dots or bars clearly show the bleeding locations.

There are two sets of magnets around the bulb neck that adjust the trajectories of the three beams so they can be made to converge at the shadow mask holes once again (Fig. 23-18). One set of magnets adjusts bleeding at screen center. The other magnets adjust for bleeding around the perimeter of the CRT. The center adjusters are permanent magnets. The perimeter magnets could be permanent magnets, electromagnets, or the deflection yoke according to the specific monitor being tested.

23-18 When the characters in a display have unwanted color fringes, the three beams are not converging at the correct shadow mask apertures. Good convergence can be adjusted back in with the convergence magnets and the deflection yoke.

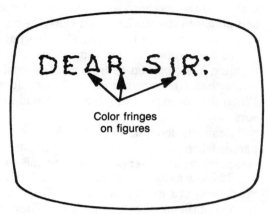

In the IBM PC monitor used as an example, the magnets are all permanent except for the deflection yoke. The following is the prescribed procedure to cure misconvergence. With an RGB dot-bar pattern entering the monitor, a dot pattern is used first. The dot pattern is handier to adjust center convergence.

There are two sets of permanent magnets on this monitor, a 4-pole and a 6-pole set. The deflection yoke is also needed for the perimeter convergence adjustments. With the dot pattern displayed, the 4-pole magnet is adjusted to converge the red and blue dots at the center of the screen. Then the 6-pole magnets are used to converge the green dots over on top of the red-blue dots. This produces white dots.

Next, a cross hatch pattern is displayed. The deflection yoke is loosened. The deflection yoke is then manipulated. The effect is, when the yoke is tilted up and down, the vertical lines at the top and bottom of the screen and the horizontal lines at the left and right of the screen can be converged.

When the yoke is tilted from side to side, the horizontal lines at the top and bottom and the vertical lines at the sides can be converged. The converged lines will be white with no bleeding. You must take your time and observe the lines carefully until you eliminate the bleeding to the best of your ability. It will never be absolutely perfect but get as close to perfection as you can. It will usually be satisfactory.

Specific computer monitors

When you are working on a computer monitor, you are in effect a TV technician. Unless the trouble is easily spotted and fixed, you will probably need the specific service notes for the unit. In the past few years as resolution and color needs have become vital, there are many kinds of monitors at all sorts of prices appearing on the market.

Since the advent of the IBM PC with its expansion slots, computers have not been limited to certain monitors. The IBM PC family and clones, as well as Apple's Macintosh and imitators do not as a rule, have the video display generators built onto the motherboard. The video generators have been installed onto cards and plug into the motherboard slots. As a result, users can easily change monitor types by purchasing the latest video output cards and plugging them in.

In the same computer you can switch from a monochrome monitor to a color monitor. You can then go from an inexpensive color monitor to a much better performer with better resolution. These advanced monitors have one drawback. When they need repairing they are found to be more complex than their predecessors.

Basically though, they are still only forms of color TVs. In order to be prepared, when you find you are getting into a complicated repair job, be sure to be equipped with TV service test instruments and the monitor's service notes.

There are two new monitor types that have become very popular in the last few years, and are worthy of specific discussion. These two types show promise of becoming the monitor of the future. They are the VGA (video-graphics array) and the Multiscan. The VGA, that has its adapter card discussed in the previous chapter, comes in both monochrome and polychrome monitor versions. The Multiscan usually is built with a color CRT.

The VGA monitor

The VGA monitor is made to display very high resolution and in the color version, to show a large number of colors. It is only able to display the VGA generated signal from the VGA adapter card. However, VGA cards have the ability to emulate both CGA and EGA signals and feed these signals to the VGA monitor in a form that will get the signals into the display. This is a convenient feature and allows many application programs that only operate with CGA and EGA monitors to be used.

Figure 23-19 is a block diagram of a typical VGA monitor. The overview is quite like the older color monitor discussed with one very important difference. Note the sync inputs. The vertical sync signal ranges between 60 to 70 Hz. That is just about conventional. However, the horizontal sync pulse of 5 V peak to peak, is running at 31,480 Hz. This is about twice as fast as the conventional 15,750 Hz. This makes the horizontal scan lines travel twice as fast in the same time putting twice as many scan lines into the display. This is one of the important reasons for the VGA high resolution

The video input signals are R, B, and G. However, they are analog inputs even though they are R, B, and G and not a composite color TV signal. With analog signals there are an infinite number of levels. Each different color shade represents a different signal level. The circuits limit the number of levels and thus the colors even though theoretically there could be an infinite number of colors. However, the input signal can still result in 256 different colors from a palette of 256,000 colors.

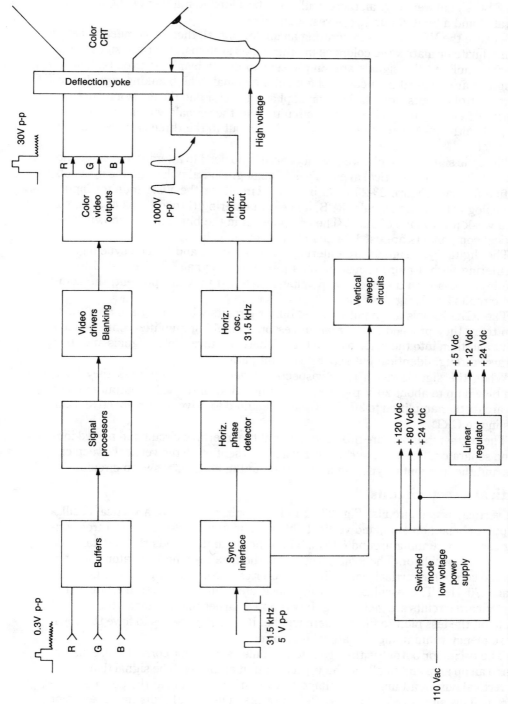

Block diagram for VGA monitor

23-19 Block diagram of a VGA type monitor. Note the 31.5 kHz horizontal frequency, twice as fast as conventional.

If the RBG signal were digital, there could only be a limited number of signal levels generated and a limited number of resultant colors.

Because the VGA card is generating an analog signal, there is no need to have to demodulate or matrix the colors as in other video systems. After the signals are properly amplified the signals are simply sent to driver blanking circuits. There the signals are blanked by a composite blanking signal. The blanking signals are generated from inputs from the horizontal phase detector and the horizontal output circuits. After that the video output circuits take the signals which are, at this point, a healthy 30 V p-p. The signals are then input to the three cathodes of the color CRT.

The sync signals though, are digital. There is no need to attempt to change the digital horizontal and vertical sync pulses to analog. Digital pulses do the sync job in a fine fashion. Figure 23-20 is an interface circuit for the VGA monitor input. The analog color video signals, R, B, and G are entering through pins 4, 5, and 1 with a weak p-p voltage of 0.3 V. The components in the blue line are shown. The identical components are used for the red and green color video lines.

The digital sync signals are entering through pins 6 and 2. The sync signals are entering with a more robust, 5 volts p-p. These signals can be tested for at these input pins with a scope or p-p voltage meter. If they are present, the computer circuits are doing their job.

The RBG signals are input to three buffer circuits where they are amplified. From there they proceed to a signal processor, a blanking amplifier, onto a video output and then into the color picture tube. There are three color signals and they all travel through identical but separate circuit paths.

When the signals reach their respective video output amplifiers they have been blown up to about 20 V p-p from the input 0.3 V. In the video output circuits they are further amplified to 30 V p-p that is required to drive their respective color guns in the CRT.

The two sync signals are mixed together at the interface circuit and placed into a sync separator. There the vertical sync signal is sent on to the vertical sweep circuits and the horizontal sync signal is sent on to the horizontal sweep circuits.

Vertical sweep circuits

The vertical sweep circuits, Fig. 23-21 in the monitor consist of a vertical oscillator, pulse shaper, op amp, and vertical output. The vertical oscillator is a free running oscillator running around 60 Hz. The sync separator sends the vertical sync pulse to the oscillator. The sync pulse locks the free running oscillator into step with the computer vertical sync. The computer can be outputting a pulse between 60 and 70 Hz. The oscillator gets into lock step with whatever frequency the adapter card circuits are generating. It was noted earlier that the faster the vertical oscillator, the less picture flicker there will be. It is advantageous to have the vertical frequency running higher rather than lower.

The oscillator output is then sent to the pulse shaper for correct pulse sizing, then to an op amp and finally to the vertical output amplifier. The signal that leaves the vertical output attains a p-p voltage of 48 V and is running at the desired vertical rate. This signal is fed to the deflection yoke. The signal pulls the three color

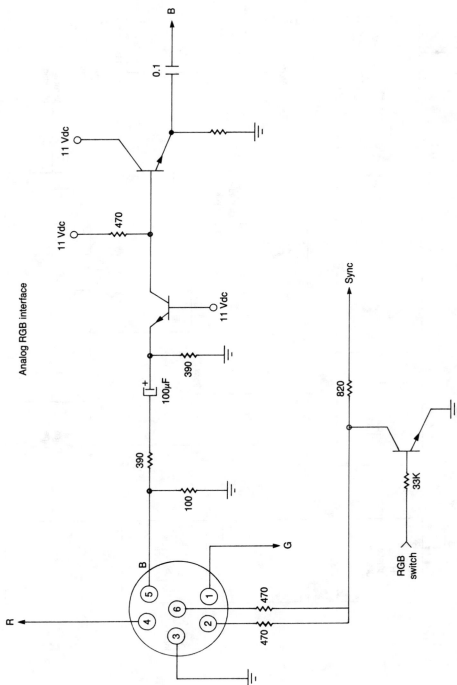

23-20 The monitor interface circuit handles the incoming analog RGB signal and separates the color video from the sync.

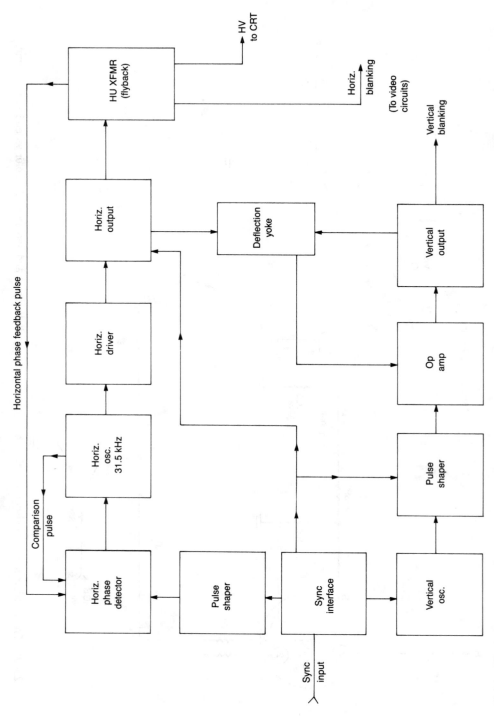

23-21   Block diagram of the sweep circuits. The vertical sweep circuits and horizontal sweep circuits are not unusual from a block diagram point of view. Actual circuit components depend on individual manufacturers design. To properly troubleshoot these circuits, the service notes and schematic must be used.

beams down and then back up at the vertical frequency after the beams pass through their centers in the neck of the CRT.

Horizontal sweep circuits

The horizontal circuits act in a similar way except they are operating at a much higher frequency. The sync separate feeds the sync signal to a horizontal phase detector, which extracts the sync signal from the sync mixture. The detector output then syncs the free running horizontal oscillator into step with the 31,480 Hz signal the adapter card is generating. The horizontal oscillator then lock steps with computer output.

The horizontal signal is then sent to the horizontal output circuit. The output circuit then develops two distinct signals. One is a horizontal pulse of about 1000 V p-p that is sent to the yoke to join the vertical yoke pulse. The 31.48 kHz horizontal pulse causes the yoke to develop an electromagnetic field that draws the three beams across the display and back. Between the horizontal yoke pulse drawing the beams across and then retracing them back, and the vertical pulling the beams down and then retracing them back up, a raster is formed on the screen.

The horizontal output circuit also takes its 1000 volt p-p signal and feeds it to a high voltage circuit. The HV circuit takes the pulse and amplifies it, rectifies it and outputs a large 26,000 V electron attraction positive voltage. This voltage is applied to the side of the CRT.

CRTs for VGA monitors

The three factors that determine the resolution of the monitor is the bandwidth, the focus and the phosphor dot pitch. The bandwidth or the speed the monitor can turn pixels off and on is determined by the frequencies that are processed in the circuitry. The color CRT can easily handle the video frequencies the monitor circuits input to it. There is no special need to improve the CRT for bandwidth considerations.

The second factor of focus, is a built-in quality of the CRT. It is important that the electron gun is made so as to form a beam that is focused to a tiny spot at the CRT faceplate. This is a given in most modern color CRTs. This is especially true for CRTs that must produce high resolution pictures.

The third factor, dot pitch of the phosphor triads, is important. As discussed earlier, the smaller the phosphor dots and the closer they are together, the better the resolution will be. Also the better the dot pitch the more expensive the CRT is and the monitor also has to be bought with more money.

As a result, there are different models of VGA monitors with varying prices. CRTs with dot pitches such as 0.41 – 0.51 millimeters are inexpensive when compared to CRTs with dot pitches of 0.21 – 0.31 millimeters. It is much more expensive to construct a phosphor laden faceplate with smaller dots than larger dots.

The different dot pitches are the only real consideration in the VGA CRTs. Otherwise, the color VGA monitors are all pretty much the same.

The multiscan monitor

The idea of the multiscan monitor is to have a monitor that is compatible with as many adapter card outputs as possible. For example, a typical multiscan could operate easily with RGB, CGA, EGA, and VGA. The important differences between these systems is two fold. One, they have different horizontal scanning frequencies. Two, they have various color signal differences. The multiscan is built to accommodate all the different systems. It was designed for users who switch applications and computers frequently. The circuitry gets very tricky and servicing can get confusing.

The horizontal scanning

The tough part of the circuitry deals with the different horizontal scanning frequencies. The easy changes are made with the different video inputs. The video circuits are only converting all the different types of information to one that the monitor can process and display.

In the sweep circuits there are many components that affect the scanning frequencies. Any frequency change in a fixed circuit is usually due to a component fault and could cause trouble. For example, a change in a component that throws the horizontal frequency off could also kill the high voltage resulting in a display blackout. Therefore, when a circuit is designed to operate at a number of different frequencies, great care must be taken. If a component failure takes place, it can be very confusing to diagnose.

The multiscan can be designed to operate at four basic frequencies. For example, 15,750 Hz the conventional home TV frequency; 21,800 Hz a CGA-EGA frequency; 24,000 Hz; and 31,480 Hz the VGA frequency. The frequencies are mostly affected by inductors and capacitances. The actual frequency the oscillator will run at is a function of the value of reactive resistance and active conductance. The multiscan activity works by adding and subtracting inductors and capacitors from the circuits. As the components are switched in and switched out, the circuit can work its way from frequency to frequency. The typical design takes the horizontal oscillator from a low of 15,000 Hz to a high of 34,000 Hz. The monitor is equipped with circuits that detect the incoming sync frequency from the computer video output and then switch the scanning frequency of the horizontal oscillator and its surrounding circuits.

The video interface

The incoming horizontal frequency can often tell the video circuits what type of interface is needed. For example, if the incoming frequency is 31.48 kHz, the video realizes a VGA card is outputting an analog RBG signal. However, this is a hit and miss type of situation. As a result, multiscan monitors are usually equipped with video input switches. Examples are an analog/digital and normal/special switches. At any rate, a horizontal sync decoder circuit detects the horizontal frequency and sends a coded signal to the video interface appraising the interface what type of video it should expect.

Figure 23-22 is a block diagram of a multiscan monitor. The video enters at a video/sync interface section. The interface has three functions. One, it sends a negative polarity sync signal to the detection circuits independent of the input polarity. Two, it acts as a digital-to-analog converter. The interface will convert a digital signal to analog or leave it digital according to need. Three, it sends a video signal to a video amplifier. The signal could be specified to be 400 mV p-p.

The video circuits

The video amplifier circuit receives composite blanking signal from the blanking amplifier. This makes sure the raster is blanked out during retrace times. The video amplifier increases the current of the signal and transfers the signal to the video output with a 200 mV p-p. There is also a contrast type control connected to the video amplifier to adjust the picture. After this processing the signal is passed on to the video output circuit.

The video output beefs up the signal to about 40 V p-p. Then the signals are sent to the color CRT cathodes. The video amplifier sets the dc bias on the CRT cathodes so the video is applied correctly. The CRT displays the three signals.

The tricky horizontal circuits

The video/sync interface sends the incoming horizontal sync signals to a sync amplifier. The sync from there goes to two different circuits that work together. They are the horizontal position select and the horizontal pulse width correction circuits. The horizontal position circuits control the horizontal phase position. This controlled phase signal is then sent to pulse width correction circuit.

The pulse width circuit then goes to work. It does four vital jobs. One, it supplies the horizontal phase detector (*AFC*) circuit with a constant pulse width sync signal. Two, it supplies the sync decoder circuit with an adjustable pulse width signal. Three, it supplies the horizontal oscillator control circuit with a varying pulse. Fourth, it supplies the raster blanking and the horizontal oscillator control circuits with a one second switching pulse.

These signal transfers will do the following when the multisync changes a mode. As the raster blanking circuit is activated, the screen will go blank. The one second pulse then takes over the horizontal oscillator control circuit and stabilizes the oscillator. The horizontal sync decoder is the one who detects the incoming sync frequency and outputs a number of switching voltages. The switching voltages will control what mode the monitor is to operate in. The switching voltages are transferred to the horizontal output section, the color mode control, the horizontal position select and the vertical size control circuits.

The horizontal oscillator control circuit is the one that actually controls the frequency the free running oscillator will run at. The incoming adapter card frequency is detected after the video interface in the horizontal sync amplifier. A control voltage is generated in the oscillator control circuit and applied to the oscillator. The oscillator then runs at the incoming sync frequency.

Once the oscillator is set to run at the incoming horizontal sync frequency, the tricky part of the circuit action is over. The oscillator is the source of the horizontal

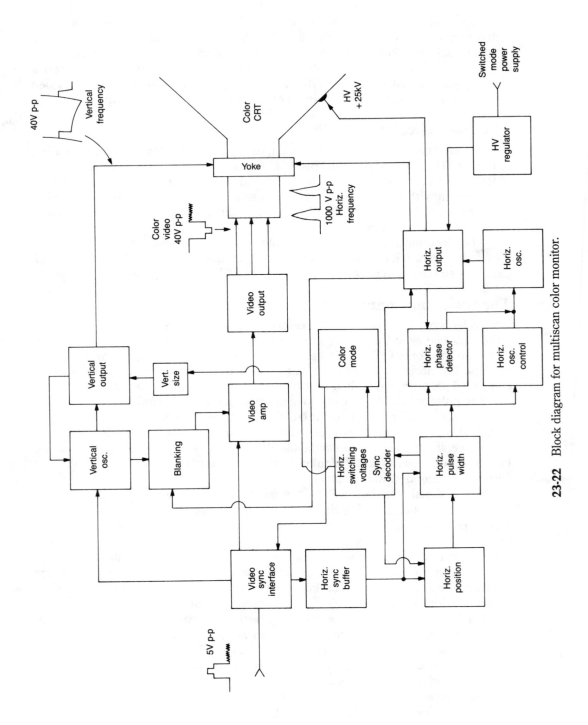

23-22 Block diagram for multiscan color monitor.

sweep signal. The rest of the horizontal sweep circuits can then do their job. The oscillator passes the phase adjusted horizontal wave shape it developed to the horizontal output circuit.

The horizontal output circuit is designed specifically for this multiscanning frequency type operation. It is going to have to operate at four or more different frequencies in the range of 15 through 34 kHz. It is going to have to switch voltages in order to tell the circuits around it what scanning mode it is in. The horizontal output generates feedback signals to indicate its mode of operation. There is one feedback signal it must send to the horizontal phase detector as a reference voltage. In the phase detector, the feedback signal is used as a comparison voltage to phase adjust and pulse width correct the developed sync signal in the sync amplifier. This correction signal is then mixed with the oscillator control voltage. The resultant voltage then locks the phase of the horizontal oscillator so it matches the incoming sync at the exact right points in time. There is a second feedback signal the horizontal output circuit sends to the horizontal blanking circuit to develop a blanking signal with the right operating frequency.

The vertical sweep circuits

A vertical sync signal is extracted from the total incoming sync at the video/interface circuit. The sync signal is then sent directly to the vertical oscillator without further ado. The oscillator is designed to be able to run at any frequency between 48 and 62 Hz. It is not difficult to design an oscillator to be able to vary this far at these low frequencies. The incoming vertical sync signal is typically in this range.

The vertical oscillator is free running in the 50 – 60 Hz range. The incoming sync signal from the computer output then phase locks the oscillator in step with the adapter card generated vertical sync signal. The oscillator then generates a sawtooth waveform and transfers it to the awaiting vertical output circuit.

Connected to the vertical output is the vertical size control circuit. The circuit has the job of changing the vertical sweep size so the sweep is not too large or too small to accommodate the resultant vertical scanning frequency. The vertical size control receives a signal from the sync decoder in the horizontal circuit complex. The sync decoder knows what mode the monitor is operating in. It passes a signal to the vertical size that controls the different vertical modes of operation.

Monitor power supplies

The low-voltage power supplies in computer monitors are quite different than the computer supplies. In some early computers, the monitor was built into the computer system and a complicated supply was used that provided both the computer and the monitor with energy. These supplies were hard to repair.

Fortunately, in today's computers, the computer has its special supply and the monitor has its own supply. The computer type supplies are discussed in the first part of chapter 25. The monitor supplies are covered in the last section of the chapter. The monitor supplies are similar to the ones found in home TV receivers and like the rest of the monitor circuits use TV repair type techniques to repair them when they go down.

24
Disk-drive maintenance and adjustments

THERE ARE SOME COMPUTERS THAT DO NOT HAVE A BUILT-IN DISK DRIVE. These diskless computers are either special purpose, being used as a smart terminal in a network, or old computers that use a cassette recorder. Whatever, most computers do have disk drives. A computer is really restricted without one. The disk drives, of course, are used to write or read data to and from disks.

There are two categories of disk drives. They are called floppy disk drives and hard disk drives. The floppies come in assorted physical sizes. The hard drives come in assorted capacity sizes. Different manufacturers build drives with various configurations that take special brackets and bolting, but in general, there are only two types—floppy and hard.

The usual floppy disk drives

These units get their name from the disks they use. The disks are somewhat flexible, but don't bend them—just let them flex on their own. Aside from the fact that a floppy drive can come as a physical full-height or half-height unit, they are for the most part physically compatible with each other. There are a number of odd-size units that are found in dedicated word processors and other dedicated machines but these odd units are a distinct minority. The floppies come in the familiar 5¹/₄ and 3¹/₂ inch sizes (Table 24-1). The majority of the 5¹/₄ inch floppies come in three general types. The 3¹/₂ inch floppy drives come in two types.

The 5¹/₄ inch drives

The most recent type is the high-density, 5¹/₄ inch floppy disk drive. These use disks that are 5¹/₄ inches in diameter. The disks are able to store 1.2Mb of data. When you buy disks for this unit, you look on the box for 1.2Mb capacity and the

Table 24-1. Common floppy-disk drive characteristics.

	5¹/₄ Inch Double Density	High Density
Initials	DD	HD
Capacity	320 Kb – 360 Kb	1.2 Mb
Tracks per side	40	80
Height	Full & half height	Full & half height
Sectors per track	9	15
Bytes per Sector	512	512

	3¹/₂ Inch Double Density	High Density
Initial	DD	HD
Capacity	720 Kb	1.44 Mb
Tracks per side	80	80
Height	Half height	Half height
Sectors per Track	9	18
Bytes per Sector	512	512

lettering *HD* (high density). Most of the time the disk box will also have the lettering *DS* (double sided), which means the 1.2Mb's of data is stored on both sides of the disk.

A nice feature of these drives is, most of the time they are able not only to read data from their 1.2Mb HD, DS disks, but also from lower-capacity types in the 5¹/₄ inch size. These floppies are quite compatible with the lower-capacity models.

A step down in capacity are the double-sided, double-density, 5¹/₄ inch drives. There are two types. One uses disks that are able to store 360 kb of data. The other uses disks that store 320 kb. The disks from these units are usually able to be read by the 1.2Mb drive, but the 360 kb or 320 kb drives are not able to read the higher density disks.

The bottom of the 5¼ inch model line are the drives that can only store 180 kb or 160 kb on a single side with double density. There are still a few of these units around. A disk made on these units can be read by the models higher in density. These drives cannot read disks made by the improved models above.

The 3¹/₂ inch drives

The most recent 3¹/₂ inch drive is the high-density, 1.4Mb type. These are double sided. These units are much younger than the 5¼ inch types. (This size drive is double-sided only; there are no single-sided 3¹/₂ inch floppy drives.) Also, there is no easy compatibility between this top-of-the-line 3¹/₂ inch drive and the lower-capacity 3¹/₂ inch models. This drive will only read its prescribed size and capacity disk. If you try to read lower-capacity disks, you will usually get an error message.

The lower-capacity 3¹/₂ inch drive is the double-sided, double-density (DS,DD), 720 kb type. It too is not compatible with any other unit. Table 24-1 lists the common types and their comparisons. If you buy disks, you'll find the lower-capacity disks are a lot cheaper compared to the higher-density types. The 3¹/₂ inch disks are, as a rule, somewhat more expensive than the 5¼ inch types. You pay for the amount of data storage space that is available on the disks. All 3¹/₂ inch drives come in half-height sizes.

Hard-disk drives

Hard-disk drives use disks, but the disks are rigid metal and are mounted and sealed permanently in the drive housing. You do not go into a store and buy hard disks as you do with floppies. If you have to change a hard disk, you have a major servicing job on your hands.

The hard-disk drive comes in many capacity sizes. The capacity a hard disk has is many times the capacity a floppy drive can handle at one time. Typical hard disks can have capacities that range from 20 Mb into hundreds of megabytes. The usual personal computer will have somewhere between 20 and 80 Mb.

A hard-disk drive is a very high precision and expensive instrument. When it must be taken apart and serviced, the job must be done in a *clean room*. A clean room is one of these special rooms where the dust, temperature, and humidity are carefully monitored. The hard drive has a number of metal disks in a sealed unit. Even a small amount of dust in the unit could cause a drive *crash* (failure) and ruin the mechanism. The hard drive is discussed further in this chapter, but they are not usually repaired in the home or in an ordinary electronic service shop.

More about floppies

Whatever the size, a floppy disk has the following characteristics. It is not like a phonograph record despite the resemblance. A record has grooves cut into its surface that a needle rubs over producing mechanical vibrations that are turned into audio frequencies and heard from speakers. The computer disk is more like magnetic tape, in that a layer of iron oxide is coated on the smooth surface of the disk. The coating can be magnetized at any spot on the coating. The spots are microscopic. Each spot becomes a tiny permanent magnet.

When a spot is magnetized, the little magnet that is formed lines up with all the other little magnets that are made. The spots that remain unmagnetized are not placed in a line and lie around in a haphazard way. If a high is installed, the magnet could be lined up in a north-south orientation. Should a low be installed, the magnets are placed in the line but in a south-north position. Therefore all the highs are lined up in one direction and all the lows pointing in the opposite direction.

Each line is called a track. There could be thousands of bits in an inch of track. An advanced system can easily have 15,000 bits per inch of track. A floppy can be laid out with 40 concentric tracks. The tracks are given numbers, 0 – 39. The outside track is 0 and the inside one is 39. The tracks are not continuous like a phonograph record. Each track is an individual closed circle.

There could be ten sectors on each track. Each sector on each track is given an address. With 40 tracks, each with ten sectors, the 400 sector addresses can be 0 – 399. Each address is able to hold 512 bytes of data. Each of the eight bits in each byte is represented by a tiny magnet. Highs point in one direction, and lows point in the other.

The disks are placed in the drive when it is time for the processor to access this form of memory. When the disk is placed in the drive, the mechanism starts rotating the disk. An inexpensive disk drive rotates the disk at 300 rpm revolutions per minute. This is a rather slow computer disk drive speed. In more expensive disk systems, rotation speeds of 1500 rpm on disks with a few thousand tracks are not uncommon.

The disk rotates continually. The disk head is on an index shaft as shown in Fig. 24-1. The shaft is arranged to move in a line from the outer edge of the disk to the center of the disk. That way the head can be positioned over any of the 40 tracks as quickly as possible. The head can access any of the tracks in one fast mechanical move. This is why the disk drive is so much faster than cassette tape. In order to access tape, the tape must be run till the place where the desired information is located finally arrives at the head.

In this disk drive, with the disk rotating at 300 rpm, the ten sectors on each track are able to pass under the head five times a second. When you address the disk, it will place the head over the sector of data in less than a second. Each sector contains the equivalent of 512 keyboard characters, which can be sent to the processor very quickly.

The disk stores data in serial form. The processor reads and writes data over a parallel data bus. Therefore, when the disk is accessed, either to read its data or to write data to it, the data must be converted. When the processor is reading, the serial data on the disk must be converted to parallel. If the processor is writing to the disk, the parallel data must be converted to serial. A disk interface system handles that chore.

Data is packaged in a special format for the disk operation. Every piece of data

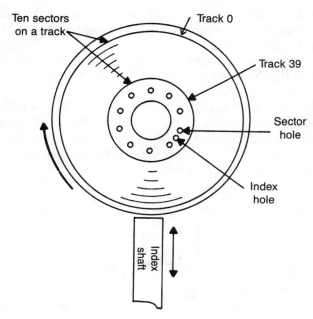

24-1 A floppy disk rotates in the drive. An index shaft with the recording heads can move over the tracks and access one quickly.

including the packaging bits is still only a high or a low, but in a special disk operating pattern. The 512 data bytes in a sector are placed into a cocoon of bytes that take care of functions such as sync and addressing. When a sector is filled with 512 bytes of data, the data is surrounded with a lot of control bytes. When the processor writes data to the disk drive, the interface circuits, along with the parallel to serial conversion, installs all of the control bytes.

The mechanical system that spins the disks and moves the index arm that holds the recording head, resembles a record player but is much faster. The mechanical pieces wear out and break down like a record player. However, the disk drive is much more critical. To repair the disk drive mechanically requires great care. The electronic repairs are not as mechanically critical. It is necessary though to understand the disk operation. The factory service manual would be very handy.

Disk control

In the IBM world, there are many manufacturers that make disk drives that fit into the IBM PCs. They also make drives that sit external to all computers and plug in or are wired in. All of these drives must be controlled by the processor of the computer.

In the IBM PC family a disk controller card is supplied that plugs into one of the port expansion slots, in the same way the monochrome and color output cards plug in. The disk controller card has a ribbon output cable that then connects to the disk drive, whatever its physical size and placement might be. The IBM card is able to support four disk drives.

The drive itself can be using disks that are single sided or double sided. The important thing is that it has 40 tracks. The sectors on the tracks must be divided by a predetermined set of bits.

The actual data that travels between the disk and the processor is controlled by an 8237 *DMA* (direct memory access) controller (Fig. 24-2) on the main board. It takes over the computer during the data transferring. It is able to move data from the disk to computer memory, from the computer memory to disk and even from one disk to another disk drive.

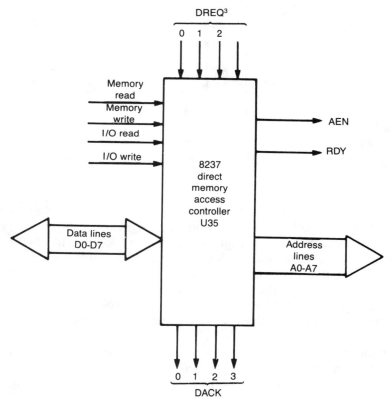

24-2   In the IBM PC, an 8237 controller chip in the computer takes over the system during data transfer between the disk and the computer.

When a disk drive wants to send data, it activates one of the four DREQ lines of the DMA controller. The chip in turn turns on one of its DACK lines. Then the chip sends out a signal to all the other I/O devices that puts them into a three-state condition.

Next the starting address and the number of bytes to be transferred are sent to the DMA controller. The data starts moving from the disk through the disk-controller card onto the data bus and into RAM. After all the bytes have been sent, the data bus control is given back to the processor.

A floppy-disk interface board

A floppy disk interface must have a chip that converts data serial-to-parallel and parallel-to-serial. On one end of the card there is an input from the data bus in the computer. At the other end of the card there is an input from disk drive. In between is the shift register chip that will convert the data.

Typically, the data bus will feed directly into a shift register like a UART. Once the data is converted from parallel to serial, then it must be conditioned into the bit pattern format required by the drive circuits. There is usually a circuit that will first divide the clock frequency and then decode the information into a 1-of-8 output. This defines each bit into a microsecond amount and synchronizes the bit with the system clock. Then the bit is passed through some logic circuits to produce the final bit pattern the floppy disk drive requires.

When data is going the other way, from the floppy disk to the computer, the bits must be conditioned on the card. As mentioned earlier, the bits are stored on the disk as tiny permanent magnets. The magnetic flux points in one direction for a high and the other for a low. Typically, each bit is bracketed with sync bits so that variations in speed of the rotating disk will not cause errors. A byte of serial data that is stored in a sector is eight bit patterns that include the sync besides the data.

During the storage operation bit 0 is stored first and bit 7 last. Whenever data is read back from the disk, bit 0 is transferred first and bit 7 last. The data is passed in serial form through some conditioning logic circuits. First, the data is separated from the clock pulses that are coming from the drive. Then the data is fed to the UART where the serial data is changed to parallel and at the same time synced firmly in step with the computer clock. Once the data transfer is complete and the data is stored in RAM, the controller turns the operation of the computer back to the processor or whatever other device is to take charge of the address and data bus lines.

Floppy-disk physical details

When you place a floppy disk into its drive slot and lock it in place, it is ready to run. It won't spin unless it is seated properly and locked. The 5$1/4$ inch drives have a locking handle. The 3$1/2$ inch drives are simply pushed into a spring loaded mechanism, are pressed downward and will click into place. The drive will then run according to command.

The disks spin inside their holders at rotation rates of either 300 or 360 rpm. The high-density drives spin the disks at 360, and the lower-density drives spin disk at 300 rpm. As the disks spin, the heads move over the top and bottom of the disk. The heads are able to move back and forth a total distance of about an inch.

The distance the heads move can cover 40 tracks on the $5^1/4$ inch, 360 kb, disks or 80 tracks on the $5^1/4$ inch, 1.2 Mb; $3^1/2$ inch 720 kb; and $3^1/2$ inch 1.4 Mb disks. The 40 tracks on the lesser density covers the same amount of disk real estate that the higher density 80 tracks do. The 80 tracks are just packed in more tightly. The width of the tracks get thinner and thinner as the density increases. For example, the $5^1/4$ inch 360 kb disk has tracks that are 0.33 millimeters wide. The $5^1/4$ inch 1.2 Mb disk has tracks that are 0.16 millimeters wide, only half the track width of the lessor density disk.

Because the heads traverse the top and bottom of the disk at the same time, the data on the top and bottom head pathways are accessed together. This dual accessing path is called a cylinder. A single cylinder is defined as that part of the tracks that are accessed together on the top and bottom of the disk. A disk is designated to possess a certain number of cylinders.

These different track widths do not present too much of a problem when data is being read with a high-density $5^1/4$ inch drive from a lower-density disk. However, trying to write to these disks can cause complications. A good rule to follow is—do not write data to disks that do not match the drive being used. It can be done, but it can cause complications and loss of data. As mentioned earlier, the different $3^1/2$ inch drives are not usually compatible at all.

Floppy-disk drive components

The heads in the drive are the link between the data stored in microscopic, permanent magnets in tracks on the disk and the electronics on the drive print board. The heads convert the magnet positions to an electronic signal. They are, gauss to voltage, converters. The old single-sided drives had a single head. The double-sided drives, which make up most of the floppies, have two heads—one for the top of the disk and one for the bottom. The two heads travel through the space encompassed by a cylinder, as defined earlier.

The heads are both a gauss-to-voltage converter and a voltage-to-gauss converter. The G-to-V occurs when the heads are reading from the disk. The V-to-G happens when the heads are writing to the disk. As a result they are called read-write heads. The heads move in and out over a straight line, over the spinning disk. The two heads are spring loaded and grip the disk through the slotted apertures on the top and bottom of the disk. They grasp the disk material between them with a very light touch. The pressure causes no problem with friction. The disks are usually coated with some sort of solid lubricating material to reduce any undue wear. The only thing that occurs is some oxide builds up over time on the heads. The oxide then must be cleaned off as described later in the chapter.

The heads are made of soft iron compounds embedded in a configuration of electromagnetic coils. Each head is actually three heads. There is one read-write coil and two erase coils. The three heads are built together as shown in Fig. 24-3 and move in over the disk with the read-write coil leading the way. The two erase heads follow the read-write coil. The read-write coil accesses the disk. The two erase coils flank the read-write coil and erase the outer bands of the accessed track. This makes the data in the track stay within a narrow area on the track. If

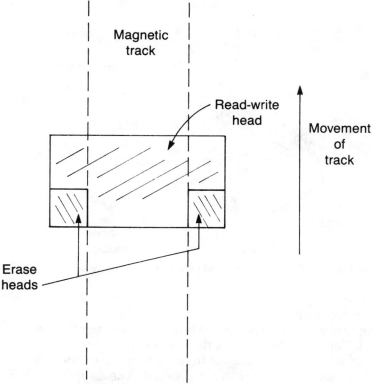

24-3 A typical recording head consists of one read-write section and two erase sections.

the data should spill off the track it could interfere with data on the adjoining tracks. The erase heads keep the data closely within the boundaries of its assigned track.

It is vital that the heads travel over the apertures in the disk and grasp the disk precisely at the right spots. If the heads should get out of line just a little bit, problems will occur. This condition, when it occurs, is an alignment problem. You can check the alignment floppies with a test alignment disk for your machine. These disks are prepared by producing a disk from a known good floppy drive of the same type you are using.

Stepper motor

The heads are mounted on some sort of arm that is connected to a stepper motor, as in Fig. 24-4. A stepper motor is one that does not rotate continually. It can only rotate a total of one revolution. However, it is built to move in steps during that one revolution. It is able to move the read-write heads in steps over the tracks. If the drive operates with 40 track disks, the stepper motor can move 40 steps, one for each track. Should the drive work on 80 track disks, the stepper moves 80 steps during its single revolution. The drive is able to move the heads over any track

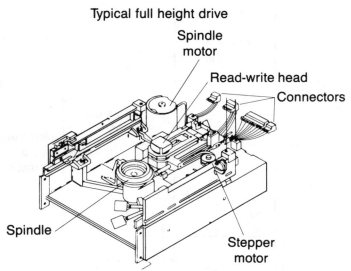

Typical full height drive

24-4　The floppy-disk drive components are installed tightly and critically in the unit.

from any other track. The stepper goes back and forth easily and can be positioned over any desired track.

A stepper motor can cause the heads to travel over all of its tracks in about $1/5$ of a second. This is from one end of the tracks to the other. If the heads only have to travel half the total track distance to reach an assigned track, it can do that in half of $1/5$ of a second which is $1/10$ of a second. The stepper motor is the determiner of a floppy disk characteristic called average access time. This is the average time that occurs for each access as the heads are reading or writing. It usually averages somewhere around $1/10$ of a second.

Spindle motor

There is another motor in the floppy drive that spins the disk at 300 or 360 rpm. It is called the spindle motor. The newer motors are direct drive. They are built to run at exactly 300 or 360 rpm and unless the motor breaks, they maintain that rotation rate.

Early spindle motors were not direct drive but were driven by a belt. The belts over time wore badly, loosened, and frayed. This caused the rotation rates to change which caused many access problems. When the rate changes and troubles occur in these belt driven motors, the cure is to reset the rotation rate. The technique to do this is discussed in this chapter.

Electronics

Also, every floppy drive needs electronics that is mounted on print boards in the drive. These print boards do a number of jobs. First of all, these boards are the interface to the controller in computer. The controller consists of special circuits that are either on an adapter card or on the motherboard in the computer. The controller connects to the special floppy drive boards. Between the controller and the floppies print board, are all the circuits that control the movement of the stepper motor, the read-write heads, the spindle motors and the other components in the drive. When these print boards develop failures, troubleshooting is the same as any other print board. Service notes and test equipment are needed. Often you can buy a new board or swap a board with a defect for a fee.

Connectors

There are two types of connectors on a floppy drive. One is needed for actual ac power to energize the drive. The second connector is needed for the transfer of data as the computer reads from or writes to the disk. You can quickly identify which connector is which. The power connector is a four inline type. The control information and data travels through a 34-pin edge connector. While these connectors are typical on a floppy drive, they could be slightly different on various makes and models. It is easy though to tell the difference. The power connector will have very few lines attached to it, perhaps three or four. The power lines are also heavy-duty wires because they conduct significant amounts of current. The data and control signal lines are more numerous and use thin types of wire. There are insignificant amounts of current when data travels over the wires. In addition, while a typical floppy drive uses a 34-pin edge connector, you could encounter special drives with different connectors and/or numbers of pins. However, the data and control signal connectors will always have many more wires attached than a power connector. All of the connections are important for servicing. They are test points where you can obtain valid voltage, current and scope readings.

A few words on floppy disks

In every instruction manual where floppy drives are involved, there are a group of do's and don'ts on handling the disks. The typical warnings are, don't spill coffee on the disk, don't bend the disk, keep the disk away from heat and magnetic fields, don't touch the actual surface of the disk with your fingers or anything else, only write on the jacket with a felt tip pen and not a ball point, etc. Of course, follow these instructions as well as you can. They are only common sense.

However, there are some booby traps around that you should try to avoid. They can ruin data on a disk without you hardly realizing it. If you recall chapter 23, in the color CRT section, it was mentioned that you could use a degaussing coil to demagnetize the metal parts of a color CRT. These degaussing coils will also demagnetize your floppy disks if they are laying nearby. In addition the coils could harm the data on a hard disk, if its electromagnetic field crosses the drive. Be careful if you use a degaussing coil. Keep it away from all disks when it is energized.

In addition, many color TV receivers and color monitors have built in degaussing coils. The coils are energized every time you turn on the TV or monitor. Fortunately, the built in degaussers are considerably weaker than the external degaussers and are installed in the monitor to cause the least amount of electromagnetic radiation. They will be harmless for the most part, just do not lay floppies full of data on top of a color monitor. The data could be ruined. Also keep floppies away from all electric devices. Be especially careful when using vacuum cleaners and telephone systems. Store floppies in a safe, cool, electromagnetic free place.

Typical floppies

Just about everyone knows what a floppy disk looks like. A close look (Fig. 24-5) reveals there are a number of details. There are, of course, two main types, the 5¼ inch and the 3½ inch. Each has a special construction of its own, besides the physical size.

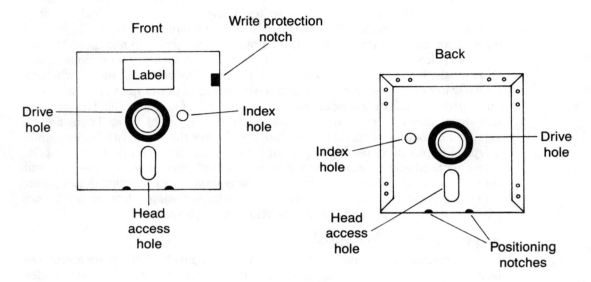

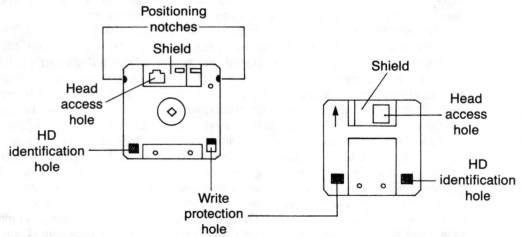

24-5   Typical 5¼-inch and 3½-inch disks. Each hole has a specific purpose.

The 5^1/$_4$ inch floppy is shown in Fig. 24-5. There is a round hole in the center of the jacket. Sticking out of the jacket is a ring of actual disk material. When you insert a disk into the drive slot and lock the latch, a cone-shaped clamp grabs the disk material sticking out of the inside of its hole and firmly places the disk into a specific position. Alongside of the hole on the right on the jacket is an index hole. If you would rotate the disk inside the jacket you would see a hole on the disk material that lines up with the jacket index hole. There are index holes on both sides of the jacket. The index hole on the disk material is used by the drive as the reference point that will indicate where all the sectors on the disk are.

Directly beneath the main hole is a slot in the jacket that exposes the disk surface. There are slots on both sides of the jacket. These slots are the entry ways for the read-write heads to grasp the disk. There is one slot for the top head and one slot for the bottom head. The heads can move forward and back in the slots as the disk material rotates inside the protective jacket. In disk drives, these slots are called the media access holes. The media of course, being the data and control signal that are read from the disk or written to the disk.

In the upper half of the disk, just to the right of the label is a little square cutout called the write-enable hole. These cutouts are only found on virgin disks. If you buy a disk that has a permanent program on it, the cutout will either be missing or be taped over. You can't write to the disk when the cutout is not there or is taped over. The disk can only be written to if the cutout is open. Then the disk is write enabled. If you want to stop a disk from ever being written to, tape over the cutout.

The only other two items on the ordinary floppy is the label and two positioning notches at the bottom of the disk. The label, of course is for your use. The two bottom notches are used by the drive to keep the disk and jacket positioned properly as the disk is rotated. The notches also act as stress relief for the jacket material as the disk spins and puts pressures on the jacket.

The 3^1/$_2$ inch floppies also shown in Fig. 24-5 are not as floppy as the 5^1/$_4$ inch. In fact, they are quite rigid. That is, their jacket is rigid, the disk inside is still flexible. There is no center hole on the top of the jacket. There is one hole on the bottom of the jacket. A round metal cover protrudes from the hole. There is a small square in the center of the metal cover. The drive enters the small square and grasps the metal, which is in turn firmly attached to the disk material. The drive can then spin the disk material inside the jacket.

Alongside the square hole on the metal hole cover is the index hole. This index hole does the same job as the one on the 5^1/$_4$ inch disk. That is, it acts as a reference for the drive to know where the sectors on the disk are. The slots that permit the read-write heads to grasp the disk material are hidden under a spring loaded shutter. The shutter is a metal device that you can move to the left. That will expose the disk material on the top and bottom of the jacket through two slots.

On the bottom left side of the jacket is a little square hole. On the other side of the jacket is a slider that can open or shut the hole. This is the write enable hole. When the hole is open the disk can be written to. If the slider is pushed to close the hole, the disk cannot be written to. It works the same way the write enable notch operates on the 5^1/$_4$ inch disk and is used in the same way. A virgin disk will have a square hole and slider for your use. A disk that you purchase with a program on it could be made without the write-enable hole so the disk won't ever be accidentally written to.

On high-density disks, there is one more hole not found on the lower double density disks. This is the high-density indicator hole. When the hole is present, the drive knows it is dealing with an HD disk. If there is no hole there the drive knows it has a DD disk in its grasp. Finally, there are two positioning holes on the bottom side of the jacket. They are drilled on the two sides of the shutter that exposes the disk material. These two holes help to keep the disk in the precise operating position as it rotates.

As a point of interest, the disk materials are composed of a plastic like mylar coated with a compound that contains magnetic substances. In the typical lower density disks the compound is based around iron oxide. For higher density disks, instead of iron, cobalt could be used. All of the materials are plentiful and relatively inexpensive. Floppy disks are sturdy, permanent data storage means. By using care during handling and only using the correct disk for the drive, floppies and their data can last for years without problems.

Floppy-disk maintenance and adjustments

The disk drive system is a computer type device on its own. It is a good idea not to attempt any electronic repairs unless you are an experienced technician equipped with the service manual for the particular unit. The repairing of the electronics of disk drives encompasses the computer, the drive controller board in the computer and the logic board in the drive. All of this information will be found in the service manuals for the computer and floppy drive.

As far as the mechanical maintenance and adjustments of the drive are concerned, there are a few things that can be done with a little care. Mechanical repairs are another story. When the mechanisms break, you must be experienced and armed with service notes and replacement parts. Otherwise have a disk drive repair shop do the honors. Evaluate the costs carefully. Quite often it would pay you to purchase a new drive instead of fixing it.

Fortunately, most of the time that floppy trouble occurs, the cure falls into the category of maintenance and adjustments. The most common trouble that happens is due to dirty drive heads. They can be cleaned without too much fuss. A second common trouble is changes in the speed of the disk rotation. In older full-height or other drives with belts that turn the spindle, the adjustments are relatively easy. In more recent half-height drives and others with direct drives, the adjustments are often difficult and not worth trying. Fortunately, direct-drive units are very reliable and do not change speeds that easily.

In all cases of floppy-drive failure, keep in mind the throw-away option. Floppy drives are a vital part of the computer and should never be operating marginally. Also floppy drives, in the scheme of things, are considered inexpensive. If a defective drive is a great chore to repair and is going to cost a lot of money, put it out of action and get a new one. Sometimes you can trade it in. If not, and the drive was not a lemon type, try to get the same make and model you had and save the old one. There are a lot of good replacement parts in it.

Cleaning dirty disk-drive heads

No matter how hard you try and how meticulous you might be, some dirt in the form of oxides will build up on your disks. They just accumulate out of the normal atmosphere. Then when you run the disks in the drive mechanism and the disk surface rotates a fraction of an inch from the read/write head, some of these oxides will deposit themselves on the head, mostly on the head side that faces the rotation. When enough oxide is collected on the head, the computer starts making read or write errors that ruins your computing. What to do? The head must be cleaned.

There are two common ways that heads can be cleaned. One way is take some medical alcohol and a cotton swab wrapped in a lint free material. You must be careful not to moisten any of the components or hardware that surround the head. Only the head is to be swabbed.

The big problem with the manual cleaning procedure is getting to the head. You must disassemble the computer and the drive mechanism. Each personal computer has its own special ways that the disassembly must be performed. It is a good idea to have the exact disassembly instructions for your machine before you attempt to take it apart.

Once you do gain access to the head and it is free and clear, then you can rub the oxides off. When you are satisfied the head is clean, step away and let the area completely dry. After it is dry you can retrace your steps and reassemble the system.

If you are not interested in taking your machine apart for the cleaning, you can purchase a disk head cleaning kit in a computer store. The kit consists of a special cleaning disk that is covered with some cleaning solvent. To clean the head, the cleaning disk is simply placed into your disk drive and turned on. The spinning action of the drive rubs the disk material against the head. The oxides are then rubbed off.

Follow the directions with the cleaning disk. However, it is a good idea to time the disk as it cleans. A good average time is 30 seconds. Do not leave the cleaning disk on more than that or else you could ruin the head from the friction.

How often should you clean your disk drive heads? Everytime you clean the heads you are exposing your drive to some possible mishap. In addition, there will be some wear and tear from the activity. Yet in order for the drive to function properly the head must be clean.

I personally feel that a regular weekly or monthly type of cleaning schedule that some manufacturers recommend is not applicable to all people. Your drive could be in any type of environment, cold, hot, high or low humidity, and with pollution, etc. The drive might be used continually or only on occasions.

Leave the drive alone until you start getting some read/write errors. Then you can clean it with a cleaning disk. If the trouble persists, perhaps a manual cleaning might then be in order. The best thing to do is keep your disk covered up when not in use and perform the tricky cleaning process only when there is a problem.

Adjusting the disk speed of rotation in belt-driven drives

Typical personal computer drives rotate at 300 rpm. If the drive speed should slow down or speed up due to mechanical wear and tear, the read/write head might not be able to perform correctly. If the speed is erratic the head will read a wrong address or the head will write to a wrong spot on the disk. The only solution is to adjust the drive so the rotation is exactly correct such as the prescribed 300 rpm.

There is a special control on belt-driven disk drive mechanisms that can be adjusted with a tiny screwdriver. Besides the screwdriver a means of noting the rpm speed is needed so the adjustment can be checked and set at the prescribed speed. The following is two ways an IBM PC drive can be speed checked.

On the bottom of the PC drive (as in Fig. 24-6) you can see the flywheel that does the rotating. Mounted on the bottom of the flywheel is a disk with lines on it. These are timing marks. The outer rows of marks is designed to time 60 Hz electricity.

To use these timing marks all you need do is shine a light on them, not a battery flashlight, but one plugged into the 60 Hz plug in your home or office. You can't tell easily but such a light is flickering at a 60 Hz rate. The timing marks are designed to appear to be standing still when the disk is running at exactly 300 rpm.

If you turn on the disk and the timing marks appear to be standing still, then your machine is rotating correctly. However, if the marks are rotating slowly either one way or the other, the disk is either slower than 300 rpm or faster. All you have to do is adjust the speed control until the marks stop moving and stand still. That is the exact speed that is prescribed for the drive.

Another way the speed could be checked and adjusted is with a disk speed program on a disk. You take the test program and run it in the drive. The display will come up and show a graph like in Fig. 24-7. The display shows the current speed setting. You then adjust the speed control until the display shows the speed at 300 rpm.

In addition to cleaning procedures and the speed-control adjusting, it is not a good idea to attempt any other extensive repairs on the disk drive without training. The disk drive system is a complicated electronic and mechanical system in its own right and it requires great skill to effect repairs.

Hard-disk drives

The most obvious difference between a floppy drive and a hard drive is, there is no entrance slot to insert a disk. The machine is completely enclosed inside the computer case. There is no way to insert a disk. The obvious reason for this is, the disks are sealed into the drive and are not easily removable. You don't have to buy disks as you must for floppy operation. The hard disks inside the unit are permanently installed. They are made of a metal like aluminum and called platters rather than disks.

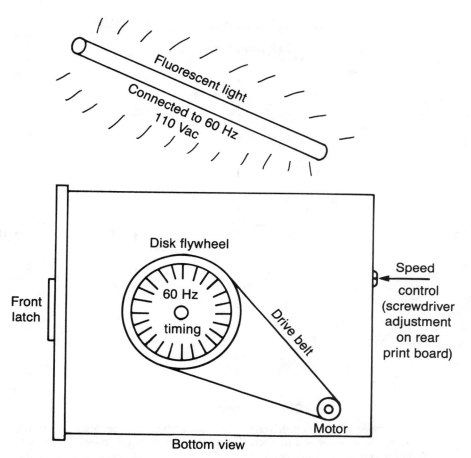

24-6 On belt-driven disk drives, the speed of rotation is typically 300 rpm (revolutions per minute). With this strobe setup of a fluorescent bulb connected to a 60 Hz voltage and with a 60 Hz timing pattern on the flywheel, the speed can be checked. If the lines appear to be moving, adjust the speed control until they stand still. They will stand still at 300 rpm.

A hard drive can be constructed with one or more platters. The platters come in the same sizes as floppy disks, 5¼ and 3½ inch and are about ⅛ inches thick. The aluminum is covered with similar magnetic materials as the floppies are. The magnetic materials are very thin and highly polished. If you look at a platter it will have a brownish shiny appearance. The process to make these platters are high tech and expensive. The platters are high-precision products with material layers that measure in the millionths of an inch. The read-write head flies closely above the material as the platters spin. By closely is meant a few millionths of an inch. The hard-drive heads do not touch the platters like the floppy heads touch the floppy disks.

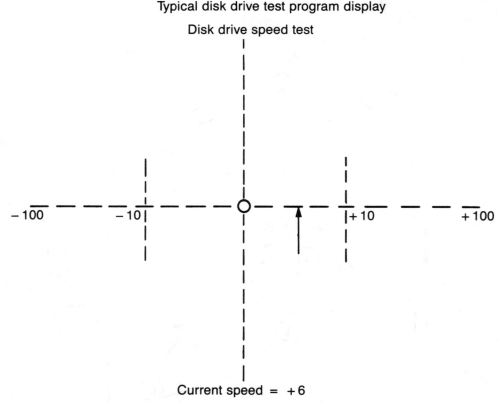

Typical disk drive test program display

Disk drive speed test

Current speed = +6

24-7 Another speed test for belt-driven disk drives can be conducted with a test program. A display like this one will be seen. The speed control can then be adjusted until the current speed error equals zero.

The drives come in full height and half height like floppies. There are both full height and half height 5¼ inch types but the 3½ inch units only come as half height. There are larger drives for special purposes, but they are not usually found in personal computers. There are smaller drives around too, often found in dedicated word processors, but not in personal computers as a rule.

How a hard-disk drive is put together

If you look inside a hard disk-drive package, there isn't too much to see. Most of the moving parts are contained in a sealed unit. The sealed unit dare not be opened in an ordinary room. There is too much dust around. The sealed unit should only be opened in a factory clean room. As mentioned, there are platters with microscopically thin magnetic coatings that spin near read-write heads that are only a few millionths of an inch away from the coatings. Unlike the floppy drives, the read-write heads do not touch the magnetic material while the platters are spinning. The heads can be made to land on the platters at assigned landing zones while the platters are still. At any rate, no dust must get into the sealed unit. Even the tiniest pieces of dust could foul the space between the heads and the platters.

If you did manage to look inside the sealed unit, you would see a mechanism somewhat like Fig. 24-8. A close look reveals all the components that are found in the floppy drive are also found in the hard drive. There are platters (disks), read-write heads, a stepper motor (in more expensive drives a voice-coil mechanism replaces the stepper motor), spindle motor, and other attachment hardware. The number of platters and their associated read-write heads varies according to available space. The small capacity half-height units could have only one platter. A larger capacity half-height $3^1/2$ inch unit could have up to about five platter systems. In the roomier full-height $5^1/4$ inch units there could be up to eight platter systems. The sealed unit is considered as a single expensive component. It cannot be repaired internally under ordinary circumstances.

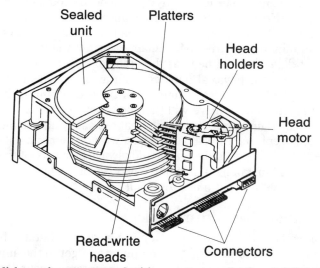

24-8 A hard disk can be constructed with one or more hard metal disks called platters. The moving mechanisms are enclosed in a sealed unit that is not easily opened up.

Outside the sealed unit are the usual drive components. You can see, the drives print board with its components, the connectors for power input and signal I/O, and the mounting hardware.

How a hard-disk drive can fail

In general, the hard drive runs in the same way a floppy drive does with a few changes. The main change is, a hard drive operates with permanent, multiple platters instead of with one removable disk. On each platter are the same kind of sectors and tracks. A set of read-write heads all ganged together are moved forward and back over the tracks simultaneously. One set of tracks, on both sides of the multiple disks, constitute a cylinder.

A second change in the hard drive is the speed of rotation that the platters spin at. The speed is typically ten times or more the floppy speed. This means the platters are typically spinning about 3600 revolutions per minute. This spinning causes a change in the position of the heads. Instead of two heads grasping a disk, the heads are made with special aerodynamic characteristics. As the platters spin, the movement of the air generated by the platters lifts the heads off the platters a few millionths of an inch. There is no friction to speak of between the platter and the heads. The heads are actually flying at a microscopically low altitude above the platters. This is high enough to eliminate friction but still close enough that the electromagnetic relationship between the platters and heads is retained.

The heads are also spring loaded. They will fly o.k. while the platters are spinning, but when the platters stop, the heads are forced to land on the platter surface. If some physical fault should happen in the platter-head area while the platters are spinning and the heads are flying, the heads could crash. If the fault is caused by dirt or specks of dust, you stand a chance of the trouble quickly stopping as the foreign matter blows away from the crash site. Most platters are hardened and lubricated to minimize head-crash damage. Most of the time, no harm is done except some lost data that had been at the crash site on the platter. On occasion though, some permanent physical damage such as a broken mechanism occurs. When it does, you will hear noises come out of the sealed unit or it will quit altogether. The unit or the entire drive will then need replacement.

Outside the sealed unit are components that are easily accessible. They can be tested, repaired, or replaced by ordinary means with test equipment, service notes and replacement parts. Here again you should always be aware of the possibility of junking the drive and installing a new one when repair parts and labor is going to cost a large percentage of what a new one will cost.

The most common hard-drive problem

The most common hard-drive problem is a physical defect, but it is fixed with software. There is no reason to open up the computer and get to the ailing hard drive. The symptoms are common, and when these symptoms occur they can almost always be cured by running a special hard-drive repair program.

When the hard disk starts having repeated read-write failures or loses data, after having operated correctly for a long time, there are problems on the platters. The platters, when first put into use, are formatted. The first part of the total format procedure is to lay the tracks and sectors onto the platters. This is accomplished with a format program. The format program writes to the virgin platter and instead of placing data bits onto the magnetic material it draws tracks and assigns sectors. The format program does a lot of other jobs too, but this condition has to do with the correct placement of the tracks and sectors.

This track degradation occurs because after time, the magnetic tracks begin to disintegrate. There are many reasons for the degradation. The little permanent magnets in the magnetic material coating can have an attraction-repulsion effect on each other and move off of the assigned track paths. There could have been some sort of electromagnetic, electrostatic, or permanent-magnet force that came close to the tracks and moved them. Perhaps some of the magnetic points on the platter loses some of its gaussian effect. Sometimes repeated head crashes would alter a track. There are many reasons that could have caused the problem.

The cure is to re-do the tracks. In the format program, the tracks are layed down in the section called *low-level format*. A new low-level format will put down fresh tracks in the correct place. There are many programs around that will reformat the hard disk. For example, in the IBM advanced diagnostics that comes with the service manuals is a low-level format program for IBM machines. There are also a few other sources of low-level format programs for this purpose. Once you reformat the off-track platters, the drive will usually start operating correctly again. To reformat, follow the program directions. You will go through the following general steps.

First of all, make sure you back up the platters. You could lose data during the process. Next run the low-level format routine. During the program run, in addition to laying tracks, the program will check for permanent defects on the platters.

Most of the time, platters have a few permanent defects in the magnetic material. The program will locate these defects and mark them so they can never be written to. Another job the program performs is setting up the interleave numbers for the particular controller and drive being used. The interleave numbers have to do with the sequence the sectors are read in one revolution. For example, if there are 17 sectors on the platters, they could be read in the following sequence on the first revolution: 1, 5, 9, 13, and 17. On subsequent revolutions, the remaining numbers are read. Each particular drive system could have different interleave numbers.

The above is the low-level format. For the complete format, the program then performs partitioning. This separates the drive memory into a number of partitions. Finally the program does the high-level formatting. This is the familiar DOS (disk-operating system), high-level format. This high-level format can be easily performed with the DOS FORMAT file. The low-level reformat software repair job on hard disks is often the only measure needed in a very large percentage of hard-drive problems.

25

Computer power supplies

ASIDE FROM BATTERY-RUN COMPUTERS ALL THE REST MUST BE PLUGGED into a wall socket and buy electrical energy from the power company. Electric companies in the U.S. provide the familiar 110 V at a 60 Hz frequency. In Europe, you might receive 220 V at 50 Hz. Whatever the power company's input, the computer power supply must receive the voltage and convert it into a form that the computer needs to use.

Inside the computer and the monitor are digital chips, op amp chips, discrete transistors, and other components that must be powered. These components need specific voltages and current capabilities that do not resemble the 110 V, 60 Hz input from the power company. The integrated-circuit chips can only operate with voltages around +5 and −5 V. The op amps and discrete transistors use voltages that range around +12 and −12 V. These voltages must be closely regulated and also be able to draw specific amounts of current. Computer monitors require TV-type supply voltages that can be around 5 V for ICs, 12 V for op amps and transistors, and voltages in the 100s or 1000s to drive the sweep circuits and CRTs. Some CRT focus voltages are around +500 V. CRT anode voltages can range from 10 – 15 kV for monochrome CRTs and up to 30 kV for color CRTs. Practically all of these required voltages are dc. They all must be derived from the original 110 V, 60 Hz rate.

The power supply for a particular computer, is for the most part, a separate unit. In the early 8-bit computers, some computers had the supply built right onto the main board. These integrated supplies are not seen much anymore. Supplies are usually separate boxes that hold all the power circuits. They bolt onto the chassis mounting assembly and plug into the motherboard. The circuits come in two versions—conventional and switching. The older conventional supply turns on when energized and applies its voltage outputs to the computer, no matter what. The switching supply is different. It turns on when energized and tests the computer to see if there is a load, that is, good operating circuits that will be energized. If the load is not present or not correct, the supply shuts itself down. There is more about switching power supplies in both the computer and the monitor in this chapter.

If you liken electric energy from the utility company to water supplies, the voltage is analogous to water pressure. The frequencies could be compared to pulsating water that comes out of the spigot. Then there is electrical current, this is like the amount of water the utility charges you for. The electric company will sell you as much current as you need. As the amperes course into your house, the meter runs and charges you. They calibrate it in kilowatt hours but they are charging you for amps. A watt is simply the voltage times amps. The voltage is fixed at 120 V but the number of amperes you draw changes every month according to your needs.

On the power supply schematic, you'll find the input plug symbol is accompanied by the voltage and the amount of current the computer system draws. For instance, the Apple II plug reads 120 V_{ac}, 290 mA. The mA means milliamps or mils. It is 0.290 A, not very much. The IBM PC reads 120 V_{ac}, 800 mA.

If you multiply 120 × .290, it equals, 34.8 W. The Apple is rated at 34.8 W. The IBM PC, 120 × .800 = 96 W. This wattage is the amount of power the supplies in these machines can deliver. The power energizes all the components in the units. The supply must also power any print cards that might get plugged into the expansion slots. The Apple has eight expansion slots, but none of the cards draw very much current. It can get by, most of the time, with a 34 W supply. The IBM PC only has five slots but the cards that plug into those slots draw a lot more current. Some of the cards have complete video systems on them, others that are heavy duty could possess a modem, memory expansions, disk, drives, and other useful accessories. Should a card be needed but draws too much current, it can't be used. For instance, a disk drive card would overload the supply. An external drive must be employed with its own power supply.

The IBM XT, as a result was built with a supply that is able to draw 130 W. The IBM AT enjoys 175 W. They are able to utilize floppy and hard disk drive cards plugged into their expansion slots. The newer PS/2 machines from IBM have a 94 W supply in the Model 50, 207 W in the Model 60 and 225 W available in the Model 80.

In a computer, the supply not only converts ac to prescribed dc levels, but the dc levels must be closely regulated. This means there cannot be any frequency ripples in the steady dc level.

dc regulation

In old vacuum tube devices, dc regulation was usually not included in the power supplies. If some ripple did get into the dc output of the supply the results were tolerable. This is not the case in microcomputers or their monitors. The lack of regulation would put interference into the digital signals and either cause errors or decimate the signal altogether.

What exactly is dc regulation? This question brings up the story of the giant storage battery. Just suppose that instead of the electric company, your neighborhood used a giant storage battery. This giant battery is able to supply all the amperes or kilowatt hours that your neighborhood needed and still have plenty more current left over.

All the electronic equipment in your neighborhood would not need complex power supplies. The battery would put out a dc voltage that would hold at the desired volt level without varying a fraction of a volt either way. Usually when equipment is first turned on, there is a sudden burst of current that flows and the voltage supply suffers a small lowering of voltage until the current flow stabilizes. When the current supply is so plentiful as in this magical battery, turning on equipment would not affect the voltage. The voltage would be regulated perfectly and not vary.

If the battery was not a giant, but much smaller, when equipment is turned on, there would be a loss of voltage for a short period of time. This loss of voltage would be a voltage spike in the steady dc output of the battery. This spike would be applied to all the chips in any computers on the line. The spike could get into a byte of signal and change the value of the byte. The program being run would have errors or even crash. Voltage regulation is essential in these sensitive electronic machines.

Because there are not giant storage batteries putting out a perfectly regulated dc voltage to energize computer systems, regulation must be installed in the power supplies. An actual regulator is discussed later in this chapter.

Voltage regulators are defined as devices that supply dc voltages to a circuit load. They automatically keep the dc voltage at or near a constant voltage. They perform this regulation no matter what the variations are in ac line voltage or the amount of current that the load draws.

In battery operated computers such as portables and laptops, batteries are used to power the units. The straight dc from the batteries are ideal and the voltage is regulated by the natural state of the battery. The ac driven computer supplies though, have to first change the ac to unregulated dc and then duplicate the dc battery regulated output with the regulator devices. Let's examine a typical small computer's power supply that is able to eliminate these unwanted ac ripples and voltage spikes that are so potentially damaging.

Power supply input

The input to most computers enters from the 120 V, 60 Hz house line through a polarized plug. The plug has two active lines that send the 120 V_{ac} to a power transformer that is fused in the high input line. The ground connection on the polarized plug is connected to the chassis ground of the computer. As shown in Fig. 25-1 there is 0.01 μF HV capacitor to ground from the high input line (120 V). There is a second HV capacitor from the low input line (0 V) to ground. There is a third HV capacitor between the high and low input lines. These bypass capacitors eliminate incoming noise spikes that might be on the power lines.

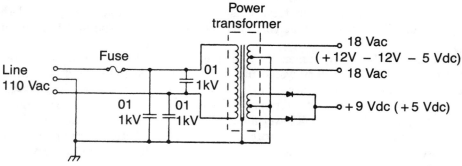

Fuse and power transformer

25-1 This computer power supply input steps down the 110 V_{ac} house current to a pair of 18 V_{ac} and +9 V_{dc} outputs.

In the transformer secondary there are two windings. Both are centertapped to the chassis ground. They are stepdown windings. The 120 V_{ac} input is stepped down to about 18 V_{ac} in the two windings. The computer can use the top winding for the +12 V, -12 V and -5 V needs. The bottom winding is then left to do the job of providing the 2 amps at +5 V the rest of the computer requires.

The power supply is one of the most common sources of trouble. It is subject to all the typical power supply troubles that technicians have become familiar with in all electronic gear. The fuse can blow, the rectifiers short or open, the transformer can open or start smoking from internal wiring shorts.

The typical symptom of power supply trouble is the dead computer. The first test, of course, is a fuse replacement. Sometimes that cures, but usually the replacement fuse will also blow and further tests must take place. Examine the circuits in detail.

+5 V line

The bottom winding of the transformer secondary is connected to the anodes of two rectifier diodes (Fig. 25-1). This provides a full wave rectification circuit. The high voltage peak of the 120 V sine wave input is rectified by one diode and the low voltage valley of the sine wave is rectified by the other diode. The cathodes of the diodes are tied together so the two rectified pulses are output together.

The twin diode output is a dc with ripple. After the rectification the dc has a voltage of +9 V. The dc has the ripple removed by being passed over the top of a 10,000 μF filter in Fig. 25-2. The smoothed out +9 V is then injected into the emitter of a discrete PNP transistor. The emitter is biased with a 68 ohm resistor from the base of the PNP.

The transistor is in charge of the amount of current the +5 V line will be permitted to have. The PNP is in turn controlled by the output of a 723C adjustable voltage regulator chip. This is a common voltage regulator that is found in a lot of computer power supplies. The regulator is vital to the correct processing of data in

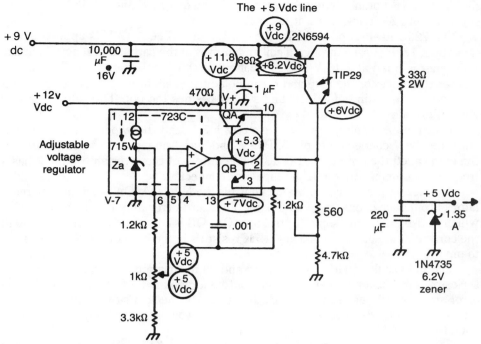

25-2 The 723C regulator chip with some buffer and pass transistors is able to output a well regulated $+5\ V_{dc}$ with heavy current abilities.

the digital circuits. Without it meaningless data bits would appear in programs and cause havoc.

The 723C is contained in a 14-pin DIP. The circuit consists of two zener diodes, two NPN transistors, and a buffer amplifier. The 723C has the job of regulating the amount of current that flows through a series-pass power transistor. It constantly samples the current flow through the transistor and automatically adjusts the flow with its connection to the base. If some ripple tends to be generated, the adjustment cancels the ripple and allows only a steady dc to power the computer components.

The regulator voltage exits pin 10 of the 723. It is connected to the base of the NPN, which in turn is driving the series-pass PNP. The output of the PNP then goes to the .33 ohm resistor. From there, the voltage passes over a 6.2 V zener diode and a 220 microfarad filter. The voltage emerges from the circuit as the desired regulated +5 V. This circuit can supply 1.35 amps without any problems. The zener diode is normally off. It is only there in case a short develops between the +5 V line and the +12 V line. It will start conducting if the voltage rises above 6.2 V and will not permit any of the higher voltages into the +5 V rated circuits. The +12 V is applied to the chip at pin 12. It passes through a coil and arrives at the cathode of zener diode Za. The zener is rated at 7.15 V and this voltage is thus applied to pin 6. This is the voltage reference for the chip and it can be adjusted slightly by a 1K pot in a voltage divider consisting of a 1.2K and a 3.3K besides the pot. The voltage divider ends at ground.

The 723C itself is powered by the +12 V line. The +12 V is applied to the chip at pin 12. It passes through a coil and arrives at the cathode of zener diode Za. The zener is rated at 7.15 V and this voltage is thus applied to pin 6. This is the voltage reference for the chip and it can be adjusted slightly by a 1K pot in a voltage divider consisting of a 1.2K and a 3.3K besides the pot. The voltage divider ends at ground.

The reference voltage is set at exactly +5 V and the wiper arm on the pot, with the +5 V connected to pin 5. Pins 4 and 5 are the inputs to a comparator on the chip called the *error amp*. Pin 13 is one output of the error amp. Pin 13 has a frequency compensating .001 μF capacitor connected.

Another output of the error amp controls the NPN QA. QA is driving the regulator output that is emerging at pin 10. The third error amp output goes to QB, which is also exercising some control over QA. QB is controlled at its base through the current limit set by the 560 and 4.7K resistors in the base of the NPN attached to pin 10.

The net result of all these controls and compensations is to adjust the PNP series-pass transistor so that it will only output a regulated +5 V up to 1.35 A. The error amp does all the sensitive work. It constantly checks its two inputs at its output. If the comparison senses a rising or falling voltage, it will adjust the output back to the +5 V.

+12 V line

The 400 mA current the +12 V line is required to supply can be regulated easily with a 7812 12 V regulator (Fig. 25-3). The 7812 is a three-pin component that resembles a power transistor. The three pins are the input, output and ground.

The input receives a +23.5 V_{dc} input from a set of bridge rectifiers that are connected to a secondary winding of the power transformer. The dc is filtered by a 1500 microfarad capacitor at 35 working volts. A diode is placed across the regulator for protection. The cathode of the diode attaches to the transformer side of the regulator. The output of the regulator is then further filtered by a pair of capacitors, a 220 μF and a .1 μF. Without further ado the +12 V leaves the supply and proceeds to its destinations.

Negative voltages

The −12 V and −5 V lines are both drawn from the same bridge diodes the +12 V line receives its input. The diodes have one output for the +12 V supply and a second output for the negative voltages. Both −12 V and −5 V use the same filter, a 470 μF at 35 WV. The bridge-filter arrangement outputs −23.5 V_{dc}.

Two leads are taken from the −23.5 V_{dc} leg. One line is for the −12 V supply and the second is to supply the −5 V needs. The −12 V lead is attached directly to a 7912 12 V regulator. The second lead goes to a 1.2K current limiting resistor and then on to a 7905 5 V regulator. The 1.2K resistor changes the −23.5 V_{dc} to −20 V_{dc}.

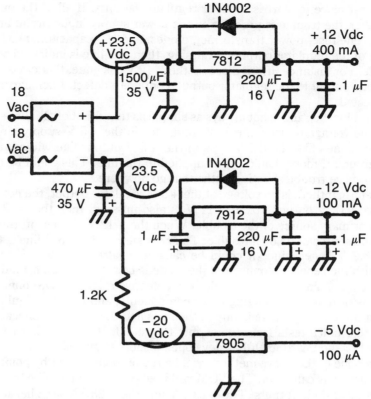

25-3 The +12, −12, and −5 V$_{dc}$ outputs are obtained from the two 18 V$_{ac}$ lines.

The −12 V circuit is like the +12 V circuit with these few changes. The regulator is 7912 in the −12 V line while the +12 V line has a 7812. The protective diode is the same one but the polarity is reversed to accommodate the minus voltage. The regulator's input filter is a μF and is wired with the + end connected to the ground. Lastly the −12 V circuit can only supply 100 mA while the +12 V line provides 400 M.

The −5 V circuit has a similar configuration, except the protective diode and the output 220 microfarad filtering are not needed. The −5 V line only has to deliver 100 microamps and the regulator can handle that without any additional components.

Troubleshooting

When the computer stops dead, the first step is to check the power supply. When a particular function of the computer fails, the first step is to test the supply voltages that are supposed to be coming to the circuit from the power supply. Power supply troubles are fairly easy to diagnose. Once the power supply is indicated as the seat of a trouble, the VOM is handy to check it out.

The best place to start is the four regulator outputs. If all of the outputs are missing, then the trouble is probably in the power supply input circuit around the fuse area. The fuse, power transformer, diodes, and HV capacitors need testing.

If one of the regulator outputs is missing, then that line is indicated as containing trouble. For instance, if you discover the -12 V_{dc} is gone, that circuit from the bridge diode output to the regulator output, contains a defect. Each part in the line must be tested.

The troubleshooting is not always as simple as that. First of all, the $+12$ V line supplies the voltage to drive the 723C regulator in the $+5$ V supply circuit. Second, zener diodes like the 6.2 V type in the $+5$ V output line will automatically short to ground if more than 6.2 V is applied to the line. This could be confusing and lead to false troubleshooting paths that go nowhere.

Therefore, if there is no voltage at the $+5$ V regulator output, the next stop is a test of the $+12$ V output. If the $+12$ V is also missing, then the $+12$ V line is really the primary source of the trouble. When the $+12$ V is present, then the $+5$ V line is the source of its own trouble. The next step in the $+5$ V line is to disconnect the 6.2 V zener, since it could be causing a false symptom. If the voltage returns with the zener disconnected, the diode is being overloaded. Find the overload before going any further. It could be a defective regulator. Disconnect the .33 Ω, 2 V resistor to avoid damaging other components, and test the regulator.

When there is no voltage in any of the lines and the fuse area checks out o.k., then run resistance tests from the supply to ground. It is possible that a bypass component or the board itself has developed a short to ground.

When none of the above methods yield a repair, then a point by point test with the computer on is called for. The VOM will read the test nodes. The bridge diodes can be tested at their outputs. The $+23.5$ V and the -23.5 V are checked. If both are missing, the bridge could be bad. If one or the other of the voltages are gone, then the filter on the regulator has broken down. The $+5$ V line can be traced by following the voltage from the $+5$ V_{dc} output. As soon as you arrive at a wrong voltage you are near the bad component.

Monitor power supply

Part of the monitor power supply works in the same way the computer's supply operated. There is a polarized plug that goes into a wall socket. Near the plug on the schematic in Fig. 25-4 are the markings, 120 V_{ac} and 340 mA. 120 $\times$ .340 = 40.8 W. This is the amount of wattage the monitor needs to operate.

Next is a step down transformer that converts the 120 V_{ac} to 22 V_{ac}. The transformer is capable of outputting 1.6 A. The 22 V_{ac} is then passed through a full-wave rectifier circuit. The 22 V_{ac} is rectified to 25.9 V, 979 mA dc. From there the dc goes to a regulator network based around a series pass transistor and an IC. The regulator output, a steady as a rock dc current flow, goes to an intersection with three roads. The top road outputs about $+15$ V_{dc}, the middle road about $+14$ V_{dc} and the bottom road, about $+5$ V_{dc}. All three outputs are dc regulated.

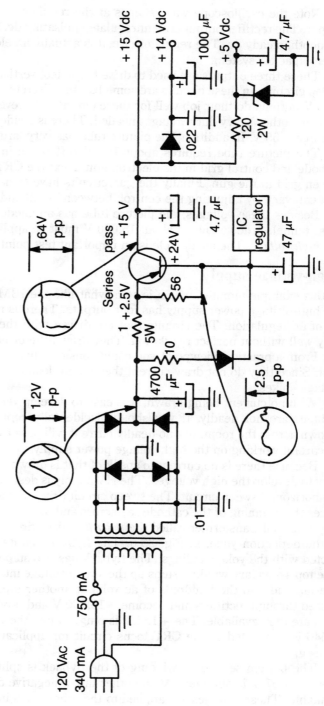

25-4 The monochrome monitor low-voltage supply produces + 15, + 14, and + 5 V_{dc}.

Note the oscilloscope wave shapes at the rectifier output, and the regulator output. The rectifier output is an unregulated pulsating dc. The regulator output is a smooth, steady dc. The regulator circuit is actually an electronic emulation of a filter capacitor system.

These three outputs are used to drive the video, vertical sweep and horizontal sweep circuits. In these circuits are some ICs and discrete transistors. The +5 and +15 V outputs do their job well for these circuits. However, in the monitor, there are some other heavy duty voltages needed. There is a video output transistor that requires +55 V. In addition, the picture tube has very large voltage needs.

The picture tube requires about 100 V difference in potential between the cathode and control grid in the electron gun. Next the CRT needs +270 V on the screen grid in the gun. Finally the gun circuits have to have a focus grid voltage that can vary, by adjusting the control, between −119 and +490 V_{dc}.

Besides these voltages, the picture tube has an anode hole in the side of the glass funnel. A dc voltage of about 15,000 V must be applied there. This is called the *high voltage*. The anode hole is an important test point.

High-voltage supply

In this example monitor, which is somewhat like the IBM monochrome monitor, the high-voltage power supply has four outputs. There is no need to go through a lot of dc regulation. The circuits that are driven with these four outputs can do very well without perfect regulation. They draw little or no current from the supply. From a practical viewpoint you could consider that they do not draw any current. Since they do not draw current they do not load down the supply and cause voltage spikes.

With no current being drawn, it is easy to develop very high voltages and the voltages are not deadly. If you should accidentally contact them you could be thrown across the room, but no deadly current will pass through you. At any rate, be careful working on the high voltage power supply.

Because there is no current to speak of that is drawn by the CRT circuits, it is easy to develop the high voltages. The HV supply is designed to be a by-product of the horizontal sweep circuit. The sweep circuit drives the deflection yoke that produces the scanning of the cathode ray across and up and down over the CRT face.

A special transformer called the *flyback* is also wired with the horizontal coils of the deflection yoke, in Fig. 25-5. The flyback has its primary windings connected with the yoke windings. The flyback has two step up secondary windings. The top secondary winding steps up the sweep voltage into the kilovolt ac range at one tap and into the hundreds of ac volts at another tap. These ac voltages are passed through rectifiers and become +15,000 V and +546 V. These two dc voltages are then available. The +15 kV is plugged into the CRT anode hole and the +546 is connected to the CRT focus circuit for application to the electron gun focus grid.

The bottom secondary winding of the flyback is split into three outputs. At one tap +57 V is obtained. At the other tap, a negative dc voltage of −167 V is available. These voltages are applied to the other grids in the electron gun input circuits and to the video output transistor's collector circuit.

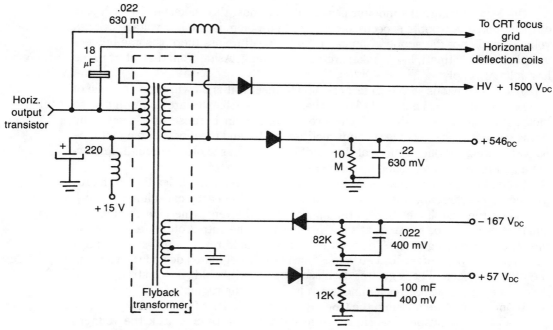

25-5 The monochrome high-voltage supply produces − 167 to + 15,000 V$_{dc}$.

The flyback transformer gets its name because of the way it handles the primary input signal. The input signal is the horizontal sweep wave shape. The wave shape is a sawtooth operating at the horizontal sweep frequency. In this monitor, that is 15,750 Hz. The sawtooth starts its movement at a low voltage and gradually increases its voltage as it draws the cathode beam across the screen. At the end of one line, the sawtooth has risen to its highest voltage. The sawtooth is then ready for its retrace. To accomplish the retrace, it drops from the highest voltage it has attained back to the low start voltage once again. The voltage drop from high to low takes place in only a fraction of the time the voltage took to rise and trace out a line.

This sudden voltage drop is called a flyback. This flyback pulse is coupled into the flyback primary winding. The suddenness of the pulse is coupled to the step up secondary windings. The top winding is able to step up the flyback pulse tremendously since no current is drawn. The flyback secondary pulse easily reaches 15,000 V for the instant the pulse is taking place. The pulse is then quickly rectified to a dc and filtered. The high voltage is thus produced. The rest of the flyback power supply voltages are developed in the same way. They are all high voltages that are fine working potentials as long as they do not draw any current.

Troubleshooting the monitor power supply

When the monitor power supply goes bad, the most common symptom is a dead monitor. It is a good idea to try another monitor and make sure the monitor is really at fault and not the computer or a video output card in a slot causing the trouble.

Once you are sure the monitor is at fault, you must then determine which part of the supply the trouble is occurring in. Is the problem in the low voltage or high voltage section of the supply? You can't tell right off unless there is some tell-tale visual or audible tipoff, like smoke, arcing, or burning. Aside from that, start in the low voltage supply.

The first obvious step is to test the ac line fuse. If it is blown, try a new one of the exact same size. That might be all that is wrong. Chances are you won't be so lucky, the fuse opened due to excessive current drain because of a short. The prime suspects then become the four rectifier diodes and the diode leading into the IC. Odds are good one or more of the rectifier diodes has shorted through. Replacing a bad rectifier diode should restore all.

Secondary suspects that could blow the ac fuse are the diode leading to the IC, the regulator transistor, the power transformer and its nearby capacitors.

When the fuse is not blown, the approach is different. Energize the monitor and take oscilloscope readings at a low frequency at the output of the rectifiers and the output of the regulator. The rectifier output should reveal a pulsating voltage with a peak to peak of one or two volts. This is the unregulated dc and the ripple in the voltage is seen. The regulator oscilloscope picture should show a straight horizontal line with a peak to peak under a volt. This is the regulated dc.

If one or both are missing, the trouble is in that section of circuits. The components all become suspect and must be tested one at a time. Check the voltages shown on the schematic. A wrong voltage will indicate a nearby defect.

When the oscilloscope pictures are present, test the three source voltages. Two of them are about $+15$ V and the third about $+5$ V. Should one of them be missing or severely incorrect, it's line and the components in the line are suspect. Check them out until you uncover the problem.

Once the low-voltage supply is exonerated, the high-voltage supply comes under suspicion. The high-voltage system is involved with the horizontal sweep circuits. Besides the components in the HV supply being possible culprits, any part of the horizontal circuit could also be under suspicion.

The first step is to see if the $+15,000$ V is being generated. This can be accomplished simply by placing a neon bulb tester near the flyback area. The flyback emanates an rf signal at 15,750 Hz. If the flyback is running, the neon will light up. If it does, then you must test the high voltage at the CRT funnel hole. This can only be done safely with a high voltage probe connected to a volt meter. Experienced technicians will draw an HV spark from the disconnected anode lead but this can be hazardous to both the circuits and the technician. The best way is with a high-voltage probe.

If the neon lights but there is no high voltage at the CRT anode, then the components from the flyback to the CRT anode are suspect. The usual problem is a defective high voltage rectifier. If you can see the rectifier it can be replaced and cure the condition. Unfortunately, in this example monitor, the rectifier is internal to the flyback. When it dies, the replacement might be too much trouble and it's best to install a new flyback.

Should the HV be present at the CRT anode but the display won't show, the electron gun circuits could be defective. Test the CRT socket for the voltages. If they are incorrect, especially the focus voltage, the trouble could be the CRT or the circuits feeding the gun. Track each voltage from the source to the gun. As soon as you lose the voltage or it becomes grossly incorrect, you probably have just passed over the defect. Test the components in that line.

When there is no HV either at the anode hole or in the flyback, then the entire horizontal sweep circuit becomes the suspect. The first test is to read the voltage on the collector of the horizontal output transistor. It should have about + 15 V, Fig. 25-6. If the voltage is missing, trace the voltage component by component back to the + 15 V source in the low voltage supply. The voltage is coming to the output transistor through the flyback primary, over a 220 μF capacitor and through a coil. Any of them could be open or defective. A tap at the collector is made by an 18 μF capacitor to the horizontal deflection yoke coils. The capacitor or the deflection yoke are possible suspects too. Also, in the line are the damper diode with its anode connected to ground and a bypass .039 capacitor. The damper diode has a history of shorting and killing HV. Once all those circuits are tested and deemed

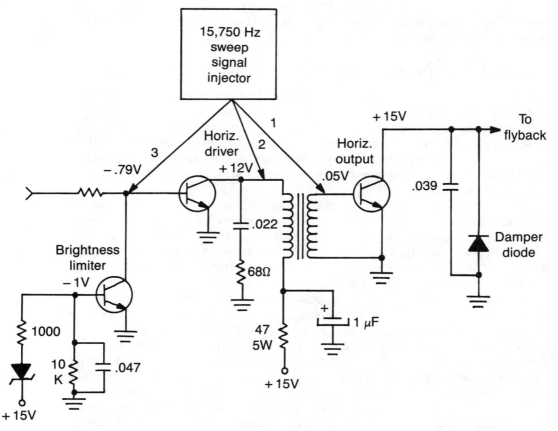

25-6 If the horizontal sweep circuits fail, the high voltage supply will shut down. A good test procedure is to isolate the trouble with a horizontal sweep signal injector.

o.k., it is time to check the horizontal sweep itself. If the horizontal sweep has died, the HV supply will too. In order to work it needs the flyback pulse generated by the sweep.

In the service shop, there is usually a piece of test equipment that generates a 15,750 Hz sweep signal. This signal must now be injected at the base of the output transistor. If the HV and screen brightness returns upon injection, then all the circuits from the base of the output transistor to the picture are cleared. The trouble is indicated to be in the horizontal drive transistor circuits. If the HV does not return, you missed something. The trouble is still in the circuits you just tested.

However, when the HV does return move the injection point backwards to the collector of the horizontal driver transistor. If the brightness returns, then the driver transformer you just passed over is o.k. When the brightness does not appear then the little transformer and the components connected to it are possible suspects and must be tested.

When the brightness did return, inject the signal into the base of the driver. If there is now no HV then the driver transistor and its adjoining components are indicated to be causing the trouble. The suspected components are tested one by one until the bad one is found. Usually there is only one defect at a time and replacing it will give you the fix.

Switching power supplies

The reason for using switching power supplies is to provide the computers and monitor with precise voltage regulation, even more exact than the circuit with the 723C regulator chip, discussed in this chapter. A switching activity works around three individual circuits, shown in Fig. 25-7. One is an oscillator. The oscillator gives the supply its "switching" name. Oscillators, as they run switch voltage levels. The oscillator therefore goes from an off condition to an on condition and back at each frequency cycle.

The second switching element is the output circuit that supplies the equipment with regulated voltage. The third part is a feedback loop circuit that samples the output and sends the voltage sample back to the oscillator for analysis. The oscillator in turn can adjust its frequency and thus generate an error pulse to make a voltage change, when needed. The width of the error pulse determines if the output voltage should be raised or lowered. The pulse controls the amount of time the filter capacitors have to charge. A longer pulse causes a longer charge time raising the voltage. A shorter pulse causes a shorter charge time lowering the voltage output. That way the final voltages hold rock steady with precise regulation.

The oscillator can consist of a discrete transistor that can run at 30,000 Hz with a p-p of about 150 V. The oscillator also is connected to a frequency-control circuit and a start-up circuit. The output is developed in some rectifier and filter networks with overload protection. The feedback loop will have some special transistors that take a sampling of the highest voltage output, and feeds the sample back to the frequency-control circuit. The frequency-control circuit is able to change the oscillator frequency if the voltage sample should rise or fall. The oscillator then adjusts the incoming voltage accordingly.

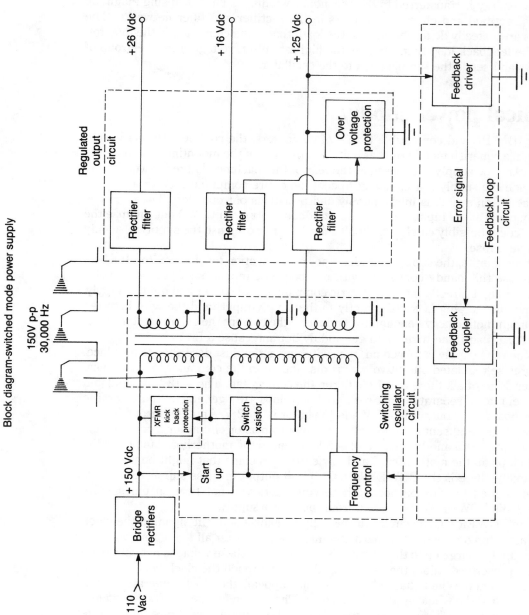

Block diagram-switched mode power supply

25-7 A switching power supply operates around three individual circuits. They are a switching oscillator, a regulated output circuit, and a feedback loop.

The oscillator drives the power transformer. As the oscillator peaks to an ON position it develops magnetic energy in the primary of the transformer. As it goes off, the energy is transferred to the secondary windings. The collapsing magnetic field is rectified and charges the filters in the rectifier and filter networks. The results are a steady dc discharge into the load, that is the computer or the monitor.

The feedback loop then samples the highest output voltage from the group of outputs and sends the sample back to the oscillator.

Typical power supply

In the IBM PC and compatible family of computers, the complete supply is contained in a squarish metal box that bolts into the rear of the mounting system of the computer. The supply is exposed at the rear of the machine. There is a ventilation fan inside the supply that is meant to cool the entire computer, motherboard and all. The off-on switch is in the supply and protrudes out one side. The supply is usually fused at the input in case of a hazardous short circuit. Without the fuse the supply could possibly catch fire. Don't ever defeat or overfuse the supply. Use only the correct fuse.

In most units, the supply provides a power connection for the monitor. It's best to only use this handy connector with monochrome monitors. If you use a color monitor, plug it directly into the electric companies wall socket and not the supply. The monitor ac plug is wired directly to the supply input, and the wire between them might not be heavy enough to conduct all the current the color monitor might need. As a result, the wire could get unduly hot and cause a fire.

When the supply is turned on, the switching action just described takes place. The precise regulated output voltage is distributed to the computer in this typical manner. First of all, there is +12 V to run the cooling fan. The +12 V is regulated so is sent to a separation network that develops two general outputs for the motherboard. One output is +5 V and the other is +12 V. Another output of −12 V is regulated and sent on to energize a driver transistor circuit for a communications adapter. Still another output of −5 V is sent to the motherboard to power the RAM chips on the motherboard and any expansion chips that might be used.

Finally, there is the POWER GOOD circuit output in these supplies. A +5 V output is used for this purpose. These computers will not turn on unless they receive this POWER GOOD signal from the power supply.

The POWER GOOD circuit in the supply sends a +5 volt signal to the clock generator chip on the motherboard 100 microseconds after all the output voltages in the supply charge up to their correct values. Should these voltages not charge up to their prescribed value, the +5 V signal does not reach the clock generator in a correct manner. When that voltage does not appear, the clock generator is not energized and the whole system shuts down. The reason for the insufficient source voltages then must be found and fixed before the computer is allowed to operate again.

While the POWER GOOD signal shuts down the computer when the output voltages are too low, there are other circuits that keep a check on the supply outputs so they do not get too high or if a short occurs that drains a lot of current. If the +5 V output should rise up above +15 V or the +12 V output rise above +36 V, or large amounts of current is drawn out of the supply, the circuits are built to immediately shut down the supply. The cause of the abnormal voltage or current must be found and fixed. One quick check you can make if the supply shuts down after warmup is the fan. If it is not running properly, it should be replaced. If it is purring along and cooling the system leave it alone.

Troubleshooting the typical power-supply shutdown

When a shutdown occurs, the first step is to determine whether the fault is in the power supply or in another section of the computer. The way to do this is disconnect the supply from the rest of the system and connect a dummy load in place of the system. When the shutdown happens, the protection circuits cause all the output voltages to drop to zero volts. If you disconnect the computer and install a dummy load and turn the supply on again, one or two things will happen. If the trouble is in the computer system the supply will come back on with correct source voltages since the fault has been disconnected. Should the trouble be in the power supply, the same condition of zero volt output will remain. This way the fault is known to be in the supply.

To disconnect the supply, pull the plugs that go to the motherboard and also pull the plugs that go to the disk drives. Next connect a dummy load, which in this case is a 47 ohm, one watt resistor. A good place to install the load is across the +5 V output to the system as shown in Fig. 25-8. Then turn the supply back on. If the output voltages return, the power supply is o.k. The system has the fault. You can then isolate which section of the system is in trouble. Remove the dummy load and start plugging the motherboard, adapter cards and disk drives back in one at a time. When you plug in the section with the fault, the supply will quit again. You then can start troubleshooting that faulty section.

When the power supply fails to provide output voltages with the dummy load in place, then the supply itself is in trouble. At this point in time you have the choice of replacing the power supply with a new and perhaps improved one, or settling down and troubleshooting it. Give this decision careful thought. Should you decide to go ahead and fix it the following are the typical steps you should take.

The first obvious step is to check the fuse. When the fuse opens, the trouble is usually not the fuse itself. There is probably a short in the supply. A common short circuit happens when one of the input diodes short out. Test them. There is one series diode and one to ground. The series diode is the one that usually conks out.

If the diodes test o.k., then test the components next in line, namely the switching oscillator circuit. That is, the oscillator IC, oscillator driver, and oscillator output transistors. If they test out o.k., check their support components.

Once the oscillator is cleared, the next circuit is the POWER GOOD. Disconnect the plugs that lead to the motherboard from the POWER GOOD circuit. Turn on the power and test for the +5 V from the circuit. If it is not there, the circuit

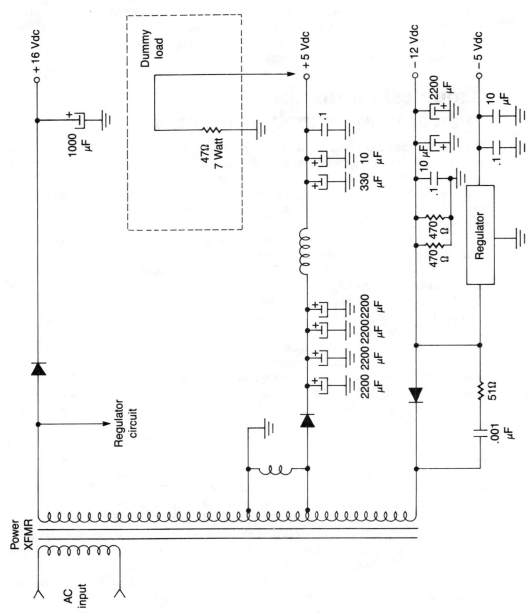

25-8   When a shutdown occurs, the first step is to determine if the problem is in the supply or the computer. Disconnect the supply and install a dummy load at the +5 V supply-output connection.

comes under suspicion. Test the POWER GOOD amp and driver transistors. Should they test good test the rest of the components in the circuit.

When POWER GOOD does output its +5 V signal, it is exonerated. Move on to the +12 V output. Should the +12 V not be there, test all its associated components. These are three +12 V transistors, the regulator driver, the regulator, and the sense amplifier. Should they be o.k., test their support components.

If the +12 V is present, next place to take a voltage reading is at the +15 V output. If it's missing, look for a diode in series with the output line. If it opens, the +15 V output will not be present. There is also a filter capacitor in the line to ground. It could be defective.

Should the +15 V be present, the next test point is at the −12 V output. If it is missing there is a series diode in that line too. An open diode could be the problem. Also test the other components in the line if the diode is o.k. When the −12 V is there the next test is to be made on the −5 V output. The −5 V line is an offshoot of the −12 V line. When the −12 V is present but the −5 V line is not, the prime suspect is the regulator IC. Next in the suspect line are the few support components.

If you go through this test routine carefully, you will have found the faulty component or connection and repaired the typical power supply. However, most supplies are not typical and could have all sorts of other exotic circuits. In order to troubleshoot an actual supply you must have the service notes for it. There are usually many deviations in the procedure due to circuit changes. The above procedure will often clue you right into the fault but other times require a lot more troubleshooting thinking and work. This test routine though, is the general way to go and gives you an idea how to go about solving power supplies failures.

26
Safety first

MICROCOMPUTERS ARE RELATIVELY SAFE MACHINES TO WORK WITH.
Their peripherals are also fairly safe. However, they operate on electricity, and
there is always a certain amount of potential danger. Electricity must be handled
properly, or else it can hurt or even kill.

Every electronic technician knows the basic safety measure to take when he or
she must put a hand into a circuit area that could possibly contain a surprise damage voltage potential. Electricity must have a closed circuit in order to have current
move through the circuit. When you get an electric shock, it's because you close
some circuit. You become a resistor in parallel or series with the circuit.

There are a number of possible paths through your body. The common ones
are from hand to hand across your chest, left hand to a leg, right hand to a leg and
from leg to leg. The paths that lead through your heart are the potentially lethal
ones. Other paths might shock or burn you, but they probably won't finish you off.

Therefore, technicians try to work in a way that if a shock does happen, the
current does not go through the heart. When working with high voltages and possible currents, keep your **left** hand in your pocket. That keeps the possible current
paths away from the heart. If you ever have to stick your hand into a circuit where
an accident could happen, remember that tip. See Fig. 26-1.

Danger while changing chips

In the single-board computer, about the only problem area is the power supply.
The machine is receiving 120 V ac, and if you get across it, a shock will result. For
instance, the handling of MOSFET chips is best performed while wearing a bracelet connected to earth ground. The bracelet is used to drain off any static electricity that develops as the technician moves around. Normal activity usually keeps a

663

26-1 When working with electricity, keep your left hand in your pocket. This poor guy could be seriously injured if he gets shocked and current flows past his heart from his left hand.

couple hundred volts of static charges in the human body. These static charges can possibly kill a chip. The bracelet keeps the static charge at near zero volts as it drains off the charge to earth ground. The chips are thus safe from the static charges during handling.

However, you are connected to earth ground. If you should accidentally get across the 120 V ac line, the voltage will push a lot of current through the bracelet to ground. This could be very dangerous and even deadly.

Therefore, a 1 mΩ resistor is installed in series between the bracelet and ground. If an accidental shock should occur, the current will be absorbed in the high resistance and not the low resistance of your body. The important thing is to avoid the possible shock. The piece of equipment that is receiving the replacement is **never** plugged into electricity while parts are being replaced.

In addition, the bracelet is only worn while handling chips that are not installed in the computer. Once the chip is plugged into a socket or soldered into place, the static charge crisis is over and the bracelet is removed before the machine is energized. It is vital that the procedure is performed in this way to avoid problems.

Other potential dangers

Electric shock, fire, CRT implosions, and X radiation are the dangers that are possible in computers, peripherals, and TV displays. The main shock sources are the house current inputs and the high voltage circuits in the TV displays. Fires can start in any electrical appliance. CRT implosions can occur with any display at any time. X radiation is a problem if you work too close with TV displays and the high voltage gets too high. Accidents can happen at any time. There are ways though that you can minimize the possibility of harm and damage.

Electrical shock

When you plug the computer system into electricity, for the most part, you are plugging in the primary of a transformer. The transformer primary is physically isolated from the secondary with heavy insulation. The ac is transferred from primary to secondary but the secondary isolates its ac from the electric company's.

This protects the computer and anyone who is working on the computer from lethal electric shock.

In general, there is the dangerous side, with the isolation transformer primary and the safer side with the transformer secondary. Refer to Fig. 26-2. On the danger side are items such as the power cord, the power plug, and possibly a fuse and some isolation high voltage capacitors. Be on the lookout for frayed insulation on the cord, cracked plugs, and cords that are stretched taut. Refer to Fig. 26-3. They are all dangerous.

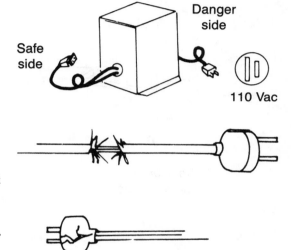

26-2 The dangerous side of an isolation transformer plugs into the wall. The safer side goes into the computer or monitor.

26-3 The ac line can be quite dangerous if you contact the copper wires inside. Be on the lookout for frayed insulation, taut lines, and cracked plugs.

Lots of units use interlocks. When you open up the machine, the power line opens up at the interlock. Refer to Fig. 26-4. If an interlock is not used, the device will probably employ a strain relief. The strain relief can take the form of an insulating bushing, clamp, strap, knotted power line, etc. It is used to keep tension off the internal connections. Do not defeat any of these measures. They are all there for your safety. Without the interlock or the strain relief, power supply trouble could eventually happen and shock or fire becomes a distinct possibility.

Most power plugs in computers are polarized. Refer to Fig. 26-5. The polarized plugs are often three wire. There is the ac high wire which contains 120 V, the ac low wire that is at 0 V, and the ground wire that goes to earth ground. It is easy to defeat the plug with adapters or other measures. **Don't do it!**

The least that could happen is a fuse will blow. The most is the computer could have all its chips blow out. Be especially careful of strip type outlets. The two wire polarized plug will fit into it. If you plug it in the wrong way, blooey!

Some monitors have their own power supply and do not use an isolation transformer. This is especially true when the monitor is a home TV. Without a transformer, the unit is entirely dependent on the polarized plug. The plug connects the print board and chassis ground to the external earth ground. The point is, never defeat the polarized plug for your sake and your equipment.

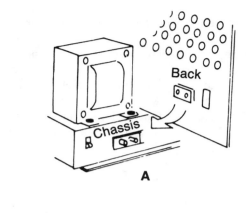

Back

Chassis

A

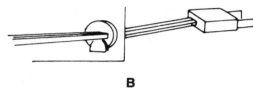

B

26-4 Many pieces of electrical equipment use interlocks (A) or strain-relief systems (B). Do not defeat any of these measures. They are carefully designed safety controls.

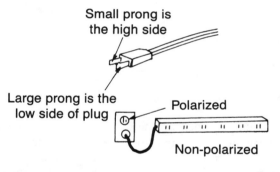

Small prong is the high side

Large prong is the low side of plug

Polarized

Non-polarized

26-5 Most computerized and other electronic equipment has polarized plugs, either three-wire or two-wire plugs. Be careful not to defeat the polarization. If you do, you could blow out the chips and transistors. You could also hurt yourself.

High voltages

There isn't any need for high voltage in the computer itself. The high voltage is only needed to be applied to the well in the side of a picture tube to attract the electron beam to the phosphor. This high voltage could be as low as 12,000 V in a monochrome monitor or as high as 30,000 V in a color TV used as a monitor.

Fortunately, this high voltage is usually not lethal. There is practically no current being drawn as it is applied to the CRT. About all that is drawn is the current in the cathode rays which is, from a danger point of view, negligible.

The danger is the high voltage will cause you to move violently and jump away. You could knock everything over and cut yourself on sharp chassis edges or bruise yourself in falls. If you have a heart condition, it could be serious.

It is a good idea not to get into the high voltage system unless you receive some training. During training, you'll become familiar with the system including the flyback transformer that produces the high voltage. The flyback is subject to heat, melting wax, cracks, and HV arcing from point to point. These are all fairly visible to the trained eye. Sometimes the problem can be repaired and other times a new flyback must be installed. Often a special type of flyback is used and must be changed only with the exact replacement. This is in the realm of TV service and should be treated as such. Just be careful in the HV circuits.

Besides those kilovoltages, there are some other voltages, not as high, but fraught with danger that are called B+. These are voltages between about 50 and 500 V. They are dc voltages produced by both the power transformer and the flyback. They are distributed throughout computer circuits and will shock you if you contact them. Needless to say, learn where they are so you won't accidentally touch them.

Fire

When your computer and peripherals leave the factory, every reasonable precaution is taken to avoid fire hazards. As time goes by the machine receives a certain amount of wear, tear, and repair. The factory safety measures could be degraded.

First of all, certain special parts are used to avoid trouble. When one of these parts breaks down, it is replaced. The replacement could be fine electronically and restore operation to the device. However, the replacement might be made by a different manufacturer whose own machines do not need certain safety measures. For instance, the part might overheat slightly in your machine while it is fine in another machine. The overheating over a period of time could result in a fire. Be sure to use only direct replacements and not one that defeats some safety measure.

Another thing to be careful of is the way the wires in your device are dressed out over the chassis. There are some components in most electronic gear that get hot. The manufacturer will dress out the leads in the machine in such a way that they do not get near the hot components. During repairs and maintenance, leads can get moved. If a lead falls on a hot component, the insulation will melt and who knows what will happen then. A fire is a good possibility.

The fuses in your equipment are carefully designed. Fuses must be replaced only with the same size and ratings. Fuses come in many different sizes, shapes, and ratings. A fuse can be a snap-in, a pig tail, a resistor or even a fusible link which is just a piece of wire. Instead of a fuse a circuit breaker is often used. Refer to Fig. 26-6. Whatever the configuration, the only right fuse is the one the factory specifies. The fuse information is usually printed right near the fuse itself.

If you install a fuse that is too small, it will keep on blowing. Should you install one too large or use a piece of wire to short it out, chances are good you'll be rewarded with a fire.

X radiation

There is a lot of confusion about X radiation from computers and their TV displays. The truth of the matter is, dangerous X radiation is possible from large picture tubes and some of the components in the HV circuits. In a color TV, the high voltage rectifier tube and the high voltage shunt regulator tubes were the villains. There are still a few of them around in old color TVs but not in the latest TV sets.

A

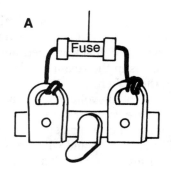

26-6 A common type of fuse is the pigtail (A). Good replacement technique dictates soldering in a new one and not jerry rigging the two connections together. Instead of a fuse, a circuit breaker could be used (B). Always replace a defective breaker with one that is rated the same. Don't take chances with a breaker that has more or less current-carrying ability.

B

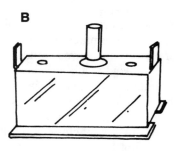

If you use an older color TV as a monitor, then stay away from those tubes while the TV is on.

X radiation is completely dependent on the level of high voltage. If the high voltage is at or near 30 kV, X radiation from the CRT and those high voltage tubes is a distinct possibility. If you must be near those items try to limit the amount of time actually exposed. Should you encounter a TV that has an HV above 30 kV, stay clear until the HV is brought down to its prescribed level.

For the most part, it has not been shown that there is any problem with today's computers and monitors as far as X radiation goes. It would be sensible though to avoid placing yourself against a lighted TV display. If you are separated from it, even by as little as 18 inches, there does not appear to be any particular hazard.

Cathode ray tubes

While the CRT is in its cabinet, the danger is minimal. CRTs can implode. They are under a great deal of atmospheric pressure. Inside the glass envelope is almost a perfect vacuum for the electron beam to travel in. If it implodes in the cabinet though, odds are, not one shred of glass will get out. The danger appears when a CRT must be removed from the cabinet. If it implodes outside its enclosure glass can fly and create a hazard. Replacing a CRT is best left to the professional.

Index